ial is re-

# Readings in the Psychology of Learning

THE LIPPINCOTT COLLEGE PSYCHOLOGY SERIES

Under the Editorship of

Dr. Carl P. Duncan, Northwestern University

and Dr. Julius Wishner, University of Pennsylvania

# Readings in the Psychology of Learning

*Edited by* **John F. Hall**

*The Pennsylvania State University*

J. B. LIPPINCOTT COMPANY

*Philadelphia & New York*

# Preface

IN TEACHING an undergraduate course in learning, I have frequently asked students to read journal articles in order to supplement the material which was found in the text and presented in lecture. Two difficulties with this procedure, however, have emerged. The first is that with large classes, students often have difficulty in securing the limited supply of articles which are available. The second problem is that the almost constant use of the journals results in their rapid deterioration so that within a short time replacement is necessary. A widely accepted solution to these problems has been to combine the articles which are used into a book of readings.

The general topics to be covered in as broad an area as learning, as well as the selection of the specific articles to be covered, are always difficult problems to be solved in a venture of this type. Inasmuch as I had recently completed a text in learning—*The Psychology of Learning*—the first problem was solved by adopting the general topical outline which I had used in writing that volume. In a sense, then, this book can be viewed as a companion text to the one which was published last year.

The selection of articles to be included within each topic was a more difficult problem to solve. My general guide was to select articles which introduced the reader to the operation of specific learning variables or processes. Once such articles were chosen, student evaluation aided in the determination of those which should be included for publication.

In order to provide some continuity among the articles, I have provided a few paragraphs at the beginning of each section in order to give the reader an overview of the general topic, as well as provide him with some orientation as to where the specific articles make their contribution.

I am particularly indebted to Carl P. Duncan and Julius Wishner, co-editors of the Lippincott College Psychology Series for their constructive comments. Special thanks are also due to my wife Jean who has been most helpful. I should like to express my thanks to all of the authors who very kindly gave me their permission to reproduce their articles and to the following organizations: Academic Press; *The American Journal of Psychol-*

v

*ogy*; The American Association for the Advancement of Science; *The American Journal of Physiology*; The American Psychological Association for its several journals; Cambridge University Press; The Journal Press; and the *Yale Journal of Biology and Medicine*.

UNIVERSITY PARK, PENNA.

JOHN F. HALL

# Contents

# SECTION TWO—(Cont.)

## General Issues in Motivation: I. The Role of Needs—(Cont.)

# SECTION THREE

# SECTION FOUR

# SECTION SEVEN

## Stimulus and Response Generalization 325

# SECTION EIGHT

## Transfer of Training 371

# SECTION NINE

## Retention and Forgetting 441

# SECTION NINE—(*Cont.*)

## Retention and Forgetting—(*Cont.*)

# Some Methodological Considerations

EW subject matters are free of methodological problems, and learning is no exception. We should like to introduce the reader to two problems which have long plagued experimenters in the field.

The first is the problem of establishing a taxonomy of learning. Why a taxonomy of learning? If each learning situation was considered as distinct and different from every other, with the principles or laws of learning which operated in one particular situation having no continuity or generality to any other, learning as an area of scientific inquiry would be impossible. An important consideration, then, is to provide some adequate classification system.

The selections of Bitterman (1962) and Grant (1964) represent two recent approaches or approximations of a taxonomy. Bitterman has confined his attention to animal learning situations, Grant to the conditioning of both animals and humans. Underwood (1964), whose paper concludes this section, presents some approaches to the establishing of a taxonomy as well as providing the reader with some background on types of verbal learning situations, a type of situation not considered by either Bitterman or Grant.

The second methodological problem concerns how learning should be measured. Currently, most investigators use either: (1) a probability of response measure, (2) an amplitude or magnitude measure, or (3) a measure which is related to time or rate of responding. It has been generally acknowledged that different experimental find-

1

ings may depend upon the response measure used. It has not always been recognized, however, that the problem of measurement is made even more complex by the fact that different experimental results may be obtained depending upon where in the apparatus the response is measured. An experiment by Goodrich (1959) illustrates this situation, while a study by Edgington (1960) reveals that the same measure taken at the same place may provide contradictory conclusions depending upon how the measure is expressed.

## REFERENCES

BITTERMAN, M. E. (1962) Techniques for the study of learning in animals: Analysis and classification. *Psychol. Bull.*, 59, 81-92.

EDGINGTON, E. S. (1960) Contradictory conclusions from two speed of performance measures. *Psychol. Bull.*, 57, 315-317.

GOODRICH, K. P. (1959) Performance in different segments of an instrumental response chain as a function of reinforcement schedule. *J. exp. Psychol.*, 57, 57-63.

GRANT, D. A. (1964) Classical and operant conditioning. In A. W. Melton (Ed.) *Categories of human learning.* New York: Academic Press.

UNDERWOOD, B. J. (1964) The representativeness of rote verbal learning. In A. W. Melton (Ed.) *Categories of human learning.* New York: Academic Press.

# 1. Classical and Operant Conditioning

## D. A. Grant

*Hilgard and Marquis in their classic text,* CONDITIONING AND LEARN-
ING, *divide conditioned response learning into classical and instrumental—a classification which many psychologists have used for
some time. Grant has used this classification as a point of departure
in providing the reader with a much more elaborate taxonomy.*

All the topics of this symposium deal with learning in the sense that they
deal with the establishment and strengthening of S—R connections or associations. It is quite appropriate to start such a discussion or symposium
with classical and operant conditioning for two reasons. First there is some
historical priority, and second, in classical and operant conditioning there
are probably fewer S—R connections involved so that these experiments
are, in a sense, simpler than most of the studies of human learning. At the
same time, we must note that no S—R connections exist in isolation; each
is embedded in a complex matrix of behavior in any experiment, and when
we isolate a particular S—R connection for logical consideration we can
never really isolate it from its matrix. And although we may consider conditioning to be simpler than most human learning, in fact, there appear to
be all sorts of processes associated with these apparently simple experiments which make their phenomena quite complicated. Indeed, so highly
efficient and developed are the verbal capacities of our human subjects (Ss)
that some of the fairly complicated forms of human learning in which verbal
functioning is especially involved actually seem to give us simpler behavior,
or at least behavior which is more regular, less variable, than that found in
our typical conditioning experiments. Also human learning occurs more
readily and more rapidly in some experiments that tap verbal functioning
than in experiments that do not. For example a simple discrimination and
discrimination reversal utilizing verbal responding occurs almost immediately and with almost perfect accuracy, whereas if the same experiment is
done, requiring a differential conditioned eyelid response of the human S,
both the initial differential conditioning and the subsequent reversal are
much slower, much less perfect, and "contaminated" with other complexities which will not be apparent when the verbal response is used (Levy,
Grant, & Clark, 1964).

The scheme of this paper is as follows: *first*, I shall present a way of

In Melton, A. W. (Ed.) *Categories of human learning*, pp. 1-13. Reprinted with
permission of the author and Academic Press, New York.

classifying classical conditioning experiments into four subclasses. The four subclasses involve, successively less and less motivation from extrinsic sources and more and more dependence upon the conditioned stimulus (CS) and unconditioned stimulus (UCS) alone. *Second*, a tridimensional classification of operant or instrumental experiments is outlined that depends upon cues, nature of the reinforcement, and nature of the response demanded of the S. The two sets of subclassifications are necessarily operational and incompletely operational at that, rather than functional, so that the *third* section of the paper points out some of the further operations and functional relations that set limits to the operational classification. Up to this point I shall not have distinguished sharply between human and animal conditioning. Then in the *fourth* section I shall discuss briefly human classical and operant conditioning, both the simple forms and more complex varieties that parallel in some respects the basic varieties of human learning that form the subject matter of this symposium. Considerations noted here lead to the *fifth* section which presents some general conclusions about our work on human learning, some of its complexities, and some of the interrelationships between different forms of human learning. So we turn, then, to the classification of conditioning experiments.

Although early workers did not make the distinction, it has proved useful for over twenty years to separate conditioning experiments into two broad classes: classical and instrumental conditioning. The Pavlovian experiment in which dogs learned to salivate to a previously neutral stimulus which had been paired repeatedly with food presentations has been taken to be the prototype of classical conditioning. Likewise the Thorndikian experiment in which hungry cats learned to manipulate latches, etc., in order to escape from a puzzle box and obtain food has been the prototype for instrumental conditioning or learning. The Skinnerian lever pressing by rats in order to obtain food is also frequently given as the prototype for instrumental conditioning, but the free operant presents special problems, so that it may be best to consider it as a class by itself.

Attempts to distinguish between classical and instrumental learning in terms of what is learned and how it is learned break down under careful analysis, and psychologists have resorted to operational definitions to separate the two classes of conditioning experiments. Thus Kimble (1961, p. 44) states:

> The basic distinction between classical and instrumental conditioning procedures is in terms of the consequences of the conditioned response. In classical conditioning, the sequence of events is independent of the subject's behavior. In instrumental conditioning, by contrast, rewards and punishments are made to occur as a consequence of the learner's response or failure to respond.

This definition serves quite well, but some precision may be gained by stating that in instrumental conditioning the *availability* of reward or punishment is contingent upon the S's behavior whereas in classical conditioning it is not.

Within the broad framework provided by these definitions the originality of numerous experimenters has led to tremendous variations in procedures. In some instances these variations in procedure tax the ingenuity of anyone attempting to classify the kind of learning involved. Nevertheless valuable classificatory schemes have been provided by Hilgard and Marquis (1940), Konorski (1948), Razran (1961a, 1961b), and Kimble (1961). Kimble's revision of the Hilgard and Marquis classic serves as an admirable point of departure from which to elaborate subclassifications of classical and instrumental conditioning.

## SUBCLASSES OF CLASSICAL AND INSTRUMENTAL CONDITIONING

### SUBCLASSES OF CLASSICAL CONDITIONING

In some respects subclassification of classical conditioning poses more problems than subclassification of instrumental conditioning. Nevertheless it will be useful to distinguish between four different kinds of classical conditioning. These will be designated Pavlovian A, Pavlovian B, Anticipatory Instructed, and Sensory Preconditioning. Although S's responses and indeed his learning may be very similar in these four subclasses of classical conditioning, the experimenter's operations are quite distinct.

*Pavlovian A conditioning.* This kind of conditioning is exemplified by the prototype of classical conditioning. In the original Pavlovian experiment the sound of a bell was repeatedly presented shortly before food was given the dog. Originally the sound of the bell elicited orientation reactions such as looking toward the sound source and pricking up the ears. When the food was presented it was ingested, eliciting the usual alimentary reflexes including buccal salivation. After repeated paired presentations of bell and food the sound of the bell came to evoke salivation and orientation movements toward the feeding cups (Pavlov, 1927, p. 22). These arrangements are diagrammed in Fig. 1. The sound of the bell is called the conditioned

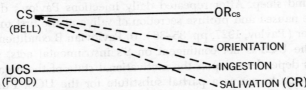

FIG. 1. Diagram for Pavlovian A classical conditioning. Pavlov selected salivation, a single component of the complex of responses forming the UCR, for study. Portions of the complex, e.g., ingestion, are absent in the CR. The CS has a signaling function. Performance of the UCR and subsequent conditioning are dependent upon food deprivation.

stimulus (CS), the response to the bell is called the orienting reflex (OR), the food is called the unconditioned stimulus (UCS) and ingestion and salivation, etc., are called the unconditioned response (UCR). Note that buccal stimulation by the UCS requires ingestion, an instrumental act by S. The new functional or learned connection is called the conditioned response (CR).

In this experiment many events occurred which Pavlov did not choose to measure. In the complex of responses to the UCS Pavlov chose to record only salivation in most of his experiments. Approach and ingestion were certainly responses to the UCS (food) and also could be noted in the CR. But it is noteworthy that the CR did not include approach to and attempts to feed upon the bell or other source of the CS (Zener, 1937). The approach and orientation movements were directed to the food source. These facts indicate that the CS does not *substitute* for the UCS as is so frequently stated. Pavlov states that the CS serves as a signal that the food is about to be presented. This position is also taken by Schlosberg (Kimble, 1961, p. 99) and seems to be a more accurate way of designating the function of the CS.

An important feature of Pavlovian A conditioning is the consummatory response, in this case, ingestion of the food. Although Pavlov's dogs had doubtless formed pre-experimental conditioned salivary responses to the sight and odor of food they did, in fact, ingest the food in his experiments, and they were brought to the experimental situation after some hours of food deprivation. It is known that conditioned salivary responses are hard to form in animals that are not hungry and, if formed, are hard to elicit from a satiated dog. It follows then that results of Pavlovian A conditioning must always be related to the motivational state of the organism during acquisition and testing of the CR.

*Pavlovian B conditioning.* This subclass of classical conditioning could well be called Watsonian conditioning after the Watson and Rayner (1920) experiment conditioning fear responses in Albert, but Pavlov has priority. The reference experiment for Pavlovian B conditioning might be that in which an animal is given repeated injections of morphine. The UCR to morphine involves severe nausea, profuse secretion of saliva, vomiting, and then profound sleep. After repeated daily injections Pavlov's dogs would show severe nausea and profuse secretion of saliva at the first touch of the experimenter (Pavlov, 1927, pp. 35–36). In Pavlovian B conditioning stimulation by the UCS is not contingent on S's instrumental acts, and hence there is less dependence upon the motivational state of the organism, and the CS appears to act as a partial substitute for the UCS. Furthermore, the UCS elicits the complete UCR in Pavlovian B conditioning whereas in Pavlovian A conditioning the organism emits the UCR of approaching and ingesting the food. Although Pavlovian B conditioning may be less affected by the motivational state of the organism, the experimenter cannot ignore the presence of concurrent antagonistic responses. For example, Watson and Rayner (1920) reported that they could not evoke conditioned fear responses as long as Albert had his thumb in his mouth. That the organism learns instrumental acts outside the paradigm for Pavlovian B conditioning is indicated by the fact that Albert evidently learned to put his thumb in his mouth when a frightening stimulus was presented. Phenomena of this sort have not been investigated to any great extent, but it is obvious that ignoring them can lead to some confusion in comparing results in different experiments.

The diagram for Pavlovian B classical conditioning is shown in Fig. 2.

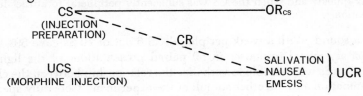

Fig. 2. Diagram for Pavlovian B classical conditioning. The CS substitutes to a great extent for the UCS, producing most if not all of the UCR. Conditioning and performance are relatively independent of motivation but probably dependent upon concurrent antagonistic responses, e.g., feeding.

The CS constitutes the preparations for the injection and insertion of the needle. There will originally be an OR to the CS. The UCS is the morphine injection itself, a very complex physiological stimulus. The UCR consists of salivation, nausea, vomiting, and other physiological changes. Many of these are readily seen as components of the CR which will be evoked by the preparations for the injection after repeated daily morphine injections. A great deal of interoceptive conditioning (Bykov, 1957; Razran, 1961b) and autonomic conditioning (Kimble, 1961) apparently follows the Pavlovian B paradigm.

*Anticipatory instructed conditioning.* Following Ivanov-Smolensky (1933) many Russian investigators have formed what they, quite legitimately, I think, call CRs based upon the voluntary squeezing of a rubber bulb in response to a sound stimulus. The sound stimulus is preceded regularly by a light or some other neutral stimulus and the Ss will learn to respond to the neutral stimulus. In effect, it is a reaction time experiment with a constant fore-period signaled by the onset of the CS. Some will doubtless balk at calling this conditioning. It is, however, similar to transferring stimulus control of an operant from one $S^D$ to another $S^D$. An excellent reference experiment for anticipatory instructed conditioning is the establishment of conditioned eyelid responses based on voluntary reinforcement by Marquis and Porter (1939). The diagram for Anticipatory Instructed Conditioning is shown in Fig. 3. The CS was a change in illumination. The Ss were instructed to blink as rapidly as possible when they

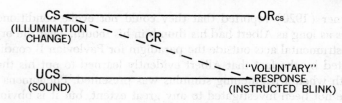

Fig. 3. Diagram for Anticipatory Instructed Conditioning. The CR appears as an anticipatory blink before the sound (UCS). Marquis and Porter (1939) found best conditioning when the instructions were to blink quickly and when the CS was sufficiently peripheral to attract little attention.

heard a sound. With a weak peripheral CS 6 out of 10 Ss gave 59% to 92% anticipatory eyelid responses in 50 paired presentations of the light and sound. The Ss were unable to verbalize the relationship between the change in illumination and the other stimuli of the experiment. Generally speaking, extinction was quite rapid following Marquis and Porter's procedures. It should be noted that of the 4 Ss who failed to show appreciable conditioning, 2 spontaneously described their attempts to inhibit blinking to the light, whereas the other 2, although they did not verbalize an inhibitory attitude, showed long reaction times. The form of the resulting CR was quite different from that obtained using the reflex wink to an air puff as the UCR. This eyelid CR closely resembled the voluntary response described by Spence and his co-workers (Spence & Taylor, 1951; Spence & Ross, 1959), i.e., the response was a complete closure with rapid recruitment and prolonged duration.

Although Russian investigators have utilized this CR a great deal and have investigated its characteristics extensively (The Israel Program for Scientific Translations, 1960) these investigations are not well known in this country, and very little work has been done with this kind of experimental procedure. It is evident, however, from the report of Marquis and Porter (1939) that this type of conditioning is heavily dependent upon stimulus arrangements, instructions, and attitude of the S.

In anticipatory instructed conditioning the CS appears to trigger a preset reaction. The response might be viewed as the false reaction to the ready signal in a reaction time experiment. It seems apparent that the CS may signal the occurrence of the UCS or may substitute for it, depending upon idiosyncrasies of the S. The sequence of events in the conditioning situation will therefore depend upon the S's interpretation of the E's instructions and the S's own self-instruction. With peripheral, scarcely noticed, conditioned stimuli and delicate time relations in the response, the S may be unaware of the fact that he is responding to the "wrong" stimulus. In the event that the S does not know that he has responded to the CS he may presumably interpret this as a "correct" or an "incorrect" response on his part. Properly instructed and properly motivated he will presumably try to increase "correct" responses and decrease "incorrect" responses. In anticipatory instructed conditioning the definition of "correct" and "incorrect" are usually left ambiguous; the E is at the mercy of the S's self-instructions.

Interpretation of instructions is important in other conditioning and learning experiments where the S believes that his responses are "voluntary." This can account for some of the anomalies found in hand-withdrawal conditioning. It is amusing but also instructive to go back to some of the earlier reports of hand-withdrawal conditioning when extensive verbal reports were taken from the Ss (e.g., Hamel, 1919; Schilder, 1929). Here we find some Ss who had to fight themselves to keep their hands down on the shocking grid in order not to spoil the E's results, whereas other Ss, as soon as they understood the relationship between the CS and the shock, withdrew their hands immediately, for to do otherwise would have been ridiculous to them. In sum, the care with which instructions are given human Ss in conditioning experiments can scarcely be overemphasized. Leaving matters up to the S results in experiments where no two Ss give the same sort of responses. The results are more likely to be confusing than enlightening. The enforced brevity of current reporting of psychological experiments puts a heavy but legitimate burden on the E. It is his responsibility to get his experiment under control.

*Sensory preconditioning.* A fourth subclass of classical conditioning is well represented by the sensory preconditioning experiment of Brogden (1939). This is diagrammed in Fig. 4. In the preconditioning phase there

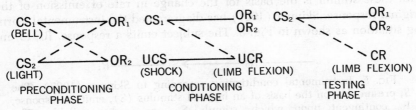

FIG. 4. Diagram for Sensory Preconditioning. The preconditioning phase produces sufficient substitution potential between $CS_1$ and $CS_2$ so that in testing phase $CS_2$ will evoke the CR previously conditioned to $CS_1$ only in conditioning phase.

were 200 paired presentations of two conditioned stimuli. During the conditioning phase, 20 daily, paired presentations of one CS with the shock to the left forelimb were presented until the criterion of 100% CRs was reached. Then, in the testing phase, the other CS was presented 20 trials per day until the forelimb flexion response disappeared. Eight out of 10 dogs produced forelimb flexion to the second CS in the testing phase and required from one to seven days to extinguish the response to the second stimulus. The preconditioning produced effective stimulus substitution and is of considerable theoretical interest because of the motivational features or lack of them in the experiment. It is by no means certain whether the preconditioning is S—S conditioning or S—R conditioning with chaining through the ORs to the two conditioned stimuli. The CS-UCS interval in the conditioning phase was 2 sec., which is quite adequate for chaining as has been demonstrated by Wickens and his co-workers (e.g., Wickens, 1959). There is evidently a good deal of published Russian research on sensory preconditioning which they call associative conditioning (cf. Razran, 1961b).

Some of the American work on sensory preconditioning has not been as successful as the original Brogden experiment (cf. Seidel, 1959). It is interesting in view of Wickens' results on compound conditioning (e.g., Wickens, 1959) to conjecture that if the $CS_2$ preceded the $CS_1$ in the preconditioning phase then more preconditioning would be demonstrated in the testing phase of the sensory preconditioning experiment. Although a good deal of sporadic work has been done on compound and chained conditioning, both in this country and in Russia (cf. references listed by Wickens, 1959; Razran, 1961b), the events and interpretations in the more complicated experiments have not been worked out in any great detail.

## SUBCLASSES OF INSTRUMENTAL CONDITIONING EXPERIMENTS

In an instrumental conditioning experiment, contingent upon the S's responses, other stimuli are made available to him, and the S's interaction with these stimuli is the basis for the change in rate of emission of the original response. Skinner (1937) has diagrammed the instrumental learning situation as shown in Fig. 5. The subject emits a response, $R_0$, to un-

$$s \text{———} R_0 \text{———} \rightarrow S_1 \text{———} R_1$$

FIG. 5. Instrumental conditioning according to Skinner (1937). The S, presumably on the basis of an internal stimulus (S), emits a response, $R_0$ contingent upon which, stimuli, $S_1$, are made available. The $S_1 \text{———} (R_1)$ complex constitutes the reinforcement. Learning is dependent upon the $R_0 \longrightarrow S_1$ contingency and is reflected in the rate of emission of $R_0$, the operant.

known stimuli, s. Contingent upon the performance of $R_0$ other stimuli, $S_1$, are made available to the subject. The $S_1$ and responses to $S_1$, ($R_1$), constitute the reinforcement. Learning is dependent upon the $R_0 \rightarrow S_1$ contingency and leads to an increase in the rate or probability of emission of the original response, $R_0$.

The extremely simple paradigm of Fig. 5 admits to many variations in experimental arrangements. Attention will be restricted to those in which only a single type of reinforcer is used. Hilgard and Marquis (1940) distinguish four types of instrumental conditioning experiments: reward training, escape training, avoidance training, and secondary reward training.

Essentially the same are mentioned by Woodworth and Schlosberg (1954, Ch. 19). To these Kimble (1961) adds omission training and punishment training. In further discussion it will be necessary to exclude secondary reward training as beyond the scope of this treatment. As a first step, the reference experiments for each form of instrumental conditioning will be described.

*Reward training.* The reference experiment for reward training might well be the free operant conditioning experiment of Skinner (1938) in which a rat is placed in a soundproof box containing a small lever which, when pressed, automatically deposited a pellet of food in a delivery cup. After a hungry rat has been placed in this situation his rate of lever-pressing will usually increase until it reaches a steady value.

*Escape training.* A good reference experiment for escape training was carried out by Sheffield and Temmer (1950). Rats were placed on a charged grill in an enclosed runway. The floor of half of the runway consisted of the charged grill, and the floor of the other half was smooth, providing a "safe" escape compartment, with a sliding door in between to prevent retracing. Speed of locomotion toward the safe compartment was used as the response measure.

Reward and escape training performance serve operationally to define reward and punishment. To parallel Thorndike's (1933) definition of satisfying and annoying states of affairs, the S will not avoid a reward and will often act so as to maintain or renew it. A punishment involves a state of affairs which the S does nothing to preserve and usually acts so as to terminate.

*Avoidance conditioning.* The conditioning phase of the Brogden sensory preconditioning experiment can serve as the reference experiment for a-voidance conditioning. The left forelimb of the dog rests on an electrode which is electrically charged upon the termination of a 2-sec. CS. On the first few trials the dog will receive the shock each time. Eventually a conditioned anticipatory response involving struggling and lifting the fore-limb from the electrode will occur before the shock is given. Finally, a regular, precise, and adaptive flexion of the forelimb will occur shortly before the electrode is charged. At this stage of learning the dog will rarely receive a shock, and conditioned flexion will be maintained with a very small number of reinforcements.

*Discriminated operant conditioning.* It is useful to differentiate discriminated operant conditioning from reward training or simple operant conditioning. The reference experiment is a slight elaboration of the experiment for reward training. An additional stimulus source is added to the rat's box, say an electric lamp. Pellets are delivered by the apparatus when the lever is depressed, if and only if, the lamp is lit. The rat soon learns to depress the lever only when the lamp is lit, and not to depress the lever when the lamp is not lit. The operant is said to come under stimulus control, and the differential stimulus, the light, is designated by Skinner as $S^D$. By clever arrangements of the contingencies between reinforcers and discriminatory stimuli, all sorts of remarkable behavior may be obtained (Ferster & Skinner, 1957).

*Omission training.* A reference experiment for omission training is that of Konorski (1948, p. 226ff). A classical salivary CR to the sound of the metronome was occasionally evoked in combination with passive flexion of the dog's leg by the experimenter, and this combination of stimulation was never reinforced with food. Very soon, it was found that concurrent raising of the leg with the sound of the metronome resulted in inhibition of the salivary flow. In addition to this, at about the same time the animal began to resist the passive flexion of the leg by actively extending it. Finally the extension movement became quite strong so that it could easily be recorded by means of a treadle arrangement. The dog had learned not only to avoid the flexion movement associated with non-reward but to make the antagonistic response. For purposes of this discussion the antagonistic response need not be overt. The situation roughly parallels that of rewarding a child when he restrains himself from some specified aggressive or destructive activity, but the use of rewards to make non-verbal animals omit responses is likely to prove difficult without Konorski's "tutoring" procedure.

*Punishment training or passive avoidance.* Another form of instrumental conditioning that Kimble derived from Konorski's valuable book was punishment training. The neat procedure used by McCleary (1961) will serve as the reference experiment. Hungry cats, placed in a two-compartment box, were trained to feed in the second compartment whenever a guillotine door was briefly raised. After initial training had brought the feeding response to a high probability level the cat was shocked as it started to feed. After two such shocks McCleary found that normal cats would no longer feed or even approach the door of the feeding compartment when the door opened. This passive avoidance was maintained in spite of several days of food deprivation.

A CLASSIFICATORY SCHEME

In spite of the ingenuity of experimenting psychologists most instrumental conditioning experiments can be fitted into the six categories previously described. Even so, there are numerous variations in procedure which will continue to defy any simple classificatory schema that may be proposed. The problem still remains of trying to work out the relationships among the six categories that have been outlined. Perhaps the most frustrating efforts to interrelate these subclasses of instrumental learning will be attempts based on what is learned. Here the intentions and observations of the *E*, the pretraining of the *S*, the specific kinds of rewards and punishments, the rate of satiation, etc., all interact to produce a bewildering sequence of behavior, some classically conditioned, some instrumentally conditioned, most of which is ignored by the psychologist who has done the experiment.

It turns out, however, that the different forms of instrumental conditioning do have a very simple tridimensional relationship if they are viewed in terms of $E$'s operations and the response-reinforcement contingencies. First of all, it will be noted that in some experiments rewards are used and in other experiments punishments are used. Typically the learned response involves attaining the reward or avoiding the punishment. Thus reward training, discriminated operant conditioning, and omission training all involve reward as the reinforcement. Escape training, avoidance conditioning, and passive avoidance all involve punishment. Furthermore, the experiments can be dichotomized in terms of whether the response of the $S$ is the performance of a positive response or the omission or inhibition of a response which already had an operant strength greater than zero. Thus, reward training, escape training, avoidance conditioning, and discriminated operant conditioning all involve the performance of a positive response in order to attain the reward or to escape the punishment. Omission training and passive avoidance conditioning both involve omission or inhibition of a response in order to achieve the reward or to avoid the punishment. Finally, the experiments can be dichotomized in terms of whether or not a cue is given as to the time that the reinforcement will be available. Thus in avoidance conditioning and discriminated operant conditioning a cue is available when the punishment or reward, respectively, is about to be presented. In reward training, escape training, omission training, and passive avoidance there is no special $S^D$ or cue to the imminence of the reinforcement. When these three independent ways of dividing the subclasses of instrumental conditioning are simultaneously applied the results are as shown in the first six lines of Table 1. Each of the six varieties of instrumental conditioning fits neatly and unambiguously into a line of the table, dependent upon whether there is a cue to the reinforcement, the positive or negative nature of the response, and the nature of the reinforcement.

Arrangement of the six types of instrumental conditioning into such a tridimensional scheme pays an interesting dividend. It will be noted that independent combinations of two possibilities as to the cue for reinforcement, two possibilities as to the response, and two possibilities as to the nature of the reinforcement yield, totally, eight possible experimental reference types. Only six were described by Kimble. It is instructive to fill out the two remaining possibilities in the table and to see if they represent plausible experiments.

If a cue to the imminence of reinforcement is given and the learned response is to omit a normally performed act in order to obtain a reward we

TABLE 1

A CLASSIFICATION OF TYPES OF INSTRUMENTAL
LEARNING EXPERIMENTS

| Instrumental types | Cue to impending reinforcement | Response | Reinforcement |
|---|---|---|---|
| Reward Training | No | Positive | Reward |
| Escape Training | No | Positive | Punishment |
| Avoidance Conditioning | Yes | Positive | Punishment |
| Discriminated Operant | Yes | Positive | Reward |
| Omission Training | No | Negative | Reward |
| Punishment (or Passive Avoidance Conditioning) | No | Negative | Punishment |
| Discriminated Omission Training | Yes | Negative | Reward |
| Discriminated Punishment Training | Yes | Negative | Punishment |

have the seventh line of the table which has been designated *Discriminated Omission Training*. If a cue is given to the imminence of reinforcement, and the appropriate response is omission or inhibition or a normally performed act in order to avoid punishment we have the eighth line of the table which has been designated *Discriminated Punishment Training*. To my knowledge, psychologists have not performed these experiments formally, but the situation envisaged by the paradigm seems to occur as a commonplace in real life. Discriminated omission training is represented by the remark of the cynic that men seek the appearance of virtue rather than virtue itself. Suppose, for example, that a parent agrees with his daughter to reward her with money, a watch, or some other valuable consideration if she stops smoking, drinking, swearing, or some such behavior. The young lady, who may be maintaining her behavior at a high operant level, may interpret this bargain to mean that the undesirable behavior must not occur at times or in places where the parent may learn of it. The result may be a well-discriminated omission of the behavior in the presence of the parent or likely informants of the parent.

Discriminated punishment training is easily exemplified by one's colleagues who may have colorful or even lurid speech in informal social contacts but whose undergraduate lectures are models of propriety. The cynical expression is, "Avoid the appearance of evil." Training animals to desist from undesirable behavior is a rich field of examples for discriminated punishment training. I have had the personally unrewarding experience of trying to train numerous generations of cats not to scratch our furniture. The carefully conducted training procedure usually consists of my throwing a paperback book or whatever is handy at the cat when he approaches the furniture with evil intent or is engaged in scratching. Not only does our scratched up furniture give mute evidence for the fact that the animals have developed a discriminated punishment pattern, but also, if I slip into the room upon hearing a cat scratch the furniture I invariably find that the cat is indeed scratching and at the same time looking around the room to see if I am coming.

In spite of the practical importance of these learning patterns in discriminated omission training and discriminated punishment training these experiments seem to have been left severely alone by psychologists. To some extent discriminated omission training has been carried out by Skinner and his associates in DRL schedules where the S is rewarded for a low operant rate. Nevertheless, in view of the tremendous diversification of instrumental learning experiments it is somewhat surprising not to find any readily at hand which conform to these patterns. They seem well worth investigating.

This particular classificatory scheme is not proposed as the ideal scheme or even a complete scheme. It seems, however, to be serviceable and relatively unambiguous as a framework within which instrumental conditioning experiments may be placed. It would, perhaps, be more desirable to classify the experiments in terms of more fundamental psychological operations involved. It will be shown, moreover, that in view of the variety and complexity of experimental arrangements and the limitations in measurement of responses that the classification given above represents only the beginning of a lengthy and difficult task.

## REFERENCES

BROGDEN, W. J. (1939) Sensory pre-conditioning. *J. exp. Psychol.*, 25, 323-332.

BYKOV, K. M. (1957) *The cerebral cortex and the internal organs.* (Translated and edited by W. H. Gantt) New York: Chemical Publ. Co.

FERSTER, C. B. and SKINNER, B. F. (1957) *Schedules of reinforcement.* New York: Appleton-Century-Crofts.

HAMEL, I. A. (1919) A study and analysis of the conditioned reflex. *Psychol. Monogr.*, 27, Whole No. 118.

HILGARD, E. R., and MARQUIS, D. G. (1940) *Conditioning and learning.* New York: Appleton-Century.

Israel Program for Scientific Translations. (1960) *The central nervous system and behavior: Selected translations from the Russian medical literature.* Bethesda, Maryland: National Institutes of Health.

IVANOV-SMOLENSKY, A. G. (1933) *Metodika issledovaniya uslovnykh refleksov u cheloveka* (methods of investigation of conditioned reflexes in man.) Moscow: Medgiz (Medical State Press).

KIMBLE, G. A. (1961) *Hilgard and Marquis' Conditioning and Learning.* New York: Appleton-Century-Crofts.

KONORSKI, J. (1948) *Conditioned reflexes and neuron organization.* Cambridge, England: Cambridge Univer. Press.

LEVY, C. M., GRANT, D. A. and CLARK, A. H. (1964) Reversal of conditioned discrimination of the eyelid response. *J. exp. Psychol.*, 67, 80-82.

MARQUIS, D. G. and PORTER, J. M., Jr. (1939) Differential characteristics of conditioned eyelid responses established by reflex and voluntary reinforcement. *J. exp. Psychol.*, 24, 347-367.

McCLEARY, R. A. (1961) Response specificity in the behavioral effects of limbic system lesions in the cat. *J. comp. physiol. Psychol.*, 54, 605-613.

PAVLOV, I. P. (1927) *Conditioned reflexes*. (Translated by G. V. Anrep) London: Oxford Univer. Press, 1927, reprinted New York: Dover, 1960.

RAZRAN, G. (1961a) The observable unconscious and the inferable conscious in current Soviet psychology: Interoceptive conditioning, semantic conditioning, and the orienting reflex. *Psychol. Rev.*, 68, 81-147.

RAZRAN, G. (1961b) Recent Soviet phyletic comparisons of classical and of operant conditioning. *J. comp. physiol. Psychol.*, 54, 357-365.

SCHILDER, P. (1929) Conditioned reflexes. *Arch. Neurol. Psychiat.*, 22, 425-443.

SEIDEL, R. J. (1959) A review of sensory preconditioning. *Psychol. Bull.*, 56, 58-73.

SHEFFIELD, F. D. and TEMMER, H. W. (1950) Relative resistance to extinction of escape training and avoidance training. *J. exp. Psychol.*, 40, 287-298.

SKINNER, B. F. (1937) Two types of conditioned reflex: A reply to Konorski and Miller. *J. gen. Psychol.*, 16, 272-279.

SKINNER, B. F. (1938) The behavior of organisms: An experimental analysis. New York: Appleton-Century.

SPENCE, K. W. and ROSS, L. E. (1959) A methodological study of the form and latency of eyelid responses in conditioning. *J. exp. Psychol.*, 58, 376-385.

SPENCE, K. W. and TAYLOR, J. (1951) Anxiety and strength of the UCS as determiners of the amount of eyelid conditioning. *J. exp. Psychol.*, 42, 183-188.

THORNDIKE, E. L. (1933) The law of effect. *Psychol. Rev.*, 40, 434-439.

WATSON, J. B. and RAYNER, R. (1920) Conditioned emotional reactions. *J. exp. Psychol.*, 3, 1-14.

WICKENS, D. D. (1959) Conditioning to complex stimuli. *Amer. Psychologist*, 14, 180-188.

WOODWORTH, R. S. and SCHLOSBERG, H. (1954) Experimental psychology (Rev. ed.). New York: Holt.

ZENER, K. (1937) The significance of behavior accompanying conditioned salivary secretion for theories of the conditioned response. *Amer. J. Psychol.*, 50, 384-403.

## 2. Techniques for the Study of Learning in Animals: Analysis and Classification

### M. E. Bitterman

*In contrast to Grant's article, which provided a taxonomy for both animals and humans, Bitterman has placed emphasis upon animals. His classification bears certain similarities to the classical-instrumental dichotomy, but there are major differences as well.*

Although many different techniques for the study of learning in animals have been developed in the 60 years or so since the problem of animal intelligence first was brought into the laboratory, their interrelations never have been carefully defined. Crude dichotomies have been proposed—"respondent conditioning" versus "operant conditioning" by Skinner (1935, 1937), "classical conditioning" versus "instrumental conditioning" by Hilgard and Marquis (1940)—and, more recently, a trichotomy—"classical conditioning" versus "instrumental conditioning" versus "selective learning" by Spence (1956)—but the diversity of method is too great to be encompassed in any such one-way analysis. While certain differences among the techniques to be classified *must* be ignored if the number of categories is to be smaller than the number of techniques, the quest for parsimony seems to have been carried too far.

Classification is not merely a matter of taste. When one can find no objective basis for evaluating the conviction that a given difference in technique should be stressed or that another safety may be disregarded, it is only because the proper experiments have not been performed. Consider, for example, the question of whether the difference between flexion conditioning with avoidable as compared with unavoidable shock should be reflected in a classification of techniques. The answer is "Yes" for Hilgard and Marquis, who emphasize the contingency of reinforcement on response. They classify flexion conditioning as "classical" when shock is unavoidable and as "instrumental" when shock is avoidable. The answer is "No" for Spence, who emphasizes the degree of control afforded the experimenter over the appearance of the response to be learned. Ignoring the contingency of shock upon failure of response to the CS, Spence treats

*Psychol. Bull.*, 1962, 59, 81-93. Reprinted with permission of the author and The American Psychological Association. This paper grows out of a program of research on the comparative psychology of learning supported by Contract Nonr 2829 (01) with the Office of Naval Research and by Grant M-2857 from the United States Public Health Service. Its reproduction in whole or in part is permitted for any purpose of the United States Government.

avoidance conditioning as a special case of classical conditioning in which the pattern of reinforcement gradually shifts from consistent to intermittent. Such a disagreement surely need not remain long in the realm of opinion. One has only to compare the behavior of an animal trained with avoidable shock and that of a control animal trained with shock that is unavoidable but simply withheld on whichever trials the first animal avoids; if response contingency is unimportant, the course of learning in the two animals should be the same.

In general, a classification of techniques may be treated as the expression of a set of hypotheses about the functional significance of differences in techniques as an assertion that they yield results which differ in some fundamental respect, and a failure to distinguish between two techniques as an assertion that they may be used interchangeably in the analysis of learning. This is not to say that a classification may not be preferred on historical, or on pedagogical, or even on esthetic grounds, but only that a functional interpretation is available which provides a basis for empirical evaluation. Methodological and functional considerations have, in fact, been linked rather closely in the past. Methodological distinctions have been taken as points of departure for dual-process analyses of learning, while striving for a unitary conception have been reflected in the blurring of methodological distinctions. One may even point to experiments designed explicitly to provide a functional comparison of different methods (Youtz, 1938a, 1938b, 1939), although the empirical study of methodological interrelations certainly has not been carried very far.

Functional considerations play a central role in the classification to be offered here, which grows out of a program of comparative research (Bitterman, 1960). The first step in the program is to assess the phyletic generality of certain theoretically significant phenomena of learning which have been established in work with the rat (hitherto the principal subject of research on learning), and to that end a variety of simple animals must be studied under conditions analogous to those which have been used for the study of the rat; but what are "analogous" conditions? Clearly, the answer to this question requires some hypotheses about the essential properties of the various techniques which have been used for the rat. As will later be indicated, the comparative enterprise not only motivates further methodological analysis but constitutes a new source of data in terms of which the outcome may be evaluated.

## THORNDIKIAN SITUATIONS

It seems reasonable to begin the analysis with a set of closely interrelated techniques which date back to the turn of the century and which have yielded most of the information on which contemporary conceptions of animal learning are based. The adjective *Thorndikian* is appropriate both because of Thorndike's pioneering role in their development and because their operation is predicated on an empirical law of effect. Familiar examples are the problem box and the maze. In each of these situations, traditionally, the experimenter sets out to change behavior by manipulating its consequences, that is, by arranging a contingency between some motivationally significant state of affairs ("reinforcement") and the behavior in question. Thus, pulling a loop in a problem box or turning to the left in a T maze may be encouraged with food or discouraged with shock. Indeed, the motivational significance of any event may be assessed in terms of its effect on the response which produces it in such a situation. An event that facilitates the occurrence of a response upon which it is contingent is called a *reward*; an event that has the opposite effect is called a *punishment*; while an event that produces no measurable change in behavior is motivationally insignificant or neutral. An aversive stimulus is one whose onset is punishing, and in what is called *escape training* the offset of such a stimulus serves as a reward.

UNITARY AND CHOICE SITUATIONS

An important distinction between two main types of Thorndikian situation may be illustrated by a comparison of the problem box and the maze. In both these apparatuses, the animal is afforded numerous possibilities for action, one of which the experimenter chooses to reward. The main difference between them has to do with the treatment of irrelevant responses. In work with the problem box, the experimenter may take some qualitative notice of the variety of fruitless activities which appear, but his interest is centered on the rewarded response and the readiness with which it comes to expression. The basic datum is time. In the maze, by contrast, the unrewarded behavior of the animal is structured more clearly; certain major alternatives to correct response are delineated, and the interest of the experimenter is centered on their decline and disappearance. The basic datum is error. Time may be recorded, but it does not as clearly reflect progress in the choice among alternative courses of action, the aspect of selective learning which the maze is so well suited to display.

The designation *unitary* Thorndikian situation (or T-1 situation) will be used here for the problem box and for any other Thorndikian situation in which but a single course of action is defined and the readiness with which it comes to expression is measured. The designation Thorndikian *choice* situation (or T-2 situation) will be used for the maze and for any other Thorndikian situation in which two or more incompatible courses of action are defined and choice among them is studied. The nature of the responses delineated and the general properties of the environments in which they appear are ignored in this classification. Thus, a problem box which offers a choice of manipulanda is classed with the maze as a T-2 situation, while the runway is classed as a T-1 situation despite its structural resemblance to the maze. The runway may, of course, provide a measure of error, as in the early works of Hicks (1911), who plotted the learning of a culless maze in terms of retracing, while the potentialities of the maze for the study of choice may be ignored, as in the early work of Thorndike (1898), who, measuring only time, used the maze as though it were just another problem box. In such cases, the classification is based on the use to which the apparatus actually is put in a given experiment. For the most part, however, contradictions between potentiality and use are rare. An investigator interested in choice among alternative courses of action is not likely to use a runway, nor, unless he is interested specifically in choice among alternative courses of action, is he likely (today) to use a maze.

Both T-1 and T-2 situations may be "chained." The most common example of a chained T-2 situation is the maze of many choice-points, once very much the mode, but rarely encountered today, perhaps because of the conviction, expressed by Lashley (1918), that the single-unit maze is quite as sensitive as the multiple-unit maze to the effects of significant variables and much less costly in time and effort. (The two kinds of apparatus are not, of course, fully equivalent; certain problems—such as that of correction versus noncorrection, first studied by Lashley—arise only when the number of choice points is reduced to one, while other problems—such as that of serial order—disappear.) Chained T-1 situations never have been widely used. An example may be found in a string of problem boxes, each presenting one manipulandum, with the first giving access to the second, the second to the third, and so on, until the reward finally is attained (Herbert & Arnold, 1947). For certain purposes, conceivably, mixed chains (composed both of T-1 and of T-2 units) might be used.

### GENERALIZED AND DISCRIMINATIVE SITUATIONS

Each of the two types of Thorndikian situation already distinguished —unitary and choice—may occur in discriminative as well as in generalized form. This new distinction, which is orthogonal to the first, will be conveyed by adding the letters g (for generalized) and d (for discriminative) to the symbols for unitary and choice: T-1g, T-1d, T-2g, T-2d. In a discriminative problem, the experimental environment is varied systematically from trial to trial, and with it the consequences of response, the capacity of the animal to discriminate the change being inferred from a corresponding variation in behavior. In a generalized problem, there may be some variation in the experimental environment from trial to trial (intentional or unintentional), and there may be some variation in the consequences of response (as in work on partial reinforcement), but there is (by definition) no correlation between the two kinds of change, and hence there is no objective basis for systematic variation in behavior.

In the simplest T-1d case, a single defined response is rewarded under one set of conditions but not rewarded (or punished) under another set of conditions, and the readiness with which the response comes to expression under the two conditions is compared. For example, response in a single-window jumping apparatus is rewarded when a white card is displayed but punished when the card displayed is black (Solomon, 1943). Performance in a T-1d problem may be expressed in terms of "error," but a temporal criterion is implied. For example, in an early experiment by Thorndike (1898), cats were fed for climbing to the top of their cage in response to the words "I must feed those cats," but not for making the same response to the words "Tomorrow is Tuesday," an error being recorded whenever they climbed up (promptly) to the second phrase or failed (in a reasonable period of time) to climb up in response to the first. Similarly, Grice (1949), working with another T-1d situation, computed the median response time for a series of trials and counted as an error any response to the negative stimulus faster than the median or any response to the positive stimulus slower than the median. A clear distinction should be made between error thus defined and erroneous choice in a T-2d situation.

In a T-2d problem, two or more alternative responses are defined—two in the simplest case. One of the responses is rewarded and the second unrewarded (or punished) under a given set of conditions, while the consequences of the two courses of action are reversed under another set of conditions, and erroneous choices are counted. For example, in a conventional jumping apparatus, a jump to the right window is rewarded when the card in the right window is white and the card in the left window is black, but a jump to the left window is rewarded when the positions of the two cards are interchanged; or, in the same apparatus, response to the right window is rewarded when two white cards are displayed, but response to the left window is rewarded when two black cards are displayed. (Problems of the first kind have been termed "simultaneous" while problems of the second kind have been termed "successive," an adjective applied as well to T-1d problems; considerable confusion has resulted from the failure to distinguish between T-1d and successive T-2d problems.) The so-called "higher order" discriminations—oddity, matching-from-sample, and multiple choice—also may be classified as T-2d problems, although they seem to make demands which go far beyond those of the simpler problems first exemplified. The T-1d and T-2d categories actually are rather coarse ones which themselves invite careful analysis and subdivision.

Like T-2g situations, T-2d situations may be "chained"—as when an animal is required to make a series of choices based on brightness before the reward is attained (Stone, 1928). Meaningful T-1d chains also are possible, although no instance of such a chain is to be found in the literature. For example, response to a manipulandum in one unit gives immediate access to the next unit when the positive stimulus is present; when the negative stimulus is present, access to the next unit is given after a predetermined period of time whether or not the animal responds.

### DISCRETE AND CONTINUOUS SITUATIONS

There has been little clarity on the relation of Skinner's technique to other techniques for the study of learning in animals. It has been asserted by Woodworth (1938), for example, that the Skinner box "bridges the gap" between the problem box and the classical conditioning situation, and a similar view is met again in Spence (1956), who places the Skinner box on a continuum at a point intermediate between the methods of Thorndike and Pavlov; but the notion of continuity is difficult to justify. Skinner (1935, 1937) certainly has succeeded very well in drawing a sharp line between his method and that of Pavlov on the basis of criteria which fail to distinguish his method from that of Thorndike.

Skinnerian situations are Thorndikian situations as the term is defined here. The original Skinner box differs from the older problem box only in that it delivers food to the response compartment (instead of admitting the animal to a separate feeding compartment) when the defined response is made, a feature which eliminates handling of the animal between trials. Equipped with a retractable lever, which is introduced to begin each trial and withdrawn after response, the Skinner box may be used in exactly the same manner as the older problem box; in fact, a retractable manipulandum which delivered food to the responding animal was developed for the monkey by Thorndike himself (1901). Skinner (1932), of course, has preferred to use his apparatus as a "repeating" problem box—his own adjective—inverting the traditional measure of performance, and substituting for time per response on discrete trials number of responses per unit time (rate of response) to a continuously available lever. Either way, a Skinner box containing one lever may be classified as a T-1 situation. A single response is delineated, its consequences are manipulated, and the readiness with which it comes to expression is measured. With two levers and the study of choice, the Skinner box becomes a T-2 situation.

It seems reasonable, nevertheless, to make a formal distinction between Thorndikian situations in which latencies or choices are measured in discrete trials and their Skinnerian counterparts in which rates of response are measured under conditions of continuous opportunity to respond.

Situations of the first kind will be designated as *discrete*, while those of the second kind will be designated as *continuous*, and for symbolic purposes the subscripts d (for discrete) or c (for continuous) will be added to the T for Thorndikian, as, for example, in $T_d$-2g (discrete, choice, generalized) or in $T_c$-1d (continuous, unitary, discriminative). The discrete-continuous distinction reflects the hypothesis that rate of response, despite its close mathematical relation to latency, has a functional significance which is to a certain extent unique, and some interesting evidence for this view comes from comparative studies of the effect of inconsistent reinforcement on resistance to extinction. In the rat, discrete and continuous techniques both give the so-called paradoxical effect (greater resistance to extinction after inconsistent than after consistent reinforcement). In the fish, initial resistance to extinction is greater after consistent reinforcement in the discrete case (Longo & Bitterman, 1960; Wodinsky & Bitterman, 1959, 1960); but some as yet unpublished data show greater resistance to extinction after inconsistent reinforcement in the continuous case. Whether the difference in outcome may be traced to a difference in the functional properties of the two techniques, or whether it is a product of certain parametric differences between the two sets of experiments, remains to be determined. The matter is introduced here only to suggest the possibility that techniques which are functionally equivalent for one species may not be so for others. In this connection it is worth noting, perhaps, that the potentialities of the rate measure seem to be realized fully only when inconsistency of reinforcement is introduced.

#### A GENERAL DEFINITION OF THORNDIKIAN SITUATIONS

In each of the Thorndikian situations considered thus far, a change in behavior is measured which springs from a contingency between some defined response and some motivationally significant state of affairs. Experiments on latent learning suggest, however, that a Thorndikian situation may be characterized without reference either to the actual occurrence of change in behavior or to the motivational significance of the consequences of response. In the T-1 case, an investigator may set out deliberately to minimize the motivational significance of the consequences of response in an effort to minimize the extent of change in behavior. For example, a hungry rat is trained in a runway which leads to an empty end box or to one which contains only water. To arrange a set of end-box conditions which are entirely without motivational significance is not, of course, always very easy, but it can be done (Gonzalez & Diamond, 1960). In the T-2 case, the consequences of alternative responses, whether motivationally significant or not, may be balanced in an effort to forestall the development of a preference for one or the other response. For example, a hungry rat is run in a simple T maze with both end boxes empty, or one empty and the other containing only water, or one containing food and the other both food and water; or a rat that is both hungry and thirsty is run in a T maze with one end box containing food and the other containing water. Such situations are intended merely to provide occasions for learning whose effects are estimated in later tests. The tests always involve a change in the motivational significance of the consequences of response: for example, food is added to a previously empty end box; or the end box is associated with food in direct feedings; or the prevailing condition of deprivation is altered, and with it the relevance of previously encountered incentives. Nevertheless, despite the careful attention which must be paid to motivational significance in evaluating the outcome of exposure to a Thorndikian situation, the situation itself may be defined without reference to motivational significance. What is essential only is *a contingency of some specified event or circumstance on some measurable bit of behavior*—a contingency arranged by an investigator who is interested in studying its effects on the animal.*

### PAVLOVIAN SITUATIONS

Well before Pavlov's experiments on conditioning became widely known, other investigators were led quite independently, by an interest in associative learning, to experiments of essentially the same kind. As far back as the turn of the century, a distinction was made between what was called "trial-and-error" or "selective learning"—the modification of behavior as a function of its consequences—and what was called "association of stimuli" or "substitution"—the acquisition by one stimulus of some of the behavioral properties of a second stimulus as a function of the pairing of the two stimuli. Primarily concerned though he was with selective learning, Thorndike (1898) himself made use of paired stimulation; when a verbal statement such as "I must feed those cats" was followed regularly by the presentation of food, he reported, the words alone would bring the animals to the feeding place. It seems fitting none-

* No treatment of Thorndikian techniques would be complete without some mention of a set of situations closely related to the problem box (calling for string-pulling, rake-wielding, box-stacking, and the like) which figured prominently in the work of certain of Thorndike's critics, beginning with Hobhouse (1901), who did not think that Thorndike's apparatus provided a representative picture of animal intelligence. Designed to be fully "surveyable" (to conceal nothing from the animal) and, although simple in principle, to render "chance" solutions unlikely, these (Hobhousian) situations present Thorndikian contingencies of a rather loose sort and *may* be used, like Thorndike's problem boxes, to study the way in which the experience of such contingencies affect subsequent behavior. Their principal use, however, has been in inquiries into the ability of animals to discover appropriate modes of behavior in advance of reinforcement—that is, in quests for evidence of "productive" or "inferential" as contrasted with "reproductive" or learned solutions.

theless—in view of the scope of Pavlov's (1927) contribution—that the method should bear his name.

In the traditional Pavlovian experiment, as in the traditional Thorndikian experiment, the behavior of the animal is altered by the introduction of some motivationally significant stimulus such as food or shock ("reinforcement"), but there are important differences. In a Thorndikian experiment, reinforcement is contingent on response; doing one thing leads to food or to shock, doing another does not. In a Pavlovian experiment, reinforcement is scheduled without regard to response; the experimenter does not set out to mold behavior in some predetermined fashion, but only to study the way in which the functional properties of one stimulus are altered by virtue of its contiguity with another. Because their introduction is not contingent on the animal's behavior, Pavlovian reinforcements cannot be treated as rewards or punishments in any meaningful manner, nor can rewards and punishments be distinguished in a Pavlovian experiment. Another difference between the two techniques is worth noting. In a Thorndikian experiment, the choice of the behavior which is to serve as the index of learning is independent of the choice of reinforcement; any of a large variety of responses which the animal is likely to make may be encouraged with food or discouraged with shock. In a Pavlovian experiment, the choice of reinforcement restricts the choice of a behavioral indicator; while the conditioned and unconditioned responses are not always (as Pavlov thought) identical, the investigator must be guided in his search for evidence of learning by the functional properties of the reinforcing stimulus. Sharp as the distinction may be between the traditional Thorndikian and Pavlovian procedures, it has been ignored very often by theorists preoccupied with the task of deriving all of the data of learning from the operation of a single process. Pavlov himself claimed, of course, that all instances of learning could be analyzed as instances of conditioning, although Thorndike, committed as he was to the generality of the law of effect, never was satisfied that Pavlov's procedure could be cast in the same mold as his own.

Coordinate with the unitary Thorndikian (or T-1) situation is the unitary Pavlovian (or P-1) situation, in which the tendency for a CS to produce some defined effect is measured in terms of latency or magnitude. The defined effect may be a response which is reflexly elicited by the US, as in the salivary conditioning experiment, or something quite different, as when the rate of fixed-interval responding in a Skinnerian situation is depressed by shock and by a stimulus paired with shock (Estes & Skinner, 1941). A P-1 situation may be generalized (P-1g) or discriminative (P-1d); in the discriminative case, the CS is varied systematically from trial to trial and with it the likelihood that the US will be presented (as, for example, when a bright light always is followed by food but a dim light never is). With two unconditioned stimuli, each eliciting a different response, it is possible to set up a P-2 situation, the Pavlovian analogue of the Thorndikian choice situation. (A T-2 situation may be constituted with but a single reinforcer, which is another interesting difference between Pavlovian and Thorndikian techniques.) The discriminative (P- 2d) case is perhaps the easier to conceive than the generalized (P-2g). For example, one CS is paired with acid introduced into the mouth of a dog, while another CS is paired with meat-powder (Pavlov, 1927). The P-2g case must involve some inconsistency of reinforcement (which is, of course, not true of T-2g). For example, a CS is paired with shock to the right forelimb on a random 75% of trials and with shock to the left forelimb on the remaining 25% of trials. This is the Pavlovian analogue of a kind of T-2 situation in which there has been much interest of late. For example, a right turn at the choice point of a maze leads to food on a random 75% of trials while a left turn leads to food on the remaining 25% of trials (Brunswik, 1939).

The discrete-continuous dichotomy, which was developed in the analysis of Thorndikian procedures, seems to have no Pavlovian parallel; Pavlovian training is an affair of discrete trials. Nor does the notion of "chaining" have any application to Pavlovian procedures.

A Pavlovian situation, like a Thorndikian situation, may serve merely as an occasion for learning whose effects are measured in subsequent tests. One such case, well known to Pavlov, is that in which the presentation of CS and US is strictly simultaneous; only when the training procedure is altered can the effects of pairing be assessed. A second is that of "sensory preconditioning"—conceived originally by Thorndike (1898) himself as a check on the existence of "representations"—which is analogous to the Thorndikian experiment with consequences of response which are lacking in motivational significance; neutral stimuli are paired, then one is given some behavioral property, and the effects of the pairing are estimated from response to the other. A third case is that in which attention is centered on the acquisition, not of response-eliciting properties, but of rewarding properties (Williams, 1929); for example, an animal is fed repeatedly in a distinctive box (that is, box and food are paired), after which access to the empty box is made contingent upon response in a Thorndikian situation. In one variety of experiment which has considerable theoretical importance, the order of these experiences is reversed; the contingency of access to the empty box upon some response is displayed, after which the animal is fed in the box, and the effect on response is measured (Gonzalez & Diamond, 1960). In general, then, a Pavlovian situation may be defined without reference either to the occurrence in that situation of any particular kind of behavioral change, or to the functional properties of the stimuli which are paired. What is essential only is *a sequence or conjunction of stimuli whose contiguity is independent of the animal's response.*

## AVOIDANCE SITUATIONS

The only learning situations which cannot be classified unequivocally as Pavlovian or Thorndikian are those which involve the avoidance of aversive stimulation. In them, Pavlovian and Thorndikian features are closely intertwined. On the one hand, a neutral stimulus is paired with an aversive stimulus, thereby acquiring certain arousing properties. The pairing is not, on the other hand, entirely independent of the animal's behavior—the aversive stimulus is introduced only if the CS fails to elicit some defined response, whose likelihood of occurrence (low at the outset) the pairing serves to increase. This contingency of reinforcement on response is not displayed on the very first trial, as it is in a pure Thorndikian situation. In avoidance training, the contingency is a negative one, which (since the mere possibility of avoidance cannot influence the animal) does not become manifest until the Pavlovian procedure has taken effect.

There is another Thorndikian contingency which operates in some (though not in all) avoidance situations, this one making itself felt from the very first trial: termination of the aversive stimulus may be contingent on some defined response, often—but not always—the same response as that which avoids the aversive stimulus. In flexion conditioning, when shock to the limb is administered through a grid on which the limb of the animal rests, and when the scheduled duration of shock is substantial, flexion both escapes and avoids shock. In the shuttle box, too, the conditions of training may be such that changing compartments both escapes and avoids shock, although, as Warner (1932) noted early, the response which escapes shock may be different from that which avoids it (for example, leaping over a hurdle as compared with crawling under). It is possible, of course, to set up an avoidance situation in which there is no escape at all. In flexion conditioning, shock may be administered through a bracelet attached to the limb, and a control circuit so arranged that the CR will forestall the shock but the UR will not alter its scheduled duration. In the shuttle box, the shock may be very brief, terminating quite independently of any response the animal may make to it (Hunter, 1935). Even without escape, however, there remains the contingency of aversive stimulation on failure of response to the CS, an essential feature of avoidance training which distinguishes it from Pavlovian training, while the paired stimulation which is responsible for the emergence of response to the CS distinguishes it from Thorndikian training. Avoidance training seems to require a major category of its own.

In its most common use, the shuttle box may be classified as an $A_d$-1g situation (A for avoidance); a single course of action is defined, and its latency is measured in discrete trials without systematic variation in sensory conditions. The corresponding discriminative ($A_d$-1d) situation also may be generated in the shuttlebox; for example, a bright light is followed by shock unless the defined response is made, but a dim light never is followed by shock. In such a situation, it may be noted, discrimination can progress only as the animal fails to respond to the dim light, since the consequences of response to the two lights are identical. (In a T-1d situation, by contrast, the consequences of response to the stimuli to be discriminated are different, and discrimination therefore is facilitated by response to the negative stimulus; in a P-1d situation, discrimination may progress quite independently of response.)

Choice among alternative courses of action also may be studied in avoidance situations. Suppose, for example, that shock from a grid in the floor of a T maze is scheduled $x$ seconds after an animal is placed in the starting box. In the generalized ($A_d$-2g) case, shock is avoided by prompt entrance into the end box on the right, but not by entrance into the end box on the left. In the discriminative ($A_d$-2d) case, a turn to the right avoids shock when the stem of the maze is black, while a turn to the left avoids shock when the stem is white. Two unconditioned stimuli are not required to generate an A-2 situation as they are to generate a P-2 situation, but two unconditioned stimuli may be used. For example, one signal is followed by avoidable shock to the right limb, while a second is followed by avoidable shock to the left limb (James, 1947).

The discrete-continuous dichotomy developed in the analysis of Thorndikian situations is applicable also to avoidance training. An $A_c$-1g situation may be constituted in a modified Skinner box or a shuttle box. In a design developed by Sidman (1953), no exteroceptive warning signal is used, but shock is scheduled every $x$ seconds by a clock which the defined response resets. (The lack of an exteroceptive signal does not, of course, subvert the definition of avoidance training as originating in a quasi-Pavlovian contiguity of stimuli; as Pavlov himself showed, internal processes correlated with the passage of time since the occurrence of a specified event may be cast in the role of CS.) In the corresponding discriminative ($A_c$-1d) case, the clock which schedules shock runs only under one of two sensory conditions. Avoidance situations of the continuous type which do involve exteroceptive signaling also are feasible. In the $A_c$-1g case, for example, shock from a grid in the floor of a Skinner box is scheduled $x$ seconds after the onset of a light and avoided by response on a variable-ratio schedule. $A_c$-2 situations, both generalized and discriminative, may be generated when alternative courses of action are defined.

Like Thorndikian situations, avoidance situations may be chained. Just as an animal may learn to run a simple T maze under threat of shock, so it may learn to run a multiple T maze. An example of chaining in an avoidance situation of the continuous type is the following: with the onset of the CS, responsive to one manipulandum is followed, on a variable-ratio schedule, by access to a second manipulandum, response to which, again on a variable-ratio schedule, terminates the CS and avoids shock.

Although the term implies threat of an aversive condition which the animal learns to forestall, avoidance training, like Thorndikian and Pavlovian training, may be characterized without reference to the nature of the stimuli employed or to the occurrence of behavioral change. It would be possible, for example, to train an animal with some neutral stimulus rather than shock in a shuttle box designed to produce a substantial frequency of spontaneous crossing, and then to test for learning after the neutral stimulus has been paired with shock. Irrespective of outcome, the conception of such an experiment is sufficient to delineate what is here regarded as the essential feature of avoidance training: *a sequence of stimuli is scheduled with the occurrence of the second contingent upon the failure of the animal to make some specified response to the first.*

## TERMINOLOGY

While there need be no detailed comparison of the classification here proposed with earlier ones, it may be worth while, in the interest of preserving whatever compatible usages may exist, to consider how well some of the broader methodological designations which now are current will serve the needs of the new classification. Since current terminology derives from earlier classifications, the major differences in emphasis must become quite apparent in the process.

The term "conditioning" usually is used for the kind of training here called Pavlovian, but that term also is used rather widely to designate techniques which are not here classified as Pavlovian, and often as a synonym for "learning" itself. The term "classical conditioning" is closer to what is here intended by Pavlovian, although in some contexts it has a narrower meaning (suggesting a harnessed animal) and in other contexts a broader one (encompassing avoidance). Avoidance remains a useful term, but "instrumental conditioning" is too ambiguous, since it has been applied indiscriminately both to avoidance training and to pure Thorndikian training. The term "operant conditioning" is even more ambiguous; it has a narrow (Skinnerian) sense in which it is tied to a questionable distinction between "elicited" and "emitted" behavior, as well as a more general sense in which it is equivalent to instrumental conditioning. The term "selective learning" has a pure Thorndikian connotation, but it seems to designate a process of learning rather than a method of studying it.

In general, there is little to salvage in the current terminology. Specific situational designations, such as maze, problem box, and runway, continue to be useful, but the broader classificatory terms are unsuitable because they are geared to methodological dichotomy rather than to trichotomy. Even if dichotomy should in time give way to trichotomy, of course, it is likely that many of the older terms will continue to be used with altered meanings and with considerable consequent confusion. The terms for the subcategories here defined—unitary and choice situations, generalized and discriminative situations, discrete and continuous situations—fortunately do not compete with established usages and therefore create less opportunity for confusion, although it is possible that a clearer notation might be found. Reflection will show, however, that complexity of notation is to a certain extent an inevitable consequence of the amount of information to be conveyed.

It is natural that a new classification should require a new terminology, although a change in classification does not, of course, necessarily imply an advance in conception. Whether the classification here proposed represents an advance in thinking about the interrelations among learning situations cannot now be told. Classification is more, ultimately, than a matter of taste, but there is little else on which to depend at the present time. It is to be hoped that a renewed concern with problems of classification will stimulate further research on methodological interrelations.

## REFERENCES

BITTERMAN, M. E. (1960) Toward a comparative psychology of learning. *Amer. Psychologist*, 15, 704-712.

BRUNSWICK, E. (1939) Probability as a determiner of rat behavior. *J. exp. Psychol.*, 25, 175-197.

ESTES, W. K. and SKINNER, B. F. (1941) Some quantitative properties of anxiety. *J. exp. Psychol.*, 29, 390-400.

GONZALEZ, R. C. and DIAMOND, L. (1960) A test of Spence's theory of incentive motivation. *Amer. J. Psychol.*, 73, 396-403.

GRICE, G. R. (1949) Visual discrimination learning with simultaneous and successive presentation of stimuli. *J. comp. physiol. Psychol.*, 42, 365-373.

HERBERT, M. J. and ARNOLD, W. J. (1947) A reaction chaining apparatus. *J. comp. physiol. Psychol.*, 40, 227-229.

HICKS, V. C. (1911) The relative values of different curves of learning. *J. anim. Behav.*, 1, 138-156.

HILGARD, E. R. and MARQUIS, D. G. (1940) *Conditioning and learning.* New York: Appleton-Century.

HOBHOUSE, L. T. (1901) *Mind in evolution.* London: Macmillan.

HUNTER, W. S. (1935) Conditioning and extinction in the rat. *Brit. J. Psychol.*, 26, 135-148.

JAMES, W. T. (1947) The use of work in developing a differential conditioned reaction of antagonistic reflex systems. *J. comp. physiol. Psychol.*, 40, 177-182.

LASHLEY, K. S. (1918) A simple maze: With data on the relation of the distribution of practice to the rate of learning. *Psychobiology*, 1, 353-367.

LONGO, N. and BITTERMAN, M. E. (1960) The effect of partial reinforcement with spaced practice on resistance to extinction in the fish. *J. comp. physiol. Psychol.*, 53, 169-172.

PAVLOV, I. P. (1927) *Conditioned reflexes: An investigation of the physiological activity of the cerebral cortex.* London: Oxford Univer. Press.

SIDMAN, M. (1953) Avoidance conditioning with brief shock and no exteroceptive warning signal. *Science*, *118*, 157-158.

SKINNER, B. F. (1932) On the rate of formation of a conditioned reflex. *J. gen. Psychol.*, *7*, 274-285.

SKINNER, B. F. (1935) Two types of conditioned reflex and a pseudo type. *J. gen. Psychol.*, *12*, 66-76.

SKINNER, B. F. (1937) Two types of conditioned reflex: A reply to Konorski and Miller. *J. gen. Psychol.*, *16*, 272-282.

SOLOMON, R. L. (1943) Latency of response as a measure of learning in a "single-door" discrimination. *Amer. J. Psychol.*, *56*, 422-432.

SPENCE, K. W. (1956) *Behavior theory and conditioning.* New Haven: Yale Univer. Press.

STONE, C. P. (1928) A multiple discrimination box and its use in studying the learning ability of rats: I. Reliability of scores. *J. genet. Psychol.*, *35*, 557-573.

THORNDIKE, E. L. (1898) Animal intelligence: An experimental study of the associative processes in animals. *Psychol. Rev. monogr. Suppl.*, *2*(4, Whole No. 8).

THORNDIKE, E. L. (1901) The mental life of monkeys. *Psychol. Rev. monogr. Suppl.*, *3*(5, Whole No. 15).

WARNER, L. H. (1932) The association span of the white rat. *J. gen. Psychol.*, *41*, 57-89.

WILLIAMS, K. A. (1929) The reward value of a conditioned stimulus. *U. Calif. Publ. Psychol.*, *4*, 31-55.

WODINSKY, J. and BITTERMAN, M. E. (1959) Partial reinforcement in the fish. *Amer. J. Psychol.*, *72*, 184-199.

WODINSKY, J. and BITTERMAN, M. E. (1960) Resistance to extinction in the fish after extensive training with partial reinforcement. *Amer. J. Psychol.*, *73*, 429-434.

WOODWORTH, R. S. (1938) *Experimental psychology.* New York: Henry Holt.

YOUTZ, R. E. P. (1938) The change with time of a Thorndikian response in the rat. *J. exp. Psychol.*, *23*, 128-140. (a)

YOUTZ, R. E. P. (1938) Reinforcement, extinction, and spontaneous recovery in a non-Pavlovian reaction. *J. exp. Psychol.*, *22*, 305-318. (b)

YOUTZ, R. E. P. (1939) The weakening of one Thorndikian response following the extinction of another. *J. exp. Psychol.*, *24*, 294-304.

## 3. The Representativeness of Rote Verbal Learning

### B. J. Underwood

*Although Underwood discusses varying approaches which may be taken to provide a taxonomy of human learning, his points have cogency for the study of animal learning as well. In addition, he has provided a description of the kinds of verbal learning situations which are in current experimental use.*

A poll taken among behavioral scientists would probably show mild firmness of belief that there is some continuity in the laws of behavior across all phyla in the animal kingdom. Were we to inquire about a family within a phylum a somewhat firmer belief in the continuity would be manifest. If we go to a given genus the belief becomes still more firm, and within the species, *Homo sapiens*, it would be firm indeed. If we follow this increasingly restrictive path one step further we arrive at one of the purposes of this conference, namely, to analyze, and eventually to make explicit how commonality of behavior is exhibited when we study the *learning* of the human organism in different situations. Assuming a positive correlation between firmness of belief and fact, it would seem that the conclusion is inescapable that there are laws of human learning which at once supersede but include the learning exhibited in any particular situation. These laws, it would seem, *must* be present and even a cursory analysis would show what they are. Chapter headings, such as Conditioning, Rote Learning, Motor Learning, and so on, we would say, are just that and no more; they should not be taken to indicate that we are dealing with human learnings. But, on second thought, perhaps the commonality is not as apparent as it appears that it should be. Perhaps if it were apparent this conference would not be required. Still, some one has to catalogue the commonality; some one has to point out the basic laws, the common dimensions, the common phenomena, or the identities of the learnings appearing under different chapter headings. Surely a careful consideration will divulge the continuity that is said to exist.

The assumption of continuity does not, of course, demand that we find evidence for complete or perfect continuity wherever we look. The manifestation of the laws may be different in different situations; certain research paradigms may not allow certain laws to be operative at all; complex interactions may mask the effects of basic laws. And that may be the

In Melton, A. W. (Ed.) *Categories of human learning*, pp. 47-56. Reprinted with permission of the author and Academic Press, New York.

situation we face. The inevitable pyramiding of research has heightened the fragmentation in the study of human learning, and it may not be easy to bring together the fundamental factors involved in all forms of human learning and thus bring concordance between belief and fact.

## APPROACHES TO A TAXONOMY OF HUMAN LEARNING

### SOME POSSIBLE APPROACHES

There are many approaches which might be used to express the relationships among research findings for all forms of human learning. Undoubtedly the most elegant way would be in terms of theory. A general theory of human learning in which the particular findings in each area are shown to be deductions from the master set of statements and relationships is clearly an ideal solution. No such system is available. Since the scientist is never content with particulars we do have many, many attempts to apply theoretical notions across areas of limited kinds of phenomena. All of the contemporary models (the favored term today) are presumed to have greater generality than the particular situation in which they have been employed, and it is quite possible that some of these will eventually provide the basis for a general theory of human learning.

Another way of attempting to express the continuity for all human learning is in terms of phenomena produced by comparable operations. Thus, can the operations defining extinction in eyelid conditioning be duplicated in verbal learning, in motor learning, in concept formation, and so on, and, if so, do the same phenomena result from these operations? This approach simply asks whether manipulable variables affect learning in the same way, regardless of the task involved. Systematic work of this nature across many variables would be of inestimable value in constructing a general theory of human learning. In fact, this approach has been rather widely used, although not in any systematic sense and not necessarily with the intent of unifying areas. The approach has certain limitations and certain elements of danger. The limitations come from the fact that there are some tasks which are simply not of such a nature that certain variables can be introduced. For example, it would seem difficult to manipulate meaningfulness on a pursuit rotor in the same sense that this variable is manipulated in verbal learning. Or, what operations in problem solving are comparable to variations in intensity of the conditioned stimulus in classical conditioning? Of course we have to say that if a given variable in one situation has no possible counterpart in another then it simply is not a relevant variable in the latter. However, if this asymmetry is widespread among tasks, any systematic program to manipulate variables across tasks becomes somewhat less than systematic.

The dangers of the method are two in number. We have no criteria for clearly specifying when operations are comparable when tasks differ. Indeed, some might say that if the tasks differ the operations cannot be comparable. The complete entertainment of such counsel would remove all hope of assessing empirically the continuity of human learning across tasks, and we should not subscribe to it. But even with less rigid criteria of saying when operations are and are not comparable, there is still an issue of concern. For example, in classical conditioning there is a body of literature on the effects of varying percentage of reinforcement, i.e., the proportion of the trials on which the unconditioned stimulus is presented. Some studies (e.g., Schulz & Runquist, 1960) have been done with paired-associate learning in which the proportion of trials on which the correct response was shown was varied. The results differ somewhat from those obtained with classical conditioning. Is this because the operations are not comparable, because the effects of the variable are different in the two situations, because measuring units are not coordinate, because other factors modify the effect, or what? Failure to obtain a comparable behavioral effect for a given variable for different tasks raises questions that are very difficult to handle when the interest is in generalizing across tasks.

A second danger may be present when equivalent results for a given variable are obtained for two or more different tasks. A compelling interpretation of such a result is that the same processes are involved in producing the effect. Thus, if distributed practice facilitates acquisition on a pursuit rotor and also on a serial list of verbal units, a ready inference is that the same fundamental process (or processes) are involved. This may or may not be true. Usually, however, these doubts can be resolved by further research in which further implications of the assumed identity of processes can be tested. Indeed, in spite of the dangers and limitations of this method, it does not seem unreasonable to suggest that the use of this approach is necessary if unification of the disparate areas of research in human learning is to be achieved.

A further way of evaluating commonality of learning in different situations is by what may be called transition experiments. An illustration would be the work of Richardson (1958). A descriptive difference between concept formation and rote verbal learning can be stated in terms of the number of identical responses to be associated with similar stimuli. Richardson translated this descriptive difference into graded operations so that continuity (or lack of it) between concept formation and rote learning could be studied directly. Probably far too little use has been made of transition experiments although there is admittedly much difficulty in working these out for certain areas. Still, the ingenious researcher may find extraordinary repayment in devising transition experiments.

At quite a different level of discourse is the procedure whereby tasks, and the behavior required of the Ss in the tasks, are analyzed along descriptive dimensions with the similarities and the differences being catalogued. Thus problem solving and verbal learning are said to differ in terms of the amount of discovery involved in determining an appropriate response, whereas free operant learning and problem solving both involve considerable discovery. There are many such descriptive dimensions which might be used (Melton, 1941). At the very minimum, such an approach has clear heuristic value in organizing the tasks used to study human learning. But whether or not the descriptive dimensions have psychological or behavioral relevance is a matter for research, and while occasional attempts have been made to determine this relevance within a given area (e.g., Riley, 1952), no concerted programs have been undertaken.

### THE PRESENT APPROACH

The search for continuity by whatever method (and there are undoubtedly others than those mentioned) may, in the writer's opinion, be superficial and perhaps even misleading until the level of analysis in a given area of study reaches a certain stage of sophistication. This statement is made from a background of research in rote verbal learning and requires explanation. The major purpose of the present paper is to look at the facts and theories of rote verbal learning with an eye toward those that reach beyond the particular situation from which they are derived. In a manner of speaking, the purpose of the paper is to view all of human learning through the window of a memory drum. To do this in any but a superficial way one cannot look at gross phenomena. To point out that retroactive inhibition occurs in motor learning, in concept learning, and in verbal learning would seem to be of little value. We need to know the comparability of the mechanisms involved in producing the retroactive inhibition for the various tasks; we need to isolate the subphenomena to see if the total effects are compounded in the same way. How far these analyses must proceed before comparabilities or continuities can be said with confidence to exist is debatable. However, one of the points to be made in the subsequent discussion is that the research in verbal learning, one of the oldest areas of research in human learning, has, in the last few years, reached a level of sophistication where we may be in a position to make rather fundamental contact with at least some other areas of human learning.

The terms "gross phenomena" and "subphenomena" have been used above. Before proceeding, it will be wise to give an illustration of how these terms are to be used. Consider a transfer situation of the A-B, C-B type (stimuli in two lists different, responses identical). An experimental group learns the two lists, a control group learns only the second. The gross phenomenon in this situation is the amount and direction of transfer which occurs in learning C-B, as determined by the difference in performance of the two groups. At the present time we know that this gross effect is constituted of a number of independently demonstrable subphenomena.

1. A positive effect produced by transfer of response learning as such. Having learned the responses in A-B, this learning will transfer and the amount of transfer will in turn depend upon certain variables, e.g., meaningfulness.

2. Transfer of response differentiation may occur in certain situations. If the responses have interfering similarity relationships, differentiation must be established in order to learn the first list and this differentiation should transfer positively for the experimental group.

3. Warm up, developed in learning the first list for the experimental group should produce a positive effect in learning the second list.

4. Learning-to-learn should produce a positive effect.

5. Backward associations should produce a negative effect.

6. Others as yet unspecified.

While we can identify these factors as being involved in the gross effect we cannot specify at the present time how they interact or go together to produce the over-all effect. Steps in this direction are clearly in order. However, even these subphenomena may be further reducible into further subphenomena. Learning-to-learn must consist of a number of components which, with appropriate research, could be broken down, whereas today it stands largely as an irritating factor to be always considered in the design of experiments. So, in fact, when a statement is made (as was made earlier), that the search for relationships among learning demonstrated on different tasks requires a certain level of analytical sophistication in the different areas to expect success, it is difficult to specify just what that level is. That we are said to have reached this level for certain phenomena in verbal learning is an expression of confidence undisciplined by any firm criteria.

## CHARACTERIZATION OF ROTE VERBAL LEARNING

Rote Learning! Let us imagine some free associations which these two words might elicit from people in psychological and educational circles, restricting the responses to those which meet standards of good taste. It is likely that the following would be among the most frequent responses: "dull," "Ebbinghaus," "narrow," "verbal learning," "sterile," "nonsense syllable," "memory drum," "serial list," and so on. Two notions can be culled from such associations. First is the notion that rote learning is closely associated with verbal learning, an association which is quite appropriate. The second notion is that rote learning, identified as the classical area of rote verbal learning, is felt to be dull, narrow, sterile, and, in a manner of speaking, deals with a form of learning that is almost intellectually demeaning. These assumed reactions to rote verbal learning may paint a somewhat exaggerated picture of an attitude toward the area, but most would probably agree that the core of such an attitude does exist. If a number of research areas in human learning were put into the cruel and grinding dimensions of the semantic differential it seems clear that rote verbal learning would come out with a "bad" profile, perhaps being pressed only by classical conditioning.

Obviously, from the writer's point of view, these attitudes are ill begot. But, perhaps these attitudes are, like so many other attitudes, representative of a cultural lag. Perhaps if the contemporary work in verbal learning were understood by all some change in attitude might occur. Perhaps it is not quite justifiable to view the nonsense syllable as the pedant's playmate. In any event, the position taken here is that the work in verbal learning—rote verbal learning—may stand squarely in the center of all human learning. Research in verbal learning is shooting out phenomena and theories which are touching, sometimes in a very fundamental way, all areas of human learning from simple conditioning to the study of the thought processes. The central nature of verbal learning will not be argued nor pressed, but there is implicit hope that its centrality may emerge obliquely but clearly from the presentation to be made.

The image of a subject in a verbal-learning experiment as being a *tabula rasa* upon which the investigator simply chisels associations, and quite against the S's wishes, is archaic. The S is far from passive and the tablet has already impressed upon it an immense network of verbal habits. Some of these habits are simple and direct and some are conceptual in their inclusiveness, i.e., they are second-order habits. A more accurate description of the verbal-learning experiment is one in which the S actively "calls upon" all the repertoire of habits and skills to outwit the investigator. Since the S is all too frequently successful in this endeavor, it is quite understandable why some investigators in the field of verbal learning do indeed wish the S were a passive and clean slate upon which the associations could be inscribed in a simple fashion. That this is not the case has several important implications, some of which will be mentioned here.

One implication is that in verbal-learning experiments we may not be dealing with "raw" learning; some might say that we never study the formation of associations uninfluenced by associations which the S already possesses. Certainly we would approach a verbal vacuum more closely if we spent more of our time studying the verbal learning of young children and less of our time on the college sophomore. But even the young child has verbal associations which will influence the learning of new ones, and investigations of verbal learning with the preverbal child poses mechanical as well as philosophical problems.

Another implication of the fact that we are dealing with organisms with an already established network of habits is that our theories of verbal learning must inevitably explain phenomena which are, in a manner of speaking, built on top of this network.

Theories aside, realization of the fact that we deal with nonpassive Ss with a vast set of habits may influence the approach we take in experimental studies of verbal learning. The preformed habits may themselves be the object of study with further attempts directed toward trying to understand how these preformed habits influence the verbal-learning phenomena under study at the moment. The fact that in rote verbal learning we must deal in some fashion with preformed habits, and the fact that these habits are of the nature that may influence learning in many other areas lends some credence to the notion that verbal learning is a transition area between simple learning and "higher" forms of learning. However this may be, let us look at some of the tasks which have been used to provide the empirical base in the area.

## TASKS

One of the defining characteristics of verbal learning is, obviously, that verbal units must in some way be presented as a part of the learning task. When the task does in fact consist of verbal units the identification is made without much ambiguity if the verbal units are symbols of the learner's language. But ambiguity may exist in certain situations. Thus, if geometrical forms are used as stimulus terms, each paired with a switch that must be closed when the stimulus term is presented, should this task be called a verbal task? The fact that many Ss will apply a verbal label to geometrical forms, and they may even do so for the so-called nonverbal response, i.e., the S may learn that this stimulus goes with the "sixth" switch in the series. Clearly, some of the studies emanating from the laboratories at Ohio State University (e.g., Alluisi & Muller, 1958), and often spoken of as perceptual-motor learning studies, may represent transition experiments between "pure" verbal learning and "pure" perceptual-motor learning. Therefore, to say that verbal learning deals with acquisition of verbal units can at best be used only as an operational distinction and, if taken too seriously, may actually hinder the development of our understanding of learning processes which might be quite the same for perceptual-motor tasks as for verbal tasks.

A second specification of a verbal-learning task is that multiple associations are required of the S. This in turn means that multiple verbal units are commonly used in the task (lists). In very recent years studies have been performed (e.g., Peterson & Peterson, 1959) in which a single verbal unit has been presented and systematic relationships determined for short-term memory. Thus, a single three-letter unit is presented to the S for a brief period of time and its recall requested at some later point in time. The most elementary unit of printed verbal material is the letter. The basic spoken or oral unit is less clear; perhaps the phoneme might be considered the unit when oral responses are required. In any event, if the letter is the basic printed verbal unit, then clearly even a single three-letter unit constitutes a three-unit list. With a three-unit list at least two associations must be formed or utilized. But this analysis may also mask the actual learning process involved since it is quite possible that for a three-letter unit the coding process (to be discussed later) makes a single unit of the three letters.

With the above two restrictions in mind, we may look at some of the tasks which are used in verbal-learning studies.

*Free learning.* In pure form this task involves presentation of a series of units to Ss under instructions to learn the units in any order. On successive trials the presentation order is varied from trial to trial. A somewhat more restricted procedure would involve a constant order of presentation on each trial but still allow the S to recall the units in any order. When in addition, however, a constant order of presentation is used and the same constant order required of the S in learning, a different task, namely, serial learning, is identified.

To those investigators who like to make specific S—R analyses of learning situations the free-learning method presents some difficulty. The difficulty is in identifying a particular stimulus for the recall of a particular unit. At the present time about all that can be said is that the stimulus for the recall of the items is the general experimental context. With certain kinds of lists it may be inferred that the recall of one item serves as the stimulus for the recall of another since the items may be known to be strongly associated. But of course the ambiguity still remains as to the stimulus for the recall of the first item. It should be clear that inability to identify a specific stimulus for each item does not prevent the determination of lawful relationships for free learning. Indeed, as will be seen later, the free-learning method has great value in studying certain subphenomena involved in the over-all learning process.

*Serial learning.* In this task the units are presented to the S in a constant order on each study trial and he is required to learn them in the order presented. In its pure form the units are discrete and the fixed order of presentation is essentially determined on a random basis. This method, dating back to Ebbinghaus, has been used in countless studies. Serial learning produces the bowed serial-position curve, a phenomenon which has tantalized theoreticians for many years. Again, investigators who like to make precise S—R analyses have, in recent years, been shying away from this method since ambiguity exists in identifying a specific stimulus for a specific response. It has probably been implicitly assumed by many that the stimulus for a response in serial learning is the immediately preceding term. However, recent considerations (Underwood, 1963) suggest that this assumption cannot be maintained with any degree of confidence. The facts seem to indicate that we cannot specify just what the stimulus is for a given response in serial learning.

Progress in a science may be identified in terms of the capacity of the investigator to break down gross phenomena into subphenomena. Regardless of the theoretical orientation involved, in the study of learning this implies in part stimulus control and stimulus analysis. It therefore seems likely that the frequency of use of serial learning as a "standard" vehicle for studying verbal learning will further diminish unless a more precise analysis of stimulus and response functions in this task is accomplished soon. It is interesting to speculate on the cause for the drop out of tasks in other areas of human learning, tasks which once were heavily used. For example, the great flood of studies using the pursuit rotor which occurred in the postwar years has essentially dried up. One possible reason for this is that the pursuit rotor is a very difficult task to break down into subcomponents for which stimulus-response functions can be specified. Investigators tend to drop a task when it will not give them the analytical power characteristic of the field as a whole.

*Serial learning with syntactical ordering of units.* In this task words vary in form class (nouns, verbs, and so on) and the ordering of the words is such as to conform to the rules of grammar. The S is required to learn the words in the order presented. The experimental unit for such a task may be a sentence and the acquisition of several such units (perhaps forming a paragraph) may constitute the task. Of course, the scoring of learning may occur at several levels, such as number of words, number of idea units, and so on. Although the items presented in this task must be words in order to realize the full effect of syntax, similar effects can be produced with nonsense words. Thus, Epstein (1961), by changing endings on various nonsense words to suggest units of various form classes in appropriate ordering, was able to show that learning was positively influenced.

It is perhaps needless to say that this learning task appears to involve properties which none of those traditionally associated with rote verbal learning have. Furthermore, the task has not been used in many studies of learning. Yet it seems likely that in the future years this task will provide an important point of contact between verbal learning, psycholinguistics, and other disciplines interested in the study of language behavior.

*Verbal discrimination.* In verbal-discrimination learning the S is presented a series of *pairs* of units. The investigator arbitrarily designates one member of each pair as the correct member, this designation being random with regard to position or any other characteristic of a conceptual nature which might obtain across pairs. Initially the S guesses one or the other units of a pair and is told in some manner whether his guess was right or wrong. The order of the pairs in "pure" verbal-discrimination learning varies from trial to trial. If the order remains constant a multiple-unit two-choice maze is simulated.

Verbal-discrimination learning emphasizes recognition learning rather than recall learning. In verbal-discrimination learning the subject does not have to learn the responses per se as in other forms of verbal learning, but clearly a discrimination of some kind must be developed between the units. However, as a task it provides a fairly close approximation to the learning required in distinguishing among stimuli of a paired-associate list and therefore should prove of considerable value in future attempts to break down stimulus functions. The fact is, however, that verbal-discrimination learning is not frequently used as a method for studying verbal learning.

*Paired associates.* Pairs of verbal units are presented to the S just as in a verbal-discrimination task. Here, however, the left-hand member of the pair is designated the stimulus term, the right-hand member the response term. The S's task is to learn to be able to recall the response term when the stimulus term is presented alone. The pairs are commonly presented in different orders on each trial. This task is by far the favorite of contemporary investigators since the stimulus for a given response can be fairly precisely specified. However, even this specification is not without ambiguity as later discussion will point out.

The above five tasks may be taken as modal tasks for the study of verbal learning. None of the procedures is fixed or immutable, nor should they be. Thus, there may be more than two choices in a verbal-discrimination task; the paired-associate list might be presented in constant order; the pairs in a paired-associate list might have minimal syntax ( e.g., the stimulus terms might be nouns, the response terms verbs), and so on.

## REFERENCES

ALLUISI, E. A., and MULLER, P. F., JR. (1958) Verbal and motor responses to seven symbolic visual codes: A study of S—R compatibility. *J. exp. Psychol.,* 55, 247-254.

EPSTEIN, W. (1961) The influence of syntactical structure on learning. *Amer. J. Psychol.,* 74, 80-85.

MELTON, A. W. (1941) Learning. In W. S. Monroe (Ed.), *Encyclopedia of educational research.* New York: Macmillan, 667-686.

PETERSON, L. R., and PETERSON, M. J. (1959) Short-term retention of individual verbal items. *J. exp. Psychol.,* 58, 193-198.

RICHARDSON, J. (1958) The relationship of stimulus similarity and number of responses. *J. exp. Psychol.,* 56, 478-484.

RILEY, D. A. (1952) Rote learning as a function of distribution of practice and the complexity of the situation. *J. exp. Psychol.,* 43, 88-95.

SCHULZ, R. W., and RUNQUIST, W. N. (1960) Learning and retention of paired adjectives as a function of percentage occurrence of response members. *J. exp. Psychol.,* 59, 409-413.

UNDERWOOD, B. J. (1963) Stimulus selection in verbal learning. In C. N. Cofer and B. S. Musgrave (Eds.), *Verbal behavior and learning: Problems and processes.* New York: McGraw-Hill.

# 4.  Performance in Different Segments of an Instrumental Response Chain as a Function of Reinforcement Schedule

## K. P. Goodrich

*Although the primary concern of Goodrich has been to examine continuous versus partial reinforcement in the instrumental reward situation, our use of this article is to illustrate how different conclusions can be obtained depending upon where in the apparatus the learning measure is obtained.*

In a review of the literature up to 1950, Jenkins and Stanley (1950) included instrumental reward conditioning in their general conclusion that continuous reinforcement leads to superior acquisition performance as compared with partial reinforcement. Although there is some evidence (Finger, 1942a, 1942b; Lewis, 1956; Lewis & Cotton, 1957; Sheffield, 1949; Wilson, Weiss, & Amsel, 1955) in support of this conclusion, the generality of these findings is made questionable by the fact that these studies employed, at most, only 30 acquisition trials.[*] Quite a different picture is suggested by the studies of Weinstock (1954) and Haggard (1956) which employed a considerably more extended acquisition period. Their findings indicate that (*a*) the initial decrement in performance under partial reinforcement is temporary and (*b*) in the case of some response measures at least, the final or asymptotic level of performance may be greater under partial than under continuous reinforcement.

While Weinstock did not find a significant advantage in the early period of training for the continuous group, or a consistent and significant advantage for his partial groups in the later stages of training, the acquisition curves of running speed did indicate an interesting pattern of initial divergence, convergence, and finally a reversal of the initial order among three of his four groups. Following up this suggestive finding, Haggard obtained further evidence which showed the same pattern (initial advantage for

*J. exp. Psychol.*, 1959, 57, 57-63. Reprinted with permission of the author and The American Psychological Association. Part of a thesis submitted to the Graduate College of the State University of Iowa in partial fulfillment of the requirements for the M.A. degree. The author is indebted to Kenneth W. Spence for advice and assistance throughout the course of the investigation. The present report was prepared while the author was a National Science Foundation Predoctoral Fellow.

[*] Four of these studies (Lewis, 1956; Lewis & Cotton, 1957; Sheffield, 1949; Wilson, Weiss, & Amsel, 1955) introduced a complication by administering 10 continuously reinforced pretraining trials in the experimental apparatus prior to the 30 subsequent acquisition trials. It is difficult to say what subsequent effects upon the relative performance of the two groups these trials may have had.

the 100% group and subsequent reversal) for curves of starting speed. In the case of these data the final superiority of the 50% group over the 100% group was significant at the .05 level. In the case of a running speed measure, Haggard found an initial advantage for the 100% group (significant at the .10 level) with the two curves finally converging at a very late stage of training. This finding suggested the possibility that the effects of variation of the reinforcement schedule in such an instrumental conditioning situation may depend upon which portion of the response chain is measured. The recent finding of Freides (1957) which showed that speed of running in the goal box end of the runway was faster for 100%-reinforced Ss than for 50%-reinforced Ss lends further support to this suggestion.

The present investigation was undertaken to obtain further information on the effects of partial reinforcement in the runway situation, particularly with respect to the questions of (a) whether the effects will vary at different points of the response chain and (b) whether, for some response measures at least, 50%-reinforced groups will respond faster at the asymptote of training than 100%-reinforced groups. The latter question has important implications for the frustration theory of Amsel (1958) and for the statistical-contiguity learning theory discussed by Weinstock (1954).

## EXPERIMENT I

### METHOD

*Subjects and apparatus.* The Ss were 30 experimentally naive female hooded rats from the colony maintained by the Psychology Department of the State University of Iowa. Ages ranged from 114 to 149 days at the beginning of the experiment.

The apparatus was a straight alley consisting of an 8-in. start box, a 13-in. alley, and a 12-in. goal box. These sections were all 2 in. wide and were covered with one continuous sheet of clear glass at a height of 3 in. Two start doors, one opaque and the other clear plastic, separated the start box from the alley. An opaque retrace door separated the alley from the goal box. These doors slid horizontally through slots in the walls. The interior of the apparatus was painted flat black, and the floor was covered with black rubber matting. Dim illumination was provided by the reflected light from two shielded 200-w. bulbs located 4 ft. overhead.

Starting, running, and goal box time measures were provided by three timing circuits activated by the interruption of infrared photocell beams located 6 in., 12 in., and 24 in., respectively, beyond the starting doors. The last beam was 1 in. from the end of the goal box and went across the top of the food cup.

*Drive maintenance and pretraining.* During the 10 days prior to the first acquisition trial the Ss were habituated to handling and a 23-hr. hunger drive cycle was established. Each S was fed 1 hr. daily in an individual feeding cage. Fresh water was always available in the home and feeding cages.

Pretraining began 6 days prior to the first acquisition trial. On Day 1, Ss ate for 30 min. in the feeding cages from a supply of the experimental 45-mg. pellets (Noyes Co.). On Days 2–6, Ss received pretraining feedings in a separate gray goal box in the experimental room. Day 2 consisted of one such 8-pellet feeding, and Days 3–6 consisted of two 4-pellet feedings each day.

*Experimental training.* Following pretraining the Ss were randomly assigned to two groups of 15 animals each. The Ss in the 100% group were reinforced on all trials with four of the 45-mg. pellets. The Ss in the 50% group were nonreinforced on two trials of every block of four trials, each block consisting of one of the following patterns: +−+−, −+−+, +−−+, −++−. One trial per day was run on Days 1 and 2, two trials were run on Day 3, and four trials per day were run beginning on Day 4. Sixty trials were run in all.

On reinforced trials Ss remained in the goal box until they turned away from the empty food cup. On nonreinforced trials (no pellets in the food cup) each S remained in the goal box after breaking the last light beam for a period equal to that S's eating time on the previous reinforced trial, or for 45 sec., whichever was shorter. The Ss were returned to individual waiting cages between trials. The intertrial interval was approximately 17 min.

RESULTS

The three time measures were converted to speeds (reciprocal time). Two additional sets of observations were recorded: (a) frequency of occurrence of stopping responses made by Ss in each section of the apparatus and (b) the time spent by each S at the food cup, i.e., the time between S's breaking the light beam over the loaded cup and his turning away from the empty cup.

*Locomotor performance.* Starting, running, and goal box speeds are plotted in Fig. 1 for the two groups by blocks of four trials. In the starting and running speed segments of the alley (a) the 50% Ss ran slower than the 100% Ss in the early blocks of trials and (b) the 50% Ss ran consistently faster than the 100% Ss during the later trials.

This reversal was expected, but prediction of the trial point at which it would occur had not been possible. Statistical evaluation of the effect must therefore depend to some extent upon the particular crossover point obtained in the data at hand. The most conservative procedure would seem to be a two-way analysis of variance with pre- and post-crossover means

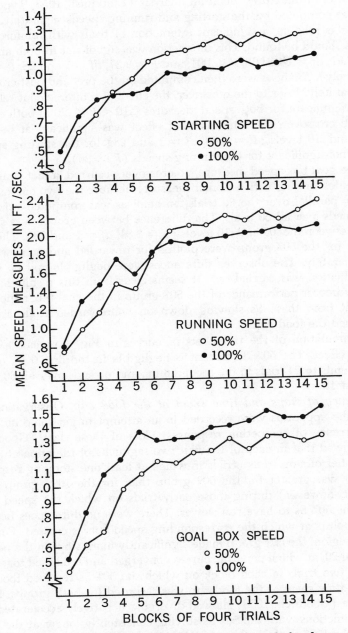

FIG. 1. Mean starting, running, and goal box speeds for the two groups in Exp. I by blocks of four trials.

as the criterion measures. Such an analysis (Lindquist, 1953, Type I design) was computed for the starting and running speeds separately. If the crossover is reliable, a significant interaction of trials with reinforcement schedule should be found. This interaction was significant in both analyses ($F = 13.91$, $df = 1$ and 28, $P < .001$, and $F = 9.37$, $df = 1$ and 28, $P < .005$, respectively). Analyses were then computed on the pre- and post-crossover data separately. Prior to the crossover, the effect of reinforcement schedule was nonsignificant for both speed measures ($.10 < P < .20$ in both cases). After the crossover, the reinforcement effect was significant at between the .05 and .10 levels ($F = 4.06$, $df = 1$ and 28) for the starting speeds, but was nonsignificant for the running speeds ($P > .20$).

For the goal box speed measure, no crossover occurred, a fact consistent with Freides' finding with a similar measure. Because the two curves were so nearly parallel over the 60 trials, an analysis was computed using the mean speeds over all 60 trials. The difference between groups was significant at between the .05 and .10 levels ($F = 3.81$, $df = 1$ and 28). The goal box data for the 50% group were plotted for rewarded and nonrewarded trials separately. The observed differences were negligible and no statistical evaluation was carried out. It seems clear from this result that the relatively poorer performance of the 50% group in the goal box region did not result from these Ss slowing down on nonrewarded trials as they approached the food cup.

An examination of the three sets of curves in Fig. 1 reveals a clear gradient effect. The 50% decrement is negligible in the first 6 in. of the alley, extends to 24 trials in the second 6 in., and extends over all 60 trials in the last 12 in.

*Frequency of stops and time spent at the food cup.* Observations of stops in the apparatus were recorded in an attempt to get some index of the occurrence of competing responses. Plots of these data (Goodrich, 1958) showed that in each of the first two segments of the apparatus the total number of stop trials (trials in which at least one stopping response occurred) was greater for the 50% group than for the 100% group (not significant, however) during those early trials on which the speed data showed the 50% Ss to have run slower. There were no differences beyond the trial points at which the corresponding speed curves crossed. For the goal box region, the 50% group made significantly more stops in the period up to Trial 20, at which point the curves converged and remained together.

On the two trials in each block on which the 50% Ss received food reward, the time spent at the food cup was recorded for both groups. Plots of the data (Goodrich, 1958) showed diverging negatively accelerated decreasing functions, with the 50% Ss staying consistently longer at the food cup than the 100% Ss throughout training. The groups differed significantly during trials 40–60 ($t = 2.27$, $df = 28$).

## EXPERIMENT II

### METHOD

*Subjects and apparatus.* The Ss were 30 experimentally naive female hooded rats from the Iowa colony, ranging in age from 114 to 149 days at the beginning of the experiment. The apparatus was identical to that used in Exp. I, except that the goal box was a 9 × 15-in. area at right angles to the alley. (Insertion of a sliding panel converted this goal box to the narrow one used in Exp. I.) Goal box walls were 11 in. high. The food cup was the same one employed in Exp. I, located in the same position straight ahead of the 2-in. alley.

*Procedure.* The drive maintenance, pretraining, and experimental training procedures were identical to those employed in Exp. I. A more detailed description of methodology and apparatus may be found elsewhere (Goodrich, 1958).

### RESULTS*

*Locomotor performance.* Starting, running, and goal box speeds are plotted in Fig. 2. As in Exp. I, we find for the starting and running measures that the 50% Ss ran slower than the 100% Ss in the early trials, and faster than the 100% Ss in the later trials.

Analyses were computed using the means over pre- and post-crossover trials as criterion measures. The interaction of trials with reinforcement schedule was significant for both the starting and running speeds ($F = 14.22$, $df = 1$ and 28, $P < .001$, and $F = 16.20$, $df = 1$ and 28, $P < .001$, respectively). Analyses were then computed for the pre- and post-crossover data separately. Prior to the crossover the group differences were nonsignificant ($F < 1$ in both cases), but following the crossover the differences were statistically reliable for both starting and running speeds ($F = 8.68$, $df = 1$ and 28, $P < .01$, and $F = 5.47$, $df = 1$ and 28, $P < .05$, respectively).

For the goal box measures, a very slight early-trial decrement occurred in the curve of the 50% group, but beyond Trial 24 the curves remained together, and no statistical evaluation was attempted. These goal box speed results are not consistent with those of Exp. I. However, a kind of gradient effect was still present in that the initial 50% decrement lasted for greater numbers of trials as performance was measured closer to the food cup. Examination of a plot (Goodrich, 1958) of the 50% data for rewarded and nonrewarded trials separately again precluded any possibility of the

* For the purposes of the present paper, Exp. II is a replication of Exp. I with a different sample of Ss and different apparatus. A discussion of the effects of goal box size variation may be found elsewhere (Goodrich, 1958).

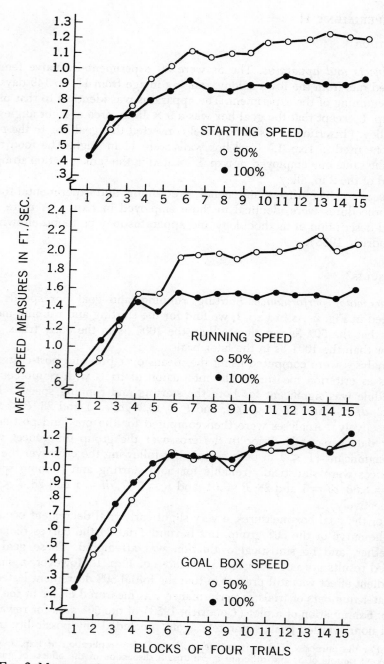

FIG. 2. Mean starting, running, and goal box speeds for the two groups in Exp. II by blocks of four trials.

relatively slow performance of the 50% Ss in the goal box region being due
to Ss slowing down as they approached the food cup on nonrewarded
trials.
*Frequency of stops and time spent at the food cup.* The results for these
measures are essentially the same as in Exp. I. In each of the three alley
segments the 50% Ss made more stops than the 100% Ss during those early
trials on which the corresponding speed data showed the 50% Ss to have
run slower. Later in training there were no differences between groups,
except for a slight tendency for the 100% Ss to make more stop responses
in the goal box region. Plots of the data (Goodrich, 1958) for time spent
at the food cup showed that the 50% Ss stayed consistently longer at the
food cup throughout training ($t = 1.67$, $df = 28$, for Trials 45–60).

## DISCUSSION

The two experiments reported here provide a consistent picture of the
effects of 50% vs. 100% reinforcement schedules upon the acquisition of an
instrumental response. They indicate that, ($a$) following an early-trial advantage for Ss in the 100% group, there occurs a reversal in the case of
starting and running speeds so that 50% Ss are responding faster at the
performance asymptote, and ($b$) the early-trial 50% reinforcement decrement persists for greater numbers of trials as performance is measured
closer to the goal region of the runway.

The finding of greatest importance for existing theoretical formulations
of instrumental conditioning is that 50%-reinforced Ss exhibit a higher
level of performance than 100%-reinforced Ss at the performance asymptote. An extension of the theoretical schema of Amsel and his students
(Amsel, 1958; Amsel & Hancock, 1957; Amsel & Roussel, 1952; Wilson,
Weiss, & Amsel, 1955) provides, to a first approximation at least, an
adequate interpretation for this phenomenon. According to this formulation, the occurrence of nonreinforcements after some minimal number of
reinforced trials produces a motivational state of "frustration" ($F$) which
may act to facilitate subsequent performance (Amsel & Hancock, 1957;
Amsel & Roussel, 1952; Wagner, 1958). Amsel further postulates that a
conditioned (antedating) form of $F$, called $r_f - s_f$, will occur back in the
alley itself. If motivational (facilitating) properties are attributed to
$r_f - s_f$ (as the formulation seems to call for but Amsel himself does not
discuss), the eventual superiority of the 50% Ss can be interpreted as being
due to a motivational increase produced by the occurrence of $r_f - s_f$.

This frustration interpretation is not without its problems. Although the
motivational effects of primary frustration ($F$) were clearly demonstrated
in studies by Amsel and Hancock (1957), Amsel and Roussel (1952), and
Wagner (1958), these facilitating effects did not show up until some 20

to 30 trials had been run. In the present study the advantage in favor of the 50% group began to develop, in the case of starting speeds, as early as the third block of trials (Trials 9–12). It is therefore necessary to hold that conditioned frustration, $r_f - s_f$, had an earlier effect in the present study than did primary frustration, $F$, in the Amsel and Wagner studies. It is quite possible that the narrow width and visual homogeneity of the starting and running sections of the runway used here discouraged competing responses, and thus enabled motivational increases to affect the instrumental running response directly. Greater numbers of competing responses in the early trials could have masked such efforts in the Amsel and Wagner studies. A more accurate index of competing responses than the crude one employed here would seem desirable for future study of these problems.

Amsel's frustration formulation attributes inferior performance under 50% reinforcement to the occurrence of competing responses elicited by the stimulus component of $r_f - s_f$. Application of this schema to the present results would require the occurrence of $r_f - s_f$ during the very early trials. However, Amsel postulates that frustration does not occur until previous rewarded trials have resulted in the growth of some minimum amount of incentive motivation, or $r_g - s_g$. Unless it is assumed that the pretraining procedures in the present study were sufficient for the growth of this $r_g - s_g$, it is doubtful whether $r_f$, and thus $s_f$, would occur early enough in training to account for the early-trial 50% decrement. An alternative, and perhaps more reasonable, interpretation would be that competing responses occur and hence are learned in the empty goal box on nonreinforced trials, and subsequently interfere with the running response (Adelman & Maatsch, 1955; Weinstock, 1954). The relationship found in the present study between the 50% decrement and the occurrence of stop responses, although only suggestive because of the statistical unreliability of the stop data, is consistent with such a view.

According to Weinstock's (1954) interpretation, which is based on a statistical-contiguity type learning theory plus an ad hoc assumption about the habituation of competing responses, a partial reinforcement schedule results most importantly in the conditioning of competing responses. Weinstock is led to conclude that, although the decrement due to these interfering responses may be small during the later acquisition trials (because of habituation), final asymptotic levels of running speed should be in direct relation to the percentage of reinforcement employed. Although competing responses may account for an early-trial 50% decrement, Weinstock's formulation is clearly inadequate as it stands to account for the fact, indicated by the available evidence, that partially reinforced Ss exhibit a higher final performance level than continuously reinforced Ss.

In both of the experiments reported here, partial reinforcement effects were found to vary with the portion of the response chain being measured, a finding consistent with the Freides (1957) and Haggard (1956) studies. No clear interpretation of the effect seems available at present. Similarly, the interpretation of the apparent relationship between the time spent at the food cup and speed of running must await additional research. The present results are ambiguous in that shorter time may represent either a faster rate of eating or merely picking up the food and moving away from the cup without actually eating the food. A measure of actual consummatory rate could be obtained more easily with a liquid incentive.

## SUMMARY

Two experiments were made to demonstrate that the relative performance of 50% and 100% reinforcement groups varies during the course of acquisition, and that these effects vary with the point in the response chain measured. In each experiment, two groups of 15 female hooded rats were given 60 acquisition trials in a straight alley, one group receiving 50% partial reinforcement and the other 100% reinforcement. The experiments differed only in the size of the goal box used.

The results of the two experiments agreed in showing that for the starting and running speed measures the 50% group was inferior in the early trials but superior at the performance asymptote. For the goal box speed measure no 50% superiority developed; the 50% Ss showed slower performance throughout training in Exp. I, and did not differ from the 100% Ss in Exp. II. In both experiments the 50% decrement lasted for greater numbers of trials as performance was measured closer to the goal region of the apparatus.

The results were discussed in relation to Amsel's frustration theory, although it was concluded that no existing theoretical schema provides an entirely adequate interpretation.

## REFERENCES

ADELMAN, H. M. and MAATSCH, J. L. (1955) Resistance to extinction as a function of the type of response elicited by frustration. *J. exp. Psychol.*, 50, 61-65.

AMSEL, A. (1958) The role of frustrative nonreward in noncontinuous reward situations. *Psychol. Bull.*, 55, 102-119.

AMSEL, A. and HANCOCK, W. (1957) Motivational properties of frustration: III. Relation of frustration effect to antedating goal factors. *J. exp. Psychol.*, 53, 126-131.

AMSEL, A. and ROUSSEL, J. (1952) Motivational properties of frustration: I. Effect on a running response of the addition of frustration to the motivational complex. *J. exp. Psychol.*, 43, 363-368.

FINGER, F. W. (1942) The effect of varying conditions of reinforcement upon a simple running response. *J. exp. Psychol.*, 30, 53-68. (a)

FINGER, F. W. (1942) Retention and subsequent extinction of a simple running response following varying conditions of reinforcement. *J. exp. Psychol.*, *31*, 120-133. (b)

FREIDES, D. (1957) Goal box cues and pattern of reinforcement. *J. exp. Psychol.*, *53*, 361-371.

GOODRICH, K. P. (1958) Acquisition of an instrumental response as a function of reinforcement schedule and goal box confinement. Unpublished master's thesis, State Univer. of Iowa.

HAGGARD, D. F. (1956) Acquisition and extinction of a simple running response as a function of partial and continuous schedules of reinforcement. Unpublished doctoral thesis, State Univer. of Iowa.

JENKINS, W. O. and STANLEY, J. C. (1950) Partial reinforcement: A review and critique. *Psychol. Bull.*, *47*, 193-234.

LEWIS, D. J. (1956) Acquisition, extinction, and spontaneous recovery as a function of percentage of reinforcement and intertrial intervals. *J. exp. Psychol.*, *51*, 45-53.

LEWIS, D. J. and COTTON, J. W. (1957) Learning and performance as a function of drive strength during acquisition and extinction. *J. comp. physiol. Psychol.*, *50*, 189-194.

LINDQUIST, E. F. (1953) *Design and analysis of experiments in psychology and education.* Boston: Houghton Mifflin.

SHEFFIELD, V. F. (1949) Extinction as a function of partial reinforcement and distribution of practice. *J. exp. Psychol.*, *39*, 511-526.

WAGNER, A. R. (1958) Motivational effects of nonreinforcement as a function of the reinforcement schedule. Unpublished master's thesis, State Univer. of Iowa.

WEINSTOCK, S. (1954) Resistance to extinction of a running response following partial reinforcement under widely spaced trials. *J. comp. physiol. Psychol.*, *47*, 318-322.

WILSON, W., WEISS, I. J., and AMSEL, A. (1955) Two tests of the Sheffield hypothesis concerning resistance to extinction, partial reinforcement, and distribution of practice. *J. exp. Psychol.*, *50*, 51-61.

# 5. Contradictory Conclusions from Two Speed of Performance Measures

## E. S. Edgington

*The Goodrich article pointed to the problem of obtaining different findings depending upon where in the apparatus the response measure was obtained. Edgington's article presents even more of a problem, that of how contradictory conclusions may be obtained depending upon how speed of performance is expressed.*

Speed of performance can be expressed in terms of amount performed per unit of time or amount of time per unit of performance. The following example will show how different the interpretation of computed statistics can be, for these two alternative measures of speed of performance. The speeds shown in Table 1 are hypothetical running speeds for two rats, each rat being sampled on two different occasions. The same observations are expressed in two ways in the table. Rat A on the average travelled more feet per second and was, therefore, faster. However, the same rat, Rat A, on the average took more seconds per foot travelled and was, therefore, slower.

TABLE 1

SPEEDS OF RATS EXPRESSED IN TWO WAYS

|          | Feet per second | | Seconds per foot (1/Feet-per-second) | |
|----------|-------|-------|-------|-------|
|          | Rat A | Rat B | Rat A | Rat B |
|          | 2     | 4     | .50   | .25   |
|          | 8     | 5     | .125  | .20   |
| Totals:  | 10    | 9     | .652  | .45   |
| Means:   | 5     | 4.5   | .3125 | .225  |

One way of settling the contradiction might be to accept the convention of physicists to express velocity only in terms of distance per unit of time, but this solution would not satisfy anyone who considered distance per unit of time and time per unit of distance to be equally valid expressions of speed.

Frequently in research the running times and latency times of rats are

*Psychol. Bull.,* 1960, 57, 315-317. Reprinted with permission of the author and The American Psychological Association.

subjected to a reciprocal transformation prior to statistical analysis; that is, the statistical analysis is carried out, using the reciprocals of the running times and the reciprocals of the latency times. However, a significant difference between means of the reciprocals of running times cannot be interpreted as indicating a significant difference between means of running times. The same is true of latency times and their reciprocals.

Furthermore, the nonlinearity of the relationship between the two reciprocally related measures ($Y = 1/X$) indicates that there can be inconsistency between them for any statistic that is derived from addition or subtraction of measurement values. Among the statistics subject to inconsistency are these conventional parametric statistics: the mean, the standard deviation, and the product-moment correlation coefficient.

Any computed significance levels that are based on addition or subtraction of the measurement numbers can be different for the two measures; thus, one of the measures might lead to the rejection of a null hypothesis while the other measure might not.

Up to this point the discussion has dealt with running times and latency times of rats, and the reciprocals of these measures. However, the statistical contradictions presented are not the result of carrying out the statistical analysis with the reciprocals instead of the original data. Either of the two reciprocally related measures is equally valid as a measure of speed of performance, and either one could be considered to be the reciprocal of the other. The point is that there are two precise measures of speed of performance which can lead to contradictory conclusions, for certain statistical computations. This fact applies to speed of performance of any kind. For example, it applies to measuring manual dexterity with a pegboard in terms of the number of pegs per unit of time or in terms of amount of time per peg. Another example is the number of nonsense syllables memorized per unit of time compared to the amount of time per nonsense syllable memorized. And, of course, verbal as well as nonverbal aptitude and achievement tests can employ as a measure of speed either amount of time per unit of performance or amount performed per unit of time. In these and other cases where speed of performance is measured, the significance level obtained can be inconsistent with what would have been obtained had the reciprocally related measure been used.

## PROPOSED SOLUTION

An obvious way to avoid the contradictions that can arise between two reciprocally related measures of speed of performance would be to confine computations to order statistics, e.g., statistics that make use only of the rank order of the original data, not the actual measurement values. The median, mode, and rank correlation coefficient are examples. The objection to this negative kind of solution is that precision of measurement is wasted, and consequently computed statistics would be less sensitive.

There is a solution in which the precision of the measurements can be fully utilized without the possibility of contradiction between the two measures for any computed statistic. A logarithmic transformation of the measurement values (either performance per unit of time or time per unit of performance) prior to statistical analysis accomplishes this result. Since the relationship between the two reciprocally related measures is $Y = 1/X$, the relationship between their logarithms is $\log Y = -\log X$; the values are identical, but have opposite signs. Since the numerical values of the logarithms are identical, all statistics computed lead to consistent conclusions. When a statistic is computed for one measure, the conclusion based on it is exactly the same as would be the conclusion based on the same statistic computed for the reciprocally related measure. Any computed level of significance would be identical for any statistic computed for the two measures.

The arithmetic mean of the logarithms is the logarithm of the number that is the geometric mean of the antilogarithms, so a significant difference of means of the logarithms corresponds to a significant difference of geometric means of the antilogarithms. But why should one test for a difference of geometric means when, instead, he is interested in the difference of arithmetic means of the measures? The answer is that he should not test for differences of geometric means instead of arithmetic means if his interest is in the difference of arithmetic means; however, the inconsistency that is associated with the arithmetic mean of speed of performance measurements casts doubt on the meaningfulness and usefulness of hypotheses about the mean speed of performance. In contrast, the geometric mean is consistent for the two measures. A similar argument can be given for the relative meaningfulness of the other statistics that may be computed from the logarithms of the measurement numbers.

Since most nonparametric statistics would lead to consistent results even without the logarithmic transformation, the principal advantage of the logarithmic transformation is in regard to parametric statistics. It is pertinent, therefore, to consider the normality of the distribution of logarithms of speed of performance measurements. Now, the reciprocal relationship between the two speeds of performance measures requires that for one to be normally distributed the other must not be. This complicates the normality assumption for the speed of performance measures themselves. On the other hand, if the logarithms of one of the two measures are normally distributed, the logarithms of the other measure also must be normally distributed. Another point in favor of the logarithmic transformation is that speed of performance measurements often show a positive skewness, which is consistent with the assumption that their logarithms are normally distributed, since a logarithmic transformation tends to reduce positive skewness.

# SECTION TWO

# General Issues in Motivation:
# I. The Role of Needs

T HE most important variable which contributes to the learning process is probably motivation. But how shall motivation be defined—what shall be included in its scope? During the past two decades, the most influential and pervasive point of view has been provided by Hull (1943, 1951), who conceptualized motivation as being comprised of primary as well as secondary needs. Primary needs were identified as the biological requirements of the organism, arising from deficiencies within the body. The fulfillment of these requirements was necessary for the health of the organism and the survival of the species. The influence of such need states was to arouse general or "spontaneous" activity, with such activity frequently measured by use of the activity wheel.

Recent experimental evidence suggests that whether or not primary needs produce activity depends upon the kind of measuring instrument. The selection by Treichler and Hall (1962) illustrates this position. The article by Stevenson and Rixon (1957), however, provides the possibility of some reconciliation of the different findings.

Secondary or acquired needs were posited to arise from primary needs through a learning process. Thus, by associating a primary need with a neutral stimulus, the stimulus could acquire motivational properties. An examination of the literature investigating the acqui-

57

sition of acquired drives reveals two general experimental procedures. The first has been to associate a neutral stimulus with a noxious stimulus, frequently electric shock. One of the early studies in this area was by Miller (1948), who trained rats to escape shock by running from a white compartment to a black one. When a door was then placed between the compartments which blocked the animal's escape, Miller found that the animals would learn to turn a wheel or press a bar which would raise the door and thus permit escape. Miller posited that fear which accompanied pain produced by the shock was conditioned to the white box; in addition, fear had stimulus characteristics which motivated the instrumental response of bar pressing or wheel turning.

The establishment of a secondary drive based upon appetitive states (i.e., food or water deprivation) has not been, in general, successful. Although Calvin, Bicknell, and Sperling (1953) did report positive findings most subsequent investigators have been unable to demonstrate the phenomenon. The selection by Siegel and MacDonnell (1954), a replication of the Calvin, Bicknell, and Sperling (1953) study, is one of the many studies which illustrate the difficulty of securing positive findings.

Dissatisfied with the primary–secondary need conceptualization of motivation, many investigators began to search for other sources of motivation and to postulate other types of needs or drive states. Two such drive states have been firmly established and have been recognized as important sources of motivation. One of these is curiosity, and Berlyne's (1950) article is one of the early contemporary studies to place emphasis upon this type of motivation. The second drive state is frustration, and the selection by Amsel and Roussel (1952) was one of the first to demonstrate unequivocally its operation.

## REFERENCES

AMSEL, A. and ROUSSEL, J. (1952) Motivational properties of frustration: I. Effect on a running response of the addition of frustration to the motivational complex. *J. exp. Psychol.*, *43*, 363-368.

BERLYNE, D. E. (1950) Novelty and curiosity as determinants of exploratory behavior. *Brit. J. Psychol.*, *41*, 68-80.

CALVIN, J. S., BICKNELL, E. A., and SPERLING, D. S. (1953) Establishment of a conditioned drive based on the hunger drive. *J. comp. physiol. Psychol.*, 46, 176-179.

HULL, C. L. (1943) *Principles of behavior.* New York: Appleton-Century-Crofts.

HULL, C. L. (1951) *Essentials of behavior.* New Haven: Yale Univ. Press.

MILLER, N. E. (1948) Studies of fear as an acquirable drive: I. Fear as motivation and fear-reduction as reinforcement in learning of new responses. *J. exp. Psychol.*, 38, 89-101.

SIEGEL, P. S. and MACDONNELL, M. F. (1954) A repetition of the Calvin-Bicknell-Sperling study of conditioned drive. *J. comp. physiol. Psychol.*, 47, 250-252.

STEVENSON, J. A. F. and RIXON, R. H. (1957) Environmental temperature and deprivation of food and water on the spontaneous activity of rats. *Yale J. Biol. Med.*, 29, 575-584.

TREICHLER, F. R. and HALL, J. F. (1962) The relationship between deprivation weight loss and several measures of activity. *J. comp. physiol, Psychol.*, 55, 346-349.

# 6.  The Relationship Between Deprivation Weight Loss and Several Measures of Activity

## F. R. Treichler and J. F. Hall

*Although the position that primary need states produce activity was supported by a number of early investigators who used the activity wheel as their measuring instrument, it has been difficult to find support for this position when other types of activity measuring devices are used. Treichler and Hall provide an example of the varying findings obtained when deprivation is measured with a variety of measuring instruments.*

In recent years, spontaneous activity has been measured as a function of a number of experimental conditions as well as with a variety of measuring instruments. Such activity has often been posited to be an expression of the energizing function of a motive.

A common method for manipulating motivation has been to place the experimental Ss under a deprivation-feeding schedule in which, within each 24-hr. period, they are given access to food and water for only an hour. Since such a schedule introduces a period of feeding following the organism's activity, it has been suggested that some of the activity occurs as a function of the reinforcement contingency (Hall, 1958).

A second problem with schedules of this kind is that the use of time implies that the changes which underlie the need state are always, and adequately, reflected by deprivation intervals. But the experimental findings of Moskowitz (1959) appear to question this assumption, for he has concluded that activity, at least as measured by the activity wheel, does not increase until body weight has decreased to levels between 85% and 90% of the S's normal weight.

A final problem relates to how activity is measured. Three general methods are typically employed: (a) activity wheels, (b) stationary cage situations which use photoelectric cells or microswitches to record movement, and (c) maze situations which measure more extended locomotor activity. The earlier evidence, summarized by Reed (1947), seems to indicate that these devices do not measure the same thing. More recently, Weasner, Finger, and Reid (1960) compared the effects of a 23-hr. deprivation–1-hr.-feeding schedule upon activity as measured with wheel and

*J. comp. physiol. Psychol.*, 1962, 55, 346-349. Reprinted with permission of the senior author and The American Psychological Association.

stationary cage techniques, and have also concluded that the two devices do not yield interchangeable data.

The present study is a further exploration of the need-activity relationship using a variety of measuring devices. To this end, two experiments were run, separated by about 3 mo. Experiment 1 was concerned with behavior in the activity wheel and stabilimetric cage as a function of continuous (a) food, (b) water, and (c) combined food and water deprivation states. Experiment 2 examined activity in a modified Dashiell maze as a function of combined food and water deprivation states. The effects of learning upon such behavior were minimized by the use of continuous deprivation schedules that would seem to preclude the operation of activity-reward contingencies. The principal concern, in keeping with the findings of the Moskowitz experiment, was to examine activity as a function of body weight rather than deprivation interval.

## EXPERIMENT 1

### METHOD

*Subjects.* The Ss were 75 male Long-Evans hooded rats of the Harlan strain, between 70 and 102 days of age at the beginning of the study. Sixty Ss were tested under varying conditions of deprivation, while the other 15 were maintained on ad libitum feeding and used as a control group in order to assess normal weight gain.

*Apparatus.* Ten Wahmann activity wheels, equated for amount of frictional torque, were used to measure wheel-running activity. Five cages of the type described by Campbell (1954) were used to measure stabilimetric activity. The stabilimeter cages were constructed by mounting a 9-in. cylindrical cage on a center pin so that each shift of S's center of gravity into a different quadrant resulted in the closing of a microswitch which pulsed an electric counter. A water-bottle holder occupied the center of the cage so as to keep the S from assuming a position such that only a very small movement could tip the cage.

*Procedure.* Animals assigned to the wheels were first adapted to them for a period of 17 days while animals tested in the stabilimeter cages were adapted for 24 hr. Measurements were then obtained for the next 3 days with all rats on ad libitum feeding, and these were considered to provide the normal base rates of activity. All further measures were expressed as percentages of the means for these 3 days. Individual weights were recorded daily and expressed as percentages of predeprivation weight adjusted for the mean percentage of weight gain shown by a group of 15 similar animals on ad libitum feeding.

The groups of 30 Ss studied in the wheels and stabilimeters, respectively, were further subdivided into three groups of 10 animals. These subgroups were then deprived of food, of water, or of both food and water. All were continuously housed in the activity devices. The deprivation conditions involved complete withdrawal of the designated dietary components, and these manipulations were maintained until the Ss died or reached 55% of their predeprivation weight.

RESULTS

The 3-day period of base-rate activity measurement afforded an opportunity to measure the reliabilities of the activity devices. Product-moment correlations of the daily scores for Days 1 and 2, and 2 and 3 were computed. For the activity wheel these yielded $r$'s of .95 and .97, respectively. A similar analysis of stabilimetric data yielded $r$'s of .78 and .75.

An analysis of activity as a function of the different kinds of deprivation conditions (food, water, and combined food and water) employed was first conducted. A Kruskal-Wallis analysis of variance of ranks was made at the following percent body weight levels: 95, 90, 85, 80, 75, 70, 65, and 60.*

Wheel-running scores as a function of the varying deprivation conditions did not significantly differ at any weight level. The scores obtained with the stabilimeter differed as a function of kind of deprivation at only the 60% level of adjusted body weight. At this point, food deprivation and combined food and water deprivation yielded an increase in activity while water deprivation did not. Since significant differences among activity scores as a function of the kind of deprivation condition imposed was found at only this one weight level, it was felt appropriate to combine all three deprivation conditions when examining activity as a function of weight loss. Figure 1 displays this relationship.

Marked differences are evident in the effects of deprivation as a function of the two kinds of measuring devices. The median running scores of Ss deprived in wheels reveal progressive increases up to 1,385% of their predeprivation base rate. The median activity scores for Ss deprived in stabilimeters do not, in contrast, yield a function of this kind. Thus, at 90% body weight, stabilimetric cage scores show a slight but significant increase ($p < 0.5$) over base-rate activity; however, the 80% and 70% body weight conditions, do not yield activity levels that differ from the mean base rate. At 60% body weight, those Ss on food deprivation and on combined food and water deprivation reveal activity scores which differ from

* Since the Ss were on continuous deprivation and their activity measured only once per day, the reader may inquire as to how the varying activity measures were obtained at these varying weight levels. All the values used in this analysis are interpolated ones. Each S's activity was plotted against its specific weight loss measured for each 24-hr. period. From the resulting plot of values, it was possible to interpolate activity scores at the specific weight levels which we have indicated.

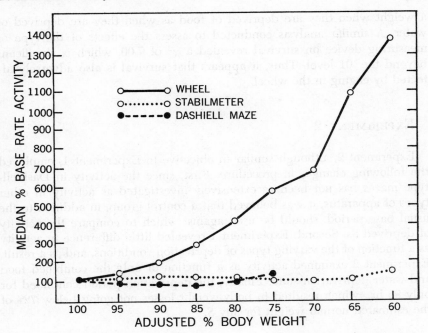

FIG. 1. Activity changes as a function of weight loss in three different measuring devices.

their base rate while Ss deprived of water seem to show no effects whatever.

Since it was possible that the different deprivation or measurement conditions might yield different rates of weight loss, which in turn might influence activity scores, an analysis of variance of weight-loss data was performed. An examination of the activity scores for the first 4 days of deprivation—the period during which all Ss survived—revealed no significant differences in weight loss attributable to either measurement conditions, deprivation conditions, or their interaction.

An interesting aspect of the study was an examination of the relationship obtained between survival to 55% body weight and (a) the type of deprivation and (b) the measuring device. Of the 10 animals per deprivation condition measured in running wheels, none on food, 8 on water, and 2 on combined deprivation survived to 55% body weight. In stabilimeters, 4 Ss on food, all 10 on water, and 7 on combined deprivation survived to this criterion.

A chi square analysis of these frequencies against the alternative frequencies from the hypothesis that an equal number of Ss should survive under all deprivation conditions yielded a $\chi^2$ value of 11.11, which is significant beyond the .01 level. Thus, we find that Ss do not survive to as low a weight when they are deprived of food as when they are deprived of water. A similar analysis conducted to assess the effects of the type of measuring device on survival revealed a $\chi^2$ of 7.00, which is significant beyond the .01 level. Thus, it appears that survival is also adversely affected by caging in the wheel.

## EXPERIMENT 2

Experiment 2, although similar in objective to Experiment 1, employed the following changes in procedure. First, since the activity in Dashiell-type mazes has not been as extensively investigated as activity in other types of apparatus, it was believed that a control group, in addition to the usual base period, should be used against which to compare the activity of deprived Ss. Second, Experiment 1 revealed little difference in activity as a function of the varying types of deprivation conditions, and as a result, Experiment 2 examined activity as a function of only the combined food and water deprivation state. Finally, the deprivation period continued for only 96 hr., which resulted in body-weight losses not going below 72% of the estimated normal weight for any S.

### METHOD

*Subjects.* The Ss were 20 male Harlan albino rats, approximately 70 days of age at the beginning of the study. One experimental S died after the first day of deprivation; as a result, its matched control was also eliminated from the study.

*Apparatus.* A modified Dashiell checkerboard maze was employed. The maze was square with each wall 25 in. long and 6 in. high. Four 5-in. by 5-in. by 6-in. blocks were placed within the square so as to form three vertical and three horizontal alleys through which S could traverse. Hardware cloth of ½-in. mesh formed the floor. The maze was placed on treated cardboard which had 5-in. squares painted on it which enabled E to determine when S moved from one square to another.

*Procedure.* Following a 7-day handling period, adaptation was begun which consisted of placing each S in the maze for 10 min. per day for 4 days. A base period was then provided which consisted of measuring the activity of each S in the maze for 4 days. The number of squares entered during each 10-min. period was recorded and constituted the measure of activity. The Ss were matched and divided into a control and an experimental group on the basis of weight and activity scores for this base period. The control group continued on ad libitum food and water conditions, while food and water were both removed from experimental Ss. Four daily sessions were conducted in which each S was first weighed and then placed in the apparatus with activity being recorded for each 10-min. session.

RESULTS

As with Experiment 1, the scores for the base period were used to assess the reliability of the modified Dashiell maze. Since 4 days were devoted to base-rate measurement in this experiment, it was possible to make three estimates of reliability by correlating scores on Days 1 and 2, 2 and 3, and 3 and 4. This procedure yielded $r$'s of .67, and .72, and .83, respectively.

In order to compare activity in this type of apparatus with activity as measured in the activity wheel and stabilimetric cage, we have placed the appropriate data in Figure 1. The necessity for using a large unit of activity measurement on the ordinate in order to accommodate the findings obtained with the wheel results in the obscuring of some of the variability of the animal's activity in the Dashiell maze. Moreover, this figure does not permit the inclusion of the control group. When these data are observed directly, the median percent base-rate activity scores for experimental animals on the four successive days of deprivation is found to be 79.7, 78.1, 112.3, and 116.5. Similar daily scores for control animals were 88.9, 108.9, 110.9, and 71.6.

Since the groups were matched, Wilcoxon $T$s were run between the daily scores of experimental and control Ss. Although certain trends, particularly for the experimental Ss, seem to be in evidence, there were no significant differences between groups at any measurement period.


DISCUSSION

The results clearly indicate that activity under deprivation differs in several measuring devices. Wheel-running shows a marked positive relation to weight loss however produced, and it also induces death at higher weights than maintenance in stabilimeters, especially when animals are food-deprived. The maze and stabilimeter show little change with increased weight loss.

The relationship that we have obtained between stabilimetric activity and degree of deprivation markedly resembles that reported by Strong (1957) with microswitch-mounted stabilimeters and a comparable extent of deprivation. Our function relating body-weight loss and wheel behavior is nearly identical to that reported by Moskowitz (1959), even though he used 1-hr. measurement periods in contrast to our 24-hr. ones and maintained his animals on an apparently less severe partial-deprivation schedule. Further, the absence of differences due to kinds of deprivation seems consistent with the conclusions of Bolles and Petrinovich (1956) that maze behavior differences are dependent upon magnitude of deprivation rather than whether the animals are deprived of food or water.

In general, the effect of deprivation upon stationary-cage activity has been minimal unless accompanied by external environmental stimulation (Campbell & Sheffield, 1953). One possibility is that the running wheel provides its own source of stimulation via kinesthetic mechanisms and, thus, allows a deprivation effect on activity to be manifest with no apparent environmental manipulation. Hall (1956) has shown that both deprivation and environmental stimulation can contribute to increased wheel activity, suggesting that stimulation effects may be cumulative.

Although increases in activity under deprivation have sometimes been used as support for the concept of an energizing function of need states, it must be noted that this application may require a consideration of particular properties of measurement devices since activity changes are not independent of methods of measurement.

## SUMMARY

Two experiments were conducted to examine some aspects of the need-activity relationship in rats when several activity measuring devices are employed.

With deprivation, activity in wheels underwent a marked increase, while maze and stabilimeter activity showed comparatively little change. No differences in weight loss during the first 4 days of deprivation were noted as a result of different kinds of deprivation or measurement in wheels or stabilimeters. However, both the deprivation and measurement variables did affect a survival criterion. Deprivations involving food withdrawal appeared more severe than only water deprivation. Deprivation in wheels appeared more severe than deprivation in stabilimeters. The different kinds of deprivation had almost no differential effect on activity when extent of deprivation was equated by a weight-loss criterion.

It was concluded that the application of activity data requires consideration of the properties of specific measurement devices.

## REFERENCES

BOLLES, R. and PETRINOVICH, L. (1956) Body-weight changes and behavioral attributes. *J. comp. physiol. Psychol.*, 49, 177-180.

CAMPBELL, B. A. (1954) Design and reliability of a new activity-recording device. *J. comp. physiol. Psychol.*, 47, 90-92.

CAMPBELL, B. A. and SHEFFIELD, F. D. (1953) Relation of random activity to food deprivation. *J. comp. physiol. Psychol.*, 46, 320-322.

HALL, J. F. (1956) The relationship between external stimulation, food deprivation and activity. *J. comp. physiol. Psychol.*, 49, 339-341.

HALL, J. F. (1958) The influence of learning in activity wheel behavior. *J. genet. Psychol.*, 92, 121-125.

MOSKOWITZ, M. J. (1959) Running-wheel activity in the white rat as a function of combined food and water deprivation. *J. comp. physiol. Psychol.*, 52, 621-625.

REED, J. D. (1947) Spontaneous activity of animals. *Psychol. Bull.*, 44, 393-412.

STRONG, P. N., JR. (1957) Activity in the white rat as a function of apparatus and hunger. *J. comp. physiol. Psychol.*, 53, 242-244.

WEASNER, M. H., FINGER, F. W., and REID, L. S. (1960) Activity changes under food deprivation as a function of recording device. *J. comp. physiol. Psychol.*, 53, 470-474.

# 7. Environmental Temperature and Deprivation of Food and Water on the Spontaneous Activity of Rats

## J. A. F. Stevenson and R. H. Rixon

*This article holds hope for reconciling the conflicting findings presented in the Treichler and Hall study. Thus, wheel running appears to arise from an attempt by the animal to keep warm, which means that running in the activity wheel is a response that does not arise spontaneously, but is, rather, a response involved in the maintenance of body temperature. Presumably those measurement devices that do not reflect activity as a function of deprivation are those that do not permit the animal to engage in the kind of free running activity provided by the wheel.*

### INTRODUCTION

Deprivation of food, water, or individual nutrients usually causes an increase in the spontaneous running activity of the rat (3, 9, 10, 17, 18, 22, 27, 28, 30) although some exceptions have been reported (2, 17, 30). The measurement of running activity has been used for investigations into motivation, for instance, as a measure of the hunger and thirst drives (9, 10, 27). Wald and Jackson (30) considered the hyperactivity of rats during nutritional deprivation an example of mammalian emigration to relieve the nutritional pressure on the home population.

*Yale J. Biol. Med.*, 1957, 29, 575-584. Reprinted with permission of the senior author and *The Yale Journal of Biology and Medicine*. This work was supported by grant 8865-02 from the Defence Research Board of Canada.

On the other hand, muscular activity is one of several means by which body temperature can be maintained through an increase in heat production (4, 5, 7, 14). If the increased activity during starvation primarily reflects some function in the maintenance of body temperature, then there should be a relation between the environmental temperature and the degree of activity in starvation.

METHODS

Male Sprague-Dawley rats (300-400 gm.) were fed a synthetic diet (4.2 cal./gm.). In this diet approximately 70 per cent of the calories were derived from sucrose, 20 per cent from crude casein and 10 per cent from corn oil. Adequate amounts of the known necessary vitamins and salts were added to the mixture (29). Food and water were provided *ad libitum*, except when one or the other was specifically restricted. The rats used in the acclimatization study were eight to nine weeks old at the beginning of the 28-week experiment. All other rats were 10 to 12 weeks old at the start of the experiments.

No other animals were kept in the experimental room and it was entered only for daily care and recording. The lights were automatically turned on at 8 a.m. and off at 8 p.m. The temperature of this room could be controlled to ± 1° C. at levels from 5° to 35° C. The relative humidity was kept at 50 per cent, except at 10° C. and below when it could not be maintained and rose to about 90 per cent.

The animals lived in individual activity cages unless otherwise specified; some control studies were made in ordinary individual cages (7 x 9 x 6 inches). The activity cage consisted of a revolving drum, 14 inches in diameter, and a small living cage separable from the drum by a sliding door.* This door was never closed during these experiments. A Veedor counter recorded each complete revolution of the drum. Twelve of these cages were arranged in three rows on a specially constructed rack. As noted by Reed (17) the animals required about 10 days to adjust to the activity cage and showed a consistent level of activity following this period.

Skin and colonic temperatures were recorded by thermocouples.† The representative skin temperature was taken as the average of readings from three areas, the back, about one inch from the base of the tail, and the "thighs" of each hind leg. Each of these areas had been shaved. The colonic temperatures were obtained by inserting a rectal thermocouple 2 to 2½ inches past the anal orifice.

---

* From Geo. H. Wahmann Mfg. Co., Baltimore, U.S.A.
† Electric thermometer manufactured by Light Laboratories, Brighton, England.

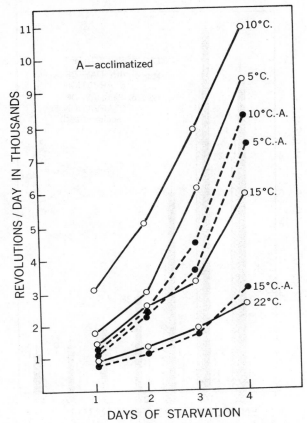

FIG. 1. The increases in spontaneous activity which occurred during four days of starvation at various environmental temperatures.

## RESULTS

Figure 1 shows the increase in activity which occurred at environmental temperatures from 5° C. to 22° C. during four days of starvation. The running activity progressively increased up to the fourth day of food deprivation. The rate of increase was dependent on the surrounding temperature and was greatest in the cold environments. Curves at higher environmental temperatures (27°, 30°, 33° C.) are not shown since they were similar to, but shallower than, that at 22° C. Since the limit of survival for those animals in the cold was about four days, the fourth day was chosen for comparison of the activity at all environmental temperatures.

Figure 2 shows the spontaneous running activity of rats during the fed state and on the fourth day of starvation at environmental temperatures

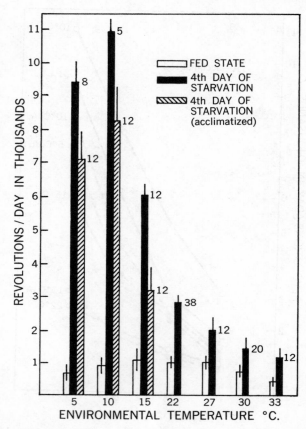

FIG. 2. The spontaneous running activity of rats in the fed state and on the fourth day of starvation at various environmental temperatures. Vertical lines represent the standard error.

ranging from 5° to 33° C. In the fed state, the activity was about 1000 rev./day at environmental temperatures from 15° to 27° C., decreasing to 450 at 33° C. and to 700 at 5° C. This decrease in warm and cool environment has been noted by Reed (17).

During starvation there were increases in spontaneous activity which varied considerably with the environmental temperature. At 22° C. the average activity had risen to 2800 rev./day by the fourth day. In warmer environments the increase was less, reaching 1,150 at 33° C. At temperatures below 22° C. the activity showed very marked increases, rising to 6,000 at 15° C., 11,000 at 10° C., but only to 9,450 at 5° C. These animals at 15°, 10°, and 5° C. were groups of rats (originally 12 in each group) not fully acclimatized to the cold. They were adjusted to the activity cages at 22° C. and then exposed to one of the lower temperatures for 10 to 15 days before starvation.

Figure 2 also contains the results from 12 animals that were exposed to all the environmental temperatures studied. These animals were taken gradually from 33° to 5° C. over a period of seven months, with intervals of adaptation, starvation, and recuperation at each of the designated temperatures. The time spent at each temperature was about four weeks. In view of the exposure to gradually decreasing temperatures and the time spent at each temperature, it is probable that these rats were fairly well acclimatized to the cold (8, 23, 24, 25, 26). No acclimatization was evident in the activity of rats at temperatures of 22° C. and above.

The acclimatized rats displayed a lower average activity in starvation at 15°, 10° and 5° C. than the corresponding nonacclimatized groups. None

TABLE 1

BODY WEIGHT LOSS DURING FOUR DAYS OF STARVATION

| | Body weight loss (gm.) | | |
|---|---|---|---|
| Env. temp. 0° C. | Activity cage | | Ordinary cage |
| | Nonacclimatized | Acclimatized | |
| 5 | 109 | 99 | 110 |
| 10 | 111 | 100 | |
| 15 | 72 | 64 | |
| 22 | 63 | | 52 |
| 27 | 48 | | |
| 30 | 48 | | |
| 33 | 42 | | 41 |

of the acclimatized animals died at any temperature during their four days of starvation, whereas in the nonacclimatized groups, seven died at 10° C. and four at 5° C. At 10° C. several of these animals were found prostrate and very cold on the fourth day of starvation after having run close to 13,000 revolutions during the previous 24 hours. Two of these animals were successfully revived by placing them in a warmer environment.

Table 1 shows the loss of body weight during the four days of starvation. Both the weight loss and the activity increased as the environmental temperature dropped. Rats of comparable weight were starved in ordinary individual cages at various environmental temperatures; these animals showed losses of body weight in four days similar to those of animals in the activity cages. At 22° C., the average length of survival in the ordinary cage was about nine days and in the activity cage about seven days. In the cold (5° C.) the survival was close to four days (19) after starvation in either type of cage.

Figure 3 demonstrates the effects of partial food restriction and com-

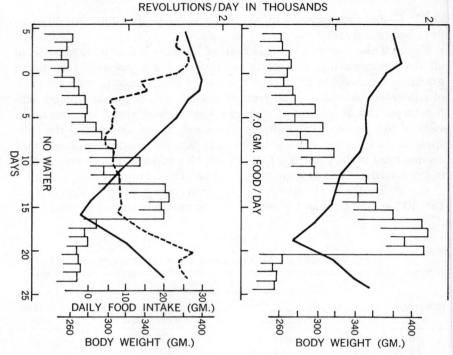

FIG. 3. The daily spontaneous activity, body weight loss, and food intake during (a) partial food and (b) complete water deprivation at an environmental temperature of 22° C. Eight rats were used in each study.

plete water deprivation on the spontaneous activity and body weight loss when rats were given one-third (7 gm./day) of their voluntary food intake at 22° C. The daily activity gradually increased over a period of 17 days, when maximal activity appeared to have been reached at slightly under 2,000 rev./day. This is lower than that observed in the completely starved rat. Refeeding resulted in an abrupt return to, or slightly below, the initial level of activity. This fall in activity on return of food was characteristic of animals at all temperatures. Finger (9) also has reported a depression of activity following restoration of food.

Complete water restriction produced a similar picture. The activity increased gradually over a period of 13 days to form a plateau at close to 1,500 rev./day. The drop in activity on the first day after the return of water has also been observed by Finger and Reid (10), but the depression below pre-thirst levels did not appear in our animals. For most of the period of water lack the food intake was about 7 gm./day, but during maximal activity it was 8 gm./day (cf. 10). This food intake may account for the slightly lower maximum activity of these animals compared to the partial food-restricted group.

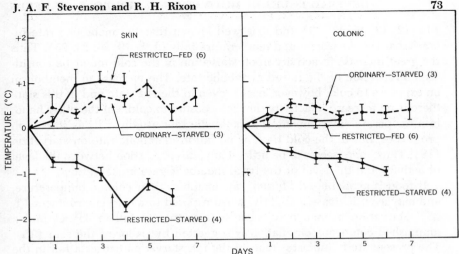

FIG. 4. The changes in skin and colonic temperatures of rats starved in canvas slings (Restricted-Starved), fed while in slings (Restricted-Fed) and starved but allowed to move freely in ordinary single cages (Ordinary-Starved). Vertical bars represent the standard error of the mean difference. Numbers in parenthesis represent number of animals. The environmental temperature was 22° C.

Preliminary experiments have been done on the skin and colonic temperatures of rats during starvation at 22° C. Figure 4 shows the temperature changes of rats in canvas slings, to minimize muscular activity, and in those allowed to move freely in ordinary individual cages (not activity cages). The animals starved in the slings showed a decline in both skin and colonic temperatures. The largest decrease was in the skin temperature. These decreases did not appear in rats which were fed during a four-day period in the slings. Rats starved but allowed to move freely maintained their skin and colonic temperatures for at least the first six days of complete food deprivation.

## DISCUSSION

Starvation causes an increase in the spontaneous activity of the rat. The inverse relation which we have observed between the level of the environmental temperature and the amount of activity supports the hypothesis that this increase in activity is related to the maintenance of body temperature in starvation. This hypothesis is further supported by our preliminary observations that the body temperature tends to fall in starvation when activity is restricted, but not when it is permitted.

A relation between activity and metabolic rate has long been considered

(11, 12, 13, 16, 17, 20) and it is well known that the metabolic rate increases as the environmental temperature falls (1, 8, 19, 23, 24, 25). Thus the great increase in activity upon starvation in the cold might be considered a reflection of the raised metabolic rate. The increase in metabolism on exposure to cold, however, occurs even in the fed state and in this state there is no increase in activity during exposure to cold. On the other hand, in a temperate environment, the metabolic rate usually falls as starvation progresses, but in the cold there is no fall in metabolic rate on starvation (19). Thus, there seems to be little, if any, direct relation between the level of activity and the level of the basal metabolic rate in starvation.

If food is available *ad libitum*, rats maintain their colonic temperature, and may even increase it slightly, when exposed to a cold environment (1, 25). Starvation in man may cause temperature to fall to 35° C. and a diminished cutaneous circulation is suggested by pallor of the skin (15). The present study indicates that, in the rat, starvation causes a fall in the core and peripheral temperature of the rat when activity is severely restricted, but not when activity is possible.

It appears from the similarity of the weight losses in the two cages that starvation increases the activity of rats in ordinary individual cages or in activity cages equally. Our methods of observation did not measure activity in the form of shivering and it is possible that the animals in the individual cages achieved a part of their increased muscular activity in this manner. Increased shivering may have decreased the running of acclimatized and nonacclimatized rats at 5° C. compared to that at 10° C (8).

Bargeton *et al.* (1) have found that the heat production of acclimatized rats is less than that of nonacclimatized rats in a cold environment. From this it may be inferred that acclimatization is associated with a reduced loss of heat. And it is the acclimatized animals which show a smaller increase in activity on starvation in the cold. The improved conservation of heat has perhaps reduced the demand for its production to maintain body temperature.

The ability of the body to conserve heat is dependent on its effective insulation and this is increased in various ways in the acclimatized animal. Starvation undoubtedly causes a deterioration in this insulation; e.g., through catabolism of the subcutaneous fat. With the progress of starvation, the ability to conserve heat may thus steadily decline and lead to an increasing demand for the production of heat to maintain body temperature. This increasing demand could be supplied, in part at least, by a steady increase in muscular activity.

Brobeck (6) has supported the hypothesis that regulation of food intake is related to the regulation of body temperature. He and his colleagues (7) have also observed that a decline in body temperature precedes the rise in running activity that occurs with estrus and that the low activity in pseudopregnancy is associated with a high body temperature. Ryan (21) has recently shown that dinitrophenol causes a marked increase in the body temperature of dogs and it is known (11, 12) that this drug, which increases the oxygen consumption and presumably the heat production, reduces activity.

Muscular activity appears to be closely related to the maintenance of body temperature, and to be interrelated with food intake in this function. The increase in activity on deprivation of water would not, at first, appear to support this conclusion, but even in this circumstance the degree of activity was related to the amount of food eaten.

## SUMMARY

1. The running activity of rats increased in starvation. This increase in activity was inversely related to the environmental temperature between 33° and 10° C. and varied from 2 to 14 times that in the fed state. The activity at 5° C., however, was lower than at 10° C.

2. Starvation did not produce as great an increase in the activity of acclimatized as in nonacclimatized rats at temperatures from 5° to 15° C.

3. The weight loss during four days of starvation in activity or in ordinary cages was similar and increased as the environmental temperature decreased.

4. Rats restricted to one-third (7.0 gm.) of their voluntary daily food intake, or completely deprived of water, increased their activity gradually and reached a maximum activity in 17 and 13 days, respectively. This activity was less than that after four days of starvation. The activity of the water deprived group was slightly less than that of the partial food-restricted animals but the food intake of the former was 8.0 gm. during maximal activity. Both groups showed a sudden drop to, or below, their initial level of activity on return of food or water *ad libitum*. This also occurred after complete starvation.

5. The rectal and skin temperatures decreased during starvation when activity was severely restricted, but not when the animals were fed and restricted simultaneously or starved with freedom of movement.

It is suggested that the increased activity during starvation is related to the maintenance of body temperature and is interrelated with food intake in this function.

## ACKNOWLEDGMENTS

We wish to thank Mr. M. Barnes and Miss L. Myiata for their technical assistance. Dr. Ruth Wolfe of Hoffmann-LaRoche kindly supplied the vitamins used in the synthetic diet.

REFERENCES

1. BARGETON, D., EON, M., KRUMM-HELLER, C., LIEBERMANN, C., and MASSON, J. (1954) Influence de l'adaptation sur les réactions thermo-regulatrices au froid chez le rat. *J. Physiol.* (Paris), *46*, 845.

2. BEVAN, W., JR., LEWIS, G. T., BLOOM, W. L., and ABESS, A. T. (1950) Spontaneous activity in rats fed an amino acid-deficient diet. *Amer. J. Physiol.*, *163*, 104.

3. BLOOMFIELD, A. L. and TAINTER, M. L. (1942-43) The effect of Vitamin B deprivation on spontaneous activity of the rat. *J. Lab. clin. Med.*, *28*, 1680.

4. BROBECK, J. R. (1945) Effects of variations in activity, food intake and environmental temperature on weight gain in the albino rat. *Amer. J. Physiol.*, *143*, 1.

5. BROBECK, J. R. (1946) Mechanism of the development of obesity in animals with hypothalamic lesions. *Physiol. Rev.*, *26*, 541.

6. BROBECK, J. R. (1948) Food intake as a mechanism of temperature regulation. *Yale J. Biol. Med.*, *20*, 545.

7. BROBECK, J. R., WHEATLAND, M., and STROMINGER, J. L. (1947) Variations in regulation of energy exchange association with estrus, diestrus, and pseudopregnancy in rats. *Endocrinology, 40*, 65.

8. BURTON, A. C. and EDHOLM, O. G. (1955) *Man in a cold environment.* London: Edward Arnold Ltd., 273 pp.

9. FINGER, F. W. (1951) The effect of food deprivation and subsequent satiation upon general activity in the rat. *J. comp. physiol. Psychol.*, *44*, 557.

10. FINGER, F. W. and REID, L. S. (1952) The effect of water deprivation and subsequent satiation upon general activity in the rat. *J. comp. physiol. Psychol.*, *45*, 368.

11. HALL, V. E. and LINDSAY, M. (1934) The effect of dinitrophenol on the spontaneous activity of the rat. *J. Pharmacol.*, *51*, 430.

12. HALL, V. E. and LINDSAY, M. (1938) The relation of the thyroid gland to the spontaneous activity of the rat. *Endocrinology, 22*, 66.

13. HOSKIN, R. G. (1927) Endocrine factors in vigor. *Endocrinology, 11*, 97.

14. HOUSSAY, B. A., LEWIS, J. T., ORIAS, O., BROUN MENENDEZ, E., HUG, E., FOHLIA, V. G., and LELOIR, L. F. (1951) *Human physiology.* 1st ed. New York, McGraw-Hill Book Company, Inc., pp. 490 *et seq.*

15. KEYS, A., BRONZEK, J., HENSCHEL, A., MICHELSON, O., and TAYLOR, H. L. (1950) *The biology of human starvation.* Rochester, Minn., University of Minnesota Press, Vol. I, pp. 612 *et seq.*

16. LEE, M. O. and BUSKIRK, E. F. VAN (1928) The effect of thyroidectomy on spontaneous activity in the rat, with a consideration of the relation of the basal metabolism to spontaneous activity. *Amer. J. Physiol.*, *84*, 321.

17. REED, J. D. (1947) Spontaneous activity of animals. *Psychol. Bull.*, *44*, 393.

18. RICHTER, C. P. and RICE, K. K. (1954) Comparison of the effects produced by fasting on gross bodily activity of wild and domesticated Norway rats. *Amer. J. Physiol.*, *179*, 305.

19. RIXON, R. H. and STEVENSON, J. A. F. (1957) Factors influencing the survival of rats in starvation: metabolic rate and body weight loss. *Amer. J. Physiol.*, *188*, 332.

20. RUNDQUIST, E. A. and BELLIS, C. J. (1933) Respiratory metabolism of active and inactive rats. *Amer. J. Physiol.*, *106*, 670.
21. RYAN, E. A. (1951) Studies on the effect of 2:4 dinitrophenol of liverless and diabetic dogs. *Amer. J. Physiol.*, *167*, 224.
22. SCHMIDT-NIELSEN, K. and SCHMIDT-NIELSEN, B. (1952) Water metabolism of desert mammals. *Physiol. Rev.*, *32*, 146.
23. SELLERS, E. A., REICHMAN, S., and THOMAS, N. (1951) Acclimatization to cold: natural and artificial. *Amer. J. Physiol.*, *167*, 644.
24. SELLERS, E. A., REICHMAN, S., THOMAS, N., and YOU, S. S. (1951) Acclimatization to cold in rats: metabolic rates. *Amer. J. Physiol.*, *167*, 651.
25. SELLERS, E. A. and YOU, S. S. (1950) Role of thyroid in metabolic responses to a cold environment. *Amer. J. Physiol.*, *163*, 81.
26. SELLERS, E. A., YOU, S. S., and THOMAS, N. (1951) Acclimatization and survival of rats in the cold: effect of clipping, of adrenalectomy and of thyroidectomy. *Amer. J. Physiol.*, *165*, 481.
27. SIEGEL, P. S. and STEINBERG, M. (1949) Activity level as a function of hunger. *J. comp. physiol. Psychol.*, *42*, 413.
28. SOUTO-MAIOR, M. G., and FOGLIA, V. G. (1944) La actividad espontanea de la rata diabetica. *Rev. Soc. Argent. Biol.*, *20*, 55.
29. STEVENSON, J. A. F. *Cold injury.* M. I. Ferrer, Ed. Transactions of the Third Conference, February 22, 23, 24, and 25, 1954. New York, The Josiah Macy, Jr. Foundation, 195 pp. 165 *et seq.*
30. WALD, G. and JACKSON, B. (1944) Activity and nutritional deprivation. *Nat. Acad. Sci. Proc.*, *30*, 255.

# 8. A Repetition of the Calvin-Bicknell-Sperling Study of Conditioned Drive

## P. S. Siegel and M. F. MacDonnell

*Although Calvin, Bicknell, and Sperling demonstrated the establishment of an acquired drive based upon an appetitive state, most experimenters have been unable to replicate these findings. The Siegel and MacDonnell study is noteworthy since these investigators have attempted to duplicate the conditions under which Calvin, Bicknell, and Sperling obtained positive findings.*

Calvin, Bicknell, and Sperling (1) recently reported a finding that is both startling to the reinforcement theorist and puzzling to the student of hunger. They employed two groups of albino rats, exposing each animal individually to a distinctive environment (a striped box) for 30 min. daily.

*J. comp. physiol. Psychol.*, 1954, *47*, 250-252. Reprinted with the permission of the senior author and The American Psychological Association. This research was supported in part by a grant from the Research Committee of the University of Alabama.

The animals of one group (high drive) were placed in this environment following 22 hr. of food privation; the animals of the other group (low drive), after 1 hr. of food privation. No animal received food or water in the distinctive environment. Rather, daily rations were administered in the home cages at a much later time. This procedure was repeated until all animals had been given 24 such daily experiences, and then the critical test was introduced. Each animal was food deprived for approximately 11½ hr. (intermediate drive level) and then placed in the distinctive environment with food present. Under these conditions, the food intake of the high-drive group was reliably greater than that of the low-drive group. The authors concluded:

> These results suggest that a previously neutral stimulus situation (the striped box) can acquire motivating properties from association with a relatively strong drive state. These results are interpreted to suggest that reinforcement is not essential for the establishment of a conditioned drive (1, p. 175).

The implications of the Calvin-Bicknell-Sperling experiment are far-reaching. The results are embarrassing to the learning theorist who holds to the principle of reinforcement. They cannot be "squared" with the psychophysiology of hunger. The present study was undertaken with the conviction that the study should be repeated.

## METHOD

With little change, we have followed the methodology employed by the original investigators. We shall note any significant variation.

Thirty-two male albino rats of the Sherman strain, varying in age from approximately 150 to 170 days, were utilized as Ss. At the beginning of the experiment, weights ranged from 208 to 364 gm.

The distinctive environment consisted of a wooden cage of triangular floor plan. The sides were fashioned of ¼-in. plywood panels, 12 in. square. The inside surface of each panel was painted with alternate black and white stripes, approximately ½ in. wide. Top and botton surfaces consisted of hardware cloth of ½-in. mesh. Illumination was afforded by a single 7-w. bulb suspended about 1 in. above the center of the cage. On the recommendation of one of the previous investigators,* the "hurdle," which was used in the original study to further the distinctiveness of the situation, was omitted as superfluous.

Sixteen of these special cages were used. Arranged in nests of four, they occupied an area roughly 2 ft. by 10 ft. During the experiment, each animal was always placed in the same box.

The procedure conveniently breaks down into three stages: adaptation

* Calvin, J. S. Personal communication, 1953.

to the feeding cycle, exposure to the unique environment, and the critical test series.

All animals were handled until docile and then placed on a once-daily feeding schedule. Rations consisted of a wet mash of ground Purina Laboratory Chow checkers and water, in the proportion of two to three by weight. The mash was administered daily to all animals in individual home cages, beginning at 6:50 P.M. A large number of food cups and a staggered order of presentation were used. This permitted precise control of the feeding interval. In the original study, the amount of mash presented to the animal was fixed at 25 gm. daily. This provides only 10 gm. of utilizable food (Purina) and was probably calorically insufficient to sustain normal weight. No weights were reported in the original study, but it is our guess that the Calvin-Bicknell-Sperling animals lost weight during the course of the experiment and probably suffered a state of semistarvation in the terminal stages. This should make for some "blurring" of the drive differential between the two groups. To avert this, we fixed the duration of the daily feeding interval rather than the amount of food. Our animals showed a steady and normal weight gain. Our procedure was to present the food mixture for 2 hr. on the first day, 1 hr. on the second, ½ hr. on the third, 15 min. on the fourth and fifth days, 30 min. on the sixth and seventh, and for 20 min. daily thereafter. Daily records of body weight and food intake were taken, and the 20-min. interval was found to be the briefest that permitted normal weight gain. This feeding interval was observed uniformly during the remainder of the experiment.

After 11 days of adaptation to the feeding schedule, the box experience was instituted. At this point it was necessary to select the two groups. To insure sensitivity in the final statistical evaluation, it was decided to match the two groups and thus control intragroup variability. The mean daily food intake for the last 4 days of the adaptation period was utilized as a provisional matching criterion. The animals were paired on the basis of this criterion, and one S of each pair was randomly assigned to either the high- or the low-drive group. For the 24 subsequent days, each animal of the high-drive group was placed in the box for 30 min. daily, 22 hr. after the daily feeding period. The animals of the low-drive group were placed in the box for 30 min., 1 hr. after their daily feeding period. Again, a staggered schedule was employed, making possible an exact control of all time intervals. In the entire experiment, the margin of error nowhere exceeded one full minute. The high-drive animals occupied the boxes between the clock hours 5:20 and 6:35 P.M.; the low-drive animals, between 8:20 and 9:35 P.M. Body weights were taken every three days, and a steady gain was noted in all animals but one. This animal very soon died.

The first critical test was conducted on the morning of the twenty-fifth day. The animals of both groups were food deprived for 11½ hr. Each was then placed in the striped box with a weighed food cup containing the

Purina paste. At the end of 10 min., the cup was removed and a second cup immediately substituted. At the end of 20 min., the animal was removed and both cups reweighed. In this fashion, we obtained a record of food intake for the first 10 min. and for the full 20 min. of the test trial. This procedure was repeated on the evening of the twenty-fifth day and on the morning and evening of the twenty-sixth day. During these three trials, a 12-hr. food privation interval was observed.

The original investigators employed food measurement intervals of 5 and 15 min. during the test trials. We elected to use longer intervals to increase reliability.

## RESULTS AND DISCUSSION

Table 1 summarizes our findings. During the first and most critical test trial, the mean food intake of the low-drive group ($N = 16$) was found to be slightly greater than that of the high-drive group ($N = 15$) for both the initial 10 min. and for the full 20-min. test interval. A comparison of mean intakes for the entire series of test trials reveals the same slight difference favoring the low-drive group.

TABLE 1

MEAN FOOD INTAKE IN GRAMS DURING TEST TRIALS

| Period | Group | | $p$ |
| --- | --- | --- | --- |
| | High drive | Low drive | |
| First 10 min. of first test | $12.7 \pm 5.7$ | $14.2 \pm 6.5$ | $.50 > p > .40$ |
| Full 20 min. of first test | $26.6 \pm 7.7$ | $28.4 \pm 7.9$ | $> .50$ |
| Total of all four test trials | $99.1 \pm 18.8$ | $105.3 \pm 13.2$ | $> .50$ |

It will be recalled that immediately following adaptation to the feeding schedule, our two groups were provisionally matched on the basis of daily food intake. Although there is strong evidence to suggest that the amount of a calorically constant diet that is ingested daily by the rat is unvarying, we re-examined our two groups at the conclusion of the experiment to make assessment of the extent to which they were matched at the time of the critical measurement series. For the four days immediately preceding the critical test series, the mean daily food intake of the low-drive group was found to be 40.3 gm. with a standard deviation of 6.65. The high-drive group yielded a mean of 41.4 with a standard deviation of 5.96. It is apparent that no significant separation of the two groups occurred during the intervening three weeks. At the time of testing, they were well matched with respect to the criterion. Mean daily food intake for the four days preceding the critical tests was found to correlate .538

with the 10-min. intake during the first test, .505 with the full 20-min. intake, and .320 with mean total intake for all four tests.

The slight mean differences favoring the low-drive group, reported in Table 1, were evaluated for significance by employing the $t$ for matched groups. In each instance the standard deviation of the difference was reduced by incorporating one of the above positive correlations into the formula. Each of the obtained $t$'s was less than 1. As the corresponding $p$ values of Table 1 clearly indicate, all our differences may be readily attributed to the operation of chance.

Our findings do not agree with those of Calvin, Bicknell, and Sperling. We can offer no explanation for the disagreement. Strain, age, and weight differences in Ss and the employment of a test interval of greater duration would seem to constitute inconsequential methodological differences. Our control of daily feeding does represent a significant procedural deviation. But, as noted earlier, by sharpening the drive differential during exposure to the distinctive environment, our operations should make for an even greater separation of the two groups during the critical test series.

## SUMMARY

Calvin, Bicknell, and Sperling have reported an experiment that suggests that in the absence of known reinforcement a neutral stimulus situation may take on motivational properties from repeated association with a strong drive state. The present study, a repetition of their experiment, failed to confirm their findings.

## REFERENCE

1. CALVIN, J. S., BICKNELL, ELIZABETH A., and SPERLING, D. S. (1953) Establishment of a conditioned drive based on the hunger drive. *J. comp. physiol. Psychol.*, 46, 173-175.

# 9. Novelty and Curiosity as Determinants of Exploratory Behaviour

## D. E. Berlyne

*Although, as Berlyne has acknowledged, Dashiell and Nissen wrote of exploration twenty-five years prior to the publication of this article, next to nothing had been done to analyze the operation of this extremely important form of motivation. This is one of the early articles which posited curiosity to be an important motivational source.*

## I. The Importance of Novelty

Psychology has so far had surprisingly little to say about stimuli which influence behaviour simply because they are new. Stimuli which owe their potency to the fact that they are not new, i.e., that they have been experienced before in certain circumstances, have given rise to the vast corpus of observations and generalizations that go to make up learning theory. But the everyday activities of both men and animals seem to attest the importance of novelty as well as familiarity in features of the environment, and novelty may, in fact, hold the key to our understanding some of the more complex levels of motivation in the human being. Few human impulses are more inexorable than the urge to escape from monotony and boredom to some new form of stimulation, as the industrial psychologist and even the psychiatrist have so frequently reason to note. An active striving to encounter new experiences, and to assimilate and understand them when encountered, underlies a huge variety of activities highly esteemed by society, from those of the scientist, the artist and the philosopher to those of the polar explorer and the connoisseur of wines. 'The instinct of curiosity', says McDougall (13), 'is at the base of many of man's most splendid achievements, for rooted in it are his speculative and scientific tendencies'.

Reactions to or towards novelty are met with in one guise after another when the problem of interest is examined (cf. Berlyne (1)); indeed, in one sense, 'interest' is used more or less as a synonym for 'curiosity'. And if one turns from interest to a closely related topic, one finds novelty figuring prominently among the qualities that can give stimuli the power to attract

*Brit. J. Psychol.,* 1950, *41,* 68–80. Reprinted with permission of the author and the British Psychological Society. The latter half of this paper, under the title 'Novelty as a Problem in Behaviour Theory', was read to a meeting of the Scottish Branch of the British Psychological Society at St. Andrews on May 6, 1950.

attention, a factor whose study has been unduly neglected (cf. Berlyne (2)). There would thus appear to be few aspects of human behaviour which might not be illuminated by some research into the effects of novel stimuli, including the question of curiosity, and yet such investigation has been remarkably lacking hitherto. One probable reason for this lack is that the relevant phenomena are so enormously complicated in man that observations of human beings cannot advance far without being supplemented by studies of the prototypes of human curiosity and response to novelty in lower animals. And the most suitable animal for such studies is undoubtedly the rat. Apart from the well-known and frequently reiterated virtues of the rat as a laboratory subject, research into his exploratory behaviour may enable us to knit the functioning of curiosity into the large body of systematized knowledge that has been acquired from rat experiments and has been shown to be pertinent in the highest degree to human psychology.

Now, a consideration of the role of novelty in the behaviour of the rat leads us to much the same conclusions as with the human being: any account of rat psychology which neglects to mention and explain curiosity and response to novelty must be seriously deficient, and yet very little has actually been done to remedy such a deficiency. One of the first facts learnt from even a few minutes' observation of rats is that they are highly inquisitive. Dashiell (3) and Nissen (18) have demonstrated the existence of an 'exploratory drive'; it is strong enough to induce a rat to cross an electrified grid in order to examine an unfamiliar environment. But next to nothing has been done to analyse the working of this extremely important form of motivation. What precisely are the adequate stimuli arousing it? What is the nature of the reactions it elicits? How does it come to be satiated? These, and a host of other questions concerning the laws of curiosity, remain unanswered, and a large body of experimental data will, no doubt, have to be painstakingly accumulated before they can be elucidated.

## II. Historical

If experimental studies of curiosity have been scanty, theoretical treatments of the question have been slightly less meagre. And before going on to report the experiment with which this paper is concerned and the hypotheses it was designed to test, it may be helpful to consider briefly the principal theories that have so far been propounded.

(1) *Shand.* According to Shand ((21), pp. 438ff.), curiosity is a 'primary emotion', consisting of 'a single impulse to know, instinctively governing and sustaining the attention, and evoking those bodily movements which will enable us to gain a fuller acquaintance with its object'. But while the end of curiosity and the stimuli arousing it are innately deter-

mined, some, at least, of the actions subserving it in the human being are acquired. Thus, apart from talk about instincts 'innately directed' towards certain ends, which is too apt to lead to confused thought for contemporary taste, we have a conception which may be reconciled with modern learning theory and bears distinct resemblances to the view we shall outline later.

Also pertinent is Shand's account of surprise. There are two varieties of this emotion: 'sensational surprise' is a reaction to 'a jar or conflict . . . between a present sensation and the memory of preceding sensations', while in 'cognitive surprise', the conflict is between 'a present cognition and a memory of preceding cognitions'. Wonder, the 'source of the love of knowledge', contains both curiosity and cognitive surprise. It is aroused by anything extraordinary and difficult to understand.

(2) *McDougall.* Curiosity, with its corresponding emotion of 'wonder', is one of McDougall's list of instincts (13, 14): '. . . its impulse is to approach and examine more closely the object that excites it. . . . The native excitant of the instinct would seem to be any object similar to, yet perceptibly different from, familiar objects habitually noticed. . . . It is . . . not easy to distinguish in general terms between the excitants of curiosity and fear . . . the two instincts, with their opposed impulses of approach and retreat, are apt to be excited in animals and very young children in rapid alternation, and simultaneously in ourselves' ((13), pp. 57–8).[1]

This treatment of the problem, with all its begged questions, is vulnerable to all the obloquy for which McDougall's doctrine of instincts was in the 1920's and 1930's such a popular target. But his description of the 'native excitant' or adequate stimulus of curiosity and his indication of a close link between curiosity and fear are extremely important and will be discussed later.

(3) *Freud.* The impulse for knowledge and investigation (*der Wiss- oder Forschertrieb*) is attributed by Freud ((4), pp. 594–5) 'on the one hand, to a sublimated form of acquisition (*Bemächtigung*)', while 'on the other hand, the energy with which it works comes from the looking impulse (*Schaulust*, scoptophilia)'. The impulse to acquire is derived from the desire to incorporate external objects, which characterizes the oral stage of psycho-sexual development, and the looking impulse, which underlies the perversion known as voyeurism, is one of the partial impulses contained in the libido. Curiosity is therefore sexual in origin; 'indeed' says Freud, 'curiosity may perhaps first be awakened by sexual problems'.

This may well be a most valuable contribution to our understanding of the development of curiosity in the individual human being, but it can hardly, for a number of reasons, be considered a complete explanation of the origins and functioning of curiosity:

(a) There is no lack of evidence that curiosity is not first awakened by sexual problems in the way that Freud meant. The fact that he goes on to

---

1 Quoted by permission of the publishers.

speak of the question 'where do children come from?' as the first problem shows that he had in mind such curiosity as makes use of language. But many observers of early childhood (e.g. Piaget (20), p. 126) report intensive curiosity and investigatory activity long before the advent of speech: the infant is busily engaged in exploring and even experimenting with his environment, thereby acquainting himself with the diversity of the phenomena it contains and the connexions between them. If he had not already equipped himself in this way with exploratory techniques and habits, he could not put them at the disposal of his sexual curiosity later on.

(b) Behaviour analogous to that characterizing human curiosity is found in the lower mammals. Although many equivalents of psycho-analytic processes and mechanisms have been found in the rat and other animals, the Freudian theory of psycho-sexual development, which depends so thoroughly on verbal and imaginal symbols, can hardly be applied to infra-human species.

(c) A tendency to explore novel aspects of an animal's surroundings is so essential biologically that it is bound to have had an earlier source than the sublimation of libidinal impulses due to their repression at the behest of human society.

(4) *Holt.* For Holt ((8), p. 216), 'exploration' is 'random movement with adience sustained'. According to his principle of adience, there is an innate tendency to approach any stimulus, although some cause injurious overstimulation and thus set up avoidance responses. When an adient movement has been elicited, the organism is attracted to the surface of the object concerned. 'And within this locus the random movements are constrained to 'explore' the surface of the object; thus chain reflexes are developed (and fixed as neurograms) which, even when the object is absent, will re-create its surface contour.'

This is an ingenious attempt to face important questions which many other neurologically minded psychologists have ignored, but it cannot be regarded as satisfactory:

(a) Holt's universal and innate adience to all stimuli has not been experimentally demonstrated.

(b) No explanation is offered of why certain stimuli attract curiosity more than others.

(c) No explanation is offered of how curiosity comes to be satiated.

(5) *Taylor.* A recent theory of exploratory activity proposed by Taylor (23) points out that an animal will find a repertoire of 'slick responses to every aspect of his environment' helpful in practically everything he does. A 'generalized habit' of learning 'to get about easily and quickly in any new environment' will therefore grow up, and this need to explore will function as a secondary drive. But stimuli which have frequently been associated with need-reduction are more likely than others to attract ex-

ploration, and behaviour-sequences leading to them will undergo secondary reinforcement.[1]

## III. The Problem of Novelty

This review of theories of curiosity reveals that several different mechanisms, motives and adequate stimuli have been alleged by different writers to call forth exploratory behaviour. And these alternative accounts are by no means necessarily incompatible; it is quite likely that superficially similar forms of exploratory behaviour may be derived from different sources at different times or even at once.

For example, there are good theoretical and empirical grounds for believing that an organism can and will learn particular investigatory response-sequences which satisfy particular motives, whether we think of the laboratory-sophisticated rat seeking the goal-box of a maze or the detective searching systematically for clues. It is even probable that exploratory habits found useful in one situation may generalize to a large variety of analogous situations, as Taylor (23) asserts (and as Miller and Dollard (16) have shown to be the case with imitation).

But besides exploration motivated and learned in this manner (which we may term *instrumental exploration*) there seems to be exploration evoked by novelty. Taylor claims that the exploratory drive is 'increased in strength by unfamiliar surroundings'. But what is there about unfamiliarity itself that could evoke a particular reaction? The role of novelty presents a difficult problem: if there are responses which new stimuli elicit but old stimuli do not elicit, these responses must be due to some quality which all new stimuli possess and all old stimuli lack. But, apart from the purely negative fact of not having occurred before, what quality is there that characterizes novel stimuli and novel stimuli only?

In the case of stimuli which influence behaviour because of the organism's previous experience of them, there is no such problem: these stimuli or similar ones have all had the opportunity in the past to acquire the power to evoke learned responses. Nor is there the same difficulty with the stimuli of innate reflexes: they have in common certain physico-chemical properties which affect receptors and the nervous system in certain ways. But novel stimuli have no physico-chemical properties to differentiate them from others; being new, they cannot owe their effects to recognition. How

---

[1] Pavlov (19) mentions the 'investigatory (or "what-is-it?") reflex'. But, although he believes that human 'inquisitiveness, the parent of . . . scientific method' has grown out of it, this can scarcely be numbered among these theories of curiosity. The adequate stimulus is not novelty, in any sense resembling those under discussion here, but any sudden change in the environment. The response is limited to orientation of receptor organs, and so it cannot account for the enormous variability of exploratory activity.

therefore is the difference between the familiar and the unfamiliar communicated to the nervous system? How does the organism distinguish between old and new and respond differentially?

To this problem there would appear to be two possible solutions:

(1) It may be that *not all* novel stimuli are effective, but only those which are familiar in some respects and novel in others—i.e., stimuli such as Shand believed responsible for 'surprise' and McDougall for 'curiosity'. This presumably means that the familiar aspects set up some sort of expectation ('fractional anticipatory response' (16), 'preparatory set' (17), etc.) with which the perception of the novel feature conflicts. Such a conflict has been stated by Isaacs (11) to be the root of our conception of truth and falsity.

Now, in the adult human being it would indeed appear that curiosity is most often aroused not by just any novel perception but by some unexpected feature in familiar material, by something that is in some degree similar and in some degree dissimilar to what is well known to him. A sideshow in a fair-ground will attract more patrons if it exhibits a two-headed but otherwise normal man or a bearded but otherwise undistinguished lady than if it offers a collection of beetles or birds' eggs, all of which may be completely new to those who inspect them.

In view of what will later be said about the relation between curiosity and fear, it is interesting to remember Hebb's findings in his studies of fear in chimpanzees (6). Expression of intense alarm was produced by such stimuli as an anesthetized ape, a model of a dismembered ape, etc.; Hebb comes to the conclusion that some strange variation in something familiar can excite fear, and he attributes the effect to a disruption of some habitual cerebral process.

But, without denying the existence of exploration induced by the unexpected (which we may term *surprise-exploration*), we shall provisionally assume that there is another type of exploration instigated by novelty pure and simple. Our reasons are as follows:

(*a*) To a human infant, very little is familiar. If the adequate stimulus for exploration is not novelty alone, but a combination of novelty and familiarity, it is difficult to see how the intensive investigatory activity of early years, which familiarizes the child with his surroundings, could occur.

(*b*) In the experiment to be described, the stimuli used—a wooden cube and a cardboard ring—do not appear to resemble anything the rats are likely to have previously encountered, let alone encountered frequently. Moreover, both cube and ring excited curiosity to a similar extent. It is highly unlikely that two stimuli selected at random would both have much the same degree of novelty in familiarity.

However, since the animals were not observed from birth, and since, in any case, there is no knowing what degree of resemblance to known objects is required, one cannot be sure.

If, as we assume, there is exploration in response to all novelty, we must resort to the second solution to the problem of novelty:

(2) The reaction may be one that *all* stimuli originally evoke, but which disappears (becomes habituated) as the organism becomes familiar with them. The crucial difference between novel and familiar stimuli that we have been seeking would then be that the former have not had time to lose their curiosity-inducing effect.

But, whatever form of novelty may ultimately turn out to be involved—whether all novelty or only the unexpected or some other form—the most urgent task would seem to be to demonstrate the influence of novelty on exploratory behaviour and to ascertain the manner of its functioning.

## IV. A Theory of Curiosity

We are now in a position to formulate the theory of curiosity that our experiment is to test. It consists of two postulates from which, when combined with the postulates of Hull's behaviour theory, three corollaries describing the functioning of exploratory behaviour may be deduced. We shall go on to describe an experiment which will verify or falsify four predictions following from our postulates and corollaries.

To some readers, what follows may seem insufficiently formal. To others, it may seem a trite and pompous re-statement of common knowledge. But more research must be carried out before the objections of the former can be removed, while to the latter we may point out that before common knowledge becomes scientific knowledge, it must be couched in a form which will enable it to be rigorously verified and related to general principles, derived from studies of a great variety of other phenomena.

*Postulate I. When a novel stimulus affects an organism's receptors, there will occur a drive-stimulus-producing response* ($R \rightsquigarrow S_D$) (*which we shall call 'curiosity'*)

*Comments*

(*a*) This postulate is put forward in this provisional form with several reservations as discussed above:

(i) It is assumed that any novel stimulus is involved, but it may concern only certain forms of novelty.

(ii) It is assumed that the curiosity-response is innate, but it may be acquired.

(iii) By 'organism' is meant, for the time being, any mammalian organism.

(*b*) We must now consider the question of the relations between curiosity and fear. McDougall (13) states that the two may be aroused by similar excitants. More recently, Whiting & Mowrer have, in the course of one of their experiments, made some observations pointing in the same direction:

> Preliminary observations showed that if animals were placed in the maze without prior habituation, they showed considerable anxiety. This was first indicated by great cautiousness of movement and excessive urination and defaecation. Later there was a great period of feverish exploration, during which animals ignored food even though they had not eaten for 24–36 hours. These observations suggest that 'curiosity' is perhaps more closely related to anxiety than is ordinarily supposed ((24), p. 236).

This impression is certainly gained from watching rats casually. The same sort of stimulus, namely anything novel, seems to excite fear or curiosity, and often an animal appears to be wavering between the two.

Now, curiosity and fear are alike in being drives motivating the organism to put an end to them, in being aroused by external stimuli, and in being aroused in particular by the novel and the unexpected. But the behaviour associated with curiosity and fear differ markedly: the one brings about approach and the other withdrawal. If novel stimuli set up a state of tension with consequent random behaviour in an organism, two classes of response-sequence are likely to be followed by tension-reduction. One is approach and exploration and the other is withdrawal until the stimulus is out of range. An individual's proneness to one or the other may depend on temperament and experience, but on the whole it may well be that withdrawal is more effective with *stronger* stimuli (since approach may mean danger) and exploration with *weaker* stimuli (since these often represent food and other goal-objects). The difference between curiosity and fear may therefore be one of intensity only. But this question must be postponed, probably till more is known about the physiological concomitants of both.

(*c*) It may be worth noting that our hypothesis that all stimuli originally set up a state of drive (in experiential language, 'are painful') receives support from psycho-analytic sources. Freud (5) asserts that external objects, apart from those which are pleasurable and therefore introjected, come to be regarded in the child as forming a hostile external world. 'Thus at the very beginning, the external world, objects, and that which was hated were one and the same thing' (p. 79). The view that during the first few weeks of life all stimuli are painful is fundamental to Melanie Klein's conception of the infantile mentality (12).[1]

---

[1] Yet another approach, this time through neurological considerations, has since led a writer to the conclusion that *all* stimuli exciting the central nervous system are to some extent drive-inducing. See Wolpe (25).

*Postulate II. As a curiosity-arousing stimulus continues to affect*
*an organism's receptors, curiosity will diminish*

## Comments

(a) It is provisionally assumed that the habituation of the curiosity-response is a process of inhibition, similar to the inhibition of learned responses according to Hull's account. 'Negative adaptation' or 'habituation' of innate responses is of course a well-known phenomenon (see (7), pp. 105ff.).

(b) We may note, with reference to the probable affinity between curiosity and fear, that Miller and his associates have observed behaviour in rats which seems to mean extinction of fear-responses by exposure to a fear-producing stimulus ((15), p. 438). Shaw has even attempted to explain the relief of anxiety in the psycho-analytic session by a similar process of extinction (22).

The following corollaries can now be deduced from these postulates plus those of the Hullian system.

*Corollary i. An organism will learn to respond to a curiosity-arousing stimulus with activity which will increase stimulation by it. (We shall call such activity 'exploration'.)* (Our Postulate II and Hull's Postulate III in *Behavior Postulates and Corollaries* (10), replacing Postulate 4 in *Principles of Behavior* (9).)

This follows from Hull's principle of reinforcement (a form of the 'law of effect'), according to which any response which is closely followed by drive-reduction (G) will tend to be repeated. Since stimulation by the curiosity-arousing stimulus leads to a decrease in the curiosity-response (and therefore in the curiosity drive-stimulus), activity increasing such stimulation will be reinforced. The organism will tend to respond to curiosity in future with such activity. 'Exploration' includes McDougall's 'approach to the object' and 'closer examination of the object by one or more channels of sense' ((14), p. 143). It will, of course, only occur if there is not simultaneously evoked an incompatible response with a higher momentary effective reaction-potential ($_s\bar{E}_R$) (e.g., withdrawal through fear).

*Corollary ii. After a time, exploration will cease.* (Our Postulate II and Hull's Postulate X in *Behavior Postulates and Corollaries* (10), replacing Postulate 8 in *Principles of Behavior* (9).)

This follows from the Mowrer-Miller hypothesis: as a response continues or is repeated there accumulates a motivation towards its cessation ('reactive inhibition' or $I_R$). The curiosity-response will therefore undergo increasing reactive inhibition until it falls below a reaction-threshold ($_sL_R$).

A particular exploratory response may, of course, succumb to reactive inhibition before curiosity ceases and may be succeeded by another, which no doubt explains why exploratory activity often takes the form of a series of varied responses. Similarly, the curiosity pertaining to one part or aspect of the unfamiliar object may be satiated, so that exploration may be directed to another part or aspect and the object investigated from one angle after another (Holt's 'random movement with adience sustained').

*Corollary iii. After a further lapse of time, if the curiosity-arousing stimulus is again affecting the organism's receptors, there will be a second spell of exploration, but this time there will be less explanation than during the first spell; such spells of exploration will recur at intervals, until exploration of the stimulus in question ceases altogether.* (Our Postulate II and Hull's Postulate X and corollary ix in *Behavior Postulates and Corollaries* (10), replacing Postulates 8 and 9 in *Principles of Behavior* (9).)

This follows from Hull's two-factor theory of inhibition. All prolonged or repeated responses are subject to (*a*) 'reactive inhibition' ($I_R$), a factor dissipating with time, which explains why extinguished responses have intermittent phases of spontaneous recovery; (*b*) 'conditioned inhibition' ($_sI_R$) which is a learned and therefore permanent factor; its gradual accumulation explains why spontaneous recovery decreases with each successive phase, until it ceases altogether.

Both the curiosity-response and individual exploratory responses will undergo these two sorts of inhibition. They will therefore show spontaneous recovery at intervals, diminishing with each recovery until they fall below a 'reaction-threshold' ($_sL_R$) and are no longer manifested.

## V. Experiment

### APPARATUS

The *'experimental box'* had an interior 25 in. long by 11 in. wide by 8 in. high. Its walls were lined with white paper, the floor consisted of a sheet of zinc; there was a roof of wire-netting through which the rats could be observed. A portion of the netting, 11 × 10 in., at one end of the box formed a hinged door, through which the rats were put into the box and taken out.

The 'stimuli' consisted of three 'cubes' (unpainted wooden cubes, 1 in. per side) and three 'rings' (hollow cylinders of brown cardboard, 1 in. in diameter and 1 in. in height, covered on the outside with black paper).

### SUBJECTS

The subjects were twelve male albino rats of the Wistar strain, aged approx. 90 days at the beginning of the experiment. They were divided randomly into an Experimental Group of six and a Control Group of six, each group being housed in one cage. Before each experimental session they were allowed to eat and drink to satiety.

PROCEDURE

(a) *Experimental Group (six rats)*

*Group habituation.* All six rats were placed together in the empty experimental box for two hours. Each rat in turn then underwent an experimental session of sixty-five minutes made up as follows:

(i) *Solitary habituation.* Twenty minutes in the empty experimental box. This was to habituate the animal still further to the experimental conditions and to satiate curiosity directed to the box itself.

(ii) Ten minutes in the home cage with the other members of the group.

(iii) *Phase I: three similar (novel) stimuli.* Five minutes in the box, where there were three similar stimuli (placed in a row across the floor, with 3 in. between neighbouring stimuli and at a distance of 11 in. from the end at which the rat entered). For three rats (the Cube Sub-Group) there were three cubes, and for the other three (the Ring Sub-Group) there were three rings.

(iv) Ten minutes in the home cage.

(v) *Phase II: three similar (familiar) stimuli.* Five minutes in the box, containing the same three stimuli as in Phase 1.

(vi) Ten minutes in the home cage.

(vii) *Phase III: two similar (familiar) stimuli and one odd (novel) stimulus.* Five minutes in the box, where one of the stimuli present in Phases I and II had been replaced by a novel stimulus—i.e., for the Cube Sub-Group, one cube had been replaced by a ring, and for the Ring Sub-Group, one ring had been replaced by a cube. For one rat of each sub-group the novel stimulus was on the left, in the middle and on the right respectively, to exclude the effects of positional preferences.

In Phases I, II and III the time spent exploring (i.e., sniffing at) each stimulus was recorded to the nearest second by a three-pen chronograph, controlled by push-buttons which the experimenter operated. If there was no exploration in the first five minutes of Phase III, the rat was left in the box for a further five minutes. But this occurred only in the case of one subject (rat D).

(b) *Control Group (six rats)*

(The procedure for this group was equivalent to that of the Experimental Group with Phases I and II omitted and Phase III repeated.)

*Group habituation.* Two hours, as for the Experimental Group. Each rat in turn then underwent an experimental session of fifty minutes made up as follows:

(i) *Solitary habituation.* Twenty minutes as for Experimental Group.

(ii) Ten minutes in the home cage.

(iii) *Phase I: two similar (novel) stimuli and one odd (novel) stimulus.* Five minutes in the experimental box, where there were two similar and one odd stimuli, arranged as for Experimental Group. For three rats (controls for Cube Sub-Group) there were two cubes and a ring, and for the other three (controls for Ring Sub-Group) there were two rings and a cube. The odd stimulus was in a different position for each rat of each subgroup, as in Phase III, Experimental Group.

(iv) Ten minutes in the home cage.

(v) *Phase II: Two similar (familiar) stimuli and one odd (familiar) stimulus.* Five minutes in the box with the same stimuli as in Phase I.

Exploration of each stimulus in Phases I and II was timed as in the case of the Experimental Group.

PREDICTIONS

In Phase III the Experimental Group face one novel stimulus and two which they have already (Phases I and II) had the opportunity to explore. They should therefore, if our Postulate II is true, have more curiosity aroused by the former than by the latter and thus spend more time exploring it.

The Control Group (Phase I) have not had a prior opportunity to familiarize themselves with the two similar stimuli, and so their behaviour will show whether the above effect is really due to the novelty of the odd stimulus.

Similarly, in Phase III, Experimental Group, the two similar stimuli are familiar, whereas in Phase I, Control Group, they are novel. If the same postulate is true, the Control Group should spend more time exploring them than the Experimental Group.

If our corollaries are correct, there should be some exploration in Phase II (both groups), when the same stimuli are presented as were explored in Phase I, but Phase II should show less exploration than Phase I.

To put our expectations in a more precise and statistically verifiable form, the following predictions follow from our theory and can be tested by our experiment:

*Prediction I.* In Phase III, Experimental Group, the mean exploration of the odd (novel) stimuli will be significantly greater than the mean exploration of the similar (familiar) stimuli.

*Prediction II.* In Phase I, Control Group, the mean exploration of the odd stimuli will *not* be significantly greater than the mean exploration of the similar stimuli.

*Prediction III.* In Phase III, Experimental Group, the mean exploration of the similar stimuli will be significantly *less* than the mean exploration of the similar stimuli in Phase I, Control Group.

*Prediction IV.* In Phase II, both groups, the mean exploration of all stimuli will be significantly *less* than the mean exploration of all stimuli in Phase I, both groups.

RESULTS

The behaviour of all rats in the experimental box followed more or less the same pattern. When first put into the box, each animal remained for some seconds in a state of tense alertness. It then advanced cautiously and, on reaching the stimuli, sniffed at them, but exploration of rings or cubes never took up more than a small fraction (maximum = 39 sec. Rat A, Phase I) of the five-minute period. After this brief and cursory investigation it invariably found some position in a corner or by a wall of the box in which to settle. It generally remained there quiescent till taken out of the box, but some animals roused themselves after a few minutes and took a second walk round, giving a few additional sniffs at the stimuli as they passed. One or two even picked up one of the rings in their mouths and played with them.

The numerical results, i.e., the seconds of exploration devoted to each stimulus, are shown in Tables 1 and 2:

TABLE 1

EXPERIMENTAL GROUP

Key: 0 = ring; X = cube (odd stimulus in italics). S = Stimuli used, from left to right; E = time of exploration of each stimulus to nearest second.

|  |  | Cube Sub-Group | | | Ring Sub-Group | | |
|---|---|---|---|---|---|---|---|
|  | Subject | A | B | C | D | E | F |
| Phase I | S | X–X–X | X–X–X | X–X–X | 0–0–0 | 0–0–0 | 0–0–0 |
|  | E | 13–13–13 | 0–1–7 | 5–4–1 | 2–3–1 | 1–3–4 | 2–8–2 |
| Phase II | S | X–X–X | X–X–X | X–X–X | 0–0–0 | 0–0–0 | 0–0–0 |
|  | E | 1–2–0 | 0–0–1 | 0–0–0 | 0–1–5 | 0–0–0 | 0–0–0 |
| Phase III | S | *0*–X–X | X–*0*–X | X–X–*0* | *X*–0–0 | 0–*X*–0 | 0–0–*X* |
|  | E | 8–7–2 | 0–*4*–1 | 0–2–*1* | *4*–1–3 | 1–*3*–1 | 1–1–*2* |

We can now see whether our predictions are fulfilled.

*Prediction I* (Phase III, Experimental Group). For each rat we take the quantity of exploration of the odd (novel) stimulus and subtract from it the mean of the quantities of exploration of the two similar (familiar) stimuli. In other words, if $O$ = exploration of odd stimulus, and $S_1 + S_2$ = exploration of two similar stimuli, we take the quantity $O - \dfrac{S_1 + S_2}{2}$. If the mean of this quantity for the six rats is positive and significant, the prediction is confirmed.

*Results.* Mean $O - \dfrac{S_1 + S_2}{2} = 2 \cdot 00;\ t = 3 \cdot 55;\ \nu = 5;\ p = 0 \cdot 017.$

The result is positive and significant at the 0·02 level and the prediction is fulfilled.

*Prediction II* (Phase I, Control Group). Again we take the mean of $O - \dfrac{S_1 + S_2}{2}$ for six rats. If this mean is positive and significant, the prediction is falsified.

*Results.* Mean $O - \dfrac{S_1 + S_2}{2} = -0 \cdot 17.$

The result is therefore not positive and significant and the prediction is fulfilled.

(The difference between the means of $O - \dfrac{S_1 + S_2}{2}$ for Phase III, Experimental Group and Phase I, Control Group is not significant ($t = 1 \cdot 48\ p = 0 \cdot 17$).)

TABLE 2

CONTROL GROUP
(Key as above)

| | Subject | Controls for cube sub-group | | | Controls for ring sub-group | | |
|---|---|---|---|---|---|---|---|
| | | A′ | B′ | C′ | D′ | E′ | F′ |
| Phase I | S | 0–X–X | X–0–X | X–X–0 | X–0–0 | 0–X–0 | 0–0–X |
| | E | 2–0–0 | 7–12–9 | 4–7–7 | 2–3–2 | 7–2–6 | 3–8–2 |
| *Phase II* | S | 0–X–X | X–0–X | X–X–0 | X–0–0 | 0–X–0 | 0–0–X |
| | E | 0–0–0 | 3–9–8 | 3–3–3 | 3–0–1 | 1–5–2 | 2–3–2 |

*Prediction III* (Phase III, Experimental Group, Phase I, Control Group). We take the mean exploration-time for the two similar stimuli of the six rats in the Experimental Group and the same for the six rats of the Control Group. If the latter is significantly greater than the former, the prediction is fulfilled.

*Results.* Mean exploration of similar stimuli (Phase III, Experimental Group), 3·33. Mean exploration of similar stimuli (Phase I, Control Group), 9·33; $t = 2 \cdot 27;\ \nu = 10;\ p = 0 \cdot 046.$

The result is therefore significant at the 0·05 level and the prediction is fulfilled.

*Prediction IV* (Phase I and Phase II, both groups). We take the mean decrease in exploration of all stimuli from Phase I to Phase II for all twelve rats. If this mean is positive and significant, the prediction is fulfilled.

*Results.* Mean decrease = 9·00. $t = 3 \cdot 40;\ v = 11;\ p = 0 \cdot 006.$

The result is therefore significant at the 0·01 level and the prediction is confirmed.

*Discussion.* All four predictions are thus fulfilled by the experiment and the theory is therefore confirmed, in the sense of 'rendered more probable.' Many problems still remain to be solved. Apart from the reservations mentioned in connexion with the postulates, we require to know more about other forms of motivation to explore, e.g., the instrumental exploration and surprise-exploration described above, and their relations to the form of motivation, due to novelty, which we have called 'curiosity.' We need to link the exploratory activity that is found in the lower animals, such as the rat, with human exploratory activity. In particular, we must investigate the symbolic processes that enable human curiosity to be satiated by an 'explanation' rather than by sensory contact with the object of curiosity.

But it is hoped that the present study will have helped to indicate some of the variables at work and thus some of the questions further research may profitably pursue.


VI. SUMMARY

The scope and importance of novelty, an unjustly neglected topic in both human and animal psychology, is discussed. Some theories of curiosity are reviewed and problems arising out of them are considered.

A new theory to deal with exploratory behaviour in response to novelty is then presented. It consists of two postulates:

*Postulate I. When a novel stimulus affects an organism's receptors, there will occur a drive-stimulus-producing response $(R \rightsquigarrow S_D)$ (which we shall call 'curiosity').*

*Postulate II. As a curiosity-arousing stimulus continues to affect an organism's receptors, curiosity will diminish.*

If these postulates are used in conjunction with Hull's behaviour theory, three corollaries follow which describe the functioning of exploratory activity.

An experiment with rats is then reported. The experiment demonstrated (*a*) that rats will spend more time exploring a novel stimulus than stimuli which they have previously been able to explore; and (*b*) that they will spend less time exploring stimuli the second time they encounter them. In particular, four predictions follow from our postulates and corollaries. All four are confirmed by the results of the experiment.

The writer wishes to express thanks to the following: the Executive Committee of the Carnegie Trust for making a grant to cover the expenses of this investigation; Mr. H. H. Ferguson for helping and supporting the project in various ways; Mr. M. J. Sweeney for invaluable technical assistance; Prof. R. Walmsley for allowing the subjects to be accommodated in the animal-house belonging to St. Andrews University, Anatomy Department.

## REFERENCES

1. BERLYNE, D. E. (1949). 'Interest' as a psychological concept. *Brit. J. Psychol.* 39, 184-95.
2. BERLYNE, D. E. (1950) Stimulus intensity and attention in relation to learning theory. *Quart. J. Exp. Psychol.*, 2, 71-5.
3. DASHIELL, J. F. (1925) A quantitative demonstration of animal drive. *J. Comp. Psychol.*, 5, 205-8.
4. FREUD, S. (1905) Three contributions to the theory of sex. In BRILL, A. A. (ed. and trans., 1938): *The Basic Writings of Sigmund Freud.* New York: Modern Library.)
5. FREUD, S. (1915) Instincts and their vicissitudes (In *Collected Papers*, IV. London: Hogarth.)
6. HEBB, D. O. (1946) On the nature of fear. *Psychol. Rev.*, 53, 259-76.
7. HILGARD, E. R. and MARQUIS, D. G. (1940) *Conditioning and Learning.* New York: Appleton-Century.
8. HOLT, E. B. (1931) *Animal Drive and the Learning Process.* London: Williams and Norgate.
9. HULL, C. L. (1943) *Principles of Behavior.* New York: Appleton-Century.
10. HULL, C. L. (1949) *Behavior Postulates and Corollaries.* November 1949. (Cyclostyled.)
11. ISAACS, N. (1949) *The Foundations of Common Sense.* London: Routledge and Kegan Paul.
12. KLEIN, M. (1932) *The Psycho-Analysis of Children.* London: Hogarth.
13. McDOUGALL, W. (1908) *An Introduction to Social Psychology.* London: Methuen.
14. McDOUGALL, W. (1923) *An Outline of Psychology.* London: Methuen.
15. MILLER, N. E. (1944) Experimental studies of conflict. (In HUNT, J. McV., *Personality and the Behavior Disorders*, I. New York: Ronald.)
16. MILLER, N. E. and DOLLARD, J. (1941) *Social Learning and Imitation.* London: Kegan Paul, 1945.
17. MOWRER, O. H. (1938). Preparatory set (expectancy)—a determinant in motivation and learning. *Psychol. Rev.* 45, 62-91.
18. NISSEN, H. W. (1930). A study of exploratory behavior in the white rat by means of the obstruction method. *J. Genet. Psychol.* XXXVII, 361-76.
19. PAVLOV, I. P. (1927). *Conditioned Reflexes.* Trans. by G. V. Anrep. Oxford University Press.
20. PIAGET, J. (1947). *La Psychologie de l'Intelligence.* Paris: Colin.
21. SHAND, A. F. (1914). *The Foundations of Character.* London: Macmillan.
22. SHAW, F. (1946). A stimulus-response analysis of repression and insight in psychotherapy. *Psychol. Rev.* LIII, 36-42.
23. TAYLOR, J. G. (1949). Behavior oscillation and the growth of preferences. *Psychol. Rev.* LVI, 77-87.
24. WHITING, J. W. M. and MOWRER, O. H. (1943). Habit progression and regression—a laboratory study of some factors relevant to human socialization. *J. Comp. Psychol.* XXXVI, 229-53.
25. WOLPE, J. (1950). Need-reduction, drive-reduction and reinforcement: a neurophysiological view. *Psychol. Rev.* LVII, 19-26.

# 10.   Motivational Properties of Frustration: I. Effect on a Running Response of the Addition of Frustration to the Motivational Complex

## A. Amsel and J. Roussel

*The authors posit frustration to be a need state which has the motivational property of energizing the organism. This study was one of the first to demonstrate unequivocally the operation of a frustration drive.*

This paper reports an attempt to test two hypotheses derived from assumptions relative to frustration. The assumptions are: (a) that frustration is a motivational condition, and (b) that strength of frustration varies with time in the frustrating situation. In this experiment, frustration is defined as a state which results from the nonreinforcement of an instrumental response which previously was *consistently* reinforced. Saying that frustration can be produced in this way does not, of course, exclude other possibilities, such as blocking of a strongly learned instrumental sequence by a physical barrier.

In a recently reported study, Rohrer (7) employed the term *frustration drive* to account for the reduction in strength of a bar-pressing response. He showed that when two groups of rats are conditioned equally strongly to bar-pressing, and each is subsequently extinguished twice under a particular degree of massing of trials, the more highly massed group takes fewer trials to the second extinction. It is our opinion that such findings do not require the introduction of the notion of a motivational frustration state to explain them. They can be handled by existing inhibition theory (3). Rohrer's results are not in our opinion a test of the motivational characteristics of frustration, nor were they probably intended to be. In order to show that frustration is a motivating condition it would seem necessary to demonstrate that its presence increases some aspect of behavior. It is not sufficient simply to show a decrease in strength of the response leading to frustration.

If frustration is to be conceived of as a need state, it would, then, seem reasonable to demonstrate, at the outset, that this state has the accepted properties of need states. Thus, Hull's treatment of motivation (3) would demand that adding frustration to a motivational complex increases the

*J. exp. Psychol.*, 1952, *43*, 363-368. Reprinted with permission of the senior author and The American Psychological Association. Supported by a grant from the Tulane University Council on Research.

strength of some ongoing response through increase in generalized drive strength, provided that the frustration drive stimulus has not become connected to a response which is antagonistic to the criterion response (1).

This experiment was designed to test the following specific hypotheses stemming from the earlier assumptions: (a) when a running response has been maximally elicited under hunger motivation, the addition of frustration to the motivational complex will result in the establishment of a new and higher maximum running speed; (b) the facilitating effect of frustration on running speed will vary with variation in the amount of time spent in the frustrating situation just preceding that running.

## METHOD

### SUBJECTS AND APPARATUS

Eighteen male albino rats of Wistar strain were $Ss$ in this experiment. Their ages were between 100–120 days at the beginning of preliminary training.

The apparatus was a modified simple straightaway consisting of a starting compartment, two runways and two goal boxes. They were arranged in a straight line in the following order: starting box, Runway A, Goal box 1, Runway B, Goal box 2. The entire apparatus, except for Goal box 2, was 2.5 in. wide and 4 in. high (inside dimensions). The starting box was 9 in. long; Runway A was 3.5 ft. long; Goal box 1, 1 ft. long; and Runway B, 10 ft. long. Goal box 2 was 11 × 7 × 10 in. Guillotine doors separated the starting compartment from Runway A, and Goal box 1 from Runway B. At the entrance to Goal boxes 1 and 2 were swing doors designed to be manipulable by S. The entire apparatus, with the exception of Goal box 2, was painted flat black. Goal box 2 was unpainted pine. The apparatus was covered with ¼-in. hardware cloth mesh. A small metal food cup was flush with the floor of Goal box 1. The food cup in Goal box 2 was a clear glass coaster.

The measurements of performance were made in Goal box 1 and Runway B. A running time measure was taken by the use of a Standard Electric Timer (.001 min.) and a microswitch arrangement. The switches were placed under hinged segments of the floor of Runway B so that the weight of the animal would trip them. The first switch was placed 1 ft. beyond Goal box 1, the second switch, 1 ft. from Goal box 2. The running time was, then, the time to traverse the middle 8-ft. portion of Runway B. The latency measure was taken with a 1/10-sec. stopwatch. This was, on each of the test trials, the elapsed time between the raising of the door of Goal box 1, and the activation of the first microswitch in the running-time circuit.

A separate swing-door and goal-box arrangement was employed during preliminary training to acquaint each S with the door-pushing response. This was of similar construction to the experimental apparatus, but was 4 in. wide and 12 in. long, and was painted gray.

### EXPERIMENTAL PROCEDURE

The entire experimental sequence required 52 days. This period was divided into three sections.

*Preliminary training.* This was a period of 12 days designed to adapt Ss to handling by E and to the apparatus. All Ss, beginning at this stage, were maintained on a 22-hr. hunger schedule. Their daily food ration was 9 gm. of Purina dog chow checkers. On each of the first seven days the Ss were handled by E. On Day 8, Ss were put into the apparatus in pairs with all doors raised, for 10 min. per pair. On Day 9 each S explored the apparatus individually for 7 min. Days 10, 11, and 12 were spent in training each S to manipulate a swing door such as those at the entrance to the goal boxes. Each S was given six trials on each of these three days. A pellet of food was given after each entrance into the goal box. After these trials none of the 18 Ss had any difficulty manipulating the door.

*Measurement of maximum running speed under 22-hr. food deprivation.* For the next 28 days, Days 13 to 40, each S was run three times per day in the apparatus under the strong hunger drive. During these trials food was in both goal boxes. The details of procedure on an individual trial are as follows: (a) S put into starting box; (b) after 3 sec., door raised; (c) S traverses Runway A, enters Goal box 1, eats one puppy pellet of chow; (d) after 30 sec. in Goal box 1, door is raised; (e) S traverses Runway B into Goal box 2, time to run this alley is measured; (f) S consumes food pellet in Goal box 2, and is returned to individual carrying cage.

The Ss were run in rotation, nine at a time, so that each of the three runs on a single day for any S was separated from the others by about 20 min.

After these 84 trials on 28 days the running speed of the Ss seemed to have reached a stable maximum.

*Measurement of latency and running speed under 22-hr. hunger with and without frustration.* During this 12-day period each S was run three times a day, a total of 36 trials. Of these, 18 trials were *frustration* trials and 18 were *reward* trials. The reward trials were identical with those in the previous period. The frustration trials differed from the reward trials in that S found Goal box 1 empty (no food or food cup), after traversing Runway A. Each S, therefore, served as its own control to test the effect of frustration on the level of the performance which immediately followed the frustrating event.

To test the second hypothesis, Ss were split into three subgroups, matched on the basis of mean running time in the preliminary running trials. These will be termed Group 5, Group 10, and Group 30. They are differentiated by the amount of time spent in Goal box 1, during these 12 test days, *on frustration trials.* Group 5 remained in the frustrating situation for 5 sec.; Groups 10 and 30 were in the frustrating situation for 10 and 30 sec., respectively. All Ss continued to remain for 30 sec. in Goal box 1 on reward trials.

During this test period, two performance measures were employed on every trial. The running time measure (time to traverse the 8-ft. segment of Runway B) was taken as before. In addition, a latency measure was obtained. This was the time interval separating the raising of the door of Goal box 1 (after 5, 10, or 30 sec.) and the activation of the first microswitch. The E raised the door of Goal box 1 only when S was oriented in that direction. This meant that on some trials, the 5-, 10-, or 30-sec. interval in Goal box 1 was slightly exceeded.

In running equal numbers of frustration and reward trials in this test period the following arrangement of daily trials was employed to control for any possible effect of order of presentation: FRF RFR FFR RRF FRR RFF. These symbols represent the order of frustration and reward trials for six days (18 trials). On the next six test days, this sequence was repeated.

## RESULTS AND DISCUSSION

*Test of two hypotheses.* Both means and medians were calculated. In all cases the general nature of the results is the same for both, except that means are higher and more variable than medians.

To evaluate the results of the test period, mean and median running time and latency scores were computed for each S under reward (R) and frustration (F) conditions. Each of these scores is an average of 18 test-trial measurements. Comparison of the R and F scores showed that for each of the 18 Ss, median running time and latency measures are lower on frustration trials than on reward trials. The means show similar results with the frustration trials producing faster subsequent running than the reward trials for 16 of 18 Ss. Seventeen of 18 Ss had shorter mean latencies on F trials than R trials. The median of individual S median reward running times was .048 min.; the corresponding frustration median was .041. The over-all means were .054 and .044 min. The over-all median R and F latencies were 1.65 and .65 sec.; the mean latencies were 4.86 and 1.69 sec. Since the raw data cannot be presented here, it should be indicated that for any given S the distribution of 18 frustration measurements overlapped very little, when at all, with the 18 reward scores. The first hypothesis—an increase in strength of performance with the addition of frustration to a motivational complex—is strongly supported.

TABLE 1

RUNNING TIME AND LATENCY AVERAGES ON REWARD AND
FRUSTRATION TEST TRIALS

|  | Running Time (Minutes) | | | | Latency (Seconds) | | | |
|---|---|---|---|---|---|---|---|---|
|  | Median | | Mean | | Median | | Mean | |
| Group | R | F | R | F | R | F | R | F |
| 5 | .053 | .042 | .056 | .045 | 1.35 | 0.65 | 4.13 | 1.87 |
| 10 | .048 | .036 | .052 | .041 | 1.30 | 0.45 | 4.25 | 1.33 |
| 30 | .046 | .041 | .053 | .046 | 3.75* | 1.25 | 6.19* | 1.90 |

* Since running times, but not latencies, were measured during the preliminary period, the groups could be equated only for running times. For this reason, it is not surprising that Group 30 deviates so greatly from the other groups in Median and Mean latency on reward test trials.

In order to test the second hypothesis, the test performance of the Ss must be considered according to whether they were in the 5-, 10-, or 30-sec. group. Table 1 shows running time and latency medians and means for each of the three groups under reward and frustration conditions. A simple analysis of variance was performed with the individual R—F scores to test whether the three conditions of time in the frustrating situation resulted in different frustration effects on running time and latency. The F ratio for running time was 3.06; the latency F ratio was 1.12. With 2 and 15 df, the 5% level of confidence requires an F ratio of 3.68. We cannot, therefore, say that time in the frustrating situation was a relevant variable in this experiment, although the average vigor of response of the Group 10 Ss on frustration trials is consistently greater than that of the other groups.

Possibly, the range from 5 to 30 sec. *in a frustrating situation* is one which produces relatively little change in the frustration effect. The performance of the Ss under 22-hr. food privation may already have been so strong as to obscure differences in frustration which may have been present in the three groups. Certainly, our groups were small for this test. It would seem reasonable, on the basis of common sense and on the basis of the typical characteristics of labile states, to expect a very rapid building up of the frustration state (perhaps almost complete by 5 sec.) followed by a gradual falling off of its intensity. This falling off would have a faster rate outside of the frustrating situation than in it.* Since, in this

* A pertinent experiment of Miller and Stevenson (5) reports an increase in agitated behavior of rats immediately following nonrewarded trials. This increased agitation was observed in the alley leading to the goal box where S has 10 sec. previously been frustrated (nonreward following consistent reward). In the Miller and Stevenson study, this frustration-motivated response was found to decrease in vigor when intervals longer than 10 sec. separated a frustration occurrence from the next run of S. By 2 min., the agitated behavior was no longer apparent. Here, time between nonreward and observation of agitated behavior was spent by S outside of the frustrating situation.

experiment, there was no significant difference between 5, 10, and 30 sec. in the frustrating situation, we offer the speculation that the period from 5 to 30 sec. is a period of relative stability of frustration before the dissipation of the state begins.

*Comparison of reward and frustration test trials with preliminary reward trials.* Figure 1 shows the median running time data for reward conditions on the initial pretest days, and for the R and F conditions during the test trials. It should be noted that the two test-trial curves represent the median running times of the same Ss under both reward and frustration conditions, so that the first F trial was the first test trial, whereas the first R trial was the second test trial, and so on in random arrangement of F and R. For this reason, at any point on the abscissa of the test-trial graph the probability of the F curve being lower than the R curve would be .5, if there were no frustration effect. Actually, the F curve is lower than the R curve at 17 of the 18 points, and at most of these points it is very much lower. Taking the appropriate term in a binomial expansion, we find that the probability of such a chance occurrence is less than .0001. This is further confirmation of our first hypothesis.

The F curve approaches an asymptote which appears to be about .010 min. lower than that of the initial R curve, and that of the test-trial R curve. This is quite striking when one considers the great stability of the initial running time curve before the introduction of the test trials. The test reward curve remains at about the same level as the pretest curve. The greater apparent variability in the test trial data than in the initial data can be attributed to the fact that the test curves were plotted from medians of individual trials while the initial curve was plotted from medians of each day's performance, and there were three trials on each of these days for each S.

Since there is, on the first four test trials, very little difference between the R and F curves, and since the difference which becomes evident by Trial 5 is due mainly to a decrease in running time on F trials, there might be some basis for arguing that the frustration effect is learned, and not simply the result of a sudden increase in motivational strength. There is, however, an explanation of this part of the data which would not involve adopting this position. Early in the test period, frustration due to nongiving of food in the first goal box is minimized because of the strong secondary-reinforcing properties of that region built up during the initial trials; later, when the secondary-reinforcing power of this goal extinguishes, the frustration effect is increased.

*Another interpretation.* There is an interpretation of the present results which does not involve the introduction of frustration as an explanatory concept, i.e., it does not apparently necessitate attributing special properties to nonreinforcement.* This would hold that the running times in Run-

* Suggested by Dr. I. E. Farber in a personal communication.

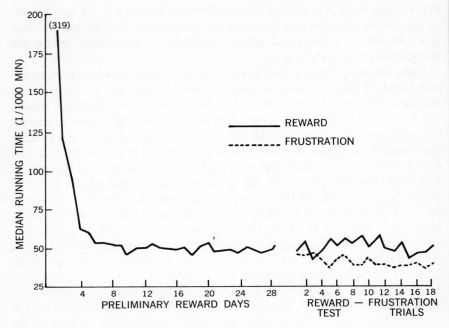

FIG. 1. Comparison of test-trial performance under reward and frustration conditions.

way B during the initial trials were actually depressed because of hunger reduction in Goal box 1 preceding those trials; and that from the beginning, the running time in Runway B would have been faster, and the final limit of performance would have been lower, if there were no eating just preceding the performance in the second runway. According to this interpretation, the increased vigor of performance which follows failure to reward a previously-rewarded response is due not to the presence of a new additional motivational component (frustration), but to the absence of a reduction in hunger tension which had consistently depressed performance before.

Actually, failure to reward in Goal box 1 changes the stimulus to running in Runway B on frustration trials, and should also, therefore, tend to *reduce* running speed on those trials. Also, there is evidence that introducing food immediately before a hunger-motivated response may actually increase the level of performance, presumably by increasing incentive motivation.* Both of these factors, if operating, would have an opposite effect to that suggested.

* Some support for this statement can be derived from certain of the early speed of locomotion experiments (2, 6). The whole question of the effect on vigor of performance of giving a small amount of reward immediately before a trial has recently been treated by Maltzman (4).

It is possible that all the factors mentioned are operating in this experimental situation, and that frustration-produced motivation is also operating. If special emergent properties are to be attributed to non-reinforcement, it remains to show, by other experiments, that the frustration effect operates independently of, and in addition to, other effects which have already been conceptualized.

## SUMMARY

This experiment was designed to test the assumptions that frustration is a motivational state, and that its strength is related to time in the frustrating situation.

Eighteen male albino rats were trained under hunger drive to run down an alley into a goal box, then leave that goal box and run down a second alley into a second goal box distinctively different from the first one. Their time to traverse the alley between Goal box 1 and Goal box 2 was measured during a preliminary period. When this time had reached a stable minimum, their running time and latency in leaving Goal box 1 were measured during test trials. In half of these trials they were frustrated in Goal box 1; in the other half, they were not. During this test period Ss were split into subgroups differentiated according to time spent in Goal box 1 on the frustration trials (5-, 10-, and 30-sec. groups).

An implication of the first assumption—that strength of performance on frustration test trials should be greater than that during the preliminary trials or that on reward test trials—was strongly supported by the data. There was, however, no statistically significant empirical support for the hypothesis of variation in strength of frustration when the time in the frustrating situation was varied between 5, 10, and 30 sec.

## REFERENCES

1. AMSEL, A. (1950) The effect upon level of consummatory response of the addition of anxiety to a motivational complex. *J. exp. Psychol.*, *40*, 709-715.
2. BRUCE, R. H. (1937) An experimental investigation of the thirst drive in rats with especial reference to the goal-gradient hypothesis. *J. gen. Psychol.*, *17*, 49-60.
3. HULL, C. L. (1943) *Principles of behavior.* New York: D. Appleton-Century.
4. MALTZMAN, I. (1952) The process need. *Psychol. Rev.*, *59*, 40-48.
5. MILLER, N. E., and STEVENSON, S. S. (1936) Agitated behavior of rats during experimental extinction and a curve of spontaneous recovery. *J. comp. Psychol.*, *21*, 205-231.
6. MORGAN, C. T., and FIELDS, P. E. (1938) The effect of variable preliminary feeding upon the rat's speed of locomotion. *J. comp. Psychol.*, *26*, 331-348.
7. ROHRER, J. H. (1949) A motivational state resulting from non-reward. *J. comp. physiol. Psychol.*, *42*, 476-485.

# General Issues in Motivation:
# II. The Role of Rewards

A SECOND topic frequently subsumed under motivation is reinforcement or reward. Contemporary considerations of reward can be traced to Hull (1943), who defined primary reinforcement as the reduction of a primary need, although subsequently this position was changed so that a reduction in the drive stimulus, rather than the need, became critical for reinforcement. A basic corollary was that primary (or secondary) reinforcement was necessary in order for learning to take place.

A number of investigators, however, demonstrated that reinforcement, at least defined in terms of reducing a primary need, was not necessary for learning to take place. The Sheffield and Roby (1950) selection was one of these early studies. Subsequently other investigators provided proof that a whole variety of stimulus conditions, i.e., light increment, light decrement, opportunity to run in an activity wheel, etc., had reinforcing properties. The result has been that Hull's law of primary reinforcement is no longer considered to be tenable.

Contemporary experimenters have spread a wide net in order to examine both behavioral as well as neurological characteristics of a reinforcing agent. On the behavioral side some investigators have demonstrated that stimuli in the form of light or sound may have reinforcing characteristics; others have placed emphasis on the role of stimulus change.

Many of the neurological inquiries on reinforcement have examined the role of brain stimulation. Olds and Milner (1954) found that a rat with an electrode implanted in its rhinencephalon would, when placed in a Skinner box in which brain stimulation followed the pressing of the bar, continue to make the bar-pressing response. Delgado, Roberts, and Miller (1954), demonstrated at about the same time that it was also possible to motivate escape or avoidance behavior by using brain stimulation. Brown and Cohen (1959), whose selection we have included in this chapter, have shown that it is possible to obtain both approach and avoidance behavior by stimulating the same brain location.

Inasmuch as Hull (1943) posited that primary reinforcement was effective for only a very short period of time in strengthening a stimulus response relationship, he found it necessary to supplement the law of primary reinforcement with the law of secondary reinforcement. This latter law stated that the power of reinforcement could be transmitted to a neutral stimulus by associating that stimulus with primary reinforcement. A large number of studies have been directed toward an examination of this principle. Thus, secondary reinforcement has been examined as a function of the frequency of primary reinforcement, the amount of primary reinforcement, the temporal relationship between the presentation of the secondary reinforcing stimulus and primary reinforcement, etc.

One puzzling feature was that although most studies indicated that secondary reinforcing stimuli could acquire reinforcing properties, such power was invariably of a temporary nature and hardly capable of sustaining protracted behavior sequences which are so frequently found in adult human behavior. A study by Zimmerman (1957), however, indicated that if a partial reinforcement procedure was used in both the original training as well as test situation, the durability issue might be at least partially solved. Unfortunately, important controls were lacking in Zimmerman's study, a defect which was corrected by Fox and King (1962), whose paper concludes this section.

## REFERENCES

BROWN, G. W. and COHEN, B. D. (1959) Avoidance and approach learning motivated by stimulation of identical hypothalamic loci. *Amer. J. Physiol.*, *197*, 153-157.

DELGADO, J. M. R., ROBERTS, W. W., and MILLER, N. E. (1954) Learning motivated by electrical stimulation of the brain. *Amer. J. Physiol.*, *179*, 587-593.

FOX, R. E. and KING, R. A. (1961) The effects of reinforcement scheduling on the strength of a secondary reinforcer. *J. comp. physiol. Psychol.*, *54*, 266-269.

HULL, C. L. (1943) *Principles of behavior.* New York: Appleton-Century-Crofts.

OLDS, J. and MILNER, P. (1954) Positive reinforcement produced by electrical stimulation of septal area and other regions of the rat brain. *J. comp. physiol. Psychol.*, *47*, 419-427.

SHEFFIELD, F. D. and ROBY, T. B. (1950) Reward value of a non-nutritive sweet taste. *J. comp. physiol. Psychol.*, *43*, 471-481.

ZIMMERMAN, D. W. (1957) Durable secondary reinforcement. Method and theory. *Psychol. Rev.*, *64*, 373-383.

## 11.   Reward Value of a Non-Nutritive Sweet Taste

### F. D. Sheffield and T. B. Roby

*This experiment was one of the early ones to discredit the Hullian position that primary reinforcement must be defined in terms of the reduction of a primary need.*

The purpose of the present experiments was to help answer the question of what constitutes a "reinforcing state of affairs" in instrumental conditioning. One of the most systematic positions on this topic (4) holds that ultimate reduction of a survival need is an essential factor, and a closely related position (5) argues for the necessity of ultimate reduction in a primary drive. However, several studies (3, 6, 1)—and at least one theory of reinforcement (10)—suggest the possibility that a sweet taste is reinforcing regardless of whether it is produced by a nutritive or non-nutritive substance. These previous studies demonstrate that sweet-flavored water is preferred to plain water by rats. They do not demonstrate, however, whether a sweet taste, per se, will operate as a reward in instrumental conditioning, uncomplicated either by a measurement of purely reflexive ingestion or by acquired reward from nutritive sweet-tasting substances. Also previous studies apparently have not related the sweet preference to the hunger state of the animal. The present experiments demonstrate that a non-nutritive sweet-tasting substance functions as a very effective reward in instrumental conditioning. They also demonstrate that the reward value depends on the degree of hunger present.

The "reward" used for instrumental conditioning in rats was a solution of saccharine in water. This substance produces a sweet taste in humans which is apparently "satisfying" to its many users (chiefly diabetics and those on reducing diets). The non-nutritive nature of saccharine is indicated by the fact that it apparently goes through the mammalian body unchanged chemically, and animals ingesting it do not diminish their food intake (3). Throughout all the present experiments the solution used was 1.30 grams of pure saccharine powder per liter of water. This value was chosen on the basis of a previous investigation of sweet preference (1) as likely to be effective with most rats.

*J. comp. physiol. Psychol.*, 1950, *43*, 471-481. Reprinted with the permission of the senior author and The American Psychological Association.

# EXPERIMENT I

### PURPOSE

The purpose of Experiment I was to determine whether a position preference in drinking behavior could be established on the basis of saccharine flavored water and whether the preference varied as a function of degree of hunger.

### METHOD

Six albino rats (age about six months at outset of experiment) were kept hungry by restricting their daily diet to eight grams (dry weight) of ground Purina Dog Chow mixed with 10 cc. of water. Six comparable control animals had food available at all times in the form of standard dry Purina Dog Chow pellets. The living cages were equipped at their rear walls with two 100 cc. graduated cylinders about four inches apart which served as water bottles. The cylinders were held in place by standard steel-clip broom holders, which permitted rapid insertion or removal without dripping of the contents. The water was taken by the rat in the usual way—by lapping from the end of a glass tube. The tips were partially sealed to a diameter small enough to prevent any spontaneous dripping. The laboratory was dimly lighted by a shielded 25-watt lamp at all times except when readings were made and when the daily food was given, at which times a bright overhead light was turned on. The procedure was as follows:
1. Two habituation days in the cages with both groups satiated for food and water, followed by a day in which the six experimental animals were not fed.
2. Five days with water in both bottles, hunger-drive regime as indicated in the Method section.
3. Nineteen days of alternate training and testing. On *training* days a saccharine solution (1.30 grams per liter) was on a given side for a given animal, water being on the other side; on the alternate *testing* days water was on both sides. The saccharine side was on the left for half of the animals of each group and on the right for the other half.

### RESULTS

*Relative consumption of water and saccharine solution:* All animals demonstrated rapid acquisition of a preference for drinking the saccharine solution as compared with the water solution on training days. Regardless of the degree of hunger, the proportion—of total liquid consumed—taken

TABLE 1

ACQUISITION OF DRINKING FROM THE SACCHARINE SIDE ON TRAINING DAYS

| | Mean per cent from saccharine side out of total intake of fluid from bottles | | | |
|---|---|---|---|---|
| | Preceding day (water in both bottles) | During first 2½ training hours | During first training day | During tenth training day |
| Hungry | 55.2 | 88.6 | 98.8 | 99.5 |
| Satiated | 59.5 | 77.3 | 95.5 | 95.8 |

from the saccharine bottle jumped to almost 100 per cent during the first training day. The relevant results are shown in table 1.

Table 1 shows that there was a slight preference in both groups for the "saccharine" side prior to the introduction of saccharine, as indicated by the per cent of water intake during the preceding day when there was water in both bottles. During the first 2½ hours with saccharine in one of the bottles, however, there was a decided preference in both groups for drinking from the saccharine bottle, and over the entire first 24 hours with saccharine both groups drank almost exclusively from the saccharine bottle. There was little difference between the first and last day of training.

Whereas there was no important difference between hungry and satiated animals in the *per cent* of total intake from the saccharine bottle, there was a large difference in *absolute* intake. Hungry animals drank far more saccharine solution than satiated animals. This is shown in table 2, which also compares saccharine drinking with water consumption prior to the first training day.

It can be seen in table 2 that both hungry and satiated rats markedly increased their fluid intake when the saccharine solution was available. Even satiated animals almost doubled their intake, while the hungry animals increased theirs by a factor of almost nine, drinking over two and

TABLE 2

EFFECT OF HUNGER ON CONSUMPTION OF SACCHARINE SOLUTION

| | Mean ccs. fluid taken | | | | |
|---|---|---|---|---|---|
| | From both water bottles before training | From saccharine bottle during training | Diff. | $t$ | df. |
| Hungry | 24.2 | 205.4 | 181.2 | 9.7 | 5 |
| Satiated | 37.8 | 78.1 | 40.3 | 4.8 | 5 |
| Diff. | −13.6 | 127.3 | | | |
| $t$ | 3.7 | 6.0 | | | |
| df. | 10 | 10 | | | |

TABLE 3

MEAN PER CENT OF WATER TAKEN FROM THE "SACCHARINE" SIDE ON
TEST DAYS DURING TRAINING

| | Mean per cent from "saccharine" side | | | |
|---|---|---|---|---|
| Day Before Training | 1st Test Day | 2nd Test Day | 3rd Test Day | 9th Test Day |
| Hungry | 55.2 | 81.1 | 82.8 | 76.7 | 72.8 |
| Satiated | 59.5 | 76.7 | 80.2 | 68.0 | 57.3 |

one-half times as much of the solution as the satiated animals. It will also
be noted that hungry animals drank significantly less water than satiated
animals during the five control days before the introduction of saccharine.
This may well merely reflect the fact that they received 10 cc. of water in
their daily ration of Purina mash. If a constant of 10 cc. is added to the
mean it becomes 34.2 and does not differ significantly from that of the
satiated group. Thus no clear relation of hunger to water intake is in
evidence.

*Position preference on test days:* All animals showed a preference for the
"saccharine" side during the nine interspersed test days on which there
was plain water in both bottles. However, the transfer of position preference was not complete, that is, while all animals drank the *majority* of
their water from the reinforced side they did not attain the 100 per cent
level. On the contrary, the transfer to test days reached a maximum on the
second test day and declined thereafter. The important trends are shown
in table 3.

It can be seen in table 3 that transfer of the reinforced position to test
days with water only increased to the second test day. At this point both
hungry and satiated animals showed reliable transfer ($p$ less than .02 in
each group). But the transfer began to decline by the third test day and
continued downward through the remainder of training. The decline from
the second to the last test day was not significant for either group but at
least the failure to progress toward 100 per cent preference indicates that
the reinforcing power of the saccharine solution was extinguishing or that
some other factor was interfering with complete transfer of the position
preference to the test days with water in both bottles. One such interfering
factor might be frustration due to failing to find a sweet taste in the
appropriate bottle on test days. Another could be acquisition of a discrimination involving drinking exclusively from the saccharine side on training
days and drinking more or less indiscriminately on the test days. The cue
for the differential behavior would be presence or absence of a sweet
taste. The critical question for the present study was whether or not the
sweet taste was losing its reinforcing power as would be the case if it

TABLE 4

POSSIBLE EXTINCTION OF SACCHARINE DRINKING

|  |  | Day of saccharine training | | |
|---|---|---|---|---|
|  |  | 1st | 2nd | 10th |
| Hungry | Mean ccs. | 244.7 | 195.5 | 194.8 |
|  | Diff. |  | 49.2 | 0.7 |
|  | t |  | 4.3 | 0.1 |
|  | df. |  | 5 | 5 |
| Satiated | Mean ccs. | 94.7 | 77.3 | 74.3 |
|  | Diff. |  | 17.4 | 3.0 |
|  | t |  | 1.6 | 0.4 |
|  | df. |  | 5 | 5 |

were an acquired reward. Evidence on this question will be considered next.

*Did the reinforcing effect extinguish?:* Perhaps the most relevant finding on this question has already been shown in table 1, in which it is obvious that an almost 100 per cent preference for the saccharine side was maintained throughout the training days for all animals. If the decline in preference on test days is due to decline of reinforcing effect, a comparable decline would be expected on training days.

Another relevant source of evidence is the course of saccharine drinking throughout the 10 training days. The finding here was an initial drop in saccharine drinking in both groups, but with little change from the second to the tenth training day. These results are shown in table 4. The table shows a significant drop between the first and second training days in the hungry group. None of the other differences shown is significant although the difference in each case is in the direction of extinction of saccharine drinking.

While the results demonstrate some initial extinction of saccharine drinking, they do not provide a convincing explanation of the failure to achieve 100 per cent transfer of position preference on test days. This preference declined *after* the saccharine drinking stabilized. Moreover, a decline in saccharine drinking is not necessarily an index of a decline in its reinforcing power—it could be acquisition of a tendency not to get too full a stomach. It should be noted that ingestion of 245 ccs. of fluid (the mean for the first day for hungry rats) involves considerable stomach distension in a 350-gram animal. The amount consumed is comparable to a 150-pound man's consuming 13 gallons of fluid in a 24-hour period.*

* The experimenters had no real check on how much of the saccharine solution was actually ingested because the cages had wire mesh floors with sawdust trays underneath. However, in Experiment III, in which drinking was done over solid floors, very little of the saccharine solution taken was found to be spilled on the floor. In any case the measure used was a good index of instrumental tongue movements.

## EXPERIMENT II

### PURPOSE

It had originally been expected that if a sweet taste was reinforcing a progressive acquisition of a position preference on test days would have been shown in Experiment I. This expectation was not borne out; instead the animals showed rapid acquisition of a moderate preference, followed by a tendency toward a decline.

The results might be interpreted as evidence that the reinforcing effect of a sweet taste was relatively weak and tended to extinguish in the course of the experiment. On the other hand the results can be interpreted as evidence that the animal was frustrated by absence of a sweet taste on test days or that a discrimination was being established such that the animals would try both bottles and drink only from the sweet side if one was sweet, but drink more indiscriminately if neither was sweet. Experiment II was designed to test further the reinforcing value of a sweet taste with both of these latter factors—frustration and discrimination—eliminated.

### METHOD

The laboratory was normally kept dimly lighted by a shielded 25-watt lamp. At 9:00 A.M., 11:00 A.M., 1:00 P.M., 3:00 P.M., and 5:00 P.M., the experimenter entered the room, turned on a bright overhead light and inserted the saccharine bottle, always on the same side for a given animal. A bottle of plain water was always present on the opposite side. The subjects were the same ones which had been used in Experiment I, the hunger regime was the same, and the saccharine solution was of the same concentration (1.30 grams per liter) and on the same side as in Experiment I. On each trial the saccharine bottle was left in position for exactly 10 minutes and the measure of instrumental behavior was the amount of the solution consumed. It was expected that if a sweet taste was reinforcing then the turning on of the light, the presence of the experimenter, the sound of the bottle being inserted, and the visual presence of the bottle would be a cue-pattern to which approach and drinking would become conditioned. The ten-minute trials were continued for 18 days—a total of 90 trials.

### RESULTS

Acquisition of instrumental drinking in response to the environmental cue-pattern appeared to continue throughout the 18-day period for hungry animals, although approaching an asymptote toward the end of training. Satiated animals on the other hand showed no signs of acquisition.

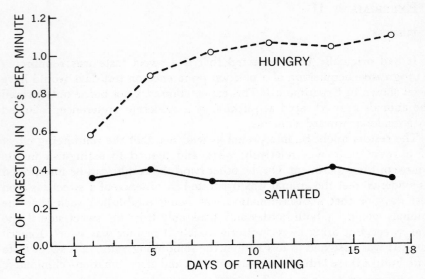

Fig. 1. Acquisition of Drinking of the Saccharine Solution (1.30 grams per liter) in Response to a Specific Cue-Pattern Accompanying Availability in the Solution.

The results are depicted in figure 1, which shows the average ccs. per 10-minute trial per rat. The results are smoothed in the figure by using successive sets of three days' trials (15 trials per rat for each point on the curve).

It is apparent in figure 1 that the satiated rats show no increase in propensity to drink saccharine whereas hungry animals show progressive acquisition. The acquisition in hungry animals is well beyond the one per cent level of confidence ($t$, for first point versus last point, $= 4.9$, df. $= 5$). Thus when the frustration and discrimination possible in Experiment I are eliminated a conventional acquisition curve is obtained. This argues against extinction of an acquired reward as an explanation of the failure to get progressive acquisition in Experiment I.

It should be borne in mind that the same animals were used in both experiments. Thus a sweet taste was shown to retain its reinforcing value for hungry animals over a lengthy period in which it could have extinguished if it were an acquired reward. Also the rate of ingestion for hungry animals was much higher by the end of Experiment II than it was even on the first day of Experiment I. Over the first day of Experiment I the hungry animals drank at a rate of 0.17 ccs. per minute, whereas the last point on the curve for hungry animals in figure 1 represents a rate of 1.09 ccs. per minute.* This difference is complicated by the fact that in

* A methodological point worth mentioning is that the hungry animals consistently drank the least at the 1:00 P.M. test, which came just before their daily feeding—at a

Experiment I the animals were asleep part of the time but it probably reflects in addition the fact that the unlimited drinking periods of Experiment I allowed any painful effects of too full a stomach to motivate avoidance of drinking behavior. The difference is in a direction opposed to the hypothesis that a sweet taste is an acquired reward which extinguishes with performance of the instrumental response. The reinforcing effect was still going strong after 10 days of unlimited drinking in Experiment I and 18 days with five 10-minute drinking periods per day in Experiment II.

## EXPERIMENT III

### PURPOSE

The main purpose of Experiment III was to test the reinforcing value of a sweet taste in a more conventional animal-learning situation than that used in Experiments I and II. A second purpose was to continue the same animals in a further learning task to give further opportunity for the reward value of a sweet taste to extinguish if it is an acquired reward. A third purpose was to get a rough idea of the order of magnitude of the reinforcing values of saccharine and food with hungry animals.

### METHOD

The same hungry animals used in Experiments I and II served as subjects in Experiment III. Of the six hungry rats used in the first two experiments, one died of whirling disease between experiments, so only five animals were available for Experiment III. The learning task was acquisition of a position habit in a standard T-maze. The stem and each arm of the maze were 21 inches long and four and one-half inches wide. The interior of the stem was painted grey, that of one arm was painted white and that of the other black. The ends of each goal box were made of wire screening to provide cues very similar to those in the animal's previous experience with drinking from the saccharine bottle in its wire-screen living cage. A Springfield timer recorded running time via a microswitch which started the timer when the door of the starting box was opened and another microswitch which stopped the clock when the animal's weight landed on a hinged floor at the far end of the arm. Retracing was prevented by dropping a door as soon as the animal entered a particular arm. The correct side for a given animal always had a bottle of saccharine

---

time when they were presumably most hungry. This runs counter to the overall relation between hunger and saccharine drinking and is interpreted by the writers as due to the conflicting habit of loitering at the front of the cage where food was soon to be introduced.

solution (1.30 grams per liter); the incorrect side had a bottle of plain water. Throughout Experiment III the animals had a supply of water from a water tray in their living cages—thus they were satiated for thirst, and the only time they drank from a glass tube during the experiment was in the maze. All trials were run in the evening, starting about 8:00 P.M.; the daily feeding of 8 grams (dry weight) of Purina flour mixed with water was given at noon. The procedure was as follows:

1. Four forced runs, two to the saccharine side and two to the water side. The forced runs were spaced over two days, one of each kind per day, balanced for order. On each trial the rat was confined in the end box for eight minutes.

2. Forty-two free-choice trials, three per day for 14 days, the trials on a given day being spaced about one half-hour apart. On each trial the rat was confined in the end box for four minutes.

RESULTS

All animals showed prompt acquisition in terms of both time and errors. The results are summarized in the three curves shown in figure 2. Curve A shows acquisition in terms of frequency of correct choice; the frequency scores plotted use per cent of correct choices on each day's set of three trials for the five animals. Thus the N at each point in the curve is 15 animal-trials. Curve B shows acquisition in terms of time to reach the end of the arm on correct choices. Every animal made at least one correct choice per day, and the value plotted in the curve is the median, over the five animals, of each animal's median daily performance. Curve C shows the mean rate of consumption of saccharine solution. The daily rate per minute was determined for each animal and these values were averaged over the five animals to get the points plotted.

An important relationship was found between rate of ingestion of saccharine solution and maze performance. Animals whose rate of drinking tended to be low during the four minutes of confinement in the goal box also tended to be poor learners both in terms of time scores and frequency scores. In other words if they did not drink the saccharine avidly they also did not perform well in getting to the solution. The relationship is depicted in figure 3.

Another interesting finding was that the average rate of consumption was much greater in Experiment III than in either of the preceding experiments. It has already been noted that the rate of ingestion was much greater in Experiment II than in Experiment I and a comparison of figure 1 and figure 2-C readily shows that the ingestion rate was much greater in Experiment III. The last point on the curve in Experiment II showed a rate of 1.09 ccs. per minute whereas the last day in Experiment III was 2.16 ccs. per minute. This result probably can be attributed to the greater

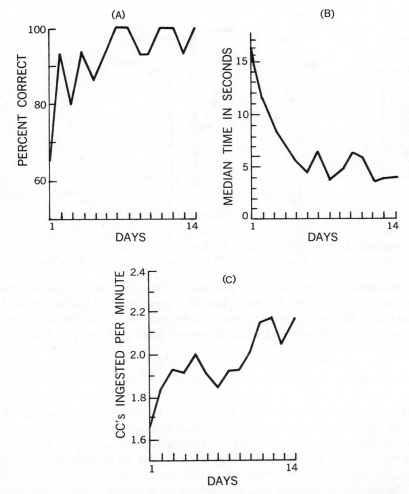

Fig. 2. Acquisition in a T-Maze with Saccharine Solution (1.30 grams per liter) as Reward: (A) Frequency of Correct Choices, (B) Time to Reach Correct Side, (C) Rate of Ingestion of Solution in the Goal Box.

specificity of the cues in the maze situation and to the fact that only four minutes of drinking were allowed at a time, thus minimizing the chance of filling up and avoiding the bottle. However, this result, like the rest of the findings in Experiment III, argues against extinction of the reward value of the non-nourishing sweet taste.

Moreover, the motivating power of the sweet taste was quite impressive. The two fastest animals appeared to run at top speed and were consistently close to two seconds at the end of training. The final median time of

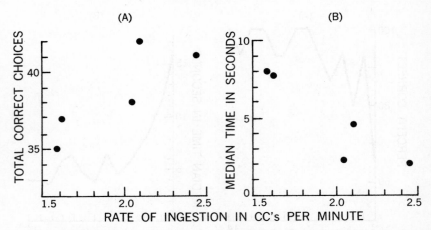

FIG. 3. Relation Between Mean Amount of Saccharine Drinking in the Four-Minute Confinement and (A) Frequency of Correct Choice on All Trials and (B) Median Running Time During the Last Half of Training.

3.8 seconds is slower than that obtained in the same apparatus by other rats rewarded with food, who achieved a median of about two seconds. However, the time is still of a low enough order of magnitude to indicate considerable reinforcement value of a sweet taste for hungry animals.

## DISCUSSION

The experiments prove that a non-nourishing but sweet-tasting substance served as a reinforcement for instrumental learning. Hunger was presumably in no way reduced by the saccharine solution, yet hungry animals clearly demonstrated acquisition in the three different learning situations in which the reward was a saccharine solution.

The possibility that the sweet taste was an acquired reward seems very unlikely—on two counts. For one thing, previously experienced sweet tastes (e.g., rat's milk, conversion of starch to sugar in the mouth, etc.) are very unlikely to have been as sweet as the concentrated saccharine solution used. Thus the sweet taste used would be at an unfavorable point on the generalization gradient as an acquired reward stimulus if we make the usual assumption that the generalization gradient falls in either direction from the stimulus intensity reinforced. Moreover, the sweet taste did not lose its reward value throughout the three experiments, with the ingestion of thousands of ccs. of saccharine solution and no doubt millions of instrumental tongue movements. Since the visual, kinesthetic, tactile, and gustatory pattern accompanying this ingestion in all three experiments (drinking from a glass tube protruding from a visible graduated cylinder through quarter-inch wire mesh) received no primary reinforcement, it would be expected that any *acquired* reward value of a sweet taste would have extinguished for this pattern.

The findings are thus at variance with the molar principle of reinforcement used by Hull (4), which identifies primary reinforcement with "need reduction." Hull admittedly chose need reduction on the grounds that from a Darwinian point of view reduction of a survival need is very likely to be accompanied by a "reinforcing state of affairs," and at the molar level this principle may be predictive in a high proportion of instances of instrumental learning. However, it does not designate the *mechanism* by which natural selection has managed to make need-reducing events reinforcing, and it is unable to predict the present results in which reinforcement is obtained in the absence of need reduction. The findings highlight the desirability of a theory concerning the mechanism (or mechanisms) by which natural selection has achieved adaptive instrumental learning.

At a more molecular level, Miller and Dollard (5) have proposed *reduction of drive* as the occasion for a reinforcing state of affairs and they tentatively identify drive with intensity of stimulation. The present findings are at variance with their position in that hunger drive, in the usual sense of the concept, is not at all reduced by the saccharine solution. Thus, as mentioned earlier, saccharine is allegedly excreted without chemical change and its ingestion has no effect on food intake (3). However, it may be postulated that part of the total stimulation in the case of hunger consists of proprioceptive return from the striped-muscle tension occasioned by the hunger state. It may further be postulated that a sweet taste relaxes the striped muscles—at the very least the animal stands still while ingesting the solution—and this innate relaxation would provide stimulus reduction and consequent acquisition of instrumental responses. Thus, a closer analysis of the physiological effects of a sweet taste may show that the present results are consistent with Miller and Dollard's position.

While the experiments were aimed mainly at providing evidence relevant to the need-reduction and drive-reduction theories, a brief comment should be made on the relation of the results to other positions on the reinforcement process. The results in no way conflict with or provide support for the relatively empirical and circular systems of Skinner (7), Thorndike (8), and Tolman (9). The results merely demonstrate that with hungry animals a saccharine solution is a "reinforcing stimulus" in Skinner's terms, is a "reward" or "satisfier" in Thorndike's terms, and probably is "demanded" in Tolman's terms. The results are also consistent with Guthrie's (2) more theoretical and less circular position involving the mechanism of stimulus change and protection of the last response from relearning. In Guthrie's terms the results demonstrate that ingesting the sweet substance innately produces a stimulus change which can be observed to be very much the same as that produced by presenting food to the hungry animal (i.e., cessation of exploration, maintained ingestion, and so forth) and it is therefore not surprising that the change is big enough to protect the instrumental response. Another theory which cannot escape mention in the present context is the unpopular "beneceptor" theory of Troland (10), which holds that the reinforcing value of a reward lies in the quality of the stimulation produced by the reward. The findings are a natural fit to his theory—which argues that stimulation of receptors for sweet is all that is needed to strengthen an instrumental act.

In conclusion the question should be answered as to whether any novel hypotheses concerning the reinforcement process are indicated by the results. The chief suggestion the authors have to make is that stimulation and performance of a consummatory response appears to be more important to instrumental learning—in a primary, not acquired, way—than the drive satisfaction which the consummatory response normally achieves. The present experiments were essentially sham-feeding experiments in which the animal was innately stimulated to ingest a substance which did not change his state of hunger, and the result was acquisition, without extinction, of the instrumental responses. Thus it would appear that *eliciting* the consummatory response of ingestion was the critical factor. This suggestion is in line with Wolfe and Kaplon's (11) finding that with total food intake held constant, the reward value of eating is a function of amount of consummatory activity required to ingest the food.

## SUMMARY

1. A non-nourishing but sweet-tasting substance was shown in three successive learning situations to be an effective reward for instrumental learning, its reward value depending on the state of hunger present.

2. The possibility that the sweet taste was an acquired reward rather than a primary reward was shown to be extremely unlikely.

3. The findings demonstrate the expected limitations of Hull's molar "need reduction" theory of reinforcement and the necessity of exploring indirect reduction of striped-muscle tension as a drive-reduction factor in Miller and Dollard's theory of reinforcement. The results are consistent with Guthrie's last-response theory of reinforcement, and demonstrate that a sweet taste is "reinforcing" in Skinner's system, "satisfying" in Thorndike's system, and "demanded" in Tolman's system.

4. It is suggested that elicitation of the consummatory response appears to be a more critical *primary* reinforcing factor in instrumental learning than the drive reduction subsequently achieved.

## REFERENCES

1. BEEBE-CENTER, J. G., BLACK, P., HOFFMAN, A. C., and WADE, MARJORIE (1948) Relative per diem consumption as a measure of preference in the rat. *J. comp. physiol. Psychol.*, *41*, 239-251.
2. GUTHRIE, E. R. (1935) *The psychology of learning.* New York: Harper.
3. HAUSMANN, M. F. (1933) The behavior of rats in choosing food. II Differentiation between sugar and saccharine. *J. comp. Psychol.*, *15*, 419-428.
4. HULL, C. L. (1943) *Principles of behavior.* New York: Appleton-Century.
5. MILLER, N. E. and DOLLARD, J. (1941) *Social learning and imitation.* New Haven: Yale Press.
6. RICHTER, C. P. and CAMPBELL, KATHRYNE (1940) Taste thresholds and taste preferences of rats for five common sugars. *J. Nutrition*, *20*, 31-46.
7. SKINNER, B. F. (1938) *The behavior of organisms.* New York: Appleton-Century.
8. THORNDIKE, E. L. (1911) *Animal intelligence.* New York: Macmillan.
9. TOLMAN, E. C. (1932) *Purposive behavior in animals and men.* New York: Appleton-Century.
10. TROLAND, L. T. (1928) *The fundamentals of human motivation.* New York: Van Nostrand.
11. WOLFE, J. B. and KAPLON, M. D. (1941) Effect of amount of reward and consummative activity on learning in chickens. *J. comp. Psychol.*, *31*, 353-361.

## 12.   Avoidance and Approach Learning Motivated by Stimulation of Identical Hypothalamic Loci

### G. W. Brown and B. D. Cohen

*The authors believe that in the brain stimulation experiment, the conditions of the experiment determine largely what behavior is learned. In this study they demonstrate that both avoidance and approach learning can be learned, although there is the stimulation of identical hypothalamic loci.*

Recent investigations involving behavioral responses associated with subcortical stimulation have supported the concept of neural 'centers' for particular emotions such as 'pleasure' and 'aversion' (1–7). In sharp contrast to 'center' concepts, we stated that the behavior patterns acquired when hypothalamic excitation is utilized as motivation depends upon the experimental situation rather than the site of stimulation (8). Thus we

*Amer. J. Physiol.*, 1959, *197*, 153-157. Reprinted with permission of the author and The American Physiological Association.

believe that the topographical locus of the stimulus governs the autonomic and skeletal muscle responses while the conditions of the experiment determine what behavior is learned.

Our hypothesis was proposed in conjunction with experiments where cats learned to avoid hypothalamic stimulation (8). Therefore, it could be argued that our experimental evidence supported the proposition that the hypothalamic areas stimulated were 'aversive' or 'punishment' centers.

If our conception of the role played by hypothalamic stimulation in learning experiments had merit we believed we could produce two antithetical types of learning in the same animals with identical localization of electrodes by altering the experimental conditions. Accordingly, the present experiments are a test of the hypothesis that a lateral hypothalamic stimulus may act as an energizing, nonassociative, drive-arousing operation to produce both avoidance and approach learning in the same cats.

METHODS

Twenty cats were prepared with electrodes implanted in the lateral hypothalamus. Two stainless steel, 22 gage, electrodes were placed in each lateral hypothalamic nucleus at Horseley-Clarke A 11 plane. The electrodes were formvar insulated except for a 1 mm² exposed tip. The distance between tips was 1.5 mm. Localization of electrode tips is illustrated in figure 1. All cats were allowed a 21-day postoperative recovery period prior to stimulation experiments.

Following the postoperative recovery period the response of all animals to 5000 cps sine wave stimulation was tested (9). To be included in the group utilized for behavioral studies each cat was required to exhibit classical 'hypothalamic rage' response to an electrical stimulus as well as random locomotion during stimulation. Thirteen of the twenty cats met this criterion. Table 1 indicates the parameters of electrical stimulation producing hissing, spitting, piloerection, pupillary dilation, snarling and random locomotion for each of the 13 cats. Thus the parameters of hypothalamic stimulation were determined prior to any behavioral experimentation. The voltage, current and frequency of stimulation so determined for each animal were the values utilized whenever that animal received a hypothalamic stimulus in any of the behavioral experiments. The stimulus duration for any particular trial in the avoidance experiments was the time from onset of hypothalamic stimulation until barrier crossing was accomplished. The duration of the stimulus in the approach situation was kept at a constant 0.3 second. This value was selected because previous experience with avoidance training had indicated that animals on a 10-day regime of avoidance training would experience a total stimulation

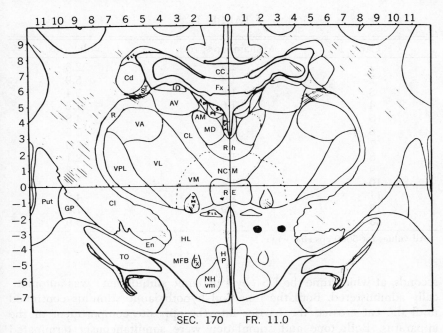

FIG. 1. Location of stimulating electrode tips (*solid circles*).

duration equivalent to 0.3 sec/trial. Therefore, the total expenditure of electrical energy in the two learning procedures would be approximately equal.

A shuttle box, figure 2, was used for the avoidance learning portion of the experiments. The apparatus was so constructed that a cat could be introduced into the box from either end. Upon entrance into the box, the subject was placed in a modified dog harness to which the electrode leads were fastened. The leads were then connected to terminals located on the animal's head, thus allowing freedom of movement within the box. A sound stimulus could be presented in either compartment of the box through loudspeakers mounted on the doors at each end. Both sound and hypothalamic stimulation could be remotely controlled from a room adjoining that in which the shuttle box was located. Observations of the animal's behavior were made through 'one-way' viewing screens.

Twenty trials per day were administered until a total of 200 trials had been accomplished. Each trial was initiated by the onset of a 'warbling' tone produced by a Clough-Brengle Audiomatic Audio Generator set to sweep through the audio frequency range (0–15,000 cps) five to six times per second. This CS (conditioned stimulus) was sounded through the speaker in the side of the shuttle box the animal happened to be occupying prior to each trial. For experimental animals the CS continued for 15

TABLE 1

| Cat | Milliamperes, rms | Volts, rms |
|-----|-------------------|------------|
| 1 | 1.4 | 2.8 |
| 2 | 1.4 | 5.9 |
| 3 | 1.8 | 5.4 |
| 4 | 1.6 | 11.2 |
| 5 | 1.4 | 4.8 |
| 6 | 1.6 | 5.5 |
| 7 | 1.5 | 4.0 |
| 8 | 1.5 | 2.1 |
| 9 | 2.1 | 4.8 |
| 10 | 1.4 | 5.9 |
| 11 | 1.5 | 4.2 |
| 12 | 1.9 | 7.0 |
| 13 | 1.3 | 3.9 |

All values for 5000 cps sine wave.

seconds, at which time the US (hypothalamic stimulation) was automatically administered. Both the tone and hypothalamic stimulus continued until the cat crossed the barrier into the opposite compartment of the apparatus. Both tone and stimulation were simultaneously terminated when the cat dropped across the barrier. Response time was automatically recorded from the initiation of the tone until the barrier was crossed. A response was counted as 'avoidance' if it occurred during the 15-second tone period prior to the onset of hypothalamic stimulation. The control procedure was similar except that tone and hypothalamic stimulation were never paired. A trial for a control cat was initiated by sounding the tone in the compartment of the apparatus the animal occupied. The tone continued until the animal either crossed the barrier or 100 seconds elapsed. Between tone trials, a hypothalamic stimulus was delivered and continued until the cat crossed the barrier. Barrier crossing terminated the stimulus. For control animals, there were 20 tone trials and 20 hypothalamic stimulation trials/day. The time required from onset of tone to barrier crossing, and onset of hypothalamic stimulus to crossing of barrier was recorded.

A runway, figure 3, was used for approach learning procedures. Control animals were introduced into the apparatus at the closed end through a door which was closed immediately. When the cat was released he was free to walk out the open end or remain in the runway. The animals were timed from the point of release until a beam of light was interrupted at the open end of the apparatus. If the animals did not traverse the runway within 100 seconds they were guided through the runway and taken to a captivity cage. Between trials, control cats were placed in an enclosure where a hypothalamic stimulus of 0.3 second duration and the same volt-

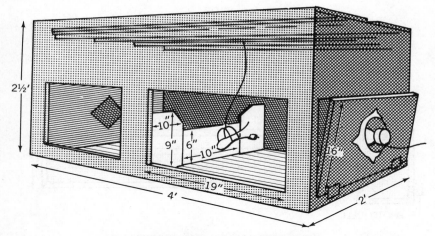

Fig. 2. Avoidance conditioning apparatus.

age, current and frequency as used for avoidance training was delivered. There were 20 complete trials/day for 10 days. Identical conditions prevailed for experimental animals except that interruption of the beam of light within 100 seconds administered the hypothalamic stimulus. If the experimental animals did not leave the runway within 100 seconds, they were treated identical to controls (i.e., led through the runway without stimulation and hypothalamic stimulation administered between trials). Experimental animals traversing the runway within 100 seconds always received hypothalamic stimulation at the end of the runway while control animals never received stimulation within the runway. However, both experimental and control animals received the same total amount of stimulation.

The 13 cats acceptable for behavioral experiments were divided into the following three groups:

| Group I | Group II | Group III |
|---|---|---|
| 4 experimental | 3 experimental | 3 experimental |
| 1 control | 1 control | 1 control |

*Group I* animals were trained with avoidance and approach procedures alternated on a daily basis (i.e. *day 1, 3, 5, 7, 9*—avoidance: *day 2, 4, 6, 8, 10*—approach). *Group II* animals received 10 days of avoidance training followed by 10 days of approach training and *group III* cats received 10 days of approach training prior to 10 days of avoidance training.

The average response time for 20 trials was utilized as a measure of performance in all cases.

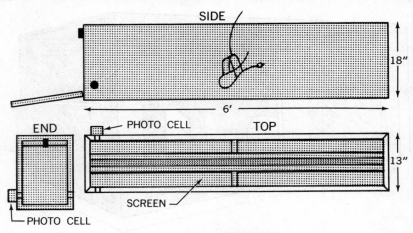

Fig. 3. Approach learning apparatus.

## Results

No significant differences could be determined between *group I, II* or *III* animals. Therefore the results have been evaluated with 10 experimental and 3 control animals.

Figure 4 is a graphical representation of the data gathered from the response times of all animals. The horizontal line on the avoidance graph represents the 15-second time interval duration of the tone. Thus, a position on the graph below this line indicates predominantly avoidance responses. The experimental group's curve on the avoidance graph remains about the 15-second line during the first 4 days of training (80 trials). Beginning on the 5th day, avoidance responses began to predominate. This is reflected on the response time curve for the experimental cats. From the 5th through 10th days of learning the mean response time becomes progressively shorter. The control animals did not cross the barrier during the 100-second tone periods. In order to yield a graphical comparison between control and experimental cats a constant 15 seconds was added to the response time of the control cats when hypothalamic stimulation was administered. Thus the control curve on the avoidance graph illustrates the mean escape time above the 15-second horizontal line.

In the approach situation, the control animals initially traverse the runway rapidly, but by the 6th day of training, their running time was distinctly slower than that of the experimental group.

The graphical representation of the approach data illustrates the difference between control and experimental animals. The experimental animals were considerably slower than the control cats during the first 5 days of approach training. They developed a 'stalking' type of behavior in

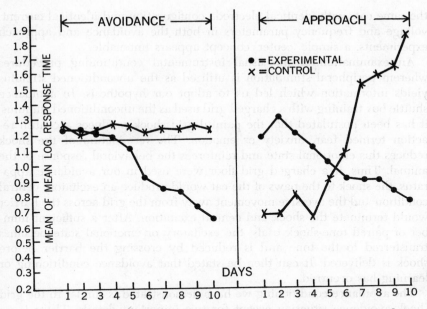

FIG. 4. Means of mean log response times on successive training days. (Experimental $N = 10$, control $N = 3$).

their approach to the beam of light at the end of the runway. The behavior pattern was strikingly similar to that of a cat stalking a bird. As training progressed, the stalking pattern did not change except for increased speed of approach to the photo cell and hypothalamic stimulation. After 120 trials (6 days) the response time of experimental cats was distinctly faster than controls. From the 6th to 10th day (120–200 trials) the control animals became slower while experimental animals became faster in traversing the runway.

## DISCUSSION

Observation of the performance or evaluation of the results obtained from the experimental cats in the avoidance experiments could easily lead to the hypothesis that the lateral hypothalamus was a 'punishment center.' The cats appeared to react similarly to cats trained in a grid-shock shuttle box. They were readily conditioned to avoid hypothalamic shock just as cats can be conditioned to avoid grid shock. Observation of the same cats in the approach experiments would as easily lead to the postulate of the lateral hypothalamus as a 'pleasure center,' particularly if the observer would interpret the stalking of a bird pleasurable to a cat. Since these are the same cats with identical electrode configuration and identical current, voltage and frequency parameters in both the avoidance and approach experiments, a simple 'center' concept appears untenable.

An examination of the usual instrumental conditioning procedures wherein peripheral stimulation is utilized as the unconditioned stimulus yields information which led us to adopt our hypothesis. In avoidance shuttle box training with a charged grid used as the unconditioned stimulus, it has been postulated that the painful grid shock produces a central reaction termed fear, anxiety or emotion. The termination of the shock reduces this emotional state and reinforces the behavioral response of the animal. Thus, if a charged grid floor were used in our avoidance apparatus, the shock to the paws of the cat would produce an excitatory central condition and the aversive movement away from the grid across the barrier would terminate the shock and central excitation. After a sufficient number of paired tone-shock trials, the excitatory or emotional state becomes transferred to the tone and is reduced by crossing the barrier before shock is delivered. It can then be stated that avoidance conditioning or learning has occurred.

The avoidance conditioning we have demonstrated is similar to the grid shock avoidance situation except for two important details. There is no painful peripheral stimulus to give direction to a response and the emotional or excitatory state is aroused by direct hypothalamic stimulation.

The barrier crossing response initially occurs as a component of the cat's random activity under hypothalamic stimulation. This response is subsequently given its specifically aversive ('escape') function by means of the experimenter's termination of the emotionally arousing central stimulus when the cat crosses the barrier. Presumably, once the tone has acquired, through conditioning, the capacity to arouse the emotional excitatory state, the animal will jump the barrier to the tone alone. Tone termination then becomes sufficient to reduce the excitatory state and maintain barrier crossing as an avoidance response. It is avoidant in that it antedates and precludes direct hypothalamic stimulation. Under these conditions, the selection of barrier crossing for reinforcement is achieved by the experimenter's actions; these actions subserve a function similar to the intrinsically aversive directional properties of peripheral pain in the grid shock situation. Viewed in this manner, it is superfluous to postulate any intrinsically aversive or punishing properties to the lateral hypothalamic stimulation itself.

The nondirectional characteristic of hypothalamic excitation as a motivational factor in learning is illustrated by the accomplishment of approach learning in the same cats that learned avoidance responses. In order to make the central stimulus function as a reinforcer for an approach response, the experimental task was changed. The initial tendency of cats to escape from a closed container and locomote through a runway (as observed in the early fast response time of controls) was utilized to provide the direction of the animal's behavior with respect to the central stimulus. The delivery of hypothalamic stimulation at the end of the runway functioned to reinforce (i.e., strengthen) this tendency. Similar results could probably be obtained by utilizing food reward at the end of the runway for hungry cats. The emotional activation involved in the anticipation and consumption of the food would function to motivate and reinforce the approach response. In the present procedure the emotional activation is produced directly by central stimulation. Also, while the food would constitute an intrinsically positive incentive for mature cats, the positive incentive value of the hypothalamic stimulation required special external conditions. It is unnecessary to postulate any intrinsic 'pleasure' meaning to the centrally produced emotional activation per se.

The emotional activation produced by direct hypothalamic stimulation provided the necessary conditions for motivating and reinforcing the animal's performance of the barrier crossing avoidance response just as it motivated and reinforced their performance of the runway approach response. When both the avoidance and approach results are considered together, one is led to the conclusion that postulation of either punishment or pleasure properties intrinsic to the excitation of lateral hypothalamic loci is not only superfluous, but is erroneous.

## REFERENCES

1. OLDS, J. and MILNER, P. (1954) *J. Comp. Physiol. Psychol.*, 47, 419.
2. OLDS, J. (1956) *Scient. Am.*, 195, 105.
3. OLDS, J. (1956) *J. Comp. & Physiol. Psychol.*, 49, 281.
4. OLDS, J. (1956) *J. Comp. & Physiol. Psychol.*, 49, 507.
5. DELGADO, J. M. R. and BURSTEIN, B. (1956) *Fed. Proc.*, 15, 143.
6. DELGADO, J. M. R., ROSVOLD, H. E., and LOONEY, E. (1956) *J. Comp. & Physiol. Psychol.*, 49, 373.
7. OLDS, J. (1958) *Science*, 127, 315.
8. COHEN, B. D., BROWN, G. W., and BROWN, M. L. (1957) *J. Exper. Psychol.*, 53, 228.
9. BROWN, G. W. (1956) *Am. J. Physiol.*, 187, 589.

# 13.  The Effects of Reinforcement Scheduling on the Strength of a Secondary Reinforcer

## R. E. Fox and R. A. King

*This study is an important one in that it demonstrates that a secondary reinforcing stimulus can acquire durability if intermittent reinforcement procedures are utilized during the training as well as the test period.*

Much experimentation has shown that the same variables which determine the strength of a response with primary reinforcement also determine the strength of secondary reinforcers. Meyers (1958) has summarized much of this work.

An important variable which affects the strength of response with primary reinforcers is the intermittency of the reinforcement (reinforcement scheduling). The concern of the present study is to investigate this variable when applied to the establishment of secondary reinforcers.

Previous work on this variable has produced conflicting results. Saltzman (1949), Notterman (1951), Dinsmoor (1952), McClelland and McGown (1953), and D'Amato, Lachman, and Kivy (1958) have presented data which may be interpreted as showing that intermittency of the pairing of primary reinforcement and the secondary reinforcing stimulus increases the strength of a secondary reinforcer. None of these experiments is a clear demonstration, however. On the other hand Dinsmoor, Kish, and Keller (1953), Melching (1954) and Clayton (1956) have shown that intermittency of pairing does not seem to affect the strength of the secondary reinforcer.

Zimmerman (1957) has suggested that intermittent or partial pairing of the primary reinforcement and secondary reinforcing stimulus will be effective if a two-stage procedure is used. In the first stage, the establishment of the secondary reinforcer, a gradually increasing ratio schedule of pairings of the secondary reinforcing stimulus with primary reinforcement was used. Zimmerman stopped when a ratio of 14/1 had been reached. In the second stage, the test for the strength of the secondary reinforcer, the "new learning" technique was used. A bar was introduced and bar-press responses were rewarded by the secondary reinforcer estab-

*J. comp. physiol. Psychol.*, 1961, 54, 266-269. Reprinted with permission of the senior author and The American Psychological Association. This report is based upon a thesis submitted in partial fulfillment of the requirements for the M.A. degree at the University of North Carolina (Fox, 1960).

lished in the first stage. Zimmerman suggests that these secondary reinforcements should also be intermittent. With this technique he was able to produce extremely strong secondary reinforcers. Perhaps the conflicting results cited above can be attributed to failure to meet the conditions outlined by Zimmerman.

While Zimmerman's work is quite suggestive, it is far from conclusive. Control groups are lacking. For instance, as Lewis (1960) has pointed out, a group trained and tested under intermittent or partial conditions should be compared with groups trained and tested under nonintermittent or continuous conditions. Other combinations of training and testing should also be compared. It is the purpose of the present experiment to do this.

## METHOD

### SUBJECTS

The Ss were 60 male albino rats of the Wistar strain. All Ss were 120 to 150 days old at the beginning of the experiment.

### APPARATUS

Two Skinner boxes placed in larger sound-attenuating chambers were used. These boxes were equipped with automatic dipper mechanisms and blowers. A 25-w. frosted lamp was used to illuminate each box. A buzzer was placed in the chamber which surrounded the Skinner box in which the S was situated. This buzzer was slightly annoying to human Os. It served as the secondary reinforcing stimulus, and, when paired with primary reinforcement, followed it by approximately .5 sec. It lasted for 3 sec.

The primary reinforcement consisted of a 16% sucrose solution (16 gm. of sucrose to 84 ml. of water). Each primary reinforcement consisted of .02 ml. of this solution.

### PROCEDURE

The experiment was done in five replications of 12 Ss each. The experiment was run on a 48-hr. cycle. Half the Ss, 6 animals, were run on the first day of the cycle, while the other 6 Ss were run on the second day of the cycle. Since the running was staggered like this, and since 2 Ss were run at a time, the maximum time of running was 3 hr. per day. All running was done between 6 P.M. and 9 P.M.

*Preliminary procedure.* Four days prior to the beginning of Stage I (the establishment of the secondary reinforcer) the Ss were deprived of food and placed on a feeding schedule which consisted of 44½ hr. of deprivation and 3½ hr. of feeding. During these four days the Ss were habituated to the Skinner boxes and tamed by gentle handling.

*Stage I*: The Establishment of the Secondary Reinforcer. This stage was begun on the fifth day. As outlined above, each S was 44½ hr. deprived at the time of running. Each S was run every other day. The buzzer and primary reinforcement were presented on several schedules during this stage. The buzzer and dipper were operated manually, independently of S's behavior, except that they were never operated when S hovered over the water-delivery aperture. The Ss had to move to the dipper when the buzzer sounded.

In the first session of this stage all Ss were given 50 pairings of buzzer and dipper. In the second session the Ss were randomly assigned to one of the two conditions under which secondary reinforcers were to be established. These were the continuous-pairing and partial-pairing conditions. The Ss of the continuous-pairing group were given 30 paired presentations of buzzer and dipper, while the partial-training Ss were given 50 buzzer presentations, 30 of which were paired with primary reinforcement. During this and subsequent partial-training days, the approach response to the buzzer did not weaken. In the third session Ss in the continuous-pairing group received 15 pairings of buzzer and dipper. The partial-pairing Ss were given 50 buzzer presentations, 15 of which were paired with primary reinforcement. In the fourth and final session of this stage the continuous group received 5 buzzer-dipper pairings, while the partial Ss were given 50 buzzer presentations, 5 of which were paired with primary reinforcement. This Stage I procedure is summarized in Table 1.

It should be noted that: ( a ) each group received 100 pairings of buzzer and primary reinforcement; ( b ) the number of buzzer presentations differed; and ( c ) the final ratio of buzzer to dipper presentations was 10/1 for the partial group.

*Stage II*: Test for the Strength of the Secondary Reinforcer. After the fourth session a bar was introduced and Ss from each Stage I group were randomly assigned to one of three Stage II groups: ( a ) Those on a con-

TABLE 1

STAGE I: THE ESTABLISHMENT OF THE SECONDARY REINFORCER

| Session | Continuous Group | | Partial Group | |
|---------|--------|--------|--------|--------|
| | Buzzer | Dipper | Buzzer | Dipper |
| 1 | 50 | 50 | 50 | 50 |
| 2 | 30 | 30 | 50 | 30 |
| 3 | 15 | 15 | 50 | 15 |
| 4 | 5 | 5 | 50 | 5 |
| Total | 100 | 100 | 200 | 100 |

TABLE 2

EXPERIMENTAL DESIGN

| Stage I Condition | Stage II Condition | | |
|---|---|---|---|
| | Partial | Continuous | No |
| Partial | PP | PC | PNo |
| Continuous | CP | CC | CNo |

tinuous schedule received the buzzer as a consequence of each bar depression. (*b*) Those on a partial schedule received the buzzer on an FI 1-min. schedule. (*c*) The control ("no") groups never received the buzzer as a consequence of bar depressions. The six groups of 10 Ss each are shown in Table 2.

Stage II was carried out in two days or sessions (Sessions 5 and 6). The number of responses made in 1 hr. was recorded in each of these sessions.

RESULTS

The mean number of responses and standard deviations for each of the six groups in Stage II (test for the strength of the secondary reinforcer) are shown in Table 3. The means and standard deviations of the logarithmic transformations of the numbers of responses are shown in Table 4. The logarithmic transformation was used in order to approximate the requirement of homogeneity of variance which is needed for further analysis.

A type III analysis of variance (Lindquist, 1953) was carried out on the transformed scores. The effect due to the Stage II variables was significant ($p < .001$); that due to the Stage I variables was significant ($p < .025$); and that due to the interaction of Stage I and Stage II vari-

TABLE 3

MEANS AND STANDARD DEVIATIONS OF RESPONSES DURING STAGE II

| Stage I Condition | Stage II Condition | | | | | |
|---|---|---|---|---|---|---|
| | Partial | | Continuous | | No | |
| | Mean | SD | Mean | SD | Mean | SD |
| Session 1 | | | | | | |
| Partial | 70.6 | 24.8 | 23.6 | 11.0 | 17.7 | SD |
| Continuous | 21.0 | 9.6 | 31.5 | 14.8 | 11.5 | 6.7 |
| Session 2 | | | | | | |
| Partial | 24.7 | 19.6 | 12.3 | 14.2 | 6.8 | 5.6 |
| Continuous | 9.8 | 7.9 | 14.6 | 10.3 | 4.2 | 2.7 |

TABLE 4

MEANS AND STANDARD DEVIATIONS OF RESPONSES DURING STAGE II
(Logarithmic Transformation)

| | Stage II Condition | | | | | |
| Stage I Condition | Partial | | Continuous | | No | |
| | Mean | SD | Mean | SD | Mean | SD |
| --- | --- | --- | --- | --- | --- | --- |
| | | | Session 1 | | | |
| Partial | 1.79 | 0.30 | 1.34 | 0.17 | 1.20 | 0.27 |
| Continuous | 1.26 | 0.27 | 1.45 | 0.67 | 0.98 | 0.29 |
| | | | Session 2 | | | |
| Partial | 1.23 | 0.49 | 1.06 | 0.19 | 0.70 | 0.38 |
| Continuous | 0.94 | 0.43 | 1.05 | 0.36 | 0.53 | 0.31 |

ables was significant ($p < .05$). The effect due to Stage II days was also significant ($p < .005$).

Since all main effects were significant, $t$ tests were made, using the transformed scores, between each pair of groups. The results are shown in Table 5.

## DISCUSSION

The conclusions to be drawn from Table 5 are: ($a$) all experimental groups gave significantly more responses than their appropriate control groups. ($b$) The PP group gave significantly more responses than any of the other three experimental groups (PC, CP, CC). ($c$) The PC, CP, and CC groups all gave about the same number of responses. In short, with regard to the experimental groups, the outcome of the experiment was $PP > CC = PC = CP$.

The first finding merely shows that the buzzer, as tested by the "new learning" technique, was a secondary reinforcer.

TABLE 5

TABLE OF $t$ TESTS BETWEEN EACH PAIR OF GROUPS (DAYS 1 AND 2 COMBINED)

| | PC | PNo | CP | CC | CNo |
| --- | --- | --- | --- | --- | --- |
| PP | 3.32** | 4.56** | 3.64** | 2.32* | 5.28** |
| PC | | 2.33* | 1.07 | 1.46 | 3.54** |
| PNo | | | 0.96 | 3.37** | 1.64 |
| CP | | | | 2.01 | 2.38* |
| CC | | | | | 4.31** |

* $p < .05$, $df = 18$.
** $p < .01$, $df = 18$.

Taken together, the second and third findings suggest that the effect of partial presentation during the establishment of a secondary reinforcer is present only under partial conditions during the test. They also suggest that partial conditions under the test do not in themselves produce the effects noted here. In short, partial conditions must be present during both the establishment of the secondary reinforcer and the test. Zimmerman (1957), whose experiment met both these conditions, obtained results in line with the ones presented here. Melching (1954) and Dinsmoor et al. (1953) did not use a two-stage procedure. Clayton's (1956) failure to obtain results was possibly due to the use of too small a ratio, 3/1, during the establishment of the secondary reinforcer.

The fact that intermittent reinforcement must be used in both parts of the experiment suggests the following ad hoc explanation. During Stage I (the establishment of the secondary reinforcer) the Ss were required to make a response to the buzzer, i.e., move to the dipper. This response was strengthened by primary reinforcement and became quite strong. Proprioceptive stimulation from this dipper-approach response was thus paired with primary reinforcement and may have come to have had the role of a secondary reinforcer. The Ss of the partial-training groups which made the response to the buzzer without primary reinforcement on the unrewarded trials were perhaps being rewarded by the secondary reinforcing properties of the proprioceptive stimulation from the response. Since stimulation from the dipper-approach response had reinforcing properties, the partial groups were being reinforced after buzzer presentations when there was no primary reinforcement. In short, Ss of the partial groups were really receiving more pairings of the secondary reinforcing stimulus (buzzer) and reinforcement of some sort. On trials when the buzzer sounded and the dipper operated there was primary reinforcement. On trials when the buzzer sounded and the dipper did not operate there was secondary reinforcement. Although they use a different explanation, Zimmerman (1957) and Dinsmoor (1950) have pointed out that a secondary reinforcer is more effective if a specific response is attached to it.

During Stage II (test for the strength of the secondary reinforcer) the Stage II partial groups might be expected to do better because the secondary reinforcing property of the buzzer would extinguish more slowly. The main reason for this is that the extinction trials, i.e., buzzer followed by no primary reinforcement, are spaced. Thus, for the partial groups in Stage II, the buzzer will retain its secondary reinforcing property longer. There is some evidence for this, in the case of the PP group at least. Most Ss (8 out of 10) of the PP group gave most of their responses in the second half of the first session, while most Ss (27 out of 30 of the other experimental groups gave most of their responses during the first half of the first session.

The combination of these effects in the two stages is thought to be necessary for an observable effect.

## SUMMARY

The present experiment was designed to discover whether scheduling of the pairing of a neutral stimulus with primary reinforcement affects the secondary reinforcing property acquired by the stimulus.

A two-stage procedure was used. In the first stage (the establishment of the secondary reinforcer) the Ss (Wistar albino rats) were given: (a) partial (variable-ratio) pairings of the neutral stimulus (buzzer) and primary reinforcement (16% sucrose solution), or (b) continuous pairings of these. In the second stage (test for the strength of the secondary reinforcer) Ss were given access to a bar. Presses of this produced the buzzer without primary reinforcement. The buzzer was presented: (a) after every bar-press for a continuous-reinforcement group; (b) on an FI schedule of 1 min. for a partial group; and (c) never for a control group. The combination of two Stage I and three Stage II conditions produced the following six groups: (a) a partial-partial group (PP); (b) a partial-continuous group (PC); (c) a partial-no buzzer group (PNo); (d) a continuous-partial group (CP); (e) a continuous-continuous group (CC); and (f) a continuous-no buzzer group (CNo). There were 10 Ss in a group.

The results were as follows: PP made significantly more responses than CC, while CC equaled PC and CC. The experimental groups always gave significantly more responses than their appropriate control groups.

The outcome is interpreted as showing that a two-stage procedure must be used to show the effects of scheduling in the establishment of a secondary reinforcer. Neither scheduling in Stage I alone nor Stage II alone is effective.

## REFERENCES

CLAYTON, F. L. (1956) Secondary reinforcement as a function of reinforcement scheduling. *Psychol. Rep.*, 2, 377-380.

D'AMATO, M. R., LACHMAN, R., and KIVY, P. (1958) Secondary reinforcement as affected by reward schedules and the testing situation. *J. comp. physiol. Psychol.*, 51, 737-741.

DINSMOOR, J. A. (1950) A quantitative comparison of the discrimination and reinforcing functions of a stimulus. *J. exp. Psychol.*, 40, 458-472.

DINSMOOR, J. A. (1952) Resistance to extinction following periodic reinforcement in the presence of a discriminative stimulus. *J. comp. physiol. Psychol.*, 45, 31-35.

DINSMOOR, J. A., KISH, G. B., and KELLER, F. S. (1953) A comparison of the effectiveness of regular and periodic secondary reinforcement. *J. gen. Psychol.*, *48*, 57-66.

Fox, R. E. (1960) The effects of reinforcement scheduling on the strength of a secondary reinforcer. Unpublished master's thesis, University of North Carolina.

Lewis, D. J. (1960) Partial reinforcement: A selective review of the literature since 1950. *Psychol. Bull.*, *57*, 1-28.

Lindquist, E. F. (1953) *Design and analysis of experiments in psychology and education*. Boston: Houghton Mifflin.

McClelland, D. C. and McGown, D. R. (1953) The effect of variable food reinforcement on the strength of a secondary reward. *J. comp. physiol. Psychol.*, *46*, 80-86.

Melching, W. H. (1954) The acquired reward value of an intermittently presented stimulus. *J. comp. physiol. Psychol.*, *47*, 370-374.

Meyers, J. L. (1958) Secondary reinforcement: A review of recent experimentation. *Psychol. Bull.*, *55*, 284-301.

Notterman, J. M. (1951) A study of some relations among aperiodic reinforcement, discrimination and secondary reinforcement. *J. exp. Psychol.*, *41*, 161-169.

Saltzman, I. J. (1949) Maze learning in the absence of primary reinforcement: A study of secondary reinforcement. *J. comp. physiol. Psychol.*, *42*, 161-173.

Zimmerman, D. W. (1957) Durable secondary reinforcement: Method and theory. *Psychol. Rev.*, *64*, 373-383.

# The Contribution of Motivational Variables to Learning

A s INDICATED in Section Three, needs have been commonly regarded as important motivational variables, and a large number of studies have shown that learning is related to need intensity or strength, particularly when a rate of response measure is used. The Trapold and Fowler (1960) article is an excellent example of this kind of study.

Our second selection is a study by Broadhurst (1957), who has shown how the intensity of the need interacts with the characteristics of the task—that is, whether the task is easy or difficult is an important determiner of how the strength of the need state contributes to learning.

Hull (1943) was responsible for calling attention to the position that reinforcement—our second motivational variable—contributed to learning in terms of: (1) the number of reinforcements provided, (2) the quantity and quality of the reinforcing agent, and (3) the time interval separating the response from the reward. An experiment by Guttman (1953), whose study we have included in this section, demonstrates the influence of the quality of the reinforcing agent on learning, while Keesey's (1962) study is an excellent example of intracranial self-stimulation in examining the delay of reward parameter.

It should not be assumed, however, that either of these characteristics represents stable parameters; a study by Schrier (1958) indicates that the quantity of reward parameter may be changed if the organism is provided some experience with the situation. Ferster (1953) has also demonstrated a similar finding with the delay of reward parameter.

Punishment represents a third motivational variable. In many ways, the literature in this area is difficult to delimit. For example, although the shock used in the Trapold and Fowler (1960) study, and the air deprivation used by Broadhurst (1957), could be thought of as being "punishing," they were not so considered by the experimenters. In an effort to provide the reader with a summary of the material that is frequently included in this general topic, we have included an overview of punishment by Solomon (1964).

## REFERENCES

BROADHURST, P. L. (1957) Emotionality and the Yerkes-Dodson law. *J. exp. Psychol.*, 54, 345-352.

FERSTER, C. B. (1953) Sustained behavior under delayed reinforcement. *J. exp. Psychol.*, 45, 218-224.

GUTTMAN, N. (1953) Operant conditioning, extinction, and periodic reinforcement in relation to concentration of sucrose used as reinforcing agent. *J. exp. Psychol.*, 46, 213-224.

HULL, C. L. (1943) *Principles of behavior.* New York: Appleton-Century-Crofts.

KEESEY, R. (1964) Intracranial reward delay and the acquisition rate of a brightness discrimination. *Science, 143,* 702-703.

SCHRIER, A. M. (1958) Comparison of two methods of investigating the effect of amount of reward on performance. *J. comp. physiol. Psychol.*, 49, 117-125.

SOLOMON, R. L. (1964) Punishment. *Amer. Psychologist, 19,* 239-253.

TRAPOLD, M. A. and FOWLER, H. (1960) Instrumental escape performance as a function of the intensity of noxious stimulation. *J. exp. Psychol., 60,* 323-326.

## 14.  Instrumental Escape Performance as a Function of the Intensity of Noxious Stimulation

## M. A. Trapold and H. Fowler

*When food or water deprivation states are employed, a number of experimenters have found that the learning of a simple task is related to the intensity of the need. This study demonstrates how the learning of a simple task is related to the intensity of the shock which was present in the startbox and alley. Note, however, the problem of response measurement, in that two different shock intensity—learning relationships are obtained depending upon which response measure is used.*

While a large amount of work has been done on the role of the primary motivational variables (e.g., food or water deprivation) in the area of instrumental appetitive conditioning, few systematic data are available on the role of motivational variables such as electric shock in instrumental escape conditioning. Moreover, as Spence (1956) has pointed out, those data which are available are quite inconsistent as to the form of the functional relationship between asymptotic escape performance and shock intensity. As these data are extensively discussed by Spence (1956) only brief mention of the inconsistencies will be made here.

While Amsel (1950) found that a group of rats receiving a strong shock ran faster than a group receiving a weak one, Campbell and Kraeling (1953) report no differences in asymptotic performance level for Ss running down a straight alley charged with shock intensities of either 200, 300, or 400 v. to an uncharged goalbox. Using much lower shock levels, Ketchel, in an unpublished study cited by Spence (1956), found that Ss escaping a 36-v. shock performed at a higher level than those escaping an 11.6-v. shock. However, Ketchel's weak-shock group showed little or no increase in performance over trials, raising the possibility that this weak shock was subthreshold and as such provided no motivation.

In view of the inconsistencies among these various results, the present study seeks to provide more extensive data on the effect of shock intensity in instrumental escape learning. A wide range of shock intensities is

*J. exp. Psychol.*, 1960, *60*, 323-326. Reprinted with permission of the senior author and The American Psychological Association. This experiment was conducted at Yale University while H. Fowler held a predoctoral fellowship from the National Institute of Mental Health, Bethesda, Maryland.

examined so as to provide a more general picture of the function relating escape performance to shock intensity.

## METHOD

*Subjects.* The Ss for this experiment were 30 male albino rats, all of which had served earlier in a food-reinforced straight alley experiment entailing the administration of a few brief and relatively weak shocks. Fifteen of these Ss were approximately 300 days old at the time of the present experiment, while the other half were approximately 180 days old. *Apparatus.* A straight alley 68 in. long, 3 in. wide, and 4 in. high served as the experimental apparatus. The alley was constructed of two L-shaped strips of galvanized sheet metal, and was covered with a transparent Plexiglas top. One of the sheet metal strips formed one side and half the floor of the apparatus; the other strip formed the other side and other half of the floor. A 1-in. gap separated the two strips at the floor.

The alley was separated into three sections; a startbox 8 in. long, an alley section 48 in. long, and a goalbox 12 in. long. These sections were separated by upward acting guillotine doors. Raising the start door operated a microswitch which started a Standard Electric clock and closed a shock circuit to the startbox and alley. Breaking a photobeam 6 in. inside the alley stopped the first clock and started a second which in turn was stopped when S broke a photobeam 2 in. inside the goalbox. Breaking this second photobeam also interrupted the shock circuit to the startbox and alley. The two time measures were recorded to the nearest .01 sec. and converted to speed scores (100/time). Hereafter these measures will be referred to as starting and running speed, respectively.

A single matched impedance 60 cps ac shock source provided shock for both the startbox and alley. In this shock system, the galvanized metal strips forming the halves of the alley were connected across the output of a power transformer through a voltage divider which provided variation in the applied voltage. In addition, a .25 megohm resistor was placed in series with S. The S received shock as long as its feet touched both of the metal strips forming the halves of the alley. The narrowness of the alley prevented S from running along only one side of the alley.

*Procedure.* The S was placed in the startbox with the startbox door closed and the goalbox door open. When S oriented toward the goal, the startbox door was opened and S could run to the goal end of the alley. When S entered the goalbox, the goalbox door was closed and S was detained in the goalbox for 20 sec. During this time, E recorded the data from that trial and reset the apparatus. At the end of the 20 sec., S was removed from the goalbox and immediately returned to the startbox for

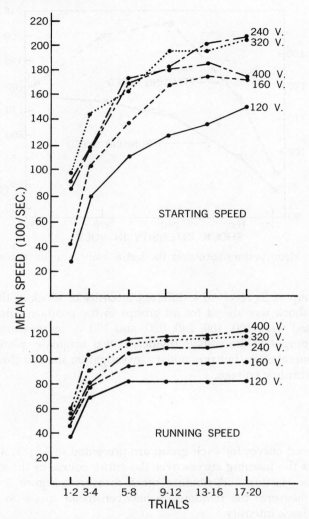

FIG. 1. Learning curves for the various shock intensity groups for both the starting speed and running speed measures.

the beginning of the next trial. In this manner each S received a total of 20 highly massed trials.

*Experimental design.* The 30 Ss were randomly assigned to five experimental groups in such a way as to randomize past experimental history as well as all other extraneous factors, with the restriction that each group contain 3 Ss from each of the two age populations. This restriction permitted isolation of the variance due to the age variable in the statistical analyses.

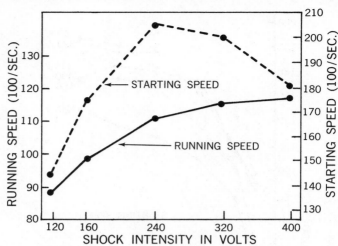

FIG. 2. Mean performance over the last 8 trials as a function of shock intensity.

Each group of Ss received a different intensity of shock in the startbox and alley; shock was absent for all groups in the goalbox. The shock intensities used were 120, 160, 240, 320, and 400 v., as measured directly across the output of the voltage divider. It was originally planned to include a group at 80 v., but preliminary investigation showed that Ss would not run at this low voltage.

RESULTS

Mean speed curves for each group are presented in Fig. 1. and 2. Figure 1 shows the learning curves over the entire course of the experiment for both the starting and running speed measures. Figure 2 shows for these two measures the relationship between mean speed on the last 8 trials and shock intensity.

The results of an analysis of variance of mean running speed over the last 8 trials showed that the young Ss ran slightly, but not significantly, faster than the old Ss ($F = 2.97$; $df = 1$, $20$; $P = .10$). The $F$ ratio for the interaction of shock intensity and age was less than 1. Because of this negligible interaction, and a similar result in the case of starting speed, the age variable, which is inconsequential to the main purposes of this experiment, was ignored in Fig. 1 and 2.

The overall $F$ for the different shock intensity conditions approached but also failed to meet conventional levels of statistical significance ($F = 2.26$; $df = 4$, $20$; $P < .10$). However, inspection of the running speed curve in Fig. 2 shows that the curve is negatively accelerated in form, with the three highest shock intensity groups being very close to one another in mean speed. The approximate equality in performance of these three groups would tend to reduce the overall shock intensity effect, thus producing the nonsignificant overall $F$. A trend analysis of these data, by orthogonal polynomial comparisons, indicates that running speed was significantly related to log shock intensity ($F = 8.53$; $df = 1, 20$; $P < .01$), with the $F$ for the residual variance after extraction of this log linear component being less than 1.

Figure 2 also shows that the form of the relationship between starting speed and shock intensity is quite different from that in the case of running speed. Starting speeds first increase with increasing shock intensity, but beyond 240 v., further increases in shock intensity lead to progressive decrements in this measure. The results of an analysis of variance of mean starting speeds on the last 8 trials showed that the overall effect of shock intensity was significant ($F = 1.61$; $df = 4, 20$; $P < .005$). However, the main effect of age was again not significant, and the Shock × Age interaction again yielded an $F$ less than 1. Analysis of the trends within these data by orthogonal polynomials showed that the functional relationship between starting speed and shock intensity contained both a significant linear component ($F = 9.29$; $df = 1, 20$; $P < .01$) and a significant quadratic component ($F = 13.18$; $df = 1, 20$; $P < .005$). The residual variance after extraction of these two components was negligible ($F < 1$).

## Discussion

In total the results show that over the range of shock intensities used in the present study, running speed is an increasing, negatively accelerated function of shock intensity, while starting speed is nonmonotonically related to shock intensity, first increasing and then decreasing with increasing shock intensities.

The results of the running speed measure are in line with the results of Amsel (1950) and Ketchel (Spence, 1956), but not those of Campbell and Kraeling (1953). While it is true that part of the inconsistency in these previous studies may have arisen from the use of different procedures and types of shock, the fact that the present study used a shock source, alley, and general procedure as close as possible to that used by Campbell and Kraeling makes this interpretation unlikely. Perhaps a more reasonable interpretation is that Campbell and Kraeling found no differences in asymptotic performance because all of their shock intensity groups were far out on the relatively flat portion of the curve relating speed to shock intensity. If it is also true that starting speed is, with this general procedure and apparatus, nonmonotonically related to shock intensity, then this factor could also have contributed to their lack of differences, as the speed measure in the Campbell and Kraeling experiment included both the starting and running speed measures of the present experiment.

## SUMMARY

Five groups of rats were trained to escape shocks of 120, 160, 240, 320, and 400 v. in a straight alley by running to an uncharged goalbox. Running speed was found to be an increasing, negatively accelerated function of shock intensity, but starting speed was nonmonotonically related to shock intensity, first increasing and then decreasing with increasing shock intensity. These results are discussed in relation to inconsistencies among the findings of several other studies pertaining to the empirical relationship between shock intensity and performance in escape conditioning.

## REFERENCES

AMSEL, A. (1950) The combination of a primary appetitional need with primary and secondary emotionally derived needs. *J. exp. Psychol.*, *40*, 1-14.
CAMPBELL, B. A. and KRAELING, D. (1953) Response strength as a function of drive level and amount of drive reduction. *J. exp. Psychol.*, *45*, 97-101.
SPENCE, K. W. (1956) *Behavior theory and conditioning.* New Haven: Yale Univer. Press.

## 15.   Emotionality and the Yerkes-Dodson Law

## P. L. Broadhurst

*Like the previous study, Broadhurst has also employed a noxious stimulus to motivate his subjects. Unlike Trapold and Fowler, however, he has investigated how the intensity of motivation is related to easy, moderate, and difficult discrimination tasks, and it is not surprising that an interaction is obtained between level of motivation and type of task. This investigation has its historical antecedents in an early study by Yerkes and Dodson, who found that the optimum motivation decreases with increasing difficulty of the learning task.*

The Yerkes-Dodson Law (17) which states that the optimum motivation for a learning task decreases with increasing difficulty has been shown to

*J. exp. Psychol.*, 1957, *54*, 345-352. Reprinted with permission of the author and The American Psychological Association.

hold for several species. See Young (18). It is the purpose of the present experiment to extend the range to include the rat. However, individual differences in drive strength are clearly important here, as may be seen from the current work showing the differential effect of anxiety on human learning (16). Recent evidence (8) supporting the identification of neuroticism as an autonomic drive (7) suggests that emotionality, as defined by defecation scores in Hall's open-field test (10), may be a relevant variable, since the lability of the autonomic nervous system probably underlies both neuroticism in humans and emotionality in rats (6, 10). Emotional rats will therefore be expected to show greater drive than nonemotionals in a situation in which the motivation used (air deprivation) is intense and of a kind likely to give rise to fear responses, and consequently to learn faster when the task is easy, but more slowly when it is hard. That is to say, the optimum drive level in the Yerkes-Dodson situation should be lower for the emotionals than for the nonemotionals. We may therefore predict an interaction between emotionality and the two variables of motivation and difficulty level which should themselves interact in the manner suggested by the Yerkes-Dodson Law.

## METHOD

*Apparatus.* The Y-shaped discrimination apparatus designed by Jonckheere (12) for surface swimming was adapted for underwater use. This is a conventional Y unit with metal walls 2 ft. high and alleys 4 in. wide. The stem of the Y is 7 in. long and the arms make an angle of 52° to the center line. Vertical partitions across each arm, 7 in. beyond the bifurcation, extend from top to bottom of the alley and contain the discrimination panels. The Ss were forced to swim through the unit completely underwater by roofing in the alleys before the partitions with stainless steel hardware cloth just below the water level (9 in.). The discrimination panels were hung vertically and hinged below the surface of the water. They were made of frosted Perspex and each presented an illuminated area, 3½ in. square, at right angles to the line of sight from the bifurcation. Either could be locked into place, or left free, to be opened underwater by S to allow escape to the part of the alleys beyond the partitions which were not roofed in below the surface. From here, hardware cloth ramps gave access to a platform above water level.

The illumination was provided by two lamps in parallel in a 24-v. circuit. One lamp was located above water level behind each discrimination panel with its filament parallel to the panel. A fixed portion of a wire resistor could be switched into the circuit of either lamp in order to dim the intensity of the light shining through the adjacent panel, the other lamp being undimmed. The S was thus presented with a choice between

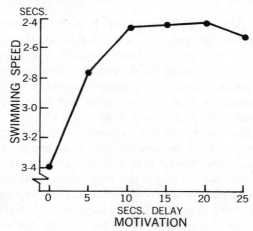

FIG. 1. The relationship between speed of swimming a 4-ft. straightaway underwater and intensity of imposed motivation (air deprivation) measured by the number of seconds delay underwater before release. Each point represents the mean time for 20 Ss; the data were collected on successive days.

a well lit and a less well lit avenue of escape from underwater. Three amounts of resistance were used; the greater the resistance the dimmer the light, yielding a greater difference between the illumination of the alleys, and an easier discrimination. Measurements with a light meter (Avo No. 2) indicated that this difference in illumination could be represented, in ascending order of difficulty, by the ratios 1:300, 1:60, and 1:15. These constitute the three levels of difficulty and are designated easy, moderate, and difficult.

A submersible cage, measuring 9 × 6 × 4½ in. wide, also made of stainless steel hardware cloth, was fitted with a sliding guillotine door which could be released from above the surface, thus allowing escape through the discrimination apparatus. Following a suggestion by Mason and Stone (14), the intensity of the air deprivation used as motivation was manipulated by detaining the Ss for different lengths of time submerged underwater before releasing them to make the discrimination on which the promptness of their escape depended. Preliminary work, using 20 female rats as Ss, gave the results shown in Fig. 1. There is clearly no advantage in using delays longer than about 10 sec., since performance is not thereby improved. Indeed, delays longer than 20 sec. result in decreased swimming speed, presumably because of the effects of anoxia. Delays were therefore kept short, and delays of 0, 2, 4, and 8 sec. before release were selected, which represent approximately equal increments in swimming speed (see Fig. 1). These constitute the four levels of motivation.

*Subjects.* Five replications of the 3 × 2 × 4 factorial design (24 treatments) were used—that is, a total of 120 Ss was required. These 120 Ss were male albino rats which formed part of the second and third generations in a selective breeding study of emotionality being conducted in this laboratory (3). When Ss averaged 105.5 days of age (SE ± .25), they were given the modified and standardized open-field test described in detail elsewhere (1). Briefly, Ss were exposed for 2 min. per day for four successive days in a circular arena 32¾ in. in diameter with white plywood walls 12½ in. high. A battery of loudspeakers and of photographic lamps above the arena provided sound ("white" noise) and light fields whose intensity at floor level in the arena averaged 78 db. (ref. .002 dynes/sq. cm.) and 165 cp., respectively. The average number of fecal boluses deposited per day constitute the emotional reactivity score, and only Ss scoring 3.3 or more were assigned to the emotional group (mean = 4.1, ± .15), and only Ss scoring 1.3 or less were assigned to the nonemotional group (mean = .8, ± .17). These two groups constitute the two levels of treatment in the emotionality variable; the difference between them is significant beyond the .1% level by t test.

The populations from which Ss were selected by virtue of their emotional elimination scores had been bred by brother × sister mating from a heterogeneous Wistar stock. They had been reared under standard conditions which are described fully elsewhere (3). In brief, these conditions featured controlled temperature and light/dark cycle in standard living quarters, standard conditions of husbandry—diet, routine care, number of animals per cage, etc.—and the minimum of handling. Some of them had been used for breeding purposes in the interval between testing in the open field and in the underwater discrimination unit, which interval itself varied with Ss' generation, but there is evidence (2) to suggest that neither the sexual experience, nor age differences of the order encountered, are likely to affect Ss' emotionality as measured. The mean age when experimentation began of the 45 Ss belonging to the second generation was 322.0 days (±6.09), and the mean age of the 75 Ss belonging to the third generation 213.4 days (±3.31). This difference is highly significant (P < .001 by t test); accordingly, the possible effect of this age difference upon the scores analyzed was investigated. There was no significant difference by t test between the over-all means of the two groups for the learning score used (discussed later), but, as might be expected, the older Ss swam significantly more slowly (P < .01, by t test). It need not, however, be anticipated that any systematic bias is thereby introduced into the analysis of the speed score, since Ss had been assigned to treatments randomly. As a check, a χ² test of the proportions of Ss of the two age groups assigned to each treatment combination showed no significant difference from that existing in the total group (45:75).

*Procedure.* The random assignments of Ss to the 24 treatment combinations was made by forming the 60 emotional Ss into 12 groups of five each, equated as far as possible with respect to defecation scores, and the 60 nonemotional Ss into a further 12 groups of five each, similarly equated. The groups thus formed were then randomly assigned, within the emotionality dichotomy, to the various treatment combinations. The Ss were tested in groups of 24 (one complete replication) on 15 successive days. The first five days were devoted to preliminary training during which Ss were successively given surface and underwater swimming practice in a 3-ft. straightaway, at which time the appropriate detention periods for the different Ss were established, then practice in the underwater discrimination unit to familiarize them with the operation of opening the doors formed by the discrimination panels. During this time the doors were unlit, and one side of the Y unit was blocked at the bifurcation by a solid partition, thus forcing the rat to one side or the other, in order to avoid the development of position habits. The side by which escape was thus permitted was varied randomly by use of a Gellerman series (9). At the end of this training all Ss were leaving the starting cage promptly on release, and opening the escape doors without difficulty.

On the next 10 days, 10 trials per day—a total of 100 trials—were given in the apparatus with a choice of alleys permitted and differences in illumination between the panels. No other illumination was present in the darkened room containing the water tank except for a small recording lamp and a radiant heat lamp above the self-draining metal boxes in which Ss were kept in the intertrial intervals. This interval was maintained relatively constant for all Ss despite the variation in delay ranging from 0 to 8 sec. by running them in larger or smaller groups, respectively. The brighter side of the unit was designated correct and kept open; an S choosing the darker side where the panel was locked was thereby forced to retrace its way to the brighter side in order to escape. That is, the correction method was used. The bright side was selected since it was constant for each of the three levels of difficulty, and because there was no tendency for Ss to prefer one side over the other. Thus, on the first trial upon which a choice was permitted, 56.7% went to the right-hand or bright side, and 43.3% to the dimmer one on the left. The difference from chance expectation yields a nonsignificant $\chi^2$. The "correct" side was randomly varied from trial to trial by use of a selection of 10 Gellerman series, the same ones being used in the same order for all Ss. The water temperature was maintained at 20° C., the air temperature during testing averaged 19.5° C. (±.21).

The time from the moment when the door of the starting cage was released until S's snout broke the surface of the water beyond the illuminated panel through which it had passed was recorded to the nearest 1/10 sec. by stop watch, and errors, defined as any entry into the "incorrect" alley of S's head and shoulders or more, noted. These constitute the time and error scores respectively.

The five replications of the experiment were tested at intervals over 4 mo. and were followed by a partial replication which supplied substitutes for the three Ss which died during experimentation and the seven whose results were excluded because they developed position habits. A position habit was defined for this purpose as the choice on two days (20 trials) or more during the last five days of testing of one side—left or right—exclusively.

## RESULTS

The number of errorless trials out of the 100 trials given was counted for each S and the data subjected to a three-way analysis of variance after Pearson and Hartley's test (15) had disclosed no significant inhomogeneity of variance. The results are presented in Table 1. The F ratios for

### TABLE 1
ANALYSES OF VARIANCE OF LEARNING AND SPEED SCORES

| | | Number of Correct Trials | | Average Time to Swim 21 In. | |
|---|---|---|---|---|---|
| Source | df | MS | F | MS† | F |
| Difficulty (D) | 2 | 2260.2 | 23.5** | 2.17 | 1.8 |
| Motivation (M) | 3 | 143.7 | 1.5 | 4.73 | 4.0** |
| Emotionality (E) | 1 | 114.1 | 3.0 | 7.21 | 6.1* |
| D × M | 6 | 96.1 | 2.5* | 1.05 | 0.9 |
| D × E | 2 | 48.9 | 1.3 | 0.73 | 0.6 |
| M × E | 3 | 77.8 | 2.1 | 2.48 | 2.1 |
| D × M × E | 6 | 54.9 | 1.4 | 1.21 | 1.0 |
| Ss | 96 | 38.0 | | 1.18 | |
| Total | 119 | | | | |

* P = .025.
** P = .01.
† Units 1/10 sec.

the difficulty and motivation main effects were calculated by using the Difficulty × Motivation interaction variance estimate, in view of the significance of the interaction between these two variables. The nature of this interaction is indicated in Fig. 2. Table 2 shows the mean scores and SD's for the various levels of the two treatments having significant main effects. These data indicate the efficacy of the experimental manipulation of these two independent variables. Thus, each increase in the difficulty of the discrimination yields a significantly lower learning score, reaching the .01 level (by 1-tail t test) in the case of the easy vs. moderate difference, and the .001 level in the case of the moderate vs. difficult one. Increasing

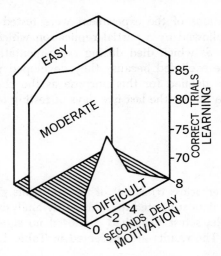

FIG. 2. A three-dimensional surface showing the relationship between learning scores in a discrimination task and (*a*) the intensity of the imposed motivation (air deprivation) measured by the number of seconds' delay underwater before release and (*b*) the level of difficulty of the task. The lamina are spaced to represent the over-all mean score for the appropriate difficulty level (see Table 2). Each point represents the mean score for 10 Ss.

the time of air deprivation first increased the mean learning score significantly (0- vs. 2-sec. delay), then caused a significant decline from the peak value (2- vs. 8-sec. delay; $P < .05$ in both cases by $t$ test). This latter finding is comparable with that of many workers reporting a curvilinear relationship between motivation and performance when increasingly intense motivation is employed (see also Fig. 1).

It is clear from these results that the Yerkes-Dodson Law may be taken as confirmed. The optimum motivation for a discrimination task demonstrably decreases with increasing difficulty of the task. This effect, repre-

TABLE 2

BREAKDOWN OF LEARNING SCORES

| Motivation Level (Air Deprivation) | Difficulty of Discrimination | | | | | | | |
|---|---|---|---|---|---|---|---|---|
| | Easy | | Moderate | | Difficult | | All | |
| | Mean | SD | Mean | SD | Mean | SD | Mean | SD |
| 0 sec. | 84.8 | 6.6 | 81.3 | 6.3 | 71.1 | 9.0 | 79.1 | 9.4 |
| 2 sec. | 86.4 | 4.7 | 84.7 | 5.9 | 79.5 | 4.8 | 83.5 | 6.0 |
| 4 sec. | 87.7 | 3.9 | 83.0 | 7.1 | 71.6 | 6.2 | 80.8 | 9.0 |
| 8 sec. | 86.8 | 3.9 | 83.2 | 5.9 | 66.1 | 6.5 | 78.7 | 10.6 |
| All | 86.4 | 5.0 | 83.1 | 6.5 | 72.1 | 8.3 | 80.5 | 9.1 |

sented by the first-order interaction between the difficulty and motivational treatments, is significant at a satisfactory level, and part of the prediction is thus verified. It is equally clear that the prediction, as made above, relating to the effects of emotional reactivity on this complex relationship is not fulfilled. The trend of the results is partly in the predicted direction. Thus emotionals learn the easy discrimination faster than nonemotionals, and are about equal on the moderately difficult one, and similarly learn faster under low motivation, and are about equal at medium levels. But on the difficult discrimination or under the most intense motivation used they again show a slight superiority. Consequently, the emotional Ss show an over-all superiority in learning, which, however, does not reach significance, and this is reflected in the failure of the one second-order and the two remaining first-order interactions, all of which involve the emotionality variable, to reach significance.

If it is conceded that the curvilinear relation involved makes such a procedure permissible, the partial success of the prediction relating to drive level and emotionality can readily be demonstrated. An analysis of variance based on the first two lowest levels of motivation only—that is, before the decline in learning associated with motivation greater than the optimum begins (see Fig. 2)—shows two significant effects. The first is the expected and highly significant one associated with level of difficulty, the second is the first-order interaction between Motivation and Emotionality ($P < .05$). This effect may be summarized by saying that the emotional Ss show superior learning under the minimal motivation used, but that this advantage disappears with the increase of motivation from 0 to 2 sec. delay before release.

Another way to investigate the relation of emotionality to drive level is to consider the *speed* of the response made to the motivational stimulus, irrespective of whether or not it resulted in improved learning. In order to derive a speed score for each S, and one which reflects its speed of swimming independent of the degree of learning attained, the time scores for the first day upon which all 10 trials were recorded as correct were averaged. In this way the individual Ss' speeds may be compared at exactly comparable points on their respective learning curves. Since the distance swum in the apparatus is essentially the same for each S making a "correct" choice (21 in.), the time scores can be used directly for the purpose, as was done in preparing Fig. 1, thus avoiding the difficulty relating to averaging time over distance scores discussed by Crespi (5). For the 13 Ss assigned to the difficult discrimination who never learned it to perfection, the average of the last day's trials was calculated, omitting times for those trials when incorrect choices were made. An analysis of variance performed on these data after no significant inhomogeneity of variance had been demonstrated gave results which are also shown in Table 1. From this analysis it will be seen that the superiority of the emotional Ss over the nonemotional Ss in speed of swimming reaches satisfactory significance. The mean time scores are 1.80 and 1.96 sec., respectively. Inserting these values on a plot of swimming speed against motivational delays (like Fig. 1)shows that the difference of .16 sec. is equivalent to the effect on over-all speed scores of an increase in motivational delay of about 4 sec. Moreover, this effect is not significantly associated with any of the other variables in the analysis, from which it can be concluded that the emotionally reactive rats display a characteristically higher level of drive, which, within the limits of the present experiment, is not affected by the intensity of the motivation imposed. It may also be noted from this analysis that the absence of a significant effect for Difficulty shows that the speed score selected was in fact independent of the degree of learning, and that the significance of Motivation confirms the efficacy of the experimental manipulation of the air deprivation variable. Thus, the mean time taken to swim 21 in. underwater decreased progressively from 1.98 sec. for 0-sec. delay to 1.97 for 2 sec., to 1.85 (4 sec.), and finally to 1.71 (8 sec.). The $SD$'s are .48, .33, .31, and .25 sec. respectively. Only the differences between each of the first three levels (0, 2, and 4 sec.) and the last one (8 sec.) reach significance (.05 level or beyond by 1-tail $t$ test).

## Discussion

The confirmation of the Yerkes-Dodson Law reported here gains in interest because it employed a different species from those hitherto used in demonstrating the principle, and because it occurred under rather different experimental conditions. The motivation in particular was very different from that used in any of the other studies of the Yerkes-Dodson Law; the electric shock previously employed as an aversive stimulus was eschewed because of the difficulty of controlling it, and because of its disruptive effect, especially when strong, upon early learning. Air deprivation as used shares with shock the quality of being a rather intense stimulus, and the advantage of being manipulable within the testing situation. It has, in addition, been shown in practice to be easily varied in intensity.

It is true that in both this and the original study a visual brightness discrimination was used as the method of varying the degree of difficulty of the learning tasks. The resemblance hardly goes beyond the semantic, however. The similarity between the actual pieces of apparatus used is slight. The Yerkes box has been described as "spectacularly inefficient" (13), whereas the underwater discrimination technique as used in this study gave rapid learning without undue preliminary training.

The results obtained from the original study and the present one are surprisingly similar. A comparison of Fig. 2 with that given by Yerkes and Dodson (17, p. 479) shows that the optimum motivation is in general slightly lower in the scale used than that encountered by them, and that there is no level of difficulty for which an optimum was never reached as was the case with their easiest discrimination. An increasing sharpness of the optimum peak with increasing difficulty is characteristic of both graphs. The dissimilarities mentioned can all be ascribed to differences in the levels of motivation selected. The relation of motivation to degree of learning is typically curvilinear, a decrease in learning following motivation more intense than the optimum, so it is not always easy to select suitable levels of motivation to reveal the optimum learning, especially if it is required to include different optima associated with different levels of difficulty, and more especially with a novel motivation like air deprivation about which little is so far known.

The confirmation of the Law is the more striking because of this difference in motivation. The needs arising from electric shock and from air deprivation are different physiologically, though they both give rise to drives mediated, in part, by fear. The further generalization of the Law must await experimentation using other situations and other drives, but the outlook is promising in view of the analogies in the human field already existing.

The possible role of anoxia must not be overlooked in connection with the use of air deprivation, since it is known (11) that it can cause learning defects comparable to those caused by electroconvulsive shock. It seems unlikely, however, that air deprivation of the duration used here can have led to anoxic damage to the nervous system sufficient to account for the curvilinear relation with learning. To the arguments which lead Mason and Stone (14) to reject this explanation of their comparable findings, we may add the following germane considerations from this experiment. Firstly, if anoxia were important in this connection, it would be reasonable to anticipate that all the groups subjected to the greatest air deprivation would show a decrement in learning. A glance at Fig. 2 shows that this is not the case. Secondly, the analysis of the speed of swimming showed no significant difference between the difficulty levels (see Table 1). Now, the Ss assigned to the difficult discrimination had, at the time when the speed scores were selected, experienced much more air deprivation than had the other groups. They had made many more errors obliging them to hold their breath longer before escape, and they had also undergone many more trials. Neither of these circumstances, likely to increase any deficit ascribable to anoxia, depressed swimming speed, however.

The drive characteristics of emotionality as defined by open-field defecation scores are only partly elucidated by this experiment. Emotionally reactive Ss have a significantly higher speed of swimming—that is, they respond more vigorously to the same degree of imposed motivation. To this extent, they may be regarded either as having a higher drive level in general or as more susceptible to drive arousal. Further work to investigate the speed of swimming of these Ss, and employing a situation designed to demonstrate the Crespi effect (5) consequent upon changes in drive level, confirms the superior speed of the emotionals and the presence of the "elation" effect but indicates that they do not respond more to a sudden increase in drive than do the nonemotionals (4). It thus seems that drive level rather than drive arousal is involved.

Yet this higher drive level did not in general effect learning in this experiment in the manner expected. It seems unfruitful to enter into detailed speculations about the reasons for this seeming paradox—suffice it to say that it is probable that the situation used here is too complex to expect that any definitive solution may be found in the present data. Nevertheless the general finding relating to drive level does have some bearing on the postulated relation between emotionality in rats and neuroticism in humans. This cross-species identification is not directly verifiable, but it can be cautiously said that the present results, at the very least, do nothing to render it improbable.

## SUMMARY

The experiment was designed to test the validity of the Yerkes-Dodson Law and to investigate some of the drive characteristics of emotionality of rats. In a 3 × 4 × 2 factorial design having five replications, 120 male albino rats were used as Ss. Three levels of difficulty of an underwater brightness discrimination, four levels of motivation deriving from different degrees of air deprivation, and two levels of emotionality defined in terms of defecation scores on the open-field test were used. Time and error scores from 100 trials were secured.

Analysis of variance of the results shows that the Yerkes-Dodson Law, as demonstrated by an appropriate interaction between difficulty and motivation, is confirmed at an acceptable level of significance. The prediction relating to the effects of emotionality on motivation is only fulfilled in part; a significantly higher drive level of emotionals as shown by their swimming speed is shown.

## REFERENCES

1. BROADHURST, P. L. (1957) Determinants of emotionality in the rat: I. Situational factors. Brit. J. Psychol., 48, 1-12.
2. BROADHURST, P. L. Determinants of emotionality in the rat: II. Antecedent factors. Brit. J. Psychol., in press.
3. BROADHURST, P. L. (1957) Emotionality in the rat: a study of its determinants, inheritance and relation to some aspects of motivation. Unpublished doctor's dissertation, Univer. London.

4. BROADHURST, P. L. A note on a "Crespi effect" in the analysis of emotionality as a drive in rats. *Brit. J. Psychol.*, in press.

5. CRESPI, L. P. (1942) Quantitative variation of incentive and performance in the white rat. *Amer. J. Psychol.*, 55, 467-517.

6. EYSENCK, H. J. (1953) The structure of human personality. London: Methuen.

7. EYSENCK, H. J. (1955) A dynamic theory of anxiety and hysteria. *J. ment. Sci.*, 101, 28-51.

8. EYSENCK, H. J. (1956) Reminiscence, drive and personality theory. *J. abnorm. soc. Psychol.*, 53, 328-333.

9. GELLERMAN, L. W. (1933) Chance orders of alternating stimuli in visual discrimination experiments. *J. genet. Psychol.*, 42, 206-208.

10. HALL, C. S. (1934) Emotional behavior in the rat. I. Defecation and urination as measures of individual differences in emotionality. *J. comp. Psychol.*, 18, 385-403.

11. HAYES, K. J. (1953) Anoxic and convulsive amnesia in rats. *J. comp. physiol. Psychol.*, 46, 216-217.

12. JONCKHEERE, A. R. (1956) A study of "fixation" behaviour in the rat. Unpublished doctor's dissertation, Univer. London.

13. McCLEARN, G. E. and HARLOW, H. F. (1954) The effect of spatial contiguity on discrimination learning by Rhesus monkeys. *J. comp. physiol. Psychol.*, 47, 391-394.

14. MASON, W. A. and STONE, C. P. (1953) Maze performance of rats under conditions of surface and underwater swimming. *J. comp. physiol. Psychol.*, 46, 159-165.

15. PEARSON, E. S. and HARTLEY, H. O. (1956) *Biometrika tables for statisticians.* Vol. 1. Cambridge, Eng.: Cambridge Univer. Press.

16. TAYLOR, J. A. (1956) Drive theory and manifest anxiety. *Psychol. Bull.*, 53, 303-320.

17. YERKES, R. M. and DODSON, J. D. (1908) The relation of strength of stimulus to rapidity of habit-formation. *J. comp. Neurol. Psychol.*, 18, 459-482.

18. YOUNG, P. T. (1936) *Motivation of behavior.* New York: Wiley.

## 16.  Operant Conditioning, Extinction, and Periodic Reinforcement in Relation to Concentration of Sucrose Used as Reinforcing Agent

### N. Guttman

*One of the reinforcement variables which Hull (1943) posited to influence learning was the quantity and quality of the reinforcing agent. A number of early experimenters demonstrated this to be so, but in such studies food, measured in weight or number of units (pellets), was employed. But when the quantity of food is varied, other changes, such as the amount of consummatory activity, the amount of time in the goal box, the stimulation derived from the food prior to, or during, ingestion, or the amount of nutrition, may take place. Guttman's study is notable because it demonstrates the influence of the characteristics of the reinforcing agent on learning, while providing at the same time a technique designed to control these extraneous factors.*

This study deals with the efforts of using various concentrations of sucrose as reinforcing agent in the bar-pressing situation. The processes investigated include conditioning, extinction, and reconditioning under continuous reinforcement and performance under periodic reinforcement (PR). The same Ss and apparatus are used throughout the series of experiments so that the findings may possess some degree of quantitative comparability.

In the investigation of the "quantity of reinforcing agent," the technique of manipulating the concentration of a soluble nutrient has distinct advantages. Previous studies which have demonstrated a relationship between the amount of food given as reinforcement and the degree to which response characteristics are changed by reinforcement have used the following methods for controlling the amount of food presented on a given trial: (a) single food particles of various weights or sizes (4, 5, 10, 13, 14, 15, 21, 23); (b) various numbers of food particles of equal size and weight (1, 6, 10, 14, 21); and (c) exposure to food for various lengths of time (9).

These methods may not be equivalent, and none is satisfactory from an analytical standpoint, since they all introduce several simultaneous sources

*J. exp. Psychol.*, 1953, 46, 213-224. Reprinted with permission of the author and The American Psychological Association. Based on the author's doctoral dissertation at Indiana University. Dr. W. K. Estes sponsored and greatly aided this research.

of variation. If quantity of food is varied by the conventional methods, concurrent changes may be produced in the following factors: (a) the amount of nutrient available for assimilation, in terms of weight, volume, or some nutritive unit; (b) the amount of consummatory activity required, i.e., the number and intensity of ingestive movements at each reinforcement; (c) the stimulation (visual, olfactory, tactile) derived from the food prior to ingestion; and (d) the stimulation from the food during ingestion.

If we vary the size or number of pieces of food given to an animal, we are varying at once the stimuli which affect its receptors, the amount of chewing and swallowing it performs, and the degree to which its metabolic state will be affected (at some later time). Methods a and b involve changes in all four of the above factors. Method c affords some control of the third and fourth factors, but even here, duration of stimulation varies along with the first and second factors.

The technique of manipulating sucrose concentration reduces the multiplicity of the variable "quantity of reinforcing agent." It controls stimulation prior to ingestion and reduces variation in required ingestive activity. It does not avoid a covariation (although presumably not a linear one) between nutritive value and stimulation at the taste receptors. Nonetheless, if relations are found between concentration and various aspects of behavior, such relations can be presumed independent of stimulation prior to ingestion, and the analysis of such relations may be focused on a more restricted set of events, those during and subsequent to ingestion.

If the stimulational aspects of the reinforcing agent are of importance, the use of a concentration scale provides a more rational metric for the scaling of gustatory stimuli than is permitted by such units as weight, volume, or number of solid food particles. Since concentration is a significant and familiar dimension of stimuli in sensory research, analysis of the mechanisms involved in reinforcement may be facilitated by being brought into relation with extant knowledge of receptor processes. Such analyses may be promoted by the additional device of using simple substances of known chemical composition, such as sucrose, about which much relevant information is already available from studies of various aspects of taste (12), as well as from research in food acceptance (22) and nutrition. The present experiments are designed to narrow the gap between the findings in these areas and that group of experiments grounded rather exclusively in contemporary theories of learning.

## METHOD

### APPARATUS

A set of four identically constructed Skinner boxes was used (7). The S was housed in a sheet metal box into which a bar could be inserted. This box was housed in a larger semi-soundproof chamber with an observation window. The liquid used as reinforcement was presented to S by a dipper-type magazine driven by a motor. The volume of liquid presented by the dipper was of the order of .05 milliliter. A manual switch controlling the magazine was mounted outside the box, and used only in training S to drink from the dipper. The bar-pressing response was recorded by means of a magnetic counter and also by means of a graphic recorder which made a cumulative plot of responses against time.

### SUBJECTS

The Ss were 80 male albino rats, ranging in age from 64 to 110 days at the start of the experiment. They were run in five successive sets of 16. Two Ss in the last set died and one became ill during the experiment, but these Ss were not replaced by others.

### PROCEDURE

*Basic design.* The Ss were assigned to four experimental groups. Treatment of the groups was identical except for the concentration of sucrose used as reinforcing agent. The four concentrations were 4%, 8%, 16% and 32% sucrose by weight,* and each group was designated by the concentration received. Each group received a single concentration throughout training, except during the last portion of the experiment in which certain Ss from each group were tested on all four concentrations.

*Habituation and feeding schedule.* Upon receipt from the supplier, Ss were placed in individual living cages and fed dry Purina pellets ad libitum for at least one day. All food was then withdrawn for 23 hr. For a minimum of three successive days, Ss were given a firm mash of ground Purina pellets for 1 hr. per day at the experimental time. Cod-liver oil was occasionally added to the mash. During feeding, Ss were picked up and handled. During all phases of the study, Ss were fed mash for 1 hr. following the experimental period, and water was available at all times in the living cages.

*Magazine training.* The S was introduced into the box and trained to approach the magazine whenever it was operated by E. The bar was retracted from the box, and the magazine was filled with the appropriate sucrose solution. All sessions were ½ hr. in length.

The magazine was operated only a few times on the first day to facilitate habituation to the rather loud noise and the slight vibration produced by

* For example, the 32% solution was prepared by mixing 32 gm. of commercial granulated table sugar with 68 ml. of tap water. The four concentrations have the values .6, .9, 1.2, and 1.5 on a log 10 scale, and this scale is used in the graphs which follow.

the operation of the magazine. On subsequent days the magazine was operated at irregular intervals until S had responded 8 to 10 times by approaching and drinking from the dipper. A completed training trial was recorded when S approached and drank within 30 sec. of the operation of the magazine. Magazine training was continued the number of days required for the S to accept 50 magazine presentations.

Any S that failed to accept more than five presentations within ten days was discarded, but this criterion was imposed in only three cases. Certain Ss, especially in the 4% and 8% groups, did not always drink after approaching the magazine; only those approaches which were followed by prolonged contact with the dipper or by the characteristic head-bobbing movements accompanying licking were counted as accepted presentations. The magazine was generally operated only when S was moving about the cage, to insure that the response of huddling near the magazine not be reinforced, and thus impede the subsequent conditioning of bar-pressing.

*Conditioning of the bar-pressing response.* On the day following the completion of magazine training, conditioning was begun. The bar was inserted into the box and set to operate the magazine with each depression. The S was permitted to obtain 250 reinforcements for bar-pressing and then was removed from the box. (It was sometimes impossible to remove the animal precisely after Response 250 if it was responding at a high rate.) On the next day, 250 more reinforcements were given. Five 4% Ss that failed to obtain more than 25 reinforcements in ten days were discarded.

Animals that were slow to respond to the bar were kept in the box a minimum of 30 min. a day and were not removed until a 15-min. period of no responding had elapsed. In general Ss that responded so slowly that 250 reinforcements were not obtained in one hour were removed at 1 hr. However, several of the first cases of this type were left in the box for arbitrary times beyond 1 hr. in order not to interrupt the course of conditioning. After these cases, a sufficient number of 1-hr. periods was given to permit the execution of a total of 500 responses.

*Extinction.* On the day following the completion of conditioning, extinction of the bar-pressing response was carried out under two conditions, first without secondary reinforcement and then with secondary reinforcement. Before S was placed in the box, the bar was inserted, the magazine was emptied of sucrose solution, and the dippers were washed and dried. The S was placed in the box, and for 5 min. following the first response, all bar-pressing responses were recorded but not reinforced. At the end of the 5-min. period, the apparatus was set to operate the empty magazine after each bar-depression. Thus, each bar-pressing response was followed by the stimulus that had previously accompanied the delivery of sucrose solution of a given concentration. The S was removed from the box 30 min. after the first response that received secondary reinforcement. One S failed to respond after the first 5-min. period and was removed from the box after a 40-min. period of no responding.

*Reconditioning.* On the day following extinction, S was subjected to the same conditions (including sucrose concentration) which had prevailed during original conditioning and was permitted to obtain 250 reinforcements for bar-pressing. Failure to recondition promptly and obtain 250 reinforcements was exceptional, but Ss that were removed from the box before obtaining 250 reinforcements were given as many periods as required to obtain this total, the same conditions prevailing each day. Five Ss required more than one day to complete reconditioning.

*Periodic reinforcements.* Two determinations of the effect of sucrose concentration on the rate of the periodically reinforced bar-pressing response were carried out. The first was a comparison of four independent groups, each receiving a single concentration. Each S received the same concentration as that received during previous training. The second determination involved testing each S repeatedly on all of the four concentrations previously used.

*PR: Independent groups.* The Ss in all four groups were given five successive daily ½-hr. experimental periods in the Skinner boxes of periodic reinforcement for bar-pressing. The first day of PR followed the last day of reconditioning under continuous reinforcement. The PR interval was 1 min., i.e., only the first bar-pressing response in each minute was reinforced, but all responses were recorded. Complete data were obtained on 42 Ss in this portion of the experiment.

*PR: Each animal as its own control.* Following the completion of the above procedure, Ss were given a series of 12 successive daily 1-hr. sessions of bar-pressing under PR. Each day each S received one 15-min. test on each of the four concentrations previously given. The same 1-min. PR schedule was maintained.

The order of presentation of concentrations was counterbalanced, such that within the first four days each S received each concentration once during the first 15-min. test interval, once during the second 15-min. interval, and so on. The order of presentation during Days 1 to 4 was repeated during Days 5 to 8 and repeated again during Days 9 to 12.

The Ss were generally run in squads of four in this procedure. On a given day each Skinner box contained one concentration, but during each four-day cycle each box contained each solution once, to control for variability among boxes. To begin a daily session, four Ss were placed in the boxes with the main switch of the apparatus turned off. The boxes were closed, and the switch was turned on and left on for 15 min. while Ss responded. Then the switch was turned off, Ss were quickly transferred to other boxes and other concentrations, and another 15-min. period was begun. Twenty Ss were used in this part of the experiment. These 20 Ss comprise 3 from the 4% group, 6 from the 8% group, 6 from the 16% group, and 5 from the 32% group.

## RESULTS

*Time to condition.* The effect of concentration of reinforcement on the time required to condition the bar-pressing response is a very striking one. The median number of experimental periods required to obtain the 500 reinforcements (counting from the period in which the first response occurred) was 2.0 for the 32% and 16% groups, 3.5 for the 8% group, and 6.5 for the 4% group. Five of the 18 Ss in the 4% group failed to condition to the bar within the ten-period criterion, but all other Ss that completed magazine training were successfully conditioned. Table 1 shows the mean

TABLE 1

MEAN TIME IN MINUTES TO OBTAIN FIRST AND SECOND 250 REINFORCEMENTS
WITH VARIOUS SUCROSE CONCENTRATIONS

| Sucrose Concen- tration | N | Reinforcements | | | |
| --- | --- | --- | --- | --- | --- |
| | | 1-250 | | 251-500 | |
| | | Mean | SD | Mean | SD |
| 4% | 11 | 252.8 | 108.4 | 87.6 | 55.0 |
| 8% | 15 | 118.7 | 92.0 | 31.8 | 25.1 |
| 16% | 16 | 71.1 | 60.4 | 21.2 | 9.8 |
| 32% | 17 | 36.5 | 10.4 | 23.8 | 10.1 |

times required by the various groups to complete the first and second 250 responses. Both the means and *SD*'s are clearly affected by concentration. The differences between pairs of groups with respect to time to obtain the first 250 reinforcements are (with the exception of the difference between the 8% and 16% groups) statistically significant at or beyond the 5% level of confidence.* For the second 250 reinforcements the differences among groups are smaller, and only the differences between the 4% group and each of the others are statistically significant. As will be seen in detail below, the 16% group obtains the second 250 reinforcements in the shortest time.

Inspection of the cumulative records obtained during conditioning reveals certain important points. Only in the 32% group do all Ss show the kind of conditioning curve that has ordinarily been obtained in the Skinner box with water or food pellets as reinforcement. In this group the first or

---

* The heterogeneity of the variances precludes the use of the analysis of variance. Therefore, the Festinger (3) and Mann-Whitney (11) tests have been used. The latter test was used for those values of *N* for which the Festinger test is not tabled.

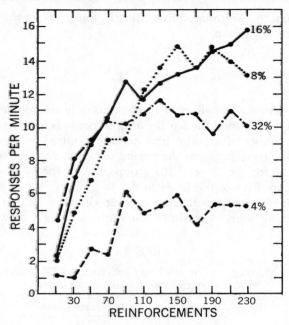

Fig. 1. Mean rate of bar-pressing of groups receiving various sucrose concentrations over the course of the first 240 continuous reinforcements.

second response is followed in the succeeding few minutes by a sustained acceleration to a high and stable rate. Most records in the 16% group are quite similar, but in a few cases the acceleration does not develop until 5–10 reinforcements have been obtained.

In the 8% group, only 4 of the 15 complete records are "typical." In the other cases, the acceleration to the final rate is very protracted, extending over as many as three or four experimental periods. The responses occur in definite bursts, separated by pauses ranging from seconds to several minutes. In the 4% group, no typical records are found, and the features seen in the 8% records are exaggerated. A steady rate of responding may not be achieved within 500 reinforcements. As conditioning progresses, the number of responses in a burst tends to increase. Within a burst, the rate of responding may reach 25 per minute, which is approximately as great as that observed in any S.

*Changes in rate during conditioning.* The graphic cumulative records were averaged by obtaining from each record the time required for successive blocks of reinforcements and converting these times to rates of responding. The averaged conditioning curves (group mean rate as a function of number of reinforcements) are shown in Fig. 1. Primarily, it may be seen that for the first 50 responses the curves are ranked in ascending order according to concentration. Beyond this point the rate

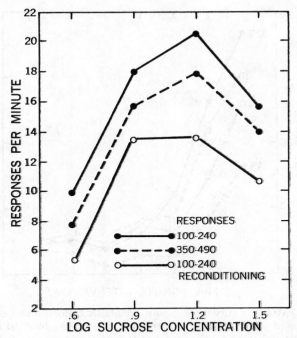

FIG. 2. Mean rate of bar-pressing under continuous reinforcement as a function of sucrose concentration at three stages of training.

of the 32% group is surpassed by that of the 16% group and later by that of the 8% group. The corresponding curves for the second 250 reinforcements and for reconditioning are essentially similar.

*Final rate of responding under continuous reinforcement.* Estimates of the asymptotic rates of responding for the various groups were obtained by taking the mean rates over the following blocks of reinforcements: ( *a* ) from Reinforcements 100 to 240; ( *b* ) from Reinforcements 350 to 490; and ( *c* ) from Reinforcements 100 to 240 of reconditioning.* These final rates are plotted against log concentration in Fig. 2. The three curves are clearly of similar form and are successively displaced upward on the ordinate. Final rate of responding increases as a function of concentration to 16% and then decreases. Separate analyses of variance for the three estimates of final rate were performed. In each case the differences among groups are significant beyond the .1% level of confidence. Differences between means of pairs of groups were tested with the *t* test. All comparisons involving the 4% group are significant beyond the .1% level. The difference between the 16% and 32% groups is significant beyond the 1% level in two instances, and it approaches the 5% level in the third instance.

* In general these blocks of reinforcements are the latter portions of given experimental periods, but for certain 4% and 8% Ss these blocks may comprise several periods.

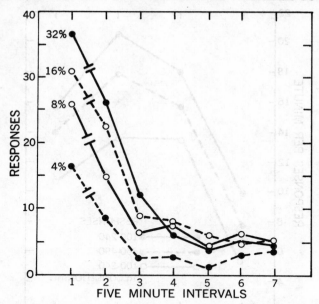

FIG. 3. Extinction curves for groups previously trained under continuous reinforcement with various concentrations. During the final 30 min., bar-pressing was followed by the sound of the magazine.

*Resistance to extinction.* In Fig. 3 are shown the mean extinction curves for the various groups. The initial points on these curves, representing 5 min. of extinction without secondary reinforcement, are ranked in ascending order according to concentration. These points are plotted as a function of concentration in the lower curve of Fig. 4. The differences among the groups are significant, in terms of the analysis of variance, beyond the 1% level of confidence. In terms of the $t$ test, all differences between non-adjacent pairs of groups are significant beyond the 2% level.

For at least the first 10 min. of the second phase of extinction, the groups are again ranked according to concentration. Beyond this point several inversions appear. The total number of responses in the second phase is plotted as a function of concentration in the upper curve of Fig. 4. The relationship is monotonic, but curvilinear. The analysis of variance for the totals indicates that the between-groups differences are not significant ($p(F) > .10$).*

*PR: Independent groups.* The mean rates of bar-pressing of the four concentration groups for all five experimental days are plotted as a func-

---

* A sampling error involving the loss of one case qualifies the findings for the second phase of extinction. The largest extinction curve for this phase (323 responses) was obtained from a 32% $S$ whose results are not included because it received six presentations of 8% sucrose by mistake during magazine training. Inclusion of this case would cause the mean extinction curve for the 32% group (Fig. 3) to be highest at all points.

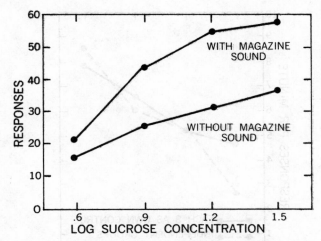

FIG. 4. Resistance to extinction as a function of sucrose concentration previously received.

tion of $\log_{10}$ sucrose concentration in Fig. 5. Rate of responding under PR is a monotonic increasing function of concentration over the range from 4% to 32% sucrose. The rate of the 32% group is more than triple that of the 4% group. In terms of the analysis of variance the over-all differences are significant beyond the .1% level of confidence. In terms of the $t$ test the differences between mean rates of pairs of groups are (with the exception of the difference between the 8% and 16% groups) significant at the 5% level, or better.

PR: *Each animal as its own control.* The over-all relationship between concentration and rate of responding in this determination is shown in Fig. 5. The empirical function is again nearly logarithmic, but the range of differences is more restricted than in the preceding determination. A statistical test of the differences among concentrations in terms of the analysis of variance indicates that the differences are significant beyond the .1% level of confidence. The $t$ tests of differences between means of pairs of concentrations are significant beyond the .1% level in all instances.

The average relationship for this determination is supported by the findings for individual Ss. In general, the rate-concentration curves for individual Ss are of the same monotonic increasing form as the mean curve, 16 of the 20 Ss showing no inversions. The differences among the individual curves are mainly in respect to their slopes and placements.

There is no indication that the concentration used in conditioning or prior PR training has a significant effect upon the results of the present determination. Rate-concentration curves were obtained for the four subgroups which were trained on different concentrations prior to this part of the experiment. These subgroup curves lie within .6 of a response per

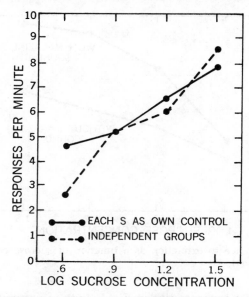

FIG. 5. Mean rate of bar-pressing under periodic reinforcement.

minute of the mean curve for the entire group of 20 Ss. A statistical test of the differences among the subgroup curves by means of the multivariate analysis of variance reveals differences at the 38% level of confidence.* The degree of similarity of the subgroup curves is striking in view of the small numbers of Ss involved.

*Comparison of the two PR procedures.* The quantitative disparity between the relationships shown in Fig. 5 is reduced when an estimate of the asymptotic rate-concentration function from the second determination is obtained. Over the 12 days of this experiment, the differences in rate among concentrations increase, the major portion of the change occurring in the first four days. During the course of the 15-min. experimental periods, the rates on various concentrations diverge as shown in Fig. 6. Estimates of the asymptotic rates for the second PR determination were derived by taking mean rates from the last 5 min. of test intervals in the last eight experimental days, when both long- and short-term changes are proceeding slowly. These values are plotted in Fig. 7, along with mean rates from the entire independent groups experiment. Straight lines have been fitted to these two sets of values by the method of least squares. The empirical points and fitted lines coincide to a marked extent, indicating a high order of stability in the underlying function. Also, it may be seen that the PR values are in agreement with the mean rates of responding for the

* Thanks are due to Dr. C. J. Burke for the suggestion that the multivariate form of the analysis of variance would be appropriate here and for the computation of the distribution function of the statistic for the parameters occurring in this application.

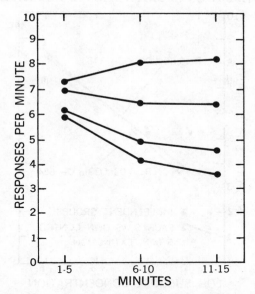

Fig. 6. Changes in rate of responding under PR during successive thirds of 15-min. test intervals. Each point is the mean of 240 5-min. intervals.

first 5 min. of extinction following continuous reinforcement. This relationship is somewhat in accordance with Skinner's notion of the "extinction ratio." Of course, the agreement of the PR and extinction values depends upon the portion of the extinction process which has been considered in the comparison, since in extinction all rates eventually go nearly to zero.

*Reinforcement threshold for sucrose.* The equations in Fig. 7 permit an estimate of the highest concentration of sucrose for which the rate of responding would not be expected to exceed the unconditioned rate, or operant level (17). This may be done by setting the equations equal to the operant level and solving for concentration. In this situation the operant level is not greatly in excess of zero, so as an approximation this value has been used. The two equations then yield 1% and 1.3% sucrose concentration as estimates of the reinforcement threshold. These values are of the same order of magnitude as the rat's sucrose taste threshold, .5% concentration, as determined by the preference method (16, 22). What importance can be attached to these findings we shall discuss below.

DISCUSSION

The concentration of sucrose used as reinforcement for bar-pressing has considerable effect upon acquisition, resistance to extinction, and perform-

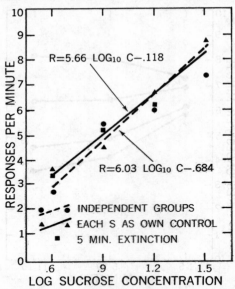

FIG. 7. Fitted rate-concentration functions for the two PR determinations. Mean rates of responding during first 5 min. of extinction following continuous reinforcement are replotted here for comparison.

ance under both continuous and periodic reinforcement. In general, the effects of concentration over the range investigated take the form of monotonic increasing functions. The exception is the case of final rate of responding under continuous reinforcement, where a consistently nonmonotonic relation to concentration is found. No satisfactory account of this relation can be given here, but various hypotheses need to be considered, and comparison must be made between other of the present findings and the results of previous experiments concerned with magnitude of reinforcing agent.

*Acquisition.* The present acquisition curves do not confirm Hull's view (8) and Zeaman's finding (23) that the number of reinforcements required to reach the performance asymptote is constant for various amounts of reinforcing agent. Figure 1 indicates that the 32% group achieves a relatively constant rate within a relatively smaller number of reinforcements than do the other groups. The initial slopes of the acquisition curves increase with concentration. In terms of *time* to reach the final rate, there is a clear effect of concentration: stable rates are always reached with the higher two concentrations within minutes, and may not be reached within hours with 4% solutions. Hull's hypothesis is not conclusively disproved by the present evidence, but it is opened to serious examination, especially for very small amounts of reinforcing agent.

It is important to note that the amounts of food used here are far smaller than those used in other studies. One reinforcement of 4% sucrose in these experiments contains about 1/5000 gm. sucrose, while Zeaman's (23) minimum was 1/20 gm. and Crespi's (1) was 1/50 gm. of solid food. The amounts used here are also far smaller than ordinarily used in bar-pressing experiments. Skinner (19) used 1/20 gm. food pellets, and typically found an almost complete transition from the unconditioned to the conditioned rate of responding as the result of a single reinforcement. Gradual conditioning curves similar to those of the present 16% and 32% groups have been reported by Estes (2) in experiments with the present apparatus, but employing water reinforcement and thirst motivation. The present results and Estes' suggest that Skinner's conditioning curves are not necessarily prototypic of operant conditioning, but whether records like Skinner's can be produced by varying magnitude of reinforcement alone remains an open experimental question.

*Resistance to extinction.* A relation between amount of reinforcement and resistance to extinction of bar-pressing has already been reported by Fitts (4), using 10 gr. and .2 gr. pellets. Reynolds (14) found no significant differences in resistance to extinction of bar-pressing among one 60 mgm., two 60 mgm., and one 160 mgm. pellets. The present results cast doubt on the generality of Reynolds' conclusions and on the "R-hypothesis" he proposes to explain the inappearance of an effect of amount of reinforcement in his study. It is suggested that all the amounts used by Reynolds were too close to the asymptote of the amount function to reveal significant differences in behavior with the N's used.

*Final rate of responding under continuous reinforcement.* In this experiment, resistance to extinction cannot be predicted from rate of responding under continuous reinforcement prior to extinction, since resistance to extinction is proportional to concentration over the entire range from 4% to 32% sucrose, and the "reflex reserve" developed with 32% is not indicated by the momentary rate of performance at a late stage of training. The most obvious hypothesis to account for the nonmonotonic form of the curves in Fig. 2 is more rapid satiation with 32% sucrose. Several facts make this hypothesis very dubious. In Fig. 1, the curve for 32% rises rapidly to a level which is below that later attained by the 16% and 8% curves, and it remains at this level with at least as much stability as is shown by the other curves. The individual 32% records do not suggest a satiation decrement, nor would a significant decrement be expected from the total amount of sucrose in 250 reinforcements of 32% solution, about .4 gm. Young (22) has found that a rat will ingest about 50 ml. of 32% sucrose in 24 hr., given no other food on the day of testing, which in his study follows a day of cafeteria feeding. What must be accounted for is that rate of responding on 32% never reaches the level obtained with 16%; if satiation is the responsible factor, its effects must be exerted before 1 ml. of liquid has been ingested.

Another explanation is suggested by Young's finding that ad libitum intake of sucrose solutions is a nonmonotonic function of concentration. He finds, however, that the maximum volume ingestion is at about 8.5%, whereas here the maximum rate of bar-pressing must be at a value somewhere above 8%. Even without this disparity, however, appeal to such a hypothesis will not account for the greater resistance to extinction of the 32% group. In reviewing the present findings, Young[*] has suggested that greater rates of adaptation of the taste receptors at higher concentrations might be involved, leading eventually to a lowered sensory effect and reduced performance. This would imply that resistance to extinction is primarily determined by the earlier rather than the later reinforcements. This possibility is not inconsistent with the present data.

As a final suggestion, it may be that there is a prolongation of drinking behavior at the higher concentrations, contrary to the intended control over this factor. It is possible that at 32% the consummatory response affords sufficient competition to bar-pressing to depress its rate of emission. No actual measurements of the time of drinking were made, and this hypothesis cannot be directly evaluated. However, indirect evidence on this point is supplied by the findings with regard to periodic reinforcement, under which condition the consummatory response might be in competition with bar-pressing during only a small fraction of the interval between reinforcements. The PR determinations were, in fact, included in the study partly as a test of this hypothesis, and the results are consistent with this interpretation of the continuous reinforcement relationship. Decisive evidence on this problem is not available, however, and it cannot be resolved at this time.

*Performance under PR.* The present data on PR, taken in relation to the findings for resistance to extinction, furnish the clearest evidence on the role of concentration of reinforcing agent. Methodologically considered, these relationships suggest that in studies of this type where an effect upon resistance to extinction is sought, the PR procedure provides virtually equivalent information with an economy of experimental effort.

The relationship between PR rate and concentration is a highly stable and reproducible one. Animals originally conditioned and given prolonged experience with various single concentrations behave very much alike when tested under PR on a number of concentrations. There is revealed no effect comparable to the "elation" or "depression" phenomena reported by Crespi (1) and Zeaman (23) occurring as the result of increases and decreases in amount of reinforcement. It is possible that these effects exist in this study in small measure but that the analysis was too gross to reveal them. If, as these writers suggest, these phenomena are emotional in nature, it is reasonable to expect that the effects should disappear through

[*] Young, P. T. Personal communication.

adaptation over the course of the numerous shifts in concentration in the second PR determination.

*Theoretical considerations.* The methods and results of this study invite a reconceptualization of the reinforcing agent in such a manner that it can be explicitly treated as a *stimulus* and its properties and functions so described. When, following current drive-reduction notions, a piece of food is thought of primarily as a nutrient agent, the fact that reinforcements are stimuli is likely to be obscured or entirely overlooked. If, on the contrary, the stimulational function of the reinforcement is taken seriously, such a fact as the semilogarithmic relation between sucrose concentration and PR rate becomes strongly suggestive of commonly found relations of the same form between stimulus intensity and receptor activity or reflex magnitude. By setting aside the drive-reduction habit of thought, and by using certain obvious extensions of methods developed for sensory and reflexological research, direct investigation of the important properties of reinforcing stimuli may be permitted.

As a move in this direction, we have suggested an extension of the notion of the threshold to cover the case of reinforcement. The reinforcement threshold for sucrose estimated by extrapolation from the present data may not be accurate and may not coincide with the threshold for acquisition, since it is based on data for performance. But in general the utility of the threshold notion as an analytic tool is great, and its place in the scheme we are outlining can be made quite determinate: the events essential to the strengthening of instrumental behavior must be considered to be those which are initiated when the reinforcement threshold is reached. Hypotheses about the nature of these events cannot be confirmed until thresholds are precisely measured and are compared with independent measurements on the supposed underlying processes. Among a priori hypotheses, there is one which is readily testable by virtue of its simplicity: that the reinforcement threshold coincides numerically with the receptive threshold of particular end-organs and that it is invariant for a wide variety of conditions, including changes in drive. This statement amounts to a quantitative interpretation of Troland's beneceptor theory (20), which has already received some indirect support (18). Other more complex hypotheses regarding reinforcement are also susceptible to interpretation in terms of the reinforcement threshold and will be so treated in a later paper.

## SUMMARY AND CONCLUSIONS

Four concentrations of sucrose, 4%, 8%, 16%, and 32%, were used as reinforcing agent with four groups of rats ($N = 80$) in a study of bar-pressing behavior. Each group received a single concentration during magazine training and conditioning under continuous reinforcement. Following extinction and reconditioning, performance was observed under periodic reinforcement for five days. Then, 20 Ss from the various groups were tested under periodic reinforcement an additional 12 times with each of the four concentrations previously used.

1. The time required to condition and to execute 500 responses decreases as concentration increases.

2. The averaged acquisition curves indicate a positive relation between concentration and the rate of approach to the asymptotic rate of responding under continuous reinforcement.

3. The relationship between concentration and rate of responding under continuous reinforcement at various stages beyond 100 reinforcements is nonmonotonic, increasing to 16% and then decreasing.

4. Resistance to extinction in terms of rate of responding in the initial 15 min. of extinction is an increasing monotonic function of the concentration used in conditioning. For the first 5 min., the relationship is approximately logarithmic.

5. Rate of responding under periodic reinforcement is an approximately logarithmic function of concentration, as determined both by comparison of independent groups and by using each S as its own control.

6. The concentration used in conditioning appears to have no effect upon the rate-concentration function for periodic reinforcement.

7. Extrapolation of the rate-concentration curves suggests a reinforcement threshold in the region of the sucrose taste threshold as determined by preference tests. Some implications of this hypothesis are discussed.

## REFERENCES

1. CRESPI, L. P. (1942) Quantitative variation of incentive and performance in the white rat. Amer. J. Psychol., 55, 467-517.

2. ESTES, W. K. (1950) Effects of competing reactions on the conditioning curve for bar-pressing. J. exp. Psychol., 40, 200-205.

3. FESTINGER, L. (1949) The significance of the differences between means without reference to the frequency distribution function. Psychometrika, 2, 97-105.

4. FITTS, P. M. (1940) The effect of a large and a small reward as indicated by the resistance-to-extinction curve for the rat. Psychol. Bull., 37, 429-430. (Abstract)

5. FLETCHER, F. M. (1940) Effects of quantitative variation of food-incentive on the performance of physical work by chimpanzees. Comp. Psychol. Monogr., 16, No. 82.

6. GRINDLEY, G. C. (1929) Experiments on the influence of the amount of reward on learning in young chickens. Brit. J. Psychol., 20, 173-180.

7. GUTTMAN, N. and ESTES, W. K. (1949) A modified apparatus for the study of operant behavior in the rat. J. gen. Psychol., 41, 297-301.

8. HULL, C. L. (1943) *Principles of behavior.* New York: D. Appleton-Century.
9. JENKINS, W. O. and CLAYTON, F. L. (1949) Rate of responding and amount of reinforcement. *J. comp. Psychol., 42,* 174-181.
10. LAWRENCE, D. H. and MILLER, N. E. (1947) A positive relationship between reinforcement and resistance to extinction produced by removing a source of confusion from a technique that had produced opposite results. *J. exp. Psychol., 37,* 494-509.
11. MANN, H. B. and WHITNEY, D. R. (1947) A test of whether one of two random variables is stochastically larger than the other. *Ann. math. Statist., 18,* 50-60.
12. MONCRIEFF, R. W. (1946) *The chemical senses.* New York: Wiley.
13. REYNOLDS, B. (1949) Acquisition of a black-white discrimination habit under two levels of reinforcement. *J. exp. Psychol., 39,* 760-769.
14. REYNOLDS, B. (1950) Resistance to extinction as a function of the amount of reinforcement present during acquisition. *J. exp. Psychol., 40,* 46-52.
15. REYNOLDS, B. (1950) Acquisition of a simple spatial discrimination as a function of the amount of reinforcement. *J. exp. Psychol., 40,* 152-160.
16. RICHTER, C. P. and CAMPBELL, K. H. (1940) Taste thresholds and taste preferences of rats for five common sugars. *J. Nutrition, 20,* 31-46.
17. SCHOENFELD, W. N., ANTONITIS, J. J., and BERSH, P. J. (1950) Unconditioned response rate of the white rat in a bar-pressing apparatus. *J. comp. physiol. Psychol., 43,* 41-48.
18. SHEFFIELD, F. D. and ROBY, T. B. (1940) Reward value of a non-nutritive sweet taste. *J. comp. physiol. Psychol., 43,* 471-481.
19. SKINNER, B. F. (1932) On the rate of formation of a conditioned reflex. *J. gen. Psychol., 7,* 274-286.
20. TROLAND, L. T. (1928) *The fundamentals of human motivation.* New York: Van Nostrand.
21. WOLFE, J. B. and KAPLON, M. D. (1941) Effect of amount of reward and consummatory activity on learning in chickens. *J. comp. Psychol., 31,* 353-361.
22. YOUNG, P. T. (1949) Studies of food preference, appetite, and dietary habit. IX. Palatability versus appetite as determinants of the critical concentrations of sucrose and sodium chloride. *Comp. Psychol. Monogr., 19,* 1-44.
23. ZEAMAN, D. (1949) Response latency as a function of the amount of reinforcement. *J. exp. Psychol., 39,* 466-483.

# 17.    Comparison of Two Methods of Investigating the Effect of Amount of Reward on Performance

## A. M. Schrier

*As we have noted from the Guttman study, most investigators have found that learning is related to the characteristics of the reinforcing agent. It should be noted, however, that the organisms' experience with rewards plays an important role in determining this effect. Schrier's study illustrates this finding.*

A large number of experiments have been concerned with the relationship between amount of food reward and frequency of correct responses on various tasks, usually visual or spatial discrimination or delayed response. The relationship obtained has always been positive and statistically significant when the Ss were monkeys or apes (1, 13, 14, 16, 20). On the other hand, the results have not been consistent when the Ss were rats, some investigators (4, 10, 11, 17) reporting no distinct relationship, others (18, 19) reporting a significant positive relationship. There is, apparently, no condition, including the type of task, common to all the studies in which reward amount influenced correct responses, which would differentiate them from those studies in which there was no such influence.

It is possible that species differences in sensitivity to the reward variable can account for the difference in the consistency of the findings of the experiments on monkeys and apes and those on rats. However, there is an alternative explanation for the difference in consistency: In the studies on rats, the amount for each S was never shifted during experimental tests, but was varied from group to group. In the experiments on monkeys and apes, the reward amount was repeatedly shifted upward and downward, so that each S would receive all levels. The method used with rats will be called the "nonshift method" here, and the one used with monkeys, the "shift method."

One advantage of the shift method is that an experimental design can be used which permits the elimination of inter-S differences as a source of error, thus increasing the precision of the experiment. In addition, the

*J. comp. physiological Psychol.*, 1958, 49, 117-125. Reprinted with permission of the author and The American Psychological Association. This experiment was reported in a doctoral dissertation, under the direction of Harry F. Harlow, submitted to the Graduate School of the University of Wisconsin in 1956, and was conducted during the author's tenure as a National Science Foundation Predoctoral Research Fellow.

results of several studies which involved reward shifts provide a basis for hypothesizing a difference in the effectiveness of the two methods independent of design considerations. In two experiments on rats (2, 21), shifts in amount of reward were introduced after a period of training under the nonshift method. Following an increase in amount, running time or response latency decreased to a level which was lower than that predicted on the basis of preshift performance. The same result was obtained, but in the opposite direction, following a decrease in amount. Zeaman (21) labeled these postshift phenomena "contrast effects." An experiment by Meyer (13) on monkeys and one by Elliott (3) on rats, the latter E employing shifts in the quality of food reward, indicated that the contrast effects can be obtained when the measure is the frequency of correct responses. Data gathered by Greene (6) on visual discrimination by rats imply a difference in the effectiveness of the two methods, but his experimental design prevents a clear-cut conclusion regarding the role played by contrast effects.

The results with reward shifts suggest the hypothesis that variation in performance as a function of reward amount may generally be greater with the shift method. This method involves repeated shifts among amounts, and, consequently, performance levels may be higher with the larger amounts and lower with the smaller than are obtained when shifts are not involved. In short, contrast effects may occur when the shift method is used. Recently, Lawson (9) reported an experiment, similar to the present, on brightness discrimination by rats which provides direct support for the hypothesis. Employing the nonshift method, Lawson found differences in the effect of a large and of a small amount of reward to be small and nonsignificant, but, employing the shift method, he found differences in the effect of the same amounts to be large and significant.

In the experiment reported here, two groups of monkeys were given the same series of object-discrimination problems. The reward amount, 1, 2, 4, or 8 food pellets, was varied from problem to problem for the Ss in one group. Identical amounts were used for the other group. However, the group was divided into four subgroups with the reward amount different for each subgroup. In accordance with the hypothesis outlined above, it was predicted that the positive slope of the function relating reward amount and discrimination performance would be greater for the former group, the group on which the shift method was used.

## METHOD

### SUBJECTS

Twenty-five experimentally naive rhesus monkeys, 3.8 to 6.8 lb., were used in the experiment. Their extra-experimental diet consisted of Chim-cracker once a day supplemented by fruit and vegetables twice a week.

APPARATUS

The Wisconsin General Test Apparatus (WGTA), described elsewhere (8), was used throughout most of the experiment. The test tray had one foodwell during pretraining and two foodwells during discrimination training. The series of discrimination problems consisted of 160 pairs of stimulus objects, differing in multiple dimensions, selected at random from the large collection at the laboratory. The food pellets used for experimental rewards weighed 65 mg. each and were pressed from Okatie Diet powder mixed with a sugar syrup, which constituted approximately 20% of each pellet. The pellets were similar in shape to small aspirin tablets.

PROCEDURE

*Incentive conditions.* The Ss were divided into five equal groups by a random procedure. Four of these were designated by the subgroups of the "nonshift group," whereas the remaining one was designated the "shift group." Reward amounts, 1, 2, 4, and 8 food pellets, were identical for both groups. The reward amount was constant for a given S in the nonshift group throughout pretraining and discrimination training, but was different for each of the four subgroups. On the other hand, the reward amount for each S in the shift group was shifted every block of four trials during pretraining and every problem during discrimination training. All four amounts were used in a new random order, different for each S in the group, every four blocks of trials or every four problems.

One S, assigned to the four-pellets subgroup of the nonshift group, died of a respiratory disorder shortly before discrimination training.

*Pretraining.* All Ss were given 16 trials per experimental period (EP), one EP a day, five days a week, for a minimum total of 45 EPs. Pretraining was carried out in three stages as follows: For at least five EPs, each S was placed in a transport cage and presented the food pellets in a small cup to which a long handle was attached. Then, for at least 10 EPs, each S was placed in a special cage, permitting close contact between E and S, and was presented the food pellets at first in the cup and later by hand. Lastly, each S was trained for at least 30 EPs in the WGTA to displace a wood block which covered the food pellets. A trial was considered balked if an S did not respond to the food pellets within 30 sec. Every S was required to reach a criterion of proficiency before advancing a stage. If, however, the criterion was attained before the indicated minimum number of EPs, training was continued until the minimum number was completed. No significant relationship between frequency of balked trials and reward amount was obtained for either group.

*Discrimination training.* All Ss received four, four-trial discrimination problems per EP, 1 EP a day, five days a week, for a total of 40 EPs. A discrimination problem consisted of a pair of objects, one of which always covered the baited foodwell. Preliminary work by the author indicated that the reward-amount effects would not be complicated by factors, such as differential reduction of the hunger drive, developing within EPs. This is also suggested by other forms of evidence (12, 15).

There are six possible positional sequences for four-trial problems in each of which the correct object appears equally often in the left and right positions. The sequences were used in a new random order every six problems.

A noncorrection technique and an intertrial interval of 25 to 30 sec. were used. Other details of the specific trial procedure have been described before (8, 13).

*Treatment of data.* Discrimination training was arbitrarily divided into a first and second practice period, EPs 1 to 20 and 21 to 40, respectively. The unit datum for an S in the shift group for each practice period was the percentage of correct responses after the first correct response on every problem with one of the reward amounts. Because of the shifts in amount, an S in this group did not have an opportunity to experience the amount on a new problem until its first correct response. Thus, the first correct response and preceding responses on a problem could not have been influenced by the amount for that problem. The unit datum for an S in the nonshift group for each practice period was the percentage of correct responses after the first correct response on every problem. The elimination of responses including and preceding each first correct response was deemed necessary for the nonshift group to achieve a greater comparability of the scores for the two groups. It was found that the percentage of eliminated responses was practically the same for each subgroup in the nonshift group, and, in the case of the shift group, for each set of problems under a different reward amount. In addition, there was little difference between the groups in the percentage of eliminated responses. For the experiment as a whole, the percentage, excluding Trial 1 of all problems, was 22 for the shift group and 23 for the nonshift.

All percentages of correct responses were subjected to an arcsin transformation before determining the means.

After transformation, three analyses of variance combined with orthogonal polynomial trend tests (5) were carried out: one on the data of the shift group alone, a second on the data of the nonshift group alone, and a third, which involved direct tests for differences between groups, on the data of the two groups. In performing the third analysis, the scores of the shift group for the different reward levels, presumably correlated, were treated as if they were independent, that is, as if they had been obtained from different subgroups. It should also be noted that each unit datum in the nonshift group was based on a greater number of trials than each unit datum in the shift group. The $F$s obtained under these circumstances tend

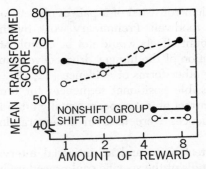

FIG. 1. Mean arcsin-transformed percentage of correct responses as a function of the amount of food reward (number of pellets). The intervals between the amounts on the abscissa are logarithmic. Each point on the curve for the nonshift group represents a different subgroup, whereas each point on the curve for the shift group represents the same Ss.

to be somewhat conservative. "Trend" here refers to fluctuation in mean performance level from log reward amount to log reward amount. By using the logs of the reward amounts, the requirement of equal spacing between levels of the independent variable was satisfied. Because an equal $n$ per cell is also required for the trend tests, it was necessary to estimate the score for a fifth S in the four-pellets subgroup of the nonshift group. The estimate was simply the mean for that subgroup.

## RESULTS

Figure 1 shows the mean arcsin-transformed percentage of correct responses as a function of amount of food reward, for discrimination training as a whole. The parameter is the method of investigating the effect of reward amount. It should be noted that the chance level is 45 as a result of the transformation. The mean performance level within the nonshift group declined slightly with increase in reward amount to two pellets, did not change appreciably with the increase to four pellets, then rose relatively sharply to the highest level within the group with the largest amount. On the other hand, the mean performance level of the shift group was positively related to reward amount throughout. The over-all difference in performance level of the two groups was small. The mean transformed percentage of correct responses by the nonshift group was 63.7, and by the shift group, 62.2.

The meaningful terms in the statistical analysis of the transformed data of the two groups were those which involved a comparison between groups, and, hence, the results of the analysis will not be reported in full. No significant difference in the over-all level of performance of the two groups was found. The linear component of the interaction between groups and rewards, that is, the difference between group slopes, was significant ($p = .05$), whereas the quadratic and cubic components were not. Thus, it can be concluded simply that the slope of the straight line best fitting the mean performance levels of the shift group, shown in Figure 1, is significantly greater than the slope of the straight line best fitting the mean performance levels of the nonshift group, also shown in Figure 1. It should be kept in mind that the interpretation here is not that the trend for each group was linear. None of the orthogonal components of the rewards-by-groups-by-practice interaction was significant.

With one exception, the probability of every $F$ interpreted as not significant in the above analysis was greater than .10, and, thus, it seems reasonable to assume that the lack of significance of these $F$s was not the result of the conservativeness of the tests. The exception was the $F$ for the linear component of the triple interaction, the probability of which fell between 5.0 and .10. This last $F$ reflected the fact that the difference between group slopes increased as a function of practice.

The statistical analysis of the transformed data of the nonshift group is summarized in Table 1. The quadratic component of the trend for discrimination training as a whole was significant, as is indicated in Table 1 by the $F$ for the subgroups-quadratic term. This implies a significant nonlinear fluctuation in mean performance level with increase in log reward amount. Although initially mean performance level declined with increase in amount, the statistical results do not imply the decrease is real. For example, a significant quadratic component could have been obtained if the first three points for the nonshift group in Figure 1 had had identical

TABLE 1

SUMMARY OF ANALYSIS OF VARIANCE AND TREND TESTS
FOR THE NONSHIFT GROUP

| Source of Variation | df | Mean Square | F |
|---|---|---|---|
| Subgroups (SG) | 3 | 148.6 | 2.5 |
| Linear | (1) | 151.3 | 2.6 |
| Quadratic | (1) | 279.6 | 4.7[a] |
| Cubic | (1) | 14.2 | $< 1$ |
| Ss/SG | 15 | 58.9 | |
| Practice (P) | 1 | 685.8 | 59.1[b] |
| P × SG | 3 | 1.9 | $< 1$ |
| Linear | (1) | .6 | $< 1$ |
| Quadratic | (1) | 2.4 | $< 1$ |
| Cubic | (1) | 2.4 | $< 1$ |
| P × Ss/SG | 15 | 11.6 | |

[a] Significant at the .05 level.
[b] Significant at the .001 level.

TABLE 2

SUMMARY OF ANALYSIS OF VARIANCE AND TREND TESTS FOR THE SHIFT GROUP

| Source of Variation | df | Mean Square | F |
|---|---|---|---|
| Rewards (R) | 3 | 446.1 | 16.2[c] |
| Linear | (1) | 1290.5 | 18.5[a] |
| Quadratic | (1) | 1.5 | < 1 |
| Cubic | (1) | 46.1 | 5.7 |
| Practice (P) | 1 | 379.8 | 23.3[b] |
| Ss | 4 | 117.8 | 17.7[c] |
| R × P | 3 | 41.2 | 6.2[b] |
| Linear | (1) | 75.0 | 6.6 |
| Quadratic | (1) | .2 | < 1 |
| Cubic | (1) | 48.6 | 16.6[a] |
| R × Ss | 12 | 27.6 | 41.5[c] |
| Linear | (4) | 69.9 | 6.1 |
| Quadratic | (4) | 4.6 | < 1 |
| Cubic | (4) | 8.2 | 2.8 |
| P × Ss | 4 | 16.3 | 2.4 |
| R × P × Ss | 12 | 6.6 | |
| Linear | (4) | 11.5 | |
| Quadratic | (4) | 5.6 | |
| Cubic | (4) | 3.0 | |

[a] Significant at the .05 level.
[b] Significant at the .01 level.
[c] Significant at the .001 level.

values on the ordinate. The main effect of practice was also significant.

The statistical analysis of the transformed data of the shift group is summarized in Table 2. The significance of the rewards-linear term indicates that the rate of improvement of the shift group as a function of log reward amount was essentially linear for discrimination training as a whole. However, the significance of the cubic component of the rewards-by-practice interaction implies a difference in curvilinearity of the function relating performance to log reward amount for each practice period. The significance of the rewards-linear term is probably a reflection of the greater tendency to a strictly linear trend of performance during the second practice period. The trend of the performance of the shift group during each practice period is illustrated in Figure 2. Although the differences between individual trends were highly significant, as revealed by the F for the rewards-by-Ss interaction, the differences could not be localized in any of the orthogonal components. The differences between individual linear trends approached significance. Additional significant sources of variation were Ss and practice.

The performance level of each subgroup of the nonshift group for the first two problems of all EPs and for the second two problems of all EPs

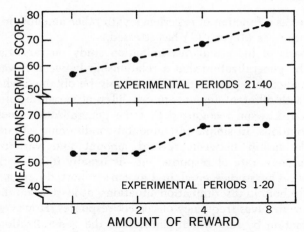

FIG. 2. Mean arcsin-transformed percentage of correct responses by the shift group as a function of amount of food reward (number of pellets). The intervals between the amounts on the abscissa are logarithmic. The lower curve is for the first practice period, and the upper curve is for the second.

was determined in order to check the influence of problem order within EPs on the results. Practically no change in the relative effects of the reward amounts within EPs was apparent in these data. Analysis of variance revealed no significant interaction of the effect of problem order within EPs and subgroups. Differential reduction of the hunger drive, therefore, did not appear to be an important factor in the results of the experiment.

## DISCUSSION

The method of investigating the effect of amount of food reward on discrimination performance by monkeys clearly influenced the outcome. The Ss in the shift group received all four levels of the reward, whereas the reward level was constant for each S in the nonshift group, different subgroups having received the different levels. The positive slope of the trend of the mean performance level with increase in reward amount was significantly greater for the shift group than for the nonshift for discrimination training as a whole. The differences between nonlinear group trends and the difference in the over-all level of performance of the groups were not significant. These findings essentially confirmed the prediction based on previous reports of contrast phenomena (2, 3, 9, 13, 21). The general implication is that the effect of a given amount of reward varies as a function of experience with other amounts in an experimental situation, as Meyer (13) has stressed.

On the basis of his visual discrimination study on rats, Lawson (9) suggested the generalization that a relationship between reward amount and performance in a given situation can only be obtained when Ss have experience with different amounts under different variations of the particular situation. Lawson recognized that the generalization does not hold for some situations. In simple instrumental conditioning situations, a significant relationship between reward amount and various response measures—latency, rate of response, etc.—is usually found with the nonshift method. The studies cited in Lawson's report do suggest that he expected it to hold in discrimination situations, at least when the performance measure involves frequency of correct responses. However, evidence on discrimination by rats which contradicts the generalization has been reported by Reynolds (18) and by Schrier (19). The problem in Reynolds' experiment was spatial discrimination and in Schrier's it was brightness discrimination. Although the nonshift method was used throughout, both Es found a significant relationship between reward amount and correct responses. A significant variation in discrimination performance as a function of reward amount was also obtained with the present nonshift group of monkeys. There is no reason to believe that the experimental situations were less unique to the Ss in the above experiments than to the Ss in Lawson's "absolute" (nonshift) groups, or to the Ss in other experiments in which, using the nonshift method, reward amount did not affect correct responses. Thus, it appears that reward amount can have a significant influence on the discrimination performance of monkeys and rats when either method is used. However, according to the present findings and Lawson's as well, other things being equal, the variation in performance levels should be greater when the shift method is used.

The findings here suggest that the uniform results of food-reward experiments on monkeys and apes can be attributed in large part to the consistent use of the shift method. If the shift method is in general more effective than the nonshift, it would follow that conditions which tend to obscure a relationship between reward amount and performance would be less likely to do so in any experiment in which the shift method is used.

Two questions regarding the contrast effects have received some attention: (a) What is the temporal course of the contrast effects during the period following a shift in reward amount? and (b) What influence have repeated shifts in reward amount on the magnitude of these effects? With respect to Question a, Crespi (2) took the view that the contrast effects are emotional phenomena and therefore transitory. Zeaman (21) seems to have accepted Crespi's view, but felt that his own data and Crespi's suggest that the rate of decay of the contrast effect following an increase in amount may be slower than that following a decrease. Guttman (7) raised Question *b* in connection with his failure to find a difference in results for the shift and the nonshift method when measuring rate of response of rats as a function of sucrose concentration. Guttman reasoned that, if the contrast effects are emotional in nature, it is to be expected ". . . that the effects should disappear through adaptation over the course of the numerous shifts in concentration . . ." (7, p. 222). However, the present experiment and Lawson's (9) indicate that, at least when measured in terms of frequency of correct responses, the contrast effects can persist over the course of a rather long series of shifts. During the present discrimination training, the magnitude of the contrast effects increased with repeated shifts and showed no sign of diminishing during the latter part of the experiment. Lawson did not report performance levels at different stages of practice. Returning to Question *a*, the possibility still remains that the contrast effects are more or less transitory in the sense of a decay following a shift in amount. There are no clear-cut data on this question as yet. Either in the manner of the design of the experiment or of the analysis of the results, the emphasis in all the experiments cited, as well as the present one, was on a demonstration of these effects rather than a study of their temporal course following a shift. If, for whatever the reason, the contrast effects do in fact tend to decay after a shift, it would follow that, other things being equal, the greater the number of trials between shifts, the less will be the difference in outcome for the shift and the nonshift method.

The discrimination performance of the shift group for the experiment as a whole was essentially a linear function of the log amount of reward. This relationship tended to become more marked with practice. In an experiment by Schrier and Harlow (20), on the other hand, performance of monkeys on color discrimination problems was an increasing and negatively accelerated function of the log amount of reward. The curvilinear trend of performance developed early in the experiment and persisted with practice. The present report was based on transformed scores, and the Schrier and Harlow report was not. This difference does not, however, appear to be critical because the transformation had little effect on the form of the curves. There is little basis at present for choosing which of a number of other differences in procedure might explain the difference in the results.

There have been no prior experiments employing the nonshift method on monkeys. The present findings indicate that increases in reward amount according to a ratio of the order of 8:1 may be required with this method to obtain appreciable increases in efficiency of performance of monkeys. By contrast, a ratio of 2:1 appears to be sufficient when using the shift method, as was shown here and also previously (14, 20).

SUMMARY

The purpose of the experiment was to compare directly two methods of investigating the effect of amount of food reward on performance. Two groups of monkeys were given four, four-trial object discrimination problems per experimental period for a total of 40 such periods. Using the "shift method" on one group, the reward amount per trial, 1, 2, 4, or 8 food pellets, was shifted for each problem, so that Ss in this group repeatedly received each of the four amounts. The amounts were identical for the second group, but the "nonshift method" was used. The group was divided into four subgroups, and the amount per trial was different for each subgroup.

Trend analyses revealed a significant, positive relationship, essentially linear, between the mean performance level of the shift-method group and reward amount for discrimination training as a whole, and a significant curvilinear relationship in the case of the nonshift-method group. Mean performance level within this latter group declined slightly with the increase in amount to two pellets, did not change appreciably with the further increase to four pellets, then rose relatively sharply to the highest level within this group with the largest amount. By testing differences between groups directly, it was found that the positive slope of the trend of the mean performance level with increase in reward amount was significantly greater for the shift-method group than for the nonshift-method group for discrimination training as a whole. There was no significant difference between nonlinear group trends. The difference in the over-all level of performance of the two groups was small and not significant.

The results essentially confirmed predictions based on previous reports of contrast effects following shifts in incentive amount. It was suggested that significant variation in discrimination performance as a function of reward amount may be obtained when using either method, but, other things being equal, the variation in performance should be greater when the shift method is used.

REFERENCES

1. COWLES, J. T. and NISSEN, H. W. (1937) Reward expectancy in delayed responses of chimpanzees. J. comp. Psychol., 24, 345-358.
2. CRESPI, L. P. (1944) Amount of reinforcement and level of performance. Psychol. Rev., 51, 341-357.
3. ELLIOTT, M. H. (1928) The effect of change of reward on the maze performance of rats. Univer. Calif. Publ. Psychol., 4, 19-30.
4. FURCHGOTT, E. and RUBIN, R. (1953) The effect of magnitude of reward on maze learning in the white rat. J. comp. physiol. Psychol., 46, 9-12.

5. GRANT, D. A. (1956) Analysis-of-variance tests in the analysis and comparison of curves. *Psychol. Bull.*, 53, 141-154.
6. GREENE, J. E. (1953) Magnitude of reward and acquisition of a black-white discrimination habit. *J. exp. Psychol.*, 46, 113-119.
7. GUTTMAN, N. (1953) Operant conditioning, extinction, and periodic reinforcement in relation to concentration of sucrose used as reinforcing agent. *J. exp. Psychol.*, 46, 213-224.
8. HARLOW, H. F. (1949) The formation of learning sets. *Psychol. Rev.*, 56, 51-65.
9. LAWSON, R. (1957) Brightness discrimination performance and secondary reward strength as a function of primary reward amount. *J. comp. physiol. Psychol.*, 50, 35-39.
10. McKELVEY, R. K. (1956) The relationship between training methods and reward variables in brightness discrimination learning. *J. comp. physiol. Psychol.*, 49, 485-491.
11. MAHER, W. B. and WICKENS, D. D. (1954) Effect of differential quantity of reward on acquisition and performance of a maze habit *J. comp. physiol. Psychol.*, 47, 44-46.
12. MEYER, D. R. (1951) Food deprivation and discrimination reversal learning by monkeys. *J. exp. Psychol.*, 41, 10-16.
13. MEYER, D. R. (1951) The effects of differential rewards on discrimination reversal learning by monkeys. *J. exp. Psychol.*, 41, 268-274.
14. MEYER, D. R. and HARLOW, H. F. (1952) Effects of multiple variables on delayed response performance by monkeys. *J. genet. Psychol.*, 81, 53-61.
15. MILES, R. C. Discrimination in the squirrel monkey as a function of deprivation and problem difficulty. *J. exp. Psychol.*, in press.
16. NISSEN, H. W. and ELDER, J. H. (1935) The influence of amount of incentive on delayed response performance by chimpanzees. *J. genet. Psychol.*, 47, 49-72.
17. REYNOLDS, B. (1949) The acquisition of a black-white discrimination habit under two levels of reinforcement. *J. exp. Psychol.*, 39, 760-769.
18. REYNOLDS, B. (1950) Acquisition of a simple spatial discrimination as a function of the amount of reinforcement. *J. exp. Psychol.*, 40, 152-160.
19. SCHRIER, A. M. (1956) Amount of incentive and performance on a black-white discrimination problem. *J. comp. physiol. Psychol.*, 49, 123-125.
20. SCHRIER, A. M. and HARLOW, H. F. (1956) Effect of amount of incentive on discrimination learning by monkeys. *J. comp. physiol. Psychol.*, 49, 117-122.
21. ZEAMAN, D. (1949) Response latency as a function of the amount of reinforcement. *J. exp. Psychol.*, 39, 466-483.

## 18.    Intracranial Reward Delay and the Acquisition Rate of a Brightness Discrimination

### R. E. Keesey

*The Olds and Milner study, which demonstrated that electrical stimulation can serve as a reward, is used to good advantage in this study by Keesey, who has employed the technique to investigate the delay of reinforcement gradient. The functional relationship between delay of reinforcement and learning which the author has obtained is quite similar to that obtained by Grice, who used food reward and a somewhat different learning situation.*

The demonstration that electrical stimulation of the brain can serve as an effective reward (1) has provided a new basis on which to approach the study of many reinforcement phenomena. Numerous investigators have, in fact, used these stimulation techniques to good advantage to study such factors as the brain structures involved in reward effects (2), the influence of various drive states on these central reward structures (3), and a variety of other related problems. Still another potentially useful application might be in studying the temporal parameters of reward and their relation to learning. Precise control of the duration of reinforcement or of the delay between the occurrence of a response and its reward is frequently complicated when food or water is the reward, since such factors are, in part, contingent upon the animal's behavior. In contrast, the techniques of electrical stimulation permit direct experimental control of such parameters and the use of a wider range of intervals than is normally possible with conventional reinforcers.

Evidence presently available indicates that brain stimulation is an effective reward in a learning situation. Rats will, for example, learn a multiple maze for such stimulation (4), and more recent evidence suggests that stimulation of certain areas of the hypothalamus is at least as effective a reward as food for the learning of a brightness discrimination (5). In the work reported here, this line of investigation was extended to study the

*Science*, 1964, *143*, 702-703. Reprinted with permission of the author and the American Association for the Advancement of Science. Copyright 1964 by the American Association for the Advancement of Science. This report is based upon a thesis submitted to the department of psychology at Brown University for the Ph.D. degree. The research was conducted during tenure of a U.S. Public Health Service predoctoral research fellowship (MF-9865) and was supported by a U.S. Public Health Service research grant (M-23371) (Cl) to J. W. Kling. The advice and encouragement of Dr. Kling is gratefully acknowledged.

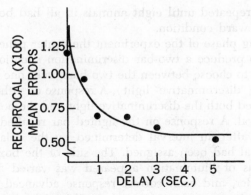

FIG. 1. Rate of learning as a function of the delay of reward. The reciprocal, times 100, of the mean number of errors in 500 trials is plotted against the delay interval. The curve has been visually fitted to the data points.

rate of learning among groups reinforced by stimulation when there are differences in the stimulation along a temporal dimension. Delay of reward (stimulation of the hypothalamus) was the parameter chosen.

Male Sprague-Dawley rats were prepared for this experiment by permanent implantation of bipolar electrodes ("chronic electrodes") aimed at the same area of the posterior hypothalamus in all the animals. Subsequent histological examination of the brains of a sample of 12 of the 48 experimental animals revealed that the majority of these electrodes terminated in the dorsomedial and posterior hypothalamic nuclei, the remainder being distributed in the more lateral region of the hypothalamus or more posteriorly in the supramammillary area. Stimulation was provided by a biphasic rectangular waveform, with the parameters held constant throughout the experiment at the following values: peak current, 2 ma; frequency, 85 pulses per second; pulse duration, 0.175 msec; train duration, 0.5 second. Prior work with stimulation of essentially these same areas of the hypothalamus has indicated that effective reward is provided by these stimulus conditions (6).

The experimental compartment was a rectangular box containing two response bars; in the penetrating phase of the experiment the box was divided into two boxes, each with one bar, by the addition of a center panel. Under this latter condition each subject was first trained to press for stimulation on one or the other of the bars. A training session followed in which each response extinguished the house lights for a 10-second period and eliminated the opportunity for reinforcement until the lights came on again. Of each group of six animals completing 100 such trials on both sides of the box, one was assigned at random to each of the following six delay conditions: 0.0, 0.5, 1.0, 2.0, 3.0, and 5.0 seconds. This procedure was repeated until eight animals in all had been assigned to each delay-of-reward condition.

In the learning phase of the experiment the center panel was removed from the box to produce a two-bar discrimination situation. The task of the subject was to choose between the two bars, over one of which there was a light (the "discriminative" light). A response on either bar immediately extinguished both the discriminative light and the house lights for a 10-second interval. A response on the lighted bar resulted in delivery of the stimulation after an interval determined by the delay condition to which the animal had been assigned. The side of the box on which the positive stimulus of illumination appeared was varied according to a prearranged order, and each correct response advanced this sequence. With this procedure, a subject was given 500 trials; for the most part these were given in two sessions—300 trials in the first and 200 in the second. In a few cases, especially under the longer delay conditions, an animal would stop responding for 15 minutes or more. When this occurred, training was terminated for that day and continued on the next, for as many daily sessions as were necessary to complete 500 trials.

The reciprocal of the mean number of errors made by each group in the 500 trials was plotted against the delay condition to produce the delay-of-reward gradient shown in Fig. 1. Statistical analysis of these data showed that the differences between the error scores for the six groups were reliable ($p < .001$). Examination of the acquisition curves (not shown) revealed that the first three groups—those subjected to 0.0-, 0.5-, and 1.0-second reward delay—attained a terminal performance level between 90 and 100 percent correct. The curves for the other three groups were still rising at the end of the 500 trials, and it is possible that they would have reached this same performance level had training continued. It is worth noting, however, that an increasing number of animals in the groups where delay was longer failed to show clear evidence of learning over the 500 trials, and three of the animals subjected to 5-second delay responded at what was close to a chance level throughout the experiment. It may be, therefore, that for a visual discrimination the 5-second delay is close to the limit for learning in the rat, as was suggested in an earlier study (7).

Much of our present knowledge concerning the relation of delayed reward to the rate of learning in rats is based upon the work of Grice (7), who used a food reward. While the work reported here resembles this earlier study in the choice of a visual discrimination task, the two do differ, both with respect to the reinforcing stimulus employed and in the use of a two-bar rather than a two-alley testing situation. In spite of these differences, comparison shows the two sets of data to be remarkably similar. It is possible, of course, that a closer examination of the relation between delayed reward and learning may reveal differences in the responses for food reward and for stimulation reward, perhaps at very short delays where, with food stimuli, the response time of the systems mediating reward may introduce a certain delay that central stimulation eliminates. On the other hand, the close similarity of the present data to those of Grice argues strongly for the essential comparability of food and stimulation as rewards for learning. This, together with the observation that group comparisons of experimental treatments are feasible in spite of the expected variation between subjects in electrode placement, offers considerable encouragement for applying these brain-stimulation techniques to studying the relation between reward and learning.

## REFERENCES AND NOTES

1. OLDS, J. and MILNER, P. (1954) *J. Comp. Physiol. Psychol.*, 47, 419.
2. OLDS, J. (1958) *ibid.*, 51, 675; PORTER, R. W., CONRAD, D. G., and BRADY, J. V. (1959) *J. Exptl. Anal. Behavior*, 2, 43; OLDS, J., TRAVIS, R.P., and SCHWING, R. C. (1960) *J. Comp. Physiol. Psychol.*, 53, 23.
3. BRADY, J. V., BOREN, J. J., CONRAD, D., and SIDMAN, M. (1957) *J. Comp. Physiol. Psychol.*, 50, 134; OLDS, J. (1958) *ibid.*, 51, 320; HODOS, W. and VALENSTEIN, E. S. (1960) *ibid.*, 53, 502; HOEBEL, B. G. and TEITELBAUM, P. (1962) *Science, 135*, 375.
4. OLDS, J. (1956) *J. Comp. Physiol. Psychol.*, 49, 507.
5. KLING, J. W. and MATSUMIYA, Y. (1962) *Science, 135*, 668.
6. KEESEY, R. E. (1962) *J. Comp. Physiol. Psychol.*, 55, 671.
7. GRICE, G. R. (1948) *J. Exptl. Psychol.*, 38, 1.

## 19.  Punishment

## R. L. Solomon

*It has been only recently that punishment has occupied an important place in the psychology of learning. In this article the author has provided an excellent overview of the area, (1) examining punishment parameters and empirical generalizations, (2) reviewing theoretical positions which have been hypothesized to explain how punishment operates, and finally, exploding some of the myths or legends which have surrounded its operation.*

First, an introduction: I will attempt to achieve three goals today. (*a*) I will summarize some *empirical generalizations and problems* concerning the effects of punishment on behavior; (*b*) I will give some demonstrations of the *advantages of a two-process learning theory* for suggesting new procedures to be tried out in punishment experiments; and (*c*) finally, I shall take this opportunity today to *decry some unscientific legends* about punishment, and to do a little pontificating—a privilege that I might be denied in a journal such as the *Psychological Review*, which I edit!

Now, for a working definition of punishment: The definition of a punishment is not operationally simple, but some of its attributes are clear. A punishment is a noxious stimulus, one which will support, by its termination or omission, the growth of new escape or avoidance responses. It is one which the subject will reject, if given a choice between the punishment and no stimulus at all. Whether the data on the behavioral effects of such noxious stimuli will substantiate our common-sense view of what constitutes an effective punishment, depends on a wide variety of conditions that I shall survey. Needless to say, most of these experimental conditions have been studied with infrahuman subjects rather than with human subjects.

### Sample Experiments

Let us first consider two sample experiments. Imagine a traditional alley runway, 6 feet long, with its delineated goal box and start box, and an

*Amer. Psychol.*, 1964, *19*, 239-253. Reprinted with permission of the author and The American Psychological Association. This is a slightly revised text of the author's Presidential Address to the Eastern Psychological Association, New York City, April 1963. The research associated with this address was supported by Grant No. M-4202 from the United States Public Health Service.

electrified grid floor. In our first experiment, a rat is shocked in the start box and alley, but there is no shock in the goal box. We can quickly train the rat to run down the alley, if the shock commences as the start-box gate is raised and persists until the rat enters the goal box. This is *escape* training. If, however, we give the rat 5 seconds to reach the goal box after the start-box gate is raised, and only then do we apply the shock, the rat will usually learn to run quickly enough to avoid the shock entirely. This procedure is called *avoidance* training, and the resultant behavior change is called *active* avoidance learning. Note that the response required, either to terminate the shock or to remove the rat from the presence of the dangerous start box and alley, is well specified, while the behavior leading to the onset of these noxious stimulus conditions is left vague. It could be any item of behavior coming *before* the opening of the gate, and it would depend on what the rat happened to be doing when the experimenter raised the gate.

In our second sample experiment, we train a hungry rat to run to the goal box in order to obtain food. After performance appears to be asymptotic, we introduce a shock, both in the alley and goal box, and eliminate the food. The rat quickly stops running and spends its time in the start box. This procedure is called the *punishment procedure*, and the resultant learning-to-stay-in-the-start-box is called *passive* avoidance learning. Note that, while the behavior *producing* the punishment is well specified, the particular behavior *terminating* the punishment is left vague. It could be composed of any behavior that keeps the rat in the start box and out of the alley.

In the first experiment, we were teaching the rat *what to do*, while in the second experiment we were teaching him exactly *what not to do*; yet in each case, the criterion of learning was correlated with the rat's receiving *no* shocks, in contrast to its previous experience of receiving several shocks in the same experimental setting. One cannot think adequately about punishment without considering what is known about the outcomes of both procedures. Yet most reviews of the aversive control of behavior emphasize active avoidance learning and ignore passive avoidance learning. I shall, in this talk, emphasize the similarities, rather than the differences between active and passive avoidance learning. I shall point out that there is a rich store of knowledge of active avoidance learning which, when applied to the punishment procedure, increases our understanding of some of the puzzling and sometimes chaotic results obtained in punishment experiments.

But first, I would like to review some of the empirical generalities which appear to describe the outcomes of experiments on *punishment* and passive avoidance learning. For this purpose, I divide the evidence into 5 classes: (*a*) the effects of punishment on behavior previously established by *rewards* or positive reinforcement, (*b*) the effects of punishment on *consummatory* responses, (*c*) the effects of punishment on complex, sequential patterns of *innate* responses, (*d*) the effects of punishment on discrete reflexes, (*e*) the effects of punishment on responses previously established by punishment—or, if you will, the effects of punishment on active escape and avoidance responses. The effectiveness of punishment will be seen to differ greatly across these five classes of experiments. For convenience, I mean by *effectiveness* the degree to which a punishment procedure produces *suppression* of, or facilitates the *extinction* of, existing response patterns.

Now, let us look at punishment for *instrumental responses or habits previously established by reward or positive reinforcers.* First, the outcomes of punishment procedures applied to previously rewarded habits are strongly related to the *intensity* of the punishing agent. Sometimes intensity is independently defined and measured, as in the case of electric shock. Sometimes we have qualitative evaluations, as in the case of Maier's (1949) rat bumping his nose on a locked door, or Masserman's (Masserman & Pechtel, 1953) spider monkey being presented with a toy snake, or Skinner's (1938) rat receiving a slap on the paw from a lever, or my dog receiving a swat from a rolled-up newspaper. As the intensity of shock applied to rats, cats, and dogs is increased from about .1 milliampere to 4 milliamperes, these orderly results can be obtained: (*a*) *detection* and *arousal*, wherein the punisher can be used as a cue, discriminative stimulus, response intensifier, or even as a secondary reinforcer; (*b*) *temporary suppression*, wherein punishment results in suppression of the punished response, followed by complete recovery, such that the subject later appears unaltered from his prepunished state; (*c*) *partial suppression*, wherein the subject always displays some lasting suppression of the punished response, without total recovery; and (*d*) finally, there is *complete suppression*, with no observable recovery. Any of these outcomes can be produced, other things being equal, by merely varying the intensity of the noxious stimulus used (Azrin & Holz, 1961), when we punish responses previously established by reward or positive reinforcement. No wonder different experimenters report incomparable outcomes. Azrin (1959) has produced a response-rate *increase* while operants are punished. Storms, Boroczi, and Broen (1962) have produced long-lasting suppression of operants in rats.* Were punishment intensities different? Were punishment durations different? (Storms, Boroczi & Broen, 1963, have shown albino rats to be more resistant to punishment than are hooded rats, and this is another source of discrepancy between experiments.)

But other variables are possibly as important as punishment intensity,

---

* Since the delivery of this address, several articles have appeared concerning the punishment intensity problem. See especially Karsh (1963), Appel (1963), and Walters and Rogers (1963). All these studies support the conclusion that shock intensity is a crucial variable, and high intensities produce lasting suppression effects.

and their operation can make it unnecessary to use *intense* punishers in order to produce the effective suppression of a response previously established by positive reinforcement. Here are some selected examples:

1. *Proximity* in time and space to the punished response determines to some extent the effectiveness of a punishment. There is a response-suppression gradient. This has been demonstrated in the runway (Brown, 1948; Karsh, 1962), in the lever box (Azrin, 1956), and in the shuttle box (Kamin, 1959). This phenomenon has been labeled the gradient of temporal delay of punishment.

2. The conceptualized *strength* of a response, as measured by its resistance to extinction after omission of positive reinforcement, predicts the effect of a punishment contingent upon the response. Strong responses, so defined, are more resistant to the suppressive effects of punishment. Thus, for example, the overtraining of a response, which often decreases ordinary resistance to experimental extinction, also increases the effectiveness of punishment (Karsh, 1962; Miller, 1960) as a response suppressor.

3. *Adaptation* to punishment can occur, and this *decreases* its effectiveness. New, intense punishers are better than old, intense punishers (Miller, 1960). Punishment intensity, if slowly increased, tends not to be as effective as in the case where it is introduced initially at its high-intensity value.

4. In general, resistance to extinction is decreased whenever a previously reinforced response is punished. However, if the subject is habituated to receiving shock together with positive reinforcement during reward training, the relationship can be reversed, and punishment during extinction can actually increase resistance to extinction (Holz & Azrin, 1961). Evidently, punishment, so employed, can functionally operate as a *secondary reinforcer*, or as a cue for reward, or as an arouser.

5. Punishments become extremely effective when the response-suppression period is tactically used as an aid to the reinforcement of new responses that are topographically *incompatible* with the punished one. When new instrumental acts are established which lead to the old goal (a new *means* to an old *end*), a punishment of very low intensity can have very long-lasting suppression effects. Whiting and Mowrer (1943) demonstrated this clearly. They first rewarded one route to food, then punished it. When the subjects ceased taking the punished route, they provided a new rewarded route. The old route was not traversed again. This reliable suppression effect also seems to be true of temporal, discriminative restraints on behavior. The suppression of urination in dogs, under the control of *indoor stimuli*, is extremely effective in housebreaking the dog, as long as urination is allowed to go unpunished under the control of *outdoor stimuli*. There is a valuable lesson here in the effective use of punishments in producing *impulse control*. A *rewarded alternative*, under discriminative control, makes passive avoidance training a potent behavioral

influence. It can produce a highly reliable dog or child. In some preliminary observations of puppy training, we have noted that puppies raised in the lab, if punished by the swat of a newspaper for eating horsemeat, and rewarded for eating pellets, will starve themselves to death when only given the opportunity to eat the taboo horsemeat. They eagerly eat the pellets when they are available.

It is at this point that we should look at the experiments wherein punishment appears to have only a temporary suppression effect. Most of these experiments offered the subject *no* rewarded alternative to the punished response in attaining his goal. In many such experiments, it was a case of take a chance or go hungry. Hunger-drive strength, under such no-alternative conditions, together with punishment intensity, are the crucial variables in predicting recovery from the suppression effects of punishment. Here, an interesting, yet hard-to-understand phenomenon frequently occurs, akin to Freudian "reaction formation." If a subject has been punished for touching some manipulandum which yields food, he may stay nearer to the manipulandum under low hunger drive and move farther away from it under high hunger drive, even though the probability of finally touching the manipulandum increases as hunger drive increases. This phenomenon is complex and needs to be studied in some detail. Our knowledge of it now is fragmentary. It was observed by Hunt and Schlosberg (1950) when the water supply of rats was electrified, and we have seen it occur in approach-avoidance conflict experiments in our laboratory, but we do not know the precise conditions for its occurrence.

Finally, I should point out that the attributes of effective punishments vary *across species* and *across stages in maturational development* within species. A toy snake can frighten monkeys. It does not faze a rat. A loud noise terrified Watson's little Albert. To us it is merely a Chinese gong.

I have sketchily reviewed some effects of punishment on *instrumental* acts established by *positive reinforcers*. We have seen that any result one might desire, from response enhancement and little or no suppression, to relatively complete suppression, can be obtained with our current knowledge of appropriate experimental conditions. Now let us look at the effects of punishment on *consummatory acts*. Here, the data are, to me, surprising. One would think that consummatory acts, often being of biological significance for the survival of the individual and the species, would be highly resistant to suppression by punishment. The *contrary* appears to be so. Male sexual behavior may be seriously suppressed by weak punishment (Beach, Conovitz, Steinberg & Goldstein, 1956; Gantt, 1944). Eating in dogs and cats can be permanently suppressed by a moderate shock delivered through the feet or through the food dish itself (Lichtenstein, 1950; Masserman, 1943). Such suppression effects can lead to fatal self-starvation. A toy snake presented to a spider monkey while he is eating can result in self-starvation (Masserman & Pechtel, 1953).

The interference with consummatory responses by punishment needs a great deal of investigation. Punishment seems to be especially effective in breaking up this class of responses, and one can ask *why*, with some profit. Perhaps the intimate temporal connection between drive, incentive, and punishment results in drive or incentive becoming conditioned-stimulus (CS) patterns for aversive emotional reactions when consummatory acts are punished. Perhaps this interferes with vegetative activity: i.e., does it "kill the appetite" in a hungry subject? But, one may ask why the same punisher might not appear to be as effective when made contingent on an *instrumental* act as contrasted with a consummatory act. Perhaps the nature of operants is such that they are separated in time and space and response topography from consummatory behavior and positive incentive stimuli, so that appetitive reactions are not clearly present during punishment for operants. We do not know enough yet about such matters, and speculation about it is still fun.

Perhaps the most interesting parametric variation one can study, in experiments on the effects of punishment on consummatory acts, is the *temporal order* of rewards and punishments. If we hold hunger drive constant, shock-punishment intensity constant, and food-reward amounts constant, a huge differential effect can be obtained when we reverse the order of reward and punishment. If we train a cat to approach a food cup, its behavior in the experimental setting will become quite stereotyped. Then, if we introduce shock to the cat's feet while it is eating, the cat will vocalize, retreat, and show fear reactions. It will be slow to recover its eating behavior in this situation. Indeed, as Masserman (1943) has shown, such a procedure is likely, if repeated a few times, to lead to self-starvation. Lichtenstein (1950) showed the same phenomenon in dogs. Contrast this outcome with that found when the temporal order of food and shock is *reversed*. We now use shock as a discriminative stimulus to signalize the availability of food. When the cat is performing well, the shock may produce eating with a latency of less than 5 seconds. The subject's appetite does not seem to be disturbed. One cannot imagine a more dramatic difference than that induced by reversing the temporal order of reward and punishment (Holz & Azrin, 1962; Masserman, 1943).

Thus, the effects of punishment are partly determined by those events that directly precede it and those that directly follow it. A punishment is not just a punishment. It is an event in a temporal and spatial flow of stimulation and behavior, and its effects will be produced by its temporal and spatial point of insertion in that flow.

I have hastily surveyed some of the effects of punishment when it has been made contingent either on rewarded *operants* and instrumental acts or on *consummatory* acts. A third class of behaviors, closely related to consummatory acts, but yet a little different, are *instinctive act sequences*: the kinds of complex, innately governed behaviors which the ethologists study, such as nest building in birds. There has been little adequate experimentation, to my knowledge, on the effects of punishment on such innate behavior sequences. There are, however, some hints of interesting things to come. For example, sometimes frightening events will produce what the ethologists call displacement reactions—the expression of an inappropriate behavior pattern of an innate sort. We need to experiment with such phenomena in a systematic fashion. The best example I could find of this phenomenon is the imprinting of birds on moving objects, using the locomotor following response as an index. Moltz, Rosenblum, and Halikas (1959), in one experiment, and Kovach and Hess (1963; see also Hess, 1959a, 1959b) in another, have shown that the punishment of such imprinted behavior sometimes depresses its occurrence. However, if birds are punished prior to the presentation of an imprinted object, often the following response will be energized. It is hard to understand what this finding means, except that punishment can either arouse or inhibit such behavior, depending on the manner of presentation of punishment. The suggestion is that imprinting is partially a function of fear or distress. The effectiveness of punishment also is found to be related to the critical period for imprinting (Kovach & Hess, 1963).

However, the systematic study of known punishment parameters as they affect a wide variety of complex sequences of innate behaviors is yet to be carried out. It would appear to be a worthwhile enterprise, for it is the type of work which would enable us to make a new attack on the effects of experience on innate behavior patterns. Ultimately the outcomes of such experiments *could* affect psychoanalytic conceptions of the effects of trauma on impulses of an innate sort.*

A fourth class of behavior upon which punishment can be made contingent, is the simple, discrete reflex. For example, what might happen if a conditioned or an unconditioned knee jerk were punished? We are completely lacking in information on this point. Can subjects be trained to inhibit reflexes under aversive motivation? Or does such motivation sensitize and enhance reflexes? Some simple experiments are appropriate, but I was unable to find them in the published work I read.

A fifth class of behavior, upon which punishment can be made contingent, is behavior *previously established by punishment procedures*: in other words, the effect of passive avoidance training on existing, active avoidance learned responses. This use of punishment produces an unexpected outcome. In general, if the same noxious stimulus is used to

* Since the delivery of this address, an article has appeared on this specific problem. See Adler and Hogan (1963). The authors showed that the gill-extension response of *Betta splendens* could be conditioned to a previously neutral stimulus by a Pavlovian technique, and it could also be suppressed by electric-shock punishment. This is an important finding, because there are very few known cases where the same response can be both conditioned and trained. Here, the gill-extension response is typically elicited by a rival fish, and is usually interpreted to be aggressive or hostile in nature.

punish a response as was used to establish it in the first place, the response becomes strengthened during initial applications of punishment. After several such events, however, the response may weaken, but not always. The similarity of the noxious stimulus used for active avoidance training to that used for punishment of the established avoidance response can be of great importance. For example, Carlsmith (1961) has shown that one can increase resistance to extinction by using the same noxious stimuli for both purposes and yet decrease resistance to extinction by using equally noxious, but discriminatively different, punishments. He trained some rats to run in order to avoid shock, then punished them during extinction by blowing a loud horn. He trained other rats to run in order to avoid the loud horn, then during extinction he punished them by shocking them for running. In two control groups, the punisher stimulus and training stimulus were the same. The groups which were trained and then punished by different noxious stimuli extinguished more rapidly during punishment than did the groups in which the active avoidance training unconditioned stimulus (US) was the same as the passive avoidance training US. Thus, punishment for responses established originally by punishment may be ineffective in eliminating the avoidance responses they are supposed to eliminate. Indeed, the punishment may strengthen the responses. We need to know more about this puzzling phenomenon. It is interesting to me that in Japan, Imada (1959) has been systematically exploring shock intensity as it affects this phenomenon.

Our quick survey of the effects of punishment on five classes of responses revealed a wide variety of discrepant phenomena. Thus, to predict in even the grossest way the action of punishment on a response, one has to know *how* that particular response was originally inserted in the subject's response repertoire. Is the response an instrumental one which was strengthened by reward? Is it instead a consummatory response? Is it an innate sequential response pattern? Is it a discrete reflex? Was it originally established by means of punishment? *Where*, temporally, in a behavior sequence, was the punishment used? How *intense* was it? These are but a few of the relevant, critical questions, the answers to which are necessary in order for us to make reasonable predictions about the effects of punishment. Thus, to conclude, as some psychologists have, that the punishment procedure is typically either effective or ineffective, typically either a temporary suppressor or a permanent one, is to oversimplify irresponsibly a complex area of scientific knowledge, one still containing a myriad of intriguing problems for experimental attack.

Yet, the complexities involved in ascertaining the effects of punishment on behavior *need not* be a bar to useful speculation ultimately leading to experimentation of a fruitful sort. The complexities should, however, dictate a great deal of caution in making dogmatic statements about whether punishment is effective or ineffective as a behavioral influence, or whether it is good or bad. I do *not* wish to do that. I would like now to speculate about the data-oriented theories, rather than support or derogate the dogmas and the social philosophies dealing with punishment. I will get to the dogmas later.

## THEORY

Here is a theoretical approach that, for me, has high pragmatic value in stimulating new lines of experimentation. Many psychologists today consider the punishment procedure to be a special case of avoidance training, and the resultant learning processes to be theoretically identical in nature. Woodworth and Schlosberg (1954) distinguish the two training procedures, *"punishment for action"* from *"punishment for inaction,"* but assume that the same theoretical motive, a "positive incentive value of safety" can explain the learning produced by both procedures. Dinsmoor (1955) argues that the facts related to both procedures are well explained by simple stimulus-response (S-R) principles of avoidance learning. He says:

If we punish the subject for making a given response or sequence of responses —that is, apply aversive stimulation, like shock—the cues or discriminative stimuli for this response will correspond to the warning signals that are typically used in more direct studies of avoidance training. By his own response to these stimuli, the subject himself produces the punishing stimulus and pairs or correlates it with these signals. As a result, they too become aversive. In the meantime, any variations in the subject's behavior that interfere or conflict with the chain of reactions leading to the punishment delay the occurrence of the final response and the receipt of the stimulation that follows it. These variations in behavior disrupt the discriminative stimulus pattern for the continuation of the punished chain, changing the current stimulation from an aversive to a nonaversive compound; they are conditioned, differentiated, and maintained by the reinforcing effects of the change in stimulation [p. 96].

The foci of the Dinsmoor analysis are the processes whereby: (*a*) discriminative stimuli become aversive, and (*b*) instrumental acts are reinforced. He stays at the quasi-descriptive level. He uses a peripheralistic, S-R analysis, in which response-produced proprioceptive stimuli and exteroceptive stimuli serve to hold behavior chains together. He rejects, as unnecessary, concepts such as fear or anxiety, in explaining the effectiveness of punishment.

Mowrer (1960) also argues that the facts related to the two training procedures are explained by a common set of principles, but Mowrer's principles are somewhat different than those of either Woodworth and Schlosberg, or Dinsmoor, cited above. Mowrer says:

In both instances, there is fear conditioning; and in both instances a way of behaving is found which eliminates or controls the fear. The only important distinction, it seems is that the stimuli to which the fear gets connected are different. In so-called punishment, these stimuli are produced by (correlated with) the behavior, or response, which we wish to block; whereas, in so-called avoidance learning, the fear-arousing stimuli are not response-produced—they are, so to say, extrinsic rather than intrinsic, independent rather than response-dependent. But in both cases there is avoidance and in both cases there is its antithesis, punishment; hence the impropriety of referring to the one as "punishment" and to the other as "avoidance learning." Obviously precision and clarity of understanding are better served by the alternative terms here suggested, namely, passive avoidance learning and active avoidance learning, respectively. . . . But, as we have seen, the two phenomena involve exactly the same basic principles of fear conditioning and of the reinforcement of whatever action (or inaction) eliminates the fear [pp. 31-32].

I like the simple beauty of each of the three unifying positions; what holds for punishment and its action on behavior should hold also for escape and avoidance training, and vice versa. Generalizations about one process should tell us something about the other. New experimental relationships discovered in the one experimental setting should tell us how to predict a new empirical event in the other experimental setting. A brief discussion of a few selected examples can illustrate this possibility.

## APPLICATIONS OF THEORY

I use a case in point stemming from work done in our own laboratory. It gives us new hints about some hidden sources of effectiveness of punishment. Remember, for the sake of argument, that we are assuming many important similarities to exist between active and passive avoidance-learning processes. Therefore, we can look at active avoidance learning as a theoretical device to suggest to us new, unstudied variables pertaining to the effectiveness of punishment.

Turner and I have recently published an extensive monograph (1962) on human traumatic avoidance learning. Our experiments showed that when a very reflexive, short-latency, skeletal response, such as a toe twitch, was used as an escape and avoidance response, grave difficulties in active avoidance learning were experienced by the subject. Experimental variations which tended to render the escape responses more emitted, more deliberate, more voluntary, more operant, or less reflexive, tended also to render the avoidance responses easier to learn. Thus, when a subject was required to move a knob in a slot in order to avoid shock, learning was rapid, in contrast to the many failures to learn with a toe-flexion avoidance response.

There are descriptions of this phenomenon already available in several published experiments on active avoidance learning, but their implications have not previously been noted. When Schlosberg (1934) used for the avoidance response a highly reflexive, short-latency, paw-flexion response in the rat, he found active avoidance learning to be unreliable, unstable, and quick to extinguish. Whenever the rats made active avoidance flexions, a decrement in response strength ensued. When the rats were shocked on several escape trials, the avoidance response tended to reappear for a few trials. Thus, learning to avoid was a tortuous, cyclical process, never exceeding 30% success. Contrast these results with the active avoidance training of nonreflexive, long-latency operants, such as rats running in Hunter's (1935) circular maze. Hunter found that the occurrence of avoidance responses tended to produce more avoidance responses. Omission of shock seemed to reinforce the avoidance running response. Omission of shock seemed to extinguish the avoidance paw flexion. Clearly the operant-respondent distinction has predictive value in active avoidance learning.

The same trend can be detected in experiments using dogs as subjects. For example, Brogden (1949), using the forepaw-flexion response, found that meeting a 20/20 criterion of avoidance learning was quite difficult. He found that 30 dogs took from approximately 200–600 trials to reach the avoidance criterion. The response used was, in our language, highly reflexive—it was totally elicited by the shock on escape trials with a very short latency, approximately .3 second. Compare, if you will, the learning of active avoidance by dogs in the shuttle box with that found in the forelimb-flexion experiment. In the shuttle box, a large number of dogs were able to embark on their criterion trials after 5–15 active avoidance-training trials. Early escape response latencies were long. Resistance to extinction is, across these two types of avoidance responses, inversely related to trials needed for a subject to achieve criterion. Conditions leading to quick acquisition are, in this case, those conducive to slow extinction. Our conclusion, then, is that high-probability, short-latency, *respondents* are not as good as medium-probability, long-latency operants when they are required experimentally to function as active avoidance responses. This generalization seems to hold for rats, dogs, and college students.

How can we make the inferential leap from such findings in active avoidance training to possible variations in punishment experiments? It is relatively simple to generalize across the two kinds of experiments in the case of CS-US interval, US intensity, and CS duration. But the inferential steps are not as obvious in the case of the operant-respondent distinction. So I will trace out the logic in some detail. If one of the major effects of punishment is to motivate or elicit new behaviors, and reinforce them through removal of punishment, and thus, as Dinsmoor describes, establish avoidance responses incompatible with a punished response, how does the operant-respondent distinction logically enter? Here, Mowrer's two-process avoidance-learning theory can suggest a possible answer.

Suppose, for example, that a hungry rat has been trained to lever press for food and is performing at a stable rate. Now we make a short-duration, high-intensity pulse of shock contingent upon the bar press. The pulse elicits a startle pattern that produces a release of the lever in .2 second, and the shock is gone. The rat freezes for a few seconds, breathing heavily, and he urinates and defecates. It is our supposition that a conditioned emotional reaction (CER) is thereby established, with its major stimulus control coming from the sight of the bar, the touch of the bar, and proprioceptive stimuli aroused by the lever-press movements themselves. This is, as Dinsmoor describes it, the development of acquired aversiveness of stimuli; or, as Mowrer describes it, the acquisition of conditioned fear reactions. Therefore, Pavlovian conditioning variables should be the important ones in the development of this process. The reappearance of lever pressing in this punished rat would thus depend on the extinction of the CER and skeletal freezing. If no further shocks are administered, then the CER should extinguish according to the laws of Pavlovian extinction, and reappearance of the lever press should not take long, even if the shock-intensity level were high enough to have been able to produce active avoidance learning in another apparatus.

Two-process avoidance theory tells us that something very important for successful and durable response suppression was missing in the punishment procedure we just described. What was lacking in this punishment procedure was a good operant to allow us to reinforce a reliable avoidance response. Because the reaction to shock was a respondent, was highly *reflexive*, and was quick to occur, I am led to argue that the termination of shock will *not* reinforce it, nor will it lead to stable avoidance responses. This conclusion follows directly from our experiments on human avoidance learning. If the termination of shock is made contingent on the occurrence of an operant, especially an operant topographically incompatible with the lever press, an active avoidance learning process should then ensue. So I will now propose that we shock the rat until he huddles in a corner of the box. The rat will have learned to *do* something arbitrary whenever the controlling CSs reappear. Thus, the rat in the latter procedure, if he is to press the lever again, must undergo *two* extinction processes. The CER, established by the pairing of CS patterns and shock, must become weaker. Second, the learned huddling response must extinguish. This combination of requirements should make the effect of punishment more lasting, if my inferences are correct. Two problems must be solved by the subject, not one. The experiments needed to test these speculations are, it would appear, easy to design, and there is no reason why one should not be able to gather the requisite information in the near future. I feel that there is much to be gained in carrying on theoretical games like this, with the major assumptions being (a) that active and passive avoidance learning are similar processes, ones in which the same variables have analogous effects, and (b) that two processes, the conditioning of fear reactions, and the reinforcement of operants incompatible with the punished response, may operate in punishment experiments.

There is another gain in playing theoretical games of this sort. One can use them to question the usual significance imputed to past findings. Take, for example, the extensive studies of Neal Miller (1959) and his students, and Brown (1948) and his students, on gradients of approach and avoidance in conflict situations. Our foregoing analysis of the role of the operant-respondent distinction puts to question one of their central assumptions—that the avoidance gradient is unconditionally steeper than is the approach gradient in approach-avoidance conflicts. In such experiments, the subject is typically trained while hungry to run down a short alley to obtain food. After the running is reliable, the subject is shocked, usually near the goal, in such a way that entering the goal box is discouraged temporarily. The subsequent behavior of the typical subject consists of remaining in the start box, making abortive approaches to the food box, showing hesitancy, oscillation, and various displacement activities, like grooming. Eventually, if shock is eliminated by the experimenter, the subject resumes running to food. The avoidance tendency is therefore thought to have extinguished sufficiently so that the magnitude of the conceptualized approach gradient exceeds that of the avoidance gradient at the goal box. The steepness of the avoidance gradient as a function of distance from the goal box is inferred from the behavior of the subject *prior* to the extinction of the avoidance tendencies. If the subject stays as far away from the goal box as possible, the avoidance gradient may be inferred to be either displaced upward, or if the subject slowly creeps up on the goal box from trial to trial, it may be inferred to be less steep than the approach gradient. Which alternative is more plausible? Miller and his collaborators very cleverly have shown that the latter alternative is a better interpretation.

The differential-steepness assumption appears to be substantiated by several studies by Miller and his collaborators (Miller & Murray, 1952; Murray & Berkun, 1955). They studied the displacement of conflicted approach responses along both spatial and color dimensions, and clearly showed that the approach responses generalized more readily than did the avoidance responses. Rats whose running in an alley had been completely suppressed by shock punishment showed recovery of running in a similar alley. Thus the inference made was that the avoidance gradient is steeper than is the approach gradient; avoidance tendencies weaken more rapidly with changes in the external environmental setting than do approach tendencies. On the basis of the analysis I made of the action of punishment, both as a US for the establishment of a Pavlovian CER and as a potent event for the reinforcement of instrumental escape and avoidance responses, it seems to me very likely that the approach-avoidance conflict experiments have been carried out in such a way as to produce inevitably the steeper avoidance gradients. In other words, these experiments from my particular viewpoint have been inadvertently biased, and they were not appropriate for testing hypotheses about the gradient slopes.

My argument is as follows: Typically, the subject in an approach-avoidance experiment is trained to perform a specific sequence of responses under reward incentive and appetitive drive conditions. He runs to food when hungry. In contrast, when the shock is introduced into the runway, it is usually placed near the goal, and no specific, long sequence of instrumental responses is required of the subject before the shock is terminated. Thus, the initial strengths of the approach and avoidance instrumental responses (which are in conflict) are not equated by analogous or symmetrical procedures. Miller has thoroughly and carefully discussed this, and has suggested that the avoidance gradient would not have as steep a slope if the shock were encountered by the rat early in the runway in the case where the whole runway is electrified. While this comment is probably correct, it does not go far enough, and I would like to elaborate on it. I would argue that if one wants to study the relative steepnesses of approach and avoidance responses in an unbiased way, the competing instrumental responses should be established in a *symmetrical* fashion. After learning to run down an alley to food, the subject should be shocked near the goal box or in it, and the shock should not be terminated until the subject has escaped all the way into the start box. Then one can argue that two conflicting instrumental responses have been established. First, the subject runs one way for food; now he runs the same distance in the opposite direction in order to escape shock. When he stays in the start box, he avoids shock entirely. Then the generalization or displacement of the approach and avoidance responses can be fairly studied.

I am arguing that we need *instrumental*-response balancing, as well as *Pavlovian*-conditioning balancing, in such conflict experiments, if the slopes of gradients are to be determined for a test of the differential-steepness assumption. Two-process avoidance-learning theory requires such a symmetrical test. In previous experiments, an aversive CER and its respondent motor pattern, not a well-reinforced avoidance response, has been pitted against a well-reinforced instrumental-approach response. Since the instrumental behavior of the subject is being used subsequently to test for the slope of the gradients, the usual asymmetrical procedure is, I think, not appropriate. My guess is that, if the symmetrical procedure I described is actually used, the slopes of the two gradients will be essentially the same, and the recovery of the subject from the effects of punishment will be seen to be nearly all-or-none. That is, the avoidance gradient, as extinction of the CER proceeds in time, will drop below the approach gradient, and this will hold all along the runway if the slopes of the two gradients are indeed the same. Using the test of displacement, subjects should stay in the starting area of a similar alley on initial tests and when they finally move forward they should go all the way to the goal box. The outcomes of such experiments would be a matter of great interest to me, for, as you will read in a moment, I feel that the suppressive power of punishment over instrumental acts has been understated. The approach-avoidance conflict experiment is *but one* example among many wherein the outcome *may have been* inadvertently biased in the direction of showing reward-training influences to be superior, in some particular way, to punishment-training procedures. Now let us look more closely at this matter of bias.

LEGENDS

Skinner, in 1938, described the effect of a short-duration slap on the paw on the extinction of lever pressing in the rat. Temporary suppression of lever-pressing rate was obtained. When the rate increased, it exceeded the usual extinction performance. The total number of responses before extinction occurred was not affected by the punishment for lever pressing. Estes (1944) obtained similar results, and attributed the temporary suppression to the establishment of a CER (anxiety) which dissipated rapidly. Tolman, Hall, and Bretnall (1932) had shown earlier that punishment could enhance maze learning by serving as a cue for correct, rewarded behavior. Skinner made these observations (on the seemingly ineffective nature of punishment as a response weakener) the basis for his advocacy of a positive reinforcement regime in his utopia, *Walden Two*. In *Walden Two*, Skinner (1948), speaking through the words of Frazier, wrote: "We are now discovering at an untold cost in human suffering—that in the long run punishment doesn't reduce the probability that an act will occur [p. 260]." No punishments would be used there, because they would produce poor behavioral control, he claimed.

During the decade following the publication of *Walden Two*, Skinner (1953) maintained his position concerning the effects of punishment on instrumental responses: Response suppression is but temporary, and the side effects, such as fear and neurotic and psychotic disturbances, are not worth the temporary advantages of the use of punishment. He said:

In the long run, punishment, unlike reinforcement, works to the disadvantage of both the punished organism and the punishing agency [p. 183].
The fact that punishment does not permanently reduce a tendency to respond is in agreement with Freud's discovery of the surviving activity of what he called repressed wishes [p. 184].
Punishment, as we have seen, does not create a negative probability that a response will be made but rather a positive probability that incompatible behavior will occur [p. 222].

It must be said, in Skinner's defense, that in 1953 he devoted about 12 pages to the topic of punishment in his introductory textbook. Other texts had devoted but a few words to this topic.

In Bugelski's (1956) words about the early work on punishment: "The purport of the experiments mentioned above appears to be to demonstrate that punishment is ineffective in eliminating behavior. This conclusion appears to win favor with various sentimentalists [p. 275]." Skinner (1961) summarized his position most recently in this way:

Ultimate advantages seem to be particularly easy to overlook in the control of behavior, where a quick though slight advantage may have undue weight. Thus, although we boast that the birch rod has been abandoned, most school children are still under aversive control—not because punishment is more effective in the long run, but because it yields immediate results. It is easier for the teacher to control the student by threatening punishment than by using positive reinforcement with its *deferred, though more powerful,* effects [p. 36.08, italics mine].

Skinner's conclusions were drawn over a span of time when, just as is the case *now,* there was no conclusive evidence about the supposedly more powerful and long-lasting effects of positive reinforcement. I admire the humanitarian and kindly dispositions contained in such writings. But the scientific basis for the conclusions therein was shabby, because, even in 1938, there were conflicting data which demonstrated the great effectiveness of punishment in controlling instrumental behavior. For example, the widely cited experiments of Warden and Aylesworth (1927) showed that discrimination learning in the rat was more rapid and more stable when incorrect responses were punished with shock than when reward alone for the correct response was used. Later on, avoidance-training experiments in the 1940s and 1950s added impressive data on the long-lasting behavioral control exerted by noxious stimuli (Solomon & Brush, 1956). In spite of this empirical development, many writers of books in the field of learning now devote but a few lines to the problem of punishment, perhaps a reflection of the undesirability of trying to bring satisfying order out of seeming chaos. In this category are the recent books of Spence, Hull, and Kimble. An exception is Bugelski (1956) who devotes several pages to the complexities of this topic. Most contemporary *introductory psychology* texts devote but a paragraph or two to punishment as a scientific problem. Conspicuously, George Miller's new book, *Psychology, the Science of Mental Life,* has no discussion of punishment in it.

The most exhaustive textbook treatment today is that of Deese (1958), and it is a thoughtful and objective evaluation, a singular event in this area of our science. The most exhaustive journal article is that by Church (1963), who has thoroughly summarized our knowledge of punishment. I am indebted to Church for letting me borrow freely from his fine essay in prepublication form. Without this assistance, the organization of this paper would have been much more difficult, indeed.

Perhaps one reason for the usual textbook relegation of the topic of punishment to the fringe of experimental psychology is the wide-spread belief that punishment is unimportant because it *does not really weaken habits*; that it pragmatically is a *poor controller* of behavior; that it is extremely *cruel* and unnecessary; and that it is a technique leading to *neurosis* and worse. This legend, and it is a legend without sufficient empirical basis, probably arose with Thorndike (1931). Punishment, in the time of Thorndike, used to be called punishment, not passive avoidance training. The term referred to the use of noxious stimuli for the avowed purpose of discouraging some selected kind of behavior. Thorndike (1931) came to the conclusion that punishment did not really accomplish its major purpose, the destruction or extinction of habits. In his book, *Human Learning*, he said:

Annoyers do not act on learning in general by weakening whatever connection they follow. If they do anything in learning, they do it indirectly, by informing the learner that such and such a response in such and such a situation brings distress, or by making the learner feel fear of a certain object, or by making him jump back from a certain place, or by some other definite and specific change which they produce in him [p. 46].

This argument is similar to that of Guthrie (1935), and of Wendt (1936), in explaining the extinction of instrumental acts and conditioned reflexes. They maintained that extinction was not the weakening of a habit, but the replacement of a habit by a new one, even though the new one might only be sitting still and doing very little.

When Thorndike claimed that the effects of punishment were indirect, he was emphasizing the power of punishment to evoke behavior other than that which produced the punishment; in much the same manner, Guthrie emphasized the extinction procedure as one arousing competing responses. The competing-response theory of extinction today cannot yet be empirically chosen over other theories such as Pavlovian and Hullian inhibition theory, or the frustration theories of Amsel or Spence. The Thorndikian position on punishment is limited in the same way. It is difficult to designate the empirical criteria which would enable us to know, on those occasions when punishment for a response results in a weakening of performance of that response, whether a habit was indeed weakened or not. How can one tell whether competing responses have displaced the punished response, or whether the punished habit is itself weakened by punishment? Thorndike could not tell, and neither could Guthrie. Yet a legend was perpetuated. Perhaps the acceptance of the legend had something to do with the lack of concerted research on punishment from 1930–1955. For example, psychologists were not then particularly adventuresome in their search for experimentally effective punishments.

Or, in addition to the legend, perhaps a bit of softheartedness is partly responsible for limiting our inventiveness. (The Inquisitors, the Barbarians, and the Puritans could have given us some good hints! They did not have electric shock, but they had a variety of interesting ideas, which, regrettably, they often put to practice.) We clearly need to study new kinds of punishments in the laboratory. For most psychologists, a punishment in the laboratory means electric shock. A few enterprising experimenters have used air blasts, the presentation of an innate fear releaser, or a signal for the coming omission of reinforcement, as punishments. But we still do not know enough about using these stimuli in a controlled fashion to produce either behavior suppression, or a CER effect, or the facilitation of extinction. Many aversive states have gone unstudied. For example, conditioned nausea and vomiting is easy to produce, but it has not been used in the role of punishment. Even the brain stimulators, though they have since 1954 tickled brain areas that will instigate active escape learning, have not used this knowledge to study systematically the punishing effects of such stimulation on existing responses.

While the more humanitarian ones of us were bent on the discovery of new positive reinforcers, there was no such concerted effort on the part of the more brutal ones of us. Thus, for reasons that now completely escape me, some of us in the past were thrilled by the discovery that, under some limited conditions, either a light onset or a light termination could raise lever-pressing rate significantly, though trivially, above operant level. If one is looking for agents to help in the task of getting stronger predictive power, and strong control of behavior, such discoveries seem not too exciting. Yet, in contrast, discoveries *already have* been made of the powerful aversive control of behavior. Clearly, we have been afraid of their implications. Humanitarian guilt and normal kindness are undoubtedly involved, as they should be. But I believe that one reason for our fear has been the widespread implication of the *neurotic syndrome* as a *necessary* outcome of all severe punishment procedures. A second reason has been the general acceptance of the behavioral phenomena of rigidity, inflexibility, or narrowed cognitive map, as *necessary* outcomes of experiments in which noxious stimuli have been used. I shall question *both* of these conclusions.

If one should feel that the Skinnerian generalizations about the inadequate effects of punishment on instrumental responses are tinged with a laudable, though thoroughly incorrect and unscientific, sentimentalism and softness, then, in contrast, one can find more than a lurid tinge in discussions of the effects of punishment on the *emotional* balance of the individual. When punishments are asserted to be ineffective controllers of instrumental behavior, they are, in contrast, often asserted to be devastating controllers of emotional reactions, leading to neurotic and psychotic symptoms, and to general pessimism, depressiveness, constriction of thinking, horrible psychosomatic diseases, and even death! This is somewhat of a paradox, I think. The convincing part of such generalizations is only their face validity. There *are* experiments, many of them carefully done, in which these neurotic outcomes were clearly observed. Gantt's (1944) work on neurotic dogs, Masserman's (1943) work on neurotic cats and monkeys, Brady's (1958) recent work on ulcerous monkeys, Maier's (1949) work on fixated rats, show some of the devastating consequences of the utilization of punishment to control behavior. The side effects are frightening, indeed, and should *not* be ignored! But there *must be* some rules, some principles, governing the appearance of such side effects, for they *do not* appear in all experiments involving the use of strong punishment or the elicitation of terror. In Yates' (1962) new book, *Frustration and Conflict*, we find a thorough discussion of punishment as a creator of conflict. Major attention is paid to the instrumental-response outcomes of conflict due to punishment. Phenomena such as rigidity, fixation, regression, aggression, displacement, and primitivization are discussed. Yates accepts the definition of neurosis developed by Maier and by Mowrer: self-defeating behavior oriented toward no goal, yet compulsive in quality. The behavioral phenomena that reveal neuroses are said to be fixations, regressions, aggressions, or resignations. But we are not told the necessary or sufficient experimental conditions under which these dramatic phenomena emerge.

Anyone who has tried to train a rat in a T maze, using food reward for a correct response, and shock to the feet for an incorrect response, knows that there *is* a period of emotionality during early training, but that, thereafter, the rat, when the percentage of correct responses is high, looks like a hungry, well-motivated, happy rat, eager to get from his cage to the experimenter's hand, and thence to the start box. Evidently, merely going through conflict is not a condition for neurosis. The rat is reliable, unswerving in his choices. Is he neurotic? Should this be called subservient resignation? Or a happy adjustment to an inevitable event? Is the behavior constricted? Is it a fixation, an evidence of behavioral rigidity? The criteria for answering such questions are vague today. Even if we should suggest some specific tests for rigidity, they lack face validity. For example, we might examine *discrimination reversal* as a test of *rigidity*. Do subjects who have received reward for the correct response, and punishment for the incorrect response, find it harder to reverse when the contingencies are reversed, as compared with subjects trained with reward alone? Or, we might try a *transfer test*, introducing our subject to a new maze, or to a new jumping stand. Would the previously punished subject generalize more readily than one not so punished? And if he did, would he then be *less discriminating* and thus neurotic? Or, would the previously punished subject generalize poorly and hesitantly, thus being *too discriminating*, and thus neurotic, too? What are the criteria for behavioral *malfunction* as a consequence of the use of punishment? When instrumental responses are used as the indicator, we are, alas, left in doubt!

The most convincing demonstrations of neurotic disturbances stemming from the use of punishment are seen in Masserman's (Masserman & Pechtel, 1953) work with monkeys. But here the criterion for neurosis is *not* based on instrumental responding. Instead, it is based on emotionality expressed in consummatory acts and innate impulses. Masserman's monkeys were frightened by a toy snake while they were eating. Feeding inhibition, shifts in food preferences, odd sexual behavior, tics, long periods of crying, were observed. Here, the criteria have a face validity that is hard to reject. Clearly, punishment was a dangerous and disruptive behavioral influence in Masserman's experiments. Such findings are consonant with the Freudian position postulating the pervasive influences of traumatic experiences, permeating all phases of the affective existence of the individual, and persisting for long time periods.

To harmonize all of the considerations I have raised concerning the conditions leading to neurosis due to punishment is a formidable task. My guess at the moment is that neurotic disturbances arise often in those cases where *consummatory* behavior or *instinctive* behavior is punished, and punished under *nondiscriminatory* control. But this is merely a guess, and in order for it to be adequately tested, Masserman's interesting procedures would have to be repeated, using discriminative stimuli to signalize when it is safe and not safe for the monkey. Such experiments should be carried out if we are to explore adequately the possible effects of punishment on emotionality. Another possibility is that the number of rewarded behavior alternatives in an otherwise punishing situation will determine the emotional aftereffects of punishments. We have seen that Whiting and Mowrer (1943) gave their rats a rewarding alternative, and the resulting behavior was highly reliable. Their rats remained easy to handle and eager to enter the experimental situation. One guess is that increasing the number of behavioral alternatives leading to a consummatory response will, in a situation where only one behavior alternative is being punished, result in reliable behavior and the absence of neurotic emotional manifestations. However, I suspect that matters cannot be that simple. If our animal subject is punished for Response A, and the punishment quickly elicits Response B, and then Response B is quickly rewarded, we have the stimulus contingencies for the establishment of a masochistic habit. Reward follows punishment quickly. Perhaps the subject would then persist in performing the punished Response A? Such questions need to be worked out empirically, and the important parameters must be identified. We are certainly in no position today to specify the necessary or sufficient conditions for experimental neurosis.

I have, in this talk, decried the stultifying effects of legends concerning punishment. To some extent, my tone was reflective of bias, and so I overstated some conclusions. Perhaps now it would be prudent to soften my claims.\* I must admit that all is not lost! Recently, I have noted a definite increase in good parametric studies of the effects of punishment on several kinds of behavior. For example, the pages of the *Journal of the Experimental Analysis of Behavior* have, in the last 5 years, become liberally sprinkled with reports of punishment experiments. This is a heartening development, and though it comes 20 years delayed, it is welcome.

## SUMMARY

I have covered a great deal of ground here, perhaps too much for the creation of a clear picture. The major points I have made are as follows: *First, the effectiveness of punishment as a controller of instrumental behavior varies with a wide variety of known parameters.* Some of these are: (*a*) intensity of the punishment stimulus, (*b*) whether the response being punished is an instrumental one or a consummatory one, (*c*) whether the response is instinctive or reflexive, (*d*) whether it was established originally by reward or by punishment, (*e*) whether or not the punishment is closely associated in time with the punished response, (*f*) the temporal arrangements of reward and punishment, (*g*) the strength of the response to be punished, (*h*) the familiarity of the subject with the punishment being used, (*i*) whether or not a reward alternative is offered during the behavior-suppression period induced by punishment, (*j*) whether a distinctive, incompatible avoidance response is strengthened by omission of punishment, (*k*) the age of the subject, and (*l*) the strain and species of the subject.

*Second*, I have tried to show the theoretical virtues of considering active and passive avoidance learning to be similar processes, and have shown the utility of a two-process learning theory. I have described some examples of the application of findings in active avoidance-learning experiments to the creation of new punishment experiments and to the reanalysis of approach-avoidance conflict experiments.

*Third*, I have questioned persisting legends concerning both the ineffectiveness of punishment as an agent for behavioral change as well as the inevitability of the neurotic outcome as a legacy of all punishment procedures.

---

\* Presidential addresses sometimes produce statements that may be plausible at the moment, but on second thought may seem inappropriate. In contrast to my complaints about inadequate research on punishment and the nature of active and passive avoidance learning are Hebb's (1960) recent remarks in his APA Presidential Address. He said: "The choice is whether to prosecute the attack, or to go on with the endless and trivial elaboration of the same set of basic experiments (on pain avoidance for example); trivial because they have added nothing to knowledge for some time, though the early work was of great value [p. 740]."

*Finally,* I have indicated where new experimentation might be especially interesting or useful in furthering our understanding of the effects of punishment.

If there is one idea I would have you retain, it is this: Our laboratory knowledge of the effects of punishment on instrumental and emotional behavior is still rudimentary—much too rudimentary to make an intelligent choice among conflicting ideas about it. The polarized doctrines are probably inadequate and in error. The popularized Skinnerian position concerning the inadequacy of punishment in suppressing *instrumental* behavior is, if correct at all, only conditionally correct. The Freudian position, pointing to pain or trauma as an agent for the pervasive and long-lasting distortion of *affective* behavior is equally questionable, and only conditionally correct.

Happily, there is now growing attention being paid to the effects of punishment on behavior, and this new development will undoubtedly accelerate, because the complexity of our current knowledge, and the perplexity it engenders, are, I think, exciting and challenging.

## REFERENCES

ADLER, N. and HOGAN, J. A. (1963) Classical conditioning and punishment of an instinctive response in *Betta splendens. Anim. Behav., 11,* 351-354.

APPEL, J. B. (1963) Punishment and shock intensity. *Science, 141,* 528-529.

AZRIN, N. H. (1956) Some effects of two intermittent schedules of immediate and non-immediate punishment. *J. Psychol., 42,* 8-21.

AZRIN, N. H. (1959) Punishment and recovery during fixed-ratio performance. *J. exp. Anal. Behav., 2,* 301-305.

AZRIN, N. H. and HOLZ, W. C. (1961) Punishment during fixed-interval reinforcement. *J. exp. Anal. Behav., 4,* 343-347.

BEACH, F. A., CONOVITZ, M. W., STEINBERG, F., and GOLDSTEIN, A. C. (1956) Experimental inhibition and restoration of mating behavior in male rats. *J. genet. Psychol., 89,* 165-181.

BRADY, J. V. (1958) Ulcers in "executive monkeys." *Scient. American, 199,* 95-103.

BROGDEN, W. J. (1949) Acquisition and extinction of conditioned avoidance response in dogs. *J. comp. physiol. Psychol., 42,* 296-302.

BROWN, J. S. (1948) Gradients of approach and avoidance responses and their relation to level of motivation. *J. comp. physiol. Psychol., 41,* 450-465.

BUGELSKI, B. R. (1956) *The psychology of learning.* New York: Holt.

CARLSMITH, J. M. The effect of punishment on avoidance responses: The use of different stimuli for training and punishment. Paper read at Eastern Psychological Association, Philadelphia, April, 1961.

CHURCH, R. M. (1963) The varied effects of punishment on behavior. *Psychol. Rev., 70,* 369-402.

DEESE, J. (1958) *The psychology of learning.* New York: McGraw-Hill.

DINSMOOR, J. A. (1955) Punishment: II. An interpretation of empirical findings. *Psychol. Rev., 62,* 96-105.

ESTES, W. K. (1944) An experimental study of punishment. *Psychol. Monogr.*, 57(3, Whole No. 263).

GANTT, W. H. (1944) *Experimental basis for neurotic behavior.* New York: Hoeber.

GUTHRIE, E. R. (1935) *The psychology of learning.* New York: Harper. (Rev. ed., 1952)

HEBB, D. O. (1960) The American revolution. *Amer. Psychologist, 15,* 735-745.

HESS, E. H. (1959) Imprinting. *Science, 130,* 133-141. (a)

HESS, E. H. (1959) Two conditions limiting critical age for imprinting. *J. comp. physiol. Psychol., 52,* 515-518. (b)

HOLZ, W. and AZRIN, N. H. (1961) Discriminative properties of punishment. *J. exp. Anal. Behav., 4,* 225-232.

HOLZ, W. C. and AZRIN, N. H. (1962) Interactions between the discriminative and aversive properties of punishment. *J. exp. Anal. Behav., 5,* 229-234.

HUNT, J. McV. and SCHLOSBERG, H. (1950) Behavior of rats in continuous conflict. *J. comp. physiol. Psychol., 43,* 351-357.

HUNTER, W. S. (1935) Conditioning and extinction in the rat. *Brit. J. Psychol., 26,* 135-148.

IMADA, M. (1959) The effects of punishment on avoidance behavior. *Jap. Psychol. Res., 1,* 27-38.

KAMIN, L. J. (1959) The delay-of-punishment gradient. *J. comp. physiol. Psychol., 52,* 434-437.

KARSH, E. B. (1962) Effects of number of rewarded trials and intensity of punishment on running speed. *J. comp. physiol. Psychol., 55,* 44-51.

KARSH, E. B. (1963) Changes in intensity of punishment: Effect on runway behavior of rats. *Science, 140,* 1084-1085.

KOVACH, J. K. and HESS, E. H. (1963) Imprinting: Effects of painful stimulation upon the following response. *J. comp. physiol. Psychol., 56,* 461-464.

LICHTENSTEIN, F. E. (1950) Studies of anxiety: I. The production of a feeding inhibition in dogs. *J. comp. physiol. Psychol., 43,* 16-29.

MAIER, N. R. F. (1949) *Frustration: The study of behavior without a goal.* New York: McGraw-Hill.

MASSERMAN, J. M. (1943) *Behavior and neurosis.* Chicago: Univer. Chicago Press.

MASSERMAN, J. M. and PECHTEL, C. (1953) Neurosis in monkeys: A preliminary report of experimental observations. *Ann. N. Y. Acad. Sci., 56,* 253-265.

MILLER, N. E. (1959) Liberalization of basic S-R concepts: Extensions to conflict behavior, motivation, and social learning. In S. Koch (Ed.), *Psychology: A study of a science.* Vol. 2. *Sensory, perceptual, and physiological formulations.* New York: McGraw-Hill. Pp. 196-292.

MILLER, N. E. (1960) Learning resistance to pain and fear: Effects of overlearning, exposure, and rewarded exposure in context. *J. exp. Psychol., 60,* 137-145.

MILLER, N. E. and MURRAY, E. J. (1952) Displacement and conflict-learnable drive as a basis for the steeper gradient of approach than of avoidance. *J. exp. Psychol., 43,* 227-231.

MOLTZ, H., ROSENBLUM, L., and HALIKAS, N. (1959) Imprinting and level of anxiety. *J. comp. physiol. Psychol., 52,* 240-244.

MOWRER, O. H. (1960) *Learning theory and behavior.* New York: Wiley.

MURRAY, E. J. and BERKUN, M. M. (1955) Displacement as a function of conflict. *J. abnorm. soc. Psychol., 51,* 47-56.

SCHLOSBERG, H. (1934) Conditioned responses in the white rat. *J. genet. Psychol.*, 45, 303-335.

SKINNER, B. F. (1938) *The behavior of organisms.* New York: Appleton-Century.

SKINNER, B. F. (1948) *Walden Two.* New York: Macmillan.

SKINNER, B. F. (1953) *Science and human behavior.* New York: Macmillan.

SKINNER, B. F. (1961) *Cumulative record.* New York: Appleton-Century-Crofts.

SOLOMON, R. L. and BRUSH, E. S. (1956) Experimentally derived conceptions of anxiety and aversion. In M. R. Jones (Ed.), *Nebraska Symposium on Motivation: 1956.* Lincoln: Univer. Nebraska Press.

STORMS, L. H., BOROCZI, C., and BROEN, W. E. (1962) Punishment inhibits on instrumental response in hooded rats. *Science, 135,* 1133-1134.

STORMS, L. H., BOROCZI, C., and BROEN, W. E. (1963) Effects of punishment as a function of strain of rat and duration of shock. *J. comp. physiol. Psychol.,* 56, 1022-1026.

THORNDIKE, E. L. (1931) *Human learning.* New York: Appleton-Century-Crofts.

TOLMAN, E. C., HALL, C. S., and BRETNALL, E. P. (1932) A disproof of the law of effect and a substitution of the laws of emphasis, motivation, and disruption. *J. exp. Psychol.,* 15, 601-614.

TURNER, L. H. and SOLOMON, R. L. (1962) Human traumatic avoidance learning: Theory and experiments on the operant-respondent distinction and failures to learn. *Psychol. Monogr., 76*(40, Whole No. 559).

WALTERS, G. C. and ROGERS, J. V. (1963) Aversive stimulation of the rat: Long term effects on subsequent behavior. *Science, 142,* 70-71.

WARDEN, C. J. and AYLESWORTH, M. (1927) The relative value of reward and punishment in the formation of a visual discrimination habit in the white rat. *J. comp. Psychol.,* 7, 117-127.

WENDT, G. R. (1936) An interpretation of inhibition of conditioned reflexes as competition between reaction systems. *Psychol. Rev.,* 43, 258-281.

WHITING, J. W. M. and MOWRER, O. H. (1943) Habit progression and regression—a laboratory study of some factors relevant to human socialization. *J. comp. Psychol., 36,* 229-253.

WOODWORTH, R. S., and SCHLOSBERG, H. (1954) *Experimental psychology.* New York: Holt.

YATES, A. J. (1962) *Frustration and conflict.* New York: Wiley.

# SECTION FIVE

# The Role of Nonreinforced
# Responses in the Learning Situation

M ANY studies examining the role of reinforcement in learning utilize a procedure in which the organism is rewarded on every trial, or reinforced after making every correct response. It is possible, of course, to introduce nonrewarded trials into the experimental situation, and when this is done, we have a procedure which has been referred to as partial or intermittent reinforcement. Partial reinforcement, as Jenkins and Stanley (1950) have written, ". . . refers to the reinforcement given at least once but omitted on one or more of the trials or after one or more of the responses in a series." The influence of partial reinforcement in the learning situation has been widely investigated; perhaps the most notable finding has been that it almost invariably results in prolonging experimental extinction. This has given rise to a number of theoretical explanations. Two of these have been proposed by Mowrer and Jones (1945), our first selection in this chapter. One of these explanations, the response unit hypothesis, has not had very much interest for investigators, but the discrimination hypothesis has provoked a considerable number of experimental tests.

A few years later, Sheffield (1950) proposed still another explanation, an aftereffects hypothesis which also resulted in a number of experimental studies designed to test its validity. One such test was provided by Wilson, Weiss, and Amsel (1955), our third selection in this section. It is interesting that these authors propose still another explanation for the effects of partial reinforcement on experimental extinction.

It must be acknowledged, however, as Lewis (1960) in a recent review has concluded, that no single theory can account for all the experimental findings that have been obtained.

A second nonreinforcement procedure is found in the discrimination learning situation. Here, in a two choice learning problem, where the correct stimulus is associated with reinforcement, and the incorrect stimulus is never associated with reward, a frequently investigated problem has been to contrast the contribution of rewarded to nonrewarded trials. More specifically, the question can be raised: does lack of reinforcement following an incorrect response contribute more to the learning of the problem than reward following the correct response? Our selection by Fitzwater (1952) explores this problem area.

## REFERENCES

FITZWATER, M. E. (1952) The relative effect of reinforcement and non-reinforcement in establishing a form discrimination. *J. comp. physiol. Psychol.*, 45, 476-481.

JENKINS, W. O. and STANLEY, J. C., JR. (1950) Partial reinforcement: A review and critique. *Psychol. Bull.*, 47, 193-234.

LEWIS, D. J. (1960) Partial reinforcement: A selective review of the literature since 1950. *Psychol. Bull.*, 57, 1-28.

MOWRER, O. H. and JONES, H. M. (1945) Habit strength as a function of the pattern of reinforcement. *J. exp. Psychol.*, 35, 293-311.

SHEFFIELD, V. F. (1950) Resistance to extinction as a function of the distribution of extinction trials. *J. exp. Psychol.*, 40, 305-313.

WILSON, W., WEISS, E. J., and AMSEL, A. (1955) Two tests of the Sheffield hypothesis concerning resistance to extinction, partial reinforcement and distribution of practice. *J. exp. Psychol.*, 50, 51-60.

## 20.  Habit Strength as a Function of the Pattern of Reinforcement

### O. H. Mowrer and H. Jones

*Humphreys, who found that a partial reinforcement procedure provided greater resistance to extinction than a continuous one, used this finding to question the Law of Effect. Mowrer and Jones have attempted to show that Humphreys' findings do not necessarily provide such an invalidation.*

It was long assumed that the basic truth concerning the psychology of learning was embodied in the Law of Exercise (Repetition, Use, Frequency), which held that every performance of a habit necessarily strengthened that habit. But evidence gradually accumulated which suggested that 'exercise,' as such, has little, if anything, to do with the strength of a habit. It was rather the presence or absence of *reward* (Law of Effect) that seemed crucial, since only rewarded responses grow stronger with repetition and non-rewarded (or punished) responses are actually inhibited thereby. Even this proposition, that every rewarded repetition of a habit strengthens it, has, however, recently been questioned. It is our purpose to consider whether the doubt which has thus been thrown on this proposition is justified.

If it be assumed that reward is the essential factor in strengthening a habit and that non-rewarded repetitions have a weakening effect, it would seem to follow that habits which are rewarded every time they occur would be strengthened more than habits which are rewarded only intermittently. But recent experimentation has brought the validity of this inference under suspicion. When 'resistance to extinction,' i.e., the extent to which a previously rewarded habit will continue to occur after reward is eliminated, is used as a measure of habit strength, it is found that a habit which has been developed on the basis of intermittent reward is, by this criterion, 'stronger' than a habit which has been continuously rewarded. The experiment here reported represents an attempt to explain this paradox and to show that the experimental facts are actually consistent with the Law of Effect.

*J. exp. Psychol.*, 1945, *35*, 293-311. Reprinted with permission of the senior author and The American Psychological Association.

## FORMULATION OF THE PROBLEM

Since the present investigation was prompted largely by Humphreys' research on intermittent vs. constant reinforcement, it is necessary to give a brief description of this work.

Humphreys performed three experiments with human subjects, in the first of which he used the conditioned eyelid response (12), in the second a verbal response (13), and in the third the conditioned psychogalvanic response (14). In all three experiments a conditioned stimulus was followed by the unconditioned stimulus 100 per cent of the time in one group, whereas in a second group, the conditioned stimulus was followed by the unconditioned stimulus only 50 per cent of the time, in a predetermined but unpredictable order (though never with more than two reinforced or two non-reinforced trials in succession).* In each experiment Humphreys found that the 50-per cent-reinforcement group showed reliably greater resistance to extinction than did the 100-per cent-reinforcement group.

Discarding Hull's 'excitatory potential' concept (10), Skinner's 'reflex reserve' theory (28), and Hovland's hypothesis of 'extinction of reinforcement' (8) as inadequate to account for his findings, Humphreys has put forward the alternative suggestion that "conditioned responses are a consequence of anticipated reinforcement, extinction [a consequence] of anticipated nonreinforcement and that the role of frequency in the repetition of reinforcement and nonreinforcement is by way of its influence on the subject's expectation of the stimuli which are to appear" (12, p. 150). Elsewhere, Humphreys says that the fact that discontinuous reinforcement produces greater resistance to extinction than does continuous reinforcement is "apparently due to difficulty in forming an hypothesis of continuous non-reinforcement after discontinuous reinforcement in acquisition" (14, p. 74).

More recent investigations by Humphreys (15) and Finger (5, 6), with rats as Ss, have likewise shown greater resistance to extinction after discontinuous than after continuous reinforcement. But Brown† has questioned whether Humphreys' 'expectation' hypothesis is scientifically meaningful at the infra-human level and has proposed an alternative interpretation. Brown suggests that an understanding of the results obtained with

---

* For Pavlov and many of his followers, the establishment of conditioned responses was assumed to involve nothing more than the paired presentation of the conditioned and the unconditioned stimulus. But it is now clear that even in avoidance conditioning of the kind employed in Humphreys' three experiments, the learning that occurs is subject to the same principles as control trial-and-error learning, where drive and reward play such an unmistakable role (18, 19, 22). Therefore, whenever we use the term 'reinforcement' we assume it to imply reward (drive reduction), even though it be in describing experiments in which the experimenter thought of reinforcement in purely Pavlovian (associationistic) terms.

† Dr. Judson S. Brown—personal communication.

intermittent reinforcement hinges on the definition of the word 'response.' Let us suppose that a hungry animal has been trained with intermittent reinforcement to press a bar as a means of obtaining food, i.e., has sometimes been rewarded after pressing the bar once, sometimes after pressing it twice, sometimes after pressing it three times. The 'response' which is thus effective in securing food consists, therefore, sometimes of one, sometimes of two, sometimes of three individual bar depressions. During extinction, animals trained to depress the bar more than once as a means of getting food might, consequently, be expected to depress the bar more times *but not necessarily to make more 'responses' as thus defined* than animals which, having been rewarded consistently rather than intermittently, have learned exclusively a 'response' consisting of *only one* depression of the bar. In other words, Brown's suggestion is that we may have been deceiving ourselves in this type of situation by equating the term 'response' to single bar depressions instead of interpreting it to mean the total sequence, or *pattern*, of behavior leading up to the reward.*

The foregoing considerations raise the following specific question: If one uses as the unit for measuring resistance to extinction the same pattern of behavior which served as the instrumental 'response,' or 'act,' during acquisition, will intermittent reinforcement still produce greater habit strength than does reinforcement that is continuous?

In order to answer this question it seemed desirable to carry out an experiment involving one group of rats in which reward would follow each bar depression, three groups whose response pattern, or unit, would always consist, respectively, of two, three, or four depressions of the bar, and a final group which would be rewarded not only discontinuously but also randomly, on the average after every two and one-half bar depressions.

The reason for this particular combination of groups is that prior experiments on intermittency of reinforcement have been to some extent confounded: groups of Ss which have been rewarded continuously and, necessarily, regularly have been compared with groups which have been rewarded discontinuously *and irregularly*. This confounding leaves open the question whether the obtained results are due to one, the other, or both of these factors. In our experiment, Group I is rewarded regularly and continuously, Groups II, III, and IV are rewarded regularly but discontinuously, and Group V is rewarded discontinuously and irregularly. In this way we have a combination of groups which makes possible all the comparisons necessary to determine whether it is to discontinuity, irregularity, or both that the phenomenon in question is attributable.†

* *Cf.* Murray's (24) similar emphasis upon the distinction between what he terms 'actones' and 'acts.'

† We are indebted to Mr. John L. Wallin for useful suggestions concerning the logic and design of this experiment.

APPARATUS

The apparatus used in this experiment has been fully described elsewhere (21). It consists, essentially, of a wooden box, approximately one foot square, with a glass front and a wire-mesh floor. Originally there were two ¼-in. brass rods which extended horizontally into the box on either side of the food trough, which was located in the center of the interior rear wall; but for the purposes of this experiment, only the bar on the right was used.

In order to avoid differential auditory cues following bar depressions which were and were not to produce food, the automatic delivery mechanism employed in earlier experiments was disconnected and the food (a small, cylindrical pellet of Purina dog chow) was manually released by E from the rear of the apparatus into the chute-like trough. However, the criterion as to when the bar had been pushed down sufficiently far to count as a full depression was standardized by a system of electrical contacts and a relay which caused a small light to flash on in E's (but not in the rat's) field of vision whenever the bar was depressed by a predetermined amount. This electrical set-up was also arranged so that each flash of the light signified a full excursion of the bar, i.e., the bar could not be depressed until the light came on and then 'jiggled' as a means of making multiple flashes of light. Once the light had come on, it would stay on until the bar was released and allowed to return to its normal position; only by means of another complete depression of the bar could the light be made to come on again.

A cumulative work recorder, which has also been separately described (20), was connected to the apparatus so that each time the light flashed, a small increment of change was registered. Records thus obtained will be reproduced on a later page.

The reasons for arranging the apparatus so that only complete, discrete bar depressions would cause the light to flash and the recorder to operate are obvious, but the precautions taken to eliminate differential cues require a word of explanation. It was felt that if bar depressions which produced food resulted in a sound (due to the automatic delivery mechanism) which was noticeably different from the sound accompanying depressions which did not produce food, the animals would simply learn to go to the bar and pump away until they got the auditory cue signifying the reward. Similarly, in extinction there would have been a tendency to keep pushing the bar until the tell-tale sound occurred. It therefore seemed desirable to circumvent the entire problem by simply eliminating all differential cues. By releasing the pellet manually, it was possible to make the accompanying sound almost imperceptible; and by withholding the pellet until the animal came and looked in the trough, we prevented even this slight noise from serving as a cue as to whether any given bar depression would or would not be followed by food. The only way an animal could 'know' when he had pushed the bar enough, without actually going and looking in the trough, was on the basis of his own kinaesthesis.*

PROCEDURE

*Habituation and acquisition.* Thirty Lashley-strain male rats (four months old) were reduced and held for the duration of this investigation to 15 per cent below normal body weight. At the outset of the experiment, each animal was given 20 pellets of food in the apparatus for purposes of habituation. On the first training day, the bar (requiring a minimum pull of five grams to depress it) was inserted into the apparatus, and the animals were required to push it in order to obtain the food. Each animal was given 20 trials. This same procedure was repeated on the second and third days. On the fourth day the animals made the first five responses with the bar requiring a downward pull of five grams as usual, but for the next five responses the bar was weighted so as to require a pull of 15 gm., and on the final 10 responses the bar required a pull of 30 gm. During the remainder of the experiment the bar was kept weighted so as to require this latter amount of downward pressure to operate it.†

On the fifth day, after the preliminary training just described, the animals were randomly divided into five groups. The animals in Group I were rewarded after every bar depression, those in Group II after every second bar depression, those in Group III after every third, those in Group IV after every fourth, and those in Group V in random order, after one, two, three, or four bar depressions but, on the average, after two and one-half. These different procedures were followed from the fifth through the eleventh day, the animals in each group being given 20 reinforcements (pellets) daily, as on days one to four. By the end of the eleventh day each animal had thus received 220 reinforcements, the first 80 of which had been received under the same preliminary conditions for all groups, and the last 140 under conditions which were distinctive for each group.

*Extinction.* Extinction began on the 12th day and continued through the

* Earlier unpublished research indicates that rats can learn to discriminate between one and two bar depressions and between two and three, but beyond this their discrimination becomes unreliable. In the present experiment, multiple bar depressions often occurred between inspections of the food trough, but the more usual procedure in all groups was to press, look; press, look; etc.

† The bar was made easy to depress during the early phase of training and reward was provided after each response in order to get the bar-pressing habit established more quickly and more reliably than would have been possible if the various conditions employed in the later part of the experiment had existed from the beginning. Our reason for increasing the effort required to depress the bar on the fourth day of training was that we wanted this act to be the major element in the total sequence of behavior involved in going back and forth between the bar and the trough, eating the food, etc.

13th and 14th days. The animals were left in the apparatus for 20 min. on each of these days, free to press the bar at will but given no food whatever. (Outside the experimental situation, they received enough food to keep them at the standard body weight mentioned previously.) The number of bar depressions made during this period was counted by the observer and recorded automatically.

## RESULTS AND INTERPRETATIONS

Groups I, II, III, and IV will be discussed first, inasmuch as the problem investigated with the animals comprising these four groups is that of the effect of continuous reinforcement (Group I) vs. discontinuous, or intermittent, reinforcement (Groups II, III, and IV). Group V poses the separate question of the importance of irregularity, or randomness, as opposed to regularity of reinforcement (Groups I–IV).

### CONTINUOUS VS. DISCONTINUOUS REINFORCEMENT

Table I gives the average number of bar depressions made by Groups I, II, III, and IV during the three days of extinction. Fig. 1 shows the actual extinction performances on Day I and Day III of typical animals in Groups I and IV. These records for individual animals give a graphic equivalent of the corresponding group averages appearing in the four corners of Table I. From Table I it is evident (*a*) that all groups made progressively fewer bar depressions on the three days of extinction and (*b*) that the animals in Groups I to IV made progressively more bar depressions on each of the three days of extinction, as well as for the three extinction days considered as a whole (see Totals). From Fig. 1 it is further evident (*c*) that, as has repeatedly been noted by other investi-

## TABLE I

AVERAGE NUMBER OF BAR DEPRESSIONS MADE ON THREE SUCCESSIVE DAYS OF EXTINCTION BY GROUPS I, II, III, AND IV

The bottom line (Totals) gives the average number of bar depressions made by each group during all three extinction days.

| Extinction | Groups | | | |
| Days | I | II | III | IV |
|---|---|---|---|---|
| I | 77.4 | 105.5 | 113.8 | 155.1 |
| II | 34.8 | 60.5 | 74.3 | 75.0 |
| III | 15.8 | 22.0 | 27.4 | 42.2 |
| Totals .... | 128.0 | 188.0 | 215.5 | 272.3 |

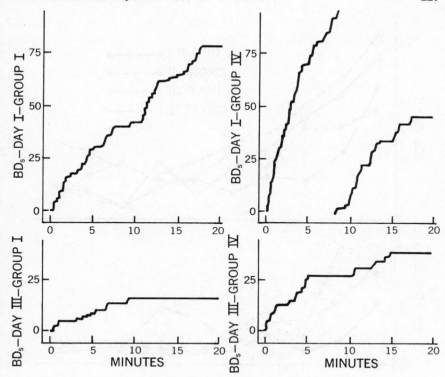

Fig. 1. Graphic recordings of the performance of a typical animal in Group I and a typical animal in Group IV on Day I and Day III of extinction. These four individual recordings, representing 79, 16, 143, and 38 bar depressions (BDs) respectively, correspond to the group averages appearing in the four corners of Table I. The two curves in the upper right-hand recording should be thought of as continuous (*cf.* 20).

gators (7, 11), the rate of bar-pressing activity was greatest at the beginning of each extinction session and was thereafter negatively accelerated.

The three sets of curves appearing in Fig. 2 present these same data in a somewhat different manner. They represent the average number of bar-depressions made by each of the four groups, by two-min. periods, during each of the three 20-min. extinction sessions. The three trends mentioned in the preceding paragraph are again evident in Fig. 2.

The relationship between resistance to extinction and the reinforcement ratio used during acquisition becomes especially clear in Fig. 3. The broken line shows (*cf.* Totals in Table I) the average number of bar depressions made during all three extinction days by the animals in Groups I, II, III, and IV. This number was 128.0 for Group I, 188.0 for Group II, 215.5 for Group III, and 272.3 for Group IV. An analysis of variance gives an $F$ of 7.18 for the differences between these groups due

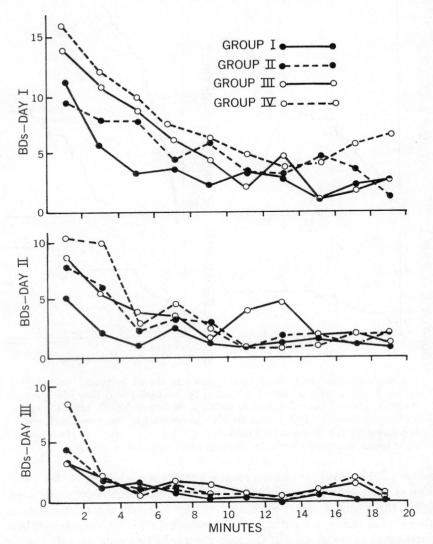

Fig. 2. Curves showing the average number of bar depressions (BDs) made by Groups I-IV on the three days of extinction. Each point on the curves represents the average number of bar depressions made in a two-min. interval.

to frequency of reinforcement, an $F$ of only 4.43 being necessary for significance at the .01 level. The $t$-test shows significant differences at the .02 level or better between the mean of Group I and the means of all other groups and between the means of Groups II and IV.

From these results it would appear, in keeping with earlier findings,

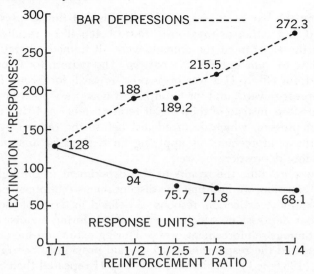

FIG. 3. Curves showing the average number of bar depressions as contrasted with response-units made by Groups I-IV (reinforcement ratio of 1/1 to 1/4) on all three days of extinction.

that not only is intermittent reinforcement reliably more effective than continuous reinforcement in establishing a tendency to depress the bar in the absence of reinforcement; it may also be said that, within the limits of this experiment, the functional relationship between these two variables is virtually linear.

Since the animals in Group I were rewarded during acquisition every time they pressed the bar, whereas the animals in Groups II, III, and IV received reinforcement only one-half, one-third, and one-fourth as often— and yet developed progressively greater apparent habit strength, as measured by resistance to extinction, it is easy to see how results of this kind might indeed seem incompatible with the assumption that every rewarded repetition of a habit strengthens it and non-rewarded repetitions weaken it. There are, however, at least two ways in which this paradox may be explained, well within the framework of effect learning theory.

*The response-unit hypothesis.* The first of these explanations has already been suggested. Various studies (7, 11) have shown that the reinforcing effects of reward apply not only to the immediately preceding behavior but also, to a diminishing extent, to the behavior which is temporarily more remote from the advent of reward. According to this principle (the 'gradient of reinforcement'), we know that under the conditions of the present experiment it was possible for an animal to be somewhat reinforced for pressing the bar even when this behavior did not immediately produce food. Thus, because an animal was, for example, rewarded only after pressing the bar twice, we should not think of this as press-failure, press-reward, but rather as press-press-reward. It will be recalled that in this part of the experiment the animals were all trained, after the fourth day, according to some one definite pattern. The pattern for Group I was press-reward; for Group II it was press-press-reward; for Group III it was press-press-press-reward; and for Group IV it was press-press-press-press-reward. Therefore, instead of thinking of reinforcement as being restricted to the bar depression which occurred just before the reward, we should rather see the reinforcement as applying, in decreasing amount, to the other preceding depressions as well.

If we now reëxamine the results of this experiment in the light of the preceding discussion, we find that the discontinuous-reinforcement groups did *not* make more extinction 'responses,' defined in terms of the pattern, or unit, of bar depressions which was rewarded during acquisition, than did the continuous-reinforcement group. During extinction the animals in Group I repeated the response-unit which had previously been rewarded 128.0 times (128.0 ÷ 1), the animals in Group II repeated their response-unit 94.0 times (188.0 ÷ 2), those in Group III, 71.8 times (215.5 ÷ 3), and those in Group IV 68.1 times (272.3 ÷ 4). By thus using as a definition of 'habit,' or 'response,' the total unit of bar depressions which was re-warded in each of the four groups of animals during acquisition, we find that the apparent advantage of so-called intermittent reinforcement dis-appears (see solid line, Fig. 2). The hypothesis that rewarded repetitions of a habit (so defined) strengthen it is, therefore, still tenable.*

A subsidiary problem remains, however. Since we are proceeding on the assumption that every rewarded repetition of a habit (defined as the total response-unit, or instrumental act) strengthens it, and since each of the groups of Ss in the present experiment made the same number of re-warded response-units during acquisition, each group might have been expected to make approximately the same number of response-units dur-ing extinction. But as Fig. 2 indicates, the average number of extinction response-units becomes progressively smaller as we go from Group I to Group IV, being 128.0, 94.0, 71.8, and 68.0, respectively. The *t*-value for

---

* Sears (27) has recently commented on the difficulty involved in precisely defining the term 'instrumental act' and has to a considerable extent anticipated the above analysis by pointing out that "all activity preceding the goal response appears to come under this heading and to undergo reinforcement. If a given *movement* must be per-formed twice before the goal is reached, then the *pair* of movements becomes the instrumental act to the goal response. If later, these acts are repeatedly performed without any reward occurring, it is to be expected that more *single* movements would occur during the extinction process if a *pair* of movements was the unit that had originally been reinforced than if a *single* movement had been the unit" (p. 84). Skinner (28) has similarly remarked: "This is fundamentally a problem in the defi-nition of a unit of behavior. As a rather general statement it may be said that when a reinforcement depends upon the completion of a number of similar acts, the whole group tends to acquire the status of a single response, and the contribution of the reserve tends to be in terms of groups" (p. 300).

the differences between the mean thus obtained for Group I and the means of the other three groups and between the mean for Group II and that for Group IV all show significance at the .05 level or better, thereby indicating that the downward slope of the solid line in Fig. 2 is statistically reliable and scientifically meaningful.

In a previous paper (21) we have shown that if a response requires more effort to perform, it will extinguish more quickly than if it requires less effort. Obviously, a response-unit consisting of four bar depressions requires more effort than a response-unit of only one depression. It is not surprising, therefore, that the former extinguishes more rapidly than the latter.

Equally plausible is an explanation based on the fact that even though all of the bar depressions involved in a response-unit of four depressions receive some reinforcement, they do not receive the same amount, since the one nearest the reward gets most, the one preceding somewhat less, the one preceding that one still less, and the original one in the series least of all.* On the other hand, if the response-unit consists of only one bar depression, it always receives the same, maximal amount of reinforcement (provided that the animal goes immediately to the trough and eats the food). Therefore, although the behavior involved in pressing the bar will be considerably more reinforced in Group IV than in Group I, it will not be reinforced *four times* as much. Consequently, when the behavior which occurs during extinction is analyzed in terms of response-units, Group I will necessarily rank highest, with Groups II, III, and IV following in order.

Whether one or both of the two mechanisms just described—greater effortfulness of multiple than of single bar-depressions, or the greater average but smaller total reinforcement received by single than by multiple depressions—were actually involved in producing the downward slope of the solid line in Fig. 3, is a question which cannot be answered on the basis of our present data.

*The discrimination hypothesis.* The second way of explaining the results obtained with intermittent reinforcement depends upon the concept of discrimination, or sign-learning. Let us, for the moment, disregard the immediately preceding analysis in terms of response-units. Viewing the continuous- and discontinuous-reinforcement procedures afresh, we see that the animals in Group IV, for example, had no means of differentiating so sharply between the acquisition situation and the extinction situation as did the animals in Group I. For the Group I animals, the act of pressing the bar had always 'meant' that food would follow, i.e., during acquisition

---

* Hull (11) has recently reported evidence that in order for a response on the part of a rat to be reinforced by a subsequent reward it must occur within 30 sec. of that event. In the present investigation, all of the bar depressions comprising a response-unit often occurred within a 30-sec. period (even in Group IV), but this was not always the case. (This statement is based on general observation; we have no systematic data.)

the kinaesthetic and other stimuli which accompanied the performance of this movement became conditioned to the responses involved in turning from the bar to the trough and consuming the food. On the other hand, in the case of the Group IV animals the kinaesthetic and other stimuli accompanying bar depression were ambiguous, since they were sometimes followed by eating responses and sometimes by pressing the bar again, once again, and still again. Therefore, with the onset of extinction, when food did not follow the first, second, or even third depression of the bar, the situation was not yet any different, psychologically, from what it had been during acquisition. Only after at least four bar depressions had occurred and not been followed by food did the 'meaning' of the situation begin to change for the Group IV rats and then probably only very slowly. One would accordingly expect that the tendency to press the bar would wane much less quickly in the discontinuous- than in the continuous-reinforcement groups.

We suspect that this explanation is essentially what Humphreys had in mind in speaking of the greater difficulty which Ss who have been trained with discontinuous reinforcement have in changing from an 'expectation,' or 'hypothesis,' of reinforcement to one of non-reinforcement than do subjects who have been trained with continuous reinforcement. Our alternative statement merely attempts to make explicit some of the intermediate steps which were apparently implicit in Humphreys' reasoning.

The plausibility of the foregoing interpretation is increased by the observation, reported by Pavlov (25) and confirmed by others, that in learning experiments in which Ss are continuously reinforced, extinguished, retrained, reëxtinguished, etc., extinction and re-learning both take place with increasing speed. This finding suggests that the receiving of the reward has psychological implications over and beyond the automatic action of the Law of Effect. It suggests that the absence of reward, on the first trial of successive extinctions, may come to signify to the S that further response is, at least for the time being, futile, i.e., the stimuli associated with the absence of reward become conditioned to resting instead of working, just as the presence of reward, on the first trial during successive re-learning periods, may come to signify to the S that the opposite situation now prevails.* Thus, in an experiment in which hunger is the principal drive, the S learns to discriminate sharply between two total patterns: hunger-(and-fatigue)-plus-stimuli-associated-with-getting-food and hun-

---

* Cook and Harris (3), Cole (4), and Mowrer (17) have shown that it is possible to produce almost instantaneous 'extinction' and 're-learning' of involuntary conditioned responses in human Ss by means of signals or verbal instruction to the Ss indicating changes in experimental conditions. All these investigators used avoidance rather than appetitive conditioning, which probably means that they were simply manipulating the secondary motive of fear symbolically instead of requiring their Ss to build up their own inductive generalizations, or 'hypotheses.' Cf. Krechevsky (16) and Brunswik (2) for a discussion of this problem as it relates to the behavior of rats.

ger-(and-fatigue)-plus-stimuli-associated-with-*not*-getting-food. To the first configuration the S learns to make food-seeking responses; to the second configuration the S learns to make resting responses.*

It is obvious that if reinforcement is discontinuous during acquisition, acquisition will be harder to discriminate from extinction (ergo, greater 'resistance to extinction') than if reinforcement has been continuous. And not only would we expect to encounter this type of confusion on the first transition from acquisition to extinction; if, as in Pavlov's experiment, we passed a number of times from the one condition to the other, we should expect less rapid discriminative learning where acquisition involved discontinuous reinforcement than where it involved continuous reinforcement.

This type of analysis turns out to have an unsuspected advantage: it suggests why it is that in previous experiments on continuous vs. discontinuous reinforcement, there has been the confounding, already noted, of the continuity-discontinuity factor with the regularity-irregularity factor. The research in this field was started by Humphreys, using college students as subjects.† Knowing that such Ss can *count*, he may have antici-

---

* In acknowledging the 'sign-function' of success and failure, one does not need to repudiate the Law of Effect, as Tolman, Hall, and Bretnall (29), for example, suggest. It would appear that we are dealing here with a mechanism which often supplements and on occasion even supersedes simple law-of-effect learning, but this is no proof that the latter is not a perfectly valid phenomenon. Our guess is that in those situations in which one non-rewarded repetition of a response (or a signal of some kind—see footnote on p. 232) causes a sudden cessation ('extinction') of response what happens is that a strong *emotion* (anticipation of many non-rewarded, futile performances of the response) is aroused which serves to counteract the habit strength, or response tendency, built up by the preceding rewarded repetitions of the response. Likewise, a single rewarded repetition of a response (or a signal from the experimenter—see footnote) may likewise serve as a kind of all-clear sign which removes the depressing effect of many antecedent non-rewarded repetitions of a response (or of an earlier signal from the experimenter) and thus releases the tendency to make the response in question. Or it may be that a single success or some other sign that reward will now follow if responses are resumed may serve, not merely to banish 'discouragement' but also to arouse an emotion of 'hope' which suddenly energizes the response tendency. Thus a single success or failure (or a signal or word with the same implications) may cause an abrupt change in behavior of the kind that has often been accepted as proof of 'insight,' 'change in hypothesis,' or 'alteration in cognitive structure' and as disproof of the Law of Effect. In our judgment this is not a real antithesis and should not cause the cleavage which exists today between those learning theorists who stress the role of effect and those who stress so-called cognition. What we are suggesting is that *emotion* is the key to the controversy and may enable us to build up a more unified structure of behavior theory, from the lower to the higher levels of complexity, than now exists. The present hypothesis would seem to have especially promising applications to discrimination learning and in resolving such paradoxes as Hull (11) has recently pointed out in connection with 'patterning.' It may also be useful in more correctly interpreting 'latent learning.'

† Skinner's work (28) on discontinuity of reinforcement with rats actually antedates that of Humphreys, but it was only with the publication of Humphreys' findings that general interest in this problem was stimulated. Brogden (1), Cole (4), and Brunswik (2) have also published data on the effects of intermittent reinforcement, showing that, in general, acquisition of a given habit occurs more slowly with intermittent than with continuous reinforcement (*cf.* also Finger, 5). Of these three writers Cole alone was

pated that the effects of discontinuity could be demonstrated only if he made the reinforcement procedure not only discontinuous, but also irregular, since, by counting, a human being can detect a change from an acquisition to an extinction situation quite as accurately if the reinforcement has been discontinuous as if it has been continuous, provided the reinforcement has been regular. In other words, for a human being who, during discontinuous but regular reinforcement, makes each unrewarded trial distinctive by performing the 'pure stimulus act' (Hull, 9) of saying, 'One,' 'Two,' 'Three,' etc., failure of reward to follow, for example, a fourth trial after three non-rewarded ones can be just as significant as the occurrence of a single non-rewarded trial following continuous reinforcement.

As Reiss (26) has pointed out, the rudimentary function of counting is to make possible the same sharpness of discrimination between 10 and 11, or 100 and 101 otherwise identical, successive events (reactions) as between 0 and 1 or 1 and 2 such events. With such precision of discrimination possible by means of counting, it is questionable whether the Humphreys' effect can be demonstrated in educated human Ss with discontinuous but regular reinforcement.

## REGULAR VS. IRREGULAR REINFORCEMENT

The foregoing discussion provides a convenient setting for the description of the results obtained from our Group V animals, which, it will be recalled, received reinforcement both intermittently and randomly, but on the average after every two and one-half depressions of the bar. These animals depressed the bar a mean number of 189.2 times during the three days of extinction. The point corresponding to this value has been indicated in Fig. 3. Dividing 189.2 by 2.5 (the figure comparable to the response-units of the other four groups), we find that the Group-V animals made 75.5 repetitions of their hypothetical average response-unit. The point corresponding to this value has likewise been indicated in Fig. 3.

From these results it is evident that the greater resistance to extinction obtained in this experiment following discontinuous (Groups II, III, and IV) than continuous (Group I) reinforcement is probably in no way contingent upon the factor of irregularity of reinforcement. In fact, as a glance at Fig. 3 will indicate, our Group V animals depressed the bar actually somewhat less frequently during extinction than would have been expected from interpolation on the curve representing the performances of the regular reinforcement groups (I, II, III, and IV).

Unfortunately, there is no way of determining whether the obtained

---

interested in the possible effects of intermittent reinforcement on resistance to extinction and he only incidentally. Insofar as his results can be compared to those of Humphreys and Finger they are, however, confirmatory.

downward deviation of the Group V results is due to the factor of irregularity or to factors which the experimenters did not attempt to control, i.e., 'chance.' If the Group V animals had been irregularly rewarded after pushing the bar either two or three times, on the average, instead of 2.5 times, their extinction scores would then have been directly comparable, statistically, to those for the Group-II or the Group-III animals.

That this procedure was not followed is now a patent defect in the design of the experiment. However, from a common-sense standpoint, our results indicate clearly enough that, for rats at least, it is discontinuity of reinforcement, rather than irregularity, that accounts for the greater resistance to extinction resulting from a training procedure involving both discontinuity and irregularity of reinforcement. Therefore, the confounding of the discontinuity and irregularity factors which has been noted in previous studies is probably unimportant and was even necessary if this phenomenon was to be demonstrated in human Ss, due to the latter's tendency to count and thereby render discontinuous and continuous reinforcement much more nearly equivalent, psychologically, than they otherwise would be.

## OTHER IMPLICATIONS

As we have seen, there are two about equally plausible ways in which the Humphreys effect can be accounted for: by the 'response-unit hypothesis' and by the 'discrimination hypothesis.' Naturally the question arises as to which of these is the more valid, and experiments can probably be devised (though not easily) which would throw light on this problem.* However, in situations of this kind we fall perhaps too easily into the practice of taking an either-or attitude, of assuming that where two or more mechanisms may account for a given result one must ultimately prove significant and the other not. Actually we know that in all but the most excessively simplified types of psychological situations the observed outcome is nearly always 'over-determined,' i.e., is a product of multiple processes acting, and interacting, simultaneously. It may well be, therefore, that both of the explanations advanced above to account for the Humphreys effect are valid.

One other implication of research on continuous vs. discontinuous rein-

* The response-unit and the discrimination hypothesis are designed to account for the greater resistance to extinction (in the sense of more "work" done) following discontinuous than continuous reinforcement. They make no assumption concerning the effect of regular vs. irregular reinforcement. That the findings of this investigation indicate that, in rats at least, the factor of regularity-irregularity is of little or no importance in this connection may have implications for the relative validity of these two hypotheses, but if so these implications are so subtle as to be obscure to the present writers.

forcement in relation to 'resistance to extinction' should be noted. In an experiment reported by Whiting and Mowrer (30), it has been discovered that when rats, previously punished for taking the shorter route to the goal on a D-shaped maze, found that the punishment (an electric shock) was no longer in force, they precipitously reverted to this route. This behavior was contrasted with the behavior of human beings, who often show life-long tendencies to refrain from doing certain things they have been taught to regard as 'wrong' even though the external sanctions originally used to set up such attitudes have long since disappeared.*

This difference between the behavior of rats and human beings raises the question as to what it is about the education, or 'socialization,' of the latter that creates conscience, character. The psychology of conscience is undoubtedly exceedingly complicated, but one consideration seems obvious: in the experiment reported by Whiting and Mowrer, the rats discovered that the punishment always occurred at a certain point along the shorter route to the goal. If they got past this point, they were safe and had no reason to feel 'guilty.' In learning to run the 'social maze' which parents and others set for them, children, on the other hand, discover at an early age that punishments, even though indefinitely delayed, may still be forthcoming; and certainly parents are likely to foster the impression on the part of their offspring that their 'sins' must ultimately be found out and that retribution will surely follow.

Thus it is that at least part of that kind of conscience which is based on fear is probably set up. But if conscience is an institution whereby the individual punishes himself (i.e., his conscience 'hurts' him) for acts, contemplated as well as actually performed, which are likely to bring external disapproval, so is there a comparable mechanism, based on hope and faith, which makes for perseverance in the face of adversity, in a word, 'morale.' Very small children display both the moral and the morale aspects of conscience in only incipient amounts, and much of their 'character training' consists of attempts to bring about development along these lines. As part of such a program they are commonly encouraged to keep plugging away

---

* Whether the originally (usual parental) sanctions become 'introjected' and form a permanent part of the personality ('super-ego') needing no further reinforcement from the external world or are subtly strengthened periodically by other (community) sanctions is one of the important and difficult psychological problems of our time. It is perhaps the central point of issue between Freudian psychoanalysis, with its emphasis upon the past (childhood), and the followers of Karen Horney and members of the Washington ('inter-personal relations') School of Psychiatry, for whom the current life situation of the individual is of greatest importance. This problem is also related to the question as to whether emotions (attitudes) are 'autonomous' (Allport) or require at least occasional reinforcement, like any other learned response. Professor F. J. Shaw (personal correspondence) has remarked, "We still face the problem of the apparent resistance of the anxiety state itself to extinction. This strikes me as a rather difficult problem for reinforcement theory whereas Guthrie's theory might have less difficulty with this particular problem."

if they do not immediately reach their (legitimate) goals and are admonished, when confronted by failure, to 'try, try again.'

Even in the course of ordinary events, children learn to carry out long sequences of action where the reward is so remote that in the beginning it can sustain endeavor for only a short time. Thus, a small child, though capable of endless activity at home, will quickly report being 'tired' if taken for a walk. But it is almost certainly not so much fatigue as it is 'extinction,' or 'loss of interest,' that is responsible for his lagging steps. He puts one foot forward, then the other, then the one, then the other, etc., etc., and nothing happens. Only gradually, with encouragement from his elders and periodic indulgences—a look at the train here, an ice cream or candy there—does the child get so he can, at the age of five or six, set out on a long walk with only a single destination or objective in mind. His 'resistance to extinction' has increased, in a manner probably not fundamentally different from that used in producing the Humphreys effect. By requiring rats to push a bar at first only a few times for a piece of food, then a larger and a larger number of times, Skinner (28) was able to get them eventually to make 192 responses for a single piece of food, and there was no indication that this number necessarily represented the limit of which the rat was capable. Did these rats have 'morale'? They certainly had 'hope,' 'faith.'

Somewhere between fear and faith—the pivotal concepts of most religions—lies the truth about conscience. Any improvement in our understanding of how they work is a contribution to the psychology of character, and character defects. Here, it would seem, is a most promising point of articulation between scientific learning theory and education, ethics, psychotherapy, and other practical problems of both a social and individual nature.

## Summary

In this paper an attempt is made to show that the Humphreys paradox—that habitual responses which are rewarded only intermittently are apparently stronger than those which are rewarded after each occurrence—does not invalidate the Law of Effect. Experimental results are reported which confirm Humphreys' empirical findings but which can be explained either by the 'response-unit hypothesis' or by the 'discrimination hypothesis,' both of which are consistent with the view that reward is the fundamental and crucial determinant of habit strength.

The response-unit hypothesis defines a 'response,' not as a single, isolated movement, but as the totality of behavior which leads to a given goal. For example, the fact that a rat has to press a bar three times in order to get a pellet of food does not mean that three separate acts, or 'responses,' have been performed; the sequence of three bar depressions is here conceived as a unitary, integrated, instrumental performance. When 'response' is thus re-defined in terms of the whole pattern of behavior which proves effective in producing reward during acquisition, the Humphreys paradox disappears. When 'response' is thus re-defined, it is found that intermittent reinforcement, far from producing greater 'habit strength,' actually produces reliably less than does continuous reinforcement.

But there is another equally plausible approach to this problem. If, during acquisition, a response (conceived as a more or less isolated movement) occurs repeatedly but is rewarded only now and then, the transition from acquisition to extinction will not be discriminated as sharply as if acquisition has involved reward for each and every response. With 'faith' thus established that failure will ultimately be followed by success, 'discouragement' is slower to set in (ergo, greater 'resistance to extinction') when there is a change in objective conditions from acquisition (occasional reward) to extinction (no reward whatever).

This second interpretation involves the introduction of *intervening variables* ('faith,' 'discouragement'), factors which disrupt the direct, one-to-one relationship observed in the simplest kinds of situations (and subjects) between reward and behavior. Here we are approaching the realm of 'ego psychology,' but it should not be supposed that there is any discontinuity between the fundamental laws of learning that can be so easily demonstrated at the lower levels of behavior and the generalizations that seem to hold best at the higher levels. The intervening variables which operate at the higher levels and which complicate the simple relationships observed at the lower levels between reward and the behavior-changes which we call learning are themselves products of former learning—i.e., 'emotions,' 'secondary drives,' 'expectations,' 'attitudes,' 'sentiments,' 'conscience.'*

Here we are dealing with a distinction similar to the one which Murray (24) has made between *viscerogenetic needs* and *psychogenic needs*. And when there are psychogenic needs (secondary drives) operating within an organism, we do not expect the viscerogenetic needs (primary drives) to produce the same results as when psychogenetic needs are absent. When these two types of 'needs,' or drives, come into opposition, there will necessarily be *conflict* (sometimes 'character'); and we know that the outcome is rarely a matter of simple algebraic summation (23). The various 'dynamisms' (Freud), or 'self-systems' (Sullivan), go into action, with the end-

---

* We do not overlook the fact that 'thoughts' and 'ideas' are also important intervening variables, but the intra-psychic use of symbols is so intimately tied up with emotions that in stressing the latter we are necessarily subsuming the former. It is a common form of human vanity to make thoughts a 'higher' and emotions a 'lower' mental process, but from a dynamic standpoint, the emotions are both genetically and energetically basic. Emotions supply the rudiments of 'reason' and remain its driving force no matter how refined or elaborated it becomes (23).

lessly complicated results which we see clinically (as well as in the 'experimental neuroses' of animals) and even in ordinary, 'normal' human behavior.

## REFERENCES

1. BROGDEN, W. J. (1939) The effect of frequency of reinforcement upon the level of conditioning. *J. exp. Psychol.*, *24*, 419-431.
2. BRUNSWIK, E. (1939) Probability as a determiner of rat behavior. *J. exp. Psychol.*, *25*, 175-197.
3. COOK, S. W. and HARRIS, R. E. (1937) The verbal conditioning of the galvanic skin reflex. *J. exp. Psychol.*, *21*, 202-210.
4. COLE, L. E. (1939) A comparison of the factors of practice and knowledge of experimental procedure in conditioning the eyelid response of human subjects. *J. gen. Psychol.*, *20*, 349-373.
5. FINGER, F. W. (1942) The effect of varying conditions of reinforcement upon a simple running response. *J. exp. Psychol.*, *30*, 53-68.
6. FINGER, F. W. (1942) Retention and subsequent extinction of a simple running response following varying conditions of reinforcement. *J. exp. Psychol.*, *31*, 120-134.
7. HILGARD, E. R. and MARQUIS, D. G. (1940) *Conditioning and learning.* New York: D. Appleton-Century Co.
8. HOVLAND, C. I. (1936) 'Inhibition of reinforcement' and phenomena of experimental extinction. *Proc. nat. Acad. Sci.* (Washington), *22*, 430-433.
9. HULL, C. L. (1930) Knowledge and purpose as habit mechanisms. *Psychol. Rev.*, *37*, 511-525.
10. HULL, C. L. (1938) The excitatory-potential hypothesis and behavior theory. On file in Institute of Human Relations, Yale Univ.
11. HULL, C. L. (1943) *Principles of behavior.* New York: D. Appleton-Century Co.
12. HUMPHREYS, L. G. (1939) The effect of random alternation of reinforcement on the acquisition and extinction of conditioned eyelid reactions. *J. exp. Psychol.*, *25*, 141-158.
13. HUMPHREYS, L. G. (1939) Acquisition and extinction of verbal expectations in a situation analogous to conditioning. *J. exp. Psychol.*, *25*, 294-301.
14. HUMPHREYS, L. G. (1940) Extinction of conditioned psycho-galvanic responses following two conditions of reinforcement. *J. exp. Psychol.*, *27*, 71-76.
15. HUMPHREYS, L. G. (1940) The strength of a Thorndikian response as a function of the number of practice trials. *Psychol. Bull.*, *37*, 571.
16. KRECHEVSKY, I. (1932) Antagonistic verbal discrimination habits in the white rat. *J. comp. Psychol.*, *14*, 263-277.
17. MOWRER, O. H. (1938) Preparatory set (expectancy)—a determinant in motivation and learning. *Psychol. Rev.*, *45*, 62-91.
18. MOWRER, O. H. (1941) Motivation and learning in relation to the National Emergency. *Psychol. Bull.*, *38*, 421-431.
19. MOWRER, O. H. and LAMOREAUX, R. R. (1942) Avoidance conditioning and signal duration—a study of secondary motivation and reward. *Psychol. Monogr.*, *54*, No. 5, 34 pp.

20. MOWRER, O. H. (1943) A cumulative graphic work-recorder. *J. exp. Psychol.*, *33*, 159-163.
21. MOWRER, O. H. and JONES, H. M. (1943) Extinction and behavior variability as functions of effortfulness of task. *J. exp. Psychol.*, *33*, 369-386.
22. MOWRER, O. H. and LAMOREAUX, R. R. Fear as an intervening variable in avoidance conditioning. *J. comp. Psychol.* (in press).
23. MOWRER, O. H. and ULLMAN, A. D. Time as a determinant in integrative learning. *Psychol. Rev.* (in press).
24. MURRAY, H. A. (1938) *Explorations in personality.* London: Oxford Univ. Press.
25. PAVLOV, I. P. (1927) *Conditioned reflexes.* (Trans. and ed. by G. V. Anrep.) London: Oxford Univ. Press.
26. RIESS, A. (1943) An analysis of children's number responses. *Harvard educ. Rev.*, *13*, 149-162.
27. SEARS, R. R. (1943) *Survey of objective studies of psychoanalytic concepts.* New York: Social Science Research Council.
28. SKINNER, B. F. (1938) *The behavior of organisms.* New York: D. Appleton-Century Co.
29. TOLMAN, E. C., HALL, C. S., and BRETNALL, E. P. (1932) A disproof of the law of effect and a substitution of the laws of emphasis, motivation and disruption. *J. exp. Psychol.*, *15*, 601-614.
30. WHITING, J. W. M. and MOWRER, O. H. (1943) Habit progression and regression—a laboratory study of some factors relevant to human socialization. *J. comp. Psychol.*, *36*, 229-253.

# 21. Extinction as a Function of Partial Reinforcement and Distribution of Practice

## V. F. Sheffield

*Like Mowrer and Jones, the author rejects Humphreys' expectancy theory as an explanation for the influence of partial reinforcement on extinction. Her experimental findings lend support to a proposed aftereffects hypothesis.*

### PURPOSE

The purpose of this study was to determine whether distribution of practice influences the effect of partial reinforcement on resistance to ex-

*J. exp. Psychol.*, 1949, 39, 511-526. Reprinted with permission of the author and The American Psychological Association. This article reports part of a dissertation submitted to the faculty of the Department of Psychology of Yale University in partial fulfillment of the requirements for the Ph.D. degree. The writer is indebted to Dr. Neal E. Miller, under whose direction the research was conducted, and to Dr. Clark L. Hull and Dr. Carl I. Hovland, who served on the advisory committee.

tinction. The problem has theoretical significance because of its bearing on a general hypothesis concerning extinction which may explain the finding that partial reinforcement results in greater resistance to extinction than reinforcement on every trial.

For some time it has been recognized that reinforcement on every trial is not essential either for the establishment or for the maintenance of a conditioned response. Pavlov (18) describes an experiment performed in his laboratory in which conditioned salivation in a dog was established with food reinforcement on every other trial and on every third trial. Others (2, 3), while not specifically studying partial reinforcement, have also obtained successful acquisition using partial reinforcement instead of reinforcement on every trial. Also it has been shown (1) that a conditioned response, established with reinforcement on every trial, may be maintained at almost its original level with relatively infrequent reinforcement.

The most striking finding with partial reinforcement, however, is that not only are conditioned responses readily acquired with partial reinforcement, but also they are considerably more resistant to extinction than when reinforcement is given on every trial. For example, Skinner (20), using bar pressing with rats, interspersed reinforcements at regular time intervals ('periodic reconditioning') or after given numbers of responses ('reinforcement at a fixed ratio'). He found that many more responses were required to produce extinction than when reinforcement had been given for each response.

Attention was particularly focused on the phenomenon of increased resistance to extinction following partial reinforcement in an experiment by Humphreys (11) using the conditioned eyelid response in human subjects. Of two groups of subjects, one trained with reinforcement on every trial and one trained with reinforcement 'randomly' on only half the trials, the latter group responded at a significantly higher level throughout extinction. Humphreys (13) later obtained the same result using the conditioned galvanic response in humans.

It has been claimed (8, 11) that the increased resistance to extinction with partial reinforcement challenges the adequacy of stimulus-response learning theory. Humphreys (11) proposed the principle of *expectancy* as an alternative theory. This 'principle' is not rigorously stated and depends on commonsense concepts in its explanation of the results. The 'expectancy' explanation may be paraphrased as follows. Conditioned responses are the consequence of the subject's expectation that reinforcement will appear. In extinction after reinforcement on every trial, the response rapidly disappears because the sudden shift from uniform reinforcement to uniform nonreinforcement makes it easy to change to an expectation of uniform nonreinforcement. But in extinction after partial reinforcement, the subject continues to expect that reinforcement will be periodic as it was during training—extinction is prolonged by his expectation that reinforcement will be reintroduced. This interpretation is contrasted with stimulus-response learning theories, which usually assume, in one form or another, that reinforcement strengthens a conditioned response and nonreinforcement extinguishes it. This suggests that the infrequent reinforcements and the interspersed nonreinforcements which characterize partial reinforcement would produce a weaker response, which would extinguish more rapidly than would be the case with uniform reinforcement.

However, it is believed that ordinary stimulus-response learning concepts, such as those used by Guthrie (7) and Hull (10), can explain the increased resistance to extinction. The present study was designed to test a theoretical interpretation which utilizes only stimulus-response concepts. The interpretation hinges on a hypothesis about a general factor in extinction which is particularly applicable in the case of partial reinforcement.

## THEORY

The basic hypothesis is that extinction necessarily involves different cues from those used during training. Omission of reinforcement alters the context and makes extinction a case of 'transfer of training' in which a certain amount of generalization decrement is expected because of the change in cues. This hypothesis would be applied in explaining the effect of partial reinforcement on extinction as follows. Occurrence of reinforcement on a given trial produces effects which, in varying degree, provide characteristic stimuli at the start of the following trial, these stimuli becoming part of the total stimulus pattern acting at the start of the next trial. When reinforcement is given on every trial, the after-effects of the reinforcement will be part of the conditioned stimulus pattern on every trial after the first. In the present experiment, where rats were trained to run in an alley to food, the after-effects of reinforcement would perhaps include continued food taste and even particles of food in the mouth, temporary relaxation, etc. When extinction is begun, the stimulus pattern is changed not only by the absence of the after-effects of reinforcement, but also by the presence of whatever new stimulation results from the absence of reinforcement, particularly from the subject's reaction to that absence. In the present experiment, the after-effects of nonreinforcement would include such new reactions as searching, conflict, frustration, slowing up, etc. This change in the conditioned stimulus pattern should result in a weakening of the conditioned response, because the cues present during extinction are at a point on the generalization gradient at which responding is expected to be weaker than to the cues present during training.

However, when training with partial reinforcement is given, the subject is exposed, on reinforced training trials that follow nonreinforced trials, to cues which are normally present only during extinction. Examples of such cues for animals reinforced with food would be lack of food particles in the mouth, a state of frustration, etc. In other situations, examples would be the absence of irritation from recent air puff to the eye or shock to the wrist, cues from any relaxation resulting from freedom from the air puff or shock, implicit verbalizations relating to nonreinforcement, etc. With these nonreinforcement cues as part of the current stimulus pattern, reinforcement is reintroduced, and the subject therefore learns to perform the response in the presence of such nonreinforcement cues. Since the response has become conditioned during training to the cues characteristic of extinction, there is less loss through a change in the conditioned stimulus pattern when reinforcement is withdrawn completely than is found after training by reinforcement on every trial.

Thus, the initiation of extinction trials produces a relatively large change in the conditioned stimulus pattern when it follows training with reinforcement on every trial, but much less change when it follows training with partial reinforcement. Because the response evoked by a generalized stimulus is weaker than that evoked by the reinforced stimulus, the conditioned response during extinction will be weaker in the former case than in the latter. The possibility of the operation of this mechanism has been recognized by other authors (4, 9, 16, 17).

## METHOD

The proposed test of this interpretation consisted of controlling some of the after-effects of reinforcement and nonreinforcement by spacing of trials. The assumption was that if animal subjects were used with trials widely spaced, most of the after-effects of reinforcement or nonreinforcement would have dissipated by the start of the next trial, making the conditioned stimulus pattern much the same whether reinforcement had or had not been received on the preceding trial. The group receiving reinforcement on every trial and the group receiving partial reinforcement would thus be trained with more similar conditioned stimulus patterns than when trials were massed. Similarly the change in conditions when extinction was started would be more nearly the same for the two groups; as a result, the difference in resistance to extinction should be reduced.

Specifically, rats were trained to go down an alley with food at the end of the alley as reinforcement. Such after-effects of reinforcement as food taste and such after-effects of nonreinforcement as frustration may reasonably be assumed to dissipate with the passage of time and the performance of other behavior. Therefore, it follows that the extent to which differentiable reinforcement and nonreinforcement cues enter into the total stimulus pattern on a given trial will be maximized if trials are spaced close together and will be minimized if trials are spaced far apart. Massing of training trials, then, should give the maximum advantage to partial reinforcement in preventing extinction as compared with reinforcement on every trial, whereas relative spacing of trials should diminish or destroy this advantage. It is this deduction which the present experiment was designed to test.

Seventy-two rats were used in the experiment. Half the animals were trained with 100 percent reinforcement for 30 trials, half with reinforcement randomly on 50 percent of the 30 training trials. Of each group, half were trained with the trials massed (15-sec. interval), half with the trials spaced (15-min. interval). The question to be answered was: would partial reinforcement have less advantage in resistance to extinction in the latter group?

It seemed probable that the spacing of trials, both during training and during extinction, would have the direct effect of increasing resistance to extinction as well as its indirect effects through interaction with partial reinforcement. At the same time, it seemed probable that a change from massed to spaced or from spaced to massed when extinction begins would have the effect of hastening extinction. In order to balance completely for these factors, each of the four training groups was divided for extinction, half receiving massed extinction trials and half spaced extinction trials. This procedure not only served as a balancing procedure in the main problem to be investigated, but also had intrinsic value in supplying data on the problem of the relative resistance to extinction when extinction trials are massed compared with when they are spaced. The results of this aspect of the experiment will be presented in a separate article (19). Table I shows the design in schematic form; each cell of the table represents a separate subgroup of the experiment.

DETAILS OF APPARATUS AND PROCEDURE

The apparatus, shown in Fig. 1, consisted of a four-foot alley connecting a starting box and a goal box. Walls throughout were nine inches high. The interior of the starting box was painted white, and the interiors of the alley and goal box were painted black. The light in the room was from a ceiling fixture directly over the center of the apparatus. The two doors were operated vertically by strings and pulleys. Small pellets of wet mash, made from powdered Purina dog chow, flour, and water, were presented in a white food cup in one corner of the goal box. On all nonreinforced trials, both during partial reinforcement and during extinction, the white food cup was removed from the goal box. A black curtain placed diagonally at the entrance to the goal box cut off sight of the food

## TABLE I

### Design of the Experiment

|  | Massed Training | | Spaced Training | |
|---|---|---|---|---|
|  | Massed Ext. | Spaced Ext. | Massed Ext. | Spaced Ext. |
| 100% Reinf. | 100% MM 9 | 100% MS 9 | 100% SM 9 | 100% SS 9 |
| 50% Reinf. | 50% MM 9 | 50% MS 9 | 50% SM 9 | 50% SS 9 |

cup from the alley, so that an animal could not tell whether the cup was present or absent until he was actually inside the goal box.

The rats were always placed in the starting box facing the closed door. After approximately two sec. the door of the starting box was raised. When the rat left the starting box, the door was lowered; when he stepped onto the floor of the goal box, the door near the goal box was lowered to prevent retracing. Microswitches mechanically operated by the animal's weight on hinged floor sections in the two end boxes activated Springfield timers which recorded starting time (time from opportunity to respond until departure from the starting box) and running time (time from leaving the starting box to entering the goal box). The starting box was covered with a glass lid to prevent animals from prematurely operating the timer switches by jumping into the air before they actually left the box. The alley and goal box had no covering. A holding relay prevented re-operation of the switches by retracing. The goal box door was set back a short distance in the alley so that once the animal's forepaws were inside the goal box and the second timer had stopped, the door could be closed even if the animal did not immediately enter the box completely.

Seventy-two male albino rats from the albino farms at Redbank, N. J. were used, their ages ranging from 83 to 107 days (average 93 days) at the time they were started in the experiment. They had never been used in any previous experimentation.

Before and during the experiment the animals lived in the experimental room. During the two weeks prior to training, the animals were given daily taming sessions, consisting of handling during feeding periods until all would eat pellets of food from the experimenter's hand. They were also given practice at eating in unfamiliar surroundings—cages unlike their living cage, a tabletop, and a large cardboard carton. During these two weeks, they were fed a restricted diet of wet mash given about noon. Two days prior to the start of the experiment, the feeding time was shifted to the time at which their training would be started, a shift ranging from zero to four hours.

On the first day of the experiment proper, all animals were given 10

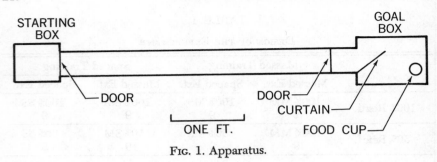

Fig. 1. Apparatus.

pre-training trials in the apparatus under constant conditions of massed trials and 100 percent reinforcement. This pre-training provided a criterion for eliminating, in advance of the application of the experimental variables, those rats too timid to explore the alley (and probably also helped insure that the rats scheduled to receive partial reinforcement would not give up on the first few training trials). If during the course of the 10 pre-training trials an animal took more than five min. to find the food or to eat it, he was discarded. On this basis, 14 rats were eliminated. Two rats were discarded after pre-training despite acceptable performance in the alley, one because he violently resisted being picked up and because he consistently bit the experimenter, the other because the apparatus broke down during experimental training. All discards were replaced to make the final group of 72 experimental animals.

The 10 pre-training trials were given on the first day; 30 training trials were given on the second day; and 30 extinction trials were given on the third day. The trials were started at the same time on each of the three successive days. The 50-percent reinforcement groups, having the same number of training trials as the 100-percent reinforcement groups, received only half as many reinforcements during training. At the end of their training trials, when the animals were given the balance of their ration for the day, this difference in amount eaten between 50-percent and 100-percent reinforcement animals was made up.

At the end of a run, animals were left in the goal box for 10 sec., or until they found and ate the food, longer times being necessary on early training trials. Ten sec. was an adequate time to eat the pellet of wet mash once the animal had learned, and this time was used whether food was present or not, during pre-training, training, and extinction. The animals were then removed to their individual living cages to await the next trial. Animals receiving massed trials were left in their living cages for 15 sec. between trials. This amount of time was required to record the time measures and reset the apparatus for the next trial. Due to variable running time, the time from the start of one trial to the start of the next was thus variable, but it very rarely ran over two min. and was usually close to

½ min. except on the first few training trials and during extinction. For spaced trials, the time from the start of one trial to the start of the next was 15 min. During extinction the animals were removed from the apparatus if either the starting time or the running time ran to two min., but all animals were given the full 30 extinction trials.

Since the training session extended over a much longer time for spaced groups than for massed groups, it was not possible, with the experimental setup used, to obtain strictly comparable hunger drive from group to group. However, the hunger drive was kept at a high enough level for all rats that it was felt that any variability in absolute level would be unimportant. In any case, whatever drive difference may have been present between certain of the groups did not enter into the basic comparisons of 50 percent and 100 percent reinforcement, for which drive was constant in groups compared. A restricted diet of seven gm. (dry weight) of the dog chow and flour mash was used before and during the experiment. Thirty pellets, the most any rat received during training, weighed about 2⅓ gm. (dry weight), which was only one-third of the restricted diet and an even smaller fraction of what any rat would eat if allowed an unlimited supply of food. Rats given massed training trials had a 23-hour hunger drive at the start of extinction. Spaced training was spread through a period of about 7¼ hours, at the end of which time the animals were given the balance of their food for that day. Extinction for space-trained animals was started 24 hours after the start of training, i.e., 16½ hours after feeding. In an attempt to make the hunger drive of space-trained animals, more comparable at the start of extinction with that of mass-trained animals, a total food ration of only six gm. was given at the end of training instead of the usual seven gm.

In preparing the orders of reinforced and nonreinforced trials for presenting 15 rewards distributed over 30 training trials, certain restrictions were used. These restrictions were selected to produce orders which contained single nonreinforced trials, and successions of two in a row, three in a row, and four in a row, which closely approximated, within *each* series of 30 trials, the distribution expected by chance in an infinite series. In other words, chance frequencies were stratified within orders. Nine orders were prepared, each order being used once in each subgroup. In each of the orders prepared:

1. Four successive nonreinforcements and three successive nonreinforcements each appeared once.

2. Three successive reinforcements appeared twice.

3. Two successive reinforcements and two successive nonreinforcements each appeared twice.

4. Isolated single reinforcements appeared five times, and isolated single nonreinforcements appeared four times.

In order to prevent partial-reinforcement animals from refusing to run in the early part of training and in order to end their training with the response at high strength, the following additional restrictions were used:

5. The first training trial was always rewarded.

6. The set of four successive nonreinforcements never appeared in the first half of training.

7. The last training trial was always an isolated single reinforcement.

Within these restrictions the distributions used were prepared from Tippett's (20) random numbers. The nine orders used were assigned randomly to the nine animals in each subgroup.

## STATISTICAL ANALYSIS

The statistical analysis of the results treated the data as nine replications of the experiment, with eight degrees of freedom for each comparison made. This treatment was partly dictated by a balancing procedure used in assigning rats to the eight conditions.

The rats used were obtained in three different shipments, each shipment upon arrival being broken down into sets of eight cage-mates. Differences in ease of taming were apparent between the shipments and between the sets of eight cage-mates within each shipment (perhaps due to the more docile being removed from the shipping crate first). These differences were balanced out by dividing the rats from each shipment equally among the eight experimental conditions and by assigning one each of the eight rats in a cage to the eight experimental conditions. The assignment of the eight rats to the eight experimental groups was done randomly, using Tippett's tables of random sampling numbers (21).

As a result of this balancing procedure, the eight rats within a replication were more homogeneous than the rats within a given experimental group. The greater precision in the experiment obtained by this procedure was taken into account in the statistical analysis by basing comparisons on the eight degrees of freedom provided by the nine replications. Thus in testing for the significances of the mean differences between two major groups, the appropriate difference was found among rats within each replication, and the mean difference was tested from the distribution of nine differences so obtained. This procedure removed from the estimated variance of mean differences any correlation due to balancing of cage differences.

## RESULTS

Although two time measures were recorded—starting time and running time—comparison of the learning and extinction curves for the eight ex-

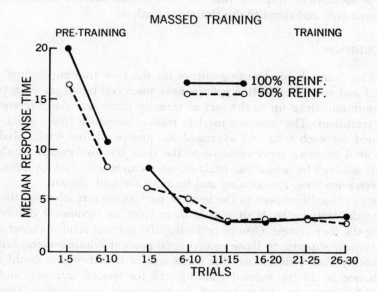

performed groups revealed that the pattern of results was the same for the two measures. Therefore the two measures were added together to make a single measure of response time, in order to increase the stability of the measurements and simplify the analysis.

ACQUISITION

In Fig. 2 the acquisition curves for the four training groups. The massed and spaced groups have been combined for the pre-training condition, since up to the end of training there is no difference in their treatment. The measure used is median response time, which was obtained for each trial and averaged for groups of five trials. Medians were used in more representative of the data, because means would be unduly affected by occasional trials on which an animal had an unusually long response time. Ho-hum and the like.

Test of the differences in the level of performance reach by the last half of the training showed that there were no significant differences among the four groups. Among the 100 percent reinforcement were very high. The squares of those reaching 50 per cent reinforcement, but the probabilities those in the subgroups would give .... would give by-chance is .20 for massed training, .15 for spaced training, and .15 overall. Chance reaching spaced training were probably superior to those receiving massed training, but the probabilities are .13 for 100 percent reinforcement, .25 for 50 percent reinforcement, and .19 overall.

DISCUSSION

Fig. 2 shows acquisition curves for the 100 percent and 50 percent reinforcement groups, and compared with the 50 per cent and 50 percent reinforcement groups, that were spaced training with massed and spaced conditions being combined for each training group. Median response time could not be used in plotting extinction data when on some trials more than half the animals were removed from the apparatus because of exceeding the two-minute time limit during the fifteen-trial extinction. Median response time over an individual animals tests also could not be used as a measure on individual animals to performance in the final set of extinction data. Further, some animals exceeded the time limit on the ... extinction trials. A frequency measure was introduced that chosen was the number of percentages of trials with...

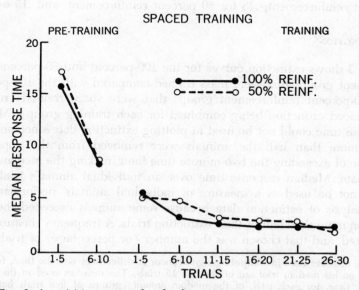

FIG. 2. Acquisition curves for the four training groups, showing median response time (averaged for groups of five trials) during the 10 pre-training trials and the 30 training trials.

perimental groups revealed that the pattern of results was the same for the two measures. Therefore, the two measures were added together to make a single measure of 'response time' in order to increase the stability of the measurements and simplify the statistical analysis.

## ACQUISITION

In Fig. 2 are shown learning curves for the four training groups. The massed and spaced extinction groups have been combined for each training condition, since up to the end of training there was no difference in their treatment. The measure used is median response time, which was obtained for each trial and averaged for groups of five trials. Medians were used as more representative of the data because means would be unduly affected by occasional trials on which an animal had an unusually long response time. Pre-training and training are both shown.

Tests of the differences in the level of performance reached on the last half of the training trials show that there were no significant differences among the four groups. Groups receiving 100 percent reinforcement were very slightly superior to those receiving 50 percent reinforcement, but the probability that a difference this large and in this direction could arise by chance is .20 for massed training, .12 for spaced training, and .15 overall.* Groups receiving spaced training were very slightly superior to those receiving massed training, but the probabilities are .13 for 100 percent reinforcement, .28 for 50 percent reinforcement, and .15 overall.

## EXTINCTION

Fig. 3 shows extinction curves for the 100-percent and 50-percent reinforcement groups that were mass trained compared with the 100-percent and 50-percent reinforcement groups that were space trained (massed and spaced extinction being combined for each training group). Median response time could not be used in plotting extinction data since on some trials more than half the animals were removed from the apparatus because of exceeding the two-minute time limit, making the median indeterminate. Median response time over an individual animal's trials also could not be used as a measure of individual animals' performance in the analysis of extinction data because some animals exceeded the time limit on more than half of their extinction trials. A frequency measure was indicated, and that chosen was the number (or percentage) of trials with

* The measure used in computing significances of differences was the time, for each *animal*, on his median *trial* out of the last 15 trials. The measure used in the curves was the time, for each *trial*, of the median *animal* (groups of five trials being averaged). This difference between the methods of obtaining the two measures probably accounts for the fact that the slight superiority of 100 percent reinforcement during massed training indicated by the significance test is not apparent in the curves.

**V. F. Sheffield**

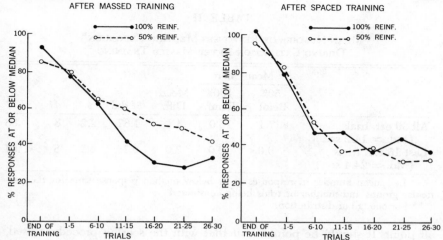

Fig. 3. Extinction curves for 100-percent and 50-percent reinforcement groups after massed training and after spaced training, showing percentage of responses in sets of five trials which were at or below 16.3 sec. (the overall median response time). The reference points at the beginning are the values for the last five training trials.

response times at or below the combined median response time for whatever groups were being compared. The median was chosen as the cut-off point partly because of its arbitrary nature and partly because it places the mean of the scores close to the middle of the range, which should give maximum sensitivity in comparing groups and at the same time avoid skewed distributions. The median time for all 72 animals on all 30 extinction trials was 16.3 sec., and it is the mean frequency of responses at or below this value for each set of five trials that is plotted in Fig. 3. The first point on the curves is the corresponding percentage value for the last five training trials, which is shown as a reference point.

*Extinction after massed training.* As can be seen in Fig. 3, the results after massed training confirm the findings of previous investigators that training with 50 percent reinforcement results in greater resistance to extinction than training with 100 percent reinforcement. The results of a significance test are shown in Table II. All groups reached approximately the same level of performance at the end of training, and performance was also similar on the early extinction trials, but the two groups diverged after the first ten extinction trials. The significance test was made separately for all extinction trials and for the last half of the trials. The means in Table II for all 30 trials used the median of 14.2 sec., obtained for the 30 extinction trials of the 50-percent and the 100-percent mass-trained groups combined, as the cut-off point in getting each animal's score. The means for the last 15 trials used the median of these 15 trials, 24.4 sec., as the cut-

TABLE II

Mean Number of Responses Meeting Criterion*
During Extinction After Massed Training

| | Mean Score | | | | | | |
| | 50% Reinf. | 100% Reinf. | Mean Diff. | $\sigma M$ diff. | $t$ | $df$ | $P$** |
|---|---|---|---|---|---|---|---|
| All 30 ext. trials (Md. = 14.2 sec.) | 17.1 | 13.0 | 4.1 | 1.87 | 2.2 | 8 | .03 |
| Last 15 ext. trials (Md. = 24.4 sec.) | 9.0 | 6.0 | 3.0 | 0.72 | 4.2 | 8 | < .01 |

* I.e., mean number of responses at or below median response time for the particular groups and number of trials being considered.
** For one tail of distribution.

off point. It should be pointed out that with the scoring procedure used, the potential range of scores is the same as the number of trials involved, so the means shown for all extinction trials and for the last half of the trials cannot be directly compared.

Table II shows that animals trained with partial reinforcement made a significantly larger number of responses during extinction which were below the median response time than did animals trained with 100 percent reinforcement, their superiority being more marked during the latter half of extinction than over all extinction trials.

*Extinction after spaced training.* When training trials were spaced 15 min. apart, greater resistance to extinction following 50 percent reinforcement as compared with 100 percent reinforcement was absent. This result can be seen in Fig. 3. A significance test is shown in Table III. As in Table II, results are shown for all extinction trials and for the last half of the extinction trials. The scores on which Table III is based used the medians of the 50-percent and 100-percent space-trained groups combined for the relevant number of trials. The theory says nothing about the direction of this difference; as trials are more and more widely spaced, the difference should become smaller and smaller, but at what interval it would become zero and whether it would become negative are questions that would have to be answered empirically. For this reason, the $P$'s shown are for a difference this large in either direction.

Table III shows that with training trials spaced, animals trained with partial reinforcement did not differ significantly during extinction from animals trained with 100 percent reinforcement. The slight difference obtained was in the reverse direction from that obtained with massed training, 100 percent reinforcement being superior.

*Effect of distribution of practice on extinction.* The results confirm the expectation from the stimulus-response analysis of partial reinforcement that the difference in resistance to extinction between groups trained with

## TABLE III

### Mean Number of Responses Meeting Criterion*
### During Extinction After Spaced Training

| | Mean Score | | | | | | |
| | 50% Reinf. | 100% Reinf. | Mean Diff. | $\sigma M$ diff. | $t$ | $df$ | $P$** |
|---|---|---|---|---|---|---|---|
| All 30 ext. trials (Md. = 19.1 sec.) | 14.7 | 15.4 | −0.7 | 2.71 | 0.3 | 8 | .77 |
| Last 15 ext. trials (Md. = 27.0 sec.) | 6.9 | 8.0 | −1.1 | 1.49 | 0.7 | 8 | .50 |

* I.e., mean number of responses at or below median response time for the particular groups and number of trials being considered.
** For both tails of distribution.

100 percent reinforcement and groups trained with 50 percent reinforcement would be greater if the training trials were massed than if they were spaced. Tables II and III show that with massed training partial reinforcement significantly retarded extinction, whereas with spaced training it did not. They do not show, however, whether this obtained difference in the effect of partial reinforcement was significant. A significance test on this point is shown in Table IV. Here the overall median response time of 16.3 sec. for all groups combined was used to obtain the scores over the 30 trials, and the median performance of 25.3 sec. for all groups combined on the last 15 trials was used in obtaining scores for this portion of extinction. The $t$-test is based on the distribution of the second-order differences indicated in the table, over the nine replications of the experiment.

Table IV shows that the difference in resistance to extinction between 100 percent and partial reinforcement is significantly greater with massed training than with spaced training. Results in same direction were obtained when the analysis shown in Table IV was performed separately for those groups whose extinction trials were massed and for those groups whose extinction trials were spaced, but the differences were not nearly

## TABLE IV

### Comparison of the Differences* Between 50% and 100% Reinforcement
### Groups During Extinction After Massed Training and
### After Spaced Training

| | Massed Training | | | Spaced Training | | | $D_1$ (massed) minus $D_2$ (spaced) | $\sigma D_1 - D_2$ | $t$ | $df$ | $P$** |
| | Mean Score | | Mean Diff. | Mean Score | | Mean Diff. | | | | | |
| | 50% | 100% | | 50% | 100% | | | | | | |
|---|---|---|---|---|---|---|---|---|---|---|---|
| All 30 ext. trials (Md. = 16.3 sec.) | 17.8 | 14.2 | 3.6 | 13.6 | 14.4 | −0.8 | 4.4 | 1.95 | 2.3 | 8 | .03 |
| Last 15 ext. trials (Md. = 25.3 sec.) | 9.1 | 6.3 | 2.8 | 6.8 | 7.8 | −1.0 | 3.8 | 1.09 | 3.5 | 8 | <.01 |

* The measure used was mean number of responses at or below the overall median response time.
** For one tail of distribution.

as reliable as in the overall analysis. For massed extinction analyzed separately, the probabilities were .07 for all extinction trials and .12 for the last half of the extinction trials that the difference obtained would arise by chance. For spaced extinction the corresponding probabilities were .20 and .11.

### DISCUSSION

As stated in greater detail in the introduction, the present experiment was based on a hypothesis which provides a stimulus-response explanation for the greater resistance to extinction that has been found after training with partial reinforcement as compared with 100 percent reinforcement. According to this explanation, the partial reinforcement technique has the effect of conditioning the response to cues normally present only during extinction. After one or more nonreinforced trials, the conditioned stimulus pattern at the start of a reinforced trial includes after-effects of the preceding nonreinforced trials, which make it much like a trial during extinction. When performance of the response in the presence of these nonreinforcement or extinction cues is now reinforced in the trial being considered, the partial reinforcement group learns to give the response to cues for extinction. When the actual extinction trials are started, the omission of reinforcement does not introduce unfamiliar cues: the response has been conditioned to nonreinforcement cues during training and continues at a relatively high level. After training with 100 percent reinforcement, on the other hand, the start of extinction introduces nonreinforcement cues for the first time. The conditioned response to the changed stimulus pattern is therefore weakened because it is at a different point on the generalization gradient from the reinforced stimulus pattern.

From this theoretical analysis it was predicted that spacing of training trials with animal subjects should reduce or destroy the advantage of partial reinforcement during extinction, because with long inter-trial intervals the after-effects of reinforcement or nonreinforcement on the preceding trials would have dissipated to some extent. The conditioned stimulus pattern at the start of a new trial would thus be more similar for the partial and 100-percent reinforcement groups during spaced training, and their performance during extinction should be more comparable. The results of the experiment bear out the prediction. Whereas after massed training, significantly greater resistance to extinction was found for 50 percent than for 100 percent reinforcement, after spaced training, there was no advantage for 50 percent reinforcement—the slight difference obtained was in the reverse direction.

The reversal obtained with spacing in the present results is not a necessary implication of the hypothesis, which implies only that the difference will be reduced. By changing the spaced intervals used, the degree of over-learning (i.e., amount of training with nonreinforcement followed by rein-forcement), and other details of the procedure, it may be possible to vary the size of the difference from a small change, with 50 percent reinforcement still showing considerably greater resistance to extinction, to a significant reversal, with 50 percent reinforcement extinguishing more rapidly. Another factor affecting the size of the difference, and one which is probably little influenced by spacing of trials, is *reinstatement* of cues for continued responding. There are undoubtedly stimuli from the animal's behavior which are reinstated each time the animal is placed in the apparatus and which become cues for continued responding in spite of non-reinforcement. For example, in addition to cues from the frustration which carries over from a nonreinforced trial to the start of the following trial with massed training, there may be cues from *conditioned* frustration aroused by apparatus cues on each trial with *both* massed and spaced training. If the latter type of cue is a big part of the stimulus pattern, spacing of trials would not reduce by much the difference between extinction following 50 percent and 100 percent reinforcement.

As stated above, the hypothesis is applied specifically to a comparison of extinction after partial and 100 percent reinforcement. It may be applied more generally as a hypothesis to explain part of the decrement that characterizes all extinction. According to this hypothesis, a response becomes conditioned during training to the after-effects of reinforcement as part of the conditioned stimulus pattern. Omission of reinforcement during extinction thus changes the conditioned stimulus pattern, not only by the removal of reinforcement cues, but also by introducing whatever new cues result from the omission, such as those that are produced by the subject's reaction to the omission. Part of the decrement in the response during extinction would thus be interpreted as a weakening of the response though generalization to the new stimulus pattern, combined with the weakening effects of any incompatible responses that might be produced by the new stimulus pattern or the omission of reinforcement.

It might be asked whether this hypothesis (as applied to partial rein-forcement) can explain cases in which experiments failed to obtain greater resistance to extinction with partial reinforcement. Humphreys (14), in a bar-pressing experiment with rats, found an advantage for partial reinforcement only if number of reinforcements was held constant. Four groups received reinforcements on (1) 18 out of 52 trials, (2) 18 out of 18 trials, (3) 7 out of 18 trials, and (4) 7 out of 7 trials. Comparison of number of responses during fixed extinction periods showed an advantage for (1) over (2) and an advantage for (3) over (4), in each case the number of reinforcements being the same and the number of trials variable. But there was no difference between (2) and (3), where number of reinforcements is variable and number of trials is constant.

The explanation of the effects of partial reinforcement proposed in the present report assumes that there must be a large enough number of occurrences of nonreinforcement followed by reinforcement during training for a stable response to be conditioned to the extinction cues. In (3) above, only seven reinforcements were given. If it is assumed that the first trial was always reinforced, there would be a maximum of six reinforced trials following nonreinforced trials. It is unlikely that a very strong response could be conditioned to the extinction cues in so few trials. If there had been a control group for (1), with 52 trials all reinforced, it is possible that a comparison of this group with (1) might have revealed a difference in resistance to extinction.

Another experiment which failed to demonstrate any difference in extinction between partial and 100 percent reinforcement is one by Denny (4), involving rats in a T-maze. However, this failure actually provides confirmation for the results of the present study, for the absence of an effect was under circumstances in which the present findings indicate there should be no effect, namely following training with widely spaced trials. Partial reinforcement groups were given one reinforced and one nonreinforced trial per day, and 100-percent reinforcement groups were given two reinforced trials per day (plus, in each case, two trials to the incorrect side, the last two trials of the day being forced to achieve this combination). But the interval between trials given on the same day was 20–30 min., and 24 hours intervened between every two correct choices. In the present study, it was shown that a 15-min. interval was sufficient to reduce to zero the difference in extinction of a running response following partial and 100 percent reinforcement.

Finger (5, 6), on the basis of his studies, concluded that partial reinforcement per se did not result in greater resistance to extinction, but his results are shown to be inconclusive in a study by Lawrence and Miller (15) because of the effects of certain aspects of Finger's technique.

The question arises as to whether other theories that have been proposed to explain the results of partial reinforcement are able to account for the results of the present study. Foremost among other explanations is the 'expectancy' interpretation proposed by Humphreys (11) and later amplified by Hilgard (8). A difficulty in this case is that the interpretation is not stated rigorously enough for its application in a new situation to be clear. In fact, its application even to Humphreys' findings is not unambiguous. The relatively higher level of responding during extinction after partial reinforcement is explained merely as due to the difficulty of shifting from an expectation of intermittent reinforcement to an expectation of complete nonreinforcement, compared with the ease (after 100 percent reinforcement) of shifting from an expectation of uniform reinforcement to an expectation of uniform nonreinforcement. One might as readily argue, at the same level of discourse, just the reverse: that after being habituated to infrequent reinforcements, the subject finds it easy to get used to the idea that there will be none at all, but after being habituated to uniform reinforcement, the subject finds it hard to believe that there will be no more reinforcements.

The point is that Humphreys' explanation did not follow from an expectancy principle; it was an ex post facto conjecture as to what the course of expectancies must have been if expectancies are to be considered the causes of the behavior. The fact that in a subsequent study (12) Humphreys showed that the course of verbal expectancies did roughly correspond to that of conditioned responses is treated by Hilgard (8) as confirmation of this conjecture and as evidence in favor of an expectancy principle. However, Humphreys' subsequent results show only that verbal responses are affected by partial reinforcement in much the same way as other responses. And the critical issue is that neither of these was deduced from the expectancy hypothesis; the course of expectancies was determined empirically, and the course of the other conditioned responses was explained as being due to the course of expectancies. One of the advantages of the present hypothesis is that it can predict the course of both kinds of responses without recourse to any empirical analysis.

Humphreys' (11, 13) initial rise in the extinction curve after partial reinforcement is attributed to high expectation of reinforcement after two extinction trials because there never were more than two successive non-reinforcements during training. This must mean that the subject is keeping track of (i.e., responding differentially to the after-effects of) the successions of reinforcements and nonreinforcements. To say that, after a series of events which has always been followed by reinforcement, the subject has a high expectation of reinforcement contributes nothing beyond the stimulus-response interpretation that to a differential cue that has always been followed by reinforcement, there is maximal probability of eliciting the conditioned response.

If expectancy is viewed as the basic principle for explaining all learning, then there would appear to be no reason for predicting anything different for resistance to extinction following spaced training from that following massed training. The fact that the animals in this study *learned* as well, if not better, with spaced as compared with massed training would indicate that the expectancies used by the expectancy principle can be set up and maintained through intervals as long as those used. Therefore, it is difficult to see why spacing of training should remove the advantage in resistance to extinction usually found with partial reinforcement. Presumably expectancies are aroused when a previously-experienced situation recurs, regardless of the time interval separating the two exposures. Distributed practice should facilitate the acquisition of an expectancy as much as it does the learning of any response, and the advantage of partial reinforcement should be increased, if anything, by the spaced practice in forming expectancies.

However, if expectancies are regarded as secondary phenomena sometimes involved in learning, then such expectancies, particularly in the form of implicit verbal responses with human subjects, would be included here as one of the after-effects of reinforcement or nonreinforcement as described in the present hypothesis. For human subjects, such verbal responses would undoubtedly be an important part of the reinforcement or extinction cues to which the response becomes conditioned. For example, human subjects who tended to verbalize what went on in Humphreys' experiments (11, 13) might, after a certain amount of practice, think to themselves the equivalents of: "Two shocks in a row, none next time," or "No shock and then shock, maybe shock again this time," or "No shock for two trials, shock for sure next time." Such verbalizations would function as after-effects and would provide distinctive cues exactly correlated with preceding patterns of reinforcement (to the extent that they correctly described the actual events of the experiment). They would also very probably be one of the cues reinstated at the start of each trial. Furthermore, they would be differential cues that had been reinforced, respectively, 0 percent, 50 percent, and 100 percent of the time in Humphreys' procedure. It is not surprising, therefore, that strength of actual responding correlated to some extent with cues so differentially reinforced. A separate expectancy principle is not required to explain why these expectancies help produce the greater resistance to extinction found by Humphreys. The subject who has always been reinforced while thinking "No shock for two times" is more likely to give the conditioned response when he thinks "No shock for three or four times" than the subject who not only has never been reinforced while thinking this but also never thought anything like it during acquisition. Such verbalizations function exactly as the presence or absence of food taste in the mouth and the state of frustration in the case of rats.

But applying the expectancy principle to animals as if they had implicit verbal cues would very probably lead to errors of prediction. Humphreys (14) himself does not attempt to apply the expectancy principle in his study of partial reinforcement with rats. In the case of human subjects, spacing of training trials would probably have much less effect of reducing the difference between partial and 100 percent reinforcement in resistance to extinction, because verbal cues could doubtless still be rearoused after long inter-trial intervals. Still, some effect similar to the present findings should show up since the advantage of partial reinforcement would partly depend, in human subjects, on their ability to remember, at any point during learning, what had happened on the last few trials, and since some forgetting would be expected with long intervals between trials.

Another proposal for explaining the effects of partial reinforcement is one by J. S. Brown, which has been tested by Mowrer and Jones (17). They have designated it the 'response-unit' hypothesis. Speaking of their bar-pressing response, they suggest that what is reinforced in the partial reinforcement situation is not the single bar-depression that immediately precedes food but the sequence of bar-depressions leading up to the reward. Defining the 'response' as a sequence or pattern of behavior rather than a single act, they propose that the behavior temporally more remote from the reward is reinforced by it to a diminishing extent according to the principle of the gradient of reinforcement. Accordingly, animals rewarded during training for several depressions of the bar would be expected during extinction to press the bar more times but not necessarily to make more 'responses' than animals whose 'response' during training was a single bar-depression.

From this hypothesis it would probably be predicted that spacing of training trials would make it difficult for a sequence of behavior to be reinforced as a 'unit' and would therefore cause a breakdown in the usual advantage of partial reinforcement in extinction. However, even with massed training, it would appear to be much easier to conceive of several bar-depressions as a response-unit than two or three runs down an alley separated by 15-second intervals in the home cage. In the latter case, the length of time involved and the possibility for variable intervening activity make the idea of a response-unit untenable.

Denny (4) has obtained evidence supporting a secondary reinforcement hypothesis for explaining the fact that *acquisition* is almost as good with partial reinforcement as with 100 percent reinforcement. He does not attempt to apply it to differences in *extinction* under the two conditions, which in fact his study does not show. Secondary reinforcement from the empty goal box unquestionably operated in the 50 percent groups in the present study, but there is no reason to expect it to operate differently when training trials are spaced from when they are massed. Secondary reinforcement not only cannot explain the differential effect on resistance to extinction obtained with massed and spaced training trials, but also it cannot account for the basic difference in extinction between partial and 100 percent reinforcement with massed training trials. In order for the secondary reinforcement principle to explain the latter, it would have to be assumed that secondary reinforcement is stronger than primary reinforcement.

## SUMMARY

1. Seventy-two rats were trained to run down an alley for food. Half received reinforcements on all training trials, and half randomly on 50 per-

cent of the trials. Half of each group were trained with a 15-sec. interval between trials and half with a 15-min. interval. Each of the four training groups was divided for extinction, half being extinguished with the 15-sec. interval and half with the 15-min. interval.

2. There were no significant differences in level of performance on the last half of the acquisition trials, either between 100 percent and 50 percent reinforcement or between massed and spaced training.

3. After massed training, resistance to extinction was significantly greater for 50-percent reinforcement groups than for 100-percent reinforcement groups.

4. After spaced training, the difference in resistance to extinction between 100-percent and 50-percent reinforcement groups was not significant; it was, in fact, slightly reversed.

5. The differential effect of partial reinforcement depending on whether training was massed or spaced was found to be significant.

6. These results verify a prediction from a hypothesis ultilizing stimulus-response learning concepts for explaining the effect of partial reinforcement on extinction.

## REFERENCES

1. BROGDEN, W. J. (1939) The effect of frequency of reinforcement upon the level of conditioning. *J. exp. Psychol.*, 24, 419-431.
2. BRUNSWIK, E. (1939) Probability as a determiner of rat behavior. *J. exp. Psychol.*, 25, 175-197.
3. COLE, L. E. (1939) A comparison of the factors of practice and knowledge of experimental procedure in conditioning the eyelid response of human subjects. *J. gen. Psychol.*, 20, 349-373.
4. DENNY, M. R. (1946) The role of secondary reinforcement in a partial reinforcement learning situation. *J. exp. Psychol.*, 36, 373-389.
5. FINGER, F. W. (1942) The effect of varying conditions of reinforcement upon a simple running response. *J. exp. Psychol.*, 30, 53-68.
6. FINGER, F. W. (1942) Retention and subsequent extinction of a simple running response following varying conditions of reinforcement. *J. exp. Psychol.*, 31, 120-133.
7. GUTHRIE, E. R. (1935) *Psychology of learning.* New York: Harper.
8. HILGARD, E. R. (1948) *Theories of learning.* New York: Appleton-Century-Crofts.
9. HULL, C. L. (1941) Notes on the Humphreys extinction paradox. Unpublished symposium notes, Midwestern Psychol. Assn.
10. HULL, C. L. (1943) *Principles of behavior.* New York: Appleton-Century.
11. HUMPHREYS, L. G. (1939) The effect of random alternation of reinforcement on the acquisition and extinction of conditioned eyelid reactions. *J. exp. Psychol.*, 25, 141-158.
12. HUMPHREYS, L. G. (1939) Acquisition and extinction of verbal expectations in a situation analogous to conditioning. *J. exp. Psychol.*, 25, 294-301.

13. HUMPHREYS, L. G. (1940) Extinction of conditioned psychogalvanic responses following two conditions of reinforcement. *J. exp. Psychol.*, 27, 71-75.

14. HUMPHREYS, L. G. (1943) The strength of a Thorndikian response as a function of the number of practice trials. *J. comp. Psychol.*, 35, 101-110.

15. LAWRENCE, D. H. and MILLER, N. E. (1947) A positive relationship between reinforcement and resistance to extinction produced by removing a source of confusion from a technique that had produced opposite results. *J. exp. Psychol.*, 37, 494-509.

16. MILLER, N. E. and DOLLARD, J. (1941) *Social learning and imitation.* New Haven: Yale Univ. Press.

17. MOWRER, O. H. and JONES, HELEN (1945) Habit strength as a function of the pattern of reinforcement. *J. exp. Psychol.*, 35, 293-311.

18. PAVLOV, I. P. (1927) *Conditioned reflexes.* (Trans. by G. V. Anrep) London: Oxford Univ. Press.

19. SHEFFIELD, VIRGINIA F. (1950) Resistance to extinction as a function of the distribution of extinction trials. *J. exp. Psychol.*, 40. (In press)

20. SKINNER, B. F. (1938) *The behavior of organisms.* New York: Appleton-Century.

21. TIPPETT, L. H. C. (1927) *Random sampling numbers.* London: Cambridge Univ. Press.

## 22. Two Tests of the Sheffield Hypothesis Concerning Resistance to Extinction, Partial Reinforcement, and Distribution of Practice

### W. Wilson, E. J. Weiss, and A. Amsel

*In this selection, Sheffield's aftereffects hypothesis is examined and found wanting. The authors propose still another hypothesis to explain the partial reinforcement effect.*

Sheffield (7) has offered a stimulus generalization interpretation of the finding that responses acquired under partial (50%) reinforcement are more resistant to extinction than those acquired under continuous (100%) reinforcement conditions. She assumes that some part of the stimulation, on any trial after the first in a series of trials, is composed of carried-over traces of goal stimulation from the previous trial; so that stimulation on

*J. exp. Psychol.*, 1955, 50, 51-60. Reprinted with permission of the author and The American Psychological Association. This article is based on the master's theses of W. W. and E.J.W. (12, 13) which were directed by A.A. The authors are indebted to Dr. E. Lee Hoffman for his advice and help in the statistical analysis.

trials following reinforcement would be unlike that during any extinction trial after the first, while stimulation on trials following nonreinforcements, in partial reinforcement training, would be similar to that during extinction trials. Consequently, there should be more generalized decrement from 100% reinforcement to extinction than from 50% reinforcement to extinction, and resistance to extinction following partial reinforcement should be greater than after continuous reinforcement.

Sheffield reasoned that if time were allowed between acquistion trials for carry-over stimulation to dissipate, increased resistance to extinction following partial reinforcement should be eliminated. In an experimental test of this interpretation, Sheffield found that 50% reinforcement resulted in greater resistance to extinction than 100% reinforcement after massed but not after spaced acquisition.

Several variations of the Sheffield experiment have been performed using different response systems or different time intervals (3, 4, 11). In each case, the partial reinforcement groups were more resistant to extinction than the continuous ones. Sheffield's finding, that partial and continuous groups were equally resistant to extinction following spaced training, has not been confirmed. Her results have been considered the most significant exception to the usual finding of increased resistance to extinction after partial reinforcement (5).

An important factor in Sheffield's generalization interpretation is the role of stimulation arising from food particles in the mouth, present on trials immediately following reinforced trials but not on any extinction trial. We have assumed that the degree of persistence of such mouth cues depends upon the kind of reinforcing agent employed. With this in mind, two repetitions of the Sheffield experiment were undertaken, varying only the kind of reinforcement. In Exp. 1, dry food was substituted for the wet mash used by Sheffield as reinforcement; this was expected to increase the persistence of traces and enhance—at least not reduce—the Sheffield effect. In Exp. 2, water was used as the reinforcing agent in an attempt to minimize the duration of the reinforcement stimulus trace since, presumably, water does not persist as a mouth cue as long as food. Therefore, following Sheffield's reasoning, not only should there be no difference in resistance to extinction between partial- and continuous-reinforcement groups after spaced training, but little or no difference even after massed training with water as the reinforcing agent, since reducing the duration of the reinforcement traces is, in this respect, the equivalent of increasing the time between trials.

These experiments also provide data pertinent to Sheffield's findings concerning massed versus spaced extinction (8). She found greater resistance to extinction with massed than with spaced extinction trials, particularly after massed acquisition.

METHOD

*Subjects.* The Ss were 144 naive rats, 72 in each experiment. These included male and female, hooded and albino, and ranged in age from 4 to 10 mo. For each of nine replications, however, the strain, sex, and age of the Ss were held as constant as possible within and between the two experiments. Twenty-two additional Ss were discarded during pretraining trials for failure to meet the criteria for service as Ss.

*Apparatus and procedure.* Except for differences in motivational-reward conditions, the two experiments duplicated as exactly as possible Sheffield's experimental apparatus, design, and procedure. Two identical straight-alley runways were used, constructed in every respect according to Sheffield's specifications (7). Each runway was illuminated by a 40-w. fluorescent tube about 4 ft. above the runway and in line with it.

The experiment was run in three stages: 10 pretraining trials on Day 1, 30 acquisition trials on Day 2, and 30 extinction trials on Day 3. The three main variables were intertrial interval in acquisition (15 sec. vs. 15 min. or M vs. S) reinforcement ratio in acquisition (50% vs. 100% or P vs. C) and intertrial interval in extinction (15 sec. vs. 15 min.). This required four acquisition groups (MP, MC, SP, SC) and eight extinction groups (MPM, MPS, MCM, MCS, SPM, SPS, SCM, SCS) for complete counterbalancing. Nine replications were run in each experiment and eight Ss were used in each replication, one S being run under each of the eight extinction conditions. Each of the two Es ran one-half of the Ss in each condition of each of the two experiments.

During a 2-week taming period, Ss were handled and adjusted to the drive regimen of the experiment. The Ss in Exp. 1 were reduced to 10 gm. of food per day until the day before the pretraining trials, when their ration was cut to 6 gm. for the 3-day experimental period. The Ss in Exp. 2 remained on a 16½-hr. water deprivation schedule from the first day of the training period until the end of the experimental period.

A feature of all experiments involving a comparison of massed and spaced practice—and accentuated in the present design—is that the massed group receives the same number of reinforcements as the spaced group in a much shorter space of time. According to the present design, the massed Ss received 30 reinforcements on Day 2 in about 15–20 min., while the spaced Ss require about 7 hr. to complete 30 trials. We would expect, therefore, the drive level on successive trials to be higher in the spaced group than in the massed group, making questionable the validity of any comparison between spaced and massed acquisition. While acquisition comparisons are not, per se, an important aspect of these experiments, we attempted to offset this factor somewhat by deviating from the Sheffield procedure in the following ways: (a) All Ss in each experiment were brought into the experimental room on the acquisition and extinction days

(Days 2 and 3) under the same conditions of deprivation. This meant that no S was given the balance of its daily ration on Day 1 or Day 2 until all Ss had completed trials for that day. (b) The running of massed Ss was stretched out over the 7-hr. period required for the spaced acquisition trials, so that some massed trials were run with the earlier spaced trials and others with the later spaced trials. For any given replication, one E ran all massed and the other all spaced acquisition trials; but which E ran the massed trials changed from one replication to the next. Since each E ran the same Ss on both acquisition and extinction, and would therefore be running both massed and spaced Ss at extinction, one-half of the massed Ss were run before and one-half after all of the spaced Ss on Day 3.

As was indicated earlier, each of the experiments employed a reinforcing agent different from Sheffield, who used a wet mash of dog chow and flour. In Exp. 1, dry dog-chow food pellets were used; 30 such pellets, given as reinforcement on the acquisition day, weighed 2 gm. The reinforcement in Exp. 2 was two drops of water at room temperature; the 60 drops which reinforced acquisition measured about 4 ml.

After all Ss had completed their trials on the pretraining and acquisition days, food deprivation groups received the remainder of the 6-gm. daily ration, and water deprivation groups had access to water for 45 min.

Response time, the dependent variable, was measured from the raising of the start-box door to entry into the goal box.

*Statistics.* Sheffield reports time scores in acquisition and frequency scores in extinction. Here, frequency scores are reported for both acquisition and extinction, although response-time medians are also reported in Tables 1 and 3. In every case, values in the graphs and in the statistical analyses are numbers of responses at or below the over-all median response time for the appropriate series. The decision to employ these frequency measures was based on three considerations: (a) to have the same type of values in all graphs and all statistical analyses; (b) to make the results more directly comparable to Sheffield's; and (c) to obtain values which could be subjected to analysis of variance and covariance—the time scores deviated from normality and homogeneity of variance even after a square-root transformation.

Instead of the t tests used by Sheffield, the acquistion data were subjected to analysis of variance, and extinction data to analysis of variance and covariance. The results of both analyses are offered particularly in regard to the partial reinforcement variable. The analysis of variance of extinction data would test the notion that partial reinforcement leads to greater resistance to extinction *despite* possibly a lower level of acquisition performance in acquisition; the analysis of covariance tests resistance to extinction following partial and continuous reinforcement adjusting for any inequality in acquisition performance.

RESULTS*

EXPERIMENT 1

This repetition of the Sheffield experiment used dry food as reinforcement instead of wet mash.

*Acquisition.* Since we were interested in the final level of acquisition performance, an analysis of variance was performed to test the equality of the four groups on the last 15 of the 30 acquisition trials. The score for each S in this analysis was its number of responses at or below the over-all median response time. The total of such responses for each group along with the group median response times on the last 15 trials are given in Table 1. The analysis indicated that variation due to difference among replications was significant beyond the .01 level. With this factor isolated, the difference between massed and spaced training groups fell just short of significance: $F$ was 4.02, significance at the .05 level required an $F$ of 4.14. Continuous reinforcement yields higher final acquisition values than partial reinforcement, but the difference is short of significance at the .05 level ($F = 2.73$). No interaction variance approaches significance at the .05 level. The picture presented by these acquisition data is similar to that of the Sheffield data. The final response-time level was about the same in both experiments.

*Extinction.* In plotting the curves of Fig. 1 and in the statistical analyses the response index employed was the frequency of scores at or below the median response time for the 30 extinction trials. Table 1 presents the

* For other graphic and tabular presentations and analyses of the data of Exp. 1 and 2, see the Wilson (13) and the Weiss (12) theses.

TABLE 1

MEDIAN RESPONSE TIME IN SECONDS FOR LAST 15 ACQUISITION TRIALS AND 30
EXTINCTION TRIALS AND NUMBER OF RESPONSES AT OR BELOW
THE OVER-ALL MEDIAN: EXPERIMENT 1

| Group | Acquisition | | Extinction | |
|---|---|---|---|---|
| | Median Response Time | Responses At or Below Median | Median Response Time | Responses At or Below Median |
| MPS | 3 | 184 | 65 | 98 |
| MPM | | | 21 | 168 |
| MCS | 3 | 167 | 80 | 88 |
| MCM | | | 38 | 148 |
| SPS | 3 | 175 | 22 | 172 |
| SPM | | | 41 | 141 |
| SCS | 2 | 235 | 42 | 133 |
| SCM | | | 42 | 138 |

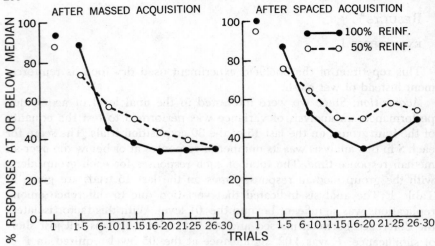

Fig. 1. Extinction curves for food-reinforcement groups after massed and spaced training, showing percentage of responses in 5-trial blocks at or below the over-all median response time. Data of Trial 1 are plotted separately.

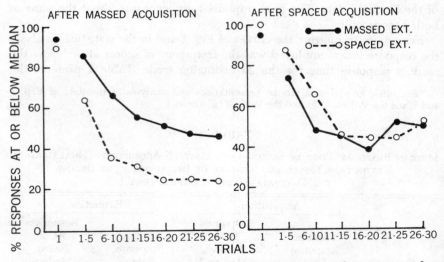

Fig. 2. Extinction curves for food-reinforcement groups showing massed and spaced extinction performance after massed and spaced acquisition. Data of Trial 1 are plotted separately.

median response-time values for each of eight extinction groups and number of responses at or below the over-all median for each group. Figure 1 shows both the massed and the spaced partial reinforcement groups more resistant to extinction than the comparable continuous reinforcement

TABLE 2

SUMMARY OF ANALYSIS OF VARIANCE AND COVARIANCE: EXPERIMENT 1

| Source of Variation | df | Analysis of Variance | | Analysis of Covariance | |
| --- | --- | --- | --- | --- | --- |
| | | Mean Square | F | Adjusted Mean Square | F |
| A. Massed and spaced acquisition | 1 | 93.36 | 2.25 | 25.32 | .... |
| B. 100% and 50% reinforcement | 1 | 72.00 | 1.74 | 221.84 | 8.19** |
| C. Massed and spaced extinction | 1 | 150.22 | 3.62 | 137.22 | 5.60* |
| D. Replications | 8 | 133.06 | 3.21** | 83.21 | 3.07* |
| A × B | 1 | 2.00 | .... | 33.85 | 1.25 |
| A × C | 1 | 338.01 | 8.15** | 168.42 | 6.22* |
| A × D | 8 | 52.01 | 1.25 | 54.43 | 2.01 |
| B × C | 1 | 9.39 | .... | 16.02 | .... |
| B × D | 8 | 56.12 | 1.35 | 30.93 | 1.14 |
| C × D | 8 | 35.28 | .... | 21.04 | .... |
| Residual† | 33 | 41.47 | .... | 27.07 | .... |

* Significant at .05 level.
** Significant at .01 level.
† Residual df are 32 for the analysis of covariance.

groups. If anything, the difference seems larger after spaced training than after massed training. The analysis of variance of extinction data, summarized in Table 2, showed only two significant sources of variation, both at the .01 level—one was for replications, as expected, and the other was a significant interaction between massed vs. spaced acquisition and massed vs. spaced extinction. This significant interaction resulted from the fact, shown graphically in Fig. 2, that the extinction performance of the massed groups was higher than that of the spaced groups after massed acquisition, but at about the same level as the spaced groups after spaced acquisition.

When extinction data were adjusted for differences in acquisition in the analysis of covariance (Table 2), partial reinforcement groups were shown to be significantly more resistant to extinction than were continuous reinforcement groups *regardless of the intertrial interval in acquisition.* The interaction (A × B) between massed and spaced acquisition and partial and continuous reinforcement was small and not statistically significant. If the difference between partial and continuous reinforcement groups in extinction depended upon the distribution of acquisition trials, this interaction would have been large. The analysis of covariance also indicated that massed extinction groups were significantly more resistant to extinction than spaced ($p < .05$). This difference is, however, complicated by the still-present significant interaction (A × C) between the massed-spaced variable in acquisition and the massed-spaced variable in extinction. As in the analysis of variance, variation due to replications was significant.

EXPERIMENT 2

This was a repetition of the Sheffield experiment using water as reinforcement instead of wet mash.

*Acquisition.* The statistical analysis was based on the number of responses in the last 15 acquisition trials for each S at or below over-all median response time. The values shown in Table 3 are, for each acquisition group, the median response time and the number of responses at or below the median response time for the last 15 trials. It will be noted that the number at or below the median was 335 for the continuous groups and 220 for the partial reinforcement groups. The analysis of variance shows that the higher level of performance attained by the continuous reinforcement groups is significant beyond the .05 level ($F = 6.98$). Distribution of trials had no significant effect on acquisition. The variation due to differences among replications was significant beyond the .05 level. No interaction variance approached statistical significance in acquisition. The final level of performance was lower (higher running time) in this experiment than in Exp. 1 or in Sheffield's study.

*Extinction.* The statistical analysis of the extinction data and the extinction curves are based on the number of responses at or below the over-all extinction median. Table 3 gives the number of such responses for each of

TABLE 3

MEDIAN RESPONSE TIME IN SECONDS FOR LAST 15 ACQUISITION TRIALS AND 30 EXTINCTION TRIALS AND NUMBER OF RESPONSES AT OR BELOW THE OVER-ALL MEDIAN: EXPERIMENT 2

| | Acquisition | | Extinction | |
|---|---|---|---|---|
| Group | Median Response Time | Responses At or Below Median | Median Response Time | Responses At or Below Median |
| MPS | 7 | 109 | 117 | 119 |
| MPM | | | 50 | 183 |
| MCS | 3 | 161 | 120 | 105 |
| MCM | | | 88 | 140 |
| SPS | 7 | 111 | 91 | 140 |
| SPM | | | 87 | 149 |
| SCS | 3 | 174 | 120 | 89 |
| SCM | | | 78 | 156 |

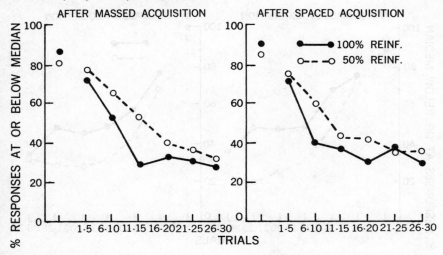

Fig. 3. Extinction curves for water-reinforcement groups after massed and spaced training, showing percentage of responses in 5-trial blocks at or below the over-all median response time. Data of Trial 1 are plotted separately.

the eight extinction groups along with the median response time of each group. Extinction curves as a function of acquisition conditions are shown in Fig. 3. After either spaced or massed training, the groups whose acquisition was with partial reinforcement were more resistant to extinction than those which had been continuously reinforced. The comparisons plotted in Fig. 3 do not suggest that the difference in extinction between partial and continuous reinforcement groups depends upon the distribution of acquisition trials. The analysis of variance of extinction data (Table 4) shows two significant sources of variation, both at the .05 level. As in Exp. 1, one is for replications, as expected; the second, in this experiment, is for the massed-spaced extinction variable. Figure 4 shows graphically the large difference in the curves for massed and spaced extinction after massed or spaced acquisition. The interaction between massed vs. spaced acquisition and massed vs. spaced extinction was very small in this experiment. Variation due to partial as against continuous reinforcement was not significant in the analysis of variance, nor was the critical interaction between massed vs. spaced and partial vs. continuous acquisition.

The analysis of covariance, summarized in Table 4, is an analysis of the extinction data adjusted for differences between groups in acquisition. When an adjustment was made for the superior performance of the 100% reinforcement groups in acquisition, the greater resistance to extinction of the 50% reinforcement groups was found to be significant beyond the .01 level. (The analysis of variance had failed to indicate significance at

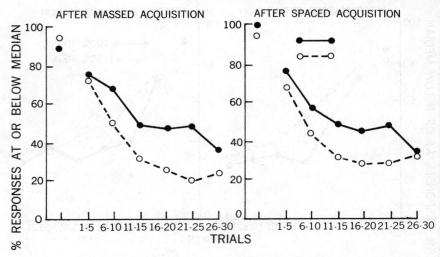

Fig. 4. Extinction curves for water-reinforcement groups showing massed and spaced extinction performance after massed and spaced acquisition. Data of Trial 1 are plotted separately.

TABLE 4

SUMMARY OF ANALYSIS OF VARIANCE AND COVARIANCE EXPERIMENT 2

| Source of Variation | df | Analysis of Variance | | Analysis of Covariance | |
|---|---|---|---|---|---|
| | | Mean Square | F | Adjusted Mean Square | F |
| A. Massed and spaced acquisition | 1 | 2.35 | .... | .11 | .... |
| B. 100% and 50% reinforcement | 1 | 141.68 | 2.32 | 413.93 | 8.88** |
| C. Massed and spaced extinction | 1 | 425.35 | 6.98* | 541.72 | 11.63** |
| D. Replications | 8 | 155.51 | 2.55* | 98.28 | 2.11 |
| A × B | 1 | 2.35 | .... | 8.72 | .... |
| A × C | 1 | 7.35 | .... | 18.42 | .... |
| A × D | 8 | 23.91 | .... | 9.68 | .... |
| B × C | 1 | 11.68 | .... | 67.93 | 1.45 |
| B × D | 8 | 81.99 | 1.35 | 37.97 | .... |
| C × D | 8 | 13.28 | .... | 10.65 | .... |
| Residual† | 33 | 60.93 | .... | 46.57 | .... |

* Significant at .05 level.
** Significant at .01 level.
† Residual df are 32 for the analysis of covariance.

the .05 level.) The analysis of covariance also demonstrated the greater resistance to extinction of the massed extinction over the spaced extinction groups ($p < .01$). No other variation and no interaction variance was statistically significant.

DISCUSSION

*Partial reinforcement and resistance to extinction.* In both experiments—with dry food or water as reinforcement—partial reinforcement groups were more resistant to extinction than continuous reinforcement groups, whether acquisition trials had been massed or spaced. This finding was not significant in the analysis of variance in either experiment, but was in the analysis of covariance. Sheffield's emphasis on the stimulus function of rapidly dissipating traces of reinforcement and nonreinforcement in the explanation of resistance to extinction following partial reinforcement is not supported in either case. To support Sheffield's interpretation it would have to be shown that massing of acquisition trials enhanced the resistance to extinction of the partial reinforcement relative to the continuous reinforcement group, particularly in Exp. 1, and that spacing of acquisition trials prevented any difference between partial and continuous groups in extinction, especially in Exp. 2. The fact that in all four extinction analyses—analysis of variance and covariance for each experiment—there was not a single significant A × B interaction (interaction between massed vs. spaced acquisition and partial vs. continuous reinforcement) argues convincingly against the Sheffield hypothesis.

It is conceivable that carried-over traces of previous goal events do affect resistance to extinction, but they would appear to be, at best, a factor of secondary importance. Crum, Brown, and Bitterman (2) found that a 50% delay-reinforcement group was more resistant to extinction than a 100% immediate reinforcement group. Tyler, Wortz, and Bitterman (10) reported that a random 50%-reinforcement group extinguished more slowly than an alternating 50%-reinforcement group. Neither of these results can be accounted for in terms of Sheffield's trace factor. Weinstock (11) spaced partial and continuous reinforcement trials at 24-hr. intervals, precluding any carry-over effect, and the advantage of partial reinforcement groups was still evident.

Slower extinction following partial reinforcement, *whether massed or spaced,* can be accounted for if a learned (associative) factor is postulated as the primary one. Such a factor must be relatively uninfluenced by the kind of reinforcement (e.g., food or water) or the distribution of trials and its effects must increase as acquisition progresses. That persistence of responding, despite nonreinforcements, develops as partial reinforcement training proceeds is recognized implicitly in the Sheffield procedure. On the first day of the experiment, 10 successive reinforced trials are run. On the second (training) day, the maximum number of consecutive nonreinforced trials is four, and these are reserved for the latter half of training "in order to prevent partial-reinforcement animals from refusing to run in the early part of training" (7, p. 516). It seems obvious, then, that by the time the extinction series is begun the partially reinforced Ss have been trained to persist in running despite nonreinforcements. The mechanism through which this persistence is developed can be conceived of as the conditioning of running to response-produced stimuli related to anticipatory frustration ($r_F \rightarrow s_F$). By this reasoning, runway stimuli are first conditioned, in the acquisition series of the partial-reinforcement groups, to fractional anticipatory goal (reinforcement) responses, $r_R \rightarrow s_R$. Then, when nonreinforcement comes to be frustrating,* the same runway stimuli are conditioned to the frustration reaction and $r_F \rightarrow s_F$ results. Although $s_F$ would tend initially to evoke responses antagonistic to running, as long as running continues in partial reinforcement training $s_F$ should become conditioned to the running response. If continued running is conditioned to stimuli produced by anticipatory frustration responses, as well as anticipatory reward responses, the partial groups would be more resistant to extinction than the continuous reinforcement groups. These implicit anticipatory conditioned mechanisms would develop under either massed or spaced acquisition conditions. Sheffield (7, p. 521) recognizes the possibility that some such mechanism might operate "in addition to cues from the frustration which carries over from a nonreinforced trial to the start of the following trial with massed training." Our results, and others cited already, suggest that the anticipatory frustration factor may be the more important of the two determining increased resistance to extinction following partial reinforcement.

*Distribution of extinction trials and resistance to extinction.* Sheffield (8) reported greater resistance to extinction with massed than with spaced extinction conditions. Stanley (9) has confirmed Sheffield's findings for a response time measure—he terms this "a vigor, and presumably a drive, measure of performance"—but has shown that an association measure of performance (percentage of correct runs) shows spaced extinction groups more resistant to extinction. In Sheffield's study and in the comparable portion of Stanley's, massed groups were significantly more resistant to extinction than spaced groups after massed acquisition; the extinction difference is in the same direction, but is not significant after spaced acquisition. This suggests that two factors are operating: (*a*) a motivational effect related to nonreward (frustration) which would show up particularly under massed conditions (1, 8, 9) and (*b*) generalized decrement due to shifting of intertrial intervals from acquisition to extinction. According to this reasoning the massed acquisition-massed extinction groups should be most highly resistant to extinction, and the massed-spaced groups should extinguish most readily.

* A study by Roussel (6) and other unpublished data from our laboratory support the notion that nonreward is not frustrating early in partial (50%) reinforcement training, but becomes more frustrating as training progresses; also, there is an indication that the degree of the frustration effect is a function of the amount of "reward expectation" which has already developed.

Our repetitions of this portion of the Sheffield analysis showed Exp. 2 in complete agreement with her finding and Stanley's; the results of Exp. 1 were in partial agreement. In Exp. 2 massed extinction groups were more resistant to extinction than spaced groups after spaced or massed training, although the difference was somewhat larger after massed acquisition. The interaction between massed-spaced acquisition and massed and spaced extinction was not significant. In Exp. 1, the massed-massed group resisted extinction significantly more than the massed-spaced group, but the difference between spaced-massed and spaced-spaced groups was slightly (not significantly) in the reverse direction. This, by itself, would not rule out the two-factor interpretation; however, in Exp. 1 there was no significant difference in resistance to extinction between spaced-spaced and massed-massed conditions, neither of which was subject to generalization decrement. This aspect of the results of Exp. 1 is contrary to the interpretation offered above.

Possibly the disagreement in this aspect of the results of our two experiments can be accounted for in terms of the general performance level attained by the food- and the water-reinforcement groups. The food-deprivation Ss showed consistently lower response times than the water-deprivation Ss in acquisition and extinction (compare Tables 1 and 3). If we take this to mean that the food-deprivation Ss were nearer to their limit of performance, it could be argued that the frustrative effect in extinction could show up more in Exp. 2 than in Exp. 1, and the generalization decrement more in Exp. 1 than in Exp. 2. Were this the case, the reversal in Exp. 1 between the spaced-massed and spaced-spaced groups —the only reversal in either experiment—could be attributed to a generalization decrement in switching from spaced acquisition to massed extinction which more than offset the facilitating frustration effect of massing extinction trials.

## SUMMARY

Two experiments were performed to test Sheffield's interpretation of resistance to extinction following partial reinforcement. Sheffield's design and procedure were duplicated and the experiments differed from hers only in the motivational-reward conditions employed. In Exp. 1 hungry Ss were rewarded with dry food, while in Exp. 2 thirsty Ss were rewarded with water. Sheffield had employed a wet mash as reinforcement.

The results were not in agreement with Sheffield's, and did not support her interpretation. Partial (50%) reinforcement groups were more resistant to extinction than continuous (100%) groups regardless of intertrial interval in acquisition or kind of reinforcement. These differences were significant only in an analysis of covariance which adjusted the groups for differences in acquisition levels of performance. An associative mechanism was postulated to account for the results.

Although, in Exp. 1, massing of trials increased resistance to extinction, the effect of distribution of extinction trials on resistance to extinction depended also upon the distribution of acquisition trials: the switched groups were less resistant to extinction than the unswitched ones. In Exp. 2, massed extinction groups were more resistant to extinction than spaced ones after both massed and spaced training and after both partial and continuous reinforcement, although here too generalization decrement seemed to be a factor.

## REFERENCES

1. AMSEL, A. and ROUSSEL, J. (1952) Motivational properties of frustration: I. Effect on a running response of the addition of frustration to the motivational complex. *J. exp. Psychol.*, 43, 363-368.
2. CRUM, J., BROWN, W. L., and BITTERMAN, M. E. (1951) The effect of partial and delayed reinforcement on resistance to extinction. *Amer. J. Psychol.*, 64, 228-237.
3. GRANT, D. A., HORNSETH, J. P., and HAKE, H. W. (1950) The influence of the intertrial interval on the Humphreys' "random reinforcement" effect during the extinction of a verbal response. *J. exp. Psychol.*, 40, 609-612.
4. GRANT, D. A., SCHIPPER, L. M., and ROSS, B. M. (1952) Effect of intertrial interval during acquisition on extinction of the conditioned eyelid response following partial reinforcement. *J. exp. Psychol.*, 44, 203-210.
5. JENKINS, W. O. and STANLEY, J. C., JR. (1950) Partial reinforcement: a review and critique. *Psychol. Bull.*, 47, 193-234.
6. ROUSSEL, J. (1952) Frustration effect as a function of repeated nonreinforcements and as a function of the consistency of reinforcement prior to the introduction of nonreinforcement. Unpublished master's thesis, Tulane Univ.
7. SHEFFIELD, V. F. (1949) Extinction as a function of partial reinforcement and distribution of practice. *J. exp. Psychol.*, 39, 511-526.
8. SHEFFIELD, V. F. (1950) Resistance to extinction as a function of the distribution of extinction trials. *J. exp. Psychol.*, 40, 305-313.
9. STANLEY, W. C. (1952) Extinction as a function of the spacing of extinction trials. *J. exp. Psychol.*, 43, 249-260.
10. TYLER, D. W., WORTZ, E. C., and BITTERMAN, M. E. (1953) The effect of random and alternating partial reinforcement on resistance to extinction in the rat. *Amer. J. Psychol.*, 66, 57-65.
11. WEINSTOCK, S. (1953) Acquisition and extinction of a partially reinforced running response at a 24 hour intertrial interval. Unpublished doctor's dissertation, Indiana Univ.
12. WEISS, E. J. (1954) Extinction as a function of water reinforcement and distribution of practice. Unpublished master's thesis, Tulane Univ.
13. WILSON, W. (1954) Extinction as a function of food reinforcement and distribution of practice. Unpublished master's thesis, Tulane Univ.

# 23. The Relative Effect of Reinforcement and Nonreinforcement in Establishing a Form Discrimination

## M. E. Fitzwater

*In getting an organism to learn to solve a discrimination problem, it is readily accepted that reinforcement must be provided for the subject's correct responses. But what role do nonreinforced trials play? And how does the nonreinforced response to the incorrect stimulus compare with a reinforced response to the correct stimulus? A number of experiments have been done in this area; Fitzwater's study is one of the early ones, and yet is quite definitive in providing an answer to this question.*

In recent years many research projects have been concerned with the independent variables related to the study of reinforcement. Most theorists have at least acknowledged the results of these studies by incorporating reinforcement as a primary or necessary condition of learning—Hull (6), Spence (9), Thorndike (10, 11); or as a secondary contributing condition —Tolman (12), Guthrie (4); or they have stressed its importance relative to specific kinds or types of learning—Skinner (8), Harlow (5).

Sufficient empirical evidence has been compiled (1, 7) to demonstrate that discrimination learning can occur as a result of nonreinforced practice, and so a study oriented only toward demonstrating the phenomenon appears unnecessary. Instead, the emphasis of the present study concerns the relative effects of differential proportions of nonreinforced and reinforced practice, other variables being equal. The primary independent variable considered was that of the proportion of preliminary practice devoted to reinforced trials and to nonreinforced trials. Along such a dimension several points were selected that were deduced as being the ones most likely to show the individual and composite effects of the two types of practice.

## PROBLEM

1. To compare the relative effectiveness of reinforced and nonreinforced single-alley practice in the establishment of a form discrimination.

*J. comp. physiol. Psychol.*, 1952, 45, 476-481. Reprinted with permission of the author and The American Psychological Association. This paper is an abstract of a dissertation submitted to the Graduate School of The Ohio State University in partial fulfillment of the requirements for the Ph.D. degree. The author wishes to thank Dr. D. D. Wickens for his advice and assistance.

2. To compare the effect of the tendency to approach the previously reinforced form with the tendency to avoid the previously nonreinforced form after discrimination has reached an asymptote.

## METHOD

### SUBJECTS

Seventy naive albino rats, aged 80 to 110 days at the beginning of the experiment, were used in the study. They were divided into seven groups, each with five males and five females, by the closed random-order technique. The rats were obtained from the colony maintained by the Department of Psychology at Bowling Green State University. The colony was developed from animals originally obtained from the Department of Psychology of the Ohio State University.

### APPARATUS

The apparatus consisted of a discrimination box similar in many ways to the one used by Grice (2, 3). It was composed of a starting box, a V-shaped choice chamber, and three goal boxes. The apparatus allowed the animal a choice between two stimulus figures appearing upon the doors at the front of each goal box. The apparatus was also used during pretraining as a single-alley apparatus. The change was effected by inserting two wedges in the choice chamber to reduce the taper and allow the presentation of one stimulus door at a time.

The over-all internal length of the discrimination box was 37 in. The walls and floors of the box were constructed from ¾-in. clear white pine. Each section of the apparatus was covered with ¼-in. hardware cloth. The entire apparatus with the exception of the stimulus figures was painted a dull black.

The stimulus cues consisted of 18-mm., alternate black and white striations. During choice training for any given rat either vertical striations were reinforced and horizontal striations were nonreinforced consistently, or vice versa. These cues were painted on push-through doors at the entrance to individual feeding chambers. Other figures used were a solid, dull black door and a 60-mm. white circle.

Door blocks were used behind the nonreinforced cue doors in such a way that the "incorrect" door could be opened only about ½ in. at the bottom.

### PROCEDURE

Before preliminary training, each rat was handled individually on four consecutive days. The animals were removed from their home cages, petted, placed upon a table, and picked up a number of times for 10 min. each day. Then they were placed in individual feeding cages for 1 hr. before being returned to their home cage.

Each rat was motivated by being deprived of food for an average of 22¾ hr. Purina Laboratory Chow was used as food throughout the experiment.

*Preliminary training.* During this training the apparatus was a single-alley, nonchoice apparatus. Each rat received a total of 40 trials, 8 trials per day for five days, in one of the following stimulus conditions: Experimental groups E-I, E-II, and E-III received 5, 10, and 20 reinforced trials to the subsequently reinforced cue, and 35, 30, and 20 nonreinforced trials to the subsequently nonreinforced cue, respectively. Groups C-V, C-VI, and C-VII were control groups for each of the above experimental groups, with the number of reinforced trials equal, respectively, to those of the experimental groups. The control groups differed in that the 35, 30, and 20 nonreinforced practice trials were to a solid, dull black door instead of the subsequently nonreinforced cue. A seventh group, Group IV, received all 40 reinforced trials to the subsequently reinforced cue.

All trials for a given rat on a given day were massed. If the nonreinforced cue confronted the animal when the starting-box door was opened, the animal was permitted to approach and nose the push-through door until it struck the block; then the rat was returned to the starting box and the apparatus was reset for the next trial. If the reinforced cue confronted the animal when the starting-box door was opened, the animal was permitted to approach and nose through the push-through door into the goal box and then to feed upon the ¾-in. square of chow for 20 sec. before being returned to the starting box for the subsequent trial.

*Choice training.* On the following day, after the last preliminary trial, the apparatus was changed to a double-choice discrimination box by removing the wedges from the choice chamber.

Choice training consisted of 16 massed trials per day for 6 days. The "correct" figure was alternated from right to left in a random fashion from trial to trial. Feeding time in the goal box was 10 sec.

During these trials the animals were confronted with one of the striated cues as consistently positive (the same cue as in preliminary training) and the opposite striated stimulus cue as consistently negative. The correction method was used.

*Substitution test trials.* After completion of the 96 choice-training trials, 16 additional trials were given. All conditions were the same as for the previous 96 choice trials except as follows: For half of the animals in each group the previously positively reinforced figure was replaced with a 60-mm. white circle. The same nonreinforced figure remained for these animals. For the other half of the animals, the same reinforced cue was presented, but the white circle was substituted for the previously nonreinforced cue. This substitution was for the purpose of measuring separately

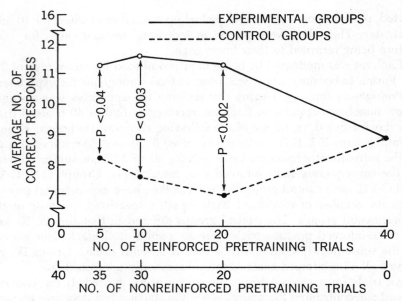

FIG. 1. Empirical curves showing the effects upon initial choice performance of differential amounts of single-alley reinforcements with and without nonreinforced practice.

the relative tendency to approach the positive cue and to avoid the negative cue after discrimination had become approximately asymptotic for all groups.

## RESULTS

### RELATIVE TO EFFECTS OF PRELIMINARY TRAINING

Performance data for successive days of choice training are presented for the three combined experimental groups E-I, E-II, and E-III and for

TABLE 1

COMPARISON OF COMBINED EXPERIMENTAL GROUPS WITH COMBINED CONTROL
GROUPS FOR SUCCESSIVE DAYS OF CHOICE TRAINING*

| Measure | Days | | | | | |
|---|---|---|---|---|---|---|
|  | 1 | 2 | 3 | 4 | 5 | 6 |
| $M_{Exp.}$ ........ | 11.40 | 12.40 | 13.73 | 13.70 | 15.03 | 14.73 |
| $M_{Cont.}$ ....... | 7.60 | 10.90 | 12.27 | 12.83 | 13.80 | 14.30 |
| $\sigma D_M$ ......... | 0.678 | 0.648 | 0.575 | 0.494 | 0.380 | 0.372 |
| $t$† ........... | 5.605 | 2.315 | 2.539 | 1.761 | 3.237 | 1.156 |
| $p$ ........... | <0.001 | <0.03 | <0.02 | <0.10 | <0.01 | <0.25 |

* Units are the number of correct responses per day; largest possible = 16.
† $Df = 58$ for all $t$'s.

the three combined control groups C-V, C-VI, and C-VII in Table 1. Note that the experimental animals receiving preliminary single-alley training with both the subsequently positive and subsequently negative cues performed significantly better than the control animals receiving preliminary training with only the positive cue. The difference between these combined groups diminishes to an insignificantly small difference by the end of the sixth day, where the two curves appear to be approaching approximately the same asymptote. This may be regarded as a verification of adequate sampling, for with prolonged practice under similar conditions of choice training the same level of proficiency should be reached.

The means of the seven groups for the first day of choice training are plotted in Figure 1. Group IV appears in a unique position both theoretically and empirically in that the rats therein received all preliminary trials to the positive cue; the group was therefore neither clearly experimental nor control. Group E-11 demonstrated the highest performance level, although not significantly higher than the other two experimental groups.

RELATIVE TO THE EFFECT OF CUE SUBSTITUTION AFTER PERFORMANCE
REACHED AN ASYMPTOTE

In Tables 2 and 3 the means and the summary of the variance analysis are presented for the four groups divided according to prior training and cue change; i.e., to run correctly, the experimental-approach or the control-approach animals would have to run toward the previously rewarded cue, and the experimental-avoidance or the control-avoidance animals would have to run toward the substituted circle or away from the previously blocked cue. Although the $F$ test is not significant at the 5 per cent level of confidence, the difference between the means still maintains a larger control vs. experimental difference than an approach vs. avoidance difference. The animals appeared to be able to perform as proficiently by avoiding the incorrect cue as by approaching the correct one.

TABLE 2

MEANS OF COMBINED EXPERIMENTAL AND COMBINED CONTROL PLUS GROUP IV

Groups were divided to test the subsequent tendency to approach the correct or avoid the incorrect cue after the alternate cue had been replaced by a neutral cue.

| Combined Group | N | Mean |
|---|---|---|
| Experimental—Approach . . . . . . . . . . . . . . . . . | 15 | 13.27 |
| Experimental—Avoidance . . . . . . . . . . . . . . . . | 15 | 12.07 |
| Control—Approach* . . . . . . . . . . . . . . . . . . . . . | 20 | 11.95 |
| Control—Avoidance* . . . . . . . . . . . . . . . . . . . . | 20 | 11.50 |

* Includes animals assigned from Group IV and treated as a control group because these animals received no preliminary practice to the later-to-be-nonreinforced cue.

TABLE 3

ANALYSIS OF VARIANCE OF RESULTS OF COMBINED GROUPS CITED IN TABLE 2

| Source of Variance | Sum of Squares | $df$ | Est. of Var. |
|---|---|---|---|
| Between groups ............... | 28.03 | 3 | 9.34 |
| Within groups ............... | 497.81 | 66 | 7.54 |
| Total ..................... | 525.84 | 69 | — |

$F = 1.239.$
$p > 0.05.$

## DISCUSSION

The significant superiority in performance of the experimental animals over the control animals on the first day of choice training after preliminary single-alley training substantiates Grice's (2) results concerning transfer of habit tendencies from a single-alley situation to a choice situation. Differences between experimental and control results along with those of the cue-substitution test indicate that apparently in a visual-discrimination task it is about as important to establish an avoidance habit as an approach habit, and that an appreciable discrimination does not seem to occur if an approach habit is established alone.

It may be noted that this study is not critical of any of the dominant theoretical systems for each can "explain" the obtained results as functions of its own theoretical constructs. The study is presented as a contribution to empirical knowledge rather than as a test of a "crucial" deduction. Inasmuch as it is demonstrated that the nonreinforced cue has acquired some deterrent quality, it appears that now problems formerly related to the reinforcing aspects of learning situations can fruitfully be studied relative to nonreinforcing situations.

## SUMMARY

This study was designed to compare the relative effectiveness of reinforced and nonreinforced single-alley practice in the establishment of a form discrimination, and the relative strength of the tendency to approach a previously nonreinforced cue after a discrimination habit had been established.

Results indicate that the combination of nonreinforced practice with reinforced practice during preliminary training was found to yield significantly better double-choice discrimination than reinforced practice alone. It was also shown that after the double-choice discrimination was established, no significant difference was found between the tendency to approach the "correct" cue and the tendency to avoid the "incorrect" cue when a neutral cue was substituted for the alternate one. The animals appeared to perform as proficiently by avoiding the incorrect cue as by approaching the correct one.

REFERENCES

1. DENNY, M. R. (1948) A demonstration of learning based solely on work inhibition drive—A substantiation of Hull's concept of $_sI_R$. Amer. Psychologist, 3, 250-251. (Abstract)
2. GRICE, G. R. (1948) The acquisition of a visual discrimination habit following response to a single stimulus. J. exp. Psychol., 38, 633-642.
3. GRICE, G. R. (1948) The relation of secondary reinforcement to delayed reward in visual discrimination learning. J. exp. Psychol., 38, 1-18.
4. GUTHRIE, E. R. (1942) Conditioning: A theory of learning in terms of stimulus, response and association. Natl. Soc. Stud. Educ., 41st yearbook, part II, 17-60.
5. HARLOW, H. F. (1950) Analysis of discrimination learning by monkeys. J. exp. Psychol., 40, 26-39.
6. HULL, C. L. (1943) Principles of behavior. New York: D. Appleton-Century Co., 57-67.
7. MOSS, EILEEN M. and HARLOW, H. F. (1947) The role of reward in discrimination learning in monkeys. J. comp. physiol. Psychol., 40, 333-342.
8. SKINNER, B. F. (1938) The behavior of organisms. New York: D. Appleton-Century Co., 167-231.
9. SPENCE, K. W. (1936) The nature of discrimination learning in animals. Psychol. Rev., 43, 427-449.
10. THORNDIKE, E. L. (1911) Animal intelligence. New York: Macmillan.
11. THORNDIKE, E. L. (1932) The fundamentals of learning. New York: Teachers College, Columbia Univer.
12. TOLMAN, E. C. (1932) Purposive behavior in animals and men. New York: D. Appleton-Century Co., 371-391.

SECTION SIX

# The Contribution of Task
# Variables to Learning

W HEN humans are used as subjects for learning tasks, experimental interest has centered primarily on an examination of the influence of task variables.

In the verbal learning task, the meaningfulness of the material has been generally recognized as a variable which is most important for learning. There have been a number of methods devised for measuring meaningfulness. A frequently used technique has been proposed by Noble (1952), who measured meaningfulness by counting the number of written associations to a stimulus word produced by an individual during a fixed interval of time—frequently 60 seconds. A great many investigators have demonstrated that learning is a function of meaningfulness as measured by this method.

Although most verbal learning studies employ lists of isolated words or trigrams or pairs of these, there has been some work done with connected discourse. Miller and Selfridge (1950) have found that the context of such material plays an important role in learning, although a more recent article by Coleman (1963) modifies somewhat Miller and Selfridge's conclusions. Both of these articles have been included in this chapter.

In the classical conditioning area, many investigators have examined the influence of the intensity of the conditioned stimulus, with mixed findings. Grice and Hunter (1964) show that whether or not the intensity of the conditioned stimulus plays an important role in ease of conditioning depends upon the type of experimental design which is used.

Finally, one of the most frequently examined task variables is the intertrial interval or the distribution of practice. Nowhere is the influence of this variable more clearly demonstrated than in the motor skills learning situation. A study by Adams (1954) demonstrates this finding with considerable clarity.

## REFERENCES

ADAMS, J. A. (1954) Psychomotor performance as a function of intertrial rest interval. *J. exp. Psychol.*, 48, 131-133.

COLEMAN, E. B. (1963) Approximations to English. *Amer. J. Psychol.*, 76, 239-247.

GRICE, G. R. and HUNTER, J. J. (1964) Stimulus intensity effects depend upon the type of experimental design. *Psychol. Rev.*, 71, 247-256.

MILLER, G. A. and SELFRIDGE, J. A. (1950) Verbal context and the recall of meaningful material. *Amer. J. Psychol.*, 63, 176-185.

NOBLE, C. E. (1952) An analysis of meaning. *Psychol. Rev.*, 59, 421-430.

## 24.   Verbal Context and the Recall of Meaningful Material

### G. A. Miller and J. A. Selfridge

*In this article, the authors have demonstrated how learning is related to varying approximations of meaningful material. A surprising finding is that when short range contextual dependencies are preserved in nonsense material, such material is as readily recalled as meaningful material.*

Communicative behavior, perhaps more than any of man's other activities, depends upon patterning for its significance and usefulness. An accidental inversion of words or letters or sounds can produce grotesque alterations of a sentence, and to scramble the elements at random is to turn a sensible message into gibberish. No attack upon the problems of verbal behavior will be satisfactory if it does not take quantitative account of the patterns of verbal elements.

We can dependably produce and distinguish only a small number of different letters or speech sounds. We must use these few elements to talk about millions of different things and situations. To stretch these few elements to cover these many needs, we are forced to combine the elements into patterns and to assign a different significance to each pattern. Since the number of possible patterns increases exponentially as the length of the pattern increases, this proves to be an efficient method of solving the problem.

Not all the possible patterns of elements are used in any particular language. In English, for example, the sequence of letters *qke* does not occur. It is reasonable to ask, therefore, why we do not exploit the available patterns more effectively. Is it not inefficient to ignore some patterns while others are greatly overworked?

The preference for some patterns at the expense of others forces us to produce more elements—letters, sounds, words, etc.—in order to make the same number of distinctions that we could make with the same elements if we used all possible patterns. To illustrate: imagine a language with 10 elementary symbols that is used to refer to 100 different things, events or situations. If we used all possible pairs of elements, we could refer to everyone of the 100 things with one of the 100 pairs of 10 symbols. If, however, we refuse to use some of the pairs and so rule them out of the language, it is necessary to make up the difference by using triads. Thus

*Amer. J. Psychol.*, 1950, 63, 176-185. Reprinted with permission of the senior author and *The American Journal of Psychology*.

the language uses patterns of three elements to make distinctions that could be made with patterns of two elements.

On further consideration, however, this kind of inefficiency does not appear a complete waste of time. By favoring some patterns rather than others the language is protected against error.[*] More specifically, in English we recognize immediately that an error has occurred if we read in our newspaper, "Man bites dxg." The pattern dxg is not admitted in English, and so we catch the error. If, however, all patterns of elements were admissible, dxg would have some semantic rule and we would not be able to catch the mistake. The number system is an example of the efficient use of ten symbols, but it is highly susceptible to mechanical errors. If a man says that his telephone number is 9236 we have no way of recognizing that he has or has not made an error.

Patterns are unavoidable, and a preference for some patterns provides insurance against errors. Thus it seems reasonable that the statistical studies of different languages all show that some patterns of elements are greatly overworked while others occur rarely or not at all.[†] The present interest in verbal patterning, however, is in the light these observations can throw upon the psychological problem of verbal context.

*Verbal context.* Psychologists use the word context to refer to the totality of conditions influencing a behavioral event. For the present discussion we want to restrict this broad definition and to consider only the antecedent verbal conditions. When a man talks, his choice of words depends upon his training, his needs and intentions, the situation and audience. These factors comprise the total context in which his words must be studied. By verbal context, as opposed to total context, we mean only the extent to which the prior occurrence of certain verbal elements influences the talker's present choice. If the talker has said "children like to," his choice for the next word in this pattern is considerably limited—*elephant, punished, loud, Bill,* and many other words are highly unlikely continuations.

By verbal context, therefore, we mean the extent to which the choice of a particular word depends upon the words that precede it. In the statistical sense, this definition of verbal context is given in terms of dependent probabilities.[‡] The probability that event $C$ will occur is not the same after $A$ as it is after $B$. The statistical dependencies between successive units form the basis for a study of verbal context.

To illustrate the operation of conditional probabilities in our verbal behavior, consider the set of all possible sequences 10 letters long. We could construct a table listing them. The first row of the table would be the

[*] C. E. Shannon, A mathematical theory of communication, *Bell Syst. Tech. J.*, 27, 1948, 379-423, 623-656.

[†] G. K. Zipf, *Human Behavior and the Principle of Least Effort*, 1949, 1-343.

[‡] G. A. Miller and F. C. Frick, Statistical behavioristics and sequences of responses, *Psychol. Rev.*, 56, 1949, 311-324.

pattern *aaaaaaaaaa*, 10 consecutive *a*'s. The second would be *aaaaaaaaab*, then *aaaaaaaaba*, *aaaaaaaabb*, *aaaaaaabaa*, etc., until all possible arrangements of letters, spaces, commas, periods, hyphens, quotes, colons, numbers, etc., were exhausted. Altogether there would be about 50 different symbols, and the table would contain $50^{10}$, or about 100,000,000,000,000,000 different patterns. Then we would examine some English writing and try to determine the relative frequencies of occurrence of the patterns. Only a small fraction of the $50^{10}$ alternatives actually occur in English. The table would show strong dependencies. For example, the letter *q* is always followed in English by the letter *u*, and so all those entries in the table that contained a *q* followed by anything but *u* would not occur in English. It is not possible to predict the relative frequency of *qe*, for instance, by multiplying the relative frequencies of *q* and of *e*.

If such a table existed, along with the relative frequencies of occurrence, it would be possible to construct sequences of letters that reflected the statistical dependencies of English verbal patterns. We can imagine similar tables constructed for shorter or longer sequences of letters. A table for all patterns of 2 symbols would represent the relative frequencies of pairs; for 3 symbols, triads, etc. The longer the sequence, the more information the table contains about the pattern of dependencies in our molar verbalizations.

To illustrate the use of such information we shall borrow a device used by Shannon. Suppose we have no knowledge at all of the relative frequencies of occurrence, but only a list of the 50 different symbols. Then, for all we know, any sequence of symbols might be permissible. If we tried to construct a message in the language, the best we could do would be to draw at random from the 50 different symbols. We have no reason to think that one sequence of symbols is more likely than another. Proceeding in ignorance to construct a message, we might produce something like this: *cplp'rzw(p".:k!)"ntegznqO?i6vlaur :8h*, etc.

Now suppose that we have a reliable tabulation of the relative frequencies of 'patterns' of one symbol. We know, therefore, that *e* and the space between words are more likely to occur than are *?* and *z*. With this information we can increase the chance of constructing a meaningful message, although our chances are still very small. If we draw successive symbols according to their relative frequencies of occurrence in English, we might produce something like this: *wli hnrooye lricocnri mae c zg 2eaya*, etc.

The next step is to imagine that we have a tabulation of relative frequencies of occurrence of patterns of two symbols. Now it is possible to improve the statistical approximation to English by drawing in the following way. Begin by drawing any likely pair. Suppose the pair is *au*. Now look at all the pairs starting with *u* and draw from them according to their relative frequencies of occurrence. Suppose the result is *ud*. Now look at all pairs starting with *d* and draw one of those, and so proceed to build up the message. Notice that each draw depends upon the preceding draw—the preceding draw determines from which set the present draw is to be made. Drawing in this way reflects the conditional probabilities of successive symbols. A message constructed in this way might read *aud ren stiofivo omerk. thed thes bllale,* etc.

If we have a tabulation of sequences of three letters, we can construct a message that reflects the conditional probabilities of English triads. First we draw a likely triplet, say *ann,* then draw next from the triplets starting with *nn* and obtain *nna,* then from the triplets beginning *na,* etc. The preceding two symbols determine from which set the next triplet is drawn. In this way a message might be produced that would read: *annation ef to the acticas. Oth rested,* etc.

With a tabulation of sequences of four letters we might produce: *influst intradio be decay, the condive,* etc. By tabulating the relative frequencies of longer sequences and drawing successive items so as to reflect these frequencies, we can construct messages that reflect the statistical dependencies of English as extensively as we please.

For convenience, we shall refer to these different ways of constructing a statistical English as orders of approximation, and shall number them from $0$ to $n$. At the zero order we have no knowledge of relative frequencies, at the first order we know the relative frequencies of individual symbols, at the second order we know the relative frequencies of pairs, at the $n$th order we know the relative frequencies of $n$.

Consider this statistical English now in terms of verbal context. With a zero-order approximation to English there are no contextual influences whatsoever on the choice of successive symbols. At the $n$th-order approximation, however, each symbol is selected in the context of the preceding $n$-symbols. As the order of approximation is increased, the amount of context for each symbol is increased, and the contextual constraints (dependent probabilities) have a chance to operate. As the order of approximation is increased, the messages we can construct become more and more familiar, reasonable, meaningful. The more we permit contextual restraints to operate, the better our chances of producing a message that might actually occur in English.

We have, therefore, a scale for what can be loosely called 'meaningfulness.' At one end are the random jumbles of symbols we customarily call nonsense, and at the other end are patterns of jumbles that could easily appear in our daily discourse. Equipped with this quantitative estimate of 'the degree of nonsense' or 'amount of contextual constraint,' we can proceed to study certain psychological problems that have been phrased in terms of meaningfulness.

*An experimental illustration.* Briefly stated, the problem to which this concept of verbal context has been applied is, How well can people remember sequences of symbols that have various degrees of contextual constraint in their composition? The experimental literature contains considerable evidence to support the reasonable belief that nonsense is harder to remember than sense. This evidence has suffered, however, from a necessarily subjective interpretation of what was sensible.

In the present experiment, the learning materials were constructed at several orders of approximation to English. These materials were presented to Ss whose recall scores were then plotted as a function of the order of approximation.*

*Learning materials.* In the preceding examples we have used patterns of letters to illustrate the effects of contextual constraints. There is, of course, no necessity to limit the argument to letters. It is possible to use words or even sentences as the component elements that are arranged according to the statistical structure of English. In the present experimental illustration the materials were constructed with words as the units of analysis.

In theory, the construction of materials to incorporate the statistical structure of English over sequences of several words requires a tabulation of the relative frequencies of such sequences. Such a tabulation would be exceedingly long and tedious to compile. An alternative method of construction is available, however, which makes the procedure practicable. Instead of drawing each successive word from a different statistical distribution indicated by the preceding words, we draw the word from a different person who has seen the preceding words.

At the second order, for example, a common word, such as *he, it* or *the,* is presented to a person who is instructed to use the word in a sentence. The word he uses directly after the one given him is then noted and later presented to another person who has not heard the sentence given by the first person, and he, in turn, is asked to use that word in a sentence. The word he uses directly after the one given him is then noted and later given to yet another person. This procedure is repeated until the total sequence of words is of the desired length. Each successive pair of words could go together in a sentence. Each word is determined in the context of only one preceding word.

For higher orders of approximation the person would see a sequence of words and would use the sequence in a sentence. Then the word he used directly after the sequence would be added, the first word of the sequence would be dropped, and the new (but overlapping) sequence would be presented to the next person. By this procedure we constructed sequences of words at the second, third, fourth, fifth and seventh orders of approximation.

* The experiment was carried out by the junior author and is presented in detail in her honor's thesis, *Investigations into the Structure of Verbal Context*, 1949. The thesis is on file in the Library of the Psychological Laboratory, Memorial Hall, Harvard University.

For the first order approximation to English a scrambling of the words in the higher orders was used. By drawing words at random from the contextually determined lists, we obtained as good an approximation to the relative frequencies of individual words in English as these higher order lists provided. The alternative method of selecting words at random from a newspaper might have given a sample quite different in difficulty (familiarity).

A zero order approximation to English could be obtained by drawing at random from a dictionary. Most dictionaries contain too many rare words, however, so we drew from the 30,000 commonest words listed by Thorndike and Lorge.* This source had the additional advantage that it listed separately all forms of the word, whereas the dictionary lists only the lexical units. Words drawn at random from this list of 30,000 words are selected independently and without any constraints due to adjacent words or the relative frequencies of appearance of the words in English.

A final set of words was taken directly from current fiction or biography. These lists represent a full contextual determination.

By these devices we constructed sequences of words with eight different degrees of contextual constraint. In the following discussion we shall refer to these lists as 0, 1, 2, 3, 4, 5, 7 and text-orders of approximation. At each order four lists of different length—10, 20, 30 and 50 words—were constructed. Thus the experimental design called for 32 different lists. Two such sets of 32 lists were constructed. Since the lists require considerable time to compile and since they may be some general interest, one of the sets of 32 is reproduced in full in the appendix to this paper.

*Experimental procedure.* Each set of 32 lists was read aloud and recorded on a wire recorder. A man's voice was used. The words were read slowly and distinctly in a near monotone, with a short pause between words. At the beginning of the recording the instructions were given and a single practice list was presented to make sure the Ss understood their task. They were to listen until a list was finished, at which time a bell sounded signalling them to begin writing what they had just heard. The Ss were instructed to write the words they remembered as nearly in their correct order as possible. Order was not used, however, as a criterion for scoring their responses. All eight of the 10-word lists were given first, proceeding from least to greatest contextual determination, then the 20-word lists in the same order, then the 30-word lists, and finally the 50-word lists. Short rest periods (5 min.) were given between the 20- and 30-word lists and between the 30- and 50-word lists.

Two groups of 10 Ss were used. One group heard and recalled one of the sets of 32 lists, the other group heard and recalled the second set. The Ss were principally students at Harvard and Radcliffe. It was E's impression that a larger number of Ss would not have reduced the irregularities

* E. L. Thorndike and I. Lorge, *The Teacher's Wordbook of 30,000 Words*, 1944.

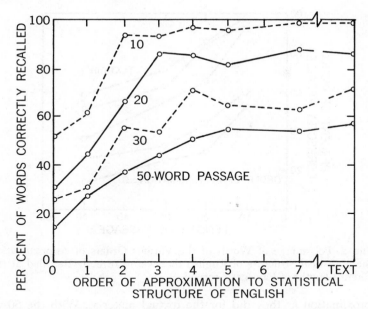

Fig. 1. Percentage of Words of the Lists of Different Lengths that were Correctly Recalled at the Various Orders of Approximation to the Statistical Structure of English.

in the results, for most of the variability seemed attributable to sampling peculiarities in the lists themselves. Several more sets of 32 lists would be needed before an accurate estimate of the functional relations could be made. The results are adequate, however, to indicate the approximate magnitudes and general trends of the functions.

S's answers were scored for the number of words that they had written that had occurred in the test material. The number recalled, regardless of order, was expressed as a percentage of the total number presented.

*Results and discussion.* The experimental data are summarized in Figs. 1 and 2. In Fig. 1 the recall-score, expressed as a percentage, is plotted as a function of the order of approximation to the statistical structure of English, with the length of the lists as the parameter. In Fig. 2 the same data are replotted to show the relation of the recall-score to the length of the list, with the order of approximation as the parameter. In both figures the functions represent the mean scores for all 20 Ss. It is clear from the results that percentage recalled increases as the order of approximation is increased and decreases as the length of the list is increased. Inspection of Fig. 1 leads to a reasonable suspicion that the two variables, length and order of approximation, interact. With the short, 10-word lists there is little to be gained from contextual bonds extending over more than two words. With the 20-word lists the Ss remembered as well at the third order

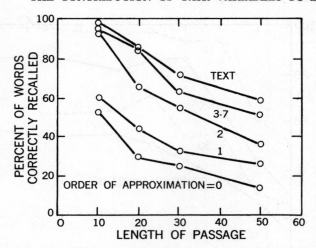

FIG. 2. Percentage of Words of the Various Orders of Approximation to the Statistical Structure of English that were Correctly Recalled at the Different Lengths of Passages Learned.

of approximation as they did for the textual material. With the 50-word lists, however, only orders 5 and 7 are comparable to the textual material in terms of percentage recalled. It would seem, therefore, that the longer the passage the greater is the usefulness of contextual associations extending over long sequences of items.

By a strict interpretation of the word 'nonsense,' one is forced to conclude that all orders of approximation less than the full text are nonsense. Consider an example from Order 5:

house to ask for is to earn our living by working towards a goal for his team in old New-York was a wonderful place wasn't it even pleasant to talk about and laugh hard when he tells lies he should not tell me the reason why you are is evident.

The experimental results show that this kind of gibberish is as easily recalled as a passage lifted from a novel. Thus there are kinds of nonsense that are as easy to recall as are meaningful passages. The significant distinction is not to be drawn between meaning and nonsense, but between materials that utilize previous learning and permit positive transfer and materials that do not. If the nonsense preserves the short range associations of the English language that are so familiar to us, the nonsense is easy to learn.

The experiment shows, therefore, that the problem of meaning vs. nonsense in verbal learning need not be approached in terms of a qualitative dichotomy, but can be studied as a functional relation between quantitative variables. The results indicate that meaningful material is easy to learn, not because it is meaningful *per se*, but because it preserves the short range associations that are familiar to the Ss. Nonsense materials that retain these short range associations are also easy to learn. By shifting the problem from 'meaning' to 'degree of contextual constraint' the whole area is reopened to experimental investigation.

Psychologists familiar with the problems of verbal learning will recognize the usefulness of the kind of material employed in this illustrative experiment. For example, is retroactive inhibition affected by interpolating different orders of approximation to English between the original learning and the recall? What is the effect of using original and interpolated materials of the same or of different orders of approximation to English? Do the higher approximations to English show the same differences between recall after sleep and recall after waking activity that the lower approximations show? Is it possible to show a continuum from the short-term reminiscence that can be demonstrated with syllables to the long-term reminiscence that can be shown with poetry? How does the span of immediate memory vary with the order of approximation? Is the superiority of distributed over massed practice a function of the order of approximation of the materials to the statistical structure of English? Can differences in learning and recalling different orders of approximation be demonstrated as a function of age?

The operational analysis of meaningfulness makes it possible to ask such questions and to see how one would proceed to answer them. The problem now is to collect the experimental data.

## SUMMARY

A quantitative definition for verbal context is given in terms of dependent probabilities. The definition is used to construct lists of words with varying degrees of contextual determination. When short range contextual dependencies are preserved in nonsense material, the nonsense is as readily recalled as is meaningful material. From this result it is argued that contextual dependencies extending over five or six words permit positive transfer, and that it is these familiar dependencies, rather than the meaning *per se*, that facilitate learning.

## APPENDIX

### LISTS USED IN RECALL EXPERIMENT

*0-order approximation*

10: byway consequence handsomely financier bent flux cavalry swiftness weather-beaten extent

20: betwixt trumpeter pebbly complication vigorous tipple careen obscure attractive consequence expedition pane unpunished prominence chest sweetly basin awoke photographer ungrateful

30: crane therewith egg journey applied crept burnish pound precipice king eat sinister descend cab Idaho baron alcohol inequality Illinois benefactor forget lethargy fluted watchtower attendance obeisance cordiality dip prolong bedraggle

50: hammer neatly unearned ill-treat earldom turkey that valve outpost broaden isolation solemnity lurk far-sighted Britain latitude task pub excessively chafe competence doubtless tether backward query exponent prose resourcefulness intermittently auburn Hawaii unhabit topsail nestle raisin liner communist Canada debauchery engulf appraise mirage loop referendum dowager absolutely towering aqueous lunatic problem

*1-order approximation*

10: abilities with that beside I for waltz you the sewing

20: tea realizing most so the together home and for were wanted to concert I posted he her it the walked

30: house reins women brought screaming especially much was said cake love that school to a they in is the home think with are his before want square of the wants

50: especially is eat objections are covering seemed the family I that substance dinner raining into black the see for will passionately anu so I after is window to down hold to boy appearance think with again room the beat go in there beside some is was after women dinner chorus

*2-order approximation*

10: was he went to the newspaper is in deep and

20: sun was nice dormitory is I like chocolate cake but I think that book is he wants to school there

30: the book was going home life is on the wall of you are ready to the waltz is I know much ado about it was a dog when it was

50: you come through my appetite is that game since he lives in school is jumping and wanted help call him well and substance was a piano is a mistake on this is warm glow in and girl went to write four turtledoves in my book is fine appearance of the

*3-order approximation*

10: tall and thin boy is a biped is the beat

20: family was large dark animal came roaring down the middle of my friends love books passionately every kiss is fine

30: happened to see Europe again is that trip to the end is coming here tomorrow after the packages arrived yesterday brought good cheer at Christmas it is raining outside as

50: came from the beginning and end this here is the top spins in a house by the library is full of happiness and love is very nice of her that fell from the window she went home from work to pass the cigarettes down to earth he picked an apple

*4-order approximation*

10: saw the football game will end at midnight on January

20: went to the movies with a man I used to go toward Harvard Square in Cambridge is mad fun for

30: the first list was posted on the bulletin he brought home a turkey will die on my rug is deep with snow and sleet are destructive and playful students always

50: the next room to mine silver in Pennsylvania is late in getting home on time my date was tremendous fun going there skiing this day would end and have no more objections to his speech on the radio last night played the viola in the orchestra and chorus performed the

*5-order approximation*

10: they saw the play Saturday and sat down beside him

20: road in the country was insane especially in dreary rooms where they have some books to buy for studying Greek

30: go it will be pleasant to you when I am near the table in the dining room was crowded with people it crashed into were screaming that they had been

50: house to ask for is to earn our living by working towards a goal for his team in old New-York was a wonderful place wasn't it even pleasant to talk about and laugh hard when he tells lies he should not tell me the reason why you are is evident

*7-order approximation*

10: recognize her abilities in music after he scolded him before

20: easy if you know how to crochet you can make a simple scarf if they knew the color that it

30: won't do for the members what they most wanted in the course an interesting professor gave I went to at one o'clock stopped at his front door and rang the

50: then go ahead and do it if possible while I make an appointment I want to skip very much around the tree and back home again to eat dinner after the movie early so that we could get lunch because we liked her method for sewing blouses and skirts is

*Text*

10: the history of California is largely that of a railroad

20: more attention has been paid to diet but mostly in relation to disease and to the growth of young children

30: Archimedes was a lonely sort of eagle as a young man he had

studied for a short time at Alexandria Egypt where he made a life-
long friend a gifted mathematician
50: the old professor's seventieth birthday was made a great occasion
for public honors and a gathering of his disciples and former
pupils from all over Europe thereafter he lectured publicly less and
less often and for ten years received a few of his students at his
house near the university

## 25. Approximations to English: Some Comments on the Method

### E. B. Coleman

*Although Miller and Selfridge demonstrated that learning was re-
lated to context, a surprising finding was that fifth order approximation material was as easily recalled as a passage lifted from a novel.
In this selection, Coleman has questioned this latter finding, pointing
to some difficulties with some of the higher order approximation
material used by Miller and Selfridge. When different material is
used, results at variance with those of Miller and Selfridge are
obtained.*

Miller and Selfridge plotted approximations to English against percentage of words recalled and got a negatively accelerated curve that became
horizontal at about a fifth-order approximation. From this they concluded
that a fifth-order approximation "is as easily recalled as a passage lifted
from a novel . . . meaningful material is easy to learn, not because it is
meaningful *per se*, but because it preserves the short range associations
that are familiar to the Ss."* Twelve years have gone by and the authors
themselves have modified their conclusions,† but the shape of the curve

*Amer. J. Psychol.*, 1963, 76, 239-247. Reprinted with permission of the author and
*The American Journal of Psychology*.
    * G. A. Miller and J. A. Selfridge, Verbal context and the recall of meaningful ma-
terial, this JOURNAL, 63, 1950, 176-185.
    † At any rate, the conclusion of this paper is little more than a paraphrase of
Miller's notion of recoding (G. A. Miller, The magic number seven; plus or minus
two: Some limits on our capacity for processing information, *Psychol. Rev.*, 63, 1956,
81-97). Also see Miller, Human memory and the storage of information, *I. R. E.
Transactions on Information Theory*, 1956, 2, 135.

and the original conclusions are still important in the literature. The curves and conclusions are quoted in general texts enjoying wide circulation,\* and the results have been replicated many times.

It is true that Marks and Jack reported conflicting results: they found that a significantly higher percentage of the prose-selections was recalled.† They used, however, a different measure, *i.e.*, the number of words recalled correctly in sequence up to the first error—the immediate memory span.

Miller and Selfridge had ignored both order and intrusions, merely counting total number of words correctly recalled. When this measure was used, many investigators have replicated the results of Miller and Selfridge: their curves became horizontal at about fifth-order approximations.‡ In fact, the Ss of one investigator (Sharp) made slightly lower scores on prose than on higher-order approximations.

Sharp's unexpected finding is not unique. Using a different measure, 'cloz' scores, Deese repeated Sharp's results.§ After fifth or sixth order, 'cloz' scores began to decrease. Thus, for two different measures and for two different samples of approximations to English, we find that after about fifth or sixth order, higher-order approximations begin to diverge from S's verbal habits.

It is really quite surprising to find that the only associations important to recall are those extending over sequences of less than six words. Language can be analyzed into units larger than words—clauses and paragraphs for instance. Surely the long-range, high-order associations between these larger units are important in recall. The mere flattening of the curve is surprising; but when both Deese and Sharp find the curve turning back downward, the implications become unreasonable enough to bring the experimental technique under suspicion. The grammatical constructions in higher-order approximations have always seemed to be more far-fetched and implausible than the constructions in lower orders. This personal impression, if it were corroborated by more objective evidence, would explain the flattening of the curve. As a matter of fact, it was corroborated by the following scaling procedure.

---

\* James Deese, *The Psychology of Learning*, 2nd ed., 1958, 177-179; E. R. Hilgard, *Theories of Learning*, 2nd ed., 1956, 381-382, Miller, *Language and Communication*, 1951, 212-213.

† M. R. Marks and Ollie Jack, Verbal context and memory span for meaningful material, this JOURNAL, 65, 1952, 298-300.

‡ Three of the most recent replications were: Leo Postman and P. A. Adams, Studies in incidental learning: VIII. The effects of contextual determination, *J. exp. Psychol.*, 59, 1960, 153-164; Patricia Richardson and J. F. Voss, Replication report: Verbal context and the recall of meaningful material, *ibid.*, 60, 1960, 417-418; H. C. Sharp, Effect of contextual constraint upon recall of verbal passages, this JOURNAL, 71, 1958, 568-572.

§ Deese, From the isolated unit to connected discourse, in C. N. Cofer (ed.), *Verbal Learning and Verbal Behavior*, 1961, 11-31.

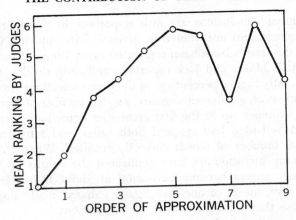

Fig. 1. Mean judges' ranking of grammaticalness plotted against order of approximation to English.

## EXPERIMENTAL I: SCALING PROCEDURE

### (A) RANKING APPROXIMATIONS AS TO GRAMMATICALNESS: JUDGES.

Twelve linguists ranked 12 sets of approximations to English as to their grammaticalness. All the judges were attending the 1961 Linguistic Institute meeting at the University of Texas. Six held doctoral degrees in either English or linguistics; six were graduate students in linguistics. None of them was familiar with approximations to English.

*Materials.* One set of approximations was drawn from the set collected by Sharp.* It consisted of a second-, a third-, and a fifth-, and a ninth-order approximation. A zero-order approximation was added by sampling at random from *The Teacher's Word Book*,† and a first-order was added by sampling randomly from Sharp's other approximations. The first 15 words of each approximation were typed on an individual card.

The other 11 sets were similar. Three were drawn from Miller and Selfridge's collection, two from Moray, and Taylor's,‡ and six from Deese's.§ The individual sequence on each card was 15 words long, and all sets were supplied with a zero- and a first-order approximation if they did not already contain them. Thus there were 12 scales represented by 12 packets of cards.

* Sharp, *op. cit.*, 568.
† E. L. Thorndike and Irving Lorge, *The Teacher's Wordbook of 30,000 Words*, 1944.
‡ Neville Moray and Ann Taylor, The effect of redundancy in shadowing one of two dichotic messages, *Language and Speech*, 1, 1958, 102-109.
§ Deese, *op. cit.*, 177.

Procedure. A judge was given a packet of cards and asked to rank them as to grammaticalness. He was instructed to use anything he knew about English grammar as a basis of his judgment.

Results and discussion. In Fig. 1, mean rank assigned by the judges is plotted against order of approximation.* The curve shows clearly that the linguists thought that the higher-order approximations deviated from English grammatical rules just as much as did the fifth-order approximations. As order of approximation becomes higher, apparently the grammatical constructions gradually become more awkward and implausible; that is, the subjects do not agree so well with their verbs, not the verbs with their direct objects, nor the modifiers with the words they modify, etc.

A gradually increasing deviation from common English is not hard to explain when the technique for generating approximations is considered. When the person who originally generated an approximation was faced with a short sequence (humble because, for instance), he could incorporate it into a short, simple sentence. On the other hand, when he was faced with a long sequence (humble because they have no electricity), sometimes he had to resort to a complex and far-fetched sentence to incorporate it. The effect was multiplied because he was not allowed to use punctuation. Thus, as order of approximation increased, the sentences from which the approximations were derived steadily diverged from common English.

The implications of Fig. 1 are obvious: its curve is almost identical to the usual curve representing recall of approximations to English. This suggests that the previous recall curves became horizontal because increasing grammatical awkwardness of some sort was counterbalancing the effect of long-range associations.

(B) WORD-COMPLEXITY OF APPROXIMATIONS.

Analyzing an extensive sample of approximations suggested that their individual words may become more uncommon and more complex after about the sixth-order.

The sample. The following approximations to English were analyzed: (a) the second-, third-, and fifth-order approximations collected by Sharp, (b) all the approximations published by Miller and Selfridge, (c) all the approximations collected by Deese. Table I shows that the sample consisted of 4100 words and represented 9 orders of approximation plus a sample of prose.

---

* This curve contradicts a statement by Chomsky, and may be of some incidental interest to linguists. N. A. Chomsky states "there appears to be no particular relation between order of approximation and grammaticalness." (N. A. Chomsky, Syntactic Structures, 1957, 17.)

*Uncommon words.* All words occurring less than 100 times per million words were counted, thus all words that were not AA words were counted.*

*Morphological complexity.* The mean number of morphemes per 100 words was computed. Only the segmental morphemes were considered, of course, and a morpheme was defined as a word-root or a derivational or inflectional affix except that suppletive and replacive inflections were not counted. For instance, *unearned* was counted as three morphemes: *un, earn, ed*; but *were* was counted as a single morpheme.

Clearly this is the same sort of complexity that Flesch is measuring less directly by counting syllables.† As a matter of fact, Flesch originally counted affixes,‡ and this is almost identical to computing the mean number of morphemes per word.

*Syllables per 100 words.* Because it is so simple and reliable, the number of syllables per 100 words was also counted as a second index of morphological complexity.

*Results.* Table I shows that the first-, third-, fourth-, fifth-, sixth-, and

TABLE I

NUMBER OF SYLLABLES, MORPHEMES, AND DIFFICULT WORDS PER 100 WORDS
FOR ORDERS OF APPROXIMATION TO ENGLISH

|  | Order of approximation | | | | | | | | | |
|---|---|---|---|---|---|---|---|---|---|---|
|  | 0 | 1 | 2 | 3 | 4 | 5 | 6 | 7 | 8 | Text |
| Words in sample | 110 | 610 | 620 | 620 | 610 | 620 | 500 | 110 | 500 | 110 |
| Syllables per 100 words | 244 | 135 | 128 | 137 | 134 | 137 | 136 | 135 | 148 | 157 |
| Morphemes per 100 words | 196 | 120 | 114 | 119 | 122 | 119 | 121 | 119 | 128 | 132 |
| Difficult words per 100 | 96 | 12 | 5 | 13 | 12 | 13 | 14 | 13 | 18 | 25 |

seventh-order approximations are about equally complex, but above the seventh-order the approximations may increase rapidly in word-complexity. The eighth-order passages jumped to 1.48 syllables per word and to 18% not AA. The indices for the prose are even higher. The prose has indices equivalent to material at the high-school level (its Flesch Reading Ease Score was 58 or 'difficult'), but the approximations have indices roughly equivalent to third-grade readers.

Two other findings in Table I deserve comment though they are not directly related to the argument of this paper. First, zero-order approximations are unusually complex because a list drawn at random from a

* Thorndike and Lorge, *op. cit.,* ix.
† Rudolf Flesch, *The Art of Readable Writing,* 1949, 214.
‡ Flesch, *Marks of Readable Style,* 1942.

dictionary contains a high proportion of morphologically complex words such as *unbeliev-able*. Secondly, the second-order approximations are unusually simple because *is* and its inflected forms occur frequently, resulting in cycles such as "*you are you are you*."

To summarize, the analysis agreed with the ranking by linguists: they both suggested that the curves of recall in previous investigations became horizontal at fifth-order approximations because increasing complexity was counterbalancing the effect of long-range associations. If the prose and all approximations were matched for word-complexity, the advantage of long-range associations might be demonstrated.

## EXPERIMENT II: RECALL OF APPROXIMATIONS TO ENGLISH

In the following two experiments (A and B) Ss attempted to recall orders of approximation to English.

These experiments differ from previous, similar studies in two respects: (1) Insofar as possible, word-complexity was held constant. All passages were matched for frequency of occurrence of words and for syllabic length. (2) Recall was scored in long sequences. Besides being scored in correct single words, recall was scored in correct two-word sequences, correct three-word sequences, and on up to correct 17-word sequences. This dimension of scoring systems will relate the findings of Marks and Jack with those of the other investigators. Essentially, Marks and Jack scored in long sequences: they used number of words recalled correctly up to the first error. By scoring in terms of single words, the other investigators may have favored the short-range associations over the long-range ones.

*Experiment IIA: Subjects.* A class of 32 students in introductory psychology served as Ss.

*Materials.* Approximations collected by Deese that were 50 words long were cut to give 30-word passages. The passages varied greatly in difficulty, but they were grouped in four sets so that within each set the passages were matched closely for syllabic length and percentage of AA words. Two of the sets were first-, third-, and fifth-order approximations; the other two were second-, fourth-, and sixth-order approximations.

A passage was drawn from modern prose to match each set, making four passages in each set. Thus each set was a scale that gradually approached the statistical structure of English, and the passages in each scale were closely matched in syllabic length and AA words. In syllabic length per word, the prose averaged 1.37 and the approximations 1.38. In percentage of words not AA, the prose averaged 15.2% and the approximations 15.0%.

*Presentation.* The approximations of a single set were presented in random order to the entire class. E selected one set, shuffled it, took the

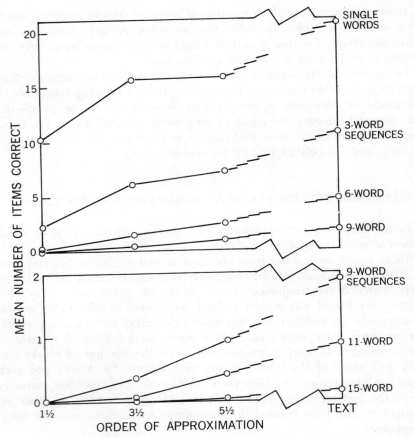

Fig. 2. Mean number of items correct plotted against order of approximation.

top passage, and read it to the class in a monotone. After he finished, the Ss wrote down all they recalled. They were instructed to write the words in order if possible, but to write all words they remembered even if they forgot the order. When all members of the class had finished, E read the second passage of the set, and so on through the set. Then he selected a second set, shuffled it, and so on through all four sets.

*Scoring.* The Ss were scored for each single word correctly recalled regardless of order, every correct two-word sequence, and so on up to correct 17-word sequences. (For instance, ABCDEF has the following three-item sequences: ABC, BCD, CDE, DEF.)

*Experiment IIB.* Experiment IIB also tested the recall of orders of approximation. Its procedures differed from IIA in the following respects:

(a) three different lengths were examined: 50-, 100-, and 150-word passages; (b) The sample of approximations was increased: there were six sets; and (c) The sample of Ss was decreased to 12. The previous experiment had suggested that most of the random error was due to the linguistic sample. (d) The Ss read the passages, which were typed on cards in solid capitals with no punctuation. They were given 0.5 sec. per word and instructed to read the passage and memorize as much as possible. Otherwise the presentation resembled that in Experiment IIA: orders of approximation were presented in random order, and immediately after reading a passage, S wrote it down.

*Results.* In Fig. 2, the mean number of items correct is plotted against order of approximation for the 30-word sequences of Experiment IIA. The curves for the longer sequences of Experiment IIB are almost identical. (In Fig. 2, note that adjacent orders of approximation were averaged together so that each point would represent four passages as did the point representing recall for prose.) All 32 Ss made higher scores for all methods of scoring on prose than on fifth-order approximations. All the Ss also made higher scores on prose than on the sixth-order approximation. Such a difference is significant, of course, at one over 2.

The curve between 5½-order and prose is staggered to remind the reader that the abscissa should actually be extended far to the right. Of course, if it were extended to its rightful position, the curves would become negatively accelerated. This seems reasonable because a twenty-ninth-order approximation should be remembered almost as well as the prose (which might be called a thirtieth-order approximation).

The rather obvious interaction between order of approximation and method of scoring is also significant. A plot similar to Fig. 2 was made for each S. For 23 Ss, the curves became more and more positively accelerated as the sequences scored became longer; for eight Ss, the curves became less positively accelerated, and the final S's curves were indeterminate. Thus the interaction is significant beyond the 0.01 level by a binomial test: the advantages of higher-order approximations increase as recall is scored in longer sequences.

Table II provides another way to interpret the effect of the scoring system. In Table II, mean score on text was divided by mean score on 5½-order, and this ratio was recorded for all scoring systems and for all lengths. Note that the proportional advantage of text over 5½-order increases as recall is scored in longer sequences. Significance of this conclusion was tested by making a similar comparison between adjacent orders of approximation for each individual and for each set of approximations (that is, sixth order was compared to fifth order, fifth to fourth, fourth to third, etc.). By the binomial test, the proportional increase was significant beyond the 0.01 level for both the sample of Ss and the sample

TABLE II

SCORE ON TEXT DIVIDED BY SCORE ON 5½-ORDER FOR ALL 17 SCORING SYSTEMS
AND PASSAGES OF ALL LENGTHS

| No. of words in sequence | 150-word passage | 100-word passage | 50-word passage | 30-word passage |
|---|---|---|---|---|
| 1 | 2.08 | 1.27 | 1.21 | 1.31 |
| 2 | 2.16 | 1.43 | 1.49 | 1.47 |
| 3 | 2.29 | 1.65 | 1.76 | 1.49 |
| 4 | 2.43 | 1.71 | 1.97 | 1.62 |
| 5 | 2.81 | 1.82 | 2.28 | 1.70 |
| 6 | 2.92 | 1.97 | 2.45 | 1.82 |
| 7 | 2.93 | 2.16 | 2.80 | 1.97 |
| 8 | 3.33 | 2.34 | 3.36 | 1.98 |
| 9 | 4.06 | 3.43 | 4.28 | 2.02 |
| 10 | 5.10 | 5.06 | 6.17 | 1.98 |
| 11 | 9.25 | 11.20 | 15.00 | 2.20 |
| 12 | 28.00 | ∞ | 25.00 | 2.42 |
| 13 | ∞ | | ∞ | 2.95 |
| 14 | | | | 4.00 |
| 15 | | | | 5.65 |
| 16 | | | | 13.00 |
| 17 | | | | ∞ |

of approximations. Again the effect of higher-level associations became more and more apparent as recall was scored in longer sequences.

## DISCUSSION AND CONCLUSIONS

In the experiments of earlier investigators, recall for prose and higher-order approximations must have been depressed because these passages were more complex and grammatically awkward than the lower-order ones. To an extent, their curves became horizontal because increasing complexity was counterbalancing the effect of long-range constraints—the constraints that package phrases, clauses, and paragraphs into familiar orders.

The present study demonstrated that when passages were matched in word-complexity higher percentages were recalled as the passages approached the statistical structure of language, and there was no leveling off at fifth-order approximations. Furthermore, as recall was scored in longer and longer sequences, the effect of long-range constraints became more and more apparent.

In recalling approximations to English, S is aided by positive transfer from his verbal habits, mainly from his habits that govern the order and coöccurrence of verbal elements. He finds adjacent elements in a familiar order, or at least the constraints upon order and coöccurrence resemble the constraints of his own habits. In zero-order approximations, the letters are ordered as familiar words. At second- and third-order approximations, additional constraints package the words into more or less familiar phrases: non-human nouns, for instance, will seldom be modified by adjectives such as *erudite*. In higher-order approximations, additional constraints package the elements into still more familiar orders: a clause (or even a paragraph) about organic farming, for instance, will seldom be adjacent to one about submarine warfare.

Clearly S has less to learn if the order of the list is already familiar, and the effect of this positive transfer from his extra-experimental ordering habits will become more and more apparent as the scoring system increases its emphasis upon order.

## SUMMARY

A ranking by linguists and an analysis of word-complexity both suggested that the technique used to generate approximations to English produce higher-order approximations that are more complex and grammatically deviant than lower-order ones. As the person who originally generates the approximations is faced with longer sequences to be incorporated into a sentence, he apparently resorts to more and more complex and far-fetched sentences.

The experiment of Miller and Selfridge was repeated with two changes: (a) the prose and all the approximations were matched in syllabic length and in word-frequency; (b) recall was scored in correct two-word, correct three-word, and on up to correct 17-word sequences. Prose was recalled significantly better than the higher-order approximations. Also the advantages for the higher-order approximations became greater as recall was scored in longer sequences.

# 26. Stimulus Intensity Effects Depend Upon the Type of Experimental Design

## G. R. Grice and J. J. Hunter

*In classical conditioning, a number of investigators have examined the role of the intensity of the conditioned stimulus. Some experimenters have found that conditioned stimulus intensity does contribute to the rapidity with which a response is conditioned, but other investigators have been unable to replicate this finding. In this study, Grice and Hunter demonstrate that the type of experimental design plays an important role in determining what effect will be obtained.*

The intensity of the CS has usually been found to be a relatively ineffective variable in human conditioning. In eyelid conditioning, Carter (1941) and Grant and Schneider (1948) found no evidence that this variable reliably affected either response strength or the associative level of conditioning. Grant and Schneider (1949) also failed to find significant CS intensity effects in GSR conditioning. The only human data cited by Hull (1949) in his presentation of the stimulus intensity dynamism (V) were studies of signal intensity in reaction time (Cattell, 1886; Piéron, 1920) and the well-known GSR study of intensity generalization by Hovland (1937). Walker (1960) reported that the intensity of an auditory CS reliably affected the frequency of eyelid responses of the voluntary form, and conditioned responses of short latency only. However, the effects which she reported were rather small. More recently, Beck (1963) has obtained a result in eyelid conditioning which, in view of this earlier literature, is quite remarkable. In an investigation of possible interaction effects between CS intensity, UCS intensity, and drive level as inferred from an anxiety scale, she included the CS intensity variable in a factorial design as a within-Ss effect. Two intensity values were used and were both administered to all Ss in an irregular order throughout 100 conditioning trials. This was done in order to achieve the statistical precision of this design, since the effect was assumed to be rather weak. The result was that the CS intensity variable not only reached statistical significance, but produced an effect which was very large in absolute terms. In fact,

*Psychol. Rev.*, 1964, 71, 247-256. Reprinted with permission of the senior author and The American Psychological Association. This work was supported by Grant G-14223 from the National Science Foundation.

the difference produced by a 50-decible difference in CS intensity was approximately the same size as that produced by values of .5 and 5.0 psi in the strength of the air-puff UCS. These represent rather extreme values of a variable well known to be highly effective in eyelid conditioning experiments. This large difference was consistent over all values of the other two variables. A rather inescapable conclusion seems to be that something more than statistical precision resulted from the within-Ss design. Apparently, the exposure of the Ss to the two intensities of the CS within the experiment served to increase the magnitude of the effect over what is obtained when S experiences only one intensity value. This is the case in the usual experiment in which a separate group of Ss is provided for each value of the variable under study.

What is required to establish this conclusion firmly, is to conduct investigations in which the two methods of studying intensity functions are directly compared. This means, in effect, the comparison of a between-Ss experiment with a within-Ss where the same values of the independent variable are used in both. This turns out to be a reasonable, but neglected, experimental design in psychological research. The use of repeated measures on the same Ss is demanded by some problems, such as the effect of increasing amounts of practice on learning. In other cases, however, within-Ss designs are used to achieve statistical precision through elimination of individual difference variance, and to effect economies in the number of Ss required. Such use of the design usually involves, often implicitly, the assumption that the treatment effects obtained are the same as would be obtained with a larger, less economical random groups design. As suggested in the case of stimulus intensity, this is not necessarily so. Even though the values of an independent variable may be the same, the two types of experiment are not investigations of the same problem. Between- and within-Ss relationships are, in principle, independent, and the laws obtained may or may not be similar. Furthermore, as in the present instance, the difference between the two types of functions may represent a problem of considerable psychological interest. Two experiments have been conducted investigating the effects of stimulus intensity under these different conditions.

## EXPERIMENT I

### METHOD

The first experiment was an investigation of CS intensity in eyelid conditioning. Conventional recording and stimulus programing equipment was used (Grice & Davis, 1960). The Ss were university undergraduate women. The basic parameters of the experiment were: a 1-psi air puff as UCS; a .5-second interstimulus interval; an average intertrial interval

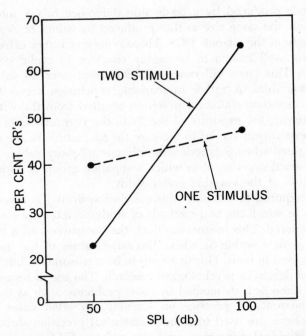

FIG. 1. Percent CRs during last 60 trials to the loud and soft tones under the one- and two-stimulus conditions.

of 20 seconds; and a buzzer warning signal at an average of 2 seconds before the CS. The CS was a 1000-cycle tone of .5-second duration, presented in earphones by means of an electronic switch with a 30-millisecond rise and decay time. Its intensity was either 50- or 100-decibel SPL. One group of Ss(Group L) was conditioned for 100 trials with the loud tone only, and a second group (S) received the soft tone. Two groups (LS-L and LS-S) received 50 conditioning trials with each tone. The order of presentation was random with the restrictions that there be no more than 4 successive trials with one intensity and that there be 10 presentations of each tone in successive blocks of 20 trials. Two orders were used, one the mirror image of the other formed by interchanging the loud and soft tones. Half of the Ss in each group had one order, and the other half, the other. Procedure for the two LS groups was identical, but for purposes of statistical analysis, the loud tone data were used for LS-L and the soft tone data for LS-S. There were 20 Ss in each group.

RESULTS

The results are presented and analyzed in terms of percentage of anticipatory CRs. The major findings of the experiment are quickly seen from

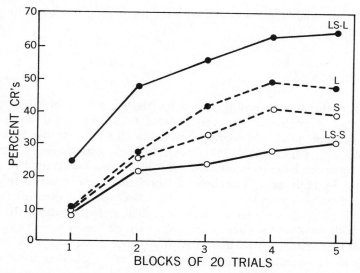

Fig. 2. Conditioning curve data showing percent CRs to each stimulus under each condition of administration during successive blocks of 20 conditioning trials.

an inspection of Figure 1. The points connected by the broken line represent percent CRs on Trials 41-100 for the two groups having only one CS. The points connected by the solid line represent the loud (LS-L) and soft (LS-S) tone data for the two groups which received both CS intensities. The magnitude of the intensity effect is more than five times as great for the condition in which Ss received both stimuli as compared with the single value condition. This interaction is also significant, $F(1, 76) = 8.32$, $p < .01$. The combined intensity effect is also significant, $F(1, 76) = 18.23$, $p < .001$, but for the single stimulus condition alone it is not, $t(76) = 0.98$. Other individual group comparisons are also of interest. For the loud tone, response frequency is significantly greater for the two-stimulus condition than for the one, $t(76) = 2.29$, $p < .05$. The inferiority of the two-stimulus condition on the soft tone does not reach significance, $t(76) = 1.79$, $.10 > p > .05$. In Figure 2 are presented the conditioning curves for the two single stimulus groups and data for the loud and soft stimuli for groups LS-L and LS-S, respectively. Data points are means of 20 trials for Groups L and S and of the appropriate 10 trials for Groups LS-L and LS-S. Basically, these curves show that the phenomena illustrated in Figure 1 begin early training and are undiminished through 100 conditioning trials. In summary, the experiment unambiguously verifies the conclusion drawn on the basis of the comparison between Beck's finding and the previous literature. The exposure of Ss to two values of CS intensity during conditioning substantially increases the effect of the variable as compared with the use of single values with separate groups.

## EXPERIMENT II

Hull's postulate concerning the dynamogenic effects of stimulus intensity was, in part, based on results from studies of signal intensity in simple reaction time, although he probably did not use the best data available, e.g., Chocholle (1945, 1948). In these experiments clear and orderly functions have been obtained. It is of interest that Cattell's (1886) data cited by Hull, as well as those of Chocholle, were obtained from repeated measures on highly practiced Ss. Chocholle, for example, would run about 20 trials with on intensity and then shift to another. In other words, both employed within-Ss designs in which the Ss were exposed to all intensities. Similar experiments with separate groups of Ss would be a tremendous undertaking, but the question as to whether they would yield similar functions is unanswered. Another question of considerable interest is the effect of using blocks of trials of various lengths with a single stimulus as opposed to the use of an unpredictable order, but this problem must await future research. In order to investigate the generality of the above finding for eyelid conditioning, a similar investigation has been conducted with simple reaction time using two intensity values of an auditory signal.

The response consisted of pressing a conventional telegraph key. Reaction signals consisted of 1000-cycle tones of 1-second duration, and of 40- and 100-decibel SPL. The 60-decibel separation was used rather than the 50-decibel of the eyelid study because Chocholle's data suggested that a wide separation was necessary in order to obtain substantial effects, if near-threshold values were to be avoided. The foreperiod signal was a buzzer and preceded the tone by 1, 1.5, and 2 seconds in an irregular order. Trials were run at approximately a rate of 4 per minute. There were 120 trials. The experimental groups were analogous to those of Experiment I. Groups L and S always received one signal intensity. Groups LS-L and LS-S received half of the trials at each intensity in an unpredictable order. For Trials 21 to 120, one of the random orders for Experiment I was used throughout. Conventional reaction time instructions were given. The Ss were women from the same population as for Experiment I. There were 20 Ss each in Groups L and S, and 10 Ss each in Groups LS-L and LS-S. Reaction latencies were recorded in milliseconds by means of an electronic counter.

The data presented in Figure 3 are means of S medians for Trials 21 to 120. Medians for the single-stimulus condition are based on all 100 trials. Those for the two-stimulus condition are based on the appropriate 50

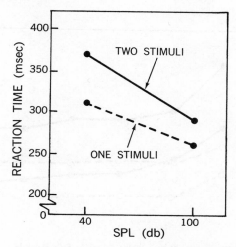

Fig. 3. Means of S median latency on the last 100 reaction time trials.

trials. It is clear that these findings are not entirely the same as those for the eyelid experiment. However, the basic finding that the intensity effect is increased by exposure to both stimuli was again obtained. The slope for the two-stimulus condition is significantly steeper than for the one-stimulus condition, $F(1, 56) = 4.48$, $p < .05$. Rather than the crossover effect found in the eyelid study, there is an overall slowing of reaction time in the two-stimulus condition. This effect is significant, $F(1, 56) = 16.59$, $p < .001$. This is produced primarily by the response to the soft tone where the difference between the two conditions is significant, $t(56) = 4.38$, $p < .01$. The difference for the loud tone is not significant. The combined intensity effect is significant, $F(1, 56) = 42.97$, $p < .001$, and even the smaller effect for the single stimulus condition alone is also significant, $t(56) = 4.13$, $p < .01$. Practice curves are presented in Figure 4. After an initial improvement, the results are quite stable, and there is no indication that the interaction between intensity and the experimental conditions is decreasing with practice. Thus, in spite of certain differences in detail in these two situations studied, both experiments confirm the general principle that differential responsiveness on the basis of stimulus intensity is increased by multiple stimulus presentation.

## Theoretical Implications

These experimental findings are of considerable theoretical interest. It is at once apparent that Hull's stimulus intensity dynamism postulate will not account for them. He assumed that V was a simple function of

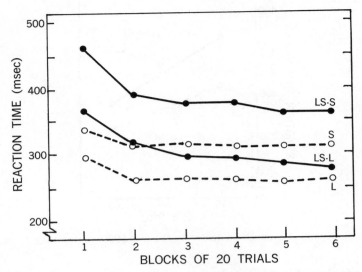

FIG. 4. Practice curves for each stimulus under the two experimental conditions in the reaction time experiment.

stimulus energy, but these experiments clearly show that the dynamogenic property of a given energy depends largely on what other stimuli are presented. It is clear, then, that there must be no invariant intensity functions.

Another hypothesis, still within the framework of Hull's theory, was independently proposed by Perkins (1953) and Logan (1954), and has been more recently elaborated by Champion (1962). These writers have suggested that the dynamism concept is superfluous in Hull's system, and that intensity effects are deducible from other portions of the theory. This view is essentially a discrimination interpretation. Making use of generalization gradients for excitation originating at the CS intensity value, and gradients of inhibition originating at the background intensity, they were able to deduce greater net excitatory strengths for stronger stimuli. There are some problems involved in the application of this theory to the present situation. If we assume, on the basis of the conditioning curves, that all habit strengths are approximately at asymptotic level, and hence about equal, the theory predicts equal differences between the two stimuli in the two situations. There is one feature of the eyelid conditioning data which is particularly embarrassing to this theory. The theory rather clearly predicts that the addition of a weaker stimulus should result in a weaker *absolute* response strength to the stronger stimulus.

This is because the inhibitory gradient from the background intensity should start at a higher level. This prediction would hold unless the strong stimulus was not within the range of this gradient, in which case, its absolute strength would be unaffected. However, in the present eyelid experiment, the response strength to the loud tone was significantly *increased* by the presence in the experiment of the soft tone. Furthermore, this occurred in spite of the fact that it received only half as many reinforced trials as in the single-stimulus situation.

These present data tend to suggest an interpretation in terms of a genuine dynamogenic effect associated with the intensity of the eliciting stimulus. Obviously, however, more than mere stimulus intensity is involved. It appears that some form of contrast effect is an important element in this phenomenon. One approach would be in terms of an adaptation-level concept similar to that of Helson (1959). This interpretation is particularly well able to handle the result of the conditioning experiment. For example, one could make the simple assumption that the dynamogenic potency of a stimulus depends upon its departure from adaptation level (AL) rather than upon absolute intensity. In the case of the single stimulus situation, then, the AL should be near the stimulus value. This would lead to the prediction of minimal intensity effects, since, irrespective of absolute intensity, departure from AL would be small. In the two-stimulus situation, however, the AL might be expected to lie between the two values. With the weak stimulus below AL and the strong above, an exaggerated intensity effect would be expected. The crossed functions of the conditioning experiment lend considerable credibility to this interpretation.

While the reaction time experiment is in agreement with the conditioning study in producing a greater intensity effect for the two-stimulus condition, it also differs in that the functions do not cross. Rather, there is a general slowing of reaction time in the two-stimulus condition, the slowing effect being greater for the soft tone. This does not fit the adaptation-level interpretation quite so neatly. However, it seems possible that, in this situation, the longer reaction times reflect a set phenomenon resulting from the unpredictability of the stimulus. There is little support for this view in the disjunctive reaction time experiments. There, the latency seems to depend upon the amount of information transmitted (Bricker, 1955), and irrelevant information in the stimulus which does not increase information transmitted has no effect, at least at high levels of practice (Morin, Forrin, & Archer, 1961). There seem to be little data, however, on this point for simple reaction time where there is no response selection, and, in this sense, no information transmitted. Mowrer, Rayman, and Bliss (1940) and Mowrer (1941) did, under some conditions, find that the occurrence of an unexpected (high informational) stimulus resulted in a slower reaction even though there was no change in the response required. The present data certainly suggest this, and the matter needs further exploration. This interpretation suggests that the intensity functions would cross except for the presence of an additive constant due to the set variable. The data of Morin, Forrin, and Archer (1961) hint that the crossing might be obtained with extremely extended practice. At least, these considerations indicate that the reaction time data can very possibly be subsumed under the adaptation-level interpretation, if the set explanation turns out to be correct.

Whether or not adaptation-level theory will provide a fully adequate explanation for these phenomena is a matter for future decision. At least a number of experimental approaches are suggested by the findings and by the interpretation. Among the experimental variables which should be of interest are: the number and range of intensity values employed; the relative frequency of occurrence of each intensity used; the length of the trial blocks in which a particular value is consecutively presented; the degree of predictability in the stimulus presentation sequence; the mere exposure of S to certain stimuli without reinforcement or requiring a response; and the role of background stimulation. Of course, experimental situations other than eyelid conditioning and reaction time should be investigated. The fact that variable stimulation leads to stronger and more persistent orienting reflexes, also suggests the possible relevance of that phenomenon. It is the intent that the present discussion be limited to situations involving human Ss. However, there is the possibility that the problem is somewhat different with animals and that stimulus intensity is a more effective variable with them (e.g., see Kimble, 1961, p. 120). If this is true, it may be that attention getting properties of strong stimuli are of more importance with animals than in most human experimentation. Perhaps this will suggest additional approaches to the problem.

A word should be added about the problem of response evocation by stimulus onset versus stimulus cessation. In general, it appears that, for a given intensity, it makes little difference whether the critical event is onset or cessation, so far as response producing potency is concerned. (Champion, 1962; Chocholle, 1948; Logan & Wagner, 1962). While the discrimination theory of Perkins and Logan will account for this similarity, the doubt cast upon this interpretation by the present data suggests that the dynamogenic property of stimuli depends upon the amount of energy change in relation to Ss' present condition of adaptation. The contention of Logan and Wagner that a dynamogenic theory implies greater effectiveness of onset is not a necessary part of such a theory. This is an interesting idea, though, since it implies that a sudden decrease in stimulus energy will have dynamogenic properties, if this event is the condition for response evocation. Certainly, the cessation condition requires exploration with the within-Ss type of experiment as well as the onset condition.

## Studies of Intensity Generalization

The present findings have a rather interesting implication for studies of generalization along intensity dimensions. Such experiments inherently involve the presentation of more than one stimulus to individual Ss. It is thus to be expected that larger intensity effects will be found in generalization studies than in independent group experiments investigating intensity directly. It is apparently no accident that Hull relied so heavily on generalization data in his discussion of the stimulus intensity dynamism, and this chief interest in the concept seemed to be its application to intensity generalization functions. It is well known that generalization tests are conducted in different ways. The Ss may be tested at only one value, either by a single test trial or by a series of extinction trials. Either of these methods involves a single intensity shift, but the extinction method then involves a series on the new intensity without further change. On the other hand, each S may be tested at all intensities, usually in an unpredictable order, counterbalanced between Ss. There may be more than one cycle of test trials. There is reason for thinking that these methods may not yield the same generalization gradients. The problem raised here suggests that they may not result in the same intensity effects either. Data are not available for adequate predictions, but a likely speculation would be that the counterbalancing procedure would produce the greatest intensity effect, and the extinction procedure the least. The experiment by Hovland (1937), using the counterbalancing method, and that by Hall

TABLE 1

Analysis of Hovland's (1937) Data on Intensity Generalization

| Source | df | F |
|---|---|---|
| Between subjects | 31 | |
| CS intensity (CS) | 1 | .56 |
| Error | 30 | (149.90) |
| Within subjects | 352 | |
| Test intensity (TI) | 3 | 27.74** |
| Cycles (Cy) | 2 | 1.81 |
| TI × Cy | 6 | .86 |
| TI × CS | 3 | 3.00* |
| Cy × CS | 2 | .50 |
| TI × Cy × CS | 6 | 1.60 |
| Error$_w$ | 330 | (27.25) |
| Error$_w$ (TI, TI × CS) | 90 | (26.22) |
| Error$_w$ (Cy, Cy × CS) | 60 | (67.91) |
| Error$_w$ (TI × Cy, TI × Cy × CS) | 180 | (14.21) |

Note.—Error mean squares in parentheses.
* p < .05.
** p < .001.

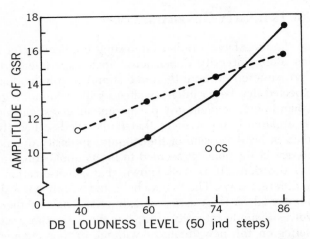

FIG. 5. Test trial data for Hovland's (1937) intensity generalization experiment. (Each point is mean of three test trials.)

and Prokasy (1961), using a single test trial, produced reliable intensity effects, while the Grant and Schneider (1948, 1949) experiments, using extinction at a single value, did not.

The most widely cited experiment using the multiple test procedure is that of Hovland (1937). This experiment is still of considerable interest for several reasons. Briefly, Hovland conditioned 16 Ss on the GSR at 40-decibel loudness level, and a second group of 16 at 86 decibels. All Ss were then tested by means of extinction trials at 40, 60, 74, and 86 decibels in counterbalanced orders. Three cycles of test trials were conducted. While appropriate methods of analysis did not exist at that time, all data were published, and a complete analysis is presented here. The basic data, averaged over the past three test cycles, are presented in Figure 5, and the summary of the analysis is presented in Table 1. The large effect of test stimulus intensity is apparent in the figure and is highly significant. This large and reliable intensity effect, as opposed to Grant and Schneider's (1949) negative finding for the GSR, is very likely due to the presentation of all stimulus intensities to each S as opposed to the Grant and Schneider procedure in which each S received only one training and one extinction intensity. This conclusion must be made with some reservation, however, since individual difference variance was not included in this comparison as it was in the Grant and Schneider experiment.* The dif-

* In the Hall and Prokasy (1961) experiment, only data for one test trial were presented. However, eight extinction trials were actually conducted with a single test intensity for each S. Unpublished data kindly provided by Hall (J. F. Hall, personal communication, 1963) indicate that the effect due to test stimulus intensity diminished during extinction. From the second trial on, the overall intensity relationship was no longer monotonic, and by the seventh trial, all traces of the effect had disappeared.

ference in slope between the two functions of Figure 5 may be interpreted as indicating true generalization decrement and is significant (TI × CS), but it accounts for a trivial portion of the variance. Hovland pointed out that the generalization gradient was flat on the first test cycle when averaged over training intensities, and that generalization decrement only appeared on the second and third test cycles. However, it turns out that this change in slope was not statistically significant (TI × CS × Cy).

Another feature of the Hovland design is that it may be regarded as a test of whether the intensity of the CS during conditioning is a determinant of the associative strength of conditioning. In this respect, it is related to the original purpose of the Grant and Schneider experiments, and to the Spence (1953) experiment of UCS intensity. This experiment, however, involves the counterbalanced presentation of four intensities to each of two CS intensity groups, rather than using a separate group for each test intensity value. The result is consistent with those of Grant and Schneider and also of Hall and Prokasy (1961) in indicating no significant effect of CS intensity. In this connection, it is significant that Hull (1951, 1952) regarded the stimulus intensity dynamism during conditioning ($V_1$) as a determiner of habit strength. Most of the data do not seem to warrant the conclusion that CS intensity does influence associative strength. However, it appears that while Hull thought of the dynamogenic properties of test stimuli ($V_2$) as dependent on stimulus energy, he apparently thought of $V_1$ as dependent only upon the age of the stimulus trace. It now appears that the dynamogenic properties of stimuli, dependent upon intensity and adaptation level, and the degree of associative efficacy, which depends on the interstimulus interval, should not be regarded as manifestations of the same concept.

## REFERENCES

BECK, SALLY B. (1963) Eyelid conditioning as a function of CS intensity, UCS intensity, and Manifest Anxiety scale score. *J. exp. Psychol.*, *66*, 429-438.

BRICKER, P. D. (1955) Information measurement and reaction time. In H. Quastler (Ed.), *Information theory in psychology*. Glencoe, Ill.: Free Press. Pp. 350-359.

CARTER, L. F. (1941) Intensity of conditioned stimulus and rate of conditioning. *J. exp. Psychol.*, *28*, 481-490.

CATTELL, J. McK. (1886) The influence of the intensity of the stimulus on the length of the reaction time. *Brain*, *8*, 512-515.

CHAMPION, R. A. (1962) Stimulus-intensity effects in response evocation. *Psychol. Rev.*, *69*, 428-449.

CHOCHOLLE, R. (1945) Variation des temps de réaction auditif en fonction de l'intensité à diverses fréquences. *Année psychol.*, *41-42*, 65-124.

CHOCHOLLE, R. (1948) Étude de la psychophysiologie de l'audition par la méthode des temps de réaction. *Année psychol.*, *44-45*, 90-131.

GRANT, D. A. and SCHNEIDER, DOROTHY E. (1948) Intensity of the conditioned stimulus and strength of conditioning: I. The conditioned eyelid response to light. *J. exp. Psychol.*, 38, 690-696.

GRANT, D. A., and SCHNEIDER, DOROTHY E. (1949) Intensity of the conditioned stimulus and strength of conditioning: II. The conditioned galvanic skin response to an auditory stimulus. *J. exp. Psychol.*, 39, 35-40.

GRICE, G. R., and DAVIS, J. D. (1960) Effect of concurrent responses on the evocation and generalization of the conditioned eyeblink. *J. exp. Psychol.*, 59, 391-395.

HALL, J. F., and PROKASY, W. F. (1961) Stimulus generalization to absolutely discriminable tones. *Percept. mot. Skills*, 12, 175-178.

HELSON, H. (1959) Adaptation level theory. In S. Koch (Ed.), *Psychology: A study of a science*. Vol. 1. *Sensory, perceptual, and physiological formulations.* New York: McGraw-Hill.

HOVLAND, C. I. (1937) The generalization of conditioned responses: II. The sensory generalization of conditioned responses with varying intensities of tone. *J. genet. Psychol.*, 51, 279-291.

HULL, C. L. (1949) Stimulus intensity dynamism (V) and stimulus generalization. *Psychol. Rev.*, 56, 67-76.

HULL, C. L. (1951) *Essentials of behavior.* New Haven: Yale Univer. Press.

HULL, C. L. (1952) *A behavior system.* New Haven: Yale Univer. Press.

KIMBLE, G. A. (1961) *Hilgard and Marquis' "Conditioning and learning."* New York: Appleton-Century-Crofts.

LOGAN, F. A. (1954) A note on stimulus intensity dynamism (V). *Psychol. Rev.*, 61, 77-80.

LOGAN, F. A., and WAGNER, A. R. (1962) Supplementary report: Direction of change in CS in eyelid conditioning. *J. exp. Psychol.*, 64, 325-326.

MORIN, R. E., FORRIN, B., and ARCHER, W. (1961) Information processing behavior: The role of irrelevant stimulus information. *J. exp. Psychol.*, 61, 89-96.

MOWRER, O. H. (1941) Preparatory set (expectancy)—Further evidence of its 'central' locus. *J. exp. Psychol.*, 28, 116-133.

MOWRER, O. H., RAYMAN, N. N., and BLISS, E. L. (1940) Preparatory set (expectancy)—An experimental demonstration of its 'central' locus. *J. exp. Psychol.*, 26, 357-372.

PERKINS, C. C., JR. (1953) The relation between conditioned stimulus intensity and response strength. *J. exp. Psychol.*, 46, 225-231.

PIÉRON, H. (1920) Nouvelles recherches sur l'analyse du temps de latence sensorielle et sur la loi qui relie le temps à l'intensité d'excitation. *Année psychol.*, 22, 58-142.

SPENCE, K. W. (1953) Learning and performance in eyelid conditioning as a function of the intensity of the UCS. *J. exp. Psychol.*, 45, 57-63.

WALKER, EVELYN G. (1960) Eyelid conditioning as a function of intensity of conditioned and unconditioned stimuli. *J. exp. Psychol.*, 59, 303-311.

# 27.  Psychomotor Performance as a Function of Intertrial Rest Interval

## J. A. Adams

*A variable of considerable interest to many experimenters is the distribution of practice or intertrial interval. In verbal learning and instrumental conditioning studies, the effect of the length of the intertrial interval on learning has been difficult to ascertain. Some studies have indicated that short intertrial intervals maximize learning, others have indicated the opposite. In the area of motor skills learning, however, the results are virtually unequivocal—learning is a function of the length of the time between trials. Adams' study illustrates this finding.*

An extensive body of research concerned with the effect of distribution of practice on performance has generally concluded that massed training results in a lower level of performance than distributed training. Although these findings have been important in furthering our knowledge of this potent performance variable, they generally have failed to provide detailed information on how distribution of practice affects general form, slope, and asymptote of performance curves. Exceptions to this are studies by Kientzle (1), Kimble (2), and Reynolds and Adams (4), which relate preasymptote performance curve characteristics to intertrial rest interval. Both Kientzle and Kimble employed the reverse alphabet printing task, whereas Reynolds and Adams used the Rotary Pursuit Test. The results of these studies differed somewhat—such as Kimble finding that performance curve slope over the later trials was positively related to intertrial interval while Reynolds and Adams found it to be independent of distribution. Task differences could account for a discrepancy such as this, but more likely it can be attributed to the portion of the total performance curve evaluated in each case. All data were obtained in relatively short practice sessions, and the curves were well below asymptote level. As a consequence, insufficient data were available to fully and carefully specify overall performance curve characteristics as a function of the distribution

*J. exp. Psychol.*, 1954, *48*, 131-133. Reprinted with permission of the author and The American Psychological Association. The experimental work for this study was performed as part of the United States Air Force Personnel and Training Research and Development Program. The opinions or conclusions contained in this report are those of the author. They are not to be construed as reflecting the views or indorsement of the Department of the Air Force.

variable. The study to be reported here augments previous research by differentiating groups on the basis of intertrial interval and by giving prolonged practice to obtain performance curves reaching an asymptote level.

## METHOD

*Apparatus.* The apparatus employed was a 15-unit Rotary Pursuit Test described elsewhere (3). Time-on-target scores were recorded in units of .001 min. on Standard Electric clocks. A buzzer sounded and the disks turned for 1.5 sec. before the clocks could be activated. Trial duration and intertrial rest were cycled automatically by Hunter Electronic Timers.

*Subjects.* The Ss were 446 basic airmen trainees selected from the population available at Lackland Air Force Base, Texas. Subgroups of 10–15 Ss were randomly assigned to five main groups.

*Procedure.* All groups received identical experimental treatment with the exception of length of intertrial rest interval. Following standard instructions (3), Ss were given 150 30-sec. trials. Each group had one of the following intertrial intervals: 0 (continuous practice), 3, 10, 20, or 30 sec.

A group is designated by the particular intertrial interval used by it, e.g., Group 3 had 3-sec. rest between trials. Instructions made no mention of the length of practice session or the concentration of the practice. This precaution was taken to avoid any possible interaction between such information and experimental treatment. Also, the possible biasing effects of hot weather on performance over the long practice session were avoided by conducting the experiment in an air-conditioned room.

The number of Ss in Groups 0, 3, 10, 20, and 30 were 72, 74, 95, 93, and 112, respectively.

## RESULTS AND DISCUSSION

Figure 1 gives a plot of the performance for the five groups. It can be seen that all curves are of the same general family of negatively accelerated increasing curves. Each group has clearly attained an asymptote, and the asymptote level is positively related to intertrial interval. The rate of approach to the asymptote is also related to intertrial interval with the larger intervals having the more rapid rate. It seems unlikely that the attainment of any asymptote is related to the possibility of some or all of the Ss reaching maximum possible score since Group 30, which has the highest performance level, is well below the .500-min. maximum possible score.

Figure 2 shows a plot of the final performance level as a function of the

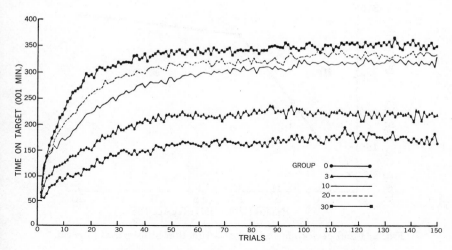

Fig. 1. Mean performance curves for the five groups.

interval between trials. The dependent measure in Fig. 2 is the mean of the last five trials. Although there are not a sufficient number of points to carefully define the nature of the relationship, the general trend suggests that it might be a negatively accelerated function.

To evaluate the hypothesis that each group had attained an asymptote and that this asymptote level differed among groups, a trend analysis was made of the measures on the last 26 trials for Groups 0, 3, 10, and 20. Group 30 was deleted because its Trials × Ss mean square was not homogeneous with those of the other four groups and therefore could not be legitimately included in the pooled Trials × Ss mean square error term. The null hypothesis for mean differences between groups was tested by using the pooled Between-Ss mean square of .141 as the error term to evaluate the Between-Groups mean square of 13.034. For 3 and 330 $df$, the obtained $F$ ratio for this test was significant beyond the 1% level and permitted rejection of the null hypothesis. To test the hypothesis that the four groups had attained an asymptote, the pooled Trials × Ss mean square of .002 was used as the error term to evaluate the Trials mean square of .001 and the Trials × Groups mean square of .002. The failure of either of these two $F$ ratios to exceed 1 makes tenable the hypothesis that trial means for all groups combined have zero slope in the population and that this trend is the same for all groups. This trend test, then, confirms the asymptote hypothesis. Although Group 30 was not included, an inspection of Fig. 1 suggests that the trend of its means over this block of trials is essentially the same as those of the other groups.

The trend of variance over trials and as a function of intertrial interval

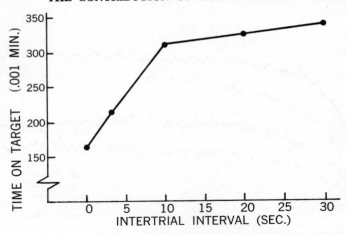

FIG. 2. Final performance level as a function of intertrial interval.

was examined. Variance over trials for each group remained essentially the same. Variance and intertrial interval were generally found to be independent. Bartlett's test for homogeneity of variance was made for the five variances on every tenth trial. Only Trials 110 and 120 had chi-square values significant beyond the 5% level.

These data extend previous research (1, 2, 4) in providing information on the quantitative aspects of extended motor performance curves as a function of practice distribution. They show that intertrial interval probably does not affect the general form of the function but is a determiner of slope and asymptote parameters. Each group rather quickly reached a steady level of responding, and this level and the rate of attaining it were defined by the conditions of distribution holding. This characteristic of human Ss will have to be considered by any theoretical schema attempting to account for distribution of practice phenomena.

## SUMMARY

Performance on a paced psychomotor task was evaluated as a function of intertrial interval. The Rotary Pursuit Test was used and 150 trials were given. Trial length was constant at 30 sec. and each group had one of the following intertrial intervals: 0, 3, 10, 20, or 30 sec.

It was found that performance curves for all groups were negatively accelerated increasing functions. Rate of approach to the asymptote was positively related to length of intertrial interval. Asymptote level appeared to be a negatively accelerated increasing function of intertrial interval.

# REFERENCES

1. KIENTZLE, M. J. (1946) Properties of learning curves under varied distributions of practice. *J. exp. Psychol.*, *36*, 187-211.
2. KIMBLE, G. A. (1949) Performance and reminiscence in motor learning as a function of the degree of distribution of practice. *J. exp. Psychol.*, *39*, 500-510.
3. MELTON, A. W. (Ed.) (1947) *Apparatus tests.* Washington: U. S. Government Printing Office. (*AAF Aviat. Psychol. Program Res. Rep.* No. 4.)
4. REYNOLDS, B. and ADAMS, J. A. (1953) Effect of distribution and shift in distribution of practice within a single training session. *J. exp. Psychol.*, *46*, 137-145.

# Stimulus and Response Generalization

S TIMULUS and response generalization have long been regarded as two basic processes in the psychology of learning. Stimulus generalization refers to the fact that a response which has been conditioned to one stimulus may also be elicited by other stimuli. A series of studies by Hovland (1937, 1937a, 1937b, 1937c) have long been considered classics in this area, and we have chosen the first of these to include in this section.

The process of stimulus generalizations invariably brings up the problem of discriminability. Does an organism generalize because it is unable to discriminate between the conditioned stimulus and the stimulus used to test for generalization? The Guttman and Kalish (1956) study addresses itself to this question. This article also deserves consideration inasmuch as the procedure these authors have used for examining generalization differs markedly from that used by Hovland.

Response generalization refers to the fact that a stimulus, which, through conditioning, is capable of eliciting one response, may also elicit other responses as well. Relatively few investigators, however, have been interested in this phenomenon. The Wickens' (1943) article is one of a number which he has published in this area. In the study cited, he was interested in examining both stimulus as well as response generalization in the finger withdrawal conditioning situation.

## REFERENCES

GUTTMAN, N. and KALISH, H. I. (1956) Discriminability and stimulus generalization. *J. exp. Psychol.*, *51*, 79-88.

HOVLAND, C. I. (1937) The generalization of conditioned responses. I. The sensory generalization of conditioned responses with varying frequencies of tone. *J. gen. Psychol.*, *17*, 125-148.

HOVLAND, C. I. (1937a) The generalization of conditioned responses. II. The sensory generalization of conditioned responses with varying intensities of tone. *J. genet. Psychol.*, *51*, 279-291.

HOVLAND, C. I. (1937b) The generalization of conditioned responses. III. Extinction, spontaneous recovery, and disinhibition of conditioned and of generalized responses. *J. exp. Psychol.*, *21*, 47-62.

HOVLAND, C. I. (1937c) The generalization of conditioned responses. IV. The effects of varying amounts of reinforcement upon the degree of generalization of conditioned responses. *J. exp. Psychol.*, *21*, 261-276.

WICKENS, D. D. (1943) Studies in response generalization in conditioning. I. Stimulus generalization during response generalization. *J. exp. Psychol.*, *33*, 221-227.

# 28. The Generalization of Conditioned Responses: I. The Sensory Generalization of Conditioned Responses with Varying Frequencies of Tone

## C. I. Hovland

*As we indicated in the introduction to this section, this is one of the early studies investigating stimulus generalization. Hovland's methodology has served as a model for many of the subsequent studies in this area. It is interesting to note that stimulus generalization was obtained for inhibition as well as excitation.*

### INTRODUCTION

An initial period of generalization,* in which the conditioned reflex occurs not only in response to the conditioned stimulus used in its establishment, but to a wide variety of similar stimuli as well, is described by Pavlov (15) as a universal phenomenon of the conditioning process. That such a period occurs during the establishment of tactile conditioned responses has been experimentally demonstrated. Anrep (2), working in Pavlov's laboratory, used dogs as experimental subjects. From his data he was able to plot the form of the spatial gradient of excitation and of inhibition. More recently, Bass and Hull (3) have supported this work, finding in adult human subjects "a definite spread of cutaneous conditioned excitatory tendency from the shoulder towards the feet and from the calf towards the head" (p. 65). There was also found "a definite analogous spread of the inhibition resulting from experimental extinction. In both cases the spread takes the form of a gradient, the magnitude of the tendency diminishing progressively with distance from the point of origin" (p. 65).

Generalization is also observed, according to Pavlov, when a tone of one frequency has been used during the establishment of the conditioned response, and adjacent tones are subsequently presented: ". . . If a tone

*J. gen. Psychol.*, 1937, 17, 125-148. Reprinted with permission of *The Journal of General Psychology* and the author's estate. The writer is greatly indebted to Professor Clark L. Hull for suggestions and assistance. The writer also wishes to thank Professor Raymond Dodge for his kindness in making available the use of a sound-proof room. This is the first of a series of studies presented as a dissertation to the faculty of the Graduate School of Yale University in partial fulfillment of the requirements for the degree of Doctor of Philosophy in psychology, 1936.

* The terms "generalization" and "generalized" are used throughout the present series of articles as they were by Bass and Hull (3, Footnote p. 47) in their experimental, rather than in their Pavlovian, neurological, connotations (*cf.* Loucks, 14).

of 1000 d.v. is established as a conditioned stimulus, many other tones spontaneously acquire similar properties, such properties diminishing proportionally to the intervals of these tones from the one of 1000 d.v." (p. 113). Direct experimental demonstration of the decrease in response with increase in distance between the frequency of the conditioned and of the adjacent tones is not given. The selected protocols which are presented serve as illustrations, but do not constitute adequate proof.

The alleged relationship between the magnitude of the response and the proximity of the test stimuli to the conditioned stimulus in frequency was investigated in the present research. This problem provides an excellent approach to the broader aspects of generalization of all types. By suitable apparatus tonal stimuli can be easily and precisely controlled, and the separation of the test tones from the conditioned stimulus in frequency can be accurately determined by psychophysical measurements, in terms of the number of just noticeable differences between them. The galvanic skin reaction provided a highly satisfactory index of the conditioned response.

The problem of generalization, which Loucks (14), in his violent attack upon certain of the studies in this field from Pavlov's laboratory, calls the "focal point" of conditioned reflex systematization (p. 44) is not only of importance in the theoretical analysis of conditioned reflex phenomena, but is related to a host of other problems as well. Students of learning, for example, whose interests are not primarily in the field of conditioned responses, see the possibility of using the data obtained from conditioning experiments as the basis for a more comprehensive theory of learning. Two recent writers have stressed the contribution which could thus be made by research on the generalization of conditioned responses. Robinson, in his book, *Association Theory Today*, states that such work may throw light upon various aspects of the Law of Assimilation, and thus reduce the circularity of reasoning now prevalent in this field (16, pp. 84-85). He poses the general problem as to when and in what degree assimilation can be expected.

Here we have an inexhaustible stock of experimental problems most of which have hardly been touched. The Pavlov school has done some work on associational spread over a series of tones and over several loci of tactile stimulation. Much more of this definite character should be done. The ideal should be to discover as many as possible of the variables of stimulation and to establish the functional relations between differences as marked off within these variables and differences in the degree of assimilative effects (pp. 86-87).

In discussing the problem of transfer of training, Hunter (12) likewise stressed the value of work on generalization at the conditioned response level:

We are still far from a satisfactory explanation of the facts of transfer. At present the theory of identical elements seems most adequate, and yet it is all but impossible to bring the theory to a rigorous experimental test. Perhaps work on conditioned reflexes may finally give us the explanatory key to the type of behavior interrelations described . . ." (p. 550).

## HISTORICAL

While no previous investigator has determined the relationship between the magnitude of response and the distance of various test tones from the conditioned tone with respect to frequency, a number of studies have been made in which generalization was studied with tonal stimuli. A still larger group of studies give incidental information concerning generalization in researches directed at the determination of the pitch discrimination of various animals [cf. e.g. Anrep (1)]. Pavlov's material on tonal generalization is largely obtained from a series of theses by Beliakov (A), Bourmakin (B), Goubergritz (C), Ivanov-Smolensky (D), Koupalov (E) and Zeliony (F).*

The principal study outside of Pavlov's laboratory on the generalization of conditioned reflexes with auditory stimuli is that of Beritoff (4). He employed the conditioned leg withdrawal technique with dogs in an attempt to obtain data on the nature of both generalization and differentiation. A recent study of auditory generalization has been reported by Ivanshina (13). The original article is not available, but the relevant material in the summary of the *Psychological Abstracts* is as follows:

Generalization of auditory C-R's in 19 5-10-year-old children was studied by the Ivanov-Smolensky grasping food technique. A C-R was formed to a sound of $e^i$ and after it was well established, other sounds ranging from $g^i$ to $d^{iv}$ were tested, with the result that the extent of the generalization was up to $d^{iv}$ in 12 children, up to $e^{iii}$ in 5, and only up to $g^i$ in the remaining 2 children. With the exception of one child, the generalization was of a wider extent in children who formed the C-R more rapidly. The magnitude of the C-R did not become consistently smaller with greater differences between the tested stimuli and the conditioned stimulus (p. 72).

## APPARATUS

The general technique of the present study involved the establishment of a conditioned galvanic skin reaction to sound stimuli. The unconditioned stimuli were faradic stimulations produced by an inductorium.

The galvanic skin response is well adapted to the study of conditioning because it is easily and quickly conditioned, can be measured with great accuracy, and, being made without the subject's knowledge, is little inter-

* Since these researches were not available to the writer the reader is referred to Pavlov's discussion of them. The references are listed as found in Pavlov (15), and appear under his name in the bibliography.

fered with by voluntary control. The technique and apparatus for recording the response were essentially the same as those employed by Switzer (17) and by Bass and Hull (3). The Tarchanoff method was employed. In this method no external source of current is employed. Switzer (18) has summarized evidence pointing to a high degree of relationship ($r = c. + .95$) between this phenomenon and that of Féré, in which the galvanometric reflections measure the "increase in the current passing through the body from an external source" (20, I, p. 219).

Silver electrodes made from polished quarter-dollars were fastened to the palm and back of the subject's hand. The electrodes were connected by means of flexible leads with a galvanometer. In series with the electrodes to the subject and with the galvanometer was a bank of variable resistances, the maximum resistance of which was 1,000,000 ohms. With high resistances in the circuit the magnitude of the galvanometric deflection is almost solely a function of the change in potential and is little affected by changes in the skin resistance of the subject [Thouless (20, II)]. A Leeds and Northrup table model D'Arsonval reflecting galvanometer was employed. This instrument (Type R, No. 2500b L. & N. catalogue 1930) has a critical damping resistance of 11,500 ohms, a sensitivity (per mm. at 1 meter) of 0.00043 microamperes, a period of 6.2 seconds, and a coil resistance of 470 ohms.

A beam of light reflected from the mirror on the moving coil of the galvanometer was focussed upon a ground glass screen. The movement of the beam on the screen was followed by the experimenter throughout the experiment by means of a movable pointer. A radio-dial vernier adjustment made possible very accurate following of the beam. The movement of the pointer was communicated, after a three to one reduction, to a recording lever on a waxed paper polygraph. The magnitude of the galvanometric deflections was maintained within a relatively narrow range from subject to subject by adjustment of a 10,000-ohm potentiometer in the galvanometric circuit.

The unconditioned stimulus was an electric shock to the right wrist. Polished silver electrodes were fastened to opposite sides of the wrist by a leather strap. The shocks were delivered from a Porter inductorium operated by two one-and-one-half volt dry cells. The voltage supplied to the inductorium was constantly maintained at 2.8 volts through the use of a rheostat and voltmeter. The shock was adjusted for each individual subject until he reported the shock as unpleasant but not painful. The secondary coil adjustment varied from 3.8 to 6.9 cm. In every case a marked galvanic response was elicited by the faradic stimulation.

The conditioned and allied stimuli were produced by the General Radio battery operated beat-frequency oscillator (Type 613-B). This apparatus has been successfully employed by Wendt (21) in determining the auditory acuity of monkeys. Sinusoidal waves of frequency from 15 to 20,000

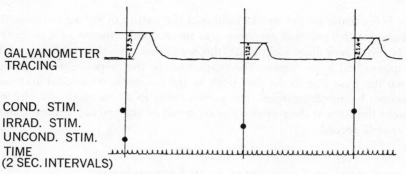

FIG. 1. Specimen Record. Sample record redrawn from waxed stylographic paper, showing galvanometric tracing, time line, spark recording of stimulus presentations, and method of measuring magnitude of response.

cycles per second can be obtained "with 3 per cent or less harmonic distortion and accuracy of frequency setting within 2 per cent" (21, p. 5). The frequency of the tones was varied by the use of the General Radio Company variable air condenser (Type 539 "p"). The intensity of the tone was regulated by adjustment of the General Radio Company 6,000-ohm 60-decibel attenuation box (Type 529-B). A double make-and-break circuit was employed in presenting the tones to prevent any possible "leakage." At the intensity of tone used in the present experiments no sudden onset of sound could be detected.

The subjects were seated in a sound-shielded room about 20 feet from the experimenter and recording apparatus. Control tests demonstrated that none of the sounds produced by the operation of the apparatus could be heard in the sound-proof room. The subjects received the tonal stimuli through a set of Western Electric earphones (Type 509 W).

The presentation of stimuli was rigidly controlled mechanically by the use of the Dodge pendulum. The period of the pendulum was about two seconds. The first rotary switch closed a relay circuit which presented the sound stimulus. Four hundred milliseconds later the second rotary switch terminated the sound stimulation. After a pause of 95 milliseconds a third switch closed a circuit which activated the inductorium; this circuit was again opened by the fourth switch 75 milliseconds later. These temporal intervals were checked by photographic methods. An accessory switch prevented the presentation of stimuli on the return swing of the pendulum. A series of knife switches permitted the experimenter to control the combination of stimuli presented by the pendulum. An electrical counter on the control board showed the number of reinforcements given.

The records were taken on waxed stylographic paper. Sparks produced by induction coils in series with the stimulus circuits pricked holes in the paper to indicate the time of presentation of the stimuli. The position of the holes made by the sparks indicated the nature of the stimulation. The tracing of the galvanic response was measured by means of a millimeter rule, after hair lines delimiting the maximum and the minimum of the response had been drawn. The magnitude of the response was measured from the base line to the first peak of the response, occasional additional maxima being disregarded. The values given in all succeeding tables represent the sizes of the responses as recorded on the tracing. Figure 1 shows a sample record.

## PRELIMINARY STANDARDIZATION EXPERIMENTS

To determine the generalization of conditioned responses to tones varying from the conditioned stimulus in frequency, four frequencies of tone were chosen. To select four equidistant frequencies of tone and equate these for loudness required several preliminary experiments. It was desired to have the four tones 25 just noticeable differences apart in frequency. Ten subjects served in the first preliminary experiment. A tone of 1,000 cycles* 40 decibels† above the subject's threshold was chosen as the standard. The standard and the variable tones were presented for a period of 400 milliseconds, to correspond with the period of stimulation in our main experiment. Two seconds elapsed between the presentations of the standard and of the variable stimuli. Twenty-five j.n.d.'s were determined by the Method of Limits (Method of Just Noticeable Difference), both above the standard and below it. Readings were taken in ascending and in descending order for each determination. The mean value for the point 25 j.n.d.'s above the standard tone of 1000 cycles was 1967 cycles. The mean value for the point 25 j.n.d.'s below was 468 cycles. The fourth value was chosen 25 j.n.d.'s below the latter value. The mean of the readings for this point was 153 cycles.

As a rough check on these values the subjects were instructed to adjust the frequency variator until they believed the distance which they selected was as much above 1000 cycles as the standard interval was below. The standard interval, previously determined to contain 25 j.n.d.'s, was from 1000 to 468 cycles. The mean of the selected values was 1864 cycles. The value selected by the subjects as being as much below 468 cycles as the interval between 468 and 1000 cycles was above, averaged 189 cycles. The approximate equivalence of the distances selected was indicated by this procedure, despite the unreliability of such a method for refined measurements.

Comparison of the present results with those of Fletcher (6) points to the fact that the method which he employed gives consistently smaller

* One cycle = 1 double vibration per second.
† For a discussion of the decibel as a unit of sound intensity see Fletcher (6).

difference limens. This is to be expected in view of the fact that in his procedure the subjects reported when they heard an apparent pulsation in the frequency of two tuned oscillators differing slightly in pitch, while in the present study the tones judged were presented at an interval of two seconds. But the results of Fletcher do tend to indicate that the distances which were selected in the present experiment are equidistant. By interpolation of the data presented by Fletcher it was found that there are about 42 just perceptible differences in pitch between 1,000 and 2,000 cycles, 37 between 500 and 1,000, and 31 between 250 and 500. These values are taken at 40 decibels above threshold at 1,000 cycles and follow the contour of equal loudness. On the above basis the number of just perceptible differences between 1,000 and 1,967, 468 and 1,000, and 153 and 468 cycles would be approximately equal.

The same group of 10 subjects was used to equate the loudness of the four different frequencies of tone. The intensity of the standard tone (1,000 cycles) was fixed by the experimenter at 40 decibels above the subject's threshold. The subjects were instructed to report whether the comparison tone was louder than, softer than, or equal to the standard. As in the previous standardization experiment the tones were presented at intervals of two seconds. The duration of the stimuli was 400 milliseconds. The attenuation box was set at 60 decibels of attenuation to produce a tone 40 db. above threshold at 1,000 cycles. The values selected by the subjects as being equally loud were the following:

| Cycles | Decibels of attenuation |
|--------|--------------------------|
| 468 | 43.7 |
| 153 | 27.9 |
| 1,967 | 42.1 |
| (1,000) | (60.0) |

On the basis of these results the number of decibels of attenuation used in the main experiments were 60 for the tone of 1,000 cycles, 44 for that of 468, 28 for 153, and 42 for 1,967 cycles. These values are quite dissimilar from those of Kingsbury reported by Fletcher (6) for tones of equal loudness. The present data show a much sharper drop in apparent loudness as the distance from 1,000 cycles increases. The difference in results is explicable in terms of the difference in the duration of the stimuli. Whereas his tones were rapidly alternated, the tones in this experiment were being judged at two-second intervals, and their duration was 400 milliseconds.

A final test of the equality of the four tones was made by conditioning all four frequencies of tone during the same experimental session, and then testing the magnitude of the conditioned responses. The tones were presented for 400 milliseconds, followed 95 milliseconds later by the electric shock which lasted 75 milliseconds. Eight paired presentations of each tone with the shock were made. Two conditioned responses were obtained to each frequency of tone in counterbalanced *a b b a* order. The magnitude of the conditioned galvanic responses to the four tones are given below:

| Frequency of tone | 153 | 468 | 1000 | 1967 |
|---|---|---|---|---|
| Attenuation setting | 28 | 44 | 60 | 42 |
| Response (in mm.) | 9.34 | 10.02 | 9.56 | 9.73 |

No consistent difference between the four tones with respect to their reflex-eliciting strength before differential conditioning is indicated by these results.*

## GENERALIZATION OF CONDITIONED EXCITATORY TENDENCIES

The procedure of this part of the experimentation involved the conditioning of one of the extreme frequencies of tone (hereinafter designated as tone *0*), and subsequently testing the response to this tone (*0*) and, in addition, the response to tones 25, 50, and 75 j.n.d.'s removed in frequency (designated as tones *1*, *2*, and *3*) not previously paired with the shock. Generalization, if present, would be revealed in the response to tones which were never given reinforcement with the shock. If Pavlov's observations are sound, a gradient is to be expected, characterized by the largest response to the conditioned stimulus and progressively smaller responses to the tones more distant from the frequency to which the conditioned response was established.

Twenty subjects, paid by the hour, were employed. They are college students and were naïve with respect to the nature of conditioned responses and the psychogalvanic reflex. Three subjects were rejected because of unsatisfactory galvanic response. Half of the group was conditioned to the tone of lowest frequency (153 cycles) and half to the highest (1,967 cycles).

In order to equate the two groups conditioned to opposite ends of the frequency scale, two responses to the shock were obtained before conditioning. The responses to the shock of the first group averaged 34.18 mm., and those of the second 35.79. No statistically significant difference between the groups was revealed.

Two tests of response to each frequency of tone before conditioning gave the following results:

* The results of L. E. Misbach. Effect of pitch and tone-stimuli upon body resistance and cardio-vascular phenomena. *J. Exper. Psychol.*, 1932, 15, 167-183, suggest that the relationship here obtained between magnitude of response and loudness does not hold for higher loudness levels.

| Tones | 153 cycles | 468 cycles | 1000 cycles | 1967 cycles |
|---|---|---|---|---|
| Response in mm. | 3.51 | 3.25 | 3.67 | 3.34 |

Here, likewise, no consistent difference between the responses before conditioning is indicated.

The complete experimental program of which the above controls were a part is presented below.

*Day 1*
    I. Test response to each of the four tones twice each.
    II. Test response to shock alone twice.
    III. Give 16 reinforcements to tone 0.
    IV. Test response to tones 0, 1, 2 and 3 twice each.
    V. Give 8 additional reinforcements to tone 0.
    VI. Test response to tones 0, 1, 2 and 3 twice each.

*Day 2*
    VII. Test response to tones 0, 1, 2 and 3 twice each.

Steps VI and VII permit comparison of the extent of generalization after the lapse of 24 hours.

Sixteen reinforcements were chosen because the writer has shown (9) that at this point the maximum degree of generalization is obtained.

A series of permutational arrangements of orders of presentation of the stimuli during the test trials was prepared in advance. Each frequency of tone was tested in the same position in the test series the same number of times as every other. Effects due to extinction, negative adaptation and the like were in this way minimized. Sample series of test orders are the following:

Conditioning to 153 cycles; testing of response to the various frequencies in the order: 468, 1967, 1000, 153, 153, 1000, 1967, 468 cycles.
Conditioning to 1967 cycles; testing of response to the various frequencies in the order: 1000, 153, 468, 1967, 1967, 468, 153, 1000 cycles.

The average values of galvanic response to two test trials with each frequency of tone following 16 reinforcements is given for the 20 subjects in Table 1. These results represent true "initial generalization" [Anrep (2)], since no differential reinforcement has been given. The exact form of the gradient can be seen by inspection of Figure 2.

Conspicuous is the fact that the degree of generalization is very marked. There is little differentiation indicated in the gradient of initial generalization, although there is a reliable difference between the response to the conditioned frequency of tone and that to any of the other frequencies:

$$\frac{\text{Diff.}}{\text{PE}_{diff}}.$$

between 0 and 1 = 5.45
between 0 and 2 = 6.29
between 0 and 3 = 10.40

## TABLE 1

### Generalization of Excitatory Tendencies

Amplitudes of galvanic response (in mm.) to conditioned tone (0) and to tones 25 (1), 50 (2), and 75 (3) j.n.d.'s removed in frequency. Each value is average of two determinations following 16 reinforcements. Subjects I-X were conditioned to one of 153 cycles; subjects XI-XX to tone of 1967 cycles.

| Subject | Tonal stimuli | | | |
| | 0 | 1 | 2 | 3 |
|---------|------|-------|-------|-------|
| I | 16.2 | 11.3 | 12.6 | 11.4 |
| II | 22.4 | 18.1 | 25.4 | 10.9 |
| III | 13.5 | 6.7 | 11.2 | 6.3 |
| IV | 15.3 | 6.4 | 3.3 | 7.6 |
| V | 19.2 | 18.5 | 22.8 | 15.3 |
| VI | 16.2 | 18.5 | 11.9 | 13.9 |
| VII | 23.7 | 17.1 | 18.0 | 16.5 |
| VIII | 11.5 | 14.1 | 9.6 | 13.8 |
| IX | 13.8 | 10.3 | 13.4 | 9.9 |
| X | 22.4 | 18.7 | 10.7 | 15.3 |
| XI | 23.7 | 21.3 | 21.1 | 10.2 |
| XII | 16.5 | 20.6 | 13.9 | 12.4 |
| XIII | 17.7 | 18.4 | 15.2 | 13.7 |
| XIV | 18.6 | 13.9 | 14.3 | 12.5 |
| XV | 15.9 | 15.5 | 13.8 | 14.2 |
| XVI | 18.8 | 12.3 | 14.6 | 9.7 |
| XVII | 21.3 | 9.7 | 10.5 | 12.3 |
| XVIII | 23.2 | 17.8 | 13.9 | 14.5 |
| XIX | 13.8 | 16.8 | 9.3 | 11.8 |
| XX | 19.9 | 12.3 | 6.9 | 15.6 |
| Mean | 18.3 | 14.91 | 13.62 | 12.89 |
| $P.E._M$ | .57 | .64 | .80 | .49 |

The critical ratio of the difference between the responses 1 and 3 is 4.21 times its $PE_M$.

The form of the gradient obtained in this experiment is quite unlike that found for tactile generalization by Bass and Hull (3). In their curve the drop from the conditioned point to the one removed one unit was very slight, but the changes with increase in distance became more and more pronounced. The curve obtained in the present study, in which the drop from frequency 0 to frequency 1 is very marked, more nearly resembles that reported by Anrep (2) for the initial generalization of excitatory tendencies. In both of the other studies, however, there was some differential reinforcement. In Bass and Hull's study the effects of the differential reinforcement can readily be observed in the ratios which they present to characterize the slope of the gradient. Unfortunately they present only the average results for the entire testing program, initial generalization and ultimate differentiation not being separated. It is difficult to ascertain from

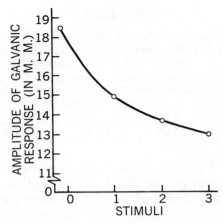

FIG. 2. Composite Curve of Generalization of Conditioned Excitatory Tendencies. Galvanic skin response to conditioned frequency of tone (0) and to other tones 25, 50 and 75 j.n.d.'s removed in frequency (1, 2 and 3 respectively). Based upon 40 values (2 determinations upon each of 20 subjects) for each point.

Anrep's results the extent to which the factor of differential reinforcement played a part. He merely states that a "new place on the skin was stimulated at intervals of seven to fourteen days, the original spot on the left thigh in the meantime being only stimulated in order to maintain the initial reflex at its maximum" (p. 408).

The form of the gradient is of considerable importance in psychological theory. If generalization is, as Hunter (12) has suggested,* related to the problem of transfer of training, the form of the relationship between the similarity of the stimulating situation and the magnitude of response or the degree of transfer should be expected to be similar. A very conspicuous feature of most transfer of training experiments is the very rapid decrement in response from the practiced to the most similar type of performance [cf. Crafts (5), Yum (23)]. Work by the writer on the theoretical analysis of rote learning (10) suggests that the present form of the gradient of generalization will very adequately form the basis of a system which will explain many of the present nonsense syllable phenomena in terms of spread, or generalization, of conditioned excitatory processes from each syllable to every other. The characteristic increase in difficulty in the middle of the lists is then explained in terms of the interaction of the forward conditioned responses with backward conditioned responses.

Pavlov has pointed out that the method employed in this study, of giving continuous reinforcement to one stimulus without contrasting presentations of the other stimuli without reinforcement, is ineffective in

* See above, pp. 328-329.

## TABLE 2

AMPLITUDE OF GALVANIC RESPONSE (IN MM.) TO CONDITIONED (0) AND
ADJACENT FREQUENCIES OF TONE (1, 2 AND 3) FOLLOWING
DIFFERENTIAL REINFORCEMENT
Based upon two determinations upon each of 20 subjects.

|          | Tonal stimuli | | | |
|----------|-------|-------|-------|-------|
|          | 0     | 1     | 2     | 3     |
| Response | 23.63 | 18.04 | 15.02 | 14.34 |

producing a high degree of differentiation. On the other hand, he has demonstrated the great efficacy of the contrast method in producing differentiation. His contrast method was utilized, after the initial testing, by giving added reinforcement to the conditioned stimulus, the adjacent frequencies of tone not being reinforced. The gradient obtained under these circumstances tends to support Pavlov's belief in the efficiency of this method. Table 2 gives a synopsis of the results for the 20 subjects. Each of the values given is based upon two readings upon 20 subjects, and was obtained with the same type of testing procedure as the data in Table 1. The increased steepness of the curve of generalization can readily be observed. The ratio of the responses to tones 0 and 1 divided by those to 2 and 3 is 1.25 before differential reinforcement. After the period of differential reinforcement of the conditioned frequency the corresponding ratio is 1.42.

The increase in differentiation which one obtains by the method of contrasted presentations of conditioned and of allied stimuli is interpreted by Pavlov in terms of an experimental extinction of the responses to the adjacent stimuli which are never reinforced. This gives rise to what he calls "differential inhibition." He describes this process as follows:

With regard to the nature of the nervous process by which the initially generalized conditioned stimulus comes to assume an extremely specialized form, we have abundant experimental evidence that it is based upon internal inhibition; in other words, we may say that the excitatory process which is originally widely spread in the cerebral part of the analyser is gradually overcome by internal inhibition, excepting only the minutest part of it which corresponds to the given conditioned stimulus (pp. 124-125).

From this explanation there follow a number of interesting implications. In the first place, the differentiation which becomes developed should decline with the passage of time as a result of the operation of spontaneous recovery of the accessory reflexes which become "inhibited." This deduction was tested in the following manner. A period of 24 hours was allowed to elapse after the differentiation produced by the differential reinforcement described above had been established. The magnitude of responses

## TABLE 3

AMPLITUDE OF GALVANIC RESPONSE (IN MM.) TO CONDITIONED (0) AND
ADJACENT FREQUENCIES OF TONE (1, 2 AND 3) 24 HOURS AFTER
TESTING FOR DIFFERENTIAL REINFORCEMENT
Based upon two determinations upon each of 20 subjects.

|          | Tonal stimulus | | | |
|----------|------|------|------|------|
|          | 0 | 1 | 2 | 3 |
| Response | 21.06 | 18.85 | 17.29 | 16.98 |

to each of the four frequencies of tone was then tested. The results are
presented in Table 3.

A pronounced decrease in the amount of differentiation is to be observed. The ratio of the responses to the tones 0 and 1 divided by those to
tones 2 and 3 declines from 1.42 obtained after differential reinforcement
on the first day to 1.16 at the beginning of testing 24 hours later.

Pavlov has pointed out that the differentiation which is developed is
subject to alteration as the result of the "disinhibition" of the differential
inhibition. The technique used in the present experiment is not well
adapted to testing a phenomenon so transitory as disinhibition. In another
experiment of the writer (8), however, this deduction was put to experimental test by a more suitable method of testing for generalization under
such conditions.

A third implication of considerable interest is suggested by Pavlov:

In differentiation as in the other types of internal inhibition the intensity of
inhibition stands in direct relation to the strength of the excitatory process on
the basis of which it was established, and can therefore be disturbed by any
increase in the intensity of the stimulus which developed the inhibitory properties, or by any change in the general or local excitability of the central nervous
system. . . . The increase in excitability of the whole alimentary nervous mechanism renders the previously established differential inhibition wholly inadequate (p. 127).

This deduction could profitably be investigated with a defensive reaction,
such as the galvanic skin response, as well as in greater detail with positive
reinforcing agents, as in the Pavlovian situation.

Any change in the activity of the nervous system should affect the degree
of generalization:

Again, if the general excitability of the central nervous system has been increased, for example by an injection of caffeine, the previously established
differentiation similarly becomes disturbed (p. 127).

Adequate testing of this principle by techniques such as were used by
Switzer (19) in investigating the effects of caffeine on extinction should
provide important data in the interpretation of a number of problems,

among them the explanation, in terms of principles of conditioning, of results such as those reported by Hull (11) on nonsense syllable learning under the influence of caffeine.

A further experimental approach to these problems which is suggested by Pavlov's theory relates to secondary extinction. If the factor operative in the reduction of the degree of generalization is an "internal inhibition" of the type described by Pavlov it should be capable of producing the secondary extinction of other responses. This problem would require considerable ingenuity for solution, but is one which has important theoretical implications as to the nature of "spread" or "generalization."

## The Generalization of Extinctive Inhibitory Tendencies

In this portion of our experimentation all four frequencies of tone were reinforced. After conditioned responses had been established to each of the four frequencies one of the extremes of frequency was presented without reinforcement until a considerable degree of experimental extinction was evident. The response to each of the four frequencies of tone was then tested. Generalization of extinctive inhibition would manifest itself by a decreased response to each of the adjacent frequencies as a result of the experimental extinction of the response to the selected tone. The tone which was repeatedly presented without reinforcement during experimental extinction is labelled tone 0. The adjacent tones were removed 25 (1), 50 (2) and 75 (3) j.n.d's in frequency as in the first part of the experiment.

From preliminary experimentation it was found that stable conditioned responses could be secured when six reinforcements were given to each of the frequencies of tone in random order (24 paired presentations in all). Sixteen unreinforced presentations were found to result in a reduction of the conditioned response to approximately a third of its original magnitude.

The experimental procedure is given below.

Step
  I. Test response to each frequency of tone twice.
 II. Test response to shock alone twice.
III. Give six reinforcements to each of the four frequencies of tone.
 IV. Test response to each tone twice.
  V. Give two additional reinforcements to each frequency.
 VI. Extinguish frequency 0 by 16 unreinforced presentations of stimulus.
VII. Test response to each of the frequencies.

Forty undergraduate subjects were used. Half of the group was given unreinforced presentations of the tone of 1967 cycles, half that of 153 cycles. The initial equality of these two groups is indicated by their response to shock before conditioning:

Group given unreinforced presentation 153 cycle tone 38.1 mm.
Group given unreinforced presentations 1967 cycle tone 40.3 mm.

The difference in response is not statistically reliable.

The magnitude of the initial responses to the tones indicates no constant gradient before conditioning:

| 0 | 1 | 2 | 3 |
|---|---|---|---|
| 4.51 | 3.89 | 4.68 | 4.01 |

Likewise after conditioning there is no reliable difference in the magnitude of respense to the four frequencies before extinction of frequency 0:

| 0 | 1 | 2 | 3 |
|---|---|---|---|
| 15.4 | 16.1 | 15.8 | 15.5 |

The principal results of this section of the experiment are given in Table 4. In this table are presented the responses to each of the frequencies after one of the conditioned responses (that to frequency 0) has been extinguished by 16 unreinforced presentations. The testing of the responses was carried out, as in the first part of the experimentation, with permutational arrangements of test orders. Some of the variability in the table is consequently to be explained as a result of the testing in the first position of responses to stimuli removed varying distances from the conditioned stimulus. The gradient obtained is of the same type as that found by Anrep (2) and Bass and Hull (3) for the generalization of extinctive inhibition. The form is the counterpart of that obtained in the first section of the present experiment on generalization of excitation, with a rapid change in slope between stimuli 0 and 1 and more gradual changes thereafter. The critical ratio of the difference between the response to frequency 0 and to 1 is 6.9 times the $PE_M$, and that between 1 and 3 is 2.4 times the PE of its mean. The form of the gradient obtained can be observed in Figure 3.

The present experiments, while determining experimentally the form of the gradient of generalization of inhibition, have thrown no light on the nature of the inhibitory process. The similarity in the form of the curves of generalization of excitation and of inhibition might suggest that the interpretations of Guthrie (7) and of Wendt (22) concerning inhibition are supported. These writers believe inhibition to be the result of learning not to respond (Guthrie), or as the competition of other action systems (Wendt). This active process would be expected to be generalized in much the same way as the analogous process of learning to respond, as in the generalization of excitation. This interpretation seems to

## TABLE 4

### GENERALIZATION OF EXTINCTION INHIBITION

Magnitude of galvanic response (in mm.) to tone (0) given repeatedly without reinforcement following conditioning, and to adjacent tones, 25 (1), 0 (2), and 75 (3) j.n.d.'s removed, conditioned but not extinguished.

| | Tonal stimuli | | | |
|---|---|---|---|---|
| Subject | 0 | 1 | 2 | 3 |
| I | 5.5 | 7.7 | 6.9 | 7.0 |
| II | 7.4 | 8.6 | 8.2 | 15.9 |
| III | 8.3 | 6.5 | 9.8 | 6.9 |
| IV | 7.0 | 7.5 | 12.1 | 10.8 |
| V | 9.1 | 9.5 | 7.2 | 8.9 |
| VI | 8.2 | 8.3 | 13.7 | 8.4 |
| VII | 8.0 | 11.0 | 16.1 | 11.6 |
| VIII | 5.6 | 7.6 | 8.1 | 9.3 |
| IX | 7.4 | 8.5 | 16.8 | 10.4 |
| X | 6.5 | 13.9 | 7.6 | 11.5 |
| XI | 10.1 | 13.9 | 11.4 | 9.6 |
| XII | 4.5 | 7.8 | 6.9 | 12.7 |
| XIII | 3.9 | 6.5 | 8.1 | 5.7 |
| XIV | 11.7 | 10.4 | 12.3 | 7.4 |
| XV | 6.8 | 7.9 | 8.6 | 8.3 |
| XVI | 5.4 | 15.5 | 6.7 | 13.2 |
| XVII | 7.5 | 6.9 | 8.6 | 4.8 |
| XVIII | 8.3 | 9.7 | 10.4 | 11.3 |
| XIX | 3.4 | 5.4 | 4.5 | 5.6 |
| XX | 5.5 | 14.3 | 7.4 | 6.4 |
| XXI | 9.0 | 14.3 | 10.7 | 13.2 |
| XXII | 10.7 | 9.1 | 11.4 | 11.1 |
| XXIII | 6.6 | 7.7 | 13.4 | 9.7 |
| XXIV | 7.3 | 8.4 | 7.5 | 4.9 |
| XXV | 11.3 | 9.0 | 14.3 | 11.2 |
| XXVI | 5.6 | 7.1 | 6.8 | 6.7 |
| XXVII | 8.2 | 6.5 | 8.5 | 13.4 |
| XXVIII | 4.4 | 8.1 | 5.9 | 10.1 |
| XXIX | 3.6 | 9.4 | 10.3 | 7.7 |
| XXX | 7.2 | 8.9 | 11.3 | 8.3 |
| XXXI | 5.4 | 10.0 | 9.8 | 4.0 |
| XXXII | 6.7 | 7.0 | 8.9 | 11.2 |
| XXXIII | 6.8 | 4.6 | 9.3 | 12.3 |
| XXXIV | 3.4 | 4.5 | 6.5 | 9.7 |
| XXXV | 6.7 | 7.9 | 9.8 | 14.5 |
| XXXVI | 5.9 | 8.1 | 9.7 | 8.2 |
| XXXVII | 6.0 | 11.4 | 8.4 | 13.6 |
| XXXVIII | 2.3 | 5.7 | 10.2 | 11.6 |
| XXXIX | 6.1 | 12.2 | 9.4 | 8.9 |
| XL | 5.6 | 7.8 | 10.0 | 18.3 |
| Mean | 6.72 | 8.88 | 9.59 | 9.86 |
| $PE_M$ | .23 | .28 | .29 | .33 |

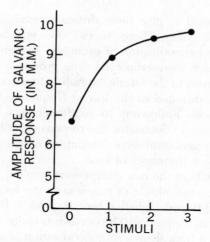

Fig. 3. Composite Curve of Generalization of Extinctive Inhibition. Galvanic skin response to tone *0*, given 6 reinforcements and then given repeatedly without reinforcement, and to tones *1*, *2* and *3* (25, 50 and 75 j.n.d.'s removed in frequency, respectively) which were conditioned but not subsequently extinguished. Each point based upon 40 values (one determination upon each of 40 subjects).

the present writer far more probable than that of a spread of an inhibitory process throughout the cerebral cortex as postulated by Pavlov, but this experiment affords no evidence opposed to his theory, and explanation of the similarity between the generalization of excitation and of inhibition, in terms of a spread of these processes over the cortex is logical, if improbable. Much further experimentation will be required, however, to establish definitely the true nature of the process.

## SUMMARY

1. The generalization stage in the formation of the conditioned response, during which a reaction occurs not only to the conditioned stimulus, but to all similar stimuli as well, was studied with the galvanic skin response. The conditioned stimuli, as well as those used in testing the extent of generalization, were auditory, produced by a beat-frequency oscillator. The subjects received the stimuli through earphones while seated in a sound-proof room. The unconditioned stimulus was faradic stimulation. All stimuli were presented automatically. The conditioned stimulus was presented for 400 milliseconds and was followed, after a pause of 95 milliseconds, by the electric shock which lasted 75 milliseconds.

2. The stimuli used in testing the extent of generalization were chosen by psychophysical methods at distances of 25 just noticeable differences.

The frequencies found to give these distances were 153, 468, 1000 (the standard) and 1967 cycles. These "tones" were equated for loudness.

3. To test for the generalization of excitatory tendencies, two groups of 20 male subjects each were employed. The groups were equated on the basis of their responses to the faradic stimuli before conditioning. The first group was then conditioned to the lowest frequency of tone, the second group to the highest. Following 16 reinforcements, both groups were given test stimulations to determine the response to all four tones. Permutational orders of presentation were determined in advance. Two responses were obtained to each frequency of tone.

4. When the results of the two groups were pooled, a curve was plotted showing the average magnitude of response to the tone to which the subject had been conditioned (labelled tone 0) and to the tones 25, 50 and 75 j.n.d.'s removed in frequency. The curve was quite smoothly negatively accelerated. While a high degree of generalization is indicated, the differences between the responses to the conditioned stimulus and to the other test stimuli are statistically significant. The curve obtained represents true *initial* generalization since no differential reinforcement had been employed.

5. The form of the curve is discussed in its relationship to other phenomena of learning, and suggestions are made for its employment in the theoretical analysis and derivation of more complex types of learning.

6. The contrast method of Pavlov, in which reinforcement of the conditioned stimulus is contrasted with unreinforced presentations of other tones, resulted in a marked diminution of the extent of generalization.

7. Following the lapse of 24 hours there was an increase in the extent of generalization as compared with that obtained immediately after the use of the contrast method. This accords with the predictions made with Pavlov's postulate that differentiation (i.e., decrease in the amount of generalization) produced by his procedure represents the experimental extinction of the generalized responses. Some further problems to test the adequacy of Pavlovian principles are suggested.

8. In the analysis of generalization of extinctive inhibition, conditioned responses were established to each of the four frequencies of tone. One extreme of the frequency range was then given repeatedly without reinforcement, until the magnitude of the conditioned response was about a third of its original size. One group was given extinction trials with the 1967 cycle tone. An equated group was given extinction on the 153 cycle tone. Forty subjects were used. Following the extinction series, responses were obtained to all four tones used in conditioning. The composite curve obtained on the entire group shows that the response is smallest to the tone given repeatedly without reinforcement (tone 0) but becomes progressively larger the further the test stimuli are removed from the conditioned

stimulus in frequency. The form of the curve is likewise negatively accelerated.

9. The similarity in the form of the curves of generalization of excitation and of inhibition supports the hypothesis of Wendt and of Guthrie that excitation and inhibition are fundamentally of the same nature, but does not constitute crucial evidence against the unsupported "neurological" theory of Pavlov.

## REFERENCES

NOTE: Four theses and two Russian articles which were not available to the writer are cited from Pavlov's bibliography and appear under the reference to his book.

1. ANREP, G. V. (1920) Pitch discrimination in the dog. *J. Physiol.*, 53, 367-385.

2. ———. (1923) Irradiation of conditioned reflexes. *Proc. Roy. Soc. London*, 94B, 404-426.

3. BASS, M. J. and HULL, C. L. (1934) The irradiation of a tactile conditioned reflex in man. *J. Comp. Psychol.*, 17, 47-65.

4. BERITOFF, J. S. (1924) On the fundamental nervous processes in the cortex of the cerebral hemispheres: I. The principal stages of the development of the individual reflex: its generalization and differentiation. *Brain*, 47, 109-148.

5. CRAFTS, L. W. (1935) Transfer as related to number of common elements. *J. Gen. Psychol.*, 13, 147-158.

6. FLETCHER, H. (1929) Speech and hearing. New York: Van Nostrand. Pp. xv + 331.

7. GUTHRIE, E. R. (1935) The psychology of learning. New York: Harper. Pp. viii + 258.

8. HOVLAND, C. I. (1937) The generalization of conditioned responses: III. Extinction, spontaneous recovery and disinhibition of conditioned and of generalized responses. *J. Exper. Psychol.*, 21, 47-62.

9. ———. The generalization of conditioned responses: IV. The effects of varying amounts of reinforcement upon the degree of generalization of conditioned responses. *J. Exper. Psychol.* (In press).

10. ———. A contribution to a conditioned-response theory of rote learning. (In prep.).

11. HULL, C. L. (1935) The influence of caffeine and other factors on certain phenomena of rote learning. *J. Gen. Psychol.*, 13, 249-274.

12. HUNTER, W. S. (1934) Learning: IV. Experimental studies of learning. In *A handbook of general experimental psychology*, ed. by C. Murchison. Worcester, Mass.: Clark Univ. Press. Pp. 497-570.

13. IVANSHINA, E. A. (1930) Isslyedovaniye staticheskoy irradiatzii razdrazhitel'nogo i tormoznogo protzesa v zvukovom analizatora u dyetey (An investigation of static irradiation of the excitatory and inhibitory processes in the auditory analyzer of children.) *Trudy Laboratorii Fiziologii Vysshey Nervnoy Deyatel'nosti Rebyonka pri Leningradskom Pedagogicheskom Institute Gertzena*, 2, 157-176. (Summarized in *Psychol. Abstr.*, 8, 72-73).

14. LOUCKS, R. B. (1933) An appraisal of Pavlov's systematization of behavior from the experimental standpoint. *J. Comp. Psychol.*, 15, 1-45.
15. PAVLOV, I. P. (1927) Conditioned reflexes. (Trans. by G. V. Anrep). London: Oxford Univ. Press. Pp. xv + 430.
  A. BELIAKOV, V. V. (1911) Contributions to the physiology of differentiation of external stimuli. Thesis, Petrograd.
  B. BOURMAKIN, V. A. (1909) Generalization of conditioned auditory reflexes in the dog. Thesis, Petrograd.
  C. GOUBERGRITZ, M. M. (1917) An improved method of developing differentiation of external stimuli. Thesis, Petrograd.
  D. IVANOV-SMOLENSKY, A. G. (1925) Irradiation of extinctive inhibition in the acoustic analyser of the dog. Collected Papers of the Physiol. Lab. of I. P. Pavlov, Vol. I, Nos. 2-3; also Pavlov Jubilee Vol., 1925.
  E. KOUPALOV, P. S. (1915) Initial generalization and subsequent specialization of conditioned reflexes. *Arch. Biol. Sci.*, 19, No. 1.
  F. ZELIONY, G. P. (1907) Contribution to the problem of the reaction of dogs to auditory stimuli. Thesis, Petrograd.
16. ROBINSON, E. S. (1932) Association theory today. New York: Century. Pp. viii + 142.
17. SWITZER, S. A. (1930) Backward conditioning of the lid reflex. *J. Exper. Psychol.*, 13, 76-97.
18. ———. (1933) Disinhibition of the conditioned galvanic skin response. *J. Gen. Psychol.*, 9, 77-100.
19. ———. (1935) The effect of caffeine on experimental extinction of conditioned reactions. *J. Gen. Psychol.*, 12, 78-94.
20. THOULESS, R. H. (1930) The technique of experimentation on the psychogalvanic reflex phenomenon and the phenomenon of Tarchanoff. *Brit. J. Psychol.*, 20, I. 219-240, II. 309-321.
21. WENDT, G. R. (1934) Auditory acuity of monkeys. *Comp. Psychol. Monog.*, 10, No. 4. Pp. 51.
22. ———. (1936) An interpretation of inhibition of conditioned reflexes as competition between reaction systems. *Psychol. Rev.*, 43, 258-281.
23. YUM, K. S. (1931) An experimental test of the law of assimilation. *J. Exper. Psychol.*, 14, 68-82.

## 29.  Discriminability and Stimulus Generalization

## N. Guttman and H. I. Kalish

*The problem of discriminability of stimuli has been invariably tied up with the stimulus generalization process. Does the organism respond to the test stimulus because it cannot discriminate it from from the conditioned stimulus? What is the relationship between the discriminability of two stimuli and stimulus generalization? In this study, the authors start out with the assumption that it is possible to produce a stimulus generalization gradient the characteristics of which reflect the discriminability of the stimuli used in the test situation.*

Three different forms for the stimulus generalization gradient have been proposed: concavity (Hull, 6), convexity (Spence, 12) and linearity (Schlosberg and Solomon, 10). In the formulation of each of these proposals, however, there has been a tacit or explicit assumption of some relationship between discriminability, in the psychophysical sense, and the generalization decrement. This assumption is manifested in Hull's postulate that generalization gradients are decreasing exponential functions on a j.n.d. scale, and also in Schlosberg and Solomon's proposal that generalization gradients are straight lines on an equal-appearing interval scale. Spence's use of a logarithmic stimulus plot appears to stem from similar considerations.

This assumption does not only appear to be intuitively reasonable, but can also be shown to have a rational basis by comparing the dimensions of the difference threshold and the generalization decrement (from which the generalization gradient can be derived by integration). The difference limen (*DL*) is ordinarily defined by the slope of the psychophysical function. For example,

$$DL = \frac{\Delta S}{[p(R) = .75] - [p(R) = .50]} = \frac{\Delta S}{\Delta p(R)}$$

*J. exp. Psychol.*, 1956, *51*, 79-88. Reprinted with permission of the senior author and The American Psychological Association. This study was supported by the Duke University Research Council and by grants M-631C and M-629C from the National Institute of Mental Health, United States Public Health Service. The research program of which this is a part is currently supported by grant MH-1002 from the National Institute of Mental Health, United States Public Health Service. The authors are indebted to Harley M. Hanson, Werner K. Honig, and Mrs. Deborah H. Nickerson for their assistance in this research.

On the other hand, the slope of the generalization gradient, i.e., the generalization decrement, is given by $\frac{\Delta p(R)}{\Delta S}$. This implies that the generalization decrement should be proportional to the reciprocal of the DL. It is a way of saying that the organism generalizes to the extent that it cannot discriminate or that generalization is the inverse of discrimination. In essence, this proposal is a reformulation of Schlosberg and Solomon's hypothesis (10).

The foregoing analysis may be subjected to empirical verification by investigating a continuum for which the discriminability function is known. For the present experiment, wave length of light was chosen as a dimension along which to test generalization because the DL for wave length ($\Delta\lambda$) is not constant over the spectrum. By an appropriate selection of CS values, therefore, it should be possible to produce a set of gradients whose slopes reflect the characteristics of the $\Delta\lambda$ function. Where $\Delta\lambda$ is small, the gradient should be sharp; where $\Delta\lambda$ is large, the gradient should be relatively flat; and if the CS is fixed at a value where $\Delta\lambda$ is either increasing or decreasing, the generalization gradient should show a corresponding asymmetry. This continuum is also interesting because of the qualitative changes which occur within it and which would lead to the expectation, on the basis of subjective experience, that generalization would occur extensively within a hue but would decrease abruptly as the transitions between spectral hues are approached.

The technique of the present study, which utilizes the aperiodically reinforced key-pecking response, permits an examination of the generalization gradients for individual Ss. Moreover, this technique makes it possible to investigate the generalization gradients at different levels of response strength during the course of extinction, as well as variations in the generalization gradient attributable to individual differences in response strength. The obtaining of generalization gradients for individual Ss in this experiment of an outcome of the fact that aperiodic reinforcement greatly increases resistance to extinction, such that the introduction of a test stimulus for a brief interval during experimental extinction reduces the response strength by a small fraction of its total extent, e.g., in a 30-sec. test, 50 responses may be subtracted from a "reserve" of several thousand.

## METHOD

*Subjects.* The Ss were 24 experimentally naive pigeons maintained by restricted feeding to 80% of their body weight under ad libitum feeding.

*Apparatus.* A modified version of the Skinner automatic key-pecking apparatus was used. The S's compartment consisted of a plywood box

14 in. high, 12 in. wide, and 12 in. long and was situated in an air-conditioned, darkened, soundproof chamber. The roof of S's box was clear Lucite and the floor was a perforated metal grating covered with a sheet of translucent plastic. The upper half of one of the walls was made of aluminum with a ⅞-in. round aperture at the center 6.5 in. above the floor of the box. The S's key, a rectangle of translucent plastic (Insurok) lightly sprung against the wall of the box, was exposed through this opening and controlled counting and reinforcing circuits.

The magazine was situated directly below the key and consisted of a metal door hinged at the top. This door was actuated by a cam on a constant-speed motor which completed a cycle in 5 sec. when a reinforcement was presented, the cam allowed the door to open abruptly, exposing the food and switching on a 7.5-w. lamp behind the food tray. The door remained open for 3.5 sec. and then closed gradually, turning off the light as it shut.

The external side of the key was illuminated by a 6-v., 18-amp. ribbon filament lamp whose beam was directed through a tunable wave-length filter and whose filament image was cast slightly out of focus on the key. The filter was a Cambridge Thermionic Corp. Monochromator (Model B). This instrument utilizes the differential rotation of quartz crystals for various wave lengths to produce dispersion of the spectrum. Its transmission spectrum at a given setting consists of a centroid of high relative intensity flanked symmetrically by a series of periodically spaced bands of lower intensity. Although the instrument may not be considered a true monochromator, it produces a stimulus patch of high apparent purity for the human observer. The band width of the centroid increases linearly from 14 to 24 M$\mu$ over the range of settings from 450 to 640 M$\mu$. The percentage transmission of incident light is approximately flat over this range, varying between 2 and 4%. No attempt was made to produce an equal energy spectrum or alternatively to equate the spectrum lights in terms of the visibility function.

*Procedure.* The procedure used in the present study derives from the work of Skinner (11) and Ferster (3), and is similar to that used by Brush, Bush, Jenkins, John, and Whiting (2). When the Ss were reduced to 80% of their ad lib. weight, they were trained to eat from the food magazine and were conditioned by the method of successive approximation to peck at the key. The 24 Ss were divided into groups of 6, and each group was trained on a given CS. The CS wave lengths were 530, 550, 580, and 600 M$\mu$. Fifty consecutive reinforcements were given on each of two days. Following this, additional sessions of aperiodic reinforcement were administered, using a mean inter-reinforcement interval of approximately 1 min. During APR, 60-sec. stimulus-on intervals were alternated with 10-sec. stimulus-off intervals, and 30 stimulus-on intervals constituted each daily training session. During the stimulus-on interval

## TABLE 1

### Generalization Test Stimuli in Mμ

| Group | −70 | −60 | −50 | −40 | −30 | −20 | −10 | CS | +10 | +20 | +30 | +40 | +50 | +60 |
|-------|-----|-----|-----|-----|-----|-----|-----|-----|-----|-----|-----|-----|-----|-----|
| | 530 | | 470 | | 490 | 500 | 510 | 520 | 530 | 540 | 550 | 560 | 570 | | 590 |
| | 550 | | 490 | | 510 | 520 | 530 | 540 | 550 | 560 | 570 | 580 | 590 | | 610 |
| | 580 | | 520 | | 540 | 550 | 560 | 570 | 580 | 590 | 600 | 610 | 620 | | 640 |
| | 600 | 530 | | 550 | 560 | 570 | 580 | 590 | 600 | 610 | 620 | 630 | 640 | | |

a shutter in the light path of the monochromator was opened and the key was illuminated with colored light. At the same time, the interior of S's box was illuminated by a 25-w. lamp reflected through the translucent plastic floor, resulting in an illuminance of <1.00 ft.-candle on the vertical walls. In the stimulus-off condition, similar to the "blackout" situation used by Ferster (4), both the key and box illumination were terminated. The blackout condition was introduced to facilitate the changing of the key color during the stimulus generalization tests.

Generalization testing was carried out under extinction and was preceded by six 30-sec. intervals of responding to the CS during which three reinforcements were administered. The wave lengths used in the generalization tests are given in Table 1. The 11 different stimuli were randomized within a series and 12 different random series were presented to each S resulting in a schedule of 132 stimulus presentations. Twelve different schedules were constructed for Ss given the 550 and 580 Mμ CS's and the same 12 schedules were subsequently used for Ss given the 530 and 600 Mμ CS's. Each stimulus presentation was 30 sec. and was followed by a 10-sec. stimulus-off interval.

Following generalization testing, three additional APR sessions were given using the original CS. After this a second generalization test identical to the first was administered. During both testings, the number of key pecks for each 30-sec. test stimulus presentation was recorded.

### RESULTS

*Characteristics of the generalization gradient.* The mean generalization gradients obtained in the first test are shown in the upper portion of Fig. 1. For each CS group (530, 550, 580, and 600 Mμ), the gradient was obtained by plotting the mean total number of responses for each test stimulus against wave length in arithmetic units.

It will be seen that the various generalization gradients have highly comparable forms. On either side of the CS, the rate of responding declines first in a nearly linear fashion, and as the rate approaches zero, the curves become negatively accelerated. The differences among the curves

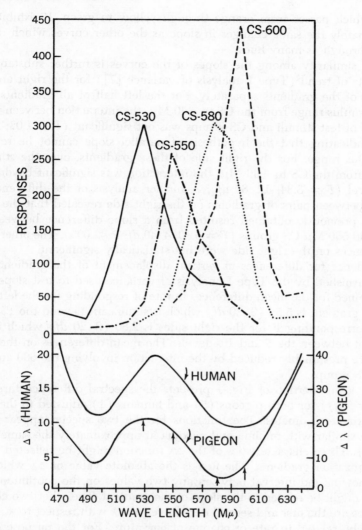

FIG. 1. Upper: Mean generalization gradients, first test. Lower: Hue discrimination as a function of wave length for pigeons (adapted from [5]), and humans (adapted from [1]).

for various CS's appear to be principally in terms of vertical displacement, i.e., total level of responding. The slopes of the generalization gradients, on the other hand, are very similar over the major portions of the curves and do not appear to conform to the expectation of marked changes corresponding to the transitions between spectral hues. The most conspicuous illustration of this point is the left half of the curve for 600

M$\mu$ which passes from orange through yellow to green. It exhibits approximately the same changes in slope as the other curves which do not pass through as many hues.

The similarity among the slopes of the curves is further substantiated by tests of trend (Type I analysis of variance [7]) for the right and left halves of the gradients separately. For the left half of all gradients, over the stimulus range from the CS to $-40$ M$\mu$, the interaction between wavelength of test stimuli and CS groups was not significant ($F = 1.02$; 12, 80 $df$), indicating that the hypothesis of parallel slope cannot be rejected over this range. For the right side of these gradients, over the stimulus range from the CS to $+40$ M$\mu$, the interaction was significant beyond the .1% level ($F = 3.84$; 12, 80 $df$). A further analysis of the differences in slope between pairs of gradients on the right side revealed that the interaction previously obtained resulted from a slope difference between the 600 and 580 M$\mu$ CS groups ($F = 5.10$; 4, 40 $df$; $P < .005$). The other slope differences on the right side were not statistically significant.

Evidence for differences in vertical displacement of the gradients was also furnished by the Type I analysis of variance used to test slope. The $F$ obtained for the mean differences in rate of responding for the left sides of the gradient is 5.55 (3, 20 $df$) which is significant beyond the 1% level. The corresponding $F$ for the right sides is 2.80 (3, 20 $df$) which is significant between the 5 and 10% levels. The mean differences on the right side are presumably reduced by the interaction involving the 600 and 580 M$\mu$ CS groups.

The lower portion of Fig. 1 presents the spectral difference threshold ($\Delta\lambda = f(\lambda)$) for both pigeons (5) and humans (1) adjusted to the same approximate ordinates. The functions for the two species appear to be highly similar with minima and maxima at approximately the same wave lengths. Three characteristics of the $\Delta\lambda$ function might be reflected in the generalization gradients. The first is the absolute value of $\Delta\lambda$ which determines the jnd interval between any two values on the continuum, and hence might be related to the slope of the gradient. The other two characteristics are the first and second derivatives of $\Delta\lambda$ with respect to $\lambda$, which might be related to rate of change of curvature. For the purpose of the present analysis, we shall be concerned mainly with the absolute value of $\Delta\lambda$.

In terms of the discriminability function for the pigeon, the generalization gradients for CS values of 530 and 580 M$\mu$ should be relatively symmetrical. For values near the CS, however, the gradient for 580 M$\lambda$ should be steeper than for any other CS. The gradients centered at 550 and 600 M$\mu$ should be asymmetrical, with 550 M$\mu$ being steeper in the direction of increasing wave length, and vice versa in the case of 600 M$\mu$.

In general, these expectations are not borne out. Figure 1 and the preceding statistical analyses of slope differences suggest that for the

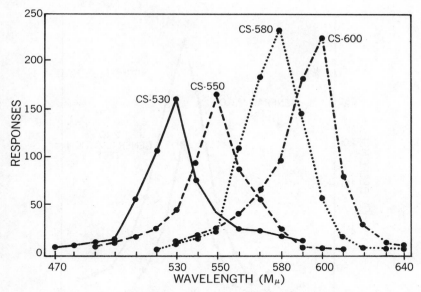

FIG. 2. Mean generalization gradients, second test.

most part the gradients are of uniform slope. The major exceptions to uniformity of slope are the relative steepness of the 600 M$\mu$ gradient and the flatness of the 580 M$\mu$ gradient, both of which features are in the direction contrary to the hypothesis based on the $\Delta\lambda$ function.

The bidirectional symmetry of the gradients was examined by means of separate analyses of variance (A × B × S [7]) for each CS group. In effect, one side of the gradient was superimposed on the other and a test of trend difference was obtained from the A × B (Right-Left Sides × Test Stimuli) interaction. The values entering into this analysis were obtained by subtracting response rate for each test stimulus from the response rate at the CS. The hypothesis of symmetry could not be rejected for the 530 and 580 gradients, since the interaction $F$ in each case was less than 1.00. This appears to conform to the $\Delta\lambda$ hypothesis. On the other hand, however, significant asymmetries contrary to the direction indicated by the $\Delta\lambda$ function are revealed in the analyses of variance for the 550 and 600 M$\mu$ groups. The interaction $F$ for the 550 M$\mu$ gradient is 8.39, which is significant beyond the .1% level for 4, 20 $df$; the $F$ for the 600 M$\mu$ gradient is 5.85, which is significant beyond the 1% level for 3, 15 $df$.*

The results of the second generalization test, shown in Fig. 2, are highly similar to those obtained in the first test. In general, all gradients are reduced in height and the differences in vertical displacement and slope are

* The number of $df$ is reduced for the 600 M$\mu$ group because only four points to the right of the CS were available for analysis.

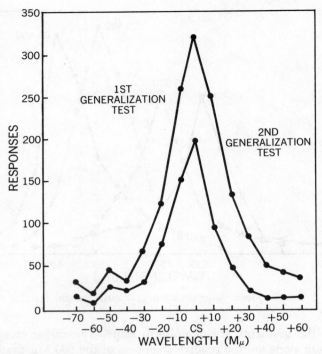

FIG. 3. Mean generalization gradients, first and second test, for all CS groups combined.

attenuated. Neither the $F$ for vertical displacement nor the $F$ for slope difference is significant ($P \lessgtr .20$). The hypothesis of symmetry can be rejected only for the 600 M$\mu$ gradient, since $F = 3.44$ (3, 15 $df$; .025 $< P$ $< .05$). The relationships among the gradients for the second generalization test are such that the curves can be nearly superimposed by translating them along the wave-length axis to a common CS point.

The relationships between the mean generalization gradient for all groups in the first test and the mean for all groups in the second test are shown in Fig. 3.

*Individual generalization gradients.* Twelve pairs of individual generalization gradients for the first and second tests are shown in Fig. 4. These gradients are arranged in order of ascending response rate, and for each CS group the Ss presented are the lowest, the highest, and the S nearest the group median. Perhaps the most salient aspect of these curves is the orderliness and reproducibility of the generalization process within the individual S. Although these gradients are summed over the individual's schedule of 132 stimulus presentations, it is interesting that a similar

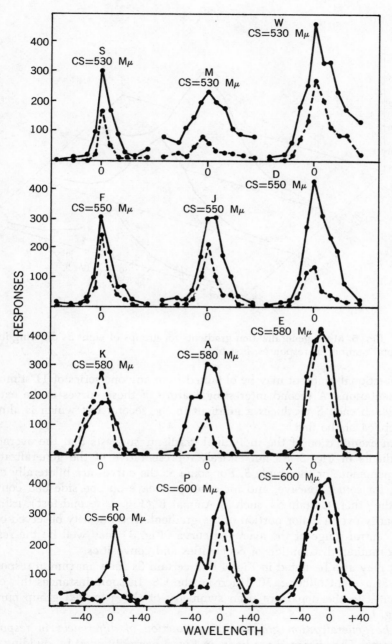

Fig. 4. Individual generalization gradients for 12 Ss representing various CS groups and levels of response strength. Solid lines designate the first test, broken lines the second test.

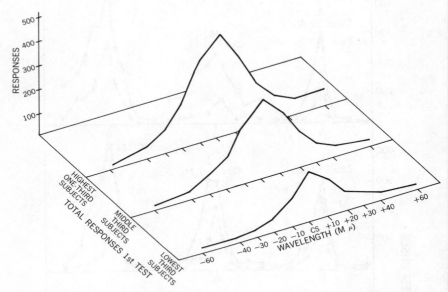

FIG. 5. Mean generalization gradients for groups of eight Ss differing in total number of responses, first test.

bidirectional gradient may be obtained from any one series of 11 stimulus presentations. A second interesting feature of these curves is the extent to which each S produces a gradient in the second test which is almost a replica of the first.

An examination of the individual gradients suggests that the averaged gradients in Fig. 3 are not entirely representative of the generalization phenomenon for the single S. For some Ss the curves are bilaterally convex, for some, concave, and for others, concave on one side and convex on the other. Certain Ss, such as Animal E (Fig. 4, second test), exhibit linearity over a major portion of the gradient. The linearity observed over the central range of the averaged curve (Fig. 3) may well be the result of a random distribution of concavities and convexities.

It may also be noted in Fig. 4 that certain Ss show maximum responding at a point either ±10 Mμ from the CS. In some instances this contributes to the departure from symmetry of the averaged group curves (Fig. 1).

*The generalization gradient as a function of differences in response strength.* The averaged gradients in Fig. 5 were obtained by dividing the 24 Ss (without respect to CS group) into three relatively homogeneous subgroups in terms of total responses for the first generalization test.

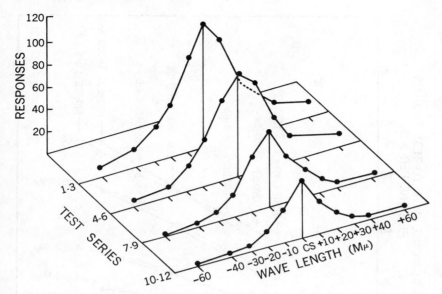

Fig. 6. Mean generalization gradients for successive fourths of first test.

As the total response level is reduced, the generalization gradient becomes uniformly flatter. Tests of trend differences over the right and left halves of the gradients separately permit rejection of the hypothesis that the curves are parallel. On the right side, the interaction $F = 22.4$ ($8, 84$ $df$; $P < .001$) while $F$ for vertical displacement is 19.8 ($2, 21$ $df$; $P < .001$). The interaction $F$ for the left halves is 5.15 ($8, 84$ $df$; $P < .001$), while the vertical displacement $F = 19.5$ ($2, 21$ $df$; $P < .001$). In a later section we shall analyze in greater detail the nature of these interactions.

Additional information concerning changes in the generalization gradient associated with changes in level of responding may be obtained from an analysis of the extinction process occurring during the generalization test. The generalization gradients in Fig. 6 are based upon the total responses of all Ss and represent the average performance for successive blocks of 33 stimulus presentations. The gradient for the first quarter of the extinction series is relatively steep, and the gradients for the succeeding quarters become progressively flatter. These changes bear a strong resemblance to those shown by the response-strength subgroups in Fig. 5. Furthermore, the gradients for the successive stages of extinction (Fig. 6) display a departure from parallelism on both sides of the CS. The interaction $F$'s for the right and left halves of the gradients are 8.22 and 6.40, both significant beyond the .1% level for 12, 276 $df$.

The similarities between the changes in the form of the generalization gradient during extinction (Fig. 6) and the changes associated with individual differences in response strength (Fig. 5) strongly suggest that

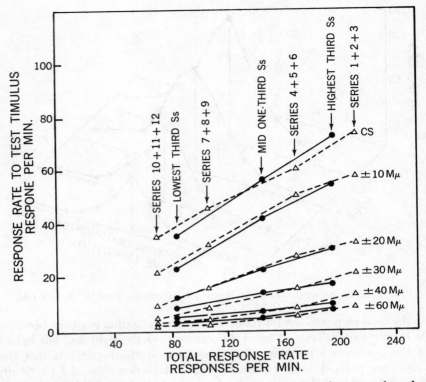

FIG. 7. Rate of responding for various test stimuli as a function of total response strength.

both sets of changes may be represented by a common function. In order to obtain a graphical comparison of these changes, each bidirectional gradient for the first generalization test in Fig. 5 and 6 was first converted to a unidirectional gradient by averaging the response rates for ±10 M$\mu$, ±20 M$\mu$, etc., and converting to a common scale of responses per minute. Next, an index* of the total rate of responding (in responses per minute) was determined for each gradient. In Fig. 7 the values from each unidirectional gradient are plotted on ordinates erected at points corresponding to the total response strength for that gradient. The lines in this figure connect the same test stimulus values for the various gradients. Thus, the

* The index used was
$$R_{CS} + \sum_{n-1}^{5} \left( \frac{[R_{+10M\mu} + R_{-10M\mu}]}{2} + \cdots \frac{[R_{+60M\mu} + R_{-60M\mu}]}{2} \right)$$
where $R$ = rate of responding in responses per minute. This index provides that the values for the CS will lie along a line with a 0,0 intercept, and permits a rescaling of the total extinction curve on a response strength axis.

uppermost pair of lines connect the CS values for the gradients in Fig. 5 and 6, the next pair of lines connect the values for $\pm 10$ M$\mu$, etc. These lines may be visualized as the contours of the surfaces in Fig. 5 and 6. The high degree of correspondence between these lines indicates that changes in generalization as a function of response strength are the same whether the response strength varies within the individual, as in the course of extinction, or whether response strength is considered as a parameter characterizing the differences between individuals.

The transformation of the data to the form shown in Fig. 7 suggests the mathematical operation necessary to predict generalization at one level of response strength given the generalization function at a different level. The operation proposed by Hull (6) is multiplication by a constant. Miller (9) has suggested, in the context of a discussion of the effect of motivational changes on the gradient, that the conversion can be accomplished by adding a constant at every point on the gradient. If the multiplicative relation holds, then all the lines in Fig. 7 should pass through the point O, O, but if the additive relation obtains, then all the lines in this figure should be parallel to each other. The present results indicate that neither hypotheses alone provides a sufficient description of the situation. The additive relation appears to hold for values near the CS, but the multiplicative relation must be invoked for values further removed from the CS.

## Discussion

The results of the present experiment do not appear to provide evidence for a correspondence between the discriminability function for wave length of light ($\Delta\lambda$ vs. $\lambda$) and the generalization process. Since some relationship is reasonable on logical and intuitive grounds, our results must be interpreted in the light of a number of possibilities. In the first place, the relationship may not, in fact, exist, because during generalization testing the S is not making a comparative judgment. In more formal terms, the analogy we have suggested between the generalization decrement and the difference limen may be misleading, because $p(R)$ in one situation refers to a simple conditioned response, while in the psychophysical experiment, $p(R)$ is associated with a complex of discriminatory responses.

The foregoing considerations, however, fall far short of excluding the possibility that a relationship does exist and that the present experiment has failed to disclose it. Our results are compatible with the notion that the wave-length discriminability function for the pigeon is much flatter than has been reported (5), flatter in fact than that for humans. It may also be that the discriminability differences in our situation are attenuated because the pigeon works in a dim light. As a check on the latter possibility a crude psychophysical experiment was performed on four human Ss using the method of minimal changes. The $\Delta\lambda$ function obtained was not appreciably different from that generally reported; it showed minima in the blue and yellow regions, a maximum in the green, and differences on the order of 5:1. The same results were obtained in the dark and in the presence of dim light.

Another factor in our experiment which might act to distort the expected relationship is brightness variation, since no attempt was made to equate the test stimuli for brightness or incident energy. This might have the consequence of increasing the slope of gradients passing into regions of lower visibility, and might account for the asymmetry of the gradient for 600 M$\mu$. If, however, brightness were an important factor over all, it would be difficult to account for the high degree of similarity among the gradients plotted on a wave-length continuum. The extent to which brightness can be invoked as a variable is inversely proportional to the degree of relationship between changes in response rate and wave length.

Finally, serious consideration must be given to the possibility that the relationship between generalization and discrimination is much more complex than we have supposed. Before any general statement can be made concerning the independence of discriminability and stimulus generalization, the problems raised by the present experiment must be explored with other continua, species, and techniques.

With respect to the issue of changes in the form of the generalization gradient with changes in response strength, our findings may be compared most directly with those of Margolius (8), who investigated changes in generalization as a function of number of conditioning trials. In terms of the rate of responding measure, Margolius found increases in the absolute and relative amounts of generalization as the number of training trials increased. Margolius' interpretation of his findings is equivalent to what we have designated as the additive relation. It will be recalled that for the present results, the additive hypothesis was tenable for the major area of the curve including values near the CS, and high response strengths, but for remote values of the stimuli and for low response strengths the additive relation fails. This suggests the possibility that the empirical gradient is comprised of two components, one which is linear on a wave-length scale and changes additively, and another which is curvilinear and changes multiplicatively. It may be that the second component is contributed by random responding and responding to extraneous stimuli accompanying the beginning of a trial. This separation of components implies that if the contribution of the second component was reduced, either experimentally or analytically, the additive relation would become more conspicuous.

## SUMMARY

An experiment was performed to test the hypothesis of a relationship between the discriminability of spectrum colors and stimulus generalization along the wave-length continuum. Four groups of six pigeons were trained to peck at a disc illuminated by monochromatic lights corresponding to 530, 550, 580, and 600 M$\mu$. Bidirectional generalization gradients were obtained from measures of response rate during extinction. These gradients were of highly comparable forms for the various spectral regions tested. The results open the possibility of an independence between the generalization decrement and the discriminability of stimuli.

Changes in the generalization gradient accompanying changes in response strength were investigated. A close correspondence was found between changes in the form of the gradient during extinction and changes associated with individual differences in response strength. In both cases the changes appear to be describable by means of a combined additive and multiplicative relationship.

## REFERENCES

1. BORING, E. G., LANGFELD, H. S., and WELD, H. P. (1948) *Foundations of psychology.* New York: Wiley.

2. BRUSH, F. R., BUSH, R. R., JENKINS, W. O., JOHN, W. F., and WHITING, J. W. M. (1952) Stimulus generalization after extinction and punishment: an experimental study of displacement. *J. abnorm. soc. Psychol., 47,* 633-640.

3. FERSTER, C. B. (1953) The use of the free operant in the analysis of behavior. *Psychol. Bull., 50,* 263-274.

4. ——— (1953) Sustained behavior under delayed reinforcement. *J. exp. Psychol., 45,* 218-224.

5. HAMILTON, W. F. and COLEMAN, T. B. (1933) Trichromatic vision in the pigeon as illustrated by the spectral hue discrimination curve. *J. comp. Psychol., 15,* 183-191.

6. HULL, C. L. (1943) *Principles of behavior.* New York: D. Appleton-Century.

7. LINDQUIST, E. F. (1953) *Design and analysis of experiments in psychology and education.* New York: Houghton Mifflin.

8. MARGOLIUS, G. (1955) Stimulus generalization of an instrumental response as a function of the number of reinforced trials. *J. exp. Psychol., 49,* 105-111.

9. MILLER, N. E. (1944) Experimental studies of conflict. In J. McV. Hunt (Ed.), *Personality and the behavior disorders.* New York: Ronald.

10. SCHLOSBERG, H. and SOLOMON, R. L. (1943) Latency of response in a choice discrimination. *J. exp. Psychol., 33,* 22-39.

11. SKINNER, B. F. (1950) Are theories of learning necessary? *Psychol. Rev., 57,* 193-216.

12. SPENCE, K. W. (1937) The differential response in animals to stimuli varying within a single dimension. *Psychol. Rev., 44,* 430-444.

# 30.    Studies of Response Generalization in Conditioning. I. Stimulus Generalization During Response Generalization

## D. D. Wickens

*This is one of a series of studies in which the author has examined the phenomenon of response generalization. In these studies, an extension response of the finger was first conditioned. Following such training, the hand was turned over and the conditioned stimulus again presented. Characteristically, the subject responded to the stimulus by flexing his finger, rather than extending it as during the original conditioning trials. The fact that a new muscle group is used in making the response to the conditioned stimulus illustrates the nature of response generalization. In the present study, the author examines response generalization as a function of the presentation of a generalized conditioned stimulus.*

## Introduction

Most investigations in the field of conditioning have been concerned primarily with the effect upon the conditioned response of variations of the two important conditioning stimuli—the conditioned and the unconditioned. Studies have been conducted to determine what conditioned and what unconditioned stimuli can be used, how variations in the frequency or consistency of presentation of the two stimuli affect the response, and how different time relations affect the response. In short, the concern of these investigations has been directed toward discovering how historical conditions affect the present conditioned response behavior. Needless to say, such researches have contributed greatly to our knowledge of behavior under certain well-defined conditions.

The very nature of these studies has demanded that all of the environmental conditions other than the conditioned and the unconditioned stimuli be held constant. The behavioral records of such experiments have pointed toward a moderately high degree of constancy in the form of the response, and toward a disturbance of the conditioning process with the introduction of new stimuli (external inhibition). As a consequence of these findings, many psychologists have been led to conceive of the con-

*J. exp. Psychol.*, 1943, 33, 221-227. Reprinted with permission of the author and The American Psychological Association.

ditioned response as a behavioral segment which is both fragile and rigid; a unit which is either shattered completely by any shift in the stimulating situation, or one which stubbornly maintains the same form in the face of wide environmental changes.

Such a view makes the conditioned response something of a psychological hot-house plant, a concept which may be amusing to play with in the laboratory, but which does not hold up in the rigors of everyday life where one finds not only variation in the environment, but equally wide variations in the response to a given stimulus. Conceiving of the conditioned response in this manner, many psychologists have rejected it as having little value in understanding behavior outside of a few restricted laboratory situations.

In the light of such criticisms of conditioning, and in view of the fact that if they are true, the conditioned response is indeed of limited theoretical value, a fruitful direction to research in the field of conditioning may be toward determining if and how the conditioned response will vary in its characteristics as a result of variations of the environment or of the subject's relation to his environment. Essentially such research would consist of developing the conditioned response, and then pressing the conditioned stimulus under altered conditions and assaying the functional relationship between these variations and the conditioned response. Only after research of this sort has been done is one in a position to appreciate the significance of the conditioned response in the extra-laboratory situation in which a constant environment is the exception rather than the rule.

Some experimental work of this sort has already been done. Thus, we know that a functional relationship exists between an already established conditioned response and motivational states (2, 14), emotional conditions (6, 7), and the general condition of the organism (11). In the case of the operant conditioned response there are data to indicate that the significance of the conditioned stimulus may carry over into a situation widely different from the one in which it acquired its significance (10).

## PROBLEM

The purpose of the present experiment was to investigate the operation of stimulus generalization during response generalization. Specifically, the experiment was designed to determine whether or not a changed response would be given to stimuli other than the one to which the S had been conditioned.

In several previous studies (12, 13) the writer has indicated that the form of the response can be radically altered by environmental changes. In these experiments an extension response of the finger was first conditioned, and then the hand was turned over and the same finger was placed on the electrode. Though the apparatus was constructed so that either an extension or a flexion could be made with equal ease, it was found that the Ss characteristically flexed, rather than extended, the finger when the conditioned stimulus alone was presented. Such a modification of the form of the response without additional training is an instance of response generalization (3, p. 350).

The facts of stimulus generalization are well known. Pavlov (7) reported that animals trained to a specific stimulus will react to others which differ from it along the same psychological dimension. More recently in this country several careful studies have been conducted on this phenomenon (1, 4, 5, 8), and have given more precise information concerning its operation. In general, these studies have indicated that generalization does occur, and that the magnitude of the generalized response is a function of the degree of similarity of the generalized to the original stimulus.

## SUBJECTS

The 59 Ss who took part in the experiment were all enrolled in the Elementary Psychology course at the University of Wisconsin. They were about equally divided as to the sexes.

## APPARATUS

The conditioning board used in the experiment was wooden, and similar to that described in a previous experiment (12). The S's arm was restrained to a board 12 in. × 30 in. by a wooden block at the elbow, a leather strap across the forearm, and a rigid wooden strap that could be clamped down across the back or the palm of the hand, depending on the position of the S's hand on the board. The location of these restrainers on the board could be adjusted to the size of the S's arm. The S's middle finger rested on an electrode about the size of a dime. This electrode was fastened to a platform supported by a spring. Since the tension of the spring was slight, the entire platform could be easily depressed by the S. Movements of the finger either upwards or downwards were recorded by means of electrical contacts. Downward movements were recorded when a bolt head attached to the electrode platform dipped into a mercury well. Upward movements were recorded when a metal strip resting on the S's finger came into contact with a brush just above the strip. Both recording mechanisms were adjustable, and were arranged so that movements of about 1/16 in. in either direction were recorded. The other electrode was strapped to the S's wrist.

The conditioned stimulus was produced by a Maico Audiometer, and was delivered into an earphone worn by the S. The unconditioned stimulus was produced by a high voltage power pack. The temporal relations between the two stimuli, as well as the duration of the individual stimuli, were controlled by lugs on a timing disk operated by a one r.p.m. synchronous motor. As the disk revolved, the lugs made contact with their appropriate brush; this closed several relay circuits which started the clock and administered the tone and the shock. The clock, which measured time in units of .01 sec., started ½ sec. before the tone was given, and continued until the S's response broke the circuit of its holding relay. The clock could be stopped by either an upward or downward response, and the direction of the response was indicated by lights on a control panel. The duration of the tone was ½ sec., and its termination coincided with the termination of the shock. The shock persisted for ⅒ sec. The control panel permitted E to adminster either stimulus independently, and to vary the inter-trial time intervals.

E and the apparatus were in adjacent rooms. The two rooms were soundproof from the rest of the building and from each other. The S could be observed, however, through a one-way-vision screen.

## I. Experimental Procedure

The general procedure used throughout the experiments for the three experimental groups was that of conditioning the Ss to one tone, turning the hand over, and testing for responses to the same tone, or to a tone differing from this by either one or two octaves.

The S was first brought into the experimental room, and the following directions were given:

"This is a conditioning experiment. During the experiment your hand will be strapped to this board, with your middle finger resting on this electrode, and the other electrode fastened to your wrist. You will receive a shock which will pass from one electrode to another. You can break the shock by lifting your finger from the electrode. During the experiment a tone will precede the shock by a regular interval of time. If you get conditioned you will develop a tendency to respond to the tone before the shock goes on. I do not want you to fight against becoming conditioned, and at the same time you are not to respond voluntarily to the tone. If your finger wants to fly up just don't inhibit it.

"I will start the experiment by obtaining your threshold to a tone. I will begin with a tone which will be clearly heard, and reduce the intensity of it until you cease to hear it. Then, using the same tone, I will increase its intensity until you hear it again. I want you to press on this button all the time you hear the tone.

"I will test for two tones in the same way.

"Following that I will test for the strength of the shock. Beginning with a weak shock, I will build it up until it is as strong as you want to take it. Let me know by calling out when it is strong enough. All I want is to have it intense enough to make you lift your finger from the electrode without thinking much about it."

E then went into the experimental room and obtained the thresholds for two different tones. The intensity of the shock was adjusted to the S's toleration. This intensity level was used throughout the experiment unless the latent times to the shock alone began to increase much beyond the average time of the first 10 responses. If this occurred, the shock was increased to the point that the latent times were reduced appropriately.

Following these various tests, the standard procedure was then begun. This procedure consisted of:

A. Three presentations of the tone alone. The intensity of the tone was set at 50 decibels above the threshold value, and the particular tone was of the frequency that would be employed in the final test. If any S's responded to the tone alone at this time, they were discarded from the experimental group. Only one S had to be eliminated from the group for this reason.

B. Three shocks alone.

C. One hundred thirty paired stimulations. The time intervals between these stimulations varied from 5 to 35 sec. Four subjects out of 63 did not show any conditioned responses as measured by anticipatory reactions during this training, and these Ss were not continued on the experiment.

D. E entered the S's room, and told him: "Now, I want to turn your hand over so that the same finger is on the electrode, but your palm is up." The hand was then turned over, and the recording contacts adjusted to the new position. If S asked any questions at this time, E replied that he would answer them later.

E. Thirty sec. after E returned to the experimental room, he began to present the tone alone. This was presented for 10 trials. Time intervals between presentation varied, and were the same for all Ss.

The Ss in the three experimental groups were conditioned or tested to tones with a frequency of 256, 512, or 1024 cycles per sec. Group I was conditioned and tested to the same tone, there being five individuals conditioned to each of the tones. The Ss in Group II were conditioned to one tone and tested to another differing from it by one octave. Half of the Ss were conditioned to the lower or the middle tones, and tested to the tone just higher, and the other half were conditioned to the highest or middle tone and tested to the tone just lower. The Ss in Group III were tested to a tone differing by two octaves from the training tone. Half of them were conditioned to the highest and tested to the lowest tone, and the reverse procedure was employed for the other half. There were 16 Ss each in Groups II and III.

## II. Control Procedure

The Control Group composed of 12 Ss was treated to the typical pseudo-conditioning procedure. They were tested to the tone and shock in the same manner as the experimental groups, but instead of being given 130 paired stimulations, they were given 130 shocks alone. They were then tested to the tone alone with the hand turned over in precisely the same manner as the experimental groups.

The directions given to this group at the beginning of the experiment differed, of course, from those given to the experimental Ss. The directions were:

"If you don't mind, I will tell you nothing much about the experiment until it is over, then I will tell you everything you may want to know.

"During the experiment your hand will be strapped to this board with your middle finger resting on this electrode, and the other electrode fastened to your wrist. You will receive a shock which will pass from one electrode to the other. You can break the shock by lifting your finger from the electrode. During the experiment you will be given a series of these shocks."

Following this the same information about obtaining the thresholds for the tones and the desired strength of shock was given.

## Results and Discussion

A. *Response Generalization.* Transference of the form of the response from extension to flexion was evident in all the experimental groups. The number of Ss who failed to show any response when the hand was turned over was 2 in Group I, 5 in Group II, and 6 in Group III. Three Ss in Group I made extension responses when the hand was turned over. One of these Ss made 5 extension responses before extinction, and the other Ss made 7 and 3 extension responses, and then changed the form of the response to flexion. No Ss in the other two groups made extension responses.

B. *Conditioning vs. Pseudo-conditioning.* The results for the three experimental groups and the control group are given in Table I. In column one the various groups are identified, column two gives the number of Ss in each group, column three indicates the mean number of responses, and column four gives the standard deviation of the distribution.

It can be readily seen from the table that the means of the experimental groups are considerably greater than the control mean. The difference between the control and each of the experimental means is significant at the one per cent level of confidence.

These results are concordant with those obtained in a previous study by the writer (12), and they indicate that the transference of the response to the new position cannot be completely accounted for by the occurrence

## TABLE I

THE MEAN NUMBER OF RESPONSES AND THE VARIABILITY OF THE TRANSFERRED
CONDITIONED RESPONSE FOR THE EXPERIMENTAL AND CONTROL GROUPS

| Group | N | M | σ |
|---|---|---|---|
| Group I | 15 | 5.87 | 3.66 |
| Group II | 16 | 3.69 | 3.45 |
| Group III | 16 | 4.19 | 4.33 |
| Group C | 12 | .16 | .37 |

of shock alone, but is primarily dependent upon the pairing of the tone and shock in the former position.

C. *Response Generalization During Stimulus Generalization.* Generalization of the generalized response is clearly indicated in the data of the experiment. In all of the experimental groups, many of the Ss gave conditioned responses to the tone alone in the new situation, whether or not they had been tested to the same tone, or to a tone one or two octaves different from the training tone. The data show some tendency for the same tone to be more effective in eliciting the transferred conditioned response than were the generalized tones, if direct comparison of the means is made. Treatment of the data by an analysis of variance, however, produces an F-ratio of less than one. Thus, there is no statistical evidence that any one of these stimuli are more effective than any of the others.

This result is probably to be expected on several counts. Humphreys (5) has shown that losses in the magnitude of the response during stimulus generalization are not great if the test tone bears an octave relationship to the training tone. Secondly, it will be recalled that the tonal stimulus was brief in duration, and had a sudden onset. This would result in a large number of similar component frequencies during the onset of each of the tones (9).

The results of the experiment militate against the narrow interpretation of conditioning previously referred to, for not only is the form of the response different from the one that was originally trained, but this generalized response may be evoked by other stimuli than those that were used in the initial training. Neither is the conditioned response in this situation stereotyped in form, nor is the varied form of the response uniquely tied to the original conditioning stimulus.

## SUMMARY

The present experiment was designed to test for the possibility of stimulus generalization of the generalized conditioned response. Three groups of subjects were conditioned to tonal stimuli. Shock served as the unconditioned stimulus, and finger extension was the conditioned response. The S's hands were then turned over and the tone alone was sounded. For one group the same tone was used, for another the test tone differed by one octave from the training tone, and for the third group a two-octave difference was employed.

A large number of Ss in all groups responded to the tone alone in the new situation, the nature of the response being characteristically flexion rather than extension. No significant difference in the frequency of the response existed in the three groups.

## REFERENCES

1. BASS, M. J. and HULL, C. L. (1934) The irradiation of a tactile conditioned reflex in man. *J. comp. Psychol.*, *17*, 47-65.
2. FINCH, G. (1938) Hunger as a determinant of conditional and unconditional salivary response magnitude. *Amer. J. Physiol.*, *123*, 379-382.
3. HILGARD, E. R. and MARQUIS, D. G. (1940) *Conditioning and learning.* New York: D. Appleton-Century Co.
4. HOVLAND, C. I. (1937) The generalization of conditioned responses. I. The sensory generalization of conditioned responses with varying frequencies of tone. *J. gen. Psychol.*, *17*, 125-148.
5. HUMPHREYS, L. G. (1939) Generalization as a function of the method of reinforcement. *J. exp. Psychol.*, *25*, 361-372.
6. LIDDELL, H. S., JAMES, W. T., and ANDERSON, O. D. (1934) The comparative physiology of the conditioned motor reflex based on experiments with the pig, dog, sheep, goat, and rabbit. *Comp. Psychol. Monogr.*, *11*, No. 1.
7. PAVLOV, I. P. (1927) *Conditioned reflexes.* London: Oxford University Press.
8. RAZRAN, G. H. S. (1938) Studies in configural conditioning. VII. Ratios and elements in salivary conditioning to various musical intervals. *Psychol. Rec.*, *2*, 370-376.
9. STEVENS, S. S. and DAVIS, H. (1938) *Hearing.* New York: John Wiley & Sons.
10. WALKER, K. C. (1942) The effect of a discriminative stimulus transferred to a previously unassociated response. *J. exp. Psychol.*, *31*, 312-321.
11. WENGER, M. A. (1936) An investigation of conditioned responses in human infants. *Univ. Ia. Stud. Child Welf.*, *12*, 9-90.
12. WICKENS, D. D. (1938) The transference of conditioned excitation and conditioned inhibition from one muscle group to the antagonistic muscle group. *J. exp. Psychol.*, *22*, 101-123.
13. WICKENS, D. D. (1939) The simultaneous transfer of conditioned excitation and conditioned inhibition. *J. exp. Psychol.*, *24*, 332-338.
14. ZENER, K. and McCURDY, H. G. (1939) Analysis of motivational factors in conditioned behavior: I. The differential effect of changes in hunger upon conditioned, unconditioned, and spontaneous salivary conditioning. *J. Psychol.*, *8*, 321-350.

# Transfer of Training

TRANSFER of training refers to the fact that the learning of one task has some influence on the learning of a second. If the learning of Task 1 aids in the learning of Task 2, we have a case of positive transfer; if Task 1 hinders the learning of Task 2, we have negative transfer.

A large number of experimenters have examined transfer from a stimulus response position, with the paired-associate learning situation being used frequently. Two transfer paradigms, or modifications thereof, have been extensively investigated: (1) attaching an old response to a new stimulus (A-B, C-B) and (2) attaching a new response to an old stimulus (A-B, A-C).

An early attempt to fit the findings into a meaningful whole was made by Robinson (1927) in the Skaggs-Robinson hypothesis. This hypothesis stated that positive transfer was maximum when the two tasks were identical; moderate degrees of similarity between the two tasks produced maximum negative transfer with such transfer decreasing as the tasks became more and more dissimilar. Unfortunately, there was no specification as to whether the hypothesis applied to similarity of stimuli, similarity of responses, or both. Some years later, Osgood (1949), whose selection we have included in this section, generated a three dimensional surface in which he attempted to resolve the problem. Although it cannot be said that all of the subsequent experiments have been consistent with Osgood's resolution, he has provided a frame of reference within which to examine the findings of others.

All transfer effects cannot be analyzed in terms of a similarity dimension existing among stimuli and responses. General factors are also important, and Harlow's (1949) classic paper on learning sets illustrates this position.

Other types of transfer situations have been frequently designated by other terms. These are: (1) familiarity, (2) stimulus predifferentiation, and (3) sensory preconditioning. A great deal of work has been done in each of these areas, but rather than attempt to provide any overview of them, we have selected the early studies of Hovland and Kurtz (1952), Gagne and Baker (1950), and Brogden (1939) to illustrate the experimental findings obtained in these areas.

## REFERENCES

BROGDEN, W. J. (1939) Sensory pre-conditioning. *J. exp. Psychol.*, 25, 323-333.
GAGNE, R. M. and BAKER, K. E. (1950) Stimulus pre-differentiation as a factor in transfer of training. *J. exp. Psychol.*, 40, 439-451.
HARLOW, H. F. (1949) The formation of learning sets. *Psychol. Rev.*, 56, 51-65.
HOVLAND, C. I. and KURTZ, K. H. (1952) Experimental studies in rote learning: X. Pre-syllable familiarization and the length-difficulty relationship *J. exp. Psychol.*, 44, 31-39.
OSGOOD, C. E. (1949) The similarity paradox in human learning: a resolution. *Psychol. Rev.*, 56, 132-143.
ROBINSON, E. S. (1927) The "similarity" factor in retroaction. *Amer. J. Psychol.*, 39, 297-312.

# 31. The Similarity Paradox in Human Learning: A Resolution

## C. E. Osgood

*The similarity between materials used in the original and transfer task has been a frequently examined variable, with many of the early studies unconcerned as to whether the similarity dimension should be applied to stimulus material, responses, or both. As Osgood points out, the law generated from these early studies—the greater the similarity, the greater the interference or negative transfer—leads to an impossible state of affairs since it means that tasks which are identical should lead to maximum amounts of negative transfer. Osgood's article is an attempt to resolve this difficulty by providing a three-dimensional surface in which the similarity of stimuli and responses are placed on different axes. It should be noted that the interference or facilitation which may be obtained in the transfer situation is believed to have applicability to proaction and retroaction situations as well, and Osgood's article points to such generality.*

Behavior is a continuous, fluid process, and activities learned in the laboratory are as much a part of it as a trip to the county fair. The segments which an experimenter arbitrarily selects for analysis are inextricably imbedded in this expanding matrix and are interpretable only in terms of its interactions. Transfer and retroaction experiments are explicit attempts to gauge these interactions, and the similarity variable—that is, the homogeneities existing among the materials successively practiced—turns out to be the most important factor as well as the most puzzling.

The classic statement of the relation between similarity and interference in human learning, as found in most textbooks in psychology, is that "the greater the similarity, the greater the interference." Although this law is traceable mainly to the work of McGeoch and his associates (10, 13, 14), there are many other experiments which superficially appear to substantiate it. When carried to its logical conclusions, however, this law leads to an impossible state of affairs. The highest degree of similarity of both stimulus and response in the materials successively practiced is that where any simple habit or S-R association is learned. The stimulus situation can never be precisely identical from trial to trial, nor can the response, but

*Psychol. Rev.*, 1949, 56, 132-143. Reprinted with permission of the author and The American Psychological Association.

they are maximally similar—and here the greatest facilitation (ordinary learning) is obtained. *Ordinary learning, then, is at once the theoretical condition for maximal interference but obviously the practical condition for maximal facilitation.* Here is the fundamental paradox, and this paper suggests a resolution.

## EMPIRICAL LAWS OF TRANSFER AND RETROACTION AS FUNCTIONS OF SIMILARITY

Transfer and retroaction in human learning are among the most extensively cultivated fields in experimental psychology, yet there are no clearcut generalizations which satisfactorily bind the data together. The difficulty may be traced in part to the bewildering variety of procedures, materials and experimental designs employed by different investigators, a phenomenon perhaps characteristic of a young science. But some of the confusion can also be laid to the fact that in a large proportion of experiments the theoretically relevant relations are patently unspecifiable: the subjects merely learn List A and then List B, or Maze I and then Maze II, and either positive or negative effects may result, depending upon quite unanalyzable conditions. The purpose of this paper is to clarify the similarity function in human learning, and to accomplish this end only those experiments can be utilized wherein the *locus* of similarities is specifiable, as being between stimulus members, response members, or both. This analytic approach, although it may be considered inappropriate by some theorists and makes use of only part of the data, does give rise to a coherent and consistent picture.

When *transfer* is studied, one is interested in the effect of a specifiable prior activity upon the learning of a given test activity. When *retroaction* is studied, one is interested in the effect of a specifiable interpolated activity upon the retention of a previously learned activity. In both cases the experimenter arbitrarily "lifts" segments of a continuing process for analysis, and it would be expected that common laws would apply to both samplings. In the present context it can be shown that identical functions of similarity apply to both transfer and retroaction data, which simplifies

Transfer and Retroaction Paradigms
TRANSFER

| Paradigm A | $S_1 \rightarrow R_1$ | $S_2 \rightarrow R_1$ | $S_1 \rightarrow R_1$ |
| Paradigm B | $S_1 \rightarrow R_1$ | $\overline{S_1} \rightarrow R_2$ | $S_1 \rightarrow R_1$ |
| Paradigm C | $S_1 \rightarrow R_1$ | $S_2 \rightarrow \overline{R_2}$ | $S_1 \rightarrow R_1$ |

RETROACTION

FIG. 1. Paradigms indicating the locus of variation among the successively practiced materials. A, stimulus variation; B, response variation; C, simultaneous stimulus and response variation.

the theoretical task considerably. Figure 1 gives symbolic representation to three basic learning paradigms, A that in which stimulus members are varied in the materials successively practiced while responses are functionally identical, B that in which responses are varied and stimuli are functionally identical, and C that in which both stimulus and response members are simultaneously varied. It will be seen that in so far as similarity relations are concerned, the test for transfer is simultaneously the interpolated activity when the entire retroactive sequence is followed. The term "functional identity" is used here to make explicit the fact that *true* identity among either stimulus or response processes is a will-o-the-wisp, approached but never attained. Functional identity of stimuli in successive trials or tasks exists when the situation is objectively constant (*i.e.*, when the same stimulus nonsense syllable appears on the screen or the same choice point is approached on repeated trials in the maze); functionally identical responses are those which the experimenter, at any given level of analysis, scores as being the same (*i.e.*, no matter how the subject says CYF or how the rat maneuvers about a turn, it is scored 'correct'). Functional identity thus becomes the limiting case of maximum similarity.

1. Let us first consider *paradigm A*, the condition in which stimulus similarity is variable and responses are functionally identical. The transfer portion of this paradigm will be recognized as nothing other than a symbolic statement of *stimulus generalization*. In Hovland's classic study (9), for example, a galvanic skin response is first conditioned to a tone of a certain frequency ($S_1-R_1$), then the test tone is presented and the extent to which the same response is made to it measured ($S_2-R_1$). Hovland found that the greater the similarity between practice and test stimuli, the greater the amount of generalization (or positive transfer). The same results are regularly found wherever this paradigm can be identified, whether the materials be motor or verbal, meaningful or nonsense, or of any other nature. McKinney (15) required subjects to respond with a correct letter upon seeing each of four geometrical designs and then measured transfer of the same responses to alterations of these designs; when Yum (25) varied the similarity of visually presented nonsense-syllable stimuli, positive transfer was the result, the magnitude increasing with stimulus similarity.

While retroaction data derived from this paradigm are not so extensive, the available evidence is consistent in revealing *facilitation*. Hamilton's (7) subjects learned lists of paired-associates in which the stimuli were geometrical forms and the responses were nonsense syllables. Although responses were 'identical' on original and interpolated lists, the stimulus forms varied from 'identity' through two degrees of similarity, as independently indexed in terms of generalization, to complete neutrality. The magnitude of retroactive facilitation decreased regularly as similarity among the stimulus members decreased, effects of approximately zero magnitude being obtained with neutral stimuli. The empirical law for this paradigm is: *where stimuli are varied and responses are functionally identical, positive transfer and retroactive facilitation are obtained, the magnitude of both increasing as the similarity among the stimulus members increases.*

2. The situation in which stimuli are constant and responses are varied, *paradigm B*, is the standard associative and reproductive inhibition paradigm and, as might be expected, a large number of experiments (*cf.* 1, 6, 21) testify to the fact that *interference* is produced under these conditions. However, there is also a large body of evidence showing positive transfer under the same conditions. The latter evidence may be discounted on two grounds: (a) In many cases the so-called transfer response has been *learned previous* to the experimental situation. In many of Tolman's sign-learning studies, for example, animals trained to traverse the route to a goal by one path or means, such as running, will shift readily to another means, such as swimming, if the original behavior is blocked. Similarly, Wickens (23) has shown that a human subject who has learned to avoid the shock which follows a tone by an extensor movement of his finger, when his palm is down, 'transfers' immediately to a flexion movement when his hand is then placed palm up. In such cases, the new learning in the experimental situation is the sign-value or meaning of the distinctive cue. A variety of overt behaviors has previously been associated with this mediation process—the human subject brings to the experiment a rich repertoire of pain-avoiding movements, and he would lift his head without new training if his nose were inserted between the electrodes! (b) In other cases what is measured as positive transfer under conditions fitting this paradigm can be shown to be attributable to '*practice effects*,' i.e., the subject is learning how to learn nonsense syllables or learning how to learn mazes, and these general skills or habits counteract the interference inherent in the design. Siipola (20), for example, obtained small amounts of positive transfer for a code-substitution task, yet concluded from the large numbers of intrusions that actual negative transfer was being masked by a general 'practice effect.'

Bugelski (2) required his subjects to learn an original list of 10 paired nonsense syllables (such as *toc-nem*) and then interpolated three additional lists, the experimental subjects having identical stimuli and varied responses (such as *toc-rul*) and the control subjects having both members varied (such as *cos-rul*). Although insignificant amounts of positive transfer to successive lists were obtained in both conditions, the inherent interfering character of the stimuli-identical paradigm was revealed in the fact that the experimental subjects showed a marked decrement upon relearning the first list while the controls showed continued facilitation. Clearest evidence for negative transfer and retroactive intereference under the conditions of this paradigm is offered in a recent monograph by Underwood (21). In measuring transfer, subjects learned 0, 2, 4, or 6 lists of meaningful paired-associates *prior* to learning a test list; in measuring retroaction, 0, 2, 4 or 6 interpolated lists were learned *after* the original learning of the same test list; in both cases, recall of the test list was measured after a delay of 25 minutes. Both negative transfer and retroactive interference were found, increasing in magnitude with the number of prior or interpolated lists having the same stimulus members but different responses.

But what about the *degree* of similarity among the varied responses in this paradigm? Perhaps because of the difficulty in defining response similarity, there are relatively few data here. In a recent experiment by Osgood (17), original learning of a set of paired letter-pairs and meaningful adjectives (such as *c.m.–elated*) was followed by three types of interpolated items, each subject serving as his own control by learning an equal number of items in each similarity relation (such as *c.m.–high, c.m.–left,* or *c.m.–low*); all subjects finally relearned the original list. Although interference was obtained under all conditions, it was significantly *less* for similar meaningful relations. One of the conditions of Bruce's (1) extensive investigation with nonsense-syllable paired-associates substantiates this finding. We may now state the empirical law for this paradigm: *where stimuli are functionally identical and responses are varied, negative transfer and retroactive interference are obtained, the magnitude of both decreasing as similarity between the responses increases.*

3. *Paradigm C,* where both stimuli and responses are simultaneously varied, is directly generated when the standard memory drum is used and lists of material are learned in constant serial order. Similarities are between items having the same serial position on successive lists, and each item serves simultaneously as a response to the preceding item and a stimulus for the succeeding item. Whatever interpolated lists are given, stimulus and response similarities must be simultaneously varied through the same degrees. McGeoch and McDonald (13) and Johnson (10) have employed this procedure with meaningful materials, finding retroactive interference to increase with the degree of similarity. Melton and Von Lackum (16) report the same result for nonsense syllables. McGeoch and McGeoch (14) and Johnson (10) find the same result to hold for transfer when this paradigm is used.

An important experiment by Gibson (6) also fits this paradigm. Her materials and procedures were identical with those reported above for Hamilton (7). The Gibson experiment was actually the first of the series. Visual stimulus forms were varied through independently measured degrees of generalization, as was the case in Hamilton's study, but here responses were different and neutral. Negative transfer and retroactive interference were obtained, their magnitudes decreasing as stimulus similarity decreased and approximating zero with neutral stimuli. It should be noted that in both studies approximately zero transfer or retroaction was found when stimuli were neutral, regardless of response identity or difference.

The empirical law for this paradigm: *when both stimulus and response members are simultaneously varied, negative transfer and retroactive interference are obtained, the magnitude of both increasing as the stimulus similarity increases.*

There are a considerable number of substantiating studies which have not been cited here, but if this writer's survey of the literature has been adequate, *there are no exceptions to the above empirical laws.* There are few studies where more than one relation is systematically explored, with the same materials, procedures and subjects, and for this reason it is difficult to quantify these relations. An exception is a study by Bruce (1). One set of nonsense pairs (such as *req-kiv*) was learned by all subjects and transfer to several variations was measured: where stimuli were varied and responses were constant (*zaf-kiv* or *reb-kiv*) positive transfer was found as compared with a control condition, the amount being greater when stimuli were more similar: where responses were varied and stimuli were constant (*req-vor*), negative transfer was found. The condition in which stimuli were constant and responses were highly similar (*req-kib*) was slightly superior to the control condition (both members neutral). Although this result appears to contradict the empirical law for this paradigm, it will be found to fit the hypothesis presented in the latter part of this paper: if ordinary learning is to be theoretically feasible, high degrees of response similarity must yield facilitation.

## ATTEMPTED INTEGRATIONS OF THE DATA

A series of attempts to integrate the facts of transfer and retroaction can be traced in the history of this problem. As early as 1919 Wylie (24) had made a distinction between stimulus and response activities, stating that the transfer effect is positive when an 'old' response is associated with a new stimulus but negative when an 'old' stimulus must be associated with a new response. "Old" in this context merely means that the member in question has previously been associated with another stimulus or response. This principle is valid, of course, within the limits of its gross differentiation. But (a) it takes account of neither stimulus nor response similarities and (b) it leaves the fundamental paradox untouched. Since successive responses are never precisely identical, even in ordinary learning, we are always associating stimuli with 'new' responses and hence should inevitably get negative transfer.

Robinson was one of the first to perceive clearly this paradox and in 1927 he offered what is now known as the Skaggs-Robinson Hypothesis as a resolution. As shown in Fig. 2, this hypothesis states that facilitation is greatest when successively practiced materials are identical (point A); facilitation is least, and hence interference maximal, with some moderate

## THE SKAGGS-ROBINSON HYPOTHESIS

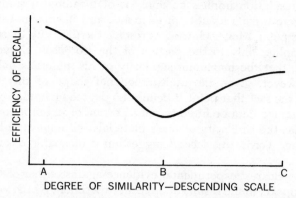

FIG. 2. The Skaggs-Robinson Hypothesis: point A specifies maximum similarity (identity) and point C minimum similarity (neutrality) among the successively practiced materials; point B merely indicates the low point in the curve for efficiency of recall.

degree of similarity (point B); and facilitation increases again as we move toward neutrality (point C) but never attains the original level. Note that while point A defines maximum similarity (identity) and point C defines minimum similarity (neutrality), point B actually specifies no degree of similarity at all, but merely says that somewhere there is a low point in the facilitation curve. Several experiments (3, 4, 8, 11, 19) combine to give rough validation to this poorly defined hypothesis, especially the A-B sector of it.

The series of studies by McGeoch and his associates (10, 13, 14) ran into direct conflict with this hypothesis and the experimental evidence supporting it. Using meaningful words, they consistently found that as the judged similarity of the original and interpolated materials increased, interference also increased. The highest degree of similarity they could obtain, where close synonyms appeared on the two serial lists, yielded the most interference. There was no evidence here of facilitation as one approached identity. In *The Psychology of Human Learning* (12) McGeoch offered two alternative rapprochements between his data and the Skaggs-Robinson Hypothesis: (1) He distinguished 'similarity of meaning' and 'degrees of identity' as two different dimensions of similarity, each having a different interference function. This distinction was suggested by the fact that some of the experiments supporting the hypothesis (8, 11, 19) had employed numeral and letter combinations with similarity indexed by the number of identical elements. Unfortunately, in other substantiating studies, materials were used in which identical elements were no more readily specifiable than with meaningful words. Dreis (4), for example, used code-substitution, and Watson (22) used card-sorting. Furthermore, this type of resolution implies an analysis of meaningful similarity that would segregate it from identity of elements, and this has not been done. (2) At a later point, McGeoch tried to resolve the difficulty by stating that his results applied only to the portion of the Robinson Curve between *B* and *C*, *i.e.*, that the maximum similarity of his materials only reached point *B*. However, given the multidirectional shape of this theoretical function and the fact that point *B* defines no degree of similarity, not only could any obtained data be fitted to some portion of it, but it could always be argued that the similarity of one's materials fell *anywhere* between *A* and *C*. In other words, this second suggestion is incapable of either proof or disproof.

Perhaps the clearest experimental evidence against either of McGeoch's resolutions appears in the results of a recent experiment by the writer (17). *Also* using meaningful materials in the traditional retroaction paradigm, interference was found to *decrease* as the meaningful similarity among the response members increased. Not only would these results seem to fit 'degrees of identity' rather than 'similarity of meaning' as the functioning dimension, despite the nature of the materials used, but they fall within the *A* to *B* sector of the theoretical curve.

Quite apart from the apparent negative evidence in the McGeoch studies, the Skaggs-Robinson Hypothesis is inadequate on several grounds. It does, to be sure, allow ordinary learning to occur. But (a) it contains a dual function of facilitation in relation to similarity without specifying at what degree of similarity the shift occurs; (b) no specification is made of the locus of similarities within the materials practiced (whether among stimulus members, response members or both), and we have seen that both the direction and the degree of either transfer or retroaction are empirically predictable from such specification. One of the most recent attempts to integrate these data has been made by Gibson (5). She followed Wylie's lead in differentiating between stimulus variation and response variation, and she added to this picture the refinement of stimulus generalization, derived from Pavlovian conditioning principles. Gibson's two theoretical laws were: (1) if responses are *identical* facilitation is obtained, its amount increasing with the degree of stimulus generalization (similarity); (2) if responses are *different* interference is obtained, its amount increasing with the degree of stimulus generalization (similarity). These hypotheses fit much of the data in the field and further serve to integrate the phenomena of human learning with those of the animal laboratory. But they are insufficient. (a) No account is given of the *degree* of response similarity, and this appears as one of the relevant variables. (b) We have one function (increasing interference) when responses are different and another (decreasing interference) when responses are 'identical'; and one would anticipate, therefore, a strange, abrupt shift in function somewhere along the line as the degree of response difference is reduced. (c) The fundamental paradox remains: responses can never be truly identical but must always be different to some degree, yet ordinary learning can occur.

## The Transfer and Retroaction Surface

The formulation proposed here makes full use of Gibson's analysis, but, utilizing data which have recently become available, goes beyond it. It is quite literally constructed from the empirical laws presented above, and this can be demonstrated by use of Fig. 3, which provides a rational framework within which the data can be integrated. The vertical dimension represents the direction and degree of *either* transfer or retroaction; degrees of response similarity are distributed along the horizontal dimension. The parenthetical numbers refer to the sequence of steps to be followed in allocating the data.

Let us first consider the ordinary learning of an association, the case in which the same materials are used for original and interpolated activities. Here functionally identical stimuli and responses are successively repeated and maximal facilitation is obtained, allowing us to locate the first point as shown (number 1). The phenomena of positive transfer (stimulus generalization) and retroactive facilitation when responses are identical and stimuli varied are represented by the series of open circles (number 2): as the degree of stimulus similarity decreases from 'identity' less and less facilitation is obtained, effects of zero magnitude being found when stimuli are neutral. Data reported by Hovland (9) and Hamilton (7) are typical. As pointed out earlier, the fact that Hamilton and Gibson (6) used the same materials and procedures, with the single exception that responses were the same in the former case and different in the latter, provides an extremely useful comparison (see number 3); where stimulus members are neutral, effects of approximately zero magnitude are obtained in both experiments, allowing us to link the Gibson and Hamilton data together on the zero-effect base line. In other words, variations in the relation between response members are of no consequence when stimulus members are completely unrelated. The Gibson experiment itself, along with other substantiating studies, provides data for the condition in which responses are different and neutral while stimulus similarity is varied. Here negative transfer and retroactive interference are regularly obtained, increasing in magnitude as the similarity of the stimulus members increases, and these data are represented by the series of solid circles (see number 4). There remains to be included the condition in which stimuli are constant and response similarity is varied. The fact that 'identity' of stimulus and variation of response yields negative transfer and retroactive inter-

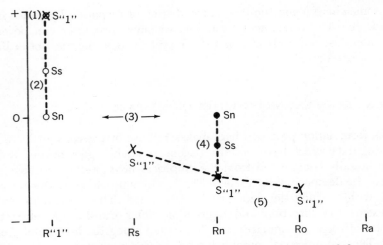

FIG. 3. Allocation of experimental data: vertical, direction and degree of either transfer or retroaction; horizontal degrees of response similarity. Numbers in parentheses refer to step in analysis followed in text.

ference is amply testified to by a number of studies (1, 6, 21). Experiments in which the *degree* of response similarity is systematically varied, as those by Bruce (1) and Osgood (17), show that interference is *less* for similar responses than for neutral ones. Since the latter study included a condition in which responses were neutral and stimuli functionally identical, thus matching the final point of the Gibson data, it is possible to link the two sets of facts together. These data are represented by the connected series of X's (number 5).

The pattern of empirical points established here sharply limits the possible theoretical functions that can be generated. By visually tracing the series of X's, for example, including the point for ordinary learning, a fairly well-defined curve becomes apparent, this curve representing the function for stimulus 'identity.' A family of such stimulus-relation curves has been constructed to fit both these empirical points and the requirements of common sense, and they appear in Fig. 4. The function for *stimulus neutrality* is a straight line of zero effect, reflecting the reasonable fact that response variations are of no consequence when successive stimulus situations are completely unrelated. Given this as a zero-effect base line, increasing the similarity among stimuli yields a progressive maximization of *both* facilitation and interference, the actual direction of the effect being dependent upon response relations. The greatest facilitation and the greatest interference are possible only with functional *stimulus identity*. Intermediate transfer and retroaction effects fall between these limits depending upon degrees of stimulus similarity. The points for antagonistic responses, showing a final, sharp increase in interference, are admittedly

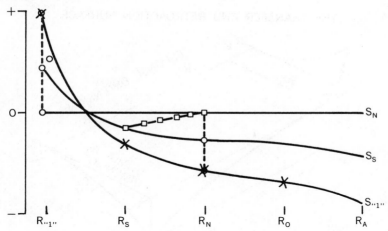

FIG. 4. Family of stimulus-relation curves constructed from data in Fig. 3; series of open squares represents data obtained by McGeoch and his associates (see text).

hypothetical. However, the writer has recently reported (18) evidence for a special form of *reciprocal inhibition* associated with the successive learning of meaningfully opposed responses. The assumption is made here that this inhibitory effect is maximal when responses are directly antagonistic.

But how do the classic findings of McGeoch and his associates fit this hypothesis? In a real sense, they serve as a crucial test of it, being both well substantiated and in apparent conflict with other results. It will be remembered that these investigators employed a method wherein the similarity of *both* stimuli and responses varied simultaneously and through the same degrees, actually from neutrality of both to high similarity (but not identity) of both. As may be seen from the row of open squares in Fig. 4, the present hypothesis *must* predict gradually increasing amounts of interference under these conditions, and this is precisely the result obtained in these studies.

Although Fig. 4 provides a useful method of demonstrating the congruence of empirical data and theoretical functions, it does not offer a clear picture of the hypothesis as a whole. To do so requires a three dimensional form, representing stimulus similarity, response similarity and degree of effect as simultaneously interrelated variables. Figure 5 presents what may be termed *the transfer and retroaction surface*. The vertical dimension represents the direction and degree of either transfer or retroaction, both having been shown to have identical functions of similarity; the width of the form represents stimulus similarity, from functional identity to neutrality; its length represents response similarity, varying from functional identity, through neutrality, to direct antagonism. The median

THE TRANSFER AND RETROACTION SURFACE

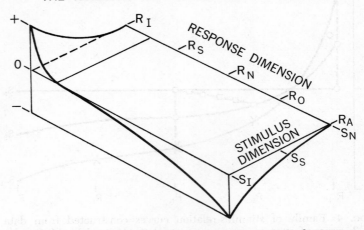

FIG. 5. The transfer and retroaction surface: medial plane represents effects of zero magnitude; response relations distributed along length of solid and stimulus relations along its width.

horizontal plane indicates effects of zero magnitude, and it may be seen that the condition of stimulus neutrality is co-extensive with this plane regardless of response variations while the remainder of the surface intersects this plane at a point between response 'identity' and response similarity. Finally, it is apparent that we have here a smooth, unbroken sequence of transfer and retroaction functions, facilitative relations rising above the median plane and interfering relations falling below it. There are no reversals in these functions nor any abrupt shifts between identity and similarity. Identity becomes merely the limiting case of maximal similarity.

## CERTAIN ADVANTAGES OF THIS HYPOTHESIS

By way of summary, certain advantages which this hypothesis offers in comparison with those which have preceded it may be indicated. (1) *All existing empirical data in the field are consistent with it and find representation upon the transfer and retroaction surface.* This statement is by necessity limited to those data wherein the locus of the similarities is specifiable and also by the adequacy of the writer's survey of the literature. The first limitation is not a serious one. If results can be shown to be lawful, and hence predictable, when such specification of the similarity relations is possible, the conflicting and confused results obtained under unspecifiable conditions are presumably attributable to unanalyzable variations in the paradigms employed. Witness the conclusive inconclusiveness on the question of formal discipline! This state of affairs illustrates why it is so difficult to make recommendations for efficient human learning in practical situations. What, for example, are the loci of similarities when the student simultaneously studies French and Spanish?

(2) *The phenomena of both transfer and retroaction are integrated within a single framework, in so far as the similarity variable is concerned.* It is common textbook procedure to study transfer under learning and retroaction under forgetting, as if these processes were somehow different in kind. The present analysis, it is felt, is a step in the direction of integrating the problems of human learning. Another step in the same direction is also suggested here: distinctions are often made in terms of meaningful vs. nonsense materials, meaningful similarity vs. degrees of identity, and so on. It should be pointed out that data substantiating each of the three empirical laws derived above have been obtained with meaningful and nonsense materials, with materials varying in terms of meaningful similarity as well as degrees of identity. There is here, of course, the underlying problem of defining similarity. It may be defined operationally in terms of generalization (*cf.* Gibson, 5) although this definition is inherently circular since the phenomenon of generalization is nothing other than a case of positive transfer with functionally identical responses. Any precise behavioral definition of similarity will require much more knowledge of the nervous system than we have at present. In practice, degrees of similarity have been specified informally by experimenters or formally by a sample of judges, which probably suffices for our present rather gross purposes.

(3) *Although constructed directly from existing empirical evidence, this hypothesis does go considerably beyond it, predicting phenomena that have not as yet been observed.* For one thing that portion of the transfer and retroaction surface where increasing similarity of response (high degrees) is accompanied by increasing facilitation remains to be explored by standard procedures, the Robinson group of studies having used a memory span technique.* It will also be noticed that the theoretical surface requires that, regardless of the degree of stimulus similarity, all functions must become facilitative at precisely the same degree of response similarity, somewhere between identity and high similarity. In other words, just as the degree of response variation is inconsequential when stimulus members are neutral, so there must exist (according to this hypothesis) some definite degree of response similarity for which all variations among stimuli will yield zero effect. This is a novel but necessary prediction from theory that sets an intriguing experimental problem. It

---

* An as yet uncompleted investigation by Mark W. Harriman at Johns Hopkins University appears to be filling in this gap in our empirical knowledge. With functionally identical stimulus members, responses on original and interpolated lists are varied by extremely small degrees, such as having the singular and plural of the same word on two lists, and the predicted results seem to be forthcoming.

is not inconceivable that this common shiftover from facilitation to interference at a certain degree of variation among responses may reflect a
basic characteristic of the nervous system,—but this is all assuming that
the present hypothesis will be found valid in terms of constantly accruing
facts.

(4) Finally, *this hypothesis resolves the fundamental paradox with
which this paper began—the fact of ordinary learning becomes theoretically feasible.* The transfer and retroaction surface describes a system of
curves within which the condition of ordinary learning, with functionally
identical stimuli and responses in the materials successively practiced, is
continuous with other relations. Identity is here merely the limiting case
of maximal similarity, and no abrupt shifts of function are required to
account for the fact that learning occurs.

## REFERENCES

1. BRUCE, R. W. (1933) Conditions of transfer of training. *J. exp. Psychol.*,
   *16*, 343-361.
2. BUGELSKI, B. R. (1942) Interferences with recall of original responses
   after learning new responses to old stimuli. *J. exp. Psychol.*, *30*, 368-379.
3. CHENG, N. Y. (1929) Retroactive effect and degree of similarity. *J. exp.
   Psychol.*, *12*, 444-449.
4. DREIS, T. A. (1933) Two studies in retroaction: I. Influence of partial
   identity. II. Susceptibility to retroaction at various grade levels. *J. gen.
   Psychol.*, *8*, 157-171.
5. GIBSON, E. J. (1940) A systematic application of the concepts of generalization and differentiation to verbal learning. *Psychol. Rev.*, *47*, 196-
   229.
6. ———. (1941) Retroactive inhibition as a function of degree of generalization between tasks. *J. exp. Psychol.*, *82*, 93-115.
7. HAMILTON, R. J. (1943) Retroactive facilitation as a function of degree
   of generalization between tasks. *J. exp. Psychol.*, *32*, 363-376.
8. HARDEN, L. M. (1929) A quantitative study of the similarity factor in
   retroactive inhibition. *J. gen. Psychol.*, *2*, 421-430.
9. HOVLAND, C. I. (1937) The generalization of conditioned responses: I.
   The sensory generalization of conditioned responses with varying frequencies of tone. *J. gen. Psychol.*, *17*, 125-148.
10. JOHNSON, L. M. (1933) Similarity of meaning as a factor in retroactive
    inhibition. *J. gen. Psychol.*, *9*, 377-388.
11. KENNELLY, T. W. (1941) The role of similarity in retroactive inhibition.
    *Arch. Psychol.*, N. Y., *37*, No. 260.
12. McGEOCH, J. A. (1942) *The psychology of human learning.* New York:
    Longmans, Green and Co.
13. ———, and McDONALD, W. T. (1931) Meaningful relation and retroactive
    inhibition. *Amer. J. Psychol.*, *43*, 579-588.
14. ———, and McGEOCH, G. O. (1937) Studies in retroactive inhibition: X.
    The influence of similarity of meaning between lists of paired associates.
    *J. exp. Psychol.*, *21*, 320-329.

15. McKinney, F. (1933) Quantitative and qualitative essential elements of transfer. *J. exp. Psychol., 16,* 854-864.
16. Melton, A. W. and von Lackum, W. J. (1941) Retroactive and proactive inhibition in retention: evidence for a two-factor theory of retroactive inhibition. *Amer. J. Psychol., 45,* 157-173.
17. Osgood, C. E. (1946) Meaningful similarity and interference in learning. *J. exp. Psychol., 36,* 277-301.
18. ———. (1948) An investigation into the causes of retroactive interference. *J. exp. Psychol., 38,* 132-154.
19. Robinson, E. S. (1927) The 'similarity' factor in retroaction. *Amer. J. Psychol., 39,* 297-312.
20. Siipola, E. M. (1941) The relation of transfer to similarity in habit-structure. *J. exp. Psychol., 28,* 233-261.
21. Underwood, B. J. (1945) The effect of successive interpolations on retroactive and proactive inhibition. *Psychol. Monogr., 59,* No. 273.
22. Watson, B. (1938) The similarity factor in transfer and inhibition. *J. educ. Psychol., 29,* 145-157.
23. Wickens, D. D. (1938) The transference of conditioned excitation and conditioned inhibition from one muscle group to the antagonistic muscle group. *J. exp. Psychol., 22,* 101-123.
24. Wylie, H. H. (1919) An experimental study of transfer of response in the white rat. *Behav. Monogr., 3,* No. 16.
25. Yum, K. S. (1931) An experimental test of the law of assimilation. *J. exp. Psychol., 14,* 68-82.

## 32.   The Formation of Learning Sets

## H. F. Harlow

*As we indicated in our introduction, transfer of training can be divided into specific as well as general factors which influence the learning of the transfer task. One such general factor is the learning set, or the learning how to learn. Harlow's paper describes the formation of learning sets in the rhesus monkey learning a series of discrimination problems.*

In most psychological ivory towers there will be found an animal laboratory. The scientists who live there think of themselves as theoretical psychologists, since they obviously have no other rationalization to explain

*Psychol. Rev.,* 1949, 56, 51-65. Reprinted with permission of the author and The American Psychological Association. This paper was presented as the presidential address of the Midwestern Psychological Association meetings in St. Paul, May 7, 1948. The researches described in this paper were supported in part by grants from the Special Research Fund of the University of Wisconsin for 1944-48.

their extravagantly paid and idyllic sinecures. These theoretical psychologists have one great advantage over those psychological citizens who study men and women. The theoreticians can subject their subhuman animals, be they rats, dogs, or monkeys, to more rigorous controls than can ordinarily be exerted over human beings. The obligation of the theoretical psychologist is to discover general laws of behavior applicable to mice, monkeys, and men. In this obligation the theoretical psychologist has often failed. His deductions frequently have had no generality beyond the species which he has studied, and his laws have been so limited that attempts to apply them to man have resulted in confusion rather than clarification.

One limitation of many experiments on subhuman animals is the brief period of time the subjects have been studied. In the typical problem, 48 rats are arranged in groups to test the effect of three different intensities of stimulation operating in conjunction with two different motivational conditions upon the formation of *an isolated* conditioned response. A brilliant Blitzkrieg research is effected—the controls are perfect, the results are important, and the rats are dead.

If this *do and die* technique were applied widely in investigations with human subjects, the results would be appalling. But of equal concern to the psychologist should be the fact that the derived general laws would be extremely limited in their application. There are experiments in which the use of naive subjects is justified, but the psychological compulsion to follow this design indicates that frequently the naive animals are to be found on both sides of the one-way vision screen.

The variety of learning situations that play an important rôle in determining our basic personality characteristics and in changing some of us into thinking animals are repeated many times in similar form. The behavior of the human being is not to be understood in terms of the results of single learning situations but rather in terms of the changes which are affected through multiple, though comparable, learning problems. Our emotional, personal, and intellectual characteristics are not the mere algebra summation of a near infinity of stimulus-response bonds. The learning of primary importance to the primates, at least, is the formation of learning sets; it is the *learning how to learn efficiently* in the situations the animal frequently encounters. This learning to learn transforms the organism from a creature that adapts to a changing environment by trial and error to one that adapts by seeming hypothesis and insight.

The rat psychologists have largely ignored this fundamental aspect of learning and, as a result, this theoretical domain remains a *terra incognita.* If learning sets are the mechanisms which, in part, transform the organism from a conditioned response robot to a reasonably rational creature, it may be thought that the mechanisms are too intangible for proper qualification. Any such presupposition is false. It is the purpose of this paper

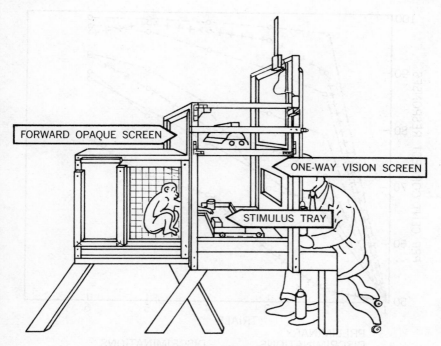

Fig. 1. Wisconsin general test apparatus.

to demonstrate the extremely orderly and quantifiable nature of the development of certain learning sets and, more broadly, to indicate the importance of learning sets to the development of intellectual organization and personality structure.

The apparatus used throughout the studies subsequently referred to is illustrated in Fig. 1. The monkey responds by displacing one of two stimulus-objects covering the food-wells in the tray before him. An opaque screen is interposed between the monkey and the stimulus situation between trials and a one-way vision screen separates monkey and man during trials.

The first problem chosen for the investigation of learning sets was the object-quality discrimination learning problem. The monkey was required to choose the rewarded one of two objects differing in multiple characteristics and shifting in the left-right positions in a predetermined balanced order. A series of 344 such problems using 344 different pairs of stimuli was run on a group of eight monkeys. Each of the first 32 problems was run for 50 trials; the next 200 problems for six trials; and the last 112 problems for an average of nine trials.

In Fig. 2 are presented learning curves which show the per cent of correct responses on the first six trials of these discriminations. The data for

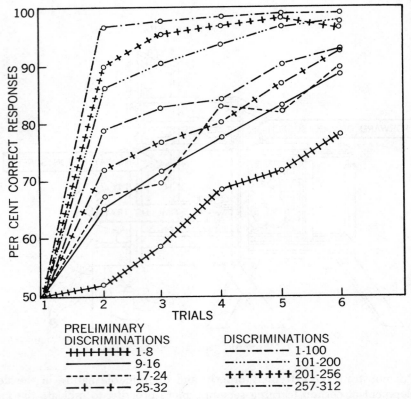

PRELIMINARY
DISCRIMINATIONS                    DISCRIMINATIONS
+++++++++ 1-8                      —⸳—⸳—⸳— 1-100
——————— 9-16                      —⸳⸳⸳—⸳⸳⸳— 101-200
------------- 17-24                +++++++ 201-256
—+—+— 25-32                       —⸳—⸳—⸳⸳— 257-312

Fig. 2. Discrimination learning curves on successive blocks of problems.

the first 32 discriminations are grouped for blocks of eight problems, and the remaining discriminations are arranged in blocks of 100, 100, 56, and 56 problems. The data indicate that the subjects progressively improve in their ability to learn object-quality discrimination problems. The monkeys *learn how to learn* individual problems with a minimum of errors. It is this *learning how to learn a kind of problem* that we designate by the term *learning set*.

The very form of the learning curve changes as learning sets become more efficient. The form of the learning curve for the first eight discrimination problems appears S-shaped: it could be described as a curve of 'trial-and-error' learning. The curve for the last 56 problems approaches linearity after Trial 2. Curves of similar form have been described as indicators of 'insightful' learning.

We wish to emphasize that this *learning to learn,* this *transfer from problem to problem* which we call the formation of a learning set, is a highly *predictable, orderly* process which can be demonstrated as long as

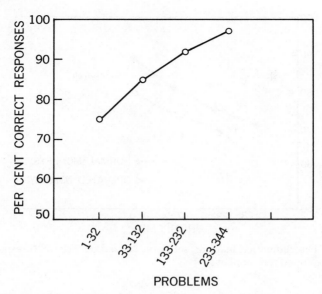

FIG. 3. Discrimination learning set curve based on Trial 2–6 responses.

controls are maintained over the subjects' experience and the difficulty of the problems. Our subjects, when they started these researches, had no previous laboratory learning experience. Their entire discrimination learning set history was obtained in this study. The stimulus pairs employed had been arranged and their serial order determined from tables of random numbers. Like nonsense syllables, the stimulus pairs were equated for difficulty. It is unlikely that any group of problems differed significantly in intrinsic difficulty from any other group.

In a conventional learning curve we plot change of performance over a series of *trials*; in a learning set curve we plot change in performance over a series of *problems*. It is important to remember that *we measure learning set in terms of problems* just as *we measure habit in terms of trials*.

Figure 3 presents a discrimination learning set curve showing progressive increase in the per cent of correct responses on Trials 2–6 on successive blocks of problems. This curve appears to be negatively accelerated or possibly linear.

Discrimination learning set curves obtained on four additional naive normal monkeys and eight naive monkeys with extensive unilateral cortical lesions, are shown in Fig. 4. Brain-injured as well as normal monkeys are seen to form effective discrimination learning sets, although the partial hemidecorticate monkeys are less efficient than the normal subjects. Improvement for both groups is progressive and the fluctuations that occur

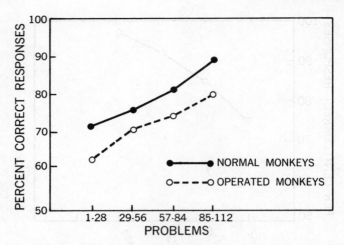

Fig. 4. Discrimination learning set curves based on Trial 2–6 responses: normal and operated monkeys.

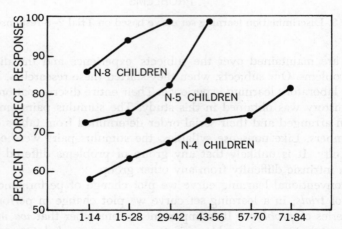

Fig. 5. Discrimination learning set curves based on Trial 2–6 responses: children.

may be attributed to the small number of subjects and the relatively small number of problems, 14, included in each of the problem blocks presented on the abscissa.

Through the courtesy of Dr. Margaret Kuenne we have discrimination learning set data on another primate species. These animals were also run on a series of six-trial discrimination problems but under slightly different conditions. Macaroni beads and toys were substituted for food rewards, and the subjects were tested sans iron-barred cages. The data for these 17 children, whose ages range from two to five years and whose intelligence quotients range from 109 to 151, are presented in Fig. 5.

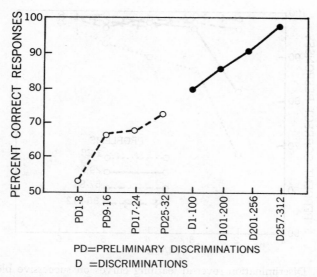

PD=PRELIMINARY DISCRIMINATIONS
D =DISCRIMINATIONS

Fɪɢ. 6. Discrimination learning set curve based on Trial 2 responses.

Learning set curves are plotted for groups of children attaining a pre-determined learning criterion within differing numbers of problem blocks. In spite of the small number of cases and the behavioral vagaries that are known to characterize this primate species, the learning set curves are orderly and lawful and show progressive increase in per cent of correct responses.

Learning set curves, like learning curves, can be plotted in terms of correct responses or errors, in terms of responses on any trial or total trials. A measure which we have frequently used is per cent of correct Trial 2 responses—the behavioral measure of the amount learned on Trial 1.

Figure 6 shows learning set curves measured in terms of the per cent correct Trial 2 responses for the 344-problem series. The data from the first 32 preliminary discriminations and the 312 subsequent discriminations have been plotted separately. As one might expect, these learning set curves are similar to those that have been previously presented. What the curves show with especial clarity is the almost unbelievable change which has taken place in the *effectiveness of the first training trial*. In the initial eight discriminations, this single paired stimulus presentation brings the Trial 2 performance of the monkeys to a level less than three per cent above chance; in the last 56 discriminations, this first training trial brings the performance of the monkeys to a level *less than three per cent* short of perfection. Before the formation of a discrimination learning set, a single training trial produces negligible gain; after the formation of a discrimination learning set, *a single trial constitutes problem solution*. These data clearly show that *animals can gradually learn insight*.

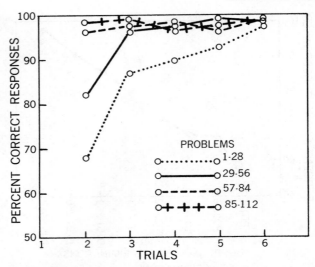

F<small>IG</small>. 7. Discrimination reversal learning curves on successive blocks of problems.

In the final phase of our discrimination series with monkeys there were subjects that solved from 20 to 30 consecutive problems with no errors whatsoever following the first blind trial,—and many of the children, after the first day or two of training, did as well or better.

These data indicate the function of learning set in converting a problem which is initially difficult for a subject into a problem which is so simple as to be immediately solvable. The learning set is the mechanism that changes the problem from an intellectual tribulation into an intellectual triviality and leaves the organism free to attack problems of another hierarchy of difficulty.

For the analysis of learning sets in monkeys on a problem that is ostensibly at a more complex level than the discrimination problem, we chose the discrimination reversal problem. The procedure was to run the monkeys on a discrimination problem for 7, 9, or 11 trials and then to reverse the reward value of the stimuli for eight trials; that is to say, the stimulus previously correct was made incorrect and the stimulus previously incorrect became correct.

The eight monkeys previously trained on discrimination learning were tested on a series of 112 discrimination reversal problems. Discrimination reversal learning curves for successive blocks of 28 problems are shown in Fig. 7. The measure used is per cent of correct responses on Reversal Trials 2 to 6. Figure 8 presents data on the formation of the discrimination reversal learning set in terms of the per cent of correct responses on Reversal Trial 2 for successive blocks of 14 problems. Reversal Trial 2 is the first trial following the 'informing' trial, i.e., the initial trial reversing the

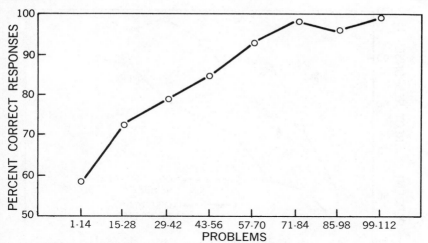

Fig. 8. Discrimination reversal learning set curve based on Trial 2 responses.

reward value of the stimuli. Reversal Trial 2 is the measure of the effectiveness with which the single informing trial leads the subject to abandon a reaction pattern which has proved correct for 7 to 11 trials, and to initiate a new reaction pattern to the stimulus pair. On the last 42 discrimination reversal problems the monkeys were responding as efficiently on Reversal Trial 2 as they were on complementary Discrimination Trial 2, *i.e.*, they were making over 97 per cent correct responses on both aspects of the problems. The eight monkeys made from 12 to 57 successive correct second trial reversal responses. Thus it becomes perfectly obvious that at the end of this problem the monkeys possessed sets both to learn and to reverse a reaction tendency, and that this behavior could be consistently and immediately elicited with hypothesis-like efficiency.

This terminal performance level is likely to focus undue attention on the one-trial learning at the expense of the earlier, less efficient performance levels. It should be kept in mind that this one-trial learning appeared only as the end result of an orderly and progressive learning process; insofar as these subjects are concerned, the insights are only to be understood in an historical perspective.

Although the discrimination reversal problems might be expected to be more difficult for the monkeys than discrimination problems, the data of Fig. 9 indicate that the discrimination reversal learning set was formed more rapidly than the previously acquired discrimination learning set. The explanation probably lies in the nature of the transfer of training from the discrimination learning to the discrimination reversal problems. A detailed analysis of the discrimination learning data indicates the operation throughout the learning series of certain error-producing factors, but with

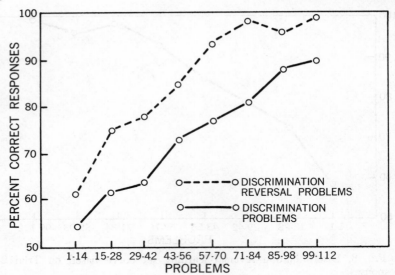

FIG. 9. Discrimination reversal and discrimination learning set curves based on Trial 2 responses.

each successive block of problems the frequencies of errors attributable to these factors are progressively decreased, although at different rates and to different degrees. The process might be conceived of as a learning of response tendencies that counteract the error-producing factors. A description of the reduction of the error-producing factors is beyond the scope of this paper, even though we are of the opinion that this type of analysis is basic to an adequate theory of discrimination learning.

Suffice it to say that there is reason to believe that there is a large degree of transfer from the discrimination series to the reversal series, of the learned response tendencies counteracting the operation of two of the three primary error-producing factors thus far identified.

The combined discrimination and discrimination reversal data show clearly how the learning set delivers the animal from Thorndikian bondage. By the time the monkey has run 232 discriminations and followed these by 112 discriminations and reversal, he does not possess 344 or 456 specific habits, bonds, connections or associations. We doubt if our monkeys at this time could respond with much more than chance efficiency on the first trial of any series of the previously learned problems. But the monkey does have a generalized ability to learn *any* discrimination problem or *any* discrimination reversal problem with the greatest of ease. Training on several hundred specific problems has not turned the monkey into an automaton exhibiting forced, sterotyped, reflex responses to specific stimuli. These several hundred habits have, instead, made the monkey

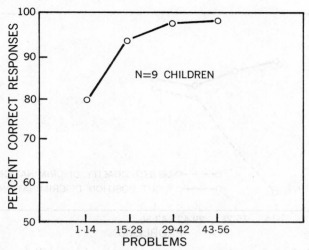

FIG. 10. Discrimination reversal learning set curve based on Trial 2 responses: children.

an adjustable creature with an *increased capacity* to adapt to the ever-changing demands of a psychology laboratory environment.

We believe that other learning sets acquired in and appropriate to the monkey's natural environment would enable him to adapt better to the changing conditions there. We are certain, moreover, that learning sets acquired by man in and appropriate to his environment have accounted for his ability to adapt and survive.

Before leaving the problem of discrimination reversal learning we submit one additional set of data that we feel merits attention. Nine of the children previously referred to were also subjected to a series of discrimination reversal problems. The outcome is partially indicated in Fig. 10 which shows the per cent of correct Reversal Trial 2 responses made on successive blocks of 14 problems. It can be seen that these three to five-year-old children clearly bested the monkeys in performance on this series of problems. Trial 2 responses approach perfection in the second block of 14 discrimination reversal problems. Actually, over half of the total Trial 2 errors were made by one child.

These discrimination reversal data on the children are the perfect illustration of set formation and transfer producing adaptable abilities rather than specific bonds. Without benefit of the monkey's discrimination reversal set learning curves we might be tempted to assume that the children's data indicate a gulf between human and subhuman learning. But the *extremely rapid* learning on the part of the children is not unlike the *rapid* learning on the part of the monkeys, and analysis of the error-

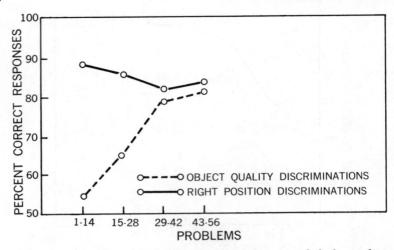

FIG. 11. Learning set curves for problem requiring shift from object-quality discrimination to right-position discrimination.

producing factors shows that the same basic mechanisms are operating in both species.

Following the discrimination reversal problem the eight monkeys were presented a new series of 56 problems designed to elicit alternation of unequivocally antagonistic response patterns. The first 7, 9, or 11 trials of each problem were simple object-quality discrimination trials. These were followed immediately by ten right-position discrimination trials with the same stimuli continuing to shift in the right-left positions in predetermined orders. In the first 7 to 11 trials, a particular object was correct regardless of its position. In the subsequent 10 trials, a particular position —the experimenter's right position—was correct, regardless of the object placed there. Thus to solve the problem the animal had to respond to object-quality cues and disregard position cues in the first 7 to 11 trials and, following the failure of reward of the previously rewarded object, he had to disregard object-quality cues and respond to position cues.

The learning data on these two antagonistic tasks are presented in Fig. 11. It is to be noted that the object-quality curve, which is based on Trials 1 to 7, begins at a very high level of accuracy, whereas the position curve, plotted for Trials 1 to 10, begins at a level little above chance. This no doubt reflects the operation of the previously well-established object-quality discrimination learning set. As the series continues, the object-quality curve shows a drop until the last block of problems, while the position curve rises progressively. In the evaluation of these data, it should be noted that chance performance is 50 per cent correct responses of the object-quality discriminations and 45 per cent for the position discriminations, since each sequence of 10 position trials includes an error

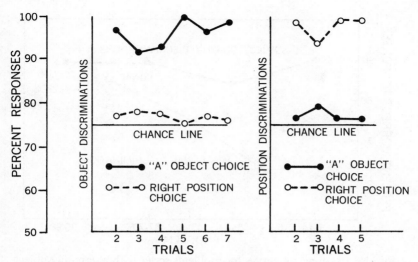

FIG. 12. Object and position choices following initial errors on both phases of object-position shift series, based on problems 42–56.

"informing" trial. It would appear that the learning of the right-position discriminations interferes with the learning of the object-quality discriminations to some extent. In spite of this decrement in object quality discrimination performance for a time, the subjects were functioning at levels far beyond chance on the antagonistic parts of the problems during the last half of the series. We believe that this behavior reflects the formation of a right-position learning set which operates at a high degree of independence of the previously established object-quality discrimination learning set.

The precision of the independent operation of these learning sets throughout the last 14 problems is indicated in Fig. 12. Since the right-position part of the problem was almost invariably initiated by an error trial, these data are limited to those problems on which the first trial object-quality discrimination response was incorrect. The per cent of correct Trial 7 responses to the 'A' object, the correct stimulus for the object-quality discriminations, is 98. The initiating error trial which occurs when the problem shifts without warning to a right-position problem, drops this per cent response to the 'A' object to 52—a level barely above chance. The per cent of Trial 7 responses to the right position during the object-quality discriminations is 52. The single error trial initiating the shift of the problem to a right-position discriminaton is followed by 97 per cent right-position responses on the next trial. In other words, *it is as though* the outcome of a single *push of an object* is adequate to switch off the 'A'-object choice reaction tendency and to switch on the right-position choice reaction tendency.

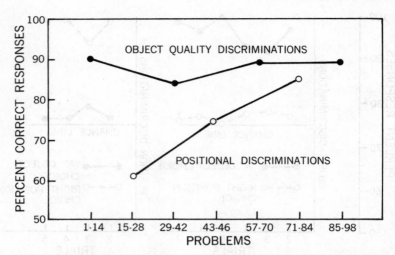

FIG. 13. Learning set curves for problems series with alternating object-quality and positional discrimination, based on total trial responses.

The cue afforded by a single trial produces at this point almost complete discontinuity of the learning process. The only question now left unsettled in the controversy over hypotheses in subhuman animals is whether or not to use this term to describe the behavior of a species incapable of verbalization.

Again, it should be remembered that both the object-quality discrimination learning set and the right-position discrimination learning set developed in a gradual and orderly manner. Only after the learning sets are formed do these phenomena of discontinuity in learned behavior appear.

Further evidence for the integrity of learning sets is presented in an additional experiment. Six monkeys with object-quality discrimination learning experience, but without training on reversal problems or position discriminations, were given seven blocks of 14 problems each, starting with a block of 25-trial object-quality discriminations, followed by a block of 14 25-trial positional discriminations composed of right-position and left-position problems presented alternately. The remaining five blocks of problems continued the alternate presentation of 14 object-quality discrimination problems and 14 right-left positional discrimination problems. Figure 13 presents curves showing the per cent of correct responses on total trials on these alternate blocks of antagonistic discriminations. The complex positional discrimination learning set curve shows progressive improvement throughout the series, whereas the object-quality discrimination curve begins at a high level of accuracy, shows decrement on the second block, and subsequently recovers. By the end of the experiment the two basically antagonistic learning sets had 'learned' to live together

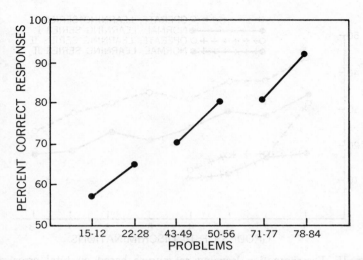

Fig. 14. Right-left positional discrimination learning set curve based on total trial responses. (Data on antagonistic object-quality discrimination problems omitted.)

with a minimum of conflict. These data are the more striking if it is recalled that between each two blocks of object-quality discriminations there were 350 trials in which no object was differentially rewarded, and between each two blocks of 14 positional discriminations there were 350 trials in which no position was differentially rewarded.

In Fig. 14 we present additional total-trial data on the formation of the positional learning set. These data show the change in performance on the first and last seven positional discriminations in each of the three separate blocks of positional discriminations. The interposed object-quality discrimination problems clearly produced interference, but they did not prevent the orderly development of the positional learning sets, nor the final attainment of a high level of performance on these problems.

We have data which suggest that educated man can face arteriosclerosis with confidence, if the results on brain-injured animals are applicable to men. Figure 15 shows discrimination learning set curves for the previously described groups of four normal monkeys and eight monkeys with very extensive unilateral cortical injury. The upper curves show total errors on an initial series of 112-six-trial discriminations. The lower curves show total errors on an additional group of 56 discriminations presented one year later. In both situations the full-brained monkeys make significantly better scores, but one should note that the educated hemidecorticate animals are superior to the uneducated unoperated monkeys. Such data suggest that half a brain is better than one if you compare the individuals having appropriate learning set with the individuals lacking them.

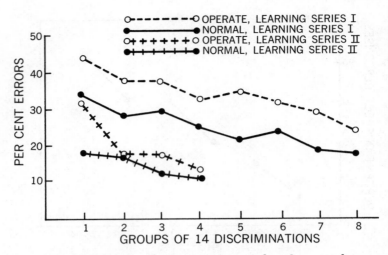

FIG. 15. Discrimination learning set curves based on total error responses: normal and operated monkeys.

More seriously, these data may indicate why educated people show less apparent deterioration with advancing age than uneducated individuals, and the data lend support to the clinical observation that our fields of greatest proficiency are the last to suffer gross deterioration.

Although our objective data are limited to the formation of learning sets which operate to give performance on intellectual problems, we have observational data of a qualitative nature on social-emotional changes in our animals. When the monkeys come to us they are wild and intractable but within a few years they have acquired, from the experimenter's point of view, good personalities. Actually we believe that one of the very important factors in the development of the good personalities of our monkeys is the formation of social-emotional learning sets organized in a manner comparable with the intellectual learning sets we have previously described. Each contact the monkey has with a human being represents a single specific learning trial. Each person represents a separate problem. Learning to react favorably to one person is followed by learning favorable reactions more rapidly to the next person to whom the monkey is socially introduced. Experience with additional individuals enables the monkey to learn further how to behave with human beings, and eventually the monkey's favorable reactions to new people are acquired so rapidly as to appear almost instantaneous.

The formation of social-emotional learning sets is not to be confused with mere stimulus generalization, a construct applied in this field with undue freedom. Actually a learning set once formed determines in large part the nature and direction of stimulus generalization. In the classic study in which Watson conditioned fear in Albert, the child developed a fear of the rat and generalized this fear, but failed to develop or generalize fear to Watson, even though Watson must have been the more conspicuous stimulus. Apparently Albert had already formed an affectional social-emotional learning set to people, which inhibited both learning and simple Pavlovian generalization.

Our observations on the formation of social-emotional learning sets have been entirely qualitative and informal, but there would appear to be no reason why they could not be studied experimentally.

The emphasis throughout this paper has been on the rôle of the historical or experience variable in learning behavior—the forgotten variable in current learning theory and research. Hull's Neo-behaviorists have constantly emphasized the necessity for an historical approach to learning, yet they have not exploited it fully. Their experimental manipulation of the experience variable has been limited to the development of isolated habits and their generalization. Their failure to find the phenomenon of discontinuity in learning may stem from their study of individual as opposed to repetitive learning situations.

The field theorists, unlike the Neo-behaviorists, have stressed insight and hypothesis in their description of learning. The impression these theorists give is that these phenomena are properties of the innate organization of the individual. If such phenomena appear independently of a gradual learning history, we have not found them in the primate order.

Psychologists working with human subjects have long believed in the phenomenon of learning sets and have even used sets as explanatory principles to account for perceptual selection and incidental learning. These psychologists have not, however, investigated the nature of these learning sets which their subjects bring to the experimental situation. The determining experiential variables of these learning sets lie buried in the subjects' pasts, but the development of such sets can be studied in the laboratory as long as the human race continues to reproduce its kind. Actually, detailed knowledge of the nature of the formation of learning sets could be of such importance to educational theory and practice as to justify prolonged and systematic investigation.

In the animal laboratory where the experimental factor can be easily controlled, we have carried out studies that outline the development and operation of specific learning sets. We believe that the construct of learning sets is of importance in the understanding of adaptive behavior. Since this is our faith, it is our hope that our limited data will be extended by those brave souls who study *real* men and *real* women.

## 33.  Experimental Studies in Rote-Learning Theory: X. Pre-Learning Syllable Familiarization and the Length-Difficulty Relationship

### C. I. Hovland and K. H. Kurtz

*In the learning of many serial or paired-associate tasks, it is necessary for a subject not only to learn to associate one verbal item with another, but also to make the units themselves a part of his response repertoire. That is, before one can learn to associate the response term XEJVOY to the stimulus term SEVEN, it is necessary for the subject to first learn XEJVOY as a response unit. In a number of studies, investigators have been interested in providing the subject with some pretraining or familiarization of verbal material so that he could have these responses available when the learning task was presented. This pretraining in the verbal learning situation has been termed familiarization, and the Hovland and Kurtz study is one of the early ones to investigate this phenomenon.*

For the determination of precise quantitative relationships in learning, Ebbinghaus (2) long ago pointed out that meaningful materials have the limitation that they involve previous associations which affect the acquiring of new relationships. His solution to the difficulty was the invention of nonsense syllables, artificial combinations of letters without previous associations. But the virtue of novelty which these materials possess is also a limitation. In learning successive pairs of such syllables or in learning lists of them in serial order one must not only learn the associations between the units but must also "learn" the units to be associated. For certain types of theoretical analysis it would be desirable to analyze the effects of these two processes separately. In studying associational interferences, for example, one may be concerned with the number of repetitions required for learning as a function of the number of units involved in a serial chain, and consequently not wish to include the effects of initial familiarization with the units to be learned serially. Here, one would need units which are free from previously learned associations, and, at the same

*J. exp. Psychol.,* 1952, *44,* 31-39. Reprinted with permission of the junior author and The American Psychological Association. The writers wish to acknowledge with thanks the assistance of Dr. Samuel Brownell of the New Haven Teachers College in securing Ss and the helpful suggestions of Drs. Fred Sheffield and Gregory Kimble in the reading of the manuscript.

time, sufficiently familiar to permit the learning trials to reflect primarily the process of serialization. Meaningful words do not meet the first requisite, while ordinary nonsense syllables fail on the second. Spelling of individual letters and the use of numerals are methods that have been used in an attempt to satisfy the requirements, but previous associations between letters or numerals may present some of the same difficulties that are involved in meaningful words. Another method is employed in the present experiment: that of using nonsense syllables which are made "familiar" by methods which do not involve forming associations between them. The Ss studied the nonsense syllables presented in constantly changing order until they knew the syllables well enough to recognize them and to supply missing letters when parts of the syllables were presented individually. Following this process of familiarization the lists were learned in the conventional manner. Under control conditions lists were learned without prior familiarization. The effects of familiarization were investigated as a methodological factor affecting the relationship between length of list and number of trials required for learning.

PROCEDURE

Three different lengths of list, consisting of 6, 12, or 24 syllables, were learned under both experimental (familiarization—Groups I, III, and V) and control (no-familiarization—Groups II, IV, and VI) conditions. Each of 12 Ss served once in each of the six conditions, with order of conditions counterbalanced between Ss for practice effects.

*Learning materials.* The experiment required that the learning materials for different lengths of list and for experimental and control conditions be as comparable as possible and that the familiarization procedure produce comparable familiarity with the units of lists of varying length. Six lists of 24 syllables each were constructed as parent-lists from which all smaller lists were derived. Each list of 24 could be considered as consisting of four sets of six syllables which could be used individually as 6-syllable lists. The first six syllables of each list were combined with the second set of six, and the third group of six with the fourth group to form two lists of 12 syllables from each of the basic lists of 24. For example, if the four lists of six syllables are designated as A, B, C, and D, the parent list of 24 would consist of ABCD and the two lists of 12 would be AB and CD. The six syllables within a segment were kept in the same order throughout.

Repetition of initial or final consonants within the lists was reduced to the practical minimum. With a single exception any given letter was not repeated within three consecutive syllables. Combinations of two letters were not repeated within any list in the same order. In applying this rule consonants grouped as phonetically similar were regarded as identical. Letters used in the first syllable of a list were not repeated in the last syllable (with one exception in a list of six). Any given syllable (or a phonetically identical one) was used only once in the entire set of lists.

The Glaze (4) association values of the individual syllables used ranged from 0% to 46.7%. The mean association value of all lengths of list was 22.7%. The range of mean association values was, for the 6-unit lists, 21.1% to 24.5%; for the 12-unit lists, 22.2% to 23.3%; and for the 24-unit lists, 22.5% to 22.8%.

*Familiarization.* Familiarization was effected by presenting a set of syllables to S one at a time, changing the order for each run through the set. To maintain uniform familiarization independently of length of list to be learned, the entire parent set of 24 syllables was used in the familiarization preceding the learning of any of its segments.

A familiarization pack was constructed for each parent set by printing the syllables individually on 3- by 5-in. index cards. For each familiarization pack three test packs were constructed in a similar fashion, substituting a dash for one of the three letters of each syllable. Each letter of a given syllable was omitted in one of the three packs. Omissions in each letter position were equally represented in any given pack.

During familiarization, E and S sat facing each other at a table. The E held the familiarization pack facing S and exposed each successive syllable at a 2-sec. rate by allowing the preceding card to fall face down on the table, timing the presentation by the sweep-second movement of a stop watch. The S read each syllable aloud as it was exposed. A trial consisted of presenting all 24 syllables once each, and required a total of 48 sec.

Trials were presented at a rate not exceeding one every 2 min. To prevent the familiarization sessions from becoming inordinately tedious, S and E engaged in spontaneous conversation between trials. Consequently, a rigid rate of presentation of trials was not maintained, and the interval between trials was allowed to exceed the minimum of 72 sec. when a break in conversation at this point would be strained and unnatural.

After every set of five trials S was given one trial with a test pack, during which he attempted to reproduce (pronounce as a unit) each complete syllable when presented with only two of its letters. If S did not give the correct response within 3 sec., the syllable was scored as incorrect and E told S the correct response. Familiarization on a given pack was continued until S responded correctly on all syllables in a single test trial. Two or more sessions were usually required to attain this criterion.

Three sets of five familiarization trials with a test after every five trials were given on the first day for any pack and four such sets on each additional day required. When S reached the criterion on the first test run of any session, the appropriate serial learning for that pack was carried out in the same session. Otherwise learning was postponed to the following session and was preceded during that session by one set of five familiarization trials and a test. This provided that learning of any familiarized list was always immediately preceded by a set of familiarization trials.

To keep the length of the experiment within reasonable limits, the familiarization procedure was slightly modified if familiarization on any pack extended beyond two sessions. If S failed to respond to a test card within the 3-sec. interval he was not corrected by the E and that card was presented again at the end of the test trial. If an incorrect response was made to any card, the procedure of correction after 3 sec. was again instituted.

*Order of presentation of conditions.* The order in which the 12 Ss learned the lists under the six conditions was arranged to counterbalance practice from session to session. Thus, each condition appeared twice (once each for two different Ss) in each practice position in a typical cross-over design. Randomization of order was further restricted by arranging the familiarized condition first in half the cases and second in the other half separately for both the 24- and 6-unit lists.

Each S reported over a series of daily sessions consisting of six serial-learning sessions and the necessary familiarization sessions. Only one list was learned serially at any learning session. Familiarization sessions for a given list were interpolated between the learning session for that list and the preceding learning session. The total number of sessions varied depending upon the number of sessions required by various Ss to reach the familiarized criterion.

*Apparatus for serial learning.* The syllables were presented by the Hull memory drum. The apparatus and E were situated behind a black screen 6 ft. high by 4 ft. wide with a 4- by 5-in. opening for displaying the syllable apertures.

Syllables were pronounced as a unit and learned serially by the anticipation method. The lists were prepared with a special typewriter on bands of semiglazed white paper in ¼-in. black uppercase letters and presented one at a time in fixed serial order at a 2-sec. rate. On each trial the first syllable was preceded by an asterisk presented for 2 sec. as a starting cue. Trials were massed, with the asterisk starting cue following immediately after the final syllable.

*Preliminary training.* Prior to serving in the experimental conditions each S was given several days' preliminary training. The first day was spent learning two lists, one each of lengths 12 and 6, both without familiarization. Preliminary training was then completed by the learning of a 24-syllable list with the familiarization procedure. The same set of preliminary lists was used for all Ss.

*Instructions.* Oral instructions were given in a uniform manner at sev-

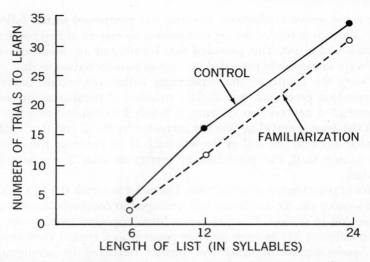

FIG. 1. The number of trials to learn to a criterion of one perfect recitation as a function of length of list under familiarization and control procedures.

eral stages of the preliminary training as each novel task was encountered.

On the first day the rationale of the experiment was explained as a comparison between learning new and learning familiar syllables. Detailed instructions for serial learning similar to those previously used in these laboratories were given before learning the first list. Following this list Ss were reassured that making mistakes was common to all Ss and that failing to follow the first perfect trial immediately with another perfect recitation was customary. The Ss were encouraged not to be upset by such occurrences.

At the first familiarization session S was instructed to ". . . *pronounce each [syllable] out loud and study it so that you get to know it and recognize it when you see it.*" It was explained they were not be learned in serial order and that the cards would be shuffled between each trial to prevent this. The test pack and procedure were then explained.

To keep initial g phonetically distinct from initial j, hard g was adopted as a standard pronunciation. Similarly, initial q was given a standard pronunciation of qw to keep it distinct from c and k. If these standard pronunciations were not spontaneously adopted by S for any particular syllable during familiarization, E suggested the standard to S.

*Subjects.* A group of 12 men, consisting of 2 University of Connecticut undergraduates, 3 Yale undergraduates, and 7 Yale graduate and professional students served as paid Ss. The median age was 25 yr. with a range of 20 to 31 yr. Two additional Ss were rejected after preliminary training because of unusual difficulty with the experimental tasks.

## TABLE 1

MEAN REPETITIONS REQUIRED TO LEARN VARYING LENGTHS OF LIST UNDER
FAMILIARIZATION AND NO-FAMILIARIZATION CONDITIONS

| Length of List | To 1 Perfect Trial | | | To 2 Suc. Perfect Trials | | |
|---|---|---|---|---|---|---|
| | Famil. | No-Famil. | p diff. | Famil. | No-Famil. | p diff. |
| 6 | 2.2 | 4.1 | .002 | 3.6 | 5.9 | .0003 |
| 12 | 11.4 | 15.9 | .04 | 14.2 | 19.5 | .01 |
| 24 | 30.2 | 33.0 | .15 | 38.7 | 45.9 | .13 |

## RESULTS

The principal results are the comparison of the number of trials to learn the 6-, 12-, and 24-unit lists with and without prior familiarization. The mean number of trials to learn the three lengths of list to one perfect recitation and to two successive perfect recitations are given in Table 1. The results for the criterion of one perfect recitation are shown graphically in Fig. 1. It will be seen that familiarization reduces the number of trials required for all three lengths by a practically constant amount but does not alter the essentially linear relationship between difficulty and length of list found in this range of lengths with the ordinary nonsense syllable procedure both in the present experiment and in previous studies by Ebbinghaus (2), Meumann (7), and others. This indicates that complications arising from the necessity of becoming familiar with units in the ordinary nonsense syllable technique does not introduce serious distortion into the length-difficulty relationship. The results for the criterion of two perfect recitations tend to indicate a somewhat greater effect of familiarization with greater length of list, but here also there is a linear relationship between length of list and difficulty with both procedures.

Another method of analyzing the results is to determine the influence of prior differentiation on the acquisition curves for each particular length. Figure 2 gives the acquisition curves with and without prior differentiation for the three lengths of list. The average number of trials to reach each syllable criterion is plotted. It will be seen that the criteria are plotted along the ordinate and the number of trials along the abscissa. This departure from the conventional use of the abscissa for the independent variable was employed to preserve the customary form of the learning curve. The effect of the familiarization will be seen to be most marked for the 6-unit lists. Calculation from the individual records shows that two-thirds of the Ss were able to get five of the six syllables correct on a single trial with the prior familiarization but only one out of the 12 Ss made a similar score under control conditions. With the 12-unit lists, half of the Ss were

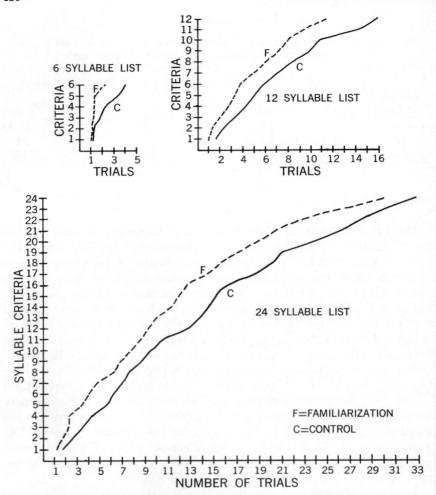

FIG. 2. The number of trials to reach successive syllable criteria in learning lists of 6, 12, and 24 syllables under familiarization (F) and control (C) conditions.

able to get three syllables correct on the first trial with the prior familiarization, but none of them reached this criterion under the control conditions.

To determine more clearly at what stage of learning the advantage of prior familiarization occurs, it is useful to compare the *rates* of learning for the two procedures throughout the course of learning. This comparison is made in Fig. 3. The values presented are obtained by computing the *difference* in number of trials required to reach successive criteria under familiarization and control procedures. The amount by which the famil-

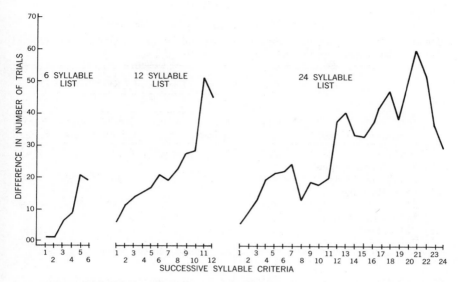

FIG. 3. The *difference* between familiarization and control procedures in the number of trials to reach successive syllable criteria.

iarization procedure is superior to the control is plotted at successive criteria of learning. Wherever the rates of learning are equal (i.e., when the increments in number of trials to go from one criterion to the next are equal) for the two procedures the plot of the differences remains horizontal. A rise in the curve indicates a more rapid rate of learning at this stage for the prior familiarization procedure, and a fall indicates a more rapid rate under the control condition. It will be seen that despite some minor irregularities a higher rate of learning for the familiarization procedure is maintained throughout learning with the 6- and 12-unit lists. With the 24-unit list the rate of learning is higher under the familiarization procedure up to the criterion of 21/24 syllables correct. From this point until mastery (24/24) the rate is higher under control conditions, although there still remains a net difference in favor of familiarization.

*Analysis of errors.* A further analysis of the data was made in terms of the number and kinds of errors made under these two conditions. All incorrect responses during serial learning were classified according to the following five categories: (*a*) Syllables belonging to the list being learned (intralist errors); (*b*) syllables belonging to a nonfamiliarized list previously learned by S; (*c*) syllables belonging to a familiarized list previously learned by S; (*d*) syllables included in a preceding familiarization procedure but not included in any serial learning; and (*e*) syllables not previously presented to S in any fashion during the experiment and, thus, "invented" by S. If a given error was repeated several times during a trial

TABLE 2

EFFECTS OF FAMILIARIZATION UPON ERRORS

Mean number of different kinds of errors under familiarization and control (nonfamiliarization) conditions for three lengths of list.

| | Length of List | | | | | |
|---|---|---|---|---|---|---|
| | 24 | | 12 | | 6 | |
| Source of Error | Con- trol | Famil- iarized | Con- trol | Famil- iarized | Con- trol | Famil- iarized |
| (1) Same list | 28.50 | 34.67 | 6.17 | 6.67 | 0.42 | 0.42 |
| (2) Prior learning non- familiarized lists) | 4.67 | 0.92* | 1.08 | 0.00 | 0.25 | 0.00 |
| (3) Prior learning (familiarized lists | 6.33 | 1.25* | 1.50 | 0.17* | 0.58 | 0.00 |
| (4) Prior familiarization | 1.17 | 0.25 | 0.08 | 0.25 | 0.33 | 0.00 |
| (5) "Invented" | 17.50 | 3.50* | 5.67 | 0.50* | 1.75 | 0.08* |

* Significant difference between control and familiarized conditions ($p < .02$).

it was counted only once, unless two occurrences were separated by a different error. Only responses which were complete syllables were included in the analysis. These constituted 78% of all errors. The mean frequency of each type of error is presented for each condition and each length of list in Table 2. The difference between the familiar and nonfamiliar conditions in number of intralist errors is not significant for any length list. The number of invented errors is reduced significantly for all lengths of list when the material learned is previously familiarized. Similarly, familiarization reduces the number of errors from previous lists, both familiarized and not familiarized. When the contributions from these two types of previous lists are combined, the difference is significant at the .01 level for the 12- and 24-unit lists, but falls slightly short of significance for the 6-unit list, where few errors are made under either condition.

## DISCUSSION

The data bearing on the relationship between length of list and difficulty confirm previous studies in showing a rough proportionality between length and number of trials required for learning, and show that this relationship is not greatly affected by prior familiarization. What is now greatly needed is information about the relationship with lists of considerably greater length. Only in this way can the formulae of Thurstone (11) and Hull et al. (5) be tested adequately. The data now available covering the greatest range of lengths are those of Lyon (6). They do not appear to follow a simple formula, but show wavelike changes somewhat analogous to the plateaus and habit hierarchies found by Bryan and Harter (1). Unfortunately, Lyon's data are based on only a single S (himself) and more research employing a wider range of Ss is needed to ascertain the length-difficulty relationship with adequate generality. Present data provide little information on individual differences, since most of the studies have been done with college students and other above-average adult Ss.

The effects of prior familiarization are clearly seen to be an increased ease of learning, both in terms of errors and trials to mastery. In the case of the shortest list only about half the number of trials is required following familiarization as under standard conditions. The present results thus do not support those of Waters (12), who concluded that prior reading of lists of syllables does not facilitate learning. In his experiment three conditions were compared: Cond. I—The Ss first read aloud three times the list to be learned. They then proceeded to the formal learning of the list. The serial order for learning was the same as for the initial reading. Cond. II—Same as Cond. I except that the order of syllables for learning was different from that during the initial reading. Cond. III—Learning without any prior reading of the list. Waters considers the comparison between Cond. II and III the crucial test for the effect of familiarization and found no difference in the number of trials to learn the lists under the two procedures. However, this comparison neglects the possibility that learning the syllables in a changed order may involve the unlearning of partly learned associative connections established during the initial reading with resulting associative interference. Thus, in Waters' experiment there was an opportunity for the factors of associative interference and familiarity to oppose and cancel one another, while in the present study the learning of associative connections during familiarization was precluded by using a constantly changing order of presentation during familiarization. A further difference between the two studies is in the amount of familiarization training given. In Waters' study familiarization consisted of only three prior readings of the lists to be learned, while in the present experiment between 30 and 70 presentations of the material were employed, the number depending upon S's speed in reaching the familiarization criterion.

Our results, then, seem to revive the possibility that Robinson's Law of Acquaintance deserves further consideration. But if, as Robinson (9) suggests, there is some advantage in familiarity with the units to be associated which can be abstracted from the many associative connections into which they enter, what is the basis for its effect?

One possible interpretation follows from the type of "communication theory" discussed by Miller (8, Ch. 5, 10, 11). He defines the amount of information conveyed by an item as dependent upon the number of alternatives from which that item is chosen, and cites evidence that learning time increases with amount of information communicated. The effect of familiarization in the present study is to sharply reduce the number of alternative items from the range of all possible nonsense syllables to the limited number to be learned. The amount of information conveyed by each syllable at the time of learning is thus greatly reduced and, accordingly, it would be expected that familiar (low-information) syllables should be learned more rapidly than the control material.

A second interpretation is suggested by Gibson (3) in her discussion of the learning of "predifferentiated" items. According to her formulation, the familiarization procedure would produce a clear discrimination among the units to be associated and between these and units learned in earlier lists. This would reduce both intra- and interlist interference and thus increase the speed of learning. However, the analysis of errors in the present study is not entirely consistent with this formulation, since there appeared to be no appreciable reduction of intralist errors under the familiarized condition, although there was the predicted decrease in interlist intrusions.

An hypothesis suggested by the present data is that in the serial learning of both familiarized and nonfamiliarized syllables there develop tendencies to make all three kinds of errors, viz., intralist intrusions, interlist intrusions, and inventions. Familiarization enables S to recognize the last two types of responses as foreign to the list being learned and, thus, as incorrect, so that the tendencies to make such responses, although present, are suppressed. On the other hand, familiarization provides no basis for knowing the correct serial order of syllables in the list being learned, and errors due to misplacing of these syllables are made with about the same frequency under familiar and nonfamiliar conditions.

This hypothesis is substantiated by the results of an unpublished study by Sheffield (10). In that study syllables were familiarized by a procedure not involving the formation of associations between syllables and were then paired with nonfamiliar syllables in a paired-associates learning procedure. The results indicate that increases in the speed of learning and decreases in intralist intrusions are more closely related to the occurrence of familiar syllables in the response position than in the stimulus position.

Further research is needed to analyze more fully the role of stimulus and response differentiation in learning and the relationship of these phenomena to the broader problem of meaningfulness in learning.

SUMMARY

1. In the serial learning of nonsense syllables the process of becoming familiar with the syllable units may be distinguished from the process of learning the serial order of these units. For research in which the primary interest is in the latter process, it would be desirable to have some method of eliminating the former. In the present study an attempt was made to compare the relationship between difficulty and length of list under ordi-

nary nonsense-syllable procedures with that under a procedure in which Ss became familiar with the syllables before learning them in serial order. In the design employed, 12 Ss learned lists of 6, 12, and 24 nonsense syllables both with and without prior familiarization of items.

2. The effect of prior familiarization with the syllables was to reduce the number of trials to mastery by a moderately constant amount for all lengths of list. In the case of the shortest lists this amounted to a reduction of approximately half the number of trials required by the ordinary procedure, while with the longer lists it amounted to a much smaller proportion. The present results on the effects of familiarization are discussed in relation to the results of Waters (12) which showed no effect of prior reading of the material to be learned.

3. The number of trials to reach the criteria of mastery employed was an approximately linear function of length of list in the range of lengths studied. This held for both criteria of learning and for both familiarization and control procedures.

4. As measured by the difference in trials to reach each syllable criterion, the rate of acquisition following familiarization was higher than that of control material throughout learning for the 6- and 12-syllable lists. Prior familiarization also produced a superior rate of learning with the 24-syllable list up until the final eighth of acquisition, when the rate of learning fell below that under control conditions. The net advantage of familiarization was thus reduced somewhat by the time that the criterion of one perfect recitation was reached.

5. Analysis of errors indicated that familiarization did not reduce the number of intralist intrusions but did reduce the number of interlist intrusions and the number of erroneous syllables "invented" by Ss.

6. The results are discussed in relation to Robinson's Law of Acquaintance (9), the generalization-differentiation analysis of Gibson (3), and the "information theory" formulation by Miller (8).

REFERENCES

1. BRYAN, W. L. and HARTER, N. (1899) Studies on the telegraphic language. The acquisition of a hierarchy of habits. *Psychol. Rev.*, 6, 345-375.
2. EBBINGHAUS, H. (1913) *Memory: A contribution to experimental psychology.* (Translated by H. A. Ruger and C. E. Bussenius.) New York: Teachers College, Columbia Univer.
3. GIBSON, E. J. (1940) A systematic application of the concepts of generalization and differentiation to verbal learning. *Psychol. Rev.*, 47, 196-229.
4. GLAZE, J. A. (1928) The association value of nonsense syllables. *J. genet. Psychol.*, 35, 255-269.
5. HULL, C. L., HOVLAND, C. I., ROSS, R. T., HALL, M., PERKINS, D. T., and

FITCH, F. B. (1940) *Mathematico-deductive theory of rote learning.* New Haven: Yale Univer. Press.
6. LYON, D. O. (1914) The relation of length of material to time taken for learning and the optimum distribution of time. *J. educ. Psychol.,* 5, 1-9, 85-91, 155-163.
7. MEUMANN, E. (1913) *The psychology of learning.* (Translated by J. W. Baird from 3rd German edition.) New York: Appleton-Century-Crofts.
8. MILLER, G. A. (1951) *Language and communication.* New York: Mc-Graw-Hill.
9. ROBINSON, E. S. (1932) *Association theory today.* New York: Appleton-Century-Crofts.
10. SHEFFIELD, F. D. (1946) The role of meaningfulness of stimulus and response in verbal learning. Unpublished Ph.D. dissertation, Yale Univer.
11. THURSTONE, L. L. (1930) The relation between learning time and length of task. *Psychol. Rev.,* 37, 44-53.
12. WATERS, R. H. (1939) The law of acquaintance. *J. exp. Psychol.,* 24, 180-191.

# 34. Stimulus Pre-Differentiation as a Factor in Transfer of Training

## R. M. Gagné and K. E. Baker

*This article reports an experiment designed to measure the effectiveness of stimulus pre-differentiation in producing transfer to a motor task. It can be noted that the operational procedures are somewhat similar to those used in familiarization.*

### INTRODUCTION

One of the important characteristics of many motor skills is that their learning appears to depend to a greater extent upon a differentiation of stimulus aspects than it does upon an improvement in precision of muscular movement. In many motor tasks the individual may learn to respond to a very complex set of sensory cues with reactions such as pressing buttons, turning cranks, or pulling levers, which in themselves are easy and well practiced movements. Practical training on a skill of this sort often emphasizes the stimulus aspects of the task, though this emphasis may be given in quite an unsystematic manner. It is a common procedure, for

*J. exp. Psychol.,* 1950, *40*, 439-451. Reprinted with permission of the senior author and The American Psychological Association. This paper is a slightly modified version of Report 316-1-7 under Contract N7onr-316, Task Order I, between Special Devices Center, Office of Naval Research, and Connecticut College.

example, to introduce a subject to the learning of a discriminative skill by giving him instructions whose main function is to point out the specific stimuli to which he must make the required reactions. In some cases a certain amount of practice in identifying these different stimuli, usually by means of verbal names, is also given before the learner undertakes to practice the motor task itself. The present experiment may be viewed as an investigation of the effectiveness for transfer of different amounts of practice of this preliminary sort, which presumably serves to make the stimuli more distinctive. The transfer of this type of training is measured in connection with a motor skill in which a number of different stimuli must be associated with the same number of different manual responses.

A number of previous experiments have been concerned with investigating the extent to which various kinds of preliminary training transfer to the learning of a motor task which was highly similar to the present one. In general these studies have interpreted the effect of preliminary training to be the reduction in the tendency of a learned response to generalize to stimuli which are similar to the one with which the given response has been associated. Thus, in one study (3), increasing positive transfer to a total skill was shown to follow increasing amounts of preliminary training on two of the four component habits of that skill. The amount of the resulting transfer was conceived to depend upon the degree to which conflicting generalized response tendencies to similar stimuli were reduced by preliminary training. In a second study (5), an analysis of the errors made in the final motor task following the same type of component training revealed that the reduction in errors was not confined to the specific S-R connections which had been practiced in the preliminary task, but applied also to S-R connections for stimuli which were only similar, in one or more aspects, to the ones used in preliminary training. Thus, it was demonstrated that discrimination training had a transfer effect which was not confined to specifically practiced responses to stimuli, but which could be interpreted as resulting from the reduction of generalization tendencies to all similar stimuli. In still a third experiment (4), the amount of transfer to a motor task was related to the amount of preliminary training on a pictured representation of the task, in which the subject was required to make pencil marks in appropriate spaces, representing positions of switches to pictures of the stimuli actually used in the final task. Increasing positive transfer to the motor task was found to be correlated with increasing amounts of practice on the preliminary 'pictured' task. In this experiment, too, the results were in accord with the idea that preliminary training reduces interference within the task by bringing about a reduction in internal generalization.

In each of these cases, the effect of preliminary training may be said to be that of increasing the distinctiveness of the discriminative habits which must be learned in the final motor task. In this sense, the preliminary training has a 'pre-differentiating' effect which, in general, increases in degree as the amount of such training is increased. But in each one of these experiments some aspects of both stimuli and responses have been common to the preliminary and the final task, so that it is impossible to distinguish completely between 'stimulus pre-differentiation' and 'response pre-differentiation,' or even to determine whether such a distinction can legitimately be made. Thus, in the two studies in which preliminary training on components was given, subjects practiced two of the four responses (to two of the four stimuli) used later in the final task. In the experiment involving preliminary practice on a pictured representation of the motor task, although the responses were quite dissimilar to those of the final task, the directional aspects of the responses were the same in the two tasks (i.e., the position of the blanks to be checked by pencil corresponded in a relative sense to the position of switches to be pressed). While the effects of different amounts of discrimination training can be compared within each of these studies, in none of them was a clear distinction drawn between the effects of pre-differentiating stimuli and of pre-differentiating responses.

The present experiment was designed to measure the effectiveness of *stimulus* pre-differentiation in producing transfer to a motor task, under conditions in which the responses employed in the preliminary training were made to be as neutral and unrelated to those of the final task as possible. The subjects first learned to make verbal responses to a set of four light stimuli, differing from each other in color and position, and subsequently proceeded to learn a task which contained the same stimuli but required the responses of pressing four switches, one for each of the lights. Three different amounts of practice on the preliminary task were given to three different groups of subjects, in order to measure the way in which this variable affected transfer. The performance of each of these experimental groups was compared with that of a control group during 60 trials of practice on the final motor task. If stimulus pre-differentiation is a significant factor in the determination of transfer of training, it was expected that the performance of the experimental groups would be superior to that of the control group, which received no 'pre-differentiating' training.

The concept of stimulus pre-differentiation appears prominently in the set of hypotheses proposed by Gibson (6) to account for certain aspects of the learning of verbal paired-associates. These hypotheses, like the analysis of discriminative motor skills we have presented in previous papers, are based upon the idea that the acquisition of each required response generates tendencies to make the same response to stimuli similar to the stimulus with which the correct response is associated. Since the stimuli of the task are to some extent similar, these generalized response tendencies conflict with the other 'correct' response tendencies which are established to each stimulus by direct practice. Continued practice may be expected to bring about a reduction in generalization, and consequently a reduction in the number of incorrect responses exhibited in the performance of the task. Some studies have found an initial increase in error occurrence to follow a small amount of practice on the task, and a subsequent decrease in errors as training is continued. This was the finding, for example, in studies of paired associate verbal learning by Gibson (7, 8) and by Gagné (1). Also, in the first of the present series of experiments (3), in which a 'paired-associate' motor task was employed, the occurrence of an initial rise in the number of overt errors at the beginning of the learning of the motor task was followed by a progressive decrease in errors as training continued.

The interpretation of these results leads to the hypothesis that any kind of preliminary training which serves to reduce the internal stimulus generalization of the task will have a facilitating effect upon the subsequent learning of the total task. Gibson's (6) proposition XV reads as follows: "*If differentiation has been set up within a list, less generalization will occur in learning a new list which includes the same stimulus items paired with different responses; and the trials required to learn the new list will tend to be reduced by reduction of the internal generalization.*" It is reasoned that if differentiation has been set up among a number of stimulus items it will be easier to differentiate them again later even though they are paired with different responses. This effect comes about because the preliminary learning has effected a reduction in the generalized response tendencies which interfere with the correct response tendencies to be established by practice. An experiment by the same author (8) showed that the number of overt errors in a second list of paired associates was smaller than the number occurring in a first list using the identical stimulus members but different responses.

With this introduction, the present experiment can be set in its proper theoretical framework. The attempt was made to reduce the internal generalization of a 'paired-associate' type of motor task by giving preliminary training on a task which utilized the same stimulus elements but quite different responses. It was expected that a small amount of such training would serve to bring about an initial increase in the internal stimulus generalization followed by a progressive reduction in generalization with continued training. A small amount of preliminary training should consequently result in an increase in the occurrence of incorrect responses, at least during the early stages of the learning of the final motor task. As the degree of pre-differentiation is increased by increased amounts of preliminary practice, a progressive reduction in errors should occur in the learning of the final task. It is to be noted that the attempt was made in this experiment to limit the effects of preliminary training to a reduction in *stimulus generalization*, by utilizing responses which were as different as possible from those of the final task. Thus, the responses were ones which were expected neither to interfere with nor to constitute practice on the final task responses. It may be said that the subject first learned to differentiate the stimuli on the basis of non-meaningful verbal 'names,' and then proceeded to utilize these same stimuli in learning a task involving motor responses of which he had no previous knowledge. We were interested in discovering the effectiveness for transfer of this process of making only the stimuli more distinctive.

## METHOD

*Subjects.* The subjects used in the experiment were 150 male undergraduate college students. Most of these men had taken a course in elementary psychology, and were aware that the experiment was concerned with learning. They had no knowledge of the nature of the task, however, before the experiment. These subjects were paid for their services on an hourly basis. The men were assigned in random fashion to four groups of approximately equal size, one of these groups being the control group, and the others the three experimental groups. After matching, each group consisted of 32 men and the data obtained for these subjects were used in the analysis.

The groups were matched on the basis of a learning score obtained from the administration of the full-page Woodworth-Wells substitution test with a time limit of 80 sec., and also on the basis of average reaction time scores obtained from 25 trials of reaction to a single green light of the apparatus by pressing a single switch given at the close of the experimental session. The multiple correlation between these two measures and the total time of all 60 learning trials in the control group was .35, and between the same measures and total errors in the control group, .23. The means and standard deviations of the scores on matching criteria are given in Table 1. Differences between these means are insignificant and in general indicate that matching of the groups was successfully carried out.

TABLE 1

SCORES ON MATCHING CRITERIA FOR THE FOUR GROUPS OF THE
EXPERIMENT. $N = 32$ FOR EACH GROUP

| Measure | Group | | | |
|---|---|---|---|---|
| | Control | 8-trial | 16-trial | 32-trial |
| Substitution Test (number right) | | | | |
| Mean | 62.87 | 62.78 | 62.69 | 62.69 |
| S.D. | 8.73 | 9.49 | 8.43 | 8.64 |
| Reaction Time (unit = 0.01 sec.) | | | | |
| Mean | 49.74 | 50.71 | 50.32 | 50.28 |
| S.D. | 6.23 | 6.12 | 5.56 | 5.18 |

*Apparatus.* The apparatus employed in the experiment was a modified form of one used in a previous experiment (3). A vertical display panel presents to the subject either a red or a green light near the top of the panel, and lights of the same color in a position near the bottom of the panel. The light stimuli are separated from each other by 7½ in. in the vertical dimension. A reaction panel which lies flat on a table contains a starting button in front on which the subject's thumb rests before each reaction, and four spring-return toggle switches, two on the left and two on the right of center. The switches within a pair are numbered 1 and 2, from left to right. The motor task requires the subject to learn to press one of the switches to each of the four different stimuli presented. The responses to be learned are as follows: Bottom red light—left switch No. 1; bottom green light—left switch No. 2; top red light—right switch No. 1; top green light—right switch No. 2. The subject is required to begin his response from a central starting button, and to respond as quickly as possible by pressing the correct switch as soon as a light appears on the display panel. An electric timer continues to run until the correct switch is pressed. The experimenter records both the time of reaction and the number and type of incorrect responses which are made.

One modification of the original apparatus makes possible the presentation of each pair of red and green lights in exactly the same position on the stimulus panel. Whereas in the apparatus previously used the two lights of each pair were placed one directly above the other, in the present apparatus both lights are behind the panel itself and illuminate a single ground-glass screen. This means that there is no longer any difference in position of the red and green lights of each pair. As has been stated, the pairs themselves are 7½ in. apart in the vertical dimension. A second modification of the apparatus was made to provide for the presentation of the letters which were used as responses in the preliminary task. In the center of the stimulus panel, between the two round openings for the lights, is a square aperture through which the response letters can be seen. Behind this square opening is mounted a shutter attached to a lever arm. This arm is tilted upward by means of a cam run by a synchronous motor mounted on the back of the panel. The motor is wired into the circuit which controls the operation of the lights, in such a way that it begins to run as soon as any light is turned on by the experimenter. After two sec., the cam pushes up the lever which operates the shutter, exposing a letter to the subject's view. The letter remains exposed for a constant interval of approximately two sec., at which time the shutter closes, the motor stops automatically, and the stimulus light goes off. The letters themselves are mounted on a disc which can be rotated from the experimenter's panel by means of a flexible cable.

In the preliminary task the subject saw only the stimulus panel of the apparatus. The response panel with its starting button and reaction switches was completely covered by a removable wooden cover. Before each trial of the preliminary task, the experimenter first set the disc containing the four letters to a position in which the appropriate one of the letters could be exposed when the shutter opened. He next gave a ready signal and depressed a button which turned on the light corresponding to this letter. At the same time this button started the motor, so that after two sec. the shutter opened and exposed the letter which was to be associated with the light. The subject was to respond before the expiration of this two-sec. interval. The subject then saw the exposed letter for a constant interval of approximately two sec., after which the shutter closed and the apparatus automatically turned itself off.

*Procedure.* At the beginning of each experimental session the full-page Woodworth-Wells substitution test was administered to each subject with a time limit of 80 sec. Following this, each subject in each experimental group was seated in a chair facing the apparatus and was given 8, 16, or 32 trials of preliminary training, depending on the particular group to which he was assigned. Subjects in the control group began the learning of the final task immediately. The preliminary task consisted of the learning of the following associations: Lower red light—'J'; lower green light—'V'; upper red light—'M'; upper green light—'S'. These particular letters were chosen to be as meaningless as possible with reference to the positions of the switches in the final motor task. Thus, such letters as 'L' which might have been associated with 'left,' or 'G' which might have been associated with 'green,' were avoided. The presentation of lights was in random order throughout each set of eight trials of preliminary training. Thus, the group given eight trials of preliminary training saw each stimulus light and its associated letter twice, the group given 16 trials saw each stimulus light and its associated letter four times, etc. The subject attempted to respond with the correct letter within two sec. after each light was turned on. Whether he responded or not at the end of two sec., the shutter opened and exposed the correct letter.

The instructions given to the subjects in each experimental group before beginning the practice of the preliminary task were as follows:

On this panel you will see a red or a green light in this round hole (point), or a red or a green light in this hole (point). Only one light will appear at a time. Your task is to learn a letter which goes with each of these lights so that you can say it as quickly as possible after the light appears. The letters are J, V, M, and S. In just a minute I will tell you which letter goes with each light. As soon as you see one of the lights, you are to try to say the letter that goes with it as quickly as possible. After each light has been on for two seconds, the correct letter will appear in this slot so that you can see whether or not you gave the correct response. You will practice saying these letters for a number of trials. At the beginning of each trial I will say 'Ready,' before I press a button which turns on one of the lights.

Now let me show you which letter goes with each light. First, you will see the light, and two seconds later the correct letter will appear in the slot. Try to remember them, so that you can say the letters fast and correctly on subsequent trials.

The four stimulus lights together with their associated letters were presented to the subject. The experimenter said the letters out loud as they appeared and he was encouraged to say them too.

Now we're ready for the practice trials. Remember, try to learn to say the correct letter as quickly as you can after seeing the light, *before* it appears in the slot. Ready?

Following the administration of the proper number of trials of preliminary training, the wooden cover was removed from the response panel, exposing the switches to which reactions were to be made during the final task. The experimenter then proceeded to give the instructions for the final task, which were essentially the same as those used in a previous study (3). The subject was told to make as rapid a reaction as possible. It was explained that the bottom lights were to be associated with switches on the left, the top lights with switches on the right; and that a red light went with switch number 1, a green light with switch number 2 in each case. The control group, which did not practice the preliminary task, was also given the same instructions before beginning the learning of the motor task. For all groups, four different random orders of 60 presentations of the lights were employed in the final task, and equal numbers of subjects within each group had the lights presented to them in each order.

The time interval between trials was maintained at the constant value of approximately 10 sec. in both preliminary and final training of all groups. The time elapsing between the end of preliminary and the beginning of practice on the final motor task was two min.

At the end of 60 practice trials on the motor task, the reaction time of each subject was measured throughout 25 trials requiring responses to switch No. 2 on the left on the appearance of the lower green light. The average of these values was used in the matching of groups.

## RESULTS

*Time of response.* Table 2 presents the average response times in successive sets of 10 trials for each of the groups of the experiment. The table also includes the standard deviations of these mean values. These data are shown graphically in Fig. 1.

It can be seen that, in general, the learning of the motor task proceeds in a negatively accelerated manner throughout its course. The learning of the control group begins at a relatively high time score value which is followed by a sharp reduction on the second set of 10 trials. Continued

TABLE 2

AVERAGE TIME OF RESPONSE PER TRIAL IN SUCCESSIVE 10–TRIAL STAGES OF
LEARNING THE MOTOR SKILL, TOGETHER WITH THE STANDARD DEVIATIONS OF
THESE VALUES, FOR EACH OF THE GROUPS OF THE EXPERIMENT

| Group | N of Scores | Trials | | | | | |
|---|---|---|---|---|---|---|---|
| | | 1–10 | 11–20 | 21–30 | 31–40 | 41–50 | 51–60 |
| Control | 320 | | | | | | |
| Mean | | 127.45 | 108.97 | 104.17 | 106.67 | 95.39 | 97.85 |
| S.D. | | 67.92 | 55.91 | 54.23 | 57.04 | 44.52 | 44.25 |
| 8-Trial | 320 | | | | | | |
| Mean | | 116.88 | 113.72 | 97.34 | 101.26 | 93.19 | 93.08 |
| S.D. | | 61.35 | 66.96 | 47.83 | 55.73 | 47.37 | 46.97 |
| 16-Trial | 320 | | | | | | |
| Mean | | 118.08 | 111.86 | 96.80 | 102.14 | 103.37 | 95.13 |
| S.D. | | 60.82 | 65.26 | 51.07 | 53.50 | 44.63 | 50.07 |
| 32-Trial | 320 | | | | | | |
| Mean | | 114.16 | 96.53 | 94.73 | 97.93 | 90.06 | 90.64 |
| S.D. | | 29.85 | 45.90 | 49.03 | 51.58 | 39.08 | 42.57 |
| t-values: | | | | | | | |
| Control–8-Trial | | 2.13* | 1.72 | 3.41* | 1.77 | 0.74 | 2.58* |
| Control–16-Trial | | 1.89* | 1.24 | 1.90* | 1.68 | 1.76 | 2.76* |
| Control–32-Trial | | 1.99* | 3.98* | 3.34* | 2.16* | 1.96* | 2.80* |

* The t-values are given for the differences between average values for control and
experimental groups on each of the ten trials at each learning stage. Starred values are
significant at the .05 level or better.

practice brings about additional improvement in performance throughout
60 trials. The experimental groups which received 8 and 16 trials of pre-
differentiating practice on the preliminary task begin the learning of the
motor task with a lower time score value than that of the control group.
Some improvement in rate of learning as a result of these amounts of preliminary training is shown on subsequent trials, particularly during the
middle stages of the 60-trial practice period. On the whole, though, the
amount of this increase is not remarkably great. The experimental group
which received 32 trials of preliminary training begins the learning of the
motor task at a still lower time score value than those of the other experimental groups. Furthermore, this group continues to exhibit relatively
large amounts of improvement in performance, compared with that of the
control group, continuing until the final stages of practice have been
reached. Thus, it would seem that 8 and 16 trials of pre-differentiating
practice have resulted in a small degree of postive transfer to the motor
task, and that 32 trials of such practice has brought about a considerably
greater degree of transfer. Taking a value of 'total possible improvement'
as the difference between the initial score of the control group and the
best final score made by any of the experimental groups ( cf. 2, Formula 6 )

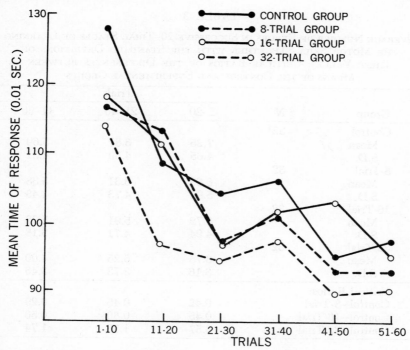

Fig. 1. Mean response time on successive 10-trial stages of learning the final motor task for groups having 0, 8, 16, and 32 trials of preliminary pre-differentiation training.

it may be seen that the 32-trial group had accomplished 84 per cent of the 'total possible improvement' by the end of 20 trials on the motor task, while the control group reached a learning level of only 50 per cent after the same amount of practice on the motor task alone.

Table 2 presents the $t$-values of the differences between the mean time scores of the control and experimental groups during each of the six successive stages of learning. These values have been obtained by computing the standard errors of the differences between the means of each of the 10 trials within each stage, using $N = 10$. Values which are starred indicate significant differences at the .05 level or better in the direction shown by the data. It will be noted that the differences in scores between the control group and the group having 32 trials of preliminary training are significant at this level throughout the course of 60 trials. About half of those of the other two experimental groups also attain this level of significance.

*Errors.* The mean number of errors for three successive stages of motor task learning in each of the four groups of the experiment is given in Table 3, together with the standard deviation of each value. These stand-

## TABLE 3

AVERAGE NUMBER OF ERRORS IN SUCCESSIVE 20–TRIAL STAGES OF LEARNING
THE MOTOR SKILL, TOGETHER WITH THE STANDARD DEVIATIONS OF
THESE VALUES. CRITICAL RATIOS OF THE DIFFERENCES BETWEEN
MEANS OF THE CONTROL AND EXPERIMENTAL GROUPS

| | | Trials | | |
|---|---|---|---|---|
| Group | N | 1–20 | 21–40 | 41–60 |
| Control | 32 | | | |
| Mean | | 7.25 | 6.81 | 5.69 |
| S.D. | | 4.65 | 4.30 | 4.31 |
| 8-Trial | 32 | | | |
| Mean | | 6.69 | 6.31 | 5.38 |
| S.D. | | 5.92 | 4.73 | 4.43 |
| 16-Trial | 32 | | | |
| Mean | | 6.72 | 5.91 | 5.22 |
| S.D. | | 4.94 | 4.71 | 3.18 |
| 32-Trial | 32 | | | |
| Mean | | 3.75 | 5.25 | 4.00 |
| S.D. | | 3.16 | 3.73 | 3.46 |
| Critical Ratios: | | | | |
| Control–8-Trial | | 0.42 | 0.45 | 0.29 |
| Control–16-Trial | | 0.45 | 0.80 | 0.50 |
| Control–32-Trial | | 3.57 | 1.56 | 1.74 |

ard deviations provide a measure of the variability in the total errors occurring during each 20-trial stage. It will be seen that the absolute number
of these errors is not large, and that the variability of the mean values is
high. This was true of the errors obtained in the previous studies (3, 4, 5).

The data of Table 3 are plotted graphically in Fig. 2, which shows the
change in average number of errors as learning proceeds throughout three
20-trial stages. This figure indicates that the groups having 8 and 16 trials
of preliminary training begin the learning of the motor task with an error
score only slightly lower than that of the control group, and continue this
trend throughout the remainder of the 60 trials of practice. The differences between these error scores on any given stage of learning are not
significant. On the other hand, the group having 32 trials of pre-differentiation training begins the learning task with an error score which is considerably below that of the control group and either of the experimental
groups. The difference between the mean values for this group and the
control, at the stage of learning denoted by trials 1–20, is a highly significant one (C.R. = 3.57). Some increase in the number of errors made by
this group occurs during the middle stage of learning, followed again by
a reduction in errors during the final stage of practice on the motor task.
The reduction in the scores of this group from those of the control group

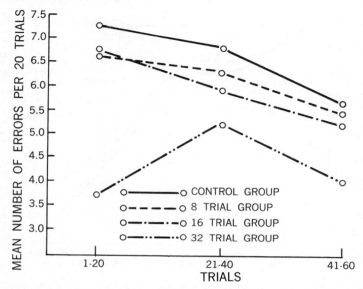

Fig. 2. Average number of errors made during successive 20-trial stages of learning the final motor task for groups having 0, 8, 16, and 32 trials of preliminary pre-differentiation training.

at the stage of learning denoted by trials 41–60 is significant at the five per cent level (C.R. = 1.74).

Fig. 3 shows the effectiveness of different amounts of pre-differentiating training in reducing errors made in the beginning stages of learning the motor task. The transfer effects of such training may be seen by comparing the average number of errors made by each of the groups on the first 20 trials. It is evident that the trend is the same as that previously described: a small, insignificant reduction in errors for the groups given 8 and 16 trials of pre-differentiation, and a considerable reduction in errors, as compared with those of the control group, for the group given 32 trials of pre-differentiating training.

Fig. 3 also shows a comparison of response time scores with the reduction in errors brought about by the different amounts of preliminary practice. The time and error measures are those obtained for each of the groups of the experiment on the first 20 trials of practice on the motor task. The high degree of correspondence between the two measures is apparent.

It will be recalled that the response-time score is the time up to the occurrence of the correct response and is inevitably increased whenever an error is made. Because of this fact, it is of interest to determine to what extent the reduction in time scores in the experimental groups may

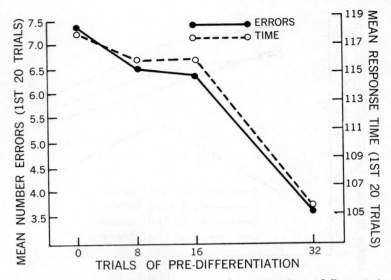

FIG. 3. The relation between number of trials of pre-differentiation training and two measures or performance on the first 20 trials of practice on the final task: (1) mean number of errors per 20 trials, and (2) mean response time per trial.

be directly attributed to the reduction in the number of occasions on which errors occur. In order to make this determination it is necessary first to find a value which can represent the increase in response time which results on any trial on which an error occurs. In the control group, the average response time for all trials on which errors occurred is found to be 188.76 hundredths of a sec.; the average response time for all trials on which no errors occur in 90.58 hundredths of a sec. The difference between these two values, 99.18, may be used as an estimate of the average amount of time taken to make an error in excess of the time taken to make the correct response only. This value may be used to determine the contribution of error reduction to response-time reduction during the first 20 trials of learning. An analysis of our data reveals that the number of error trials during this initial stage of learning is reduced by 7 in the 8-trial experimental group, by 25 in the 16-trial experimental group, and by 75 in the 32-trial experimental group. If the control group had made as few errors as the experimental groups, the total response-time for 20 trials would be reduced by an amount equal to the difference in number of error-trials times the estimated time taken to make an error. The average response time scores, then, would be 116.2, 113.4, and 105.8 hundredths of a second, respectively. The fact to be noted is that these values of estimated time scores correspond closely with the *obtained* values on the first 20 trials for each of the experimental groups, which are respectively 115.3, 114.9, and 105.4 hundredths of a sec. This supports the contention that all of the transfer which occurred following different amounts of preliminary training can be attributed to the reduction in number of error-trials. Consequently, the results indicate not only a high correlation between error reduction and transfer in terms of response time, as Fig. 3 shows, but also lead to the conclusion that the response-time scores were reduced in the final task solely because the number of errors was reduced by the preliminary training.

## DISCUSSION

The results which have been described show that preliminary practice in which the stimuli of a motor task are associated with verbal 'names' has the effect of differentiating these stimuli and consequently reducing both errors and response time for the learning of the motor task. This reduction occurred to an insignificant degree following 8 and 16 trials of preliminary practice, but was found to be significant following 32 trials of preliminary practice. Thus, a considerable amount of positive transfer to the learning of a motor task was found for pre-differentiation training when given in large enough amounts.

In line with the hypothesis previously stated, these results may be viewed as the effect of stimulus pre-differentiation on the generalization tendencies within the task. Presumably, the number of 'incorrect' responses to stimuli provides a measure of the amount of internal generalization within the task. The results seem to indicate that generalization has been progressively reduced with increasing amounts of stimulus pre-differentiation. Evidently the procedure of learning verbal 'names' for each of the stimuli of the task has had the effect of making these stimuli more distinctive, so that when they are used in a motor task, the connections which must be established between them and the required motor responses exhibit a smaller degree of interference with each other.

It may be noted that while small amounts of stimulus pre-differentiation training do not bring about significant reductions in errors, neither do they produce an increase in internal generalization. Such an increase in internal generalization, shown by an initial increase in overt errors, has been found to follow small amounts of training in both verbal and motor tasks (3, 8). The reason that this phenomenon does not appear in this case cannot be determined directly from the data. However, it is possible that in the case of this relatively simple task, eight trials of pre-differentiation plus the amount which may have been provided by the instructions, represents an amount of training which is sufficient to reduce the internal generalization of the task from its maximum point. Thus, the point of maximum generalization may already have been passed in the learning of the group which received eight trials of preliminary practice. However, marked reduction in generalization from the amount existent without training requires more than 16 trials of practice, according to these results.

In general the effect of preliminary training has been to bring about decreased 'confusability' of the stimuli, thereby reducing the number of errors, and, in turn, decreasing the response-time measure. The finding that reduction in response time may be accounted for by error reduction alone confirms the notion that transfer depends upon reduction in internal generalization among the stimuli of the motor task, when, as in our experiment, preliminary training provides no practice on the motor responses of the final task.

It is of some interest to compare the effectiveness of *stimulus* pre-differentiation, produced in this experiment, with the sort of pre-differentiation resulting from practice on a pictured representation of a motor task, used in a previous study (4). In that experiment the subjects practiced a preliminary task composed of pictures of the actual stimuli employed, together with responses which were similar to the responses of the motor task in their directional aspects, though they consisted of making pencil marks rather than pressing switches. It was found that 8 and 16 trials of preliminary practice on the pictured representation brought about a significant amount of positive transfer, while additional trials of preliminary training produced somewhat less marked increases about this amount. The results of the present study contrast with these in that they show only a very small amount of transfer following 8 and 16 trials of stimulus pre-differentiation, and a far greater amount of transfer following 32 trials. Thus, although the results of the two studies cannot be compared quantitatively because of apparatus and subject differences they suggest that an amount of preliminary training of as much as 16 trials on the pictured representation is a much more effective kind of pre-differentiation than is the strictly 'stimulus' pre-differentiation provided in the present experiment.

This comparison of results leads to the conclusion that something more than stimulus pre-differentiation must be involved in the kind of preliminary practice provided in a pictured representation of a motor task. It seems possible that the importance of providing preliminary practice on making responses in the correct directions was not sufficiently emphasized in the discussion of the previous experiment. When the stimuli are differentiated by being paired with verbal responses which do not include this directional aspect, as in the present study, more than 16 trials of preliminary practice appear to be required before significant positive transfer effects occur in the learning of the motor task.

It has been pointed out previously that the learning of motor skills in practical situations often includes preliminary practice, one function of which may be to differentiate the stimuli of the task. The results of this experiment indicate two things concerning the usefulness of such training.

In the first place they show that the procedure of requiring the learner to identify the stimuli of a motor task by name does not have an adverse effect on the subsequent learning of the motor task. Secondly, these results show that if such pre-differentiating practice is carried on systematically throughout a number of trials, it may have a significant positive transfer value for the learning of the motor task. In practical terms, this implies that if a training aid is designed to depend for its effectiveness on the practice it provides in differentiating the stimuli of a motor task, a brief period of such practice is of little value. On the other hand, if a large enough amount of systematic practice in differentiating the stimuli is given, a considerable degree of positive transfer to the subsequent learning of the motor task may be expected.

## SUMMARY

The transfer of training effects of different amounts of preliminary training in 'stimulus pre-differentiation' were measured for a discriminative motor task. Four matched groups of 32 subjects were given respectively 0, 8, 16, and 32 trials of training in which they practiced the association of the letters 'J,' 'V,' 'S,' and 'M' to four different light stimuli on a panel. Following this, time and error scores were obtained for each subject during 60 trials of practice on a motor task in which the identical stimuli were paired with manual responses to four. different switches.

1. The response-time scores in successive sets of 10 trials show that 8 and 16 trials of pre-differentiating practice bring about slightly faster learning of the motor task than shown by the control group (0 trials). However, marked facilitation of learning throughout the 60 trials occurs after 32 trials of preliminary training on stimulus pre-differentiation.

2. The error scores after 8 and 16 trials of pre-differentiating training is slightly and insignificantly reduced from those of the control group. A considerable, and significant, reduction in errors occurs in the group given 32 trials of preliminary practice, the greatest error-reduction occurring during the first 20 trials of learning.

3. The amount of transfer exhibited by the various experimental groups, measured in terms of response-time scores on the first 20 trials of learning, is closely correlated with the amount of error reduction on the same 20 trials. This result is consistent with the hypothesis that training on stimulus pre-differentiation brings about a reduction in the internal generalization of the task, thus reducing the number of incorrect responses and thereby bringing about facilitation of learning.

4. The results indicate that preliminary training which requires the subject to differentiate the stimuli of a motor task by learning their 'names' has a certain degree of effectiveness for transfer to the learning of the

motor task. More than a small amount of such training is apparently required, however, in order for significant degrees of positive transfer to be obtained.

## REFERENCES

1. GAGNÉ, R. M. (1950) The effect of sequence of presentation of similar items on the learning of paired associates. *J. exp. Psychol.*, 40, 61-73.
2. GAGNÉ, R. M., FOSTER, HARRIET, and CROWLEY, MIRIAM E. (1948) The measurement of transfer of training. *Psychol. Bull.*, 45, 97-130.
3. GAGNÉ, R. M. and FOSTER, HARRIET (1949) Transfer of training from practice on components in a motor skill. *J. exp. Psychol.*, 39, 47-68.
4. GAGNÉ, R. M. and FOSTER, HARRIET (1949) Transfer to a motor skill from practice on a picture representation. *J. exp. Psychol.*, 39, 342-355.
5. GAGNÉ, R. M., BAKER, KATHERINE E., and FOSTER, HARRIET. Transfer of discrimination training to a motor task. (To be published)
6. GIBSON, E. J. (1940) A systematic application of the concepts of generalization and differentiation to verbal learning. *Psychol. Rev.*, 47, 196-229.
7. GIBSON, E. J. (1941) Retroactive inhibition as a function of degree of generalization between tasks. *J. exp. Psychol.*, 28, 93-115.
8. GIBSON, E. J. (1942) Intra-list generalization as a factor in verbal learning. *J. exp. Psychol.*, 30, 185-200.

## 35. Sensory Pre-Conditioning

## W. J. Brogden

*Brogden's article was the first to demonstrate the phenomenon of sensory preconditioning, and since this early study, a large number of investigators have set about investigating its parameters.*

### INTRODUCTION

The present investigation was designed to answer the following question: if an organism be given successive experiences of two temporally simultaneous stimuli exciting two sense modalities without evoking any observable response, and if after this contiguous sensory experience, one stimulus be made a conditioned signal for the activity of a given behavior-system by appropriate training, will the other elicit a similar conditioned response without the usual training?

*J. exp. Psychol.*, 1939, 25, 323-332. Reprinted with permission of the author and The American Psychological Association.

Several studies have been reported which bear closely upon this problem. Prokofiev and Zeliony (4) presented human subjects with the sound of a metronome for 10 seconds and immediately afterwards gave a rhythmical pressure on the skin of the fore-arm for an additional 10 seconds. This procedure was followed at intervals of from 3 to 15 minutes, from 5 to 10 times per day for several days. In addition, a whistle was blown for 5 to 10 seconds from time to time. The tactile stimulus was then presented without the metronome and followed by an electric shock to the hand. Within a few trials, reflex retrogression of the arm became conditioned to the tactile stimulus. When this conditioned response had been firmly established, the metronome was now presented alone. Two of the three subjects responded to the metronome with retrogression of the arm. None of the subjects made any response to the whistle. In the same paper, these authors report the following experiment with a dog. Salivation, evoked by the introduction of hydrochloric acid into the mouth, was conditioned to the sound of a metronome. With this conditioned response firmly established, the introduction of acid into the mouth (without the sounding of the metronome) was then followed immediately by an electric shock to the foot, evoking flexion. When this combination had been presented a sufficient number of times to establish firmly conditioned flexion to the introduction of acid into the mouth, the metronome was given. To this stimulus, the animal salivated, but made no foot withdrawal.

Unfortunately, this investigation does not give a complete answer to the question proposed. There was no control over generalization of response. So, it is possible that human subjects conditioned to reflex retrogression of the arm to a tactile stimulus, without any prior experience of the tactile stimulus being associated with the sounding of the metronome, would respond to the sound of the metronome with arm-withdrawal. The long duration of the stimuli might tend to predispose the subject to respond to the stimulus not associated with shock. Furthermore, does response to the stimulus not associated with shock occur because the sound of the metronome functions as the equivalent of the tactile stimulus, or because the subject expects the tactile stimulus to follow the metronome?

Shipley (5) conditioned the eye wink, evoked by a sudden tap on the cheek, to the faint flash of an electric light. The tap on the cheek was now paired with shock to the finger, until it became an effective stimulus for finger-withdrawal. The subsequent presentation of the flash produced sudden withdrawals of the finger in 9 out of 15 subjects. When the tap on the cheek was given alone, then paired with shock, the presentation of the light did not evoke finger-withdrawal in any of 10 subjects. In a second control group the light and tap on the cheek were first associated; then shock to the finger was given alone. One of the 11 subjects in this group responded to the light by finger-flexion. Later, Shipley (6) put two groups of 10 subjects each through an experimental program consisting of two discrete conditioning steps. In the first step the eye wink was conditioned to a buzz and a light with one group; the buzz alone was used with the other group. In the second step, withdrawal of the finger was conditioned to the flash of a light. When the buzz was presented alone, it evoked finger-withdrawal in the subjects of both groups, the percentage of subjects responding being 60 and 70 respectively. Two control groups reveal that finger-withdrawal did not occur at the test point unless the test stimulus was one that had been previously used in one of the two steps in the experiment; and that finger-withdrawal occurred in but a small percentage of subjects when the shock employed in the second step had not been paired with an extra stimulus.

Shipley's experiments do not answer our question, for as in the case of the experiment of Prokofiev and Zeliony, the test-stimulus preceded the stimulus through which the association was made. Light and buzz preceded the tap to the cheek, just as the sound of the metronome preceded the tactile stimulus. Shipley's results are further complicated for an answer to the present problem. Light, buzz, and tap to the cheek all produced a definite motor response, an eye wink. We seek evidence of a relationship between sensory stimuli, evoking no phasic activity.

Our problem is stated specifically as follows: if dogs be given successive stimulations of sound and light in combination contiguously, and if either sound or light be made a conditioned signal for forelimb flexion from an electrically-charged grid, will the stimulus not involved in conditioning evoke flexion without being combined with shock?

## EXPERIMENTAL PROCEDURE

To answer this question, eight mongrel dogs, unselected in any manner, were placed in the stock of a sound-proofed, light-shielded experimental chamber and presented with the sound of a bell and the flash of a light in combination for 2 seconds. The sound was produced by an electric doorbell and the flash of light by a 150 watt unfrosted electric lamp. Twenty such stimulus combinations were given daily for 10 successive days. The eight animals were then arbitrarily divided into two groups of four animals each. Left forelimb flexion, with shock the unconditioned stimulus, was conditioned to bell in one group (group BE). The bell was 2 seconds in duration and was followed immediately by the shock which lasted for $\frac{1}{10}$ of a second. The second group (group LE) was conditioned to light in a similar manner. Conditioning proceeded normally, with 20 trials per day as the test-unit; the conditioned stimulus (either light or bell, as the case might be) evoking flexion with subsequent shock-avoidance more and more frequently. The day after conditioned flexion reached 100 percent (20 shock-avoiding flexion-responses in one test-period), group BE (conditioned to bell) was given 20 trials per day of the light alone, until a score of zero-flexion was reached. Group LE (conditioned to light) was given bell alone until flexion to bell was extinguished to zero. In order to check on generalization, two control groups of four animals each were trained. With one group (group BC), forelimb flexion was conditioned to bell. When 100% flexion to bell was attained, the light was presented alone. With the other group (group LC), forelimb flexion was conditioned to light and when conditioning reached the 100 per cent level, bell was

TABLE 1

RESULTS OBTAINED FROM THE EXPERIMENTAL ANIMALS

The percent scores represent the number of times conditioned flexion occurred to the conditioned stimulus. Twenty stimulus-presentations were given during each test-period.

| Animal | Group BE | | | | Group LE | | | |
|---|---|---|---|---|---|---|---|---|
| | No. 1 | No. 2 | No. 3 | No. 4 | No. 5 | No. 6 | No. 7 | No. 8 |
| Bell and light given in combination for 2 seconds, 20 times per day for 10 days | | | | | | | | |
| | Bell + shock to left forepaw | | | | Light + shock to left forepaw | | | |
| 1 | 10% | 0% | 0% | 15% | 0% | 0% | 10% | 0% |
| 2 | 0% | 0% | 0% | 20% | 0% | 0% | 0% | 15% |
| 3 | 0% | 50% | 0% | 20% | 20% | 35% | 15% | 10% |
| 4 | 35% | 85% | 50% | 30% | 20% | 25% | 0% | 0% |
| 5 | 90% | 85% | 75% | 40% | 75% | 15% | 0% | 0% |
| 6 | 95% | 95% | 90% | 75% | 50% | 20% | 35% | 0% |
| 7 | 95% | 95% | 95% | 85% | 55% | 30% | 70% | 15% |
| 8 | 90% | 95% | 75% | 75% | 65% | 10% | 55% | 10% |
| 9 | 90% | 95% | 95% | 70% | 95% | 55% | 75% | 40% |
| 10 | 100% | 95% | 95% | 80% | 100% | 60% | 90% | 60% |
| 11 | | 100% | 90% | 95% | | 30% | 90% | 75% |
| 12 | | | 95% | 90% | | 65% | 85% | 90% |
| 13 | | | 100% | 95% | | 70% | 100% | 85% |
| 14 | | | | 100% | | 95% | | 90% |
| 15 | | | | | | 90% | | 90% |
| 16 | | | | | | 85% | | 100% |
| 17 | | | | | | 90% | | |
| 18 | | | | | | 100% | | |
| Critical Tests | | | | | | | | |
| | Light alone | | | | Bell alone | | | |
| 1 | 55% | 0% | 15% | 0% | 40% | 25% | 10% | 20% |
| 2 | 30% | | 10% | | 5% | 0% | 0% | 20% |
| 3 | 10% | | 10% | | 5% | | | 45% |
| 4 | 5% | | 0% | | 0% | | | 20% |
| 5 | 0% | | | | | | | 30% |
| 6 | | | | | | | | 25% |
| 7 | | | | | | | | 10% |
| 8 | | | | | | | | 0% |

given alone. Needless to say, neither of these two groups were given the experience of bell and light in combination, prior to the conditioning procedure.

## QUANTITATIVE RESULTS

The conditioning of one of the two stimuli did make the other an effective stimulus for flexion. The four animals in group BE, conditioned to bell, responded to light a total of 27 times in the 11 test-periods required to reach zero-response (Table 1). Animals No. 2 and No. 4 made no response to light. The control animals for this group, group BC, made no response to light in a total of 4 test-periods (Table 2). Group LE, conditioned to light, responded to bell a total of 56 times in the 16 test-periods needed to produce zero-response (Table 1). All of the animals in this group made some response to bell. The control animals for this group, group LC, responded to bell 4 times in 5 test-periods (Table 2). Animal No. 15 alone showed generalization by responding to bell. The experimental animals, grouped together, responded to the stimulus never associated with shock a total of 78 times, whereas the control animals, similarly grouped, responded to the stimulus never associated with shock nor with the conditioned stimulus only 4 times. The mean frequency of response for the experimental group is 9.75 (S.E. = 4.17) and the mean frequency of response for the control group is 0.50 (S.E. = 0.50). The mean difference of 9.25 flexion-responses (S.E. = 4.20 flexion-responses), when subjected to Fisher's test for the significance of differences between small samples, is significant; such a difference could be expected to occur by chance not more than twice in 100 random samples.* The experimental animals required a total of 27 test-periods (a mean of 3.75 test-periods; S.E. = 0.85 test-periods) to reach the zero-response criterion. The control animals required a total of 9 test-periods (a mean of 1.12 test-periods; S.E. = 0.12 test-periods) to reach the same criterion. The mean difference, 2.63 test-periods (S.E. = 0.86 test-periods) in favor of the experimental group, is highly significant. When subjected to Fisher's technique, such a difference could be expected by chance only thrice or less in 1000 samples drawn at random. Therefore, animals given 200 successive experiences of two discrete sensory stimuli in contiguous combination will respond with forelimb flexion to one of them, when the other one *alone* has been made a conditioned stimulus for forelimb flexion by appropriate training with shock. The differences both in frequency and persistence

---

* The ratio of any difference to its own standard error is called *t*. With the *t* value one can enter 'Student's' tables and find the *p* value. When *p* is .02 (which signifies that the difference in question might be expected twice in 100 samples drawn at random from a homogeneous population) or less, the difference is regarded as significant. A complete description of this statistical approach is given by Fisher (2).

## TABLE 2

### Results Obtained from the Control Animals

The percent scores represent the numbers of times conditioned flexion occurred to the conditioned stimulus. Twenty stimulus-presentations were given during each test-period.

| Animal | Group BC | | | | Group LC | | | |
|---|---|---|---|---|---|---|---|---|
| | No. 9 | No. 10 | No. 11 | No. 12 | No. 13 | No. 14 | No. 15 | No. 16 |
| | Bell + shock to left forepaw | | | | Light + shock to left forepaw | | | |
| 1 | 30% | 5% | 10% | 5% | 5% | 0% | 10% | 5% |
| 2 | 40% | 30% | 35% | 30% | 0% | 0% | 10% | 5% |
| 3 | 15% | 80% | 25% | 75% | 10% | 0% | 40% | 0% |
| 4 | 30% | 85% | 65% | 95% | 15% | 0% | 20% | 0% |
| 5 | 30% | 85% | 95% | 85% | 80% | 0% | 5% | 20% |
| 6 | 25% | 40% | 95% | 95% | 60% | 0% | 45% | 20% |
| 7 | 90% | 90% | 90% | 85% | 85% | 0% | 75% | 25% |
| 8 | 90% | 85% | 95% | 95% | 90% | 0% | 80% | 35% |
| 9 | 85% | 90% | 85% | 95% | 75% | 70% | 85% | 65% |
| 10 | 95% | 90% | 100% | 100% | 80% | 75% | 85% | 85% |
| 11 | 95% | 95% | | | 85% | 90% | 95% | 75% |
| 12 | 90% | 100% | | | 100% | 80% | 95% | 75% |
| 13 | 100% | | | | | 90% | 100% | 95% |
| 14 | | | | | | 90% | | 90% |
| 15 | | | | | | 85% | | 100% |
| 16 | | | | | | 85% | | |
| 17 | | | | | | 95% | | |
| 18 | | | | | | 95% | | |
| 19 | | | | | | 95% | | |
| 20 | | | | | | 100% | | |
| | Critical Tests | | | | | | | |
| | Light alone | | | | Bell alone | | | |
| 1 | 0% | 0% | 0% | 0% | 0% | 0% | 20% | 0% |
| | | | | | | | 0% | |

of response to the stimulus never presented with shock are of statistical significance in favor of the experimental animals.

It is apparent that all of the animals of group LE responded to bell in the critical tests whereas only two of the animals of group BE responded to light. Group LE, then, responded a mean of 6.00 (S.E. = 8.94) times more often and a mean of 1.25 test-periods (S.E. = 1.79 test-periods) longer to bell, than the animals of group BE responded to light. These differences, while not significant, both being expected by chance 25 in 100 times, do, however, point to a greater effect from the bell than from the light. This tentative conclusion becomes strengthened when we find that the animals conditioned to light (both experimental and control) required a mean of 60 trials more to attain the 100 percent conditioned response-criterion than did the animals conditioned to bell. This difference is statistically significant and gives evidence of the greater strength of the bell. Furthermore, the bell is rung against a background of silence, while the light, although emitted by an unfrosted 150 watt bulb, appears upon a background of high luminous intensity. The sound differential is thus considerably greater than is the differential in visual brightness. Therefore it is assumed, that because of the disparity in the intensity of the two stimuli, the measures of sensory preconditioning (frequency and persistence of flexion-response) are greater when a test is made with the stronger of the paired stimuli (bell) than with the weaker one (light).

The experience of 200 trials of bell and light did not effect the rate of conditioned response acquisition. The animals of group BE required a mean of 15 more trials to reach 100 percent conditioning than did those of group BC. The animals of group LE required a mean of 15 trials less to reach the 100 percent response-criterion than their controls, group LC. In both cases, the differences are of chance expectancy.

## DISCUSSION

That the flexion-response is elicited by the simulus not associated with shock must be due to an association formed when the bell and the light were presented contiguously, prior to the conditioning of flexion to one of them. For the control animals, which were given identical treatment except for the 200 trials of bell and light in combination, did not respond, or responded very infrequently to the stimulus which had never been presented with shock. Some 'bond' must have been formed between the bell and the light, and some 'trace' of this bond retained. Such a 'bond' and its 'trace' can only be inferred, for the phenomenon observed experimentally is essentially this. Flexion becomes conditioned to a stimulus which has never been associated with shock, the normal procedure which produces this conditioning. This phenomenon is dependent upon two preceding events. First, this stimulus must be presented contiguously with a second stimulus for a number of times. Then, the second stimulus must be combined with shock until forelimb flexion to it has been firmly established. When these two conditions have been fulfilled, the first stimulus when given alone will evoke flexion. Therefore, we infer a sensory conditioning between the bell and light from the behavior observed experimentally, sensory preconditioning.*

It is difficult to make a conjecture as to the nature of the relationship between the bell and the light. It is extremely unlikely that an artificial synæsthesia was produced, for Kelley (3) was unable to develop an arti-

---

* Cason (1) has used the term sensory conditioning to describe the effect of conditioning one of two sensory stimuli upon the judgment of their relative intensities.

ficial chromæsthesia in humans by presenting tones of different pitches simultaneously with lights of various colors. Even under the most favorable conditions for the appearance of chromæsthesia (startle, fatigue, and mescal intoxication), no evidence of a conditioned chromæsthesia was procured. Suffice it to say that since one of the stimuli will elicit flexion, when the other alone has been combined with shock, some relationship must have been established between the two stimuli when they were presented together.

Since sensory pre-conditioning is a phenomenon of phasic activity, it is of importance as a form of behavior-modification. It is a basic principle of psychology that organisms are capable of making responses in the light of past experience. Much of this modification in behavior takes place under circumstances which fit the principles of conditioning. It is likely that in the commonplace environment of any organism, the conditions of the experiment on dogs herein reported will be fulfilled in nature. The experience of two contiguous sensory stimuli completely divorced from any phasic activity is frequent to any organism. If one of these stimuli becomes the signal for the response of a given reaction-pattern, the other will then elicit a similar response.

## CONCLUSIONS

1. Dogs given 200 successive combinations of bell and light will respond with flexion to one of these when the other has been a conditioned stimulus for flexion by appropriate training with shock.

2. The response to the stimulus not associated with shock is due to the prior association of this stimulus with another stimulus, this other stimulus having been made a conditioned stimulus for flexion; for the control animals, which were not given bell and light in combination, did not respond, or responded very infrequently to the stimulus never presented with shock.

3. There is some evidence that the bell is a stronger stimulus than the light, and therefore will elicit flexion more often and for a longer time, once bell and light have been given in combination, and flexion then conditioned to light.

4. The 200 trials of bell and light given in combination before conditioning did not effect the rate of conditioned response acquisition.

## REFERENCES

1. CASON, H. (1936) Sensory conditioning, *J. exper. Psychol.*, 19, 572-591.
2. FISHER, R. A. (1925) Application of 'Student's' distribution, *Metron*, 5, 90-104.

3. KELLEY, E. L. (1934) An experimental attempt to produce artificial chromaesthesia by the technique of the conditioned response. *J. exper. Psychol.*, *17*, 315-341.
4. PROKOFIEV, G. and ZELIONY, G. (1926) Des modes d'associations cerebrales chez l'homme et chex les animaux, *J. de Psychol.*, *23*, 1020-1028.
5. SHIPLEY, W. C. (1933) An apparent transfer of conditioning. *J. gen. Psychol.*, *8*, 382-391.
6. SHIPLEY, W. C. (1935) Indirect conditioning, *J. gen. Psychol.*, *12*, 337-357.

# Retention and Forgetting

I T is difficult to separate learning from retention. Any learning trial reflects that which has been retained from past trials or previous experiences as well as the learning which takes place on that trial. Following Melton (1963) a change from Trial N to N + 1 is considered to represent a change when the variable of interest is the ordinal number of Trial N. A change arising from N to N + 1, on the other hand, is considered to be a retention change when the variable of interest is the interval itself and/or the events which fill this interval.

Can we differentiate retention from forgetting? There is no basic difference between these constructs since retention refers to the amount of material which has been retained by the subject while forgetting refers to the amount which has been lost. One distinction which many have used, however, is that forgetting denotes interest in the characteristics of the environmental events which fill the temporal interval between Trial N and N + 1, whereas retention refers to the examination of those variables which appear to be related to the persistence of material which has been learned.

When we examine the experimental work done in the area of retention, we find two sub-areas of inquiry. One has been to examine retention as a function of many of the variables that have been shown to play a role in learning. For example, an investigator might be interested in determining the role of meaningfulness on retention.

In so doing, he would have two groups of subjects learn meaningful and nonmeaningful material to the same learning criterion, and then sometime later, i.e., 48 hours, would provide a retention test. Primary concern would involve an examination of meaningfulness as it influenced the test for retention. Illustrating this approach is the inclusion in the section of a study by Postman (1962), who examined retention as a function of the degree of overlearning, replicating an earlier study by Krueger (1929).

A second sub-area of retention has been to examine how the subject codes or organizes the material which is being learned so that it is available for subsequent use. Cofer's (1965) article summarizes the findings from a number of experiments in which organizational variables have been investigated.

Let us now turn to the area of forgetting. Some years ago it was believed that all forgetting took place as a result of disuse or simply the elapsing of time between the learning and the test for recall. But McGeoch (1932) rejected this position in a classic paper and proposed that the basic contributor to forgetting was retroactive inhibition. This construct, it will be recalled, refers to the decrement in retention resulting from activity which has been interpolated between the original learning and the test for retention. The experimental design utilized to examine its operation has been as follows:

| Exp. Group: | Learn Task A | Learn Task B | Recall Task A |
| Control: | Learn Task A | Rest | Recall Task A |

What is the nature of the events which contribute to the forgetting of Task A? One factor appears to be the blocking of Task A responses during recall occasioned by competition from Task B responses. Another factor appears to be the unlearning or extinction of Task A responses during the learning of Task B. In the Barnes and Underwood (1959) study which we have included in this section, the nature of this unlearning factor is examined.

But all forgetting cannot be attributed to retroactive inhibition. Events which have taken place prior to the learning of Task A may also provide interference during the subsequent recall of this material. This is the proactive inhibition situation and the experimental design used to examine such effects is as follows:

Exp. Group:   Learn Task B   Learn Task A   Recall Task A
Control:      Rest           Learn Task A   Recall Task A

Although many investigators have held the position that retroactive inhibition makes a greater contribution to forgetting than proactive inhibition, recent evidence indicates that this may not be the case. The selection by Underwood (1957) presents this point of view.

Before the reader embarks on his reading, however, we should like to acquaint him with some methodological considerations, inasmuch as they are as prevalent in the area of retention and forgetting as they are in the area of learning. Two articles of this variety are presented. One is by Bahrick (1964), who discusses the nature of the varying measures of retention and forgetting, while the second is by Peterson and Peterson (1959), who introduce the reader to an interesting retention methodology—that of short term memory.

## REFERENCES

BAHRICK, H. P. (1964) Retention curves: Facts or artifacts? *Psychol. Bull.*, *61*, 188-194.
BARNES, J. M. and UNDERWOOD, B. J. (1959) "Fate" of first-list associations in transfer theory. *J. exp. Psychol.*, *58*, 97-105.
COFER, C. N. (1965) On some factors in the organizational characteristics of free recall. *Amer. Psychologist, 20,* 261-272.
KRUEGER, W. C. F. (1929) The effect of overlearning on retention. *J. exp. Psychol., 12,* 71-78.
McGEOCH, J. A. (1932) Forgetting and the law of disuse. *Psychol. Rev.*, *39*, 352-370.
MELTON, A. W. (1963) Implications of short-term memory for a general theory of memory. *J. verb. Learn. and verb. Behav., 2,* 1-21.
PETERSON, L. R. and PETERSON, M. J. (1959) Short term retention of individual verbal items. *J. exp. Psychol., 58,* 193-198.
POSTMAN, L. (1962) Retention as a function of degree of overlearning. *Science, 135,* 666-667.
UNDERWOOD, B. J. (1957) Interference and forgetting. *Psychol. Rev., 64,* 49-90.

# 36.   Retention Curves: Facts or Artifacts?

## H. P. Bahrick

*Retention curves are frequently plotted with the abscissa measuring varying amounts of time between the last learning trial and the test for retention. Response measurement has been usually confined to either a recall or recognition method, although other measures may sometimes be used. This selection by Bahrick indicates some problems with the traditional methods of comparing retention measures.*

Ambiguity regarding the interrelations among commonly used response indicants creates serious methodological as well as theoretical problems. If these interrelations are not well understood, overgeneralizations and misinterpretations of experimental findings are unavoidable (Bahrick, Fitts, & Briggs, 1957). The classic study establishing the interrelations among measures of retention was performed by Luh (1922). Postman and Rau (1957) recognized certain inadequacies of Luh's method. They collected extensive new data and thoroughly reviewed the literature on this topic. One of the principal differences between the findings of Luh and of Postman and Rau pertains to the curves based upon recognition measures. Postman and Rau found practically no decline of recognition scores over a 2-day period when subjects originally learned the material to a criterion of one perfect anticipation trial. They report: "For all practical purposes the method of recognition shows no forgetting at all during the time interval used in the present study [Postman & Rau, 1957, p. 291]." They suggest that the decline of recognition performance over the same period reported by Luh was the result of methodological errors of interpolating tests of reproduction, as well as other uncontrolled interference effects which tended to lower subsequent performance on recognition tests. In regard to the interrelation between indicants of recall and recognition Postman and Rau (1957) concluded: "The one fact for which there is substantial experimental evidence is that tests of recognition yield higher scores than do tests of recall [p. 218]." This conclusion has extensive documentation (e.g., Achilles, 1920; Clarke, 1934; Hollingworth, 1913; Miler, 1957; Myers, 1914; Stalnaker, 1935). No comparable support exists for Postman and Rau's finding that recognition shows no retention

*Psychol. Bull.*, 1964, *61*, 188-194. Reprinted with permission of the author and The American Psychological Association. This research was supported by United States Public Health Service Grant MH-05685-02. The writer wishes to thank Louis Herman for his many helpful comments.

loss at all over a 2-day period, but it is generally held that recognition curves show a more gentle slope and do not exhibit the negative acceleration observed in the classical recall and anticipation retention curves (Luh, 1922; Miler, 1957).

It is the principal purpose of this article to show that both of the above conclusions regarding the superiority of recognition to recall performance, and regarding the slope of retention curves are overgeneralizations, and therefore misleading, because the findings on which they are based do not represent intrinsic differences between indicants of recognition and recall. Rather, the findings reflect the exclusive use of experimental designs which fail to control the variable of overlearning, the exclusive use of "easy" recognition tests in which correct and incorrect alternatives are highly differentiated, and artifacts arising from the use of dichotomous scoring procedures.

## EXPERIMENTAL DESIGNS AND OVERLEARNING

In most studies of retention, stimulus material, rather than retention measures per se, have been the subject of investigation. Two general types of experimental design are conventionally used when retention of different stimulus material is investigated: (a) an equal amount of training is given to subjects in the various conditions to be compared and (b) subjects are trained to a comparable criterion under the various conditions. To illustrate the advantage of using both types of design let us suppose it is desired to compare retention for nonsense syllables high and low in association value. Following Design a an equal number of training trials is administered to the groups learning the two kinds of material, and retention is tested after suitable intervals. Following Design b the two groups are trained until they reach a comparable response criterion, such as the first trial on which all responses are correct. If only Design a is used, and it is found that retention is better for the syllables high in association value, it is not possible to determine if this is true just because the material is "easier," and was therefore learned to a higher degree. By supplementing this comparison with data from Design b one can determine whether the high association value affected retention, independent of the degree of original learning.

Investigations in which comparisons of retention measures rather than of stimulus material are the subject of interest have made use of two variations of Design a, but have failed to supplement this with information from Design b. In the traditional version of Design a investigators have given all subjects a constant number of training trials and have later compared performance on recognition and recall tests. In the second version all subjects are trained to the same criterion, usually the first trial of correct anticipation, followed by the comparison between recall and recognition performance on later retention tests. At first blush it would appear that this second version corresponds exactly to the design of Type *b*, and should therefore yield the same kind of information, but this is not so.

To compare retention measures by Design *b*, subjects of various groups must be trained until they have reached a comparable criterion on the *same* task on which retention is tested later. This, of course, entails administering different numbers of training trials for the various groups, similar to the case described earlier in which different numbers of training trials were administered to the groups learning nonsense syllables high or low in association value. In the second version of Design *a* described above, the subjects in the recall and recognition groups receive *equal* amounts of training, and are not brought to a comparable criterion on the recognition and recall tasks on which retention is later measured. Thus, the degree of original learning with respect to the condition being tested during retention has not been controlled. As a consequence this type of study does not yield the information usually available from designs of Type *b*, and as a matter of fact, does not add much to the information already available from the traditional version of Design *a*.

To compare retention for recall and recognition by Design *b*, it is necessary to train one group of subjects until all of their recall responses are correct, and another group of subjects until all of their recognition responses are correct. The general conclusion that tests of recognition yield higher scores than do tests of recall has not been based upon any such comparison and is, therefore, limited to situations in which the degree of original training is not comparable. Because investigators have used only those recognition tests in which correct and incorrect alternatives were highly differentiated, the degree of learning with respect to the recognition task was generally much higher than the degree of learning with respect to the recall task when training was interrupted. The better performance on later retention tests, as well as the difference in slope of the retention curves based upon recall and recognition measures, reflects this difference in the degree of original learning. Thus, Postman, Jenkins, and Postman (1948) reported that after six trials of exposure to 48 nonsense syllables subjects were immediately able to make an average of 24.33 correct recognition responses, but only 7.20 correct recall responses if the recall test was administered first. They reported 27.66 and 9.09 correct responses, respectively, if the recognition test as taken first. Similarly, Achilles (1920) reported that subjects who were given 50 seconds to study a list of 25 nonsense syllables were immediately able to recall an average of only 12% of the list, but correctly recognized 42%. Hollingworth (1913) found that the number of trials needed to reach the threshold of recall was larger than the number of trials needed to reach the recognition threshold, and the ratio between the two was larger for meaningful than for meaningless material. Such data have led Andreas (1960, p. 447), Miler (1957), and others to conceptualize a hypothetical threshold of recognition which is lower than a hypothetical threshold of recall, so that the strength of a given memory trace may be below the recall threshold, but above the recognition threshold.

It has long been known (Ebbinghaus, 1913) that material which is overlearned will be retained better, or, more precisely, that indicants of retention are not sensitive to early retention losses if the material has been overlearned with respect to the threshold of that indicant. Thus, when material has been sufficiently overlearned with respect to the recall criterion, recall scores may continue for long periods of time near the 100% correct level. We cannot demonstrate a classical retention curve by the recall measure for the words in the Lord's Prayer or the National Anthem for most adult Americans. A somewhat analogous situation may occur when performance on easy recognition tests shows little or no decline for several days after associations have been learned to the threshold of anticipation. This does not serve as a valid basis for contending, however, that recognition measures, per se, do not yield classical, that is, negatively accelerated, retention curves. The effect of the variable of overlearning upon the slope of recognition curves is apparent if we examine results from those investigations in which the degree of overlearning was more limited.

Luh also trained subjects to lesser criteria, such as 67% and 33% of the trials needed for the threshold of anticipation. He obtained recognition curves which showed significantly more loss during the early postlearning interval.

Strong (1913) reported a negatively accelerated curve for recognition scores in a situation in which training seems to have interrupted near the threshold of recognition. His data also tend to support the present view that failure to obtain substantial decline of recognition scores in the immediate postlearning interval is a result of overlearning. A more precise interpretation of his curves is difficult, however, because training was not interrupted precisely at the threshold of recognition, and because additional variables were introduced by requiring his subjects to indicate various degrees of confidence concerning their recognition responses. The negatively accelerated curve was obtained for the responses made with the greatest degree of confidence.

The generally accepted conclusion that performance on recognition tests is less affected by retroactive inhibition than performance on recall tests (Britt, 1935; Hollingworth, 1913; Postman & Rau, 1957) is also limited by the above considerations. Overlearning makes material less vulnerable to interference effects, and therefore needs to be controlled for a valid comparison of such effects. The studies on which such comparisons are based have generally employed common rather than comparable criteria of original learning for the recall and recognition groups (Postman, 1952).

## EASY OR DIFFICULT RECOGNITION TESTS

In discussing recognition measures Deese (1958) pointed out that the recognition scores depend upon various artifacts of testing: "The probability of a correct selection on the part of the S is at the mercy of the particular choices he has to make [p. 240]." Similarly, Underwood (1949) pointed out:

> If we required S to learn a list of adjectives and then place the adjectives among a group of nonsense syllables, S would probably show very small loss in retention. Obviously the similarity of the test material to the other material is an important variable which determines the recognition score [p. 512].

Everyone who has given multiple-choice tests of recognition in academic courses knows that one can manipulate the difficulty level of an item simply by varying the incorrect alternatives. The effect of degree of differentiation among correct and incorrect alternatives upon the threshold of recognition and upon recognition retention curves has not been investigated systematically, but relevant data were reported by Lehmann (1888-89). He showed that net recognition scores for identification of gray colors declined from 87% correct to 17% correct as the wrong stimuli presented to S became more similar to the correct ones. Similarly, Seward (1928) showed that frequency, speed, and confidence of correct recognition responses depended upon the similarity of incorrect to correct items. Postman, Jenkins, and Postman (1948) showed that when one of the alternatives offered on a recognition test is more similar to the correct alternative, it receives a disproportionate share of the error choices. These data suggest that the number of trials needed to reach the threshold of a recognition test may be increased by increasing the similarity among the right and wrong alternatives of the test. Verbal material offers limited opportunities for manipulating the variable of similarity among responses along a continuum. Other symbolic material presents better opportunities for this and is therefore more suitable for an investigation of this variable. In a study comparing retention curves for recall and recognition measures (Bahrick & Bahrick, in press), differentiation among the correct and incorrect stimuli and responses in a paired-associates learning task was varied. The paired-associate method of presentation was used during training. Stimulus material consisted of 8 × 8 matrices in which 1 of the 64 cells was colored black, the remainder left blank. The responses to be matched with the stimuli were randomly chosen 3-digit numbers. One group of subjects was trained to the threshold of anticipation, that is, the first trial on which they correctly listed the 3-digit numbers paired with each of the matrices. The other two groups were trained, respectively, to an easy and to a difficult recognition threshold, as determined by two different recognition tests. In both the easy and the difficult recognition tests subjects were required to identify the correct matrix (stimulus) among five matrices presented in one row of the test blank, and to identify the associated number among five 3-digit numbers in the same row. In the easy recognition test the four wrong matrices differed from the correct one in that the stimulus position was displaced by a distance of three cells; in the difficult recognition test the displacement was only one cell removed. Similarly, the easy recognition test provided incorrect response numbers which shared none of the 3 digits with the correct number, whereas the alternative response numbers for the difficult test shared 2 out of 3 digits with the correct number. The recognition tests were administered during each 130-second intertrial interval. The same intertrial interval was used for the anticipation group, but this group took no recognition tests during the intervals. The mean number of trials required to reach the easy recognition threshold was 8.0, the anticipation threshold 9.3, the difficult recognition threshold 11.5. The group differences were significant ($p < .01$). The data thus provided an instance in which a threshold of recognition lies above the threshold of anticipation for the same material.

In the Bahrick and Bahrick study retention was measured after 2 hours, 2 days, or 2 weeks by the same method used during the training of each group. All three groups showed negatively accelerated retention curves, and the percentage correctly retained by the Anticipation group was lower than for the Easy Recognition group, but higher than for the Difficult Recognition group. This was true for all three time intervals.

This study clearly showed that thresholds for anticipation are not necessarily higher than for recognition, and the results suggest that differences in the slopes of retention curves are determined by overlearning with respect to the threshold level, rather than by the retention measurement per se. The following examination of artifacts produced by dichotomous scoring procedures makes this even more apparent.

## CHANGING SENSITIVITY OF DICHOTOMOUS SCORES

It has been demonstrated that the slope of learning curves based upon dichotomous scores is a predictable artifact of the changing sensitivity of the indicants at different stages of training (Bahrick et al., 1957). The slopes of such curves therefore can not provide a valid index of relative amounts of learning at different stages of training. An analogous situation exists with respect to retention curves. Measures of anticipation, recall, and recognition are dichotomous indicants in that they tell us only which associations are above and which are below the threshold reflected by the response measure. A subject either recalls a nonsense syllable or he does not recall it. No further differentiation of associative strength is obtained with a recall score. The same is true for indicants of anticipation and recognition, though the particular threshold dividing correct from incorrect responses may be different for each of these indicants, and in the case of recognition scores will depend upon the difficulty of the differentiation required by a particular test. The sensitivity of each of these measures to losses of associative strength changes in time. When material has been greatly overlearned with respect to a given measure, so that most of the associations are far above threshold strength, the measure is insensitive. This means that the strength of the associations may weaken considerably in time, but the slope of the curve based upon this measure will not show it because only a few of the originally weakest associations will be weakened sufficiently to pass below the threshold. The slope of the curve does not directly reflect the *amount* by which associations are weakened in time. The slope of the curve simply reflects the number of associations passing below the threshold per unit of time. Assuming greatest frequency for associations which are originally of medium strength, the measure will become more sensitive as time passes and these associations are further weakened. Still later, when the bulk of the distribution has already passed below the threshold, the measure again loses sensitivity, and the curve flattens out. If the anticipation and recognition thresholds for a particular task are widely separated, the time periods of maximal sensitivity for the respective curves will differ greatly, and as a consequence the slopes of the respective curves during a given time period will be very different. This has been commonly observed and has led to the mistaken conclusion that recognition measures yield curves which differ, per se, from those obtained by means of free recall or anticipation measures. If threshold level and the degree of learning with respect to the threshold are comparable, however, as is the case for the data reported by Bahrick and Bahrick, the slopes of the resulting anticipation and recognition curves are comparable also.

Retention curves based upon anticipation, recognition, or free recall reflect the changing sensitivity of dichotomous measures. No general conclusions regarding relative amounts of forgetting at different periods of time are permissible on the basis of such a curve. Such conclusions are valid only if they are based upon equal-interval scales. A dichotomous measure based upon a low threshold might show maximal forgetting over a time period during which the curve based upon a higher threshold has already approached an asymptote of zero.

A completely comparable analysis has been made for learning curves based upon time-on-target scores and other dichotomous indicants (Bahrick et al., 1957). The slopes of these curves should be predicted with good precision because evidence was available regarding empirical (near normal) error-amplitude distributions. The distribution of the strength of associations is not precisely known for any stage of forgetting, but it is probably not normal if learning is terminated on the first trial on which all associations are above threshold strength. Precise prediction of the slopes of retention curves based upon dichotomous measures will have to wait until empirical distributions of associative strengths reflecting inter- and intra-individual differences are obtained for various types of material and for different degrees of original learning.

It would follow from the preceding analysis, however, that the degree of homogeneity, as reflected by the combined inter- and intraindividual variance of the strength of various associations in a list, would partly determine the slope of retention curves based upon dichotomous indicants. The greater the variance, the fewer associations would pass through the threshold per unit of time, and thus the less steep the slope of the retention curve. Conversely, if all associations in a list had exactly the same strength, that is, if the variance were zero, a step-function drop from 100% to 0% retention would be predicted for a curve of an individual subject regardless of the rate at which associations are actually weakened in time. The time of this drop would of course depend upon the height of the particular threshold.

The strength of various associations within a list does not necessarily weaken equally in time. Rather, inter- and intraindividual variance may change as a function of differential interference processes, and in this way bring about curves of different slope for material of varying length, similarity, and meaningfulness. The interpretation of these curves, however, must take into account the scoring artifacts which have been discussed. This analysis cannot be directly applied to curves based upon savings scores, the only nondichotomous indicants of retention.

## REFERENCES

ACHILLES, E. M. (1920) Experimental studies in recall and recognition. *Arch. Psychol.*, 6, No. 44.

ANDREAS, B. G. (1960) *Experimental psychology.* New York: Wiley.

BAHRICK, H. P. and BAHRICK, P. O. A re-examination of interrelations among measures of retention. *Quart. J. exp. Psychol.*, in press.

BAHRICK, H. P., FITTS, P. M., and BRIGGS, G. E. (1957) Learning curves: Facts or artifacts? *Psychol. Bull.*, 54, 256-268.

BRITT, S. H. (1935) Retroactive inhibition: A review of the literature. *Psychol. Bull.*, 32, 381-440.

CLARKE, H. M. (1934) Recall and recognition for faces and names. *J. appl. Psychol.*, 18, 757-763.

DEESE, J. (1958) *The psychology of learning.* New York: McGraw-Hill.

EBBINGHAUS, H. (1913) *Memory: A contribution to experimental psychology*. (Trans. by H. A. Ruger and C. E. Bussenius.) New York: Teachers College, Columbia University.

HOLLINGWORTH, H. L. (1913) Characteristic difference between recall and recognition. *Amer. J. Psychol.*, *24*, 533-544.

LEHMANN, A. (1888-89) Ueber Wiedererkennen. [Concerning recognition.] *Phil. Stud. (Wundt)*, *5*, 96-156.

LUH, C. W. (1922) The conditions of retention. *Psychol. Monogr.*, *31* (3, Whole No. 142).

MILER, ADRIENNE (1957) Vergleich der Vergessenskurven für Reproduzieren und Wiedererkennen von sinnlosem Material. [Comparing retention curves for recall and recognition of meaningless material.] *Z. exp. angew. Psychol.*, *7*, 29-38.

MYERS, G. C. (1914) A comparative study of recognition and recall. *Psychol. Rev.*, *21*, 442-456.

POSTMAN, L. (1952) Retroactive inhibition in recall and recognition. *J. exp. Psychol.*, *44*, 165-169.

POSTMAN, L. and RAU, L. (1957) Retention as a function of the method of measurement. *U. Calif. Publ. Psychol.*, *8*, 217-270.

POSTMAN, L., JENKINS, W. O., and POSTMAN, D. L. (1948) An experimental comparison of active recall and recognition. *Amer. J. Psychol.*, *61*, 511-520.

SEWARD, G. H. (1928) Recognition time as a measure of confidence. *Arch. Psychol.*, *N.Y.*, No. 99.

STALNAKER, J. M. (1935) Recognition and recall in a vocabulary test. *J. gen. Psychol.*, *46*, 463-464.

STRONG, E. K. (1913) The effect of time-interval upon recognition memory. *Psychol. Rev.*, *20*, 339-372.

UNDERWOOD, B. J. (1949) *Experimental psychology*. New York: Appleton-Century-Crofts.

## 37.   Short-Term Retention of Individual Verbal Items

## L. R. Peterson and M. J. Peterson

*In the measurement of retention, it has been a common practice to separate the final learning or criterion trial from the test for retention with intervals measured in days or minutes. The Peterson and Peterson article is unusual in that retention was measured over an interval of seconds. It is interesting to note that this methodology has been responsible for opening a new and exciting research area—short-term memory.*

It is apparent that the acquisition of verbal habits depends on the effects of a given occasion being carried over into later repetitions of the situation. Nevertheless, textbooks separate acquisition and retention into distinct categories. The limitation of discussions of retention to long-term characteristics is necessary in large part by the scarcity of data on the course of retention over intervals of the order of magnitude of the time elapsing between successive repetitions in an acquisition study. The presence of a retentive function within the acquisition process was postulated by Hull (1940) in his use of the stimulus trace to explain serial phenomena. Again, Underwood (1949) has suggested that forgetting occurs during the acquisition process. But these theoretical considerations have not led to empirical investigation. Hull (1952) quantified the stimulus trace on data concerned with the CS-UCS interval in eyelid conditioning and it is not obvious that the construct so quantified can be readily transferred to verbal learning. One objection is that a verbal stimulus produces a strong predictable response prior to the experimental session and this is not true of the originally neutral stimulus in eyelid conditioning.

Two studies have shown that the effects of verbal stimulation can decrease over intervals measured in seconds. Pillsbury and Sylvester (1940) found marked decrement with a list of items tested for recall 10 sec. after a single presentation. However, it seems unlikely that this traditional presentation of a list and later testing for recall of the list will be useful in studying intervals near or shorter than the time necessary to present the list. Of more interest is a recent study by Brown (1958) in which among other conditions a single pair of consonants was tested after a 5-sec. inter-

*J. exp. Psychol.*, 1959, 58, 193-198. Reprinted with permission of the senior author and The American Psychological Association. The initial stages of this investigation were facilitated by National Science Foundation Grant G-2596.

val. Decrement was found at the one recall interval, but no systematic study of the course of retention over a variety of intervals was attempted.

## EXPERIMENT I

The present investigation tests recall for individual items after several short intervals. An item is presented and tested without related items intervening. The initial study examines the course of retention after one brief presentation of the item.

### METHOD

*Subjects.* The Ss were 24 students from introductory psychology courses at Indiana University. Participation in experiments was a course requirement.

*Materials.* The verbal items tested for recall were 48 consonant syllables with Witmer association value no greater than 33% (Hilgard, 1951). Other materials were 48 three-digit numbers obtained from a table of random numbers. One of these was given to S after each presentation under instructions to count backward from the number. It was considered that continuous verbal activity during the time between presentation and signal for recall was desirable in order to minimize rehearsal behavior. The materials were selected to be categorically dissimilar and hence involve a minimum of interference.

*Procedure.* The S was seated at a table with E seated facing in the same direction on S's right. A black plywood screen shielded E from S. On the table in front of S were two small lights mounted on a black box. The general procedure was for E to spell a consonant syllable and immediately speak a three-digit number. The S then counted backward by three or four from this number. On flashing of a signal light S attempted to recall the consonant syllable. The E spoke in rhythm with a metronome clicking twice per second and S was instructed to do likewise. The timing of these events is diagrammed in Fig. 1. As E spoke the third digit, he pressed a button activating a Hunter interval timer. At the end of a preset interval the timer activated a red light and an electric clock. The light was the signal for recall. The clock ran until E heard S speak three letters, when E stopped the clock by depressing a key. This time between onset of the light and completion of a response will be referred to as a latency. It is to be distinguished from the interval from completion of the syllable E to onset of the light, which will be referred to as the recall interval.

The instructions read to S were as follows: "Please sit against the back of your chair so that you are comfortable. You will not be shocked during this experiment. In front of you is a little black box. The top or green

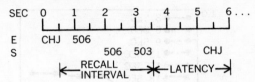

FIG. 1. Sequence of events for a recall interval of 3 sec.

light is on now. This green light means that we are ready to begin a trial. I will speak some letters and then a number. You are to repeat the number immediately after I say it and begin counting backwards by 3's (4's) from that number in time with the ticking that you hear. I might say, ABC 309. Then you say, 309, 306, 303, etc., until the bottom or red light comes on. When you see this red light come on, stop counting immediately and say the letters that were given at the beginning of the trial. Remember to keep your eyes on the black box at all times. There will be a short rest period and then the green light will come on again and we will start a new trial." The E summarized what he had already said and then gave S two practice trials. During this practice S was corrected if he hesitated before starting to count, or if he failed to stop counting on signal, or if he in any other way deviated from the instructions.

Each S was tested eight times at each of the recall intervals, 3, 6, 9, 12, 15, and 18 sec. A given consonant syllable was used only once with each S. Each syllable occurred equally often over the group at each recall interval. A specific recall interval was represented once in each successive block of six presentations. The S counted backward by three on half of the trials and by four on the remaining trials. No two successive items contained letters in common. The time between signal for recall and the start of the next presentation was 15 sec.

RESULTS AND DISCUSSION

Responses occurring any time during the 15-sec. interval following signal for recall were recorded. In Fig. 2 are plotted the proportions of correct recalls as cumulative functions of latency for each of the recall intervals. Sign tests were used to evaluate differences among the curves (Walker & Lev, 1953). At each latency differences among the 3-, 6-, 9-, and 18-sec. recall interval curves are significant at the .05 level. For latencies of 6 sec. and longer these differences are all significant at the .01 level. Note that the number correct with latency less than 2 sec. does not constitute a majority of the total correct. These responses would not seem appropriately described as identification of the gradually weakening trace of a stimulus. There is a suggestion of an oscillatory characteristic in the events determining them.

The feasibility of an interpretation by a statistical model was explored

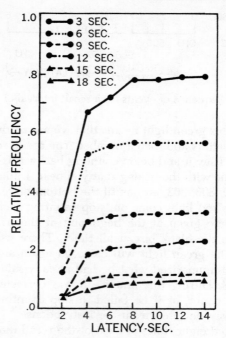

FIG. 2. Correct recalls as cumulative functions of latency.

by fitting to the data the exponential curve of Fig. 3. The empirical points plotted here are proportions of correct responses with latencies shorter than 2.83 sec. Partition of the correct responses on the basis of latency is required by considerations developed in detail by Estes (1950). A given probability of response applies to an interval of time equal in length to the average time required for the response under consideration to occur. The mean latency of correct responses in the present experiment was 2.83 sec. Differences among the proportions of correct responses with latencies shorter than 2.83 sec. were evaluated by sign tests. The difference between the 3- and 18-sec. conditions was found to be significant at the .01 level. All differences among the 3-, 6-, 9-, 12-, and 18-sec. conditions were significant at the .05 level.

The general equation of which the expression for the curve of Fig. 3 is a specific instance is derived from the stimulus fluctuation model developed by Estes (1955). In applying the model to the present experiment it is assumed that the verbal stimulus produces a response in S which is conditioned to a set of elements contiguous with the response. The elements thus conditioned are a sample of a larger population of elements into which the conditioned elements disperse as time passes. The proportion of conditioned elements in the sample determining S's behavior thus de-

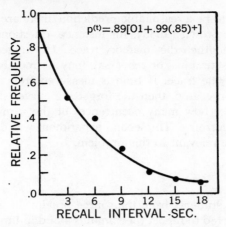

Fig. 3. Correct recalls with latencies below 2.83 sec. as a function of recall interval.

creases and with it the probability of the response. Since the fitted curve appears to do justice to the data, the observed decrement could arise from stimulus fluctuation.

The independence of successive presentations might be questioned in the light of findings that performance deteriorates as a function of previous learning (Underwood, 1957). The presence of proactive interference was tested by noting the correct responses within each successive block of 12 presentations. The short recall intervals were analyzed separately from the long recall intervals in view of the possibility that facilitation might occur with the one and interference with the other. The proportions of correct responses for the combined 3- and 6-sec. recall intervals were in order of occurrence .57, .66, .70, and .74. A sign test showed the difference between the first and last blocks to be significant at the .02 level. The proportions correct for the 15- and 18-sec. recall intervals were .08, .15, .09, and .12. The gain from first to last blocks is not significant in this case. There is no evidence for proactive interference. There is an indication of improvement with practice.

## EXPERIMENT II

The findings in Exp. I are compatible with the proposition that the after-effects of a single, brief, verbal stimulation can be interpreted as those of a trial of learning. It would be predicted from such an interpretation that probability of recall at a given recall interval should increase as a function of repetitions of the stimulation. Forgetting should proceed at differential rates for items with differing numbers of repetitions. Although this seems to be a reasonable prediction, there are those who would predict otherwise. Brown (1958), for instance, questions whether repetitions, as such, strengthen the "memory trace." He suggests that the effect of repetitions of a stimulus, or rehearsal, may be merely to postpone the onset of decay of the trace. If time is measured from the moment that the last stimulation ceased, then the forgetting curves should coincide in all cases, no matter how many occurrences of the stimulation have preceded the final occurrence. The second experiment was designed to obtain empirical evidence relevant to this problem.

### METHOD

The Ss were 48 students from the source previously described. Half of the Ss were instructed to repeat the stimulus aloud in time with the metronome until stopped by E giving them a number from which S counted backward. The remaining Ss were not given instructions concerning use of the interval between E's presentation of the stimulus and his speaking the number from which to count backward. Both the "vocal" group and the "silent" group had equated intervals of time during which rehearsal inevitably occurred in the one case and could occur in the other case. Differences in frequency of recalls between the groups would indicate a failure of the uninstructed Ss to rehearse. The zero point marking the beginning of the recall interval for the silent group was set at the point at which E spoke the number from which S counted backward. This was also true for the vocal group.

The length of the rehearsal period was varied for Ss of both groups over three conditions. On a third of the presentations S was not given time for any repetitions. This condition was thus comparable to Exp. I, save that the only recall intervals used were 3, 9, and 18 sec. On another third of the presentations 1 sec. elapsed during which S could repeat the stimulus. On another third of the presentations 3 sec. elapsed, or sufficient time for three repetitions. Consonant syllables were varied as to the rehearsal interval in which they were used, so that each syllable occurred equally often in each condition over the group. However, a given syllable was never presented more than once to any S. The Ss were assigned in order of appearance to a randomized list of conditions. Six practice presentations were given during which corrections were made of departures from instructions. Other details follow the procedures of Exp. I.

### RESULTS AND DISCUSSION

Table 1 shows the proportion of items recalled correctly. In the vocal group recall improved with repetition at each of the recall intervals tested. Conditions in the silent group were not consistently ordered. For purposes

## TABLE 1

PROPORTIONS OF ITEMS CORRECTLY RECALLED IN EXP. II

| Group | Repetition Time (Sec.) | Recall Interval (Sec.) | | |
|---|---|---|---|---|
| | | 3 | 9 | 18 |
| Vocal | 3 | .80 | .48 | .34 |
| | 1 | .68 | .34 | .21 |
| | 0 | .60 | .25 | .14 |
| Silent | 3 | .70 | .39 | .30 |
| | 1 | .74 | .35 | .22 |
| | 0 | .72 | .38 | .15 |

of statistical analysis the recall intervals were combined within each group. A sign test between numbers correct in the 0- and 3-repetition conditions of the vocal group showed the difference to be significant at the .01 level. The difference between the corresponding conditions of the silent group was not significant at the .05 level. Only under conditions where repetition of the stimulus was controlled by instructions did retention improve.

The obtained differences among the zero conditions of Exp. II and the 3-, 9-, and 18-sec. recall intervals of Exp. I require some comment, since procedures were essentially the same. Since these are between-S comparisons, some differences would be predicted because of sampling variability. But another factor is probably involved. There were 48 presentations in Exp. I and only 36 in Exp. II. Since recall was found to improve over successive blocks of trials, a superiority in recall for Ss of Exp. I is reasonable. In the case of differences between the vocal and silent groups of Exp. II a statistical test is permissible, for Ss were assigned randomly to the two groups. Wilcoxon's (1949) test for unpaired replicates, as well as a t test, was used. Neither showed significance at the .05 level.

The 1- and 3-repetition conditions of the vocal group afforded an opportunity to obtain a measure of what recall would be at the zero interval in time. It was noted whether a syllable had been correctly repeated by S. Proportions correctly repeated were .90 for the 1-repetition condition and .88 for the 3-repetition condition. The chief source of error lay in the confusion of the letters "m" and "n." This source of error is not confounded with the repetition variable, for it is S who repeats and thus perpetuates his error. Further, individual items were balanced over the three conditions. There is no suggestion of any difference in responding among the repetition conditions at the beginning of the recall interval. These differences developed during the time that S was engaged in counting backward. A differential rate of forgetting seems indisputable.

The factors underlying the improvement in retention with repetition were investigated by means of an analysis of the status of elements within the individual items. The individual consonant syllable, like the nonsense

TABLE 2

Dependent Probabilities of a Letter Being Correctly Recalled in the
Vocal Group When the Preceding Letter was Correct

| Repetition | Recall Interval (Sec.) | | |
|---|---|---|---|
| Time (Sec.) | 3 | 9 | 18 |
| 3 | .96 | .85 | .72 |
| 1 | .90 | .72 | .57 |
| 0 | .86 | .64 | .56 |

syllable, may be regarded as presenting S with a serial learning task.
Through repetitions unrelated components may develop serial dependencies until in the manner of familiar words they have become single units.
The improved retention might then be attributed to increases in these
serial dependencies. The analysis proceeded by ascertaining the dependent
probabilities that letters would be correct given the event that the previous letter was correct. These dependent probabilities are listed in Table 2.
It is clear that with increasing repetitions the serial dependencies increase. Again combining recall intervals, a sign test between the zero condition is significant at the .01 level.

Learning is seen to take place within the items. But this finding does
not eliminate the possibility that another kind of learning is proceeding
concurrently. If only the correct occurrences of the first letters of syllables
are considered, changes in retention apart from the serial dependencies
can be assessed. The proportions of first letters recalled correctly for the
0-, 1-, and 3-repetition conditions were .60, .65, and .72, respectively. A
sign test between the 0- and 3-repetition conditions was significant at
the .05 level. It may tentatively be concluded that learning of a second
kind took place.

The course of short-term verbal retention is seen to be related to learning processes. It would not appear to be strictly accurate to refer to retention after a brief presentation as a stimulus trace. Rather, it would seem
appropriate to refer to it as the result of a trial of learning. However, in
spite of possible objections to Hull's terminology the present investigation
supports his general position that a short-term retentive factor is important
for the analysis of verbal learning. The details of the role of retention in
the acquisition process remain to be worked out.

## Summary

The investigation differed from traditional verbal retention studies in
concerning itself with individual items instead of lists. Forgetting over
intervals measured in seconds was found. The course of retention after a

single presentation was related to a statistical model. Forgetting was found to progress at differential rates dependent on the amount of controlled rehearsal of the stimulus. A portion of the improvement in recall with repetitions was assigned to serial learning within the item, but a second kind of learning was also found. It was concluded that short-term retention is an important, though neglected, aspect of the acquisition process.

## REFERENCES

BROWN, J. (1958) Some tests of the decay theory of immediate memory. *Quart. J. exp. Psychol., 10,* 12-21.

ESTES, W. K. (1950) Toward a statistical theory of learning. *Psychol. Rev., 57,* 94-107.

ESTES, W. K. (1955) Statistical theory of spontaneous recovery and regression. *Psychol. Rev., 62,* 145-154.

HILGARD, E. R. (1951) Methods and procedures in the study of learning. In S. S. Stevens (Ed.), *Handbook of experimental psychology.* New York: Wiley.

HULL, C. L., HOVLAND, C. I., ROSS, R. T., HALL, M., PERKINS, D. T., and FITCH, F. B. (1940) *Mathematico-deductive theory of rote learning: A Study in scientific methodology.* New Haven: Yale Univ. Press.

HULL, C. L. (1952) *A behavior system.* New Haven: Yale Univer. Press.

PILLSBURY, W. B. and SYLVESTER, A. (1940) Retroactive and proactive inhibition in immediate memory. *J. exp. Psychol., 27,* 532-545.

UNDERWOOD, B. J. (1949) *Experimental psychology.* New York: Appleton-Century-Crofts.

UNDERWOOD, B. J. (1957) Interference and forgetting. *Psychol. Rev., 64,* 49-60.

WALKER, H. and LEV, J. (1953) *Statistical inference.* New York: Holt.

WILCOXON, F. (1949) *Some rapid approximate statistical procedures.* New York: Amer. Cyanamid Co.

# 38.   Retention as a Function of Degree of Overlearning

## L. Postman

*A variable which has assumed primary importance in influencing retention has been overlearning, defined as practice beyond the point of some arbitrary criterion set by the experimenter. Although Krueger performed the classical study in this area, Postman's study is noteworthy because he replicated Krueger's experiment under somewhat better controlled conditions.*

This study reexamines the effects of overlearning, that is, practice past the point of complete mastery, on the retention of verbal materials. A classical experiment by Krueger (1) led to the conclusion that overlearning favors retention but yields diminishing returns when it is carried beyond a moderate level. With lists of 12 nouns as learning materials and retention intervals from 1 to 28 days, Krueger found that recall and saving scores increased sharply at first, and then much more slowly, as degree of overlearning was varied from 0 through 50 to 100 per cent.

In the light of recent analyses of the conditions of retention, the generality of these results is open to question. Krueger used well-practiced subjects who served in several conditions of the experiment. It is now known that the amount recalled by practiced subjects is drastically depressed by the cumulative effects of proactive interference from prior lists learned in the laboratory (2). As a case in point, Krueger's subjects retained less than 2 per cent of a list 7 days after learning to criterion. When interference is massive, practically all items must be overlearned in order to be recalled. A moderate amount of overlearning will be sufficient for the easiest items in the list, whereas more difficult items will require extensive additional practice. Hence, retention will increase with overlearning at a negatively accelerated rate. In the absence of heavy proactive interference, on the other hand, only relatively difficult items will require overlearning. The beneficial effects of overlearning on retention may then be expected to develop gradually and to show initial positive acceleration. To test this prediction, naive subjects who learned and recalled a single list were used in the present study.

The experimental lists consisted of 12 two-syllable nouns. The word fre-

*Science,* 1962, *135,* 666-667. Reprinted with permission of the author and the American Association for the Advancement of Science. Copyright 1962 by the American Association for the Advancement of Science. This research was supported by a grant from the National Science Foundation.

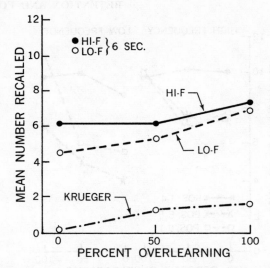

FIG. 1. Mean numbers of items recalled 7 days after the end of original learning as a function of word frequency and degree of overlearning. Points marked "6 sec" show amounts recalled on the first trial after criterion was reached. Krueger's data for the same retention interval are also shown.

quency of the items was varied in order to assess the interaction between pre-experimental language habits and the effects of overlearning. There were two types of lists drawn from the extremes of the frequency range in the Thorndike-Lorge word count (3). For the words in the high-frequency lists the number of occurrences in the "L" count was between 1000 and 3300 in 4.5 million; for the low-frequency lists the range was between 1 and 3 in 4.5 million. At each level of frequency there were two lists and two different serial orders of each list. The lists were presented on a Hull-type memory drum at a 2-second rate, with a 6-second interval between trials. Learning was by the method of serial anticipation. There were three degrees of overlearning: 0 percent, 50 percent, and 100 percent. For 0-percent overlearning, practice was terminated at a criterion of one perfect recitation. For 50-per cent overlearning, practice was continued beyond the point of mastery for half as many trials as had been required to reach criterion; for 100-per cent overlearning the number of trials was doubled. The lists were relearned to criterion 7 days after the end of original learning.

There were no significant differences in speed of learning to criterion among the groups tested with a given type of list. The mean number of trials to criterion was 19.25 for the high-frequency lists, and 25.48 for the low-frequency lists. This difference is significant ($t = 3.42$, $df = 94$, $P < .01$). Figure 1 shows the mean numbers of items recalled on the first trial of relearning. (Krueger's data for a 7-day retention interval are included for comparison.) Since associative strength at criterion varies di-

*(handwritten in left margin)* ? still true if corrected for # presentations of easier items ?

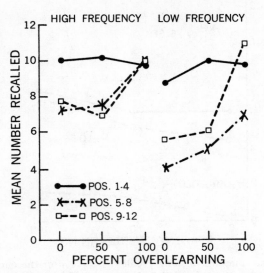

FIG. 2. Mean numbers recalled from the initial, middle, and terminal sections of the serial lists after different degrees of overlearning. The numbers of subjects giving correct responses are averaged over the four serial positions in each section.

rectly with speed of learning (4), the appropriate base line for measuring forgetting of the two types of material after 0-per cent overlearning is the amount recalled immediately (6 sec) after attainment of the criterion. These base-line measures were obtained from the protocols of the 50-per cent and 100-per cent groups. The interaction, time × word frequency, is not significant ($F = 1.80$, $df = 1/92$), that is, retention loss does not vary as a function of word frequency when associative strength at criterion is taken into account (5).

There was no change in the amount of recall for the high-frequency lists, and only a small increase for the low-frequency lists, after 50-per cent overlearning. There were clear increases in the retention of both types of material after 100-per cent overlearning. Degree of overlearning is a significant source of variance ($F = 4.15$, $df = 2/90$, $.02 < P < .05$) but does not interact with word frequency ($F < 1$). As Fig. 2 shows, the gains in retention are almost entirely a function of positively accelerated increases in the recall of the relatively difficult middle and terminal sections of the serial lists

The mean numbers of trials to relearn the high-frequency lists to criterion were 6.12, 4.69, and 3.69 after 0-, 50-, and 100-per cent overlearning, respectively. The corresponding means for the low-frequency lists were 7.31, 5.44, and 3.75. The numbers of trials in relearning decrease steadily with the degree of overlearning. The decreases are significant ($F = 11.71$,

$df = 2/90$, $P < .01$) but do not interact with word frequency ($F < 1$). Comparison between the two measures of retention indicates that speed of relearning is more sensitive than amount of recall to increases in associative strength produced by moderate amounts of overlearning.

While progressive increases in degree of overlearning must eventually yield diminishing returns, this point will be reached slowly when the beneficial effects of continuing practice are measured by the amount of recall for relatively difficult items. This conclusion applies to verbal series composed of items of high as well as low frequency of linguistic usage (6).

## REFERENCES

1. KRUEGER, W. C. F. (1929) *J. Exptl. Psychol., 12*, 71.
2. UNDERWOOD, B. J. (1957) *Psychol. Rev., 64*, 49.
3. THORNDIKE, E. L. and LORGE, I. (1944) *The Teacher's Wordbook of 30,000 Words*, Teachers College, Columbia Univ., New York.
4. UNDERWOOD, B. J (1954) *Psychol. Bull., 51*, 276.
5. This conclusion is in agreement with that of an earlier study. See L. Postman, *J. Exptl. Psychol., 61*, 97 (1961).

## 39. On Some Factors in the Organizational Characteristics of Free Recall

### C. N. Cofer

*The author has provided us with the findings of a number of studies that demonstrate, at least in part, how the individual goes about organizing material which is presented to him vis-a-vis the free recall learning situation.*

In recent years, much of my research has been concerned with the free-learning or free-recall situation. This is the case in which a list of words

*Amer. Psychol.*, 1965, *20*, 261-272. Reprinted with permission of the author and The American Psychological Association. Address of the retiring President, Eastern Psychological Association, presented at Philadelphia, April 17, 1964. Much of the work reported here was supported by contracts Nonr 595(04), Nonr 285(47) and Nonr 656(30) between the Office of Naval Research and the University of Maryland, New York University, and the Pennsylvania State University, respectively. This paper is Technical Report No. 1, under contract Nonr 656(30). Reproduction in whole or in part is permitted for any purpose of the United States Government. Assistance was also provided by a faculty research grant from the University of California, Berkeley, during 1962-63. I am indebted to the following colleagues and students for reading and criticizing a draft of this paper: David Palermo, John Hall, Lowell Schipper, James J. Jenkins, David Wicklund, Darryl Bruce, and John Robinson.

of some length is presented to a subject, and he is asked to recall the items in any order in which they occur to him. Interest in the recall performance has centered on two of its features and the variables related to them. One of these features is the total number of words correctly recalled, and the other one, which I shall emphasize here, is the order or *organization* of the recall as compared to the organization present among the items as originally presented. The general procedure was first developed by Bousfield and reported in 1953, and has been extensively explored by him and his students as well as by Jenkins and Russell (1952) and their associates. In this paper I shall review interpretations which have been made of clustering, data which pertain to these analyses, and suggest a formulation which I now find plausible.

Perhaps the major reason for studying this situation arises from the finding that subjects do, in fact, reorganize the material so that the recalls differ in sequential properties from those of the original list. My attention was first engaged by this phenomenon because of its seeming relation to the changes found in the recall of complex materials by Bartlett (1932). It appeared to offer a more convenient and simpler experimental situation for the study of such changes than the ones he used. In addition, however, and equally important, is the fact that features of verbal organization seem to be reflected in the ways in which subjects order their recalls in this free situation.

The first experiments by Bousfield employed lists which contained categorized subgroups of words. For example, a list of 40 items might be composed of 10 animals, 10 weapons, 10 cities, and 10 articles of clothing. These 40 items were presented to the subject in a random order, and the extent to which, in his recall, the subject put together the animals, the cities, and so on, represents a reorganization or *clustering* of categorized items. I shall refer to this procedure as *category clustering.* Jenkins and Russell (1952; see also Jenkins, Mink, & Russell, 1958) selected pairs of items from their standardization (Russell & Jenkins, 1954) of the Kent-Rosanoff Word Association Test. They took stimuli, say TABLE and MOUNTAIN, and frequent responses to the stimuli, e.g., CHAIR and HILL, respectively. Words selected in this manner were presented in a random order to subjects for recall. What I shall call *associate clustering* was found when in their recalls the subjects put together in sequence the stimuli and their responses which had been separated at list presentation. Category clustering and associative clustering represent operational definitions of the terms "organization" or "reorganization" in recall, as I shall use them here.

The interpretation which Bousfield at first gave to category clustering involved the activation of superordinates by the instances which were presented. Thus, the occurrence of various items, such as DOG, CAT, LION, MONKEY, would activate the superordinate "animal." This superordinate, in combination with other factors, controlled the emission of items in

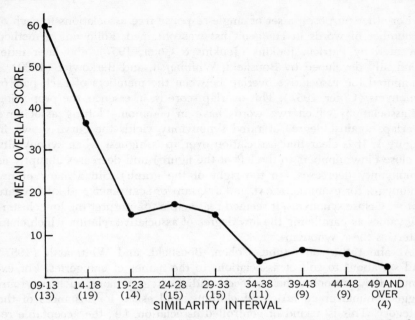

Fig. 1. Associative overlap in pairs of words as a function of judged synonymity between the members of the pair. (Synonymity ranges from high—0.9–1.3—to low—4.9+. The numbers in parentheses along the abscissa indicate the number of pairs represented in the mean overlap score for the synonymity interval.)

recall so that they appeared in clusters; the number of words recalled, also, was augmented by the superordinate. Jenkins and Russell, on the other hand, did not use superordinate concepts. Since the clustering they obtained was based on and related to the preexperimental associative strength between the members of the pairs, they had no need to go beyond the associative factor to account for the clustering they obtained.

My first experiment on clustering (Cofer, 1959) represented an attempt to show that logical relations in the language would mediate clustering. My list of 40 words consisted of eight groups of 5 words each, each group being composed of synonymous words. The words were taken from Haagen's (1949) materials which provide groups of items whose degree of synonymity to another item was rated. For example, the items REGAL, SCEPTERED, STATELY, and KINGLY are all to some degree synonyms of the word ROYAL, and these five items made up one of the word groups. When I scrambled the 40 words and, after presentation, obtained recall, I did get clustering, but it was unexpectedly minimal. Synonymity, in other words, did not provide a very good basis for clustering, at least as measured. This was a puzzling finding, but it seemed to clear up when associational data on these items were examined.

For other purposes, a set of single-response free associations to each of a number of words in Haagen's list was obtained. Following a method invented by Patricia Jenkins (Jenkins & Cofer, 1957), and later independently developed by Bousfield, Whitmarsh, and Berkowitz (1960), I computed the associative overlap between the members of each pair of synonyms (Cofer, 1957). This overlap score is, in essence, the proportion of associations which two words have in common. Plotting associative overlaps against degree of rated synonymity yields the curve shown in Figure 1. It is clear that association overlap is highest when synonymity is close (low numbers to the left of the figure) and decreases abruptly as synonymity decreases (to the right of the graph). Since many of my synonyms, for example, REGAL and STATELY, or SCEPTERED and KINGLY, are not very close synonyms, it seemed reasonable to interpret the low clustering values as paralleling the low degree of associative relation which characterizes these synonyms.

At about the same time, Cohen, Bousfield, and Whitmarsh (1957) had set about to collect associations to the names of categories. For example, they presented their subjects with a category name, such as a four-legged animal or an article of clothing, and asked for instances of the category. This is a kind of controlled association, i.e., the acceptable responses are restricted to a given class. Tabulation of the responses showed a frequency distribution such that some responses occur very frequently in a group of subjects, and others infrequently. Thus to ANIMAL, DOG and CAT are frequent responses, whereas PLATYPUS, AARDVARK, and VICUÑA are infrequent. Bousfield, Cohen, and Whitmarsh (1958) then studied clustering for lists in which the items were high-frequency associates of category names and for lists in which the items were low-frequency associates of the same names. The differences were striking, with the high-frequency associates showing marked clustering and the low-frequency lists relatively little. This finding (and other data), I think, shifted Bousfield away from superordinates to associations as responsible for the mechanics of clustering. The success of Deese (1959) in predicting free-recall scores for lists of words differing in interitem associative strength may also have been a factor. The synonym data, Bousfield's findings, and Deese's success combined to shift me also to an associative interpretation of clustering along with Jenkins, Russell, and Bousfield.

Meanwhile, Gonzalez and I (Gonzalez & Cofer, 1959) were exploring the effects of modifiers on the tendency of nouns to cluster. We used the following situation: A list of 40 nouns, representing four categories, was selected, which, unmodified, showed significant clustering. Then, with other subjects, we presented lists in which each of these nouns was modified by an adjective. For example, the unmodified nouns, LION, HORSE, DRESS, and SHIRT, representing two categories, might be presented as STRONG LION, POWERFUL HORSE, RED DRESS, BLUE SHIRT. At presentation, the

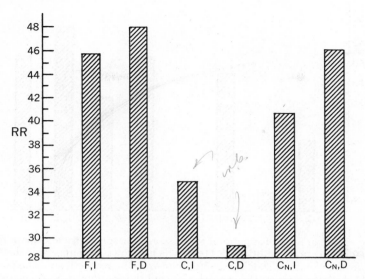

Fig. 2. Mean ratio of repetition recall scores for facilitation and conflict conditions. (F refers to facilitation, C to conflict, and $C_N$ to control conditions; I and D refer to immediate and delayed—5-minute—recalls, respectively.)

subject did not always know which of the pair members he would be asked to recall. Typically, however, he was asked to recall the nouns, and, after a 5-minute, filled interval, to recall them a second time.

We set up four conditions, as follows. In two, the adjectives, as well as the nouns, were categorized. One of these we called the facilitation condition, in which nouns of a given category were always modified by adjectives from one category. The example I just gave was one in which all animals were modified by adjectives indicating strength (STRONG and POWERFUL modifying LION and HORSE) and all articles of clothing were modified by color adjectives (RED and BLUE modifying DRESS and SHIRT). This illustrates the arrangement of modifiers in the facilitation condition. The second condition, the *conflict* condition, used the same words but here the nouns of a category were modified by adjectives drawn from all the categories used. For example, HORSE might still be modified by POWERFUL but LION by TAWNY; DRESS might be modified by a size adjective like LONG and perhaps SHIRT by STRONG, a strength-class adjective. The adjective categories were distributed *across* the noun categories in the conflict condition.

The other two conditions did not use categorized adjectives although the nouns were categorized. One of the cases we called the *specificity* condition. Here each adjective could appropriately modify only 1 noun among the 40, and it shared no category with any other adjective. For example,

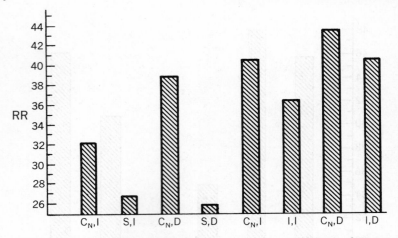

FIG. 3. Mean ratio of repetition recall scores for specificity and inappropriate-modification conditions. (The I which follows a comma and the D refer to immediate and delayed—5-minute—recalls, respectively. The four bars to the left represent the control—$C_N$—and the specificity—S—conditions of the specificity experiment. The four bars to the right represent the control—$C_N$—and the inappropriate-modification (I before the comma) conditions of the inappropriate-modification experiment. The two experiments employed different materials, so the four bars to the left cannot be compared directly to the four on the right.)

CABINET, CHAIR, and STICK may all be wooden objects; when the 3 words were modified they became LIQUOR CABINET, ROCKING CHAIR, and WALKING STICK; none of these modifiers appropriately modified a noun in the list other than the one with which it was paired. The final condition employed categorized nouns which were modified *inappropriately*. Using the nouns LION, HORSE, DRESS, and SHIRT, we can represent this condition by the pairs PURPLE LION, LEAFY HORSE, WISE DRESS, and ANGRY SHIRT.

The results of the facilitation and conflict conditions on clustering are shown in Figure 2. In this plot, the ordinate shows the ratio of repetition, which is the proportion of words recalled which are recalled in clusters. The graph shows, in order along the abscissa, the mean values for the facilitation (F) condition for both immediate and delayed recall (after 5-minute, filled interval), the conflict condition (C), and the unmodified (control) condition ($C_N$).

Figure 2 shows an increment in clustering for the facilitation condition for both recalls, as compared to the controls; the conflict condition is inferior to the control at immediate recall and becomes more inferior at delayed recall. Remember that these two lists contained identical words but in different pairings. Figure 3 presents results for the specificity and inappropriate-modification conditions. It shows a marked reduction of clustering for both specificity (S,I) and inappropriate-modification (I,I) conditions (in comparison with their controls, first $C_N,I$ and second $C_NI$), with no recovery for the specificity condition (S,D) at the second recall. Rises in clustering at second recall are often seen in other cases. Word recall, not shown in these figures, was augmented under the facilitation condition but suppressed under the other conditions, relative to their controls.

These results showed marked effect of modification in the arrangements we employed. In order to have a further basis for their interpretation, I (Cofer, 1960) then collected single-word free-association data for the nouns alone, the adjectives alone, and the adjective-noun pairs. The associational findings for the specificity, conflict, and inappropriate-modification conditions were relatively clear. For example, the unmodified nouns CABINET, CHAIR, and STICK all elicit WOOD with some frequency in free association. These common associations, however, drop out when the associations to the word *combinations* LIQUOR CABINET, ROCKING CHAIR, and WALKING STICK are compared. One might say, for the specificity and also the inappropriate modifications, that the modifiers had eliminated the associational basis for clustering which the unmodified nouns possessed. A similar but somewhat different effect was seen in the conflict condition. As indicated, CHAIR, alone, may elicit WOOD as a response. But the phrase BROKEN CHAIR might yield responses like OLD—responses similar to some of those yielded by a pair like TATTERED DRESS. Thus, associationally, CHAIR and DRESS, modified by these adjectives, might cluster together rather than with other wooden objects and with articles of clothing, respectively. That is, clustering might occur on the basis of the categories of the modifiers rather than on the basis of the noun categories. We do not actually know that this happened enough here to account for the decline of clustering under the conflict condition, but it is a distinct possibility, and another experiment shows clearly that it can happen. I will mention it in a moment.

While associational changes due to modification offer a plausible basis for the effect of the conflict, specificity, and inappropriate-modification conditions, there were *no* aspects of the association data which paralleled the augmentation of clustering and recall seen in the facilitation condition.

Gonzalez and I (Gonzalez & Cofer, 1959) also performed an investigation which was concerned with whether a clustering effect present in either adjectives or nouns would carry over through pairing to other nouns or adjectives which, by themselves, do not cluster. We prepared four lists of words: a list of categorized adjectives, a list of uncategorized adjectives, a list of categorized nouns, and a list of uncategorized nouns. In one half of the experiment, the categorized adjective list was set to modify the uncategorized nouns; nouns were recalled, and clustering was scored for the nouns on the basis of the categories of the adjectives which had modified the nouns during presentation. Recalls for a control group which was given the uncategorized nouns were also scored for clustering on this

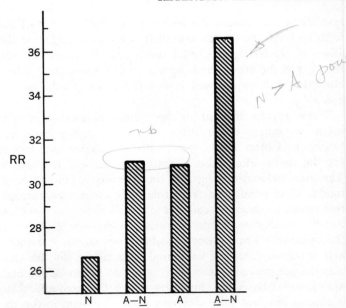

Fig. 4. Mean ratio of repetition recall scores in the mediation effect.
(The bar A-N represents the clustering obtained in the recalls of uncategorized nouns when clustering was scored on the basis of the categories
of the adjectives which modified the nouns at presentation; the bar N
gives the values for the same nouns, not modified at presentation, scored
in the same way. A-N indicates clustering in the recall of adjectives on the
basis of the nouns they modified during presentation; A is the control
for the A-N group.)

basis. The other half of the experiment represented the reverse case:
Uncategorized adjectives modified categorized nouns; adjectives were recalled, and clustering among the adjectives was scored on the basis of the
categories of the nouns they had modified during presentation. Recalls of
a control group for the uncategorized adjectives alone were scored in the
same way. The results are shown in Figure 4.

Clearly, the uncategorized nouns clustered on the basis of the categories
of the adjectives which had modified them at presentation (A-N), as compared to the noun control (N), and the uncategorized adjectives clustered
more highly on the basis of the categories of the nouns they had modified
at presentation (A-N), relative to the adjective control (A). These findings, which we have called the *mediation effect*, seem difficult to account
for on the basis of simple transfer of associations between pair members,
and, together with the data from the facilitation condition in the previous
experiments, constitute a limitation on obvious associational interpretations of clustering. The name, mediation effect, is a descriptive one, indicating that the clustering occurs through categories not well represented
in the list in which clustering is found.

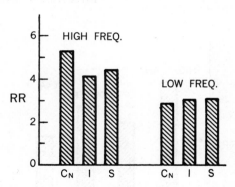

Fig. 5. Mean ratio of repetition immediate-recall scores for high-frequency and low-frequency associates of category names under inappropriate (I) and specificity (S) conditions. (The two control conditions are designated $C_N$.)

Another problematic finding concerning the associational mechanism of clustering comes from the comparison of high-frequency and low-frequency associates to the category names. We have done several experiments on the hypothesis that low-frequency associates, which, as I have said before, do not cluster very strongly, should be more affected by conditions which impair clustering than high-frequency associates. We have compared the effects of modifiers on the clustering of low-frequency and high-frequency associates to the same category names but in different lists (Cofer & Segal, 1959b). Figure 5 shows the results. The surprising outcome here is that clustering is not significantly different for the low-frequency associates in the control ($C_N$, unmodified) condition from what it is for the specificity (S) and inappropriate-modification (I) conditions. On the other hand, there is a clear effect for high-frequency associates, comparable to the results which I showed in Figure 3. A similar finding emerged when the context effects were achieved by embedding categorized nouns in sentences at presentation, and the subjects were asked to recall only the nouns (Cofer, 1961a). As Figure 6 shows, clustering in high-frequency nouns was reduced by this context (S), and this effect has been achieved in several experiments employing slightly different conditions (Cofer, 1961b; Cofer & Segal, 1959a). However, with the low-frequency associates of category names no effect of sentence context (S) has been observed.

An alternative approach for the comparison of high-frequency and low-frequency associates is to use conditions designed to augment clustering. We have not used the facilitating modification condition as yet to achieve these effects, but last year, at Berkeley, Reicher and I (Cofer & Reicher, 1963) employed a different method of presentation designed to facilitate clustering. This method we have called the block method. In this procedure, all the items belonging to a category occur one after another, i.e.,

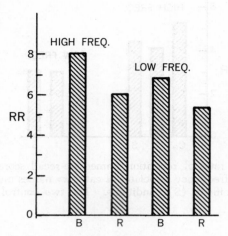

FIG. 6. Mean ratio of repetition immediate-recall scores for high-frequency and low-frequency associates of category names under sentence context conditions (S). (The two control conditions are designated $C_N$.)

together, during list presentation, rather than being randomized with items from other categories. Our hypothesis was that block presentation would augment clustering, and that the augmentation would be greater for low-frequency than for high-frequency associates of the category names. We expected this result on the ground that high-frequency items might cluster maximally after random presentation. In other words, we were expecting to find an interaction between the frequency level of the nouns and the method of presentation—block or random. Figure 7 shows that block presentation did augment clustering for items from both frequency levels, but there was no significant interaction. Block presentation affected both types of items to about the same degree, rather than affecting one more than the other. Yet to be evaluated is a possible ceiling effect on the high-frequency associates. Perhaps I should also observe that these findings can be said to represent a failure by the subject to show as much clustering in his recall as the list provides (RR of .92). This failure is greater for low-frequency than for high-frequency associates.

Let me summarize so far. Measured association seems to explain associative clustering as Jenkins and Russell (and also Bousfield) have studied it, and category clustering in the work of Bousfield. Alteration of within-category-associational relations by means of adjective modification reduced clustering in the specificity, conflict, and the inappropriate-modification conditions. The synonym findings are consistent with the limited associative overlap among the words used. On the other hand, associative changes did not parallel the increase in clustering seen in the facilitative-

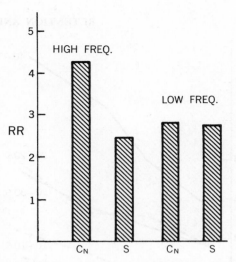

Fig. 7. Mean ratio of repetition immediate-recall scores for high-frequency and low-frequency associates of category names under block (B) and random (R) presentation procedures.

modification condition. Items which are weak associates of category names are resistant to conditions which alter the clustering of strong associates of the categories such as certain modification conditions and sentence context. Yet block presentation did not augment clustering of strong and weak associates differentially. The mediational effects occur among items that are neither clearly categorized nor probably interassociated.

Another aspect of the association-nonassociational variable in clustering came to view when, largely at the instigation of George Marshall, a student at New York University, we began to look more closely than we had before at the stimuli and their associated responses in the association norms. It is clear, when one does this, that there may be a number of relations between a stimulus and its associated responses. Such relations appear, for example, as one of common category membership, in the case BED-CHAIR, where both are items of furniture, in contrast to cases in which a common category is not easy to see. BED-SLEEP or BED-DREAM would illustrate this latter situation. Let me put it this way: It is not as easy to find a concise, specific category to link BED with SLEEP, or with DREAM, as it is in the case of BED and CHAIR. The question may be raised, of course, whether this difference matters. Marshall and I (Marshall & Cofer, 1961) and, then, Marshall (1963) for his dissertation, conducted several experiments to find out.

What we wished to do was to compare clustering for categorized words with clustering for uncategorized words, with strength of normative association between the pair members equated. To do this, we obtained free associations on a variety of stimuli (Marshall & Cofer, in press), and then

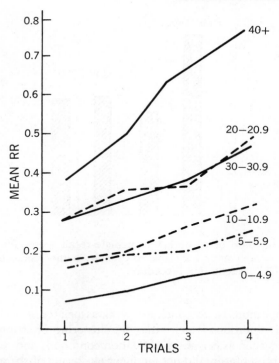

FIG. 8. Mean ratio of repetition scores for recall at each of four successive trials of lists composed of pairs varying in degree of associative overlap from 0–4.9 to 40+.

we were able to select categorized pairs and uncategorized pairs with equal or nearly equal associative overlap scores. The score here was the mutual relatedness index, or MR, which includes all of the associations which two words have in common expressed as a proportion of all of their associations. For example, if BED and DREAM both elicit SLEEP, NIGHT, and NIGHTMARE as associates, these would figure in their overlap (see Marshall & Cofer, 1963). However, CHAIR, which BED might elicit, would probably not be evoked by DREAM; CHAIR would count as one of the associates in the total given to BED, but not as a common or overlapping associate. The direct elicitation of one item by the other, as in the case BED → DREAM or DREAM → BED, would be counted in the overlap score.

An experiment was performed with six groups of subjects (Marshall, 1963, pp. 23–70). Each group was presented a scrambled list of 24 words. In the list were six categorized pairs and six uncategorized pairs at a given MR level, and there were six such lists, one per group, each representing an MR level, from low to high. Clustering was scored when the pair members appeared together in the recalls. Figure 8 shows the clustering score

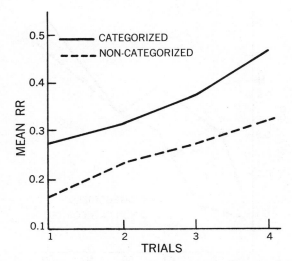

Fɪɢ. 9. Mean ratio of repetition scores for recall at each of four successive trials for pairs with equal associative overlap, but classified as either categorized or noncategorized.

over four trials (the items were rescrambled each time they were presented) with MR level as the parameter. It is clear that MR level is a very potent variable so far as clustering is concerned. Figure 9 shows clustering over trials for the categorized and uncategorized pairs, and the superiority of the categorized pairs at each trial is evident. There is no interaction with trials, however.

Figure 10 shows clustering for categorized and uncategorized pairs plotted against MR level. Remember that associative overlap is balanced here. What the figure suggests is an interaction of the categorization factor with MR level. At high MR levels categorization makes no difference to clustering, but at intermediate and to some extent at low values there is a difference in favor of the categorized pairs. This interaction is significant.

As a part of the experiment which I have just summarized, Marshall gave his subjects, after they had finished their learning trials, what he called a Recognition Association Test. This test consisted of the 24 items with which the subject had just been working, randomly arranged in a 6 × 4 matrix. The subject was asked to select and to designate pairs of words which he felt were related in some way. Marshall then tabulated these designations into three groups: One represented the categorized pairs which Marshall had put into the list. The second represented the uncategorized but associated pairs which had been placed in the list. The third consisted of pairings which had not been placed in the list—they were inventions by the subjects and were called *idiosyncratic pairs*. (They *are* idiosyncratic in that few common pairings are achieved by more than

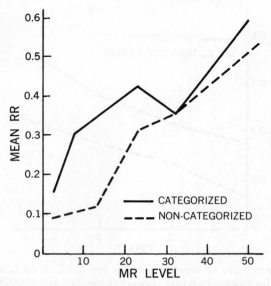

Fig. 10. Mean ratio of repetition scores for recall of categorized and noncategorized pairs as a function of associative overlap (MR level).

two subjects.) Figure 11 shows the number of these three kinds of pairs as a function of MR level. It is clear that at the three lowest MR levels idiosyncratic pairings are "recognized" frequently by the subjects but that, as MR increases, these pairings drop out. The "recognition" of uncategorized pairs provides almost a mirror image of the curve for the idiosyncratic pairs, being infrequent at first and rising rapidly as MR level increases above intermediate values. Although the recognition scores for categorized pairs start fairly high, even at low MR levels, they do show a substantial rise with MR value to the point where the curve for these pairs is virtually identical to the one for uncategorized pairs.

We can also ask, do the idiosyncratic pairs cluster? This question was answered by searching the recall protocols for each subject for instances of clustering involving the idiosyncratic pairs he had designated on the Recognition Association Test. Figure 12 shows a plot of the proportion of the clustering obtained at each MR level which is attributable to each kind of pair—categorized, uncategorized, and idiosyncratic. As could be expected, the idiosyncratic pairs account for from 20% to 40% of the clustering obtained at the three lowest MR levels, but account for virtually none of it at the higher MR values. The other curves show that the categorized pairs account for much more clustering at low and intermediate MR levels than the uncategorized pairs, a fact with which we are already familiar.

Another experiment of Marshall's (1963, pp. 71–95) adds some further information both concerning categorized and uncategorized pairs and con-

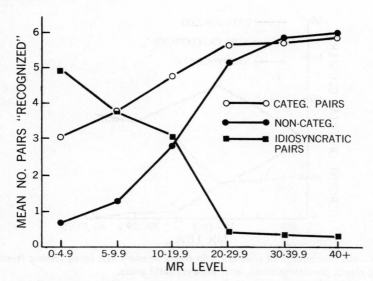

FIG. 11. Mean number of categorized, noncategorized, and idiosyncratic pairs "recognized" as a function of MR level of the pairs.

cerning idiosyncratic pairings. In this experiment, a further associative factor was included: the extent to which the associative overlap of pair members is due to their elicitation of each other as associates (what we call direct) or to their joint elicitation of other responses as associates in common (nondirect). For example, DOCTOR and LAWYER each elicits the other as an associate, and these direct associates account for 74% of their common associations. ROBIN and PARROT, on the other hand, do not elicit each other as associates, but achieve their substantial associative overlap by eliciting BIRD as a common (nondirect) associate. For this experiment, two lists were made up, equal in MR index (mean about that of the third level in the prior experiment). One of them was composed of directly and nondirectly associated *categorized* pairs, the other of directly and nondirectly *uncategorized* pairs. Thus, the lists here were homogeneous as to the presence of categorized or uncategorized pairs, whereas in the prior experiment all lists were mixed, containing both categorized and uncategorized pairs.

Figure 12 shows clustering over trials for the four types of pairs the two lists contained. It is clear that uncategorized, nondirectly associated pairs show little clustering over the trials and that the directly associated, uncategorized pairs do only a little better. Much higher scores occur with categorized pairs of both types, and the improvement over trials is marked. There is a significant interaction of the categorization-noncategorization

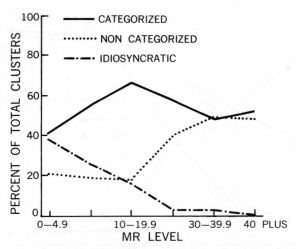

Fɪɢ. 12. Percentage of clustering in recall at each MR level arising from categorized, noncategorized, and idiosyncratic pairs.

variable with trials for these homogeneous lists, whereas there was no interaction of these variables for a mixed list of about the same MR level in the preceding experiment.

Results from the Recognition Association Test show that the categorized pairs are clearly recognized here—in fact the mean number of idiosyncratic pairings for the homogeneous categorized list is only .52. For the uncategorized pair list, however, 4.63 of the pairings are idiosyncratic, and this is a substantially higher value than was obtained for either type of categorized pair. Direct comparison of these values for the comparable mixed list of the prior experiment is not possible, but it seems likely that the homogeneity of the lists made the categorization factor more salient in the categorized pair list, and the uncategorized pairings less salient in the uncategorized list, than was true in the mixed lists. This may be why an interaction of categorization and trials appears with homogeneous lists and does not do so with mixed lists.

I believe that there is some parallel between the idiosyncratic pairings we have found under certain conditions and Tulving's (1962) notion of subjective organization in free recall. Tulving has used a list of unrelated words presented in different orders over a number of trials. Free-recall instructions were used, but Tulving has found that the same sequences of words do appear, despite these instructions, over a number of the recalls. He suggests that these sequences among words, which the experimenter has selected as unrelated, indicate that subjects can find bases for organization in such unrelated items and that recall scores rise as these sequences become more pronounced. Perhaps our idiosyncratic pairings rep-

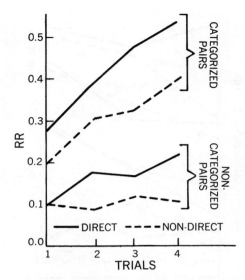

Fig. 13. Mean ratio of repetition scores for recall at successive trials of categorized and noncategorized pairs, directly or nondirectly associated.

resent the subjects' identification of relationships among the words which they use to achieve clustering. But it is worth noting that when strong, measured associative relations are prominent, as they are at high MR levels, these associations are used, and idiosyncratic pairings drop out. Similarly, categorical relations also provide an alternative to subjective or idiosyncratic pairings and are effective over a wide range of MR levels. What we perhaps have here may be stated as follows: Subjects will, themselves, find relationships among items which will confer organization on recall. But when certain relationships among items in the list are prominent, as they are among categorized words and among highly associated items, the subject uses the ones provided, and subjective organization falls to low levels.

We have a little data (Marshall & Cofer, 1961, Exp. III), presented in Figure 14, which appear to be consistent with this interpretation. In this experiment, mixed lists of categorized and uncategorized word pairs at two levels of MR were presented under either a set or a no-set condition. The set was induced by telling the subjects that they might notice relations among some of the words, and that such relations would help in the recall of the words. The data show that the set augmented clustering for both the categorized and uncategorized pairs at the high MR level but had no differential effect on these kinds of pairs at the low MR level used. Given word relations of some prominence, then, set, so far as these results go, guides the subject to identify and use them in his recall.

Resulting from the experiments with word pairs, an interpretation which

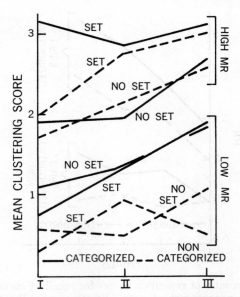

Fig. 14. Mean ratio of repetition values for the recalls at successive trials of categorized and noncategorized pairs of words with high and low associative overlap (MR) under set and no-set conditions.

makes some sense is as follows: Category relations and, in uncategorized pairs, strong associative tendencies may operate to exclude idiosyncratic bases of organization. Probably, a word tends to suggest other words to subjects. When one of the suggested words is also on the list, as is the case with highly associated pair members, and the subject discovers the other word, a "unit" is completed and a selection from among the alternatives which the first word suggests is achieved, blocking out the other alternatives. Such a mechanism is consistent, at least, with the repeated finding that intrusions are infrequent in immediate free recall. But when the pair on the list represents a low-strength association the subject may not respond to the other word as related to the one he hears or sees first; the items provided do not form a unit and the subject goes about constructing units of his own devising. Another way of saying this might be that highly associated words are integrated units (Underwood & Schulz, 1960) or are structures (Mandler, 1962).

The same things may be said for categorized words. They appear to function as integrated units or as structures, but do so over a wide range of associative levels. How do they do this? One possibility is that the category name serves to unite them. However, free-association data to each member of a categorized pair do not always support this interpretation. The words EAGLE and CROW do individually elicit in common the response BIRD, and this category name may link them into a unit or structure for the subject. But VIOLIN and PIANO do not elicit INSTRUMENT often, and are linked, associatively, through words like MUSIC and PLAY, neither of which is as precise or restrictive a category designation as BIRD is for EAGLE and CROW. There may, however, be a more restricted *domain* of associations between categorized words than is the case with uncategorized words of equal associative overlap. The uncategorized words SMOOTH and SILK, for example, are linked mainly by SOFT. It is perhaps less likely that one would get back to either SMOOTH or SILK if he had coded them as SOFT than it is that he would get back to VIOLIN and PIANO from code words like PLAY or MUSIC. This is, however, entirely a matter of conjecture at the present time.

It should not be forgotten that in our recall experiments with pairs *both* words are always presented, though not together. This is a condition which may affect the ways in which the words are related. Dolinsky (1963) has shown that when subjects are presented with two words and are asked to write in another word that logically connects the two, the word written is not typically one which is a dominant association of both the words. Often the word the subject supplies is not an association to either word at all (7 of 17 cases), sometimes it is a dominant response to one of the words (3 instances), and sometimes it is a nondominant association to one or both of the words (7 cases). It may be that, in the process of list presentation or at recall, the occurrence of the two categorized words instigates a linking response on the part of the subject, a response which is not high in associational frequency to either word alone. Or it may be that some process like "priming" of low-strength associations (Segal, 1962; Storms, 1958) may be involved. We do not know, although the findings for the set condition and for homogeneous lists, which I have already mentioned, suggest that clustering is augmented when the subject is directed to look for relationships. Whatever the value of associational or categorical relations for predicting characteristics of recall, we need much more information than we have on how such factors function to affect recall in the way they seem to do.

I have formulated the proposition that: When sufficiently prominent, experimenter-provided associational and categorical relations between members of a word pair provide a basis for clustering in free recall alternative to the bases—associational or otherwise—the subject will use to effect subjective organization or idiosyncratic pairing. Does this proposition apply as well to the other instances of clustering I have discussed? Let me try to answer this question in a few brief statements.

1. The associative clustering reported by Jenkins and Russell seems to fit; relatively highly associated pairs probably carried most of the clustering they found (Jenkins, Mink, & Russell, 1958), though category relations were also present, in all likelihood.

2. So far as category clustering is concerned, there seems to be no problem, as both prominent category and associational relations are present to provide bases for clustering.

3. The synonyms possessed few associations in common and did not represent effective categorical groups. The limited clustering obtained is consistent with these characteristics.

4. With modifiers in the specificity, conflict, and inappropriate-modification designs it seems likely that both associational and category relationships are disrupted, thus decreasing clustering.

5. I have said that the augmented clustering in the facilitation condition was not accompanied by consistent associative changes. Perhaps the subject in this case constructed units, like strong animals and colored clothing, as codes by which to organize and augment his recall.

6. That low-frequency associates of category names are resistant to conditions disruptive of clustering remains a puzzle. Recall is not as high for such items as it is for high-frequency associates. Perhaps because the number of the recalled units here is small they can somehow withstand disruption when some relations, categorical or associational, are recognized. This may be consistent with the failure of the low-frequency items to be augmented more by block presentation than they were.

7. The mediational effects are even less tractable to interpretation than are other phenomena I have listed. Somehow the subject must achieve noun units in terms of adjective categories or, in the other case, adjective units on the basis of the noun categories. We need more information to decide how he accomplishes this.

I have, throughout this paper, contrasted associational and categorical bases for clustering. It now seems to me, and this represents a change of heart, that such a contrast is neither useful nor heuristic. In free recall, our evidence suggests, subjects will use either or both of these bases to accomplish their recalls and will find ways to organize recalls even though the experimenter has not provided means in the list he presents. Free recall can tell us something of the way verbal organization is set up, but we are largely in the dark as to how this organization acts to bring related items together whatever the basis of their relationship. How do associations and category relations lead the subject to put this with that?

This is perhaps a different way of asking the same question the Würzburgers raised 60 years ago. But an approach which it suggests, at least to me, is an exhaustive study of situations and tasks. (Jenkins, 1963) in an effort to uncover the variables which augment and those which diminish the effects of preestablished association and category relations on intellectual processes. Tasks can vary from discrimination learning, on the one hand, to free recall, on the other, in terms of the opportunity they give for interword relationships to display their effects. We have seen that an induced set and the factor of homogeneity of lists can apparently influence the use of certain interword relations. We should examine the entire range of this "intentionality" variable—from incidental learning to specific, induced sets—in interaction with task and materials variables, in order, by a kind of triangulation, to fix precisely the conditions under which preestablished associations and categories will work and will not work. Thomas Hobbes said, in a discussion of trains of association around 300 years ago, that "the mind can lead from almost anything to anything." We have learned, in this discussion, that the word *almost* is a critical term in this quotation, and the work of the future can best be described, perhaps, as the search for its further explication.

## REFERENCES

BARTLETT, F. C. (1932) *Remembering*. New York: Cambridge Univer. Press.

BOUSFIELD, W. A. (1953) The occurrence of clustering in the recall of randomly arranged associates. *Journal of General Psychology, 49*, 229-240.

BOUSFIELD, W. A., COHEN, B. H., and WHITMARSH, G. A. (1958) Associative clustering in the recall of words of different taxonomic frequencies of occurrence. *Psychological Reports, 4*, 39-44.

BOUSFIELD, W. A., WHITMARSH, G. A., and BERKOWITZ, H. (1960) Partial response identities in associative clustering. *Journal of General Psychology, 63*, 233, 238.

COFER, C. N. (1957) Associative commonality and rated similarity of certain words from Haagen's list. *Psychological Reports, 3*, 603-606.

COFER, C. N. (1959) A study of clustering in free recall based on synonyms. *Journal of General Psychology, 60*, 3-10.

COFER, C. N. (1960) An experimental analysis of the role of context in verbal behavior. *Transactions of the New York Academy of Sciences, 22*(Ser. 2), 341-347.

COFER, C. N. (1961) Further studies of clustering in the recall of nouns embedded during presentation in sentences. Technical Report No. 2, New York University, Contract Nonr 285(47), Office of Naval Research. (a)

COFER, C. N. (1961) Some effects of modifiers on the clustering of nouns embedded during presentation in sentences. Technical Report No. 6, New York University, Contract Nonr 285(47), Office of Naval Research. (b)

COFER, C. N. and REICHER, G. M. (April 1963) The effects of grouping during presentation and of an immediate recall on clustering in free recall. Paper read at Western Psychological Association, Santa Monica, California.

COFER, C. N. and SEGAL, E. (1959) Certain modifier effects with nouns varying in degree of clustering tendency. Technical Report No. 29, University of Maryland, Contract Nonr 595(04), Office of Naval Research. (a)

COFER, C. N. and SEGAL, E. (1959) An exploration of clustering in the recall of nouns embedded during presentation in sentences. Technical Report No. 27, University of Maryland, Contract Nonr 595(04), Office of Naval Research. (b)

COHEN, B. H., BOUSFIELD, W. A., and WHITMARSH, G. A. (1957) Cultural norms for verbal items in 43 categories. Technical Report No. 22, University of Connecticut, Contract Nonr 631(00), Office of Naval Research.

Deese, J. (1959) Influence of inter-item associative strength upon immediate free recall. *Psychological Reports, 5,* 305-312.

Dolinsky, R. (April 1963) Word association, mediation, and conceptual category. Paper read at Eastern Psychological Association, New York City.

Gonzalez, R. C. and Cofer, C. N. (1959) Exploratory studies of verbal context by means of clustering in free recall. *Journal of Genetic Psychology, 95,* 293-320.

Haagen, C. H. (1949) Synonymity, vividness, familiarity, and association value ratings of 400 pairs of common adjectives. *Journal of Psychology, 27,* 453-463.

Jenkins, J. J. (1963) Mediated associations: Paradigms and situations. In C. N. Cofer and B. S. Musgrave (Eds.), *Verbal behavior and learning.* New York: McGraw-Hill. Pp. 210-245.

Jenkins, J. J., Mink, W. D., and Russell, W. A. (1958) Associative clustering as a function of verbal association strength. *Psychological Reports, 4,* 127-136.

Jenkins, J. J. and Russell, W. A. (1952) Associative clustering during recall. *Journal of Abnormal and Social Psychology, 47,* 818-821.

Jenkins, Patricia M. and Cofer, C. N. (1957) An exploratory study of discrete free association to compound verbal stimuli. *Psychological Reports, 3,* 599-602.

Mandler, G. A. (1962) From association to structure. *Psychological Review, 69,* 415-427.

Marshall, G. R. (1963) The organization of verbal material in free recall: The effects of patterns of associative overlap on clustering. Unpublished doctoral dissertation, New York University.

Marshall, G. R. and Cofer, C. N. (1961) Associative, category and set factors in clustering among word pairs and triads. Technical Report No. 4, New York University Contract Nonr 285(47), Office of Naval Research.

Marshall, G. R. and Cofer, C. N. (1963) Associative indices as measures of word relatedness: A summary and comparison of ten methods. *Journal of Verbal Learning and Verbal Behavior, 1,* 408-421.

Marshall, G. R. and Cofer, C. N. Single-word free association norms for 328 responses from the Connecticut Cultural norms for verbal items in categories. In L. Postman (Ed.), *Norms of word association.* New York: Academic Press, in press.

Russell, W. A. and Jenkins, J. J. (1954) The complete Minnesota norms for responses to 100 words from the Kent-Rosanoff Word Association Test. Technical Report No. 11, University of Minnesota, Contract Nonr 66216, Office of Naval Research.

Segal, S. J. (1962) *The effect of different contextual conditions on the priming of free and continued word associations.* (Doctoral dissertation, New York University.) Ann Arbor, Mich.: University Microfilms. No. 2223.

Storms, L. H. (1958) Apparent backward association: A situational effect. *Journal of Experimental Psychology, 55,* 390-395.

Tulving, E. (1962) Subjective organization in free recall of "unrelated" words. *Psychological Review, 69,* 344-354.

Underwood, B. J. and Schulz, R. W. (1960) *Meaningfulness and verbal learning.* Chicago: Lippincott.

# 40.  "Fate" of First-List Associations in Transfer Theory

## J. M. Barnes and B. J. Underwood

*An early experiment by Melton and Irwin was instrumental in pointing out that during the learning of Task B in the retroactive inhibition paradigm, there was the unlearning or extinction of first list items found in Task A. Other hypotheses have been proposed as to what happens to Task A responses during Task B learning. The Barnes and Underwood article is an attempt to examine the "fate" of these first-list associations.*

Theorists who attempt to arrive at an accounting of the facts of transfer and retroactive inhibition in verbal materials must inevitably make a decision concerning "what happens" to first-list associations when a second list is learned. The present study was designed to gather data which would make such decisions easier. Two transfer paradigms were used. One of these, A-B, A-C, is normally associated with production of negative transfer. In the other paradigm, A-B, A-B', stimuli are identical with responses highly similar; such an arrangement normally produces positive transfer.

The data from the present study allow an evaluation of three different conceptions concerning the fate of first-list (hereafter called List 1) associations during the learning of the second list (hereafter called List 2). These three positions will be examined first as they apply to the A-B, A-C paradigm.

1. List 1 associations are unlearned or extinguished during the learning of the second list. While A-B, A-C is more comparable to the operations of counterconditioning than to extinction of conditioned responses, the term extinction will be used here in keeping with past practice. As a theoretical position, the unlearning or extinction hypothesis is associated with Melton and Irwin (1940) who used it to explain certain facts of RI. They suggested that at least part of RI could be accounted for by the loss of associative strength of List 1 responses resulting from extinction. It might also be assumed that negative transfer results from the interference accompanying the extinction process. A rather impressive amount of evidence could be marshalled in support of this extinction hypothesis. For present purposes, however, only an illustration of this evidence will be given.

*J. exp. Psychol.*, 1959, 58, 97-105.  Reprinted with permission of the author and The American Psychological Association.

At various points in learning the second list, Briggs (1954) presented the stimuli common to both lists, one at a time, and asked S to give the first of the two responses which came to mind. The results showed that during the learning of List 2 there is a gradual decrease in frequency of List 1 responses, the curve being not unlike an extinction curve. A phenomenon analogous to spontaneous recovery of the List 1 responses was also found when retention was measured at various intervals of time after List 2 learning. Such evidence appears quite in line with the extinction hypothesis. However, as Briggs points out, a certain amount of ambiguity remains; the extinction curve does not necessarily mean that List 1 associations are extinguished in the sense that they are no longer available for recall. His results may mean only that List 2 associations become stronger than List 1 associations, hence, occur more and more frequently in recall. Such an increase in frequency of List 2 associations must necessarily be accompanied by a decrease in frequency of List 1 associations at recall. The question still remains, therefore, as to whether or not the A-B association is available after A-C is learned and this one question the present study attempts to answer.

2. The system of associations in List 1 (A-B) remains relatively independent and intact throughout the learning of the associations in List 2 (A-C). This will be referred to as the independence hypothesis. The verbal stimuli are, of course, identical in the A-B, A-C paradigm, but there are other possible differentiating cues (e.g., first list vs. second list) which would provide a means of having two independent response systems attached to the same apparent stimulus. Negative transfer could be said to occur in the process of establishing the independent response systems early in learning A-C. Retroactive inhibition could be attributed to loss of differentiation so that response competition occurs.

3. A third possible conception makes use of mediation. Having learned A-B in List 1, S retains this association so that List 2 items are learned with B as the mediator; S learns A—B—C. Negative transfer and RI could occur as a consequence of confusion on the part of S as to which response is used as the mediator and which response is mediated.

In the present study, different groups of Ss were stopped at various points in learning List 2 and were asked to give *both* List 1 and List 2 responses to each stimulus. If (as degree of List 2 learning increases) there is an increasing inability to give List 1 responses (over and above normal forgetting), the extinction hypothesis would be favored. If there was no such loss either the independence hypothesis or the mediation hypothesis would be favored. Provisions were included in the design to choose between these latter two if it became necessary. For example, if the mediation hypothesis is tenable it should be found that B is given before C more frequently than C before B when S is asked to write down both responses. The independence hypothesis would not predict such an ordering in response recall.

Turning next to the paradigm in which stimuli are identical but responses highly similar (A-B, A-B'), the present study should again provide bases for choice among the three hypotheses.

1. Because retroactive facilitation is expected with this paradigm (e.g., Young, 1955) it might appear that an extinction hypothesis is not tenable. However, by the use of extinction plus other factors it is possible to account for retroactive facilitation. It is a fact that more List 1 intrusions occur in the learning of List 2 for this paradigm than for the A-B, A-C paradigm. Thus, the nonreinforcement of these responses makes extinction a very plausible mechanism. So, it could be assumed that in learning A-B', A-B is extinguished. Retroactive facilitation could then be accounted for by mediation. It is known that highly similar items have high associative connection (Haagen, 1949). When S is asked to recall A-B after learning A-B', even if A-B is extinguished the mediation sequence in recall could be A—B'—B, since there has been no extinction of the strong association between B' and B. However, without the addition of still more factors the positive transfer in learning A—B' cannot be accounted for. Since the results of the present procedures do not make the extinction hypothesis a reasonable one for this paradigm, no attempt will be made here to suggest the additional factors needed to account for the positive transfer produced by this paradigm.

2. The independence hypothesis, used in conjunction with a theory of response generalization (Underwood, 1951), can be employed to account for both positive transfer and retroactive facilitation in the A-B, A-B' paradigm.

3. The mediation hypothesis also provides an attractive alternative for this positive transfer paradigm. As noted above, items which have high similarity have high associative connection. Thus, having learned A-B, the learning of A-B-B' should be very simple since B and B' are already strongly connected. Therefore, positive transfer should occur. In learning List 2, if mediation occurs S will be given additional practice on A-B; hence, this association will be further strengthened during List 2 learning, and retroactive facilitation would be expected to occur.

In summary, two paradigms are used, one associated with the production of negative transfer, the other with production of positive transfer. By requiring S to recall both List 1 and List 2 responses at various points in the learning of List 2, it was expected that choice could be made among three conceptions (extinction, independence, mediation) of the fate of List 1 associations during the learning of List 2.

## METHOD

*General.* Two parallel experiments were conducted, one using the A-B, A-C transfer paradigm and one using the A-B, A-B' paradigm. Within each experiment there were four groups of Ss. All Ss learned a first paired-associate list (List 1) of eight pairs to one perfect trial. Then List 2 was presented for a specified number of trials, namely 1, 5, 10, and 20 anticipation trials for the four groups in each experiment. After the specified number of trials for a given group, the memory drum was stopped, S was provided a sheet of paper on which the eight stimuli were printed, and he was asked to write down the two responses (one from the first list and one from the second) which were associated with each stimulus. This written recall provided the major source of data.

*Lists.* Eight nonsense syllables of from 60% to 73% association value (Glaze, 1928) were used as stimuli for all lists. Intrastimulus similarity was low in that no consonant was repeated, and four vowels were used twice each. The responses were two-syllable adjectives taken from Haagen (1949). In the A-B, A-C lists there was no apparent interlist response similarity and intralist response similarity was as low as careful inspection procedure will produce. In the A-B, A-B' lists the responses again had low intralist response similarity but high interlist response similarity. The responses from each list which were paired with the same stimulus had similarity ratings ranging from .9 to 1.4 by Haagen's scale. These high-similarity response pairs were as follows: *insane—crazy; barren—fruitless; complete—entire; royal—regal; double—twofold; afraid—scared; tranquil—peaceful; spoken—verbal.* Three different pairings of stimuli and responses were used for both experiments to avoid the possibility that fortuitous associations between stimulus and response would bias the results. An equal number of Ss in each group was given each pairing. For each experiment for each condition a given list was used as List 1 for half the Ss and as List 2 for the other half. Four orders of items were used to minimize serial learning.

The lists were presented on a Hull-type drum at a 2:2-sec. rate. The intertrial interval was 4 sec. Anticipation learning was used for List 1 and for List 2 to the point at which written recall was given (after 1, 5, 10, or 20 anticipation trials). A 1-min. interval separated the learning of the two lists.

*Subjects.* A total of 192 Ss was used. There were 24 Ss in each condition for each experiment, the conditions being the point at which S was asked for written recall. All Ss had previously served in at least one verbal-learning experiment. However, no other experiment had been run in which S was asked to recall responses from both lists, so there is no reason to believe that S anticipated that he would be asked for such recall. It should be emphasized that each S was asked for written recall only once so that it is not believed that Ss made any special attempt to remember List 1 responses. In assigning Ss, a listing of 192 entries was made such that each of the eight conditions occurred 24 times. Within these limits the ordering was random and Ss were successively assigned in order of their appearance at the laboratory.

*Written recall.* When the specified number of trials on List 2 had been given, the memory drum was stopped and the sheet for written recall given to S. The stimuli were listed on the sheet with two blank spaces under each. The Ss were first instructed to write down the responses from the two lists below the appropriate stimuli. They were further told to write these down as they came to mind, and not to attempt to recall all the responses from one list first and then all those from the other. Two minutes were then allowed for this initial recall. Following this, they were instructed to go through the responses they had written, and indicate, by assigning the numbers 1 and 2, from which list the responses had come. An additional 2 min. were allowed for this. The Ss were also told to write down any additional responses which they might think of while they were assigning list numbers.

After the recall papers were collected, a series of questions was asked to determine: (*a*) if S had written the responses as they came to mind or if there was deliberate attempt to recall the adjectives from a given list first, (*b*) whether or not S had used first-list responses to mediate the learning of the second-list responses.

## RESULTS

*Transfer.* The major concern in the present paper is with the written recall results. However, it will be worthwhile to note briefly the transfer facts and to show that random assignment of Ss to groups was effective. For all eight groups combined, the mean number of trials to learn List 1 to one perfect trial was 10.36, with the means for groups ranging from 9.17 to 12.00 trials. The F was less than 1. Lacking a precise control for transfer, some indication of the effects can be obtained by comparing the learning of List 1 with that of List 2. The total correct responses for the first three trials of the two lists were used as the response measure for the three groups having 5, 10, and 20 trials on List 2. For the A-B, A-B' paradigm, more correct responses were given on List 2 than on List 1, indicating positive transfer. For all three groups combined, the mean number correct on the first list was 9.84, and for the second, 14.35. The t was 8.55. For A-B, A-C the mean number correct on the first list was 9.64, and on the second, 8.57. This t was 1.67. This result indicates that in a statistical sense no negative transfer was present, but this is not an unusual finding for this type of comparison since learning-to-learn and warm-up would counteract the negative effect. Finally, in keeping with previous studies (e.g., Underwood, 1951), the number of overt intrusions of List 1 responses during the learning of List 2 was much greater for A-B, A-B' than for A-B, A-C.

*Written recall.* There were several alternative ways by which the written recall could be scored. The most stringent method would be to count a response as correct only if it were placed with the appropriate stimulus and also correctly identified as to list. The most liberal method would be to count an adjective correct if recalled, regardless of whether it was placed with the correct stimulus and correctly identified as to list. The results for both methods are shown in Table 1. An inspection of this table will show that the differences produced by the two scoring methods are relatively small. The implication is that if S wrote down a response, he usually identified it correctly with stimulus and list.

Turning first to the results for the A-B, A-C paradigm, the results for the stringent scoring method have been plotted in Fig. 1. As would be expected, as the number of learning trials on List 2 increases, the number of correct responses given from this list increases. Responses from the first or A-B list, however, show a gradual decline as the number of trials on List 2 increases. It is as if the A-B associations are weakened or extinguished during the learning of A-C. The loss as a function of number of A-C trials cannot be attributed to a few Ss losing many responses since most Ss showed the decline. An analysis of variance of the four recall points for A-B gave an $F$ of 8.86 ($F = 4.88$ for $P = .01$ with 3 and 92 $df$).

It was noted that Fig. 1 suggests that the A-B associations are extinguished. It might be suggested, furthermore, that not only are these as-

TABLE 1

MEAN NUMBER OF RESPONSES RECALLED FROM EACH LIST FOR EACH TRANSFER PARADIGM AS SCORED BY TWO METHODS[a]

| Method | List | Point of Written Recall (Trials) | | | |
|--------|------|------|------|------|------|
| | | 1 | 5 | 10 | 20 |
| Paradigm A-B, A-C | | | | | |
| 1 | 1 | 6.67 | 5.38 | 5.00 | 4.12 |
| | 2 | 3.46 | 6.29 | 7.33 | 7.38 |
| 2 | 1 | 6.96 | 5.58 | 5.42 | 4.29 |
| | 2 | 4.12 | 6.71 | 7.71 | 7.42 |
| Paradigm A-B, A-B' | | | | | |
| 1 | 1 | 7.67 | 7.21 | 7.12 | 6.92 |
| | 2 | 7.21 | 7.25 | 7.83 | 7.79 |
| 2 | 1 | 7.75 | 7.33 | 7.25 | 7.08 |
| | 2 | 7.38 | 7.29 | 7.96 | 7.83 |

[a] In Method 1 the response is counted correct only if correctly identified with stimulus and list. In Method 2 it is counted correct if merely recalled.

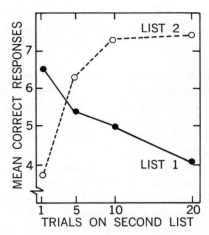

Fig. 1. Mean number of responses correctly recalled and identified with stimulus and list in the A-B, A-C paradigm.

sociations extinguished, but also that the response per se is not available. This could be deduced from the fact that the two scoring methods did not differ much, implying that if S knew the response, he also knew what stimulus and what list it went with. However, this conclusion cannot be reached with complete confidence. The reason is that the instructions to S stressed the recall of the responses to the specific stimuli; he was never told to put down a response even if he didn't know with which stimulus it was paired. It is therefore possible that Ss did not put down responses unless they were reasonably confident of its stimulus.

The objection might be raised that the decline in A-B associations seen in Fig. 1 is not to be attributed to the learning of A-C but rather represents simple forgetting. To make sure that this would not be a valid objection, a control group of 12 Ss was run. This group learned List 1 to one perfect trial and then rested for a period of time equivalent to that spent in learning A-C by the group given 20 trials. This period was 13 min. (including the 1 min. between lists). The rest interval was filled with S working on a pyramid puzzle. After the rest, Ss were given a written recall for the responses to the stimuli in the list they had learned. Counting only those responses which were appropriately paired with their stimuli, the mean recall was 7.75. Hence, it can be concluded that the decrement in recall of A-B associations as a function of trials on A-C cannot be attributed to simple forgetting, but must result from the learning of A-C.

The results for the A-B, A-B′ paradigm as given in Table 1 are quite different from those of A-B, A-C. It may first be noted that the recall of List 2 responses (A-B′) is nearly perfect after only one anticipation trial and, of course, remains high throughout 20 trials. Indeed, by both scoring methods the median recall for all groups at all points is 8.0 items. The first-list associations (A-B) show no appreciable decline. By the stringent scoring method the mean recall, even after 20 trials on A-B', is nearly seven.

*Order of recall.* The facts concerning the order of recall of the two responses can be used as evidence for or against a mediation hypothesis, as this hypothesis was discussed in the introduction. If S tends to recall List 1 responses first, it could be taken as evidence in support of a mediation hypothesis. Contrariwise, it would be evidence against mediation if List 2 responses tend to be recalled first. In this analysis data were not used from 12 Ss who admitted under questioning that they attempted to write down all responses from one list first and then all from the other. Of these, seven had learned A-B, A-C, and five, A-B, A-B'. Obviously, only cases in which both responses were recalled could be used. For A-B, A-B', there were 161, 159, 170, and 162 pairs of responses recalled for 1, 5, 10, and 20 trials, respectively. The corresponding percentages for the List 1 response being recalled before the List 2 response are 79%, 62%, 58%, and 53%. For A-B, A-C, the number of cases where both responses were recalled was 79, 113, 109, and 95 for 1, 5, 10, and 20 trials, respectively. The percentages of List 1 responses recalled first are 81%, 49%, 40%, and 43%. Assuming chance order as 50%, it can be seen that (excepting the conditions where only one trial was given on List 2 and where List 1 would be much stronger than List 2) with A-B, A-C the List 1 responses tend to be recalled first with chance or less than chance frequency. For A-B, A-B' first-list responses are recalled with greater than chance frequency although after 20 trials this frequency has nearly reach 50%.

*Subject reports.* Of the 96 Ss who learned the A-B, A-B' paradigm, 94 said they had used the List 1 responses to mediate the learning of List 2. These Ss further reported that they tended to drop the use of these mediators as List 2 learning progressed. Of those 96 Ss who had learned A-B, A-C, only two reported attempts to use the B response to mediate A-C learning; both Ss further reported that this merely confused them.

## DISCUSSION

*The A-B, A-C paradigm.* Three conceptions of what might "happen" to A-B during the learning of A-C were given in the introduction. These three conceptions were extinction or unlearning, the maintenance of two independent S-R systems, and mediation. The present data give strong support to the conception of extinction and at the same time argue against the other two conceptions. The recall of List 1 associations decreased progressively throughout the learning of A-C with nearly a 50% loss after

20 trials on A-C. A hyperbolic equation fitted to this curve predicts an asymptote at 3.46. Thus, it does not seem that all items would be extinguished, even with an extremely large number of trials on A-C. This conforms to the fact that forgetting in the RI paradigm has not been shown to be complete with very high degrees of interpolated learning. Thus, while the present data strongly support an extinction hypothesis they do not indicate why all items are not, nor are likely not to be, extinguished.

It seems reasonable to reject the independence hypothesis. If this hypothesis is to be retained, some mechanism will have to be added to account for the loss in the A-B associations over and above normal forgetting. If it is said that the A-C associations were so dominant that S was unable to recall the A-B associations, then the conception becomes very similar to an extinction hypothesis.

The mediation hypothesis cannot be seriously considered in light of the evidence. If List 2 responses are learned through mediation of B (A—B—C) the A-B association should not be lost from S's repertoire. If it is said that the mediators drop out, then something like extinction must also be added to account for their loss from S's repertoire. Furthermore, Ss' reports did not indicate that mediation had taken place (as was true of the reports for A-B, A-B'). All in all, the results give strong support to an extinction-like process; they do not give much support to an hypothesis of independence nor one of mediation.

It was noted that if S could recall a response he could usually identify it correctly as to list. On the surface, such evidence seems contrary to conceptions which say that some RI may be attributed to competition resulting from a lack of differentiation as to which response belongs in which list (e.g., Underwood, 1949). However, two additional facts must be noted which are relevant to this matter. First, in the present study essentially unlimited recall time was given so that identification of responses with lists should be more accurate than when recall is paced by a memory drum at a 2-sec. rate. Secondly, this differentiation is assumed to be very high when recall is given immediately after interpolation; differentiation is assumed to decrease as a function of time between interpolated learning and recall (Underwood, 1949). It is quite possible that the high accuracy of identifying responses with lists would be lost even with the present method if, say, a 24-hr. interval occurred between interpolation and written recall. Nevertheless, the present results would strongly suggest that nearly all RI could be accounted for by unlearning or extinction if unlimited recall time is given immediately after interpolated learning. The lack of differentiation, leading to competition between responses, should become an additional component in RI only after the passage of time since interpolated learning. Indeed, in view of the findings suggesting spontaneous recovery of extinguished associations (Briggs, 1954), it can be held that after the recovery is complete, all RI is due to competition. This two-component conception of RI will incorporate the major facts.

*The A-B, A-B' paradigm.* The data for this paradigm have shown that the A-B associations were maintained at a high level throughout the learning of A-B'. The very slight decline noted over 20 trials could be attributed to the extinction of the A-B responses for those cases in which Ss did not know the meaning of a word or words, hence, similarity of the responses was ineffective and the results were the same as an A-B, A-C paradigm. However, while accepting this possibility, it can be omitted from further consideration. The question still remains as to whether it is or is not likely that the A-B associations were extinguished while S learned A-B' even when similarity was effective. It was noted in the introduction that such an hypothesis was a plausible one; indeed, looking only at the basic results it remains plausible.

The possibility that A-B could be extinguished and the present results still be obtained (no apparent loss in the A-B associations) may be handled by mediation in which after learning A-B' (and extinguishing A-B), S recalled the B response because of its high associative connection with B'. Thus, when asked to recall, the associations were A to B' and then B' to B. If this took place, A-B could be extinguished and the present basic results would still be obtained. However, other findings argue against this interpretation and tend instead to support mediation in which A leads to B and B leads to B' at recall.

1. If B is recalled via B', B' should be recalled before B. The data indicate that B is more often recalled first. It is true that after 20 trials B and B' were recalled first about equally often. So, it is still possible that with high degrees of A-B' learning, some extinction of A-B did occur.

2. Nearly all Ss report using B as a mediator to learn A-B'; none reported that B' was used as a mediator in the recall of B. However, they did report that the use of B as a mediator tended to drop out as learning of A-B' proceeded. Some extinction of A-B might have been a concomitant or cause of this drop out. But, the fact that the percentage of times in which A-B was recalled first (before A-B) never drops below 50% suggests that if extinction was occurring it was much less in amount than that which occurred in A-B, A-C.

The conclusion is, therefore, that while the possibility of extinction of A-B in the A-B' paradigm cannot be completely ruled out, it does not appear as compelling an interpretation as does the mediation hypothesis in which A-B mediates B'.

Finally, what about the hypothesis of independent response systems in which response generalization is used to account for positive transfer and retroactive facilitation? The use of response generalization to explain certain facts of transfer has been of considerable help in organizing the facts of transfer. One particular statement of this formulation can be briefly summarized (Underwood, 1951). It is assumed that when A-B is being learned, all responses similar to B likewise develop some associative strength to A. The amount of such strength, developed through what has been called parasitic reinforcement, is directly related to similarity of the response with the B response. Positive transfer occurs, therefore, because less learning has to occur in the second list than in the first. Thus, in the present situation, if A-B' develops some associative strength as a consequence of learning A-B, positive transfer should occur when S is asked to learn A-B'. Retroactive facilitation would occur, since during the learning of A-B' the A-B association would be further strengthened. It should be noted that this hypothesis deals only with the associations between A and B, and between A and B'; it does not deal in any way with the already well-established association between B and B' which forms a central part of the mediation hypothesis.

The present evidence suggests that the response-generalization accounting of certain facts of transfer may well be abandoned in favor of a mediation hypothesis. The mediation hypothesis will account for the same general facts as will response generalization; furthermore, certain facts of the present experiment seem difficult to reconcile with the response-generalization hypothesis.

1. Almost without exception, Ss report mediation. While it may be possible to extend the theory of response generalization to account for this fact that Ss report mediation, the mediation per se can be used to account for the results, without further elaboration.

2. It was noted that after only one anticipation trial, recall of List 2 was nearly perfect. The theory of response generalization assumes a generalization gradient decreasing rather sharply as similarity decreases. The generalized association is not assumed to grow in associative strength at a rate comparable at all to the directly-reinforced association (A-B). To account for the extraordinarily rapid learning of A-B' would mean that there is essentially no gradient between B and B', or to say this another way, the gradient is flat. In previous experiments, no such rapid learning of A-B' was noted; learning was more rapid than for a control condition but nothing like that shown here in the written recall. Indeed, in the present study for the groups having 5, 10, and 20 trials (before written recall), the mean number of items recalled on the second anticipation trial (comparable to the point at which written recall was asked for in the group having only 1 anticipation trial) was 5.04. This is to be contrasted with 7.75, obtained on written recall at the same point. The reason for this discrepancy, it is believed, is that under the standard procedures of anticipation learning S does not have time to mediate all items. Given more time, recall is nearly perfect right at the start of "learning" the second list. This finding is not compatible with the theory of response generalization.

The conclusion is that mediation of B′ through A-B is a more appropriate formulation than response generalization to account for positive effects in transfer and retention when response similarity is involved with identical stimuli. As similarity between responses decreases, the associative connection between them will likewise decrease; thus, a gradient-like phenomenon will appear in transfer. With moderate similarity between responses, the associative connection between the two will be less than in the present case, and additional strengthening of the associative connection will be necessary before mediation is completely effective. Thus, positive transfer will be less than when the responses are highly similar. It is apparent that since no evidence for mediation could be found in A-B, A-C, the mediation hypothesis must be abandoned when the responses reach a certain level of disimilarity (or a low level of similarity). It is at this point that extinction begins to occur with consequent negative transfer.

## SUMMARY

The A-B, A-C and the A-B, A-B′ transfer paradigms were studied in order to evaluate three conceptions concerning the fate of first-list associations in learning a second list; namely: extinction of first-list associations, maintenance of two independent S-R systems, and mediation of the learning of the second-list response by the first-list association. For each paradigm, different groups of 24 Ss each were stopped after 1, 5, 10, or 20 anticipation trials on List 2 and were asked to write down *both* List 1 and List 2 responses to the stimuli. Both lists contained eight pairs of nonsense syllables and two-syllable adjectives. List 1 learning was carried to one perfect trial.

For the A-B, A-C paradigm there was a gradual reduction in reproduction of List 1 responses as degree of List 2 learning increased. A control condition showed that this reduction could not be accounted for by normal forgetting. No successful mediation of the C response via A-B was reported. It was concluded that of the three alternative conceptions, extinction of the List 1 responses was clearly to be preferred. It appears that nearly all retroactive inhibition measured immediately after interpolated learning may be due to extinction or unlearning of first-list responses during the learning of the second list.

For the A-B, A-B′ paradigm, the List 1 responses showed no appreciable loss over 20 trials and List 2 was given nearly perfectly after one anticipation trial. Of 96 Ss, 94 reported the use of the A-B association to mediate the B′ response. The rapid learning of List 2 is understandable by the mediation hypothesis, but some extinction of the A-B association in the A-B, A-B′ paradigm cannot be ruled out completely by the present data.

The A-B association may be extinguished and then mediation of the List 1 response occurs via A-B′-B. However, considering all evidence, it seemed most probable that mediation occurs most frequently in the order A-B-B′. Finally, the evidence suggests that transfer effects produced by variation in response similarity can be more simply accounted for by mediation than by a theory using response generalization.

## REFERENCES

BRIGGS, G. E. (1954) Acquisition, extinction, and recovery functions in retroactive inhibition. *J. exp. Psychol.*, 47, 285-293.

GLAZE, J. A. (1928) The association value of nonsense syllables. *J. genet. Psychol.*, 35, 255-269.

HAAGEN, C. H. (1949) Synonymity, vividness, familiarity, and association-value ratings for 400 pairs of common adjectives. *J. Psychol.*, 30, 185-200.

MELTON, A. W. and IRWIN, J. McQ. (1940) The influence of degree of interpolated learning on retroactive inhibition and the overt transfer of specific responses. *Amer. J. Psychol.*, 53, 175-203.

UNDERWOOD, B. J. (1949) Proactive inhibition as a function of time and degree of prior learning. *J. exp. Psychol.*, 39, 24-34.

UNDERWOOD, B. J. (1951) Associative transfer in verbal learning as a function of response similarity and degree of first-list learning. *J. exp. Psychol.*, 42, 44-53.

YOUNG, R. K. (1955) Retroactive and proactive effects under varying conditions of response similarity. *J. exp. Psychol.*, 50, 113-119.

# 41.   Interference and Forgetting

## B. J. Underwood

*For some time, many psychologists considered retroactive inhibi-
tion to be the major variable operating in the forgetting process. Thus,
as the author points out, if a single task is learned in the laboratory
and retention of that material is measured 24 hours later, the forgetting that takes place is attributed to interference arising from
activities interpolated between the learning of the material and the
subsequent test for retention. It is this general assumption that the
author questions.*

I know of no one who seriously maintains that interference among tasks
is of no consequence in the production of forgetting. Whether forgetting
is conceptualized at a strict psychological level or at a neural level (e.g.,
neural memory trace), some provision is made for interference to account
for at least some of the measured forgetting. The many studies on retroactive inhibition are probably responsible for this general agreement that
interference among tasks must produce a sizable proportion of forgetting.
By introducing an interpolated interfering task very marked decrements
in recall can be produced in a few minutes in the laboratory. But there is
a second generalization which has resulted from these studies, namely,
that most forgetting must be a function of the learning of tasks which
interfere with that which has already been learned (19). Thus, if a single
task is learned in the laboratory and retention measured after a week, the
loss has been attributed to the interference from activities learned outside
the laboratory during the week. It is this generalization with which I am
concerned in the initial portions of this paper.

Now, I cannot deny the data which show large amounts of forgetting
produced by an interpolated list in a few minutes in the laboratory. Nor
do I deny that this loss may be attributed to interference. But I will try
to show that use of retroactive inhibition as a paradigm of forgetting (via
interference) may be seriously questioned. To be more specific: if a subject learns a single task, such as a list of words, and retention of this task

*Psychol. Rev.*, 1957, *64*, 49-60. Reprinted with permission of the author and The
American Psychological Association. Address of the president, Midwestern Psychological Association, St. Louis, Missouri, May, 1956. Most of the data from my own
research referred to in this paper were obtained from work done under Contract N7
onr-45008, Project NR 154-057, between Northwestern University and The Office
of Naval Research.

is measured after a day, a week, or a month, I will try to show that very little of the forgetting can be attributed to an interfering task learned outside the laboratory during the retention interval. Before pursuing this further, I must make some general comments by way of preparation.

Whether we like it or not, the experimental study of forgetting has been largely dominated by the Ebbinghaus tradition, both in terms of methods and materials used. I do not think this is due to sheer perversity on the part of several generations of scientists interested in forgetting. It may be noted that much of our elementary knowledge can be obtained only by rote learning. To work with rote learning does not mean that we are thereby not concerning ourselves with phenomena that have no counterparts outside the laboratory. Furthermore, the investigation of these phenomena can be handled by methods which are acceptable to a science. As is well known, there are periodic verbal revolts against the Ebbinghaus tradition ( e.g., 2, 15, 22 ). But for some reason nothing much ever happens in the laboratory as a consequence of these revolts. I mention these matters neither by way of apology nor of justification for having done some research in rote learning, but for two other reasons. First, it may very well be true, as some have suggested ( e.g., 22 ), that studies of memory in the Ebbinghaus tradition are not getting at all of the important phenomena of memory. I think the same statement—that research has not got at all of the important processes—could be made about all areas in psychology; so that the criticism ( even if just) should not be indigenous to the study of memory. Science does not deal at will with all natural events. Science deals with natural events only when ingenuity in developing methods and techniques of measurement allow these events to be brought within the scope of science. If, therefore, the studies of memory which meet scientific acceptability do not tap all-important memorial processes, all I can say is that this is the state of the science in the area at the moment. Secondly, because the bulk of the systematic data on forgetting has been obtained on rote-learned tasks, I must of necessity use such data in discussing interference and forgetting.

Returning to the experimental situation, let me again put in concrete form the problem with which I first wish to deal. A subject learns a single task, such as a list of syllables, nouns, or adjectives. After an interval of time, say, 24 hours, his retention of this list is measured. The explanatory problem is what is responsible for the forgetting which commonly occurs over the 24 hours. As indicated earlier, the studies of retroactive inhibition led to the theoretical generalization that this forgetting was due largely to interference from other tasks learned during the 24-hour retention interval. McGeoch (20) came to this conclusion, his last such statement being made in 1942. I would, therefore, like to look at the data which were available to McGeoch and others interested in this matter. I must repeat that the kind of data with which I am concerned is the retention of a list without formal interpolated learning introduced. The interval of retention with which I am going to deal in this, and several subsequent analyses, is 24 hours.

First, of course, Ebbinghaus' data were available and in a sense served as the reference point for many subsequent investigations. In terms of percentage saved in relearning, Ebbinghaus showed about 65 per cent loss over 24 hours (7). In terms of recall after 24 hours, the following studies are representative of the amount forgotten: Youtz, 88 per cent loss (37); Luh, 82 per cent (18); Krueger, 74 per cent (16); Hovland, 78 per cent (11); Cheng, 65 per cent and 84 per cent (6); Lester, 65 per cent (17). Let us assume as a rough average of these studies that 75 per cent forgetting was measured over 24 hours. In all of these studies the list was learned to one perfect trial. The percentage values were derived by dividing the total number of items in the list into the number lost and changing to a percentage. Thus, on the average in these studies, if the subject learned a 12-item list and recalled three of these items after 24 hours, nine items (75 per cent) were forgotten.

The theory of interference as advanced by McGeoch, and so far as I know never seriously challenged, was that during the 24-hour interval subjects learned something outside the laboratory which interfered with the list learned in the laboratory. Most of the materials involved in the investigations cited above were nonsense syllables, and the subjects were college students. While realizing that I am viewing these results in the light of data which McGeoch and others did not have available, it seems to me to be an incredible stretch of an interference hypothesis to hold that this 75 per cent forgetting was caused by something which the subjects learned outside the laboratory during the 24-hour interval. Even if we agree with some educators that much of what we teach our students in college is nonsense, it does not seem to be the kind of learning that would interfere with nonsense syllables.

If, however, this forgetting was not due to interference from tasks learned outside the laboratory during the retention interval, to what was it due? I shall try to show that most of this forgetting was indeed produced by interference—not from tasks learned outside the laboratory, but from tasks learned previously in the laboratory. Following this I will show that when interference from laboratory tasks is removed, the amount of forgetting which occurs is relatively quite small. It then becomes more plausible that this amount could be produced by interference from tasks learned outside the laboratory, although, as I shall also point out, the interference very likely comes from prior, not interpolated, learning.

In 1950 a study was published by Mrs. Greenberg and myself (10) on retention as a function of stage of practice. The orientation for this study was crassly empirical; we simply wanted to know if subjects learn how to recall in the same sense that they learn how to learn. In the conditions

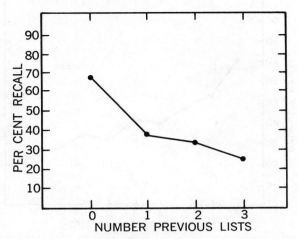

Fig. 1. Recall of paired adjectives as a function of number of previous lists learned (10).

with which I am concerned, naive subjects learned a list of ten paired adjectives to a criterion of eight out of ten correct on a single trial. Forty-eight hours later this list was recalled. On the following day, these same subjects learned a new list to the same criterion and recalled it after 48 hours. This continued for two additional lists, so that the subjects had learned and recalled four lists, but the learning and recall of each list was complete before another list was learned. There was low similarity among these lists as far as conventional symptoms of similarity are concerned. No words were repeated and no obvious similarities existed, except for the fact that they were all adjectives and a certain amount of similarity among prefixes, suffixes, and so on must inevitably occur. The recall of these four successive lists is shown in Fig. 1.

As can be seen, the more lists that are learned, the poorer the recall, from 69 per cent recall of the first list to 25 per cent recall of the fourth list. In examining errors at recall, we found a sufficient number of intrusion responses from previous lists to lead us to suggest that the increasing decrements in recall were a function of proactive interference from previous lists. And, while we pointed out that these results had implications for the design of experiments on retention, the relevance to an interference theory of forgetting was not mentioned.

Dr. E. J. Archer has made available to me certain data from an experiment which still is in progress and which deals with this issue. Subjects learned lists of 12 serial adjectives to one perfect trial and recalled them after 24 hours. The recall of a list always took place prior to learning the next list. The results for nine successive lists are shown in Fig. 2. Let me say again that there is no laboratory activity during the 24-hour interval;

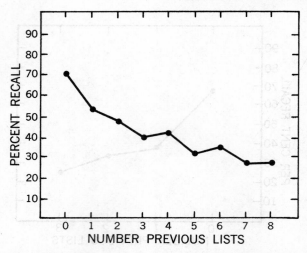

Fig. 2. Recall of serial adjective lists as a function of number of previous lists learned. Unpublished data, courtesy of Dr. E. J. Archer.

the subject learns a list, is dismissed from the laboratory, and returns after 24 hours to recall the list. The percentage of recall falls from 71 per cent for the first list to 27 per cent for the ninth.

In summarizing the more classical data on retention above, I indicated that a rough estimate showed that after 24 hours 75 per cent forgetting took place, or recall was about 25 per cent correct. In viewing these values in the light of Greenberg's and Archer's findings, the conclusion seemed inescapable that the classical studies must have been dealing with subjects who had learned many lists. That is to say, the subjects must have served in many conditions by use of counterbalancing and repeated cycles. To check on this I have made a search of the literature on the studies of retention to see if systematic data could be compiled on this matter. Preliminary work led me to establish certain criteria for inclusion in the summary to be presented. First, because degree of learning is such an important variable, I have included only those studies in which degree of learning was one perfect recitation of the list. Second, I have included only studies in which retention was measured after 24 hours. Third, I have included only studies in which recall measures were given. (Relearning measures add complexities with which I do not wish to deal in this paper.) Fourth, the summary includes only material learned by relatively massed practice. Finally, if an investigator had two or more conditions which met these criteria, I averaged the values presentation in this paper. Except for these restrictions, I have used all studies I found (with an exception to be noted later), although I do not pretend to have made an

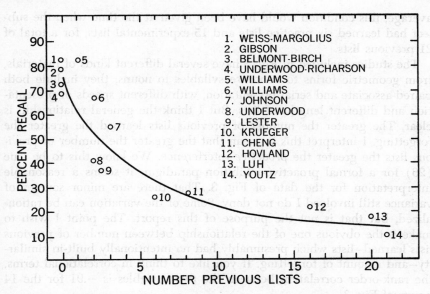

FIG. 3. Recall as a function of number of previous lists learned as determined from a number of studies. From left to right: Weiss and Margolius (35), Gibson (9), Belmont and Birch (3), Underwood and Richardson (33), Williams (36), Underwood (27, 28, 29, 30), Lester (17), Johnson (14), Krueger (16), Cheng (6), Hovland (11), Luh (18), Youtz (37).

exhaustive search. From each of these studies I got two facts: first, the percentage recalled after 24 hours, and second, the average number of previous lists the subjects had learned before learning the list on which recall after 24 hours was taken. Thus, if a subject had served in five experimental conditions via counterbalancing, and had been given two practice lists, the average number of lists learned before learning the list for which I tabulated the recall was four. This does not take into account any previous experiments in rote learning in which the subject might have served.

For each of these studies the two facts, average number of previous lists learned and percentage of recall, are related as in Fig. 3. For example, consider the study by Youtz. This study was concerned with Jost's law, and had several degrees of learning, several lengths of retention interval, and the subjects served in two cycles. Actually, there were 15 experimental conditions and each subject was given each condition twice. Also, each subject learned six practice lists before starting the experimental conditions. Among the 15 conditions was one in which the learning of the syllables was carried to one perfect recitation and recall was taken after 24 hours. It is this particular condition in which I am interested. On the average, this condition would have been given at the time when the subject had learned six practice lists and 15 experimental lists, for a total of 21 previous lists.

The studies included in Fig. 3 have several different kinds of materials, from geometric forms to nonsense syllables to nouns; they include both paired-associate and serial presentation, with different speeds of presentation and different lengths of lists. But I think the general relationship is clear. The greater the number of previous lists learned the greater the forgetting. I interpret this to mean that the greater the number of previous lists the greater the *proactive* interference. We know this to be true (26) for a formal proactive-inhibition paradigm; it seems a reasonable interpretation for the data of Fig. 3. That there are minor sources of variance still involved I do not deny. Some of the variation can be rationalized, but that is not the purpose of this report. The point I wish to make is the obvious one of the relationship between number of previous lists learned—lists which presumably had no intentionally built-in similarity—and amount of forgetting. If you like to think in correlational terms, the rank-order correlation between the two variables is −.91 for the 14 points of Fig. 3.

It may be of interest to the historian that, of the studies published before 1942 which met the criteria I imposed, I did not find a single one in which subjects had not been given at least one practice task before starting experimental conditions, and in most cases the subjects had several practice lists and several experimental conditions. Gibson's study (1942) was the first I found in which subjects served in only one condition and were not given practice tasks. I think it is apparent that the design proclivities of the 1920s and 1930s have been largely responsible for the exaggerated picture we have had of the rate of forgetting of rote-learned materials. On the basis of studies performed during the 1920s and 1930s, I have given a rough estimate of forgetting as being 75 per cent over 24 hours, recall being 25 per cent. On the basis of modern studies in which the subject has learned no previous lists—where there is no proactive inhibition from previous laboratory tasks—a rough estimate would be that forgetting is 25 per cent; recall is 75 per cent. The values are reversed. (If in the above and subsequent discussion my use of percentage values as if I were dealing with a cardinal or extensive scale is disturbing, I will say only that it makes the picture easier to grasp, and in my opinion no critical distortion results.)

Before taking the next major step, I would like to point out a few other observations which serve to support my general point that proactive inhibition from laboratory tasks has been the major cause of forgetting in the more classical studies. The first illustration I shall give exemplifies the point that when subjects have served in several conditions, forgetting after relatively short periods of time is greater than after 24 hours if the subject has served in only one condition. In the Youtz study to which I have already referred, other conditions were employed in which recall was taken after short intervals. After 20 minutes recall was 74 per cent, about what it is after 24 hours if the subject has not served in a series of conditions. After two hours recall was 32 per cent. In Ward's (34) well-known reminiscence experiment, subjects who on the average had learned ten previous lists showed a recall of only 64 per cent after 20 minutes.

In the famous Jenkins-Dallenbach (13) study on retention following sleep and following waking, two subjects were used. One subject learned a total of 61 lists and the other 62 in addition to several practice lists. Roughly, then, if the order of the conditions was randomized, approximately 30 lists had been learned prior to the learning of a list for a given experimental condition. Recall after eight waking hours for one subject was 4 per cent and for the other 14 per cent. Even after sleeping for eight hours the recall was only 55 per cent and 58 per cent.

I have said that an interpolated list can produce severe forgetting. However, in one study (1), using the A-B, A-C paradigm for original and interpolated learning, but using subjects who had never served in any previous conditions, recall of the original list was 46 per cent after 48 hours, and in another comparable study (24), 42 per cent. Thus, the loss is not nearly as great as in the classical studies I have cited where there was no interpolated learning in the laboratory.

My conclusion at this point is that, in terms of the gross analysis I have made, the amount of forgetting which might be attributed to interference from tasks learned outside the laboratory has been "reduced" from 75 per cent to about 25 per cent. I shall proceed in the next section to see if we have grounds for reducing this estimate still more. In passing on to this section, however, let me say that the study of factors which influence proactive inhibition in these counterbalanced studies is a perfectly legitimate and important area of study. I mention this because in the subsequent discussion I am going to deal only with the case where a subject has learned a single list in the laboratory, and I do not want to leave the impression that we should now and forevermore drop the study of interference produced by previous laboratory tasks. Indeed, as will be seen shortly, it is my opinion that we should increase these studies for the simple reason that the proactive paradigm provides a more realistic one than does the retroactive paradigm.

When the subject learns and recalls a single list in the laboratory, I have given an estimate of 25 per cent as being the amount forgotten over 24 hours. When, as shown above, we calculate percentage forgotten of lists learned to one perfect trial, the assumption is that had the subjects been given an immediate recall trial, the list would have been perfectly recalled. This, of course, is simply not true. The major factor determining how much error is introduced by this criterion-percentage method is probably the difficulty of the task. In general, the overestimation of forgetting by the percentage method will be directly related to the difficulty of the task. Thus, the more slowly the learning approaches a given criterion, the greater the drop on the trial immediately after the criterion trial. Data from from a study by Runquist (24), using eight paired adjectives (a comparatively easy task), shows that amount of forgetting is overestimated by about 10 per cent. In a study (32) using very difficult consonant syllables, the overestimation was approximately 20 per cent. To be conservative, assume that on the average the percentage method of reporting recall overestimates the amount forgotten by 10 per cent. If we subtract this from the 25 per cent assumed above, the forgetting is now re-estimated as being 15 per cent over 24 hours. That is to say, an interference theory, or any other form of theory, has to account for a very small amount of forgetting as compared with the amount traditionally cited.

What are the implications of so greatly "reducing" the amount of forgetting? There are at least three implications which I feel are worth pointing out. First, if one wishes to hold to an interference theory of forgetting (as I do), it seems plausible to assert that this amount of forgetting could be produced from learning which has taken place outside of the laboratory. Furthermore, it seems likely that such interference must result primarily from proactive interference. This seems likely on a simple probability basis. A 20-year-old college student will more likely have learned something during his 20 years prior to coming to the laboratory that will interfere with his retention than he will during the 24 hours between the learning and retention test. However, the longer the retention interval the more important will retroactive interference become relative to proactive interferences.

The second implication is that these data may suggest greater homogeneity or continuity in memorial processes than hitherto supposed. Although no one has adequately solved the measurement problem of how to make comparisons of retention among conditioned responses, prose material, motor tasks, concept learning, and rote-learned tasks, the gross comparisons have indicated that rote-learned tasks were forgotten much more rapidly than these other tasks. But the rote-learning data used for comparison have been those derived with the classical design in which the forgetting over 24 hours is approximately 75 per cent. If we take the revised estimate of 15 per cent, the discrepancies among tasks become considerably less.

The third implication of the revised estimate of rate of forgetting is that the number of variables which appreciably influence rate of forgetting must be sharply limited. While this statement does not inevitably follow from the analyses I have made, the current evidence strongly supports the statement. I want to turn to the final section of this paper which will consist of a review of the influence of some of the variables which are or have been thought to be related to rate of forgetting. In considering these variables, it is well to keep in mind that a variable which produces only a small difference in forgetting is important if one is interested in accounting for the 15 per cent assumed now as the loss over 24 hours. If appropriate for a given variable, I will indicate where it fits into an interference theory, although in no case will I endeavor to handle the details of such a theory.

*Time.* Passage of time between learning and recall is the critical defining variable for forgetting. Manipulation of this variable provides the basic data for which a theory must account. Previously, our conception of rate of forgetting as a function of time has been tied to the Ebbinghaus curve. If the analysis made earlier is correct, this curve does not give us the basic data we need. In short, we must start all over and derive a retention curve over time when the subjects have learned no previous materials in the laboratory. It is apparent that I expect the fall in this curve over time to be relatively small.

In conjunction with time as an independent variable, we must, in explanations of forgetting, consider why sleep retards the processes responsible for forgetting. My conception, which does not really explain anything, is that since forgetting is largely produced by proactive interference, the amount of time which a subject spends in sleep is simply to be subtracted from the total retention interval when predicting the amount to be forgotten. It is known that proactive interference increases with passage of time (5); sleep, I believe, brings to a standstill whatever these processes are which produce this increase.

*Degree of learning.* We usually say that the better or stronger the learning the more or better the retention. Yet, we do not know whether or not the *rate* of forgetting differs for items of different strength. The experimental problem is a difficult one. What we need is to have a subject learn a single association and measure its decline in strength over time. But this is difficult to carry out with verbal material, since almost of necessity we must have the subject learn a series of associations, to make it a reasonable task. And, when a series of associations are learned, complications arise from interaction effects among associations of different strength. Nevertheless, we may expect, on the basis of evidence from a wide variety of studies, that given a constant degree of similarity, the effective interference varies as some function of the strength of associations.

*Distribution of practice.* It is a fact that distribution of practice during acquisition influences retention of verbal materials. The facts of the case seem to be as follows. If the subject has not learned previous lists in the laboratory, massed practice gives equal or better retention than does distributed practice. If, on the other hand, the subject has learned a number of previous lists, distributed practice will facilitate retention (32). We do not have the theoretical solution to these facts. The point I wish to make here is that whether or not distribution of learning inhibits or facilitates retention depends upon the amount of interference from previous learning. It is reasonable to expect, therefore, that the solution to the problem will come via principles handling interference in general. I might also say that a theoretical solution to this problem will also provide a solution for Jost's laws.

*Similarity.* Amount of interference from other tasks is closely tied to similarity. This similarity must be conceived of as similarity among materials as such and also situational similarity (4). When we turn to similarity within a task, the situation is not quite so clear. Empirically and theoretically (8) one would expect that intratask similarity would be a very relevant variable in forgetting. As discussed elsewhere (31), however, variation in intratask similarity almost inevitably leads to variations in intertask similarity. We do know from a recent study (33) that with material of low meaningfulness forgetting is significantly greater with high intralist similarity than with low. While the difference in magnitude is only about 8 per cent, when we are trying to account for a total loss of 15 per cent, this amount becomes a major matter.

*Meaningfulness.* The belief has long been held that the more meaningful the material the better the retention—the less the forgetting. Osgood (21) has pointed out that if this is true it is difficult for an interference theory to handle. So far as I know, the only direct test of the influence of this variable is a recent study in which retention of syllables of 100 per cent association value was compared with that of zero association value (33). There was no difference in the recall of these syllables. Other less precise evidence would support this finding when comparisons are made among syllables, adjectives, and nouns, as plotted in Fig. 3. However, there is some evidence that materials of very low meaningfulness are forgotten more rapidly than nonsense syllables of zero association value. Consonant syllables, both serial (32) and paired associates (unpublished), show about 50 per cent loss over 24 hours. The study using serial lists was the one mentioned earlier as knowingly omitted from Fig. 3. These syllables, being extremely difficult to learn, allow a correction of about 20 per cent due to criterion overestimation, but even with this much correction the forgetting (30 per cent) is still appreciably more than the estimate we have made for other materials. To invoke the interference theory to account for this discrepancy means that we must demonstrate how interference from other activities could be greater for these consonant syllables than for nonsense syllables, nouns, adjectives, and other materials. Our best guess at the present time is that the sequences of letters in consonant syllables are contrary to other well-established language habits. That is to say, letter sequences which commonly occur in our language are largely different from those in consonant syllables. As a consequence, not only are these consonant syllables very difficult to learn, but forgetting is accelerated by proactive interference from previously well-learned letter sequences. If subsequent research cannot demonstrate such a source of interference, or if some other source is not specified, an interference theory for this case will be in some trouble.

*Affectivity.* Another task dimension which has received extensive attention is the affective tone of the material. I would also include here the studies attaching unpleasant experiences to some items experimentally and not to others, and measuring retention of these two sets of items. Freud is to a large extent responsible for these studies, but he cannot be held responsible for the malformed methodology which characterizes so many of them. What can one say by way of summarizing these studies? The only conclusion that I can reach is a statistical one, namely, that the occasional positive result found among the scores of studies is about as frequent as one would expect by sampling error, using the 5 per cent level of confidence. Until a reliable body of facts is established for this variable and associated variables, no theoretical evaluation is possible.

*Other variables.* As I indicated earlier, I will not make an exhaustive survey of the variables which may influence rate of forgetting. I have limited myself to variables which have been rather extensively investigated, which have immediate relevance to the interference theory, or for which reliable relationships are available. Nevertheless, I would like to mention briefly some of these other variables. There is the matter of *warm-up* before recall; some investigators find that this reduces forgetting (12); others, under as nearly replicated conditions as is possible to obtain, do not (23). Some resolution must be found for these flat contradictions. It seems perfectly reasonable, however, that inadequate set or context differences could reduce recall. Indeed, an interference theory would predict this forgetting if the set or context stimuli are appreciably different from those prevailing at the time of learning. In our laboratory we try to reinstate the learning set by careful instructions, and we simply do not find decrements that might be attributed to inadequate set. For example, in a recent study (33) subjects were given a 24-hour recall of a serial list after learning to one perfect trial. I think we would expect that the first item in the list would suffer the greatest decrement due to inadequate set, yet this item showed only .7 per cent loss. But let it be clear that when we are attempting to account for the 15 per cent loss over 24 hours, we should not overlook any possible source for this loss.

Thus far I have not said anything about forgetting as a function of characteristics of the subject, that is, the personality or intellectual characteristics. As far as I have been able to determine, there is not a single valid study which shows that such variables have an appreciable influence on forgetting. Many studies have shown differences in learning as a function of these variables, but not differences in rate of forgetting. Surely there must be some such variables. We do know that if subjects are severely insulted, made to feel stupid, or generally led to believe that they have no justification for continued existence on the earth just before they are asked to recall, they will show losses (e.g., 25, 38), but even the influence of this kind of psychological beating is short lived. Somehow I have never felt that such findings need explanation by a theory used to explain the other facts of forgetting.

Concerning the causes of forgetting, let me sum up in a somewhat more dogmatic fashion than is probably justified. One of the assumptions of science is finite causality. Everything cannot influence everything else. To me, the most important implication of the work on forgetting during the last ten years is that this work has markedly *reduced* the number of variables related to forgetting. Correspondingly, I think the theoretical problem has become simpler. It is my belief that we can narrow down the cause of forgetting to interference from previously learned habits, from habits being currently learned, and from habits we have yet to learn. The amount of this interference is primarily a function of similarity and associative strength, the latter being important because it interacts with similarity.

## SUMMARY

This paper deals with issues in the forgetting of rote-learned materials. An analysis of the current evidence suggests that the classical Ebbinghaus curve of forgetting is primarily a function of interference from materials learned previously in the laboratory. When this source of interference is removed, for getting decreases from about 75 per cent over 24 hours to about 25 per cent. This latter figure can be reduced by at least 10 per cent by other methodological considerations, leaving 15 per cent as an estimate of the forgetting over 24 hours. This estimate will vary somewhat as a function of intratask similarity, distributed practice, and with very low meaningful material. But the overall evidence suggests that similarity with other material and situational similarity are by far the most critical factors in forgetting. Such evidence is consonant with a general interference theory, although the details of such a theory were not presented here.

## REFERENCES

1. ARCHER, E. J. and UNDERWOOD, B. J. (1951) Retroactive inhibition of verbal associations as a multiple function of temporal point of interpolation and degree of interpolated learning. *J. exp. Psychol.*, 42, 283-290.
2. BARTLETT, F. C. (1932) *Remembering: a study in experimental and social psychology.* London: Cambridge Univer. Press.
3. BELMONT, L. and BIRCH, H. G. (1951) Re-individualizing the repression hypothesis. *J. abnorm. soc. Psychol.*, 46, 226-235.

4. BILODEAU, I. McD. and SCHLOSBERG, H. (1951) Similarity in stimulating conditions as a variable in retroactive inhibition. *J. exp. Psychol., 41,* 199-204.

5. BRIGGS, G. E. (1954) Acquisition, extinction, and recovery functions in retroactive inhibition. *J. exp. Psychol., 47,* 285-293.

6. CHENG, N. Y. (1929) Retroactive effect and degree of similarity. *J. exp. Psychol., 12,* 444-458.

7. EBBINGHAUS, H. (1913) *Memory: a contribution to experimental psychology.* (Trans. by H. A. Ruger, and C. E. Bussenius) New York: Bureau of Publications, Teachers College, Columbia Univer.

8. GIBSON, ELEANOR J. (1940) A systematic application of the concepts of generalization and differentiation to verbal learning. *Psychol. Rev., 47,* 196-229.

9. GIBSON, ELEANOR J. (1942) Intra-list generalization as a factor in verbal learning. *J. exp. Psychol., 30,* 185-200.

10. GREENBERG, R. and UNDERWOOD, B. J. (1950) Retention as a function of stage of practice. *J. exp. Psychol., 40,* 452-457.

11. HOVLAND, C. I. (1940) Experimental studies in rote-learning theory. VI. Comparison of retention following learning to same criterion by massed and distributed practice. *J. exp. Psychol., 26,* 568-587.

12. IRION, A. L. (1948) The relation of "set" to retention. *Psychol. Rev., 55,* 336-341.

13. JENKINS, J. G. and DALLENBACH, K. M. (1924) Oblivescence during sleep and waking. *Amer. J. Psychol., 35,* 605-612.

14. JOHNSON, L. M. (1939) The relative effect of a time interval upon learning and retention. *J. exp. Psychol., 24,* 169-179.

15. KATONA, G. (1940) *Organizing and memorizing: studies in the psychology of learning and teaching.* New York: Columbia Univer. Press.

16. KRUEGER, W. C. F. (1929) The effect of overlearning on retention. *J. exp. Psychol., 12,* 71-78.

17. LESTER, O. P. (1932) Mental set in relation to retroactive inhibition. *J. exp. Psychol., 15,* 681-699.

18. LUH, C. W. (1922) The conditions of retention. *Psychol. Monogr., 31,* No. 3 (Whole No. 142).

19. MCGEOCH, J. A. (1932) Forgetting and the law of disuse. *Psychol. Rev., 39,* 352-370.

20. MCGEOCH, J. A. (1942) *The psychology of human learning.* New York: Longmans, Green.

21. OSGOOD, C. E. (1953) *Method and theory in experimental psychology.* New York: Oxford Univer. Press.

22. RAPAPORT, D. (1943) Emotions and memory. *Psychol. Rev., 50,* 234-243.

23. ROCKWAY, M. R. and DUNCAN, C. P. (1952) Pre-recall warming-up in verbal retention. *J. exp. Psychol., 43,* 305-312.

24. RUNQUIST, W. (1956) Retention of verbal associations as a function of interference and strength. Unpublished doctor's dissertation, Northwestern Univer.

25. RUSSELL, W. A. (1952) Retention of verbal material as a function of motivating instructions and experimentally-induced failure. *J. exp. Psychol., 43,* 207-216.

26. UNDERWOOD, B. J. (1945) The effect of successive interpolations on retroactive and proactive inhibition. *Psychol. Monogr., 59,* No. 3 (Whole No. 273).

27. UNDERWOOD, B. J. (1952) Studies of distributed practice: VII. Learning and retention of serial nonsense lists as a function of intralist similarity. *J. exp. Psychol.*, *44*, 80-87.
28. UNDERWOOD, B. J. (1953) Studies of distributed practice: VIII. Learning and retention of paired nonsense syllables as a function of intralist similarity. *J. exp. Psychol.*, *45*, 133-142.
29. UNDERWOOD, B. J. (1953) Studies of distributed practice: IX. Learning and retention of paired adjectives as a function of intralist similarity. *J. exp. Psychol.*, *45*, 143-149.
30. UNDERWOOD, B. J. (1953) Studies of distributed practice: X. The influence of intralist similarity on learning and retention of serial adjective lists. *J. exp. Psychol.*, *45*, 253-259.
31. UNDERWOOD, R. J. (1954) Intralist similarity in verbal learning and retention. *Psychol. Rev.*, *3*, 160-166.
32. UNDERWOOD, B. J. and RICHARDSON, J. (1955) Studies of distributed practice: XIII. Interlist interference and the retention of serial nonsense lists. *J. exp. Psychol.*, *50*, 39-46.
33. UNDERWOOD, B. J. and RICHARDSON, J. (1956) The influence of meaningfulness, intralist similarity, and serial position on retention. *J. exp. Psychol.*, *52*, 119-126.
34. WARD, L. B. (1937) Reminiscence and rote learning. *Psychol. Monogr.*, *49*, No. 4 (Whole No. 220).
35. WEISS, W. and MARGOLIUS, G. (1954) The effect of context stimuli on learning and retention. *J. exp. Psychol.*, *48*, 318-322.
36. WILLIAMS, M. (1950) The effects of experimentally induced needs upon retention. *J. exp. Psychol.*, *40*, 139-151.
37. YOUTZ, ADELLA C. (1941) An experimental evaluation of Jost's laws. *Psychol. Monogr.*, *53*, No. 1 (Whole No. 238).
38. ZELLER, A. F. (1951) An experimental analogue of repression: III. The effect of induced failure and success on memory measured by recall. *J. exp. Psychol.*, *42*, 32-38.

# Name Index

**515**

# Subject Index